NEW ENGLAND CAMPING

The Complete Guide to More Than 82,000 Campsites for Tenters, RVers, and Car Campers

by Carol Connare
and Stephen Gorman

Foghorn Press
BOOKS BUILDING COMMUNITY™

ISBN 1-57354-020-X

To order individual books, visit the Foghorn Press Web site at www.foghorn.com,
or call 1-800-FOGHORN (364-4676) or (707) 773-4260. Foghorn Press
titles are distributed to the book trade by Publishers Group West, based
in Emeryville, California. To contact your local sales representative, call
1-800-788-3123.

Although the authors and publisher have made every effort to ensure that
the information in this book was correct at press time, the authors and
publisher do not assume and hereby disclaim any liability to any party for
any loss or damage caused by errors, omissions, or any potential travel
disruption, whether such errors or omissions result from negligence,
accident, or any other cause.

Library of Congress ISSN Data:
June 1997

New England Camping
*The Complete Guide to More Than 82,000 Campsites for Tenters, RVers,
and Car Campers*
First Edition
ISSN: 1093-2739

> **Leave No Trace, Inc.,** is a program dedicated to main-
> taining the integrity of outdoor recreation areas through
> education and public awareness. Foghorn Press is a
> proud supporter of this program and its ethics.

The Foghorn Press Commitment

Foghorn Press is committed to the preservation of the environment.
We promote Leave No Trace principles in our guidebooks. Additionally,
our books are printed with soy-based inks on 100 percent recycled
paper, which has a 50 percent post-consumer waste content.

Printed in the United States of America

*To my brother John, who was the first
person to take me by the hand and
lead me outdoors.*

—C. C.

*For Tasha, friend and confidant who kept me
company for five thousand miles of frost-heaves and
washboards while researching this volume. Half
collie, half German shepherd, she's one
fine traveling companion.*

—S. G.

Preface

Why camp in New England? Campgrounds are frugal, friendly, and located near all the things you want to see and do. Whether you seek to find the bricks and mortar of American history or to relish the solitary calm of a rippleless pond at sunset, you'll find the opportunity to do it here, as well as much more in between.

New England has been called the nation's attic, tucked away up here in the eaves atop all the other states. And like any good attic, New England holds a wealth of cherished memories and treasured antiques—family heirlooms, if you will—reminders of who we are and where we come from.

Poke around a bit and you turn up the Pilgrims and the first Thanksgiving, Paul Revere's midnight ride, the Battle of Bunker Hill. Look around a little more and you come across the first flourishes of our nation's literature, the founding of American education, the flowering of American art and music. Before long you discover curious artifacts scattered about, like the House of the Seven Gables, Plymouth Rock, the Old North Church, covered bridges, and the tall ships of the Yankee whaling fleet.

In New England life goes on much as it used to: lobstermen still set their traps in the frothy swells; farmers still harvest a bumper crop of rocks in the fall (the raw material for all those stone walls snaking through the woods); students still sit reading under the oaks in Harvard Yard.

But New England is much more than a richly endowed repository for our collective past. Nature is truly in charge here, and no matter where you go in New England, you are never far from the out-of-doors. This is an uncompromising landscape—an Old Testament kind of place: mostly harsh and demanding, sometimes benevolent, always

stern. Whether in downtown Boston or in the high White Mountains, nature touches everyone's lives, as she has for many generations. As a result, most Yankees feel a closeness to the land born of familiarity and respect. Perhaps more than any other region, nature has molded the New England character, dictating who the people are, what they do, and when they do it.

Though it seems winter lasts forever in New England ("nine months of snow and three months of damn poor sleddin'" is a phrase commonly heard in the north), nature furnishes a medley of seasons. Autumn, though glorious in its extravagant hues, is a time of hurried preparation for the fierce winter to come. Winter is actually four or five months of ice, cold, and snow. Spring is an explosion of rebirth. And, though short, summer is a cool, sunny reward for making it through another year.

Not only does New England have well-defined seasons, it has a rich palette of landscapes as well. From the Arctic tundra of the high mountain summits, through the heavily forested uplands, to the gleaming granite islands off the Maine coast and the sandy shores of Cape Cod, New England packs the greatest variety into the smallest package. Though New England is a small geographic area (the entire region is only one-third the size of California, for example), it looms large in the national consciousness. Nowhere else will you find the marvelous array of cultural and natural amenities within easy reach of each other.

Perhaps New England *is* like an old farmhouse attic—seasoned by the years, a bit quaint, perhaps a little drafty, yet full of fascinating nooks and crannies. The trick is to get up here and poke around a bit. Who knows what you'll find?

New England Camping

The Complete Guide to More Than 82,000
Campsites for Tenters, RVers, and Car Campers

Contents

Introduction

In the middle of the night, as indeed each time that we lay on the shore of a lake, we heard the voice of the loon, loud and distinct, from far over the lake. It is a very wild sound, quite in keeping with the place and the circumstances of the traveller, and very unlike the voice of a bird. I could lie awake for several hours listening to it, it is so thrilling. When camping in such a wilderness as this, you are prepared to hear sounds from some of its inhabitants which will give voice to its wildness. Some idea of bears, wolves, or panthers runs in your head naturally. . . .

—Henry David Thoreau,
The Maine Woods

Let us tell you about the New England camping experience: It's sharing a crackling campfire with friends as the brightest stars you've seen in years pulse overhead. It's hearing the rushing sound of a wild river. It's the snug shelter of a tent in a thunderstorm. It's a peaceful feeling of freedom and renewal.

Camping in New England provides a chance to get in touch with yourself after a long absence, to remember who you really are. With no schedules or demands except self-imposed ones, camping helps you feel calm, unhurried, and self-reliant for a change. You can put distance between yourself and the crowds, the pressures, and the hassles of everyday life. Camping is a chance to feel free. And it really doesn't get any better than right here.

New England Camping is about having access to all you want to do. Pack your bags and retreat to the Allagash Wilderness Waterway in Maine for a sense of solitude. Pull up your motor home next to the Atlantic Ocean and fish for striped bass. Park your RV just south of Boston and ride the T into the city, where you can take in a ball game, go to a concert, or eat dinner in a restaurant that touches the sky. Pack up the kids and a camper for a week in the White Mountains

of New Hampshire, where you'll find exciting theme parks next to breathtaking vistas. Strap your bikes onto the back of the car and head to the Berkshires or Connecticut's Litchfield Hills for pastoral landscapes and two-wheeled tours of vineyards, antique trails, and town greens. Pitch your tent in the Green Mountains and let wildlife put on an evening performance. It's all here, and it's not hard to find.

As outdoors writers we travel a lot in search of wildness. This quest has taken us to the highest peaks of the Rockies, to the great deserts of the Southwest, to the vast canoe country of Canada, and to the immense wilderness of Alaska and the Yukon. But no matter how far we roam, New England beckons.

Like many others we heed New England's call because everything an outdoors lover seeks is here, within easy reach. Yankees have such a rich and varied menu of places to go and things to do, visitors and residents alike sometimes feel as if New England is one large outdoor amusement park, overstocked with opportunities for adventure. Whether it's fly-fishing or white-water rafting, backpacking or canoe camping, sea kayaking, rock climbing, or bicycling down a country lane, New England is perhaps the nation's premier outdoor playground and a camper's paradise.

As we write these words one scene comes to mind. Steve was once camped at the Wadleigh Stream shelter on the Appalachian Trail, deep in the section of the Maine Woods known as the 100-Mile Wilderness. That night he listened to the rain drum on the tin roof of the lean-to as he bundled up in his sleeping bag, poured a steaming mug of cocoa, and read the shelter register, listening to the testimony of others who had passed this way. As his headlamp cut the cavelike darkness of the night he scanned these lines:

"I'm just lovin' this wilderness. The loons have taken my soul. I will never forget this time, place, or all the friends and folks I've met along the way."

Precisely. That's why we camp.

How to Use This Book

New England Camping is divided into six chapters: Maine, New Hampshire, Vermont, Massachusetts, Rhode Island, and Connecticut. Maps at the beginning of each chapter show where all the campgrounds in that state are located.

For Maine campgrounds:
see pages 31–166

For New Hampshire campgrounds:
see pages 167–278

For Vermont campgrounds:
see pages 279–352

For Massachusetts campgrounds:
see pages 353–426

For Rhode Island campgrounds:
see pages 427–446

For Connecticut campgrounds:
see pages 447–491

You can search for the ideal campsite in two ways:

1. If you know the name of the specific campground where you'd like to stay, or the name of the surrounding geographical area or nearby feature (town, national or state park or forest, mountain, lake, river, etc.), look it up in the index beginning on page 492 and turn to the corresponding page. Page numbers for campgrounds featured in this book are listed in the index in boldface type.

2. To find a campground in a particular part of a state, turn to the maps at the beginning of that chapter. You can identify entry numbers in the area where you would like to camp, then turn to the chapter table of contents to find the page numbers for those campgrounds.

See the bottom of every page for a reference to corresponding maps.

What the Ratings Mean

Each campground in this book has been rated on a scale of 1 to 10 for its scenic beauty. Ratings are based solely on scenic appeal and do not reflect quality issues such as the cleanliness of the camp or the temperament of the management, which can change from day to day.

What the Symbols Mean

Most listings in this book feature one or more symbols that represent the recreational offerings at or near the campground. Other symbols identify whether there are sites for RVs or any wheelchair-accessible facilities. Wheelchair accessibility has been indicated when it was advertised by campground managers, and concerned persons should call the contact number to ensure that their specific needs will be met. The hunting symbol has been included to remind campers that they need to be aware of the hunting season in a particular state and that they may be near hunters when camping in some state parks or in the backcountry. Hunting is a popular sport throughout New England; the season varies from state to state but generally extends from fall into early winter. Call the state departments of Fish and Game or park and forest offices to find out actual dates.

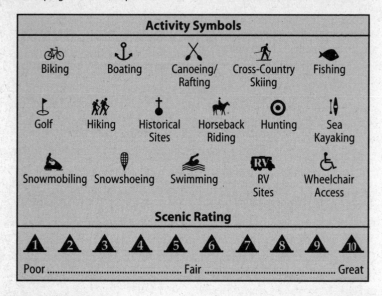

Note to Tent Campers

If the RV symbol **RV** appears in a campground listing, that does not mean that the camp is an exclusive RV resort or is unsuitable for tent campers. Many camps offer quality sites for both tent and RV camping.

About Maps

The maps in this book are designed to show the general location of campgrounds and are not meant to substitute for more detailed road maps. Readers are advised to take additional maps when heading out to any campground, particularly when venturing into the wilderness (for instance, many of the sites in the northern part of Maine).

Every effort has been made to ensure that the information in *New England Camping* is as up-to-date as possible. However, details such as fees and telephone numbers are subject to change. Please contact the campgrounds you plan to visit for current information.

Camping Tips

Keep It Simple

The first sound I heard when I shut off the engine was the flutelike song of the wood thrush. Then I caught a whiff of sunshine and soil wafting through the open window. I shut my eyes for a moment and breathed deeply. Still jittery from a harried drive, I got out and cinched my pack with trembling hands (too much coffee? too many close encounters with tractor-trailers?), then locked and shut the car door. Casting a quick glance at my companions, I thought they looked a bit tense, too. But soon, I knew, our careworn expressions would brighten as Vermont's Green Mountains worked their magic on us.

We left the trailhead lot, turned toward the forest, and confronted a dense canopy, an impenetrable green thicket as mysterious as any Amazonian jungle. I thought about machetes—the vegetation was that thick. But probing the foliage was a slight opening leading in then disappearing around a bend: the Long Trail. Our trail. That rough footpath to Canada was all the invitation we needed. We strode through the slim gap into the obscure half-light of the north woods and slipped from view.

The track lured us upward through a cool understory of hobblebush and moosewood. The worries I had carried from home vanished around the time I noticed scrolls of peeling birch bark unfurling like banners in the soft breeze. Among the birches stood silver beech trees with smooth trunks scarred by the claws of foraging bears. Through gaps in the canopy I caught glimpses of a long blue gash in the valley below: Lake Champlain. Beyond the lake the high peaks of the Adirondack Mountains in New York state scratched the sky. Barely half an hour on the trail and I had shed most of my late-twentieth-century, information-age anxieties, trading them for the peace and tranquillity I can only find outdoors.

Our greatest escape artist, Henry David Thoreau, wrote, "I think I cannot preserve my health and spirits, unless I spend four hours a day at least—and it is commonly more than that—sauntering through the woods and over the hills and fields, absolutely free from all worldly engagements." Modern saunterers, we practice what he preached, seeking the simple pleasures offered by the woods and hills. These outings restore us, they provide a necessary counterbalance to the pressures of daily life.

For me, replenishing mind and body after a hard week means spending at least a night and preferably two on the trail. I find the trick is to get out there as quickly as possible. But getting away for more than a day introduces the problem of toting adequate food and shelter. The answer: "Simplify," said Thoreau.

In a lifetime of wilderness wandering, I've concluded that the Master was quite correct. The simpler the outfit, the faster we can get out and leave our worries behind. John Muir was reportedly a genius at this: leaving all the heavy gear behind, he stuffed his pockets full of bread crumbs and hopped the back fence. Muir was on to something.

Personally, I'd rather lose myself in the color of the sunset than focus on my aching shoulders. And if I don't have to expend precious energy microtuning some equipment "design breakthrough" of dubious merit, I am happiest. I value my outfit most if I am utterly unaware of it. The gear is a means to an end, and the end is to get out there as quickly and easily as possible.

The joys of traveling light are many. For starters, it's easier on your back. It's also a lot easier on your wallet. And it's easier to hit the trail when there's less to organize. But the key to intelligent paring away isn't to do without; it's to do without excess. Your needs are shaped by where you travel. Climate and terrain aren't constant, so a Vermonter would be foolish to mimic a Californian's load. And vice versa.

Think about where you're going, then take a look at your gear. Can you go with the light sleeping bag if you wear extra clothes to sleep? Will a mug do double duty as a bowl? Will a light tarp serve instead of a tent?

Lighten up, and the effect amplifies: Leave the heavy wafflestompers behind and hike in comfortable lightweight boots. Then you can ditch the comfy camp shoes as well!

Some load-paring is done for us by the gear manufacturers, who consistently turn out new, lightweight materials weighing a fraction of what their bloated ancestors did. As an added bonus, these new materials are often stronger and perform better. By being a smart shopper who buys well-made, lightweight designs—especially those that serve more than one purpose—and little else, you will reduce your load and still bring everything you need.

Finally, to keep it simple, plan ahead. Everything you do before you hit the trail makes your time out there less hectic and much more enjoyable. Here's a checklist to help speed you on your way. Copy it and post it on your refrigerator, on your closet door, in the garage, or wherever it will be most helpful.

- Obtain maps, permits, and emergency contact numbers.
- Plan your route. Notify a friend where you are going and when you will be back.
- Prepare your menu and purchase camping food during the week when you do your regular shopping.
- Top off your car's gas tank the night before you depart.
- Run any errands, such as using an ATM machine, the night before.
- Check gear and clothing to be sure it's in good repair.
- Make a personal gear, group gear, clothing, and food checklist (see the sample on page 29). Post it wherever you store your equipment and check off items as you pack.
- Pack the evening before you plan to depart. Make sure everything fits comfortably inside your pack.
- Bring your pack with you to work on Friday so you can go directly to the trailhead or campground after work.

—*S. G.*

Food and Cooking Gear

All the wisdom I have gained during my lifetime has funneled down into a simple understanding. There is one chief human desire driving our existence on the planet: Humans live to eat. This is never more true than when outdoors and camping. Our bodies need the right fuel at the right time to keep operating smoothly. And food really does seem to taste better when eaten outdoors or after a long day on the trail.

With some forethought and an open mind, you will be a well-fed, and therefore happy, camper. Vittles are vital to our emotional well-being. Time spent in the planning reduces your food-related chores in the field and lets you concentrate on what's really important—the Great Outdoors.

Four of us once skied out of the wintry wilderness after a seven-day hut tour in a northeast mountain range with smug, slightly self-righteous grins. We had planned our food needs so closely that between us there remained a small sack of cheese, a few packets of oatmeal, some dried milk, and tea. In the course of our tour we encountered below-zero windchills, whipping winds, blistering sun, relentless snow, and meddlesome rain. We covered nearly 60 miles of mountainous terrain on telemark skis carrying full backpacks. Starting out, we shouldered four days worth of food and met up with our second installment at a mountaintop hut on the fourth night. How did we achieve such a near-perfect ratio of food consumption to food carried? Careful, pretrip meal-by-meal planning.

Of course, there is a universal law of "out there" grubbing that allowed us to achieve this noshing nirvana—if it is edible, a hungry camper will eat it. Along the way, we helped ourselves to food other campers had left behind in the huts—instant mashed potatoes, mixed nuts, pasta—but we had enough to be comfortable without these bonus calories. Granted, we all agreed we could have carried a few more candy bars, tequila, and popcorn, but space and weight were so essential given our mode of travel, we pared down our meals to the essentials.

Planning your camp food this successfully is not rocket science. There is no mystery other than planning ahead and anticipating your needs. Food and cooking gear vary given your style of camping. There are big differences in what's needed for car camping, backpacking, and camping in extreme conditions. Start out with a basic mess kit you can adapt to every situation, and make a meal-by-meal plan.

A basic cooking kit should consist of the following: a pair of nesting pots (they should be sizable but not so large that they dwarf your stove), a coffeepot, a frying pan (all of light-gauge aluminum), a metal pot grabber, plastic bowls, insulated cups, matches, a lighter, a knife, and spoons. A word about the pots: there are some excellent designs out there nowadays made out of lightweight aluminum with nonstick surfaces and grooved bottoms to prevent topples. Hurray for technology. Another advance is in insulating thermoses. Invest in the most lightweight model you can find— hot drinks on the trail are equally useful to revive flagging spirits and chilled bodies. Most experienced outdoor eaters find it essential to bring a spice kit with seasoned salt, pepper, hot pepper, garlic, olive oil, and other flavor enhancers in small sealed plastic bottles.

The most important piece of cooking gear is your stove. Pull-in tent and camper sites will likely have a fire pit or ring or permanent hibachi for cooking over an open flame. There is nothing like a grilled dinner under the stars in the shadow of a mountain or by a lake, but even during the most favorable conditions, a stove is always a better way to cook anything in a pot and to boil water. More on water later.

Gasoline stoves are the most evolved species available. They are reliable in bad weather, and gasoline has the highest heat output of all stove fuels. Generally, gasoline stoves take "white gas" or Coleman fuel—it's not safe to burn leaded gas in them. It's safer to use additive-free white gas than unleaded gas that you can get at any drive-up pump, as white gas is less volatile. You'll have to make a trip to your nearest sporting goods store to get white gas, but if you camp with any kind of frequency, it's worth it.

If you are purchasing a stove, there's no reason to get anything other than a gasoline-burning rig. But if you are borrowing someone else's equipment, here are a few words about lesser fuels: Kerosene burns as hot as gas and is much less volatile. But it smells, and stoves that use it must be primed with alcohol or gasoline. Watch out if your fuel spills or leaks, too—you won't be able to get rid of the odor anytime soon. Propane is inexpensive, but the heavy steel cylinders it comes in are too cumbersome for anything but a four-wheeled outfit. Butane simply stops working at freezing temperatures, but stoves that take it need no pumping, priming, or filling—just attach a new cylinder.

There are a few other considerations when choosing a stove.

Stability: Take the stove out of the box and give it a tip test. I ruined a breakfast of perfectly delicious buckwheat pancakes with just-gathered wild red raspberries because of a precariously balanced stove. The unfortunate incident cast a cloud over the whole day.

Startability: Get a stove with a built-in fuel pump. They start faster and put out more heat.

Simmerability: Try to buy a model that offers some kind of flame adjustability so you don't end up with burnt crud in the bottom of all your pans.

Old Man Wind: Some stoves come with wind protection—usually a metal guard that surrounds the stove—or you can buy windstops à la carte (thin aluminum works best), and these also help to conserve fuel on trips where that's a concern.

Allow your salesperson to demonstrate how particular stoves work if they are willing. If not, read all the directions and try your stove outside in the relatively innocuous location of your backyard, not once, but several times. Get to know your stove. Most times, it's the only thing standing between you and a good hot meal and safe drinking water.

Lots of campgrounds have safe drinking water readily available from nearby spigots. However, in the winter and when backcountry camping, you'll have to find sources for water to cook and clean. You can pack in drinking water or become a backcountry chemist and treat the wild stuff. If you choose the latter, make sure there is water where you are camping! Consulting maps is sometimes not enough—try to talk to a ranger or a local. In the heat of summer, certain streambeds might dry up.

The two readily available treatments used by most campers to eliminate the health threats posed by microorganisms lurking in most streambeds are iodine tablets (funny tasting) or pump filters (awkward, not foolproof). Option three is to boil all your drinking and cooking water for at least one minute. This kills giardia and any other vile critters waiting to make you sick. Then fill your water bottles, cap them tightly, and set them in the stream—voilà! cold, delicious, safe drinking water. In case of stove failure, always pack a bottle of iodine tablets for backup.

If you're camping with a group, it's wise to invite along that friend who likes nothing better than to linger in camp all day cooking up a feast to regale his or her fellow campers upon their return from the hinterlands. But most of us are out there for a reason—to get away from convention, to subsist without all the hindrances of our workaday lives. Domestically inclined campers are somewhat of an oxymoron. Thus, ideal meal planning results in hearty, good tasting meals without a lot of fuss. I like to start off the day with a hot drink and some oatmeal or granola, munch a cold lunch on the trail, and put the bulk of my culinary efforts into dinner.

Except for the dog days of summer, a hot drink in the morning, whether tea, coffee, or hot chocolate seems to hit the spot. Cereals are lightweight and can be packaged in plastic bags with powdered milk already added. Just add water and you've got breakfast in your bowl. If it's going to be a scorcher, you might make your tea the night before and set it out to cool for a refreshing drink in the morning.

Hopefully, your lunch will be taken on a lake, atop a mountain, beside a clear stream, or while you're docked on an island off the coast. Flat "mountain breads" are a smart lunch choice—they hold up well and can be filled and rolled (to minimize napkin use) with anything from peanut butter and jelly to pepperoni and cheese to smoked salmon and capers. Personally, lunch is when my sweet tooth gets ornery, so I like to have cookies or some kind of chocolate midday. Hard crackers and cured meats make for excellent luncheon foods, too. Make tea or coffee at breakfast and fill your thermos. Hot or cold, that extra boost will fuel you through the afternoon. Dried or fresh fruit, cookies, energy bars, nuts, and the like make smart snacks to boost energy between meals.

Back at camp, with the bugs at bay and the long light of day giving into the blue-black of night, it's time for dinner. Time to replenish all those calories expended cavorting outdoors all day. If you've converted the trunk of your car into a food pantry, home cooking is in order. When you are a little deeper into the woods, you've got to get a little more creative. Certainly, if you're willing to shell out the bucks, a fine array of prepared freeze-dried meals are available at sporting goods stores. But many inexpensive choices exist on the shelves of your local market.

Macaroni and cheese, couscous, chili, and rice dishes are lightweight choices. Check the diet food section of the market for just-add-water soups and stews and the gravy isle for packets of powdered sauces. Embellishing is encouraged. Dried meats and vegetables go a long way toward dressing up a meal. Health food stores carry a variety of alternative grains including quinoa, bulgur, millet, and barley, which also carry well into the woods. Be careful to note cooking times and water needs for anything you buy in bulk.

Don't be afraid to pack a little extra treat or two. My favorite sin food to sneak along is a tin of smoked oysters.

It may seem like overkill, but spread out your food and package it meal by meal, day by day. Discard all packaging and mix up your ingredients ahead of time in plastic bags. Double-bagging is strongly encouraged anytime the food will go some distance. Be sure to compress and remove air if you are using ziplocks. Remember to include instructions and label the meal with an indelible marker to avoid confusion.

Pack a stuffsack or a large ziplock each with breakfasts, lunches, dinners, and snacks, or pack one day's worth in a sack. That way you won't have to tear through all your food just to find that one item.

—C. C.

Clothing and Weather Protection

Did anyone ever stop to think that Adam and Eve, those intrepid, foraging, biblical campers, may well have wanted to wear clothes? They take all the blame for our agony over having to cover up our bodies, but who would really want to be doing all that gardening in Eden unprotected, especially in blackfly season? They might have been darn relieved when they were told to get dressed.

Camping in the wilderness sometimes provides ideal opportunities to bare all. The thrill of midnight skinny-dipping, the wild abandon of hiking without a top on, feeling the wind at every part of your back, sweat drying instantly in a cool breeze—these are some of the moments campers live for. They bring us closer to our untamed selves. But wind, water, snow, cold, and sun are forces to be reckoned with. New England is notorious for its sudden and vast changes in weather; when it's 80 degrees and sunny at the base of a mountain, it could be stormy and freezing by the time you reach the top. Likewise, the temperature on the beach is usually much warmer than out on the water. The good news is, having the right apparel in most cases makes you equal to the challenge of the elements.

There are several rules of thumb to dress by: Wear layers, dress for comfort, and carry a spare set of dry clothes in case you land in the drink or get caught in a downpour. Cotton garments are only appropriate in warm weather or when you have something dry to change into. Know the weather forecast before you go into the backcountry, whether for a day or for a week.

Contrary to the cliché, I rarely call my women friends to inquire what they are wearing to a certain event. Outdoor pursuits are the exception. My friend Mary and I were headed up to Mount Mousilauke in New Hampshire for a spring telemark ski. I called her to confer about her outfit. The day was sunny and warm, and we thought we'd be fine in Lycra pants but decided to pack our

GoreTex gear just in case. We would be skinning up on our skis—adhering a strip of moleskin to the base of the boards allows telemarkers to ascend a slope as if on snowshoes. Once at the top, we would remove our skins and make turns all the way back down. Our climb would put us well above 4,000 feet, and the area had just received a fresh foot or so of powder.

It was so warm out we could have worn short-sleeved shirts on the way up, the most exerting part of our trek. But once we got above tree line, the wind turned the temperatures to frigid. We had to don full wind gear—GoreTex pants and jackets, fleece vests, and our warmest hats and gloves to make it to the summit. It was so cold we stayed there only a few minutes. We both wore polypropylene shirts, which kept us dry underneath our jackets. Then, five minutes after we began our descent, we were shedding the same gear, back to spring-skiing mode.

The point is, no matter where you are in New England, no matter what season, plan to be surprised. This doesn't mean you need to spend a fortune on clothing and weather gear. But you will need a few essentials to be comfortable and to prevent hypothermia.

Hypothermia is the lowering of the body's core temperature, usually below 95 degrees Fahrenheit. Most frequently this affliction occurs when a camper gets wet—either by rainfall or falling into cold water. The first symptom of hypothermia is uncontrollable shivering. Then your speech thickens and you become disoriented. If these signs are ignored, your body will give in about an hour later. Shivering stops, muscles become stiff, and skin turns puffy white. If you don't warm up, death is just around the corner. To treat mild hypothermia, the vic-

tim needs to dress in warm, dry clothing, exercise to stimulate blood flow, and drink hot liquids. More advanced cases may require being wrapped in blankets soaked in hot water.

When suiting up for any length outing, think layers. What you wear closest to your skin and the exterior layer braving the elements are the most important. What comes in between is subject to endless personal preference and experience.

In the doggiest days of summer, you won't want much more than a pair of roomy shorts, a tank top or bathing suit, and a supply of bug repellent to be comfortable during the daytime. But even when it's hot out, if you're in the water, especially the ocean, bring dry clothes along. At night, even in the summertime, New England can get quite chilly. Always bring long pants and long-sleeved shirts.

Polypropylene, capilene, and several other fancy names are the best outdoor-garb fabrics invented to date in terms of undergarments, aka long underwear or long johns. This lightweight, synthetic material wicks moisture away from the skin, keeping your epidermis dry and comfortable. It's available in a variety of weights, colors, and styles. You'll find it incomparable for dry warmth during outdoor winter activities and will also find it useful as pajamas in all seasons. This miracle fabric does have one significant drawback, however. While wicking away all that dampness, it also soaks up body odor. After a few very active days, your polypropylene becomes an odiferous nightmare. Some blends are less smelly than others, but the comfort of this fabric, believe it or not, far outweighs its aromatic inconvenience. I have found that polypropylene actually reaches a stasis point; once it gets to a certain ripeness, you can continue wearing it without increasing its stench. What a bonus.

You know your favorite jeans—the ones that get worn first right out of the dryer? You'll probably want to bring these camping, but more for hanging around the fire at night than for daytime romping. In good weather, loose cotton/canvas blend pants or Lycra/cotton blend stretch pants will be far more comfortable and have another distinct advantage over jeans: when they get wet, they'll dry fairly quickly. Dungarees hang on to every last bit of moisture as long as possible. Not a fun state of affairs in the event of an unanticipated soaking. On top, you'll be most comfortable with a cotton or cotton/wool blend shirt over your interior garments, with additional layers added according to the temperature and your activity.

Another miracle fabric now widely available is Polartec fleece. This environmentally correct stuff (it's often made from recycled plastic bottles) is warm and fuzzy—and pervasive. It is sewn into coat liners, crafted into natty long-tailed caps, and made into mittens, scarves, vests, pullovers, jackets, pants, socks, jog bras, shorts, and skirts. Different weaves and weights and a host of colorful patterns make this a versatile, funky fabric. If you are wearing a wicking material underneath, it won't get wet from the inside. In the event of moisture, fleece can still provide some insulation like wool. My most-used fleece item is a vest. It provides that extra little layer of warmth on top. I also favor a thick pair of fleece gloves under mitten shells for skiing or snowshoeing on cold days. Fleece is an alternative to the traditional insulating fabric—wool. Both will retain heat when wet, but fleece weighs much less than

wool in this compromised state. I find fleece garments have a lot more give than wool and they are also machine washable and dryable.

Cotton is made out to be the bad guy of outdoor garb. True enough—it actually takes heat away from your body when it gets wet. In summertime, cotton is comfy in the hot sun. When it gets wet from perspiration, it actually helps your body cool down. In extreme winter conditions, I always wear polypropylene when active, but like to carry a cotton turtleneck for nighttime.

In all seasons, a camper's biggest foe is water. A freezing downpour is not only a pain in the neck for the ill-prepared, it's dangerous. Ideally, your camping trip will be sunny, clear, and dry. But even if the forecast doesn't call for a drop of precipitation, pack your rain gear anyway. The hills of New England sometimes have weather patterns all their own.

If you can afford them, GoreTex (lightweight, breathable waterproof fabric) pants and jacket shells will serve you well in most rainy situations. If caught in a freezing, sleety April shower that could last for days, you can layer underneath a roomy shell system. If the August sky unleashes a hellish thunder and lightning drencher, you can stay dry for the brief but fierce duration by donning your shells. GoreTex doesn't have to be out of your price range if you are willing to bargain shop. February is a good time to check the sales racks for GoreTex items. You might not find a matching set, but you can often find excellent quality separates for half the price, about $100 and up apiece.

If you're strictly a summer camper, any coated nylon rain gear will suffice. Nylon is only troublesome below about 20 degrees when it becomes brittle and stiff.

Another lower priced alternative is a rubber pants and jacket set. These are fine for short periods of time or longer periods of inactivity, but they don't breathe at all and you'll be clammy and uncomfortable if you work up any kind of sweat.

When packing your clothing, don't forget to bring a hat. Wind can cause the air temperature to plummet and a cold, unrelenting gust can bring about an "ice cream headache" lickety-split. Covered skin is also less prone to windburn and frostbite. Hats with visors provide good sun protection, but you'll want to pack sunglasses. Sunscreen is another necessity except during fall and the early winter months. Late winter, spring, and summer sun will burn your skin to a crisp if given the chance.

When the snow flies and the rivers freeze, you're going to have to add some extra insulation to your get-up. Down garments—vests and parkas—offer the best quality heat retention for the weight and space. But don't bother with down unless you're willing to make the commitment to quality rain gear. If down gets wet, it's useless. Less serious campers will be comfortable with synthetic-filled versions—they cost less and can still provide insulation when soggy.

—C. C.

Sleeping Bags and Tents

My parents gave me my first sleeping bag when I was eight. It was pink cotton, soft and fluffy, decorated with pictures of little girls in bonnets picking flowers. It came with a matching suitcase. This special set served me perfectly for years of sleepover parties. Hot fudge and popcorn butter came out in the wash.

When I turned 13, my parents presented me with a Coleman mummy bag. That worked pretty well for tenting in the summer and fall. Its heyday was during a four-day excursion with my eighth grade class to Mount Cardigan in New Hampshire. Our group of 25 was caught in a torrential downpour, so we had to hike several extra miles to sleep in a cabin for the night. Many of my campmates hadn't adequately wrapped their bags in plastic, so we had to share. I shared my dry Coleman with Matt Avery, the cutest boy in our school. I was only willing to make such a sacrifice because his survival depended on it, of course.

Once I became an avid backpacker and winter camper, I had to retire the Coleman and find something warmer and lighter. Sleeping bags are as individual as the people who use them and the environments in which they find themselves. The first stop on the road to successful snoozing is assessing your own personal slumberology. Take a good look at yourself. Are you shivering to death while your companion dozes dreamily in a similar bag? Do you constantly find yourself hanging five out the zippered side to cool down even when the mercury dips below freezing?

Next, consider your typical destination. For sea kayaking on the Maine coast, you'll need a different bag than you would when RVing on Cape Cod. In the first case, a warm, lightweight, quick-drying, compressible bag is essential. In the latter, almost any bag will do. Certain sleeping environments demand a more specialized tool than others.

Remember, though, that the bag itself does not provide warmth, rather it's an insulator. When all the fish have been caught, all the miles have been hiked, and all the rapids have been run, it's your own body heat that keeps you warm. To choose the proper insulation for your body, you've got to consider the shape, size, fill, and temperature rating of sleeping bags, always keeping in mind your intended usage.

Shapes and Sizes

A bag that's too roomy will be cooler than a tailored one because less interior space needs to be warmed up. On the other hand, if the bag's shape is too tight for your frame, you'll compress the insulation and sleep colder.

Mummy bags are narrow at the foot, wider at the shoulders, and tapered to an insulated hood. Their snug fit makes them the efficient favorite of wilderness travelers in all regions and climates. But this shape is also the most restrictive. There is little room to roll over, toss, and turn. If you're a nocturnal pugilist, you might feel like you are in a straitjacket.

Rectangular bags offer plenty of room for the to-and-fro of sleeping. But this luxury has a cost: heat escapes from the head and shoulder area and there is more dead space for your body to keep warm. And generally, these bags are too bulky and heavy for travelers who need to be weight and space conscious, such as backpackers and bicyclists. Rectangular bags are suited to car camping and RVs.

In between these two extremes are shapes, styles, and accessories enough to suit individual needs. One aid for sleeping in colder climes is a liner bag or overbag. These protect and prolong the life span of your traveling boudoir and increase insulation. Both interior and exterior liners can add about 20 degrees of warmth to your bag's temperature rating.

Extreme campers should consider a bivy sack. This uninsulated waterproof envelope fits over your regular bag and acts like a mini-tent, warding off most of the big, bad elements. A bivy sack won't keep you totally dry in extended heavy downpour, but it will allow you to forgo a tent in less than terrible conditions. Insist on factory-sealed seams for best weather resistance.

Most bags come in a couple of lengths; some are sized almost as closely as shoes. Look for enough length to stretch out your frame without too much extra airspace inside to warm up. Go ahead and zip yourself into the bag right there on the showroom floor.

Experienced cold-weather campers prefer a larger bag for storing water bottles or boots in the foot area to keep them from freezing overnight. The extra room leaves space for a liner bag or added clothing layers to extend the bag's range.

Temperature ratings are like speed limits—they sometimes seem arbitrary. That's because there is no industry standard, so you will have little luck when comparing these ratings across manufacturer lines. Only one thing about them is universal: the lower the temperature rating, the higher the price of the bag.

For most purposes, the best all-around backpacking bag for spring/summer/fall in New England is a roomy mummy in the 20-degree range. You'll be cursing your "summer bag" rated at 40 or 50 degrees on those cool late-August nights in the Green Mountains. Only winter camping diehards headed for northern New England need bother with 20-below bags or even warmer "maximum mummies," which are simply too hot to sleep in above freezing. For car campers or those who plan to rent an RV or cabin, the flannel-lined rectangular bags are the next best thing to bringing your real bed. They're plump, cozy, and roomy.

The Anatomy of Sleeping Gear

Sleeping bags aren't hard to dissect. Remember the worm from biology lab? There's the outer shell and the filling. Unless you are willing to shell out the dough for a bag with a GoreTex or other waterproof/breathable exterior, plan on taking some measures to keep your bag dry. All fillings lose at least some of their ability to insulate when they get wet, but the synthetic fills can still keep you warm when soggy.

Down fill is light, cozy, warm, and ultimately packable. It requires careful cleaning and storage, but a well-kept down bag retains its loft about three times longer than most synthetic creations. When wet, down is about as warm and comfy as a damp paper towel. Down also field-dries painfully slowly. Keep it dry with a waterproof stuffsack, bivy bag, and/or waterproof shell.

Efforts to counterfeit down still haven't quite matched the warmth, loft, and space-efficiency of lightweight natural feathers, but several new-generation synthetics have narrowed the gap. Synthetic fills retain most of their insulating value when wet, dry quickly, and are relatively inexpensive. They are also, unfortunately, bulkier, heavier, and lose their loft more quickly than down. Synthetic bags excel for cool, wet climes like northern New England's. Canoeists and kayakers should have solid personal reasons not to choose synthetics for camping around watery environs.

When getting outfitted with your perfect bedroll, consider where it will be unfurled. If you are tenting, you'll need a sleeping pad or the ground will suck out all your body heat. When in a motor home, consider the proximity of your neighbors. Some RV parks are little more than parking lots with shade where you'll be camping "wheel to wheel." You might want to pull the shades or wear earplugs if you don't sleep soundly. If you've made a dozing den out of your pickup truck, you'll want to line the bed with something to prevent the cold metal from cutting short your z's.

Choosing a good tent and using it correctly presents more challenges for the New England camper. Sporting goods manufacturers are more than ready to peg you into a certain niche: there are summer/screen tents, three-season tents, all-season tents, and mountaineering tents. Pyramids, domes, hoops, A-frames, and freestanding are just some of the available shapes and styles on the market.

When choosing a tent, consider some of the following issues: First find out the tent's ability to keep you dry. Make sure the rainfly is long enough to cover the bottom sidewalls of the tent. Seal the seams to prevent leakage. To do this properly, pitch the tent, put the rainfly on upside down (sealer bonds best to the coated side), and run a bead of sealer down every line of stitching. Apply several thin coats instead of a single goopy one. You can also treat the outer surface of the fly for extra protection, but be aware that sealer may discolor dark fabrics. It's also wise to seal both sides of the floor seams as well as all reinforcement areas (corners, pole tabs, etc.). Let the sealer dry overnight.

You'll want to choose a tent that's easily assembled even in low light. When possible, opt for aluminum poles. Fiberglass poles are heavier and easier to break. You can usually spot better-quality, tempered aluminum poles by their bright anodized finish.

Another factor to consider is what size tent you'll need. Sleeping capacity ratings are an inexact guideline only; a "two-person" tent does not allow space for two people and their gear, nor room to cook when seeking refuge from a storm. For cooking under cover you'll need a vestibule. For ample gear storage or winter expeditions, try a tent capacity rated one person beyond your intended number; plan on about 20 square feet per person and their gear.

Finally, check the weight of your pop-up home. If you're traveling long distances on foot, every pound makes a difference. Think about how much it will weigh if it gets wet.

Armed with the right bag and tent, all that's left is scouting out a good site. Pick a level spot facing west to catch the sunset or east to greet dawn's light. Just remember that cold air settles into valley floors, so in winter be sure to pitch camp partway up a slope or ridge. Try not to pitch your tent in a low-lying area or in a runoff drainage; seek higher, well-drained ground instead. Look for signs of prevailing wind directions by checking for bent trees, scoured ground around rocks, or snowdrifts. In nasty weather seek out windbreaks—a boulder, clump of trees, or a big bush—and place the tent close but not so close that the fly will be scraped if the wind blows. Finally, look up and check that there are no broken branches waiting to fall on you.

A groundcloth absorbs the wear and tear of rocky, rough campsites so your tent won't have to. Use a lightweight nylon tarp or sheet of polyethylene. The groundsheet should be slightly smaller than the floor of your tent. Place your tent directly over the groundsheet. Groundsheets that stick out will catch water and funnel it directly under the tent, where it will inevitably soak your sleeping bag and you.

Sleep-conscious campers have every excuse to snack before bedtime. Food is fuel, and fuel warms the body. Be sure to drink liquids, too, as dehydration leaves you cold, cranky, and listless. To know if you're getting enough liquid, do a simple urine test: Clear pee at night, camper's delight. Gold urine in morning, campers take warning and drink some water!

Many New England campgrounds offer rental RVs or cabins in addition to traditional tent and RV sites. Amenities differ from place to place, but if you rent an RV, linen rentals are often included in the price so you don't need to bring your own. On the other hand, cabins are not usually equipped with bed linens. Again, each place is different—just remember to find out before you arrive.

—C. C.

Of Bugs and Beasts

Canoeing Maine's Allagash Wilderness Waterway one gorgeous June day, my friend Dan and I soaked up the bright sunshine as we paddled under a flawless blue sky. Effortlessly, we put miles of sparkling water behind us as a gentle tailwind eased us down Eagle Lake.

In late afternoon, just as we were beginning to think about camping, the most exquisite site came into view. Situated on a grassy point jutting into the water, the campsite offered sumptuous views for miles up and down the lake. There were beautiful beaches, great swimming spots, and good fishing off the point. Not only that, but the site promised the luxury of both late afternoon and early morning light. Perfect.

Still congratulating ourselves on our good fortune, we had barely finished setting up the tent when the wind died. It was then that our perfect day came crashing to an end as we were instantly enveloped in a storm of blackflies. We literally dove into the tent and watched in horror through the bug-netting as the bloodthirsty beasts swirled around our little sanctuary like a black cyclone.

We were stuck inside for hours—to go out would have been madness. As the sun went down the blackflies retired, only to be replaced by their equally fiendish cousins, the North Woods mosquitoes.

There are billions and billions of reasons why much of northern New England has never been settled, and they hatch every year around the end of May. Biting flies are the main reason Native Americans migrated to the seashore in the summer, there to dine on lobster and clams on breezy beaches and rocky points, far from the madding swarms of voracious forest insects.

Mosquitoes and no-see-ums—those infinitesimally tiny winged horrors that rise in vaporous clouds in the night and whose bite feels like a burning ember—multiply in stagnant pools and low-lying swampy areas. They like humidity and are most active on damp days and in the evening, as the relative humidity increases. The blackfly breeding cycle takes place not in swamps but in swift running streams and rapids. Blackflies prefer hot, dry, sunny days and they vanish when the sun goes down. Fortunately, because of their different preferences, you almost never have to deal with mosquitoes and blackflies at the same time. Unfortunately, the changing of the guard at sundown takes place with such efficiency, you may only have a few minutes of blessed peace.

Northern New England, and especially Maine, has plenty of both flat and quick water. That's what makes it such an exceptional place to canoe-camp. But as a prolific breeding ground for bugs it's hard to beat. What can you do?

Well, you can go to the beach, lie in the sand, and read trashy romance novels. Or you can stay out of the woods and waters until the height of the bug season is over and the little devils start thinning out—most years around the end of July. Or you can cop an attitude, arm yourself with a little knowledge, and beat the pests at their own game.

Your first line of defense is to use your head. Remember mosquitoes and no-see-ums enjoy things cool, damp, and shady, so stay away from these areas as much as possible. Make sure to have all outside camp chores done before sunset. Recall that wind helps keep the blackflies down, so look for open, sunny, breezy areas where your chances of being relatively bug free are best.

Your next strategy is to adopt the garb of the traditional Maine Guide. Not only will this apparel protect you from bugs, sun, and chilly weather, but you're going to look authentic. Here's what you need to wear, plus a couple of extra items:

- A broad-brimmed hat
- A tightly woven long-sleeved cotton or light wool shirt
- Light cotton twill or wool pants
- A brightly colored bandanna worn around the neck

- Rubber-bottomed, leather-topped boots of the sort made famous by native son L.L. Bean, high enough to tuck your pant leg into (keeps bugs from biting your ankles and legs)
- A bug headnet for those times when you just can't take it anymore
- Earplugs, for those nights when the whiiinnniiinnnggg of the skeeters keeps you from falling asleep

A word about bug dope. Cover up with appropriate clothing that bugs can't bite through instead and only use the stuff (it's poison, after all) in situations of extreme discomfort. You can reduce direct contact with the toxins in effective repellents by dabbing a little dope on your bandanna, on your shirt and pant cuffs, and on the brim of your hat.

Your final refuge, your last bastion against an all-out bug assault, is your trusty tent.

I once worked for an internationally known outdoor education program that for some crackpot reason decided not to issue tents for its summer programs in Maine. It's hard to know what the directors were thinking—I guess their goal was to make sure none of the students would ever go camping again as long as they lived.

The best tents for bug season in northern New England are the inexpensive, extremely lightweight, easy-to-use "bug shelters" offered by various tent manufacturers. These ultralight havens are essentially domes of fire-resistant no-see-um netting suspended over collapsible alloy poles. You can set them up in less than a minute and relax inside, laughing at the little winged fiends as they fly their insane traffic patterns around your neighborhood.

Nice features offered by the bug shelters include lots of ventilation, good headroom, feather weight (less than a pound and a half for a two-person model), and a view of the stars at night. And what about rain, you ask? During inclement weather simply place the shelter under a lightweight tarp.

Unlike some other parts of the country, New England is comparatively free of creatures that doubtless serve a noble purpose in the grand scheme of things but are nonetheless grouped by humans in a category called "pests." This company includes, but isn't limited to, scorpions, gila monsters, kissing bugs, black widows, tarantulas, coral snakes, cottonmouths, pygmy rattlers, and many other reasons to shake out your boots in the morning. Still, even up here there are a few critters to keep in mind when exploring the back of beyond. After all, Lyme disease, carried by the tiny deer tick, is named for its place of origin, Lyme, Connecticut. For the most part, however, most dangers are far more imagined than real.

Lyme disease, a bacterial infection transmitted by the bite of a deer tick, is certainly a reason to be vigilant. On a recent hour-long walk in the Connecticut woods I picked up a half-dozen deer ticks while my dog managed to acquire another five or six. As a precaution, wear the same outfit that helps ward off the mosquitoes and blackflies—long sleeves and pants, a hat, and sturdy boots. Avoid pants with upturned cuffs that provide a hiding place for ticks. Brush off your clothing before entering your tent or RV, and be sure to thoroughly check yourself and your pet.

Poisonous snakes are extremely rare in northern New England and are totally absent from Maine, northern New Hampshire, and northern Vermont. Elsewhere in New England they are so rare many people who spend most of their lives outdoors never see one, so you might consider yourself lucky if you do.

The northern copperhead is native to southwest New England and is usually associated with deciduous forests, rocky ledges, areas with damp leaf litter, rotting woodpiles, boulder fields, in short, anywhere and everywhere. In the summer the snakes sometimes frequent the vicinity of swamps, ponds, and streams.

The eastern timber rattlesnake is a bit more widespread (but no more common), reaching up into southern New Hampshire and Vermont, and seems to prefer the same types of environments as the copperhead. The timber rattler is also associated with a few other habitats, such as old stone walls and cellar holes. Both the copperhead and the timber rattler avoid contact with humans and will flee if given the chance. They are active at night during the summer, a hunting strategy that further reduces the chance of encounters with humans.

No chapter on bugs and beasts would be complete without a mention of bears. Yes, there are bears in New England, lots of them, especially in Vermont, New Hampshire, and Maine. These are black bears—there are no grizzlies here—and for the most part they are shy, secretive forest dwellers, wary of humans and aspiring only to be left alone. If you are fortunate enough, you might see a flash of black fur crashing off through the brush away from you at warp speed.

But let's not overgeneralize bear behavior. They are, after all, highly evolved and intelligent creatures, and like people each bear is an individual. So while their natural tendency may be toward flight at the first sign of humans, some bears have been trained by sloppy campers (the most dangerous animals in the forest) that people can provide them with food in the form of garbage or poorly stored supplies.

Unfortunately, slob campers may lose their food and sometimes equipment when a bear taught to rob camps tears through their gear. But it's usually the bear that ends up paying the heavy price by being relocated or destroyed.

Your best protection in bear country is to keep a spotless camp. When RV or car camping make sure all coolers, containers, equipment, and utensils that come in contact with food are properly stored and put away for the night inside your vehicle. When backpacking or canoeing, make sure all dishes, pots, pans, and cooking gear are washed and stored in your food bags. Burn all leftover food or store it in plastic bags with the rest of your food supplies. Hang your food from a tree, suspended at least 15 feet off the ground and 10 feet away from any tree trunks or extending branches. An easy way to do this is to tie a rock to a rope, then toss the rock over an appropriate branch. Untie the rock, tie on your food bag, then hoist the bag up into the air. When the food bag is hanging out of reach, tie off the loose end of the rope to a nearby tree.

One of the best parts about camping is the chance to spend time in the company of fellow creatures. Most often these shared moments in the wild are delightful—the cow and calf moose we saw feeding in midstream, or the hawk soaring overhead. Some interactions are somewhat less pleasant but no less memorable—the skeeters buzzing in my ear, or the time old Shep came back to camp with a half-dozen ticks. It's really up to us. By learning about wildlands and the habits of the creatures who live there we can make sure more of these encounters are of the pleasant kind.

—S. G.

Camping with Kids

Camping is a terrific way to introduce a child to the world of nature. Everything—playing, eating, sleeping, learning—is done under the sun and the clouds and the moon and the stars. More than a fun vacation (although it should be that, too), it's a chance to learn lifelong skills and experience nature outside of the everyday routine.

In addition, camping is one of the more affordable trips families can take. Sleeping in campgrounds is much less expensive than staying at a motel or hotel, and activities such as hiking, fishing, and exploring nature are not as pricey as amusement-park admission fees. And since you're cooking your meals at the campsite, the high cost of eating in a restaurant is avoided.

When planning a camping trip with the kids, remember a few simple rules: Tailor the trip to their capabilities; focus on their interests; and adjust to their limitations, which are generally defined by their age and development level.

Babies can be great campers, as long as you're prepared to limit your outdoor activities and can address their special requirements (crib, stroller, formula, diapers, etc.). Toddlers especially appreciate exploring a new environment. They love to get dirty and wet, collect leaves and rocks, and watch wildlife and insects.

Elementary school–age children are typically enthusiastic campers, anxious to learn about the outdoors, help with the chores, and participate in all camping activities. They like to swim, hike, build fires, and roast hot dogs. And they can't resist hearing a good ghost story or tall tale about falling stars or wild animals.

Teenagers? Well, you're on your own there. Some teens like to camp, especially if it's an annual family vacation routine. Others consider it a drag and will take every opportunity to remind you of it. Try to involve teens in every aspect of the trip: deciding where to go, what to take, what to eat, what to do. Let them bring a friend and give them a little more freedom than they get at home. They'll be much better company during group activities and meals if they know they'll be able to go off and hike, fish, or swim on their own later.

Here are some tips on how to ensure that a fun, rewarding vacation is had by all:

• Expect short attention spans. By staying a step or two ahead of the kids in the planned activities department, you can keep them from getting bored or into trouble. Unlike adults, the kids need action on a vacation. Plan activities and games to keep them occupied. That means staying prepared by knowing what the next fun event will be—an activity that will inspire or distract a restless child.

• Bring the right gear and games. What you pack partly depends on where you'll be camping and what your children like to do. Are you camping at a sandy lake with toddlers? Then buckets, shovels, sieves, toy trucks, and plastic molds are in order. Will you be sleeping on top of a mountain? Then binoculars, a telescope and star chart, a magnifying glass, and an altimeter are ideal. Will there be a river nearby? Then bring along a fishing rod. No matter where you go, pack along a ball, a Frisbee, a pack of cards, pens and paper, or crayons and coloring pads for younger kids.

- Have a still or video camera ready to capture the moment. Photographs or videos of your family in the outdoors—hiking up a mountain, catching a fish, taking down the tent—will go a long way toward helping your kids hang on to memories of the last trip and build up a head of steam for the next.

- Let your kids help with the practical stuff. When you're camping, there are essential campground tasks that must be done—such as setting up camp, building a fire, cooking dinner—and kids would rather be involved than just watch you do everything. Show them how to help put up the tent, collect sticks for the campfire, add water and stir the pancake mix, read a compass.

- Help your children learn, but also let them play. Spending time outdoors provides the opportunity to teach them outdoor skills and safety, campground ethics, even some lessons about life. While teaching them to pick up after themselves (and others) and to respect the outdoors is very important, remember that taking your children to the woods, mountains, or desert doesn't have to be strictly an educational experience. This is first and foremost a vacation—and kids need to relax, too.

- Let them have a say in the agenda. It's everybody's trip. Listen to what the kids want to do and don't want to do. If a hike is planned and they want to spend the day swimming or tossing a Frisbee instead, let the majority rule. Follow their lead sometimes, go with their flow, let the adventure happen.

- Set rules for acceptable behavior. Giving the youngsters a say in the agenda doesn't mean letting them run wild. Rules and limits are essential to ensure kids' safety and their consideration for other campers. Let them know what behavior is acceptable around a campfire, how close they can come to a cliff or wildlife, and why it's important to stay within sight.

- Prepare kids for the ups and the downs. Enthusiasm is a key ingredient for a successful camping trip, but letting children become excessively excited can backfire when things don't go their way. If it rains or is unseasonably cold, if the fish aren't biting, or if one of them twists an ankle or catches a cold, it could ruin the whole experience for them. Tell them about the possible negative as well as the positive aspects of the trip—that way they'll be better prepared for whatever little disasters or disappointments come their way.

A Guide to Campground Ethics

As America's cities and towns become increasingly crowded, a growing number of people are turning to the outdoors for serenity, simplicity, and solitude. That's the good news. The bad news is that as urban centers become increas-

ingly crowded, a growing number of people are bringing their bad habits—primarily thoughtlessness toward fellow campers and a disrespect for the land—into the backcountry. Even folks who have the best intentions sometimes unwittingly go awry, taking the "great" out of the Great Outdoors for others.

You may wonder what is meant by "campground ethics." It's simply another way of saying use common sense and consideration while camping. Common sense in a campground means keeping quiet; noise is the most common breach of campground ethics. It arrives in a variety of amplitudes, from the laughter of children sitting at a campfire roasting marshmallows at midnight to an all-out brawl between drinking buddies at the next campsite in the wee hours. A gas-powered electrical generator that can't be heard inside a well-insulated RV is torture for tent campers up to six sites away. A group that breaks up camp the moment the sun rises—rattling pots and pans, shouting orders, and running the car (or, worse, motorcycle) engine—can wake up everyone in the campground.

Other ways in which disrespect is manifested in the Great Outdoors are through carelessness with litter, spur-of-the-moment vandalism, and destruction of the natural environment. Litter—from trash left on a picnic table or strewn around a campsite to aluminum foil, beer cans, and glass tossed into a campfire pit—can be unsightly and annoying. It can also be a health hazard: have you ever been greeted by sewage left by an RVer who was too lazy to dispose of it at a dump station?

Vandalism and malicious destruction are increasing in the backcountry, too. Vandalism is immediately identifiable: marker and spray-paint graffiti; picnic tables and tree trunks carved with knives; and signs, garbage cans, and outhouses shot up for target practice. Considering recent and looming cuts in the budgets of the state and federal government agencies that oversee public lands, vandalized facilities may never be repaired or replaced. Worse, if picnic tables are smashed or cut up for firewood, toilets are removed from privies, and water pumps are knocked over by vehicles, the campground itself may be in danger of being closed permanently.

What can be done? Here are some suggestions:

• Leave No Trace. Public-land agencies and concerned environmentalists are mounting campaigns to publicize the principles of "minimum-impact" or "leave-no-trace" camping. For specific Leave No Trace guidelines, see page 30.

• Take personal responsibility for backcountry ethics. When entering a campground, even if only for a night, read the posted rules and observe them closely. Be sure to register and pay your camping fees promptly. This enables campground hosts and park rangers to spend their time maintaining the facilities, instead of informing you of campground rules and regulations or making sure you've paid your fees.

• Observe quiet hours. Many campgrounds have established quiet hours, usually between 10 P.M. and 7 A.M. During this time, campers should speak softly, use headphones for music, refrain from running generators, and keep children under complete control—in other words, be courteous to other campers. When setting up or breaking down camp, make as little noise as possible and, if it's dark, try to avoid shining bright flashlights or headlights everywhere.

• Dispose of your litter. Litter is pollution. Whenever you're tempted to leave garbage behind, think of how you feel when you find other people's plastic bags, tin cans, or aluminum foil in your yard. If you packed it in, pack it out. Properly dispose of your trash in frequently emptied public dumpsters. Even organic refuse, such as apple cores, orange peels, and eggshells (which take months to decompose), is trash. Always leave your campsite in better condition than when you found it, even if it means picking up the litter of those who came before you.

- Keep rest-room facilities clean. Tidy up messes you make when brushing your teeth, shaving, or using toiletries. Do not put any kind of garbage in vault toilets; trash, such as plastic bags, sanitary napkins, and diapers, cannot be pumped and have to be picked out, piece by piece, by some unfortunate soul. If there is running water, use a biodegradable soap for washing dishes and cleaning up. If showers are available, bathe quickly so others can use the facilities.

- Respect the land. Leave the foliage and natural setting around the campground intact. Do not cut down limbs or branches or remove leaves from trees. If you want to build a fire, bring your own wood or buy some from a store or concessionaire. Before leaving a campsite, always make sure the fire is completely out.

- Respect the animals that inhabit the area. Don't feed or harass animals that visit your campground. Animals need to stick to their natural diets or else they might become ill. Keep your camp area clean, especially if you're in or near bear country, so you don't tempt any animals to visit your site.

- Camp and hike in established areas. Camp only in designated campsites, which are usually selected because they are resistant to constant use. Stay on the trails when walking to and from rest rooms, visitors centers, or stores, or when venturing into the backcountry.

- Avoid conflict and respect fellow campers. If a situation arises with inconsiderate or uncooperative neighbors, try to avoid confrontations, which can easily escalate and turn ugly, especially when alcohol is involved. Talk to a campground host, park ranger, or someone with authority and let him or her address the problem. Meanwhile, make sure nobody has cause to complain about you. Show your camping neighbors the same respect that you expect from them and everyone will camp happily ever after.

Canoe Camping

In western Maine, hard against the mountainous border with Quebec, a clear little river comes tumbling down from the high country and meanders through a thick dark forest of spruce and fir. Along the way the river splashes over a series of rapids, plunges down a magnificent 40-foot waterfall, and eventually empties into a beautiful, island-studded lake at the base of a high mountain ridgeline. This is the Moose River, and it's a classic canoe trip, one of many in the region. The lakes here are lovely, with beautiful beaches and campsites offering striking vistas down the waterway. The rapids are thrilling but not dangerous. And even the portage around the cascade is neither excessively long nor rugged, but rather more of a chance to stretch your legs.

For knocking around in the New England wilds, you really can't beat canoe travel. Light, simple, elegant, and strong enough to carry heavy loads, the canoe is the vehicle of choice for exploring a region laced by countless rivers and streams.

In fact, the canoe was invented here in the northeastern woodlands by Algonquian craftsmen, who built the nimble little vessels out of birch bark. Small wonder European explorers adopted the canoe when they set out to explore the continent; their heavy rowboats were useless on inland waters, and the swift Indian canoes paddled circles around them. Not only that, but the natives could see where they were going. The Old World took a bow to superior technology.

Today, the best camping canoes are 17 to 18 feet long and are made of strong synthetic material such as ABS Royalex, fiberglass, or Kevlar. These boats are designed to carry two people plus their gear. Experienced paddlers may choose to paddle their own, smaller canoes.

The secret to the canoe's beauty, grace, and ability to whisk you to the heart of the wild is its simplicity. The long, tapered lines ending in a gentle upsweep at bow and stern are a classic marriage of form and function. It's wonderful: you get in one end, your partner gets in the other, and you keep the boat roughly parallel to the shoreline (it helps to know the basic strokes). Soon, a deep sense of well-being blossoms as you drift along. You settle into a soothing rhythm of wilderness travel. Deadlines and commitments fade into irrelevance. This is the real world. You're on river time now.

A canoe trip in the New England wilds is a chance for viewing wildlife. Seeing a moose is a highlight of many trips here, especially in Maine, but the forest is home to other creatures as well. Deer are plentiful, as are bear, bobcat, beaver, raccoon, and porcupine. In the north, sharp-eyed paddlers may see a rare Canada lynx or a pine marten. Sometime in your travels you are likely to be serenaded by coyotes. The haunting sound of the loon is the voice of this northern wilderness.

Besides loons, canoe campers also have an excellent chance of seeing terns, gulls, kingfishers, great blue herons, ruffed grouse, ospreys, bald eagles, and a rich assortment of ducks and songbirds. Canoe parties that move quietly, especially at dawn and dusk, stand the best chance of encountering wildlife.

In northern Maine, especially, the fishing is superb, and unlike most other parts of the country, the fish populations are wild, not stocked. Clearly, canoe camping parties are well positioned to take advantage of the angling opportunities. Brook trout, known locally as "squaretails," are found in nearly all the lakes, rivers, and streams. Lake trout, called "togue," inhabit the cold, deep waters of the larger lakes.

The canoe is to New England what the horse is to the West, and in this part of the country, canoeing gets you farther into the wilderness faster and lets you stay out there longer than any other form of nonmotorized transportation. Many people find they are more limited by time than by what they can bring along in a canoe.

Here's what to bring: In the clothing department, place the emphasis on covering up from the sun, bugs, and brush while staying cool and comfortable. A broad-brimmed hat and lightweight cotton clothing are great for blue sky days. Bring along the polypropylene, wool, and pile for cool days and cold nights, and be sure to pack the rain gear. As in most outdoor pursuits, layering is the key to comfort.

For footwear on warm-weather trips where you don't plan to do any portaging or lining, river sandals or some mesh-topped slippers are fine. Rubber-bottomed, leather-topped boots are your best bet elsewhere.

Most any backpacking tent will suffice, but take advantage of the canoe's cargo capacity and feel free to bring a larger version and leave the ultralight sensory deprivation chamber at home. Also, a 10-by-12-foot tarp for cooking and lounging under on rainy days is a luxury that quickly becomes a necessity.

Bring a sleeping bag, sleeping pad, and a folding camp chair for relaxing by the fire or camp stove. And speaking of stoves, you can bring your lightweight backpacking stove or again take advantage of the canoe's capacity and pack a larger two-burner stove. That way you can keep the hot drinks coming while you cook your dinner—a nice option on a wet, windy day. And while you're at it, why not bring along a gas lantern for when the sun goes down? As for fires, dry driftwood is usually plentiful, as are dry fallen trees and branches in the surrounding forest.

Pack your clothing and equipment in heavy-duty waterproof rubber gear bags or traditional canvas Duluth-style packs waterproofed with heavy-duty plastic liners. Traditional rigid ash pack baskets are excellent for transporting hard-edged or fragile items. Small rubber dry bags are very useful for keeping little items handy; stash your sunscreen, shades, and bug repellent in a day pack. The day pack will come in handy if you take time off from paddling to do any day hiking.

Your gear should be packed low and in the center of the canoe, below the gunwales. There it will stay dry and won't catch the wind.

On most of the big rivers and lakes in northern Maine the water is pure and drinkable, and locals keep a cup handy for dipping while they paddle—one of the last places in the continental United States you can experience the pleasure of drinking directly from a natural source. However, if you aren't sure about the water quality, treat it with iodine or a water purifier.

Sometimes, as on the Connecticut River, or most waterways in southern New England, you have to bring water with you. Haul your own in new, unused, and clearly marked five-gallon plastic gasoline jugs.

Don't forget your life jacket, one extra paddle per boat, and a large sponge to swab the decks. Lastly, bring along a camera, film, binoculars, fishing gear, and a well-worn paperback copy of *Deliverance*. Happy paddling!

—*S. G.*

Winter Camping

Old-timers call it "termination dust." Wake up on a crisp fall morning and there it is, sprinkled sugar on the mountaintops: the first snow of the season. Another summer gone. Another camping season coming to a close.

In the mountains of northern New England, the first snows dust the high peaks anytime after mid-September. By Thanksgiving the ski season is well under way, rivers and lakes are freezing solid, and warm-weather campers have stored their gear for the winter. The land and people are settling in for the long dark silence.

For many folks up here, winter is a time to reflect on past camping adventures, to sit around the stove reliving shared moments in the outdoors, to anticipate the return of the sun. But other folks have a different, some might say peculiar, attitude toward winter. When the days grow short, when the cold winds blow and the snow piles high, these people spring into action. The fact that the mercury is curling into a tight little ball at the bottom of the thermometer doesn't faze them. These zealots think winter is the best time of all to head outdoors.

And why not? After all, in northern New England especially, winter lasts half the year or longer. And hidden under the snowy forest canopy, locked beneath frozen lakes, and tucked away in the hollows of fallen trees, life goes on despite winter's cold. Nature can't afford to wait for the big spring thaw: there's too much to do.

The same goes for us humans. Days spent traversing crystalline landscapes renew us in hardy ways unknown to the fair-weather crowds of summer. Learn the techniques for coming to terms with the cold and snow and you'll discover a whole new bright shining world of camping adventure.

If you are planning your first trip, the best time to go is after the brutally cold days of December and January. A midwinter trip can be cruelly cold. By February and March the days are longer, the temperatures are more moderate, and snow and sunshine are plentiful. Gain some experience before you tackle an early-season trip.

Fortunately, New England is blessed with a variety of terrain perfect for winter camping. We have it all here—the snowy summits of Acadia National Park overlooking the Atlantic Ocean, the elegant forests of the interior, the frosty crags of Mounts Washington and Katahdin—perhaps no other region offers so many diverse experiences to the winter adventurer. Don't overlook favorite hiking areas, which can be great places for winter camping. Becoming familiar with a small wilderness is sometimes as satisfying as trekking across a vast, expansive tract.

Spreading out maps and choosing a route is part of the fun. Most veteran winter campers can daydream for hours, linking trails and connecting routes they would love to explore. A primitive urge to go takes hold: a longing to see what lies beyond the next ridge.

Next, gather information on the area you wish to explore. Maps, guidebooks, and advice from experienced travelers will help you prepare and add to your enjoyment. The more you know about an area, the more you can seek out its rewards—the best views, camping spots, and trails—and avoid its hazards—dangerous stream crossings, impassable trails, or unwanted human intrusion such as roads or new development.

How far to go will depend upon many factors, such as the steepness of the terrain, the weather, the weight of your pack, and the pace of your slowest companion. If the snow is either slush or deep powder, you can expect tough going. If the snow has settled or is firm and wind-packed, you will be able to pick up the pace. In New Hampshire's White Mountains, covering five miles might make for an exhausting day. In a valley or on a lake or river, you may well cover that distance in a couple of hours. Beginners should start with short trips over easy terrain.

Because you will heat up while climbing and cool down while descending or when standing in camp, adjusting your clothing to suit the needs of the moment will be critical. The key to comfort is a system of layers you can add to or subtract from quickly.

A wool hat, wool or synthetic long underwear, wool pants, a wool shirt or sweater, a pile jacket, a down parka with hood, and a waterproof shell are the essential components of a layer system. When in camp on a cold night, you may need to wear all of these items to stay warm. While active you will probably leave the heavy insulating layers in the pack. Keep these layers accessible—when you stop for lunch along the trail, put them on before you start to cool down.

A note of caution: cotton has no place in your winter wardrobe. Experts call it "killer cotton" because the material absorbs moisture and actually conducts cold to your skin.

The layer system applies to hands and feet, too. A warm hand combination includes thin liner gloves worn under wool mittens with waterproof shells. If your hands are too hot, just hike along with the liners until you stop and then add more layers.

Depending upon your method of travel, you will probably be wearing ski boots or insulated shoepacs. Regardless, cold feet are no fun on a winter trip, so make sure that you can fit a liner sock and a thick wool sock comfortably in your boot. Tight boots are iceboxes: they constrict the blood flow to your feet, making it impossible for them to warm up. For a real treat for your feet, bring along a soft pair of polarguard booties to slip into when you get to camp. Never underestimate the simple pleasures.

Whether to ski or snowshoe is really a matter of personal preference. Skis are faster, but snowshoes may be more versatile when the going gets rugged. Unless you are an expert skier able to handle steep descents through the woods while wearing a pack, snowshoes are probably a better choice for most trips in New England.

For overnights you will want a sturdy tent. Domes and pyramids offer the best designs and most efficient use of space, but any summer backpacking tent will do. Some people prefer tarps, which are lighter and easier to carry, but do not offer nearly the warmth and protection of tents.

A sleeping bag with plenty of loft will ensure a good night's sleep. A mummy bag is the best for winter use. Make sure the bag is roomy enough for you to sleep in several layers of clothing, and long enough to keep your boots warm inside (but not on your feet) at the bottom of the bag.

All sleeping bags come with a temperature rating, but use this only as a guideline. While a friend sleeps soundly in a bag rated at -10 degrees Fahrenheit, you may shiver the night away in an identical bag. A hefty three-season bag may suffice if you wear plenty of clothing to bed. If you aren't sure, go with a thicker bag. The extra warmth won't hurt. Always put a thick pad of closed-cell foam under your sleeping bag or the cold ground will suck the warmth right out of you. Keep some food handy to nibble on at night.

Changing into dry long underwear will help you stay warm in the evenings and so will eating well. On a winter camping trip you'll need to consume some 5,000 calories to keep you going all day. Food is fuel, so eat plenty of fats and carbohydrates. Keep your meal preparation simple—one-pot meals are easiest and fastest. Add cheese, nuts, butter, and raisins to your meals for a fuel boost, and don't forget to bring spices for adding a little zip to your creations.

You can cook your meals over a fire or a stove. While you will most likely have a fire for warmth and cheer, bring along a reliable backpacking stove in case of rain or thaw. Become familiar with how to use the stove before you leave on your trip. Starting stoves in cold weather can be tricky. Be sure not to bring a butane stove on a winter trip. Below 32 degrees Fahrenheit, butane is simply not reliable.

As important as eating lots of food, drinking plenty of water is critical in winter. Despite the presence of snow, the winter environment is extremely dry, and breathing the cold, dry air can cause you to become dehydrated much faster than in more moderate temperatures. Also, you lose heat through sweating, perspiration, and even breathing. In order to maintain a comfortable body temperature and avoid dehydration, you must constantly replace this lost moisture. Drink plenty of water every time you stop for a short rest.

Planning a trip takes careful preparation, but for many campers, the winter wilderness is irresistible. There is a quality to the silence, the fresh, trackless snow, and the sense of solitude and space that more than makes up for any hardships.

But winter can be a hard master, and there is no avoiding an apprenticeship as you learn winter's ways. Hopefully you won't repeat my first experience, huddled around a campfire on a January Wyoming night in a place literally named the Freeze-Out Range, dressed in cowboy boots and blue jeans, waiting for the sun to show.

That wasn't fun, but something about the frozen moonlight on the peaks and snowy plains, the yipping coyotes filling the night with song, and the simple fact that I was out there, doing it, kept luring me back. I know it will bring you back, too.

—S. G.

WINTER GEAR

Clothing

Ski boots or insulated pacs
Gaiters
Several pairs of wool socks
Liner socks
Wool or synthetic long
  underwear
Wool or synthetic pants
Wool or synthetic shirt
  or sweater
Synthetic pile jacket
Down parka with hood
Wind- and waterproof
  pants and jacket
Wool or synthetic hat
Glove liners
Wool or synthetic pile mittens
Wind- and waterproof
  mitten shells

Equipment

Backpack
Skis/snowshoes
Ski poles (for skiing and
  snowshoeing)
Sleeping bag
Foam pad
Tent
Stove, fuel, and repair kit
Two pots with lids/pot scrubber
Snow shovel (grain scoops
  work well)
Maps
Compass
Water bottles (wide-mouthed)
Matches/lighter
Bowl/cup/spoon
Flashlight/extra batteries
First aid kit

Personal Items

Camera/film
Sunglasses/sunscreen
Moleskin (for blisters)
Duct tape (for general repairs)
Reading material/journal

Leave No Trace

Leave No Trace, Inc., is a program dedicated to maintaining the integrity of outdoor recreation areas through education and public awareness. Foghorn Press is a proud supporter of this program and its ethics. Here's how you can Leave No Trace:

Plan Ahead and Prepare
- Learn about the regulations and special concerns of the area you are visiting.
- Visit the backcountry in small groups.
- Avoid popular areas during peak-use periods.
- Choose equipment and clothing in subdued colors.
- Pack food in reusable containers.

Travel and Camp with Care
On the trail:
- Stay on designated trails. Walk single file in the middle of the path.
- Do not take shortcuts on switchbacks.
- When traveling cross-country where there are no trails, follow animal trails or spread out your group so no new routes are created. Walk along the most durable surfaces available, such as rock, gravel, dry grasses, or snow.
- Use a map and compass to eliminate the need for rock cairns, tree scars, or ribbons.
- If you encounter pack animals, step to the downhill side of the trail and speak softly to avoid startling them.

At camp:
- Choose an established, legal site that will not be damaged by your stay.
- Restrict activities to areas where vegetation is compacted or absent.
- Keep pollutants out of the water by camping at least 200 feet (about 70 adult steps) from lakes and streams.
- Control pets at all times, or leave them at home with a sitter. Remove dog feces.

Pack It In and Pack It Out
- Take everything you bring into the wild back out with you.
- Protect wildlife and your food by storing rations securely. Pick up all spilled foods.
- Use toilet paper or wipes sparingly; pack them out.
- Inspect your campsite for trash and any evidence of your stay. Pack out all trash— even if it's not yours!

Properly Dispose of What You Can't Pack Out
- If no refuse facility is available, deposit human waste in catholes dug six to eight inches deep at least 200 feet from water, camps, or trails. Cover and disguise the catholes when you're finished.
- To wash yourself or your dishes, carry the water 200 feet from streams or lakes and use small amounts of biodegradable soap. Scatter the strained dishwater.

Keep the Wilderness Wild
- Treat our natural heritage with respect. Leave plants, rocks, and historical artifacts as you found them.
- Good campsites are found, not made. Do not alter a campsite.
- Let nature's sounds prevail; keep loud voices and noises to a minimum.
- Do not build structures or furniture or dig trenches.

Minimize Use and Impact of Fires
- Campfires can have a lasting impact on the backcountry. Always carry a lightweight stove for cooking, and use a candle lantern instead of building a fire whenever possible.
- Where fires are permitted, use established fire rings only.
- Do not scar the natural setting by snapping the branches off live, dead, or downed trees.
- Completely extinguish your campfire and make sure it is cold before departing. Remove all unburned trash from the fire ring and scatter the cold ashes over a large area well away from any camp.

For more information on Leave No Trace Ethics, call 1-800-332-4100.

SAMPLE CAMPING GEAR CHECKLIST

Sleeping Gear

Groundcloth
Tent
Sleeping pad
Sleeping bag
Pillow
Extra blankets

Cooking Utensils

Stove
Fuel
Matches
Cooler
Spatula
Plates
Aluminum foil
Coffee
Forks, knives, and spoons
Cooking Kit
Grill
Charcoal
Water jugs
Can opener
Cups
Salt and pepper
Hot chocolate

Packing and Cleaning Supplies

Cloth towels
Paper towels
Plastic bags (large and small)
Dish soap
Sponge

First Aid

Acetaminophen, ibuprofen, or aspirin, for pain relief
Adhesive tape
Aloe vera–based burn ointment
Antibiotic ointment, for minor cuts and scrapes
Band-Aids, for minor cuts and scrapes
Betadine solution, for disinfection
Elastic bandages, to wrap sprains
Extractor, for snake venom
Gauze pads (extra thick and at least four inches square) or sanitary napkins, to reduce the flow of blood from major wounds
Insect repellent
Moleskin, to treat blisters
Notebook and pencil, to record the details of any accident or injury that might be needed by a physician
Sunscreen (at least SPF 15), to prevent sunburn
Syringe (10cc to 50cc), to flush wounds
Thermometer
Tweezers

Recreational Gear

Binoculars
Books and magazines
Camera and film
Car games for kids
Deck of cards
Field guides
Fishing rod, reel, and tackle box
Journal
Portable stereo and tapes

Miscellaneous

Camp chairs
Daypack
Flashlight
Lantern
Mosquito-net tent
Portable table
Propane heater
Compass
Firewood
Extra batteries
Maps

Resource Guide

Maine

Acadia National Park, Bar Harbor, ME 04609; (207) 288-3338.

Baxter State Park Authority, 64 Balsam Drive, Millinocket, ME 04462; (207) 723-5140.

Maine Appalachian Trail Club, P.O. Box 283, Augusta, ME 04330

Maine Bureau of Parks and Lands, 22 State House Station, Augusta, ME 04333; (207) 287-3821.

Maine Campground Owners Association (MECOA), 655 Main Street, Lewiston, ME 04240; (207) 782-5874.

North Maine Woods, P.O. Box 421, Ashland, ME 04732; (207) 435-6213.

White Mountain National Forest, Evans Notch Ranger District, Bethel, ME 04217; (207) 824-2134.

New Hampshire

The Appalachian Mountain Club, 5 Joy Street, Boston, MA 02108. For reservations, contact P.O. Box 298, Gorham, NH 03581; (603) 466-2727.

Hanover Chamber of Commerce, Hanover, NH 03755; (603) 643-3115.

The Lakes Region Association, P.O. Box 589, Center Harbor, NH 03226; (603) 253-8555.

Monadnock Travel Council, Keene, NH 03431; (603) 352-1308 or (800) 432-7864.

Mount Washington Valley Chamber of Commerce, North Conway, NH 03860; (603) 356-3171 or (800) 367-3364.

New Hampshire Division of Parks and Recreation, 172 Pembroke Road, P.O. Box 856, Concord, NH 03302-0856; (603) 271-3254.

New Hampshire Fish and Game Department, Two Hazen Drive, Concord, NH 03301; (603) 271-3421.

North Country Chamber of Commerce, Colebrook, NH 03576; (603) 237-8939.

Office of Travel and Tourism Development, P.O. Box 1856, Concord, NH 03302-1856; (603) 271-2343.

Seacoast Council on Tourism, 235 West Road, Suite 10, Portsmouth, NH 03801-5600; (603) 436-7678 or (800) 221-5623.

Southern New Hampshire Convention and Visitors Bureau, Windham, NH 03087; (603) 635-9000 or (800) 932-4CVB.

White Mountain National Forest, P.O. Box 638, Laconia, NH 03274; (603) 528-8721.

Vermont

Addison County Chamber of Commerce, 2 Court Street, Middlebury, VT 05753; (802) 388-7951.

Appalachian Trail Conference, P.O. Box 807, Harper's Ferry, WV 25425; (304) 535-6331.

Central Vermont Chamber of Commerce, P.O. Box 336, Barre, VT 05641; (802) 229-4619.

Fall Foliage Hot Line (early September through late October): (802) 828-3239.

Green Mountain Club, Route 100, RR 1, Box 650, Waterbury, VT 05677; (802) 244-7037.

Green Mountain National Forest, 231 North Main Street, P.O. Box 519, Rutland, VT 05701; (802) 747-6700.

Lake Champlain Regional Chamber of Commerce, 60 Main Street, Suite 100, Burlington, VT 05401; (802) 863-3489.

Northeast Kingdom Travel and Tourism Association, 30 Western Avenue, St. Johnsbury, VT 05819; (800) 639-6379.

Smuggler's Notch Area Chamber of Commerce, P.O. Box 364, Jeffersonville, VT 05464; (802) 644-2239.

Vermont Department of Fish and Wildlife, 103 South Main Street, Waterbury, VT 05671; (802) 241-3700.

Vermont Department of Forests, Parks, and Recreation, Division of State Parks, 103 South Main Street, Waterbury, VT 05671; (802) 241-3655.

Vermont Department of Travel and Tourism, 134 State Street, Montpelier, VT 05602; (802) 828-3236.

Massachusetts

Berkshire Hills Visitors Bureau, Berkshire Common Plaza Level, Pittsfield, MA 01201; (413) 443-9186 or (800) 237-5747.

Bristol County Convention and Visitors Bureau, 70 North Second Street, P.O. Box 976, New Bedford, MA 02741; (508) 997-1250 or (800) 288-6263.

Cape Cod Chamber of Commerce, Hyannis, MA 02601; (508) 362-3225.

Fall Foliage Hot Line (early September through late October): (800) 632-8038.

Franklin County Chamber of Commerce, 395 Main Street, Greenfield, MA 01301; (413) 773-5463.

Greater Boston Convention and Visitors Bureau, Prudential Tower, Suite 400, Box 490, Boston, MA 02199; (800) 888-5515.

Greater Merrimack Valley Convention and Visitors Bureau, 18 Palmer Street, Suite 200, Lowell, MA 01852-1818; (800) 443-3332.

Martha's Vineyard Chamber of Commerce, P.O. Box 1698, Vineyard Haven, MA 02568; (508) 693-0085.

Massachusetts Association of Campground Owners, P.O. Box 548, Scituate, MA 02066; (617) 544-3457.

Massachusetts Division of Fisheries and Wildlife, 1 Rabbit Hill Road, Westboro, MA 01581; (508) 792-7270.

Massachusetts Office of Travel and Tourism, 100 Cambridge Street, 13th Floor, Boston, MA 02202; (617) 727-3201.

Mohawk Trail Association, Box 722, Charlemont, MA 01339; (413) 664-6256.

Office of Environmental Management, Division of Forests and Parks, 100 Cambridge Street, 19th Floor, Boston, MA 02202; (617) 727-3180.

Plymouth County Development Council, P.O. Box 1620, Pembroke, MA 02359; (800) 231-1620.

Rhode Island

Rhode Island Division of Tourism, 1 West Exchange Street, Providence, RI 02903; (800) 556-2484.

Connecticut

Bureau of Outdoor Recreation, Connecticut Department of Environmental Protection, 79 Elm Street, Hartford, CT 06106-5127; (860) 424-3200. Division of Wildlife, (860) 424-3011; Fisheries Division, (860) 424-FISH/3474.

Connecticut Campground Owners Association, P.O. Box 27, Hartford, CT 06141-0027; (860) 521-4704.

Connecticut Department of Economic and Community Development, Tourism Division, 865 Brook Street, Rocky Hill, CT 06067-3405; (860) 258-4355.

Connecticut's Mystic & More, Southeastern Connecticut Tourism District, 470 Bank Street, New London, CT 06320; (860) 444-2206.

Housatonic Valley Tourism District, P.O. Box 406, 46 Main Street, Danbury, CT 06810; (203) 743-0546.

Litchfield Hills Travel Council, P.O. Box 968, Litchfield, CT 06759; (860) 567-4506.

Northeast Connecticut Visitor's District, P.O. Box 598, Putnam, CT 06260; (860) 928-1228.

Maine

Activity Symbols

Biking	Boating	Canoeing/ Rafting	Cross-Country Skiing	Fishing
Golf	Hiking	Historical Sites	Horseback Riding	Hunting	Sea Kayaking
Snowmobiling	Snowshoeing	Swimming	RV Sites	Wheelchair Access

Scenic Rating

1 2 3 4 5 6 7 8 9 10

Poor .... Fair .... Great

Northern Maine

Adjoining Maps: South: Southern Maine .... *page 33*

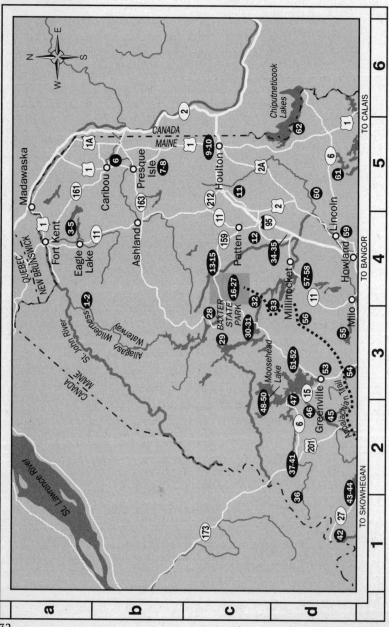

Southern Maine

Adjoining Maps: North: Northern Maine .... *page* 32
West: New Hampshire .... *pages* 168-169

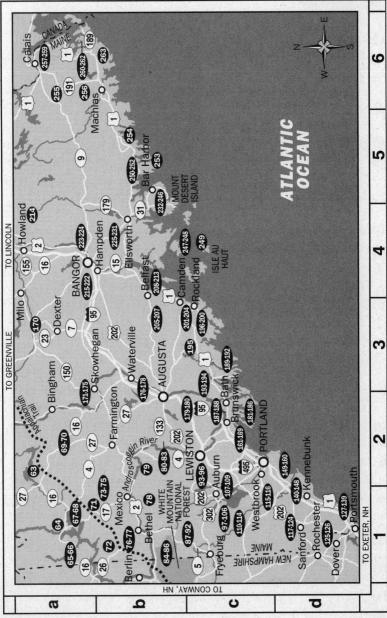

Maine features:

❶ Allagash Wilderness Waterway

Location: Along the Allagash River; Northern Maine map page 32, grid a4.

Campsites, facilities: There are 80 primitive tent sites along this section of the waterway. Each site has a pit toilet, a fire ring and grate, and a picnic table. Pets are allowed.

Reservations, fees: Sites are available on a first-come, first-served basis. The fee is $4 a night per person.

Contact: Maine Bureau of Parks and Lands, 22 State House Station, Augusta, ME 04333; (207) 287-3821.

Directions: The 100-mile-long Allagash Wilderness Waterway flows from Telos Lake in the south to near Allagash Village in the north.

Trip notes: Northern Maine is a canoe camper's paradise, and the Allagash Wilderness Waterway flows right through the heart of it. With miles of undeveloped wildlands and several enormous wilderness lakes to paddle through, canoe tripping just doesn't get any better than this. The watershed of the Allagash River and the nearby St. John River is the largest uninhabited region in the lower 48 states, so if you are looking for solitude, you've found the right place. Taking a side trip up Allagash Stream to mountain-rimmed Allagash Lake is highly recommended. And there's a wonderful nine-mile stretch of moderate white water below the ranger station at Churchill Dam. Cast a line for togue in the bigger lakes or fly-fish for trout along the riverbank, always keeping your eyes open for moose. In the winter, a few hardy wilderness travelers who don't mind deep snow and fierce cold venture out to these parts.

No matter when you come to explore the Allagash Wilderness Waterway, remember to plan ahead, as supplies and services are unavailable.

Open: Year-round.

❷ Deboullie Management Unit

Location: South of St. Francis; Northern Maine map page 32, grid a4.

Campsites, facilities: There are 13 primitive tent sites located on the lakes and streams encompassed by the management unit. Picnic tables, fire rings, and pit toilets are provided. Several of the lakes have boat ramps. Pets are allowed.

Reservations, fees: Sites are available on a first-come, first-served basis. There is no fee.

Contact: Maine Bureau of Parks and Lands, 22 State House Station, Augusta, ME 04333; (207) 287-3821.

Directions: From Fort Kent on the northern border of Maine, drive west on Route 161 to St. Francis. At the paper company checkpoint, head south on one of the logging roads for approximately 10 miles to access the management unit.

Trip notes: This remote slice of Maine is extraordinarily beautiful, a land graced with forests, lakes, and rolling hills. Unsullied and little-visited, the Deboullie Management Unit is a fine example of what the heart of the Maine Woods can offer those intrepid souls willing to venture far off the beaten path. The rewards, in terms of solitude and superior wilderness recreation, are many. With access to lakes and streams, campers can paddle around in a canoe or boat or take a refreshing dip. And for anglers looking for a place to cast out a line, the native brook trout fishery is exceptional. To gain some perspective on the land, hit the hiking trail that leads to the fire tower atop Deboullie Mountain.

Open: Year-round.

❸ Birch Haven Campground

Location: On Eagle Lake, south of the hamlet of Soldier Pond; Northern Maine map page 32, grid a4.

Campsites, facilities: There are 80 sites for tents and RVs, many with full hookups and the remainder with water and electric. Facilities include picnic tables, fireplaces, flush toilets, hot showers, a general store, laundry, and a dump station. For recreation there's a swimming beach, boat dock, canoe and paddleboat rentals, a basketball court, horseshoe pit, sports field, volleyball, an arcade, and a pool table. Leashed pets are permitted.

Reservations, fees: Reservations are accepted. Sites are $15 to $20 a night.

Contact: Ron and Jacky Roy, Birch Haven Campground, Sly Brook Road, Soldier Pond, ME 04781; (207) 444-5102.

Directions: From Fort Kent on the northern border of Maine, drive south on Route 11 and turn left at the hamlet of Soldier Pond. After crossing the Fish River, turn right on Sly Brook Road and travel approximately five miles south to the campground.

Trip notes: Life at Birch Haven Campground—located on the long, narrow, and largely undeveloped Eagle Lake—revolves around the waterfront, making this a good choice for campers who enjoy swimming, fishing, and boating. The lake empties into the Fish River, which meanders north to Fort Kent then joins the St. John River before flowing into Canada. The fishing here

is excellent, as these waters are teeming with trout, salmon, smelt, and togue, and you'll certainly find many spots where you can try your luck.

Open: Memorial Day through Labor Day.

❹ Eagle Lake Management Unit

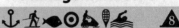

Location: Near the small town of Eagle Lake; Northern Maine map page 32, grid a4.

Campsites, facilities: There are nine primitive tent sites set along the shores of Eagle Lake and nearby Square Lake. Picnic tables, fire rings, and pit toilets are provided. Pets are allowed.

Reservations, fees: Sites are available on a first-come, first-served basis. There is no fee.

Contact: Maine Bureau of Parks and Lands, 22 State House Station, Augusta, ME 04333; (207) 287-3821.

Directions: From Fort Kent on the northern border of Maine, drive south on Route 11 and turn left at the hamlet of Soldier Pond. After crossing the Fish River, turn right on Sly Brook Road and travel approximately six miles south to the management unit. You can also access the area by boat from the hamlet of Eagle Lake.

Trip notes: The Eagle Lake Management Unit encompasses some 23,000 acres of northern woods and waters, including most of Eagle Lake. In addition, the land abuts Square Lake, another large freshwater pond connected to Eagle Lake by a small stream, or "thoroughfare," as such connecting waterways are commonly called in Maine. As is the case with most of the state's management units, Eagle Lake is used primarily by hunters and anglers during the spring and autumn months.

Open: Year-round.

❺ Winterville Lakeview Camps

Location: On St. Froid Lake in Winterville; Northern Maine map page 32, grid a4.

Campsites, facilities: There are 16 sites for tents and RVs with partial hookups. Facilities include a boat dock, playground, and horseshoe pit. Pets are allowed.

Reservations, fees: Reservations are not necessary. Sites are $12 to $14 a night.

Contact: The Hagenmillers, Winterville Lakeview Camps, Route 11, P.O. Box 397, Eagle Lake, ME 04739; (207) 444-4581.

Directions: From Fort Kent, drive south on Route 11 to the hamlet of Eagle Lake, then continue south for another 2.5 miles. At the campground sign, turn right onto a private dirt road and travel half a mile west.

Trip notes: Set alongside St. Froid Lake, the Winterville campground caters to the outdoorsmen and women who flock to this part of northern Maine to fish for trout, salmon, and togue in the summer; hunt deer, bear, moose, and grouse in the fall; and go snowmobiling, snowshoeing, cross-country skiing, or ice fishing in the winter. The lake itself is crystal clear, with many sheltered coves and inlets, and is surrounded by hundreds of square miles of woodlands for hiking.

Open: Year-round.

❻ Arndt's Aroostook River Lodge and Campground

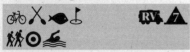

Location: On the Aroostook River near the town of Presque Isle; Northern Maine map page 32, grid b5.

Campsites, facilities: There are 55 sites for RVs, most with water and electric hookups and some without hookups, plus 20 tent sites. Facilities include a store, laundry machines, flush toilets, free hot showers, and a dump station. You'll also find a rec hall, in-ground swimming pool, canoe and bike rentals, basketball and badminton courts, a sports field, and hiking and mountain biking trails on the property. Leashed pets are permitted.

Reservations, fees: Reservations are recommended. To reserve, you must stay at least two nights and make a deposit of up to 50 percent of the list rate. Sites are $14 to $22 a night.

Contact: Clare and Ken Arndt, Arndt's Aroostook River Lodge and Campground, 95 Parkhurst Siding Road, Route 205, Presque Isle, ME 04769; (207) 764-8677.

Directions: From the junction of Route 167 and U.S. 1 in Presque Isle, drive three miles east on Route 167 to the intersection with Route 205. Turn left (north) on Route 205 and drive less than a mile to the campground.

Trip notes: From your campsite at Arndt's River Lodge and Campground, you'll be perched on a hillside overlooking the pretty Aroostook River. The campground provides good access to the water for swimming, fishing, and canoeing enthusiasts. And for mountain bikers, the Vicious Cycle bike shop in Presque Isle rents mountain bikes for use on local trails and logging roads as well as on the biking and hiking trail system on the property.

Arndt's is located just outside of downtown Presque Isle and pretty close to the Maine–New Brunswick border. For more information on the surrounding area, see the trip notes for Aroostook State Park (campground number 7).

Open: May 15 through October 15.

➐ Aroostook State Park

Location: On Echo Lake, south of Presque Isle; Northern Maine map page 32, grid b5.

Campsites, facilities: There are 30 sites for tents or RVs up to 24 feet in length. Non-flush toilets, fire grills, and picnic tables are provided. On the waterfront, you'll find a boat ramp, canoe rentals, and a swimming area with a lifeguard on duty. Leashed pets are permitted.

Reservations, fees: Reservations are accepted, although the State of Maine does allocate some sites on a first-come, first-served basis. Contact the Maine Bureau of Parks and Lands at the number below. Sites are $8 a night for Maine residents and $10 a night for nonresidents.

Contact: Aroostook State Park Ranger, (207) 768-8341. Maine Bureau of Parks and Lands, 22 State House Station, Augusta, ME 04333; (207) 287-3821.

Directions: From the junction of Route 163 and U.S. 1 in Presque Isle, drive 3.75 miles south on U.S. 1, then turn right on Spragueville Road and drive two miles west to the park entrance.

Trip notes: The quiet, wooded campground at Aroostook State Park is nestled at the base of a small mountain range in Maine's northernmost county, which also happens to be the largest county east of the Mississippi River. Aroostook County is the heart of the state's potato-growing region, in addition to being a heavily forested area. Sparsely populated, the county retains a strong frontier flavor. It was settled largely by French Canadians, and the French influence is still pervasive: conversations in local establishments are as likely to be spoken in French as in English. Campers at the state park may spend time swimming or fishing in Echo Lake or hiking the trail to the sum-

mit of nearby Quaggy Joe Mountain. The campground also puts you close to Presque Isle, the largest community in the county, and just minutes from the New Brunswick border.

Open: May 15 through October 15.

➑ Neil E. Michaud Campground

Location: On the southern outskirts of Presque Isle; Northern Maine map page 32, grid b5.

Campsites, facilities: There are 45 sites for tents and RVs, six with full hookups and 39 with water and electric. Flush toilets, hot showers, picnic tables, fireplaces, laundry facilities, a dump station, and a store are provided, as are a rec room, basketball and volleyball courts, and a playground. Leashed pets are permitted.

Reservations, fees: Reservations are not necessary. Sites are $15 to $17 a night.

Contact: Bob and Barb Kinney, Neil E. Michaud Campground, 164 Houlton Road, Presque Isle, ME 04769; (207) 769-1951.

Directions: From Presque Isle, drive south on U.S. 1 for 2.5 miles to the campground on the left (east) side of the road.

Trip notes: Located just outside the town of Presque Isle, this campground puts you within minutes of plenty of places where you can fish, swim, canoe, and boat. A popular hike to the summit of nearby Quaggy Joe Mountain leaves from nearby Aroostook State Park. In the fall, make this your base camp for hunting excursions, as you try to bag bear, moose, deer, duck, and grouse. In the winter, the area is crisscrossed with hundreds of miles of snowmobile trails. Cross-country skiing and snowshoeing are other popular pursuits. For more information on the area, see the trip notes for Aroostook State Park (campground number 7).

Open: Year-round.

---

❾ Wilde Pines Campground

Location: In Monticello; Northern Maine map page 32, grid c5.

Campsites, facilities: There are 88 sites for tents and RVs with full, partial, and no hookups. Flush toilets, hot showers, laundry facilities, tables, fireplaces, a dump station, and a store are provided. There's also a rec room and pool. Leashed pets are permitted.

Reservations, fees: Reservations are accepted. Sites are $14 to $17.50 a night.

Contact: Jack and Angela Wilde, Wilde Pines Campground, Lake Road, Monticello, ME 04760; (207) 538-9004.

Directions: From Houlton, drive north on U.S 1 for 12 miles, then turn left on Gentle Road. At the road's end, take Hill Siding Road north for less than a mile, then drive two miles west on Lake Road.

Trip notes: A new campground just north of Houlton, Wilde Pines is set in a plantation of tall, mature red pine trees. The place is so new, in fact, it's still under construction, and definitely does not have a rustic, worn-in feeling. However, don't let that deter you, for the owners are friendly and obliging and you'll have easy access to the various streams and ponds of the region where you can cast out a fishing line.

Open: Early May through October.

---

❿ My Brother's Place

Location: In Houlton near the New Brunswick border; Northern Maine map page 32, grid c5.

Campsites, facilities: There are 100 sites for tents and RVs, 40 with full hookups, 40 with water and electric, and 20 with none. Flush toilets, hot showers, picnic tables, fireplaces, laundry facilities, and a dump station are provided. Amenities also include a pond for swimming, boating, and fishing; a rec room and playground; and basketball, volleyball, and horseshoes. Leashed pets are permitted.

Reservations, fees: Reservations are recommended. Sites are $11.50 to $15.50 a night.

Contact: Art and Sally Nickel, My Brother's Place, RR 3, Box 650, Houlton, ME 04730; (207) 532-6739.

Directions: From Houlton, drive two miles north on U.S 1 to the campground on the right (east) side of the road.

Trip notes: My Brother's Place is a small, quiet retreat set on open, well-maintained fields just off the county's major north-south highway. Although the campground is not a resort in its own right and there are few activities available at the campground, you will have access to a small pond where you can toss out a fishing line, swim, or paddle around in a canoe. This is a good place to stay if you are on your way to or from Canada, as the line separating us from our northern neighbor is only four miles away.

Open: May 15 through October 15.

⓫ Birch Point Campground

Location: On Pleasant Lake, north of the town of Island Falls; Northern Maine map page 32, grid c5.

Campsites, facilities: There are 65 sites for tents and RVs, some with full hookups including cable TV and the rest with water and electric hookups. Eight housekeeping cottages equipped with hot showers, kitchenettes, and cable TV are also available. Facilities include laundry, hot showers, flush toilets, a store, and a dump station. A boat ramp, a rec room, and volleyball, basketball, and horseshoe courts are on the property as well. Canoes, paddleboats, and motorboats are available for rent. Leashed pets are permitted.

Reservations, fees: Reservations are recommended and require a 50 percent deposit. Sites are $16 to $18.25 a night, plus $1 per pet.

Contact: Steve and Joey Edwards, Birch Point Campground, P.O. Box 120, Pleasant Lake, Island Falls, ME 04747; (207) 463-2515.

Directions: From Island Falls, drive east on Route 159 for half a mile, then go three miles northeast on U.S. 2. Turn right on Pleasant Lake Road and travel 1.5 miles east to the campground.

Trip notes: Sites at Birch Point line the shore of Pleasant Lake, a large, undeveloped body of water rimmed by forest. The campground waterfront is the park's most attractive feature, and the view over the lake to the woods along the far shore is expansive. Fishing, boating, canoeing, and swimming are the main activities enjoyed by summer campers. In the fall, the campground is open for bear, deer, moose, duck, and grouse hunting.

Open: May 1 through October 31, but cottages can be rented year-round.

---

⑫ Wassataquoik Management Unit

Location: Along Wassataquoik Stream; Northern Maine map page 32, grid c4.

Campsites, facilities: There are two primitive campsites with pit toilets. Pets are permitted.

Reservations, fees: Reservations are not accepted, and the sites are available on a first-come, first-served basis. There is no fee.

Contact: Maine Bureau of Parks and Lands, 22 State House Station, Augusta, ME 04333; (207) 287-3821.

Directions: From Patten, drive south on Route 11 to Stacyville. Continue approximately six miles west on logging roads to the management unit.

Trip notes: The small preserve incorporates several miles of scenic shoreline along the splendid East Branch of the Penobscot River as well as Wassataquoik Stream, which flows through the forest down from the heights along the eastern border of Baxter State Park. Though there's no formal trail system here, the woods are a lovely place to walk.

Open: Year-round.

---

⑬ Shin Pond Village

Location: North of Patten; Northern Maine map page 32, grid c4.

Campsites, facilities: There are 25 sites for tents and RVs, 13 with water and electric hookups and 12 with no hookups. Flush toilets, hot showers, picnic tables, fireplaces, a dump station, and laundry facilities are provided. You'll also find a playground, a TV room, and a store with a snack bar. Canoes are available for rent. Leashed pets are permitted.

Reservations, fees: Reservations are accepted and require a 50 percent deposit. Sites are $14 to $18 a night.

Contact: Craig and Terry Hill, Shin Pond Village, RR 1, Box 280, Patten, ME 04765; (207) 528-2900.

Directions: From Patten, drive west on Route 159 for 10 miles to the campground.

Trip notes: Shin Pond Village is an ideal getaway for folks seeking a choice of accommodations. You can pitch a tent or pull up in an RV at one of the large and uncrowded campsites, rent an 80-year-old log cabin with modern furnishings, or bed down in a guest room at the lodge. Both Upper and Lower Shin Ponds offer excellent trout and salmon fishing, and Baxter State Park—home to many other lakes, rivers, and streams—is only minutes away. Like numerous other camps in northern New England, Shin Pond caters to hunters in search of deer, moose, bear, and grouse in the fall, and lures ice fishers, skiers, and snowmobilers in the winter. Hundreds of miles of groomed snowmobile trails leave from the campground.

Open: Year-round.

⓮ Scraggly Lake Management Unit

Location: Northeast of Baxter State Park; Northern Maine map page 32, grid c4.

Campsites, facilities: There are five primitive tent sites along the shore of Scraggly Lake. Each site has a picnic table, fire ring, and pit toilet. There's also a boat ramp. Pets are permitted.

Reservations, fees: Reservations are not accepted, and the sites are available on a first-come, first-served basis. There is no fee.

Contact: Maine Bureau of Parks and Lands, 22 State House Station, Augusta, ME 04333; (207) 287-3821.

Directions: From Patten, drive 10 miles northwest on Route 159 to Shin Pond, then continue about 18 miles north of Shin Pond on logging roads to access the unit.

Trip notes: Scraggly Lake is the center-

piece of this 10,000-acre public landholding in the North Woods. Characterized by rolling hills, heavily forested terrain, and numerous lakes, ponds, brooks, and bogs, the area provides excellent habitat for more than 200 species of wildlife, while the lakes and ponds are home to healthy populations of trout and salmon. This is a very remote region, so be sure to bring adequate supplies of food, gasoline, spare tires, and emergency equipment, especially in winter. No supplies are available in the vicinity.

Open: Year-round.

⓯ Matagamon Wilderness Campground

Location: Northwest of Patten; Northern Maine map page 32, grid c4.

Campsites, facilities: There are 36 sites for tents and RVs, all without hookups. Pit toilets, hot showers, picnic tables, fire rings, a dump station, boat ramp, and store are provided. Motorboats and canoes may be rented. Heated cabins are also available. Leashed pets are permitted.

Reservations, fees: Reservations are recommended. Payment in full is required for one or two nights; for stays of three or more nights, a $20 deposit is required. Sites are $12 a night.

Contact: Matagamon Wilderness Campground, Box 220, Patten, ME 04765; (207) 528-2448.

Directions: From the junction of Routes 11 and 159 in Patten, travel northwest on Route 159 for 24 miles to the campground.

Trip notes: These remote, wooded sites offer campers a sense of privacy. Situated on the East Branch of the Penobscot River just outside the northern entrance to Baxter State Park and immediately south of

Grand Lake Matagamon, the campground is ideally located for anyone who loves the outdoors. From here, summer visitors have easy access to river and lake water for fishing, canoeing, and swimming. Other local activities include hiking in the remote northern portion of Baxter State Park and exploring the miles of waterways accessible from the campground by canoe. In the fall, this is a popular spot for deer, bear, grouse, and moose hunters. And in the winter, more than 100 miles of groomed trails for snowmobilers and cross-country skiers await hardy souls. If you are feeling more sedentary, go ice fishing in one of the nearby lakes.

Open: Year-round; fully operational May 1 through November 1.

⑯ Trout Brook Farm Campground

Location: In Baxter State Park; Northern Maine map page 32, grid c4.

Campsites, facilities: This group camping area holds 18 tent sites. Picnic tables, fire rings, and pit toilets are provided. No vehicle larger than 9 feet high, 7 feet wide, and 22 feet long may enter Baxter State Park. Pets are not allowed in the park.

Reservations, fees: Reservations are strongly recommended and may be made either by mail or in person. The full fee must accompany reservations made by mail. Sites are $6 a night per person, with a minimum fee of $12 per site.

Contact: Baxter State Park, 64 Balsam Drive, Millinocket, ME 04462-2190; (207) 723-5140.

Directions: From the intersection of Routes 11 and 159 in Patten, travel northwest on Route 159 for 24 miles to the

Matagamon Gatehouse. Continue approximately two miles west on Perimeter Road to the campground. There is an $8 road-use fee for out-of-state vehicles.

Trip notes: The park's northernmost campground is situated, not surprisingly, along Trout Brook, a lovely stream that flows into Grand Lake Matagamon, where fishers can try to catch brook trout, togue, and salmon. Behind the campground looms Trout Brook Mountain. The Freezeout Trail, a beautiful long-distance hiking route, leaves from the campground. For more information on Baxter State Park, see Abol Campground (campground number 27).

Open: May 15 through October 15 and December 1 through April 1.

⑰ South Branch Pond Campground

Location: In Baxter State Park; Northern Maine map page 32, grid c4.

Campsites, facilities: There are 12 lean-tos, each of which can accommodate up to four people, a bunkhouse with a six-person capacity, and 21 tent sites. Picnic tables, fire rings, and pit toilets are provided. No vehicle larger than 9 feet high, 7 feet wide, and 22 feet long may enter Baxter State Park. Pets are not allowed in the park.

Reservations, fees: Reservations are strongly recommended and may be made either by mail or in person. The full fee must accompany reservations made by mail. Tent sites and lean-tos are $6 a night per person, with a minimum fee of $12 per site. The bunkhouse costs $7 per person.

Contact: Baxter State Park, 64 Balsam Drive, Millinocket, ME 04462-2190; (207) 723-5140.

Directions: From the intersection of

Routes 11 and 159 in Patten, travel northwest on Route 159 for 24 miles to the Matagamon Gatehouse. Continue nine miles west on Perimeter Road. There is an $8 road-use fee for out-of-state vehicles.

Trip notes: South Branch Pond is a large campground situated at the tip of a long, narrow lake nestled in a cleft between high mountains. The scenery is absolutely sensational. Trails to the surrounding heights fan out in all directions from the campground. If you prefer to paddle, you can rent a canoe right here. For more information on Baxter State Park, see the trip notes for Abol Campground (campground number 27).

Open: May 15 through October 15 and December 1 through April 1.

---

⑱ Russell Pond Campground

Location: In Baxter State Park; Northern Maine map page 32, grid c4.

Campsites, facilities: There are two lean-tos for up to four people each, one lean-to with a six-person capacity, one lean-to with an eight-person capacity, a bunkhouse for up to 13 people, and four tent sites. Picnic tables, fire rings, and pit toilets are provided. No vehicle larger than 9 feet high, 7 feet wide, and 22 feet long may enter Baxter State Park. Pets are not allowed.

Reservations, fees: Reservations are strongly recommended and may be made either by mail or in person. The full fee must accompany reservations made by mail. Tent sites and lean-tos are $6 a night per person, with a minimum fee of $12 per site. The bunkhouse costs $7 per person.

Contact: Baxter State Park, 64 Balsam Drive, Millinocket, ME 04462-2190; (207) 723-5140.

Directions: From the junction of Route 11/157 and the Baxter State Park Road in Millinocket, drive 18 miles west on the Baxter State Park Road to the Togue Pond Gatehouse. Continue approximately eight miles north on the Roaring Brook Road to the parking lot at Roaring Brook Campground, then hike seven miles north on the Russell Pond Trail to the campground. There is an $8 road-use fee for out-of-state vehicles.

Trip notes: In the very heart of Baxter State Park there's a hike-in campground at Russell Pond, a worthy destination for the adventurous traveler seeking an-off-the-beaten-path experience. North of the highest peaks surrounding Katahdin, Russell Pond sits nestled among low mountains. Trails that ascend the surrounding heights radiate in all directions from the campground. For more information on Baxter State Park, see the trip notes for Abol Campground (campground number 27).

Open: May 15 through October 15 and December 1 through April 1.

---

⑲ Nesowadnehunk Field Campground

Location: In Baxter State Park; Northern Maine map page 32, grid c4.

Campsites, facilities: There are 10 lean-tos that can accommodate up to four people each, one lean-to with a three-person capacity, and 12 tent sites. Picnic tables, fire rings, and pit toilets are provided. No vehicle larger than 9 feet high, 7 feet wide, and 22 feet long may enter Baxter State Park. Pets are not allowed in the park.

Reservations, fees: Reservations are strongly recommended and may be made either by mail or in person. The full fee must accompany reservations made by mail. Tent sites and lean-tos are $6 a night per person, with a minimum fee of $12 per site.

Contact: Baxter State Park, 64 Balsam Drive, Millinocket, ME 04462-2190; (207) 723-5140.

Directions: From the junction of Route 11/157 and the Baxter State Park Road in Millinocket, drive 18 miles west on the Baxter State Park Road to the Togue Pond Gatehouse. Continue about 17 miles west of the park entrance on the Perimeter Road to the campground. There is an $8 road-use fee for out-of-state vehicles.

Trip notes: Nesowadnehunk, pronounced by locals as "Sow-Dee-Hunk," is a large group campsite in a grassy, open area surrounded on all sides by strikingly beautiful scenery. Especially noteworthy are the views to the east toward Katahdin. Campers can swim and fish in Nesowadnehunk Stream, as well as in nearby lakes, ponds, and rivers. A trail leads south from the campground to the summit of Doubletop Mountain. For more information on Baxter State Park, see the trip notes for Abol Campground (campground number 27).

Open: May 15 through October 15 and December 1 through April 1.

20 Chimney Pond Campground

Location: In Baxter State Park; Northern Maine map page 32, grid c4.

Campsites, facilities: There are nine lean-tos that can accommodate up to four people each and one bunkhouse with a 12-person capacity; there are no tent sites. Pit toilets are provided. No vehicle larger than 9 feet high, 7 feet wide, and 22 feet long may enter Baxter State Park. Pets are not allowed in the park.

Reservations, fees: Reservations are strongly recommended and may be made either by mail or in person. The full fee must accompany reservations made by mail. Lean-tos are $6 a night per person, with a minimum fee of $12 per site. The bunkhouse costs $7 per person.

Contact: Baxter State Park, 64 Balsam Drive, Millinocket, ME 04462-2190; (207) 723-5140.

Directions: From the junction of Route 11/157 and the Baxter State Park Road in Millinocket, drive 18 miles west on the Baxter State Park Road to the Togue Pond Gatehouse. Continue approximately eight miles north on the Roaring Brook Road to the parking lot at Roaring Brook Campground, then hike 3.3 miles to Chimney Pond Campground. There is an $8 road-use fee for out-of-state vehicles.

Trip notes: Chimney Pond is a glacial tarn set amid some of the most spectacular high-mountain scenery in the United States. On all sides of the campground, jagged rocky summits swoop toward the sky. Mountain adventure beckons in all directions, and hikers will find myriad trails that leave from here. For more information on Baxter State Park, see Abol Campground (campground number 27).

Open: May 15 through October 15 and December 1 through April 1.

21 Roaring Brook Campground

 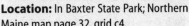

Location: In Baxter State Park; Northern Maine map page 32, grid c4.

Campsites, facilities: There are seven lean-tos that can accommodate four people each, three lean-tos with a three-person capacity, two lean-tos with a six-person capacity, and 10 tent sites. A bunkhouse can hold 12 people. Picnic tables, fire rings, and pit toilets are provided. No vehicle larger than 9 feet high, 7 feet wide, and 22 feet long may enter Baxter State Park. Pets are not allowed in the park.

Reservations, fees: Reservations are strongly recommended and may be made either by mail or in person. The full fee must accompany reservations made by mail. Tent sites and lean-tos are $6 a night per person, with a minimum fee of $12 per site. The bunkhouse costs $7 per person.

Contact: Baxter State Park, 64 Balsam Drive, Millinocket, ME 04462-2190; (207) 723-5140.

Directions: From the junction of Route 11/157 and the Baxter State Park Road in Millinocket, drive 18 miles west on the Baxter State Park Road to the Togue Pond Gatehouse. Continue approximately eight miles north of the park entrance on the Roaring Brook Road to the campground. There is an $8 road-use fee for out-of-state vehicles.

Trip notes: Perched above a tumbling, boulder-filled mountain stream, Roaring Brook is a good spot for hikers who want to get an early start on Katahdin's infamous Knife Edge Trail, a walk along a sharp spine of rock with precipitous drops on either side. This is also a good camp for skiers heading to Chimney Pond from the park entrance. For more information on Baxter State Park, see the trip notes for Abol Campground (campground number 27).

Open: May 15 through October 15 and December 1 through April 1.

㉒ Avalanche Field Campground

Location: In Baxter State Park; Northern Maine map page 32, grid c4.

Campsites, facilities: There are two lean-tos, each with a four-person capacity, and nine tent sites. Picnic tables, fire rings, and pit toilets are provided. No vehicle larger than 9 feet high, 7 feet wide, and 22 feet long may enter Baxter State Park. Pets are not allowed in the park.

Reservations, fees: Reservations are strongly recommended and may be made either by mail or in person. The full fee must accompany reservations made by mail. Tent sites and lean-tos are $6 a night per person, with a minimum fee of $12 per site.

Contact: Baxter State Park, 64 Balsam Drive, Millinocket, ME 04462-2190; (207) 723-5140.

Directions: From the junction of Route 11/157 and the Baxter State Park Road in Millinocket, drive 18 miles west on the Baxter State Park Road to the Togue Pond Gatehouse. Continue approximately six miles north of the park entrance on the Roaring Brook Road. There is an $8 road-use fee for out-of-state vehicles.

Trip notes: This small campsite lies on the eastern side of the Katahdin massif. It's a great place to spend the night before hiking the infamous Knife Edge Trail, a strenuous trek that traces the precipitous rim of Katahdin—not for those who suffer from a fear of heights. For more information on Baxter State Park, see the trip notes for Abol Campground (campground number 27).

Open: May 15 through October 15 and December 1 through April 1.

㉓ Foster Field Campground

Location: In Baxter State Park; Northern Maine map page 32, grid c4.

Campsites, facilities: There are five group tent sites. Picnic tables, fire rings, and pit toilets are provided. No vehicle larger than 9 feet high, 7 feet wide, and 22 feet long may enter Baxter State Park. Pets are not allowed in the park.

Reservations, fees: Reservations are strongly recommended and may be made either by mail or in person. The full fee must accompany reservations made by mail. Tent sites are $6 a night per person, with a minimum fee of $12 per site.

Contact: Baxter State Park, 64 Balsam Drive, Millinocket, ME 04462-2190; (207) 723-5140.

Directions: From the junction of Route 11/157 and the Baxter State Park Road in Millinocket, drive 18 miles west on the Baxter State Park Road to the Togue Pond Gatehouse. Continue approximately 12 miles west of the park entrance on the Perimeter Road until you reach the campground. There is an $8 road-use fee for out-of-state vehicles.

Trip notes: The group tenting area known as Foster Field is well situated for those who want to embark on hikes to some of the less visited peaks near Katahdin. Try following the O-J-I Trail to the summit of Mount O-J-I, or continue on a loop that includes Mount Coe and the Brothers. For more information on Baxter State Park, see Abol Campground (campground number 27).

Open: May 15 through October 15 and December 1 through April 1.

24 Kidney Pond Campground

Location: In Baxter State Park; Northern Maine map page 32, grid c4.

Campsites, facilities: There are five cabins with a two-person capacity, four cabins with a four-person capacity, and two cabins with a three-person capacity. Pit toi-

lets are provided. No vehicle larger than 9 feet high, 7 feet wide, and 22 feet long may enter Baxter State Park. Pets are not allowed in the park.

Reservations, fees: Reservations are strongly recommended and may be made either by mail or in person. The full fee must accompany reservations made by mail. Fees start at $17 a night per person in a small cabin to $50 a night at a larger cabin.

Contact: Baxter State Park, 64 Balsam Drive, Millinocket, ME 04462-2190; (207) 723-5140.

Directions: From the junction of Route 11/157 and the Baxter State Park Road in Millinocket, drive 18 miles west on the Baxter State Park Road to the Togue Pond Gatehouse. Continue approximately 13 miles west of the park entrance. There is an $8 road-use fee for out-of-state vehicles.

Trip notes: Cabins at this old-style North Woods fishing resort overlook Kidney Pond and, in the distance, mile-high Katahdin. A spectacularly pretty, peaceful spot, it combines the best elements of the park: woods, waters, mountains, and wildlife. For more information on Baxter State Park, see Abol Campground (campground number 27).

Open: May 15 through October 15 and December 1 through April 1.

25 Katahdin Stream Campground

Location: In Baxter State Park; Northern Maine map page 32, grid c4.

Campsites, facilities: There are five lean-tos that can accommodate up to four people each, four lean-tos with a five-person capacity, three lean-tos with a three-person capacity, and 10 tent sites. A bunkhouse holds six people. Picnic tables, fire rings, and pit toilets are provided. No vehicle larger than 9 feet high, 7 feet wide, and 22 feet long may enter Baxter State Park. Pets are not allowed in the park.

Reservations, fees: Reservations are strongly recommended and may be made either by mail or in person. The full fee must accompany reservations made by mail. Tent sites and lean-tos are $6 a night per person, with a minimum fee of $12 per site. The bunkhouse costs $7 per person.

Contact: Baxter State Park, 64 Balsam Drive, Millinocket, ME 04462-2190; (207) 723-5140.

Directions: From the junction of Route 11/157 and the Baxter State Park Road in Millinocket, drive 18 miles west on the Baxter State Park Road to the Togue Pond Gatehouse. Continue approximately eight miles west of the park entrance on the Perimeter Road until you reach the campground. There is an $8 road-use fee for out-of-state vehicles.

Trip notes: Katahdin Stream is a popular campground with a prime location alongside its namesake stream at the point where the water pours down the mountainside and through the woods before joining the Penobscot River. Here the final stretch of the Appalachian Trail—called the Hunt Trail at this point—begins to ascend the summit of Katahdin. For more information on Baxter State Park, see Abol Campground (campground number 27).

Open: May 15 through October 15 and December 1 through April 1.

26 Daicey Pond Campground

Location: In Baxter State Park; Northern Maine map page 32, grid c4.

Campsites, facilities: There are two lean-tos for Appalachian Trail hikers, five cabins with a four-person capacity, four cabins with a two-person capacity, and one cabin for up to three people. Pit toilets are provided. No vehicle larger than 9 feet high, 7 feet wide, and 22 feet long may enter Baxter State Park. Pets are not allowed in the park.

Reservations, fees: Reservations are strongly recommended and may be made either by mail or in person. The full fee must accompany any reservation made by mail. Tent sites and lean-tos are $6 a night per person, and there's a minimum fee of $12 per site.

Contact: Baxter State Park, 64 Balsam Drive, Millinocket, ME 04462-2190; (207) 723-5140.

Directions: From the junction of Route 11/157 and the Baxter State Park Road in Millinocket, drive 18 miles west on the Baxter State Park Road to the Togue Pond Gatehouse. Continue approximately 11 miles west to the campground turnoff, then turn left and drive about a mile to Daicey Pond. There is an $8 road-use fee for out-of-state vehicles.

Trip notes: Before Baxter State Park assumed control, these cabins at Daicey Pond were part of a fishing resort, and they still maintain that rustic North Woods camp flavor that so many outdoors lovers have come to appreciate in this part of Maine. While staying in one of the cabins, you'll enjoy views over the spruce- and fir-rimmed lake to the summit of mile-high Katahdin. The park rents canoes at Daicey Pond, and a day spent on these waters fishing for togue under the shadow of the Katahdin massif will not soon be forgotten. For more information on Baxter State Park, see Abol Campground (campground number 27).

Open: May 15 through October 15 and December 1 through April 1.

㉗ Abol Campground

Location: In Baxter State Park; Northern Maine map page 32, grid c4.

Campsites, facilities: There are 12 lean-tos that can accommodate up to four people each, plus nine tent sites. Picnic tables, fire rings, and pit toilets are provided. No vehicle larger than 9 feet high, 7 feet wide, and 22 feet long may enter Baxter State Park. Pets are not allowed in the park.

Reservations, fees: Reservations are strongly recommended and may be made either by mail or in person. The full fee must accompany reservations made by mail. Tent sites and lean-tos are $6 a night per person, with a minimum fee of $12 per site.

Contact: Baxter State Park, 64 Balsam Drive, Millinocket, ME 04462-2190; (207) 723-5140.

Directions: From the junction of Route 11/157 and the Baxter State Park Road in Millinocket, drive 18 miles west on the Baxter State Park Road to the Togue Pond Gatehouse. The campground is approximately six miles west of the park entrance. There is an $8 road-use fee for out-of-state vehicles.

Trip notes: For many people who venture into the interior of Maine, Baxter State Park is the focal point of their travels. Established in 1931, the park is surrounded by timber company landholdings that extend to the Canadian border. The views in any direction from the 5,267-foot summit of Katahdin, Maine's highest peak, are of unbroken forest, rivers, and lakes. More than 170 miles of trails have been blazed throughout the park, allowing visitors to take short day hikes or more extended backpacking trips in the interior. For many Mainers, a trek up the summit of Katahdin is almost a right of passage. Hiking the Knife Edge on Katahdin is not for the faint of heart: this narrow ridge—in places less than one yard wide—is flanked on each side by 2,000-foot precipices. (If you plan to day hike in the park, be sure to pick up the "Day Use Hiking Guide" at park headquarters.) For those who prefer water-based activity, there are numerous lakes, rivers, and streams within park boundaries as well as plentiful opportunities for boating and fishing just outside the park.

You'll find this popular campground at the southern edge of the park. Some of the sites have lean-tos, while others offer simply a place to pitch your tent.

Open: May 15 through October 15 and December 1 through April 1.

㉘ Telos Management Unit

Location: Northwest of Baxter State Park; Northern Maine map page 32, grid c3.

Campsites, facilities: There are three primitive tent sites, each with a picnic table, fire ring, and pit toilet. Pets are permitted.

Reservations, fees: Reservations are not accepted, and sites are available on a first-come, first-served basis. The fee is $4 a night per person.

Contact: Maine Bureau of Parks and Lands, 22 State House Station, Augusta, ME 04333; (207) 287-3821.

Directions: To access the unit, drive 30 miles west from Millinocket on the Golden Road to Ripogenus Dam, then bear right on the Telos Road and head 16 miles north.

Trip notes: A remote region of lakes, forests, and gently rolling hills is home to the Telos Management Unit, where intrepid campers will find a few primitive tent sites and a bounty of recreational offerings, from paddling a canoe on a lazy summer day to strapping on the snowshoes and exploring the surrounding terrain. Telos and Chamberlain Lakes are outstanding fisheries for togue and brook trout. Telos Lake is the most popular starting point for canoeists who plan to travel the Allagash Wilderness Waterway (campground number 1).

Open: Year-round.

㉙ Gero Island Management Unit

Location: West of Baxter State Park on Chesuncook Lake; Northern Maine map page 32, grid c3.

Campsites, facilities: Six primitive campsites are located along the shore of the island and are accessible by canoe. Picnic tables, fire rings, and pit toilets are provided. Pets are permitted.

Reservations, fees: Reservations are not accepted, and the sites are available on a first-come, first-served basis. The fee is $4 a night per person.

Contact: Maine Bureau of Parks and Lands, 22 State House Station, Augusta, ME 04333; (207) 287-3821.

Directions: Access to the unit is gained via water routes connecting Chesuncook Lake, the West Branch of the Penobscot River, and the Allagash Wilderness Waterway. The nearest launch sites are at Chesuncook Dam at the southern end of the lake and at the North Maine Woods campsite on Umbazooksus Stream.

Trip notes: Gero Island is a 3,100-acre island at the northern tip of Chesuncook Lake, a large and undeveloped body of water in the heart of the Maine Woods. The land is used primarily by fishers, hunters, and canoeists retracing Henry David Thoreau's canoe journey down the West

Branch of the Penobscot River. Most of the historic logging village of Chesuncook, on the mainland, is incorporated into this unit as well.

Open: Year-round.

㉚ Frost Pond Camps

Location: On Frost Pond near Ripogenus Lake; Northern Maine map page 32, grid c3.

Campsites, facilities: There are 10 sites for tents and RVs, all without hookups. Eight rustic cabins are also available. Each site has a pit toilet, and some have Adirondack-style shelters. Hot showers, picnic tables, fireplaces, a playground for small children, a boat launch, and short hiking trails are provided. Canoes, motorboats, and rowboats are rented out. The maximum RV length is 18 feet. Leashed pets are permitted.

Reservations, fees: Reservations are recommended. A deposit of one night's fee is required. The Bowater/Great Northern Paper Company requires a special permit for single or combined vehicles measuring 44 feet or longer; for a permit call (207) 723-2106 with registration numbers of all vehicles, as well as arrival and departure dates. Sites are $13 a night.

Contact: Rick and Judy Given, Frost Pond Camps, Box 620, Star Route 76, Greenville, ME 04441; (207) 695-2821 (radio phone at Folsom's seaplane base in Greenville; leave a message between 8:15 A.M. and 5 P.M.). Off-season: Rick and Judy Given, 36 Minuteman Drive, Millinocket, ME 04462; (207) 723-6622.

Directions: From the junction of Route 11/157 and the Baxter State Park Road in Millinocket, drive 9.75 miles northwest on the Baxter State Park Road. At the junction with the Golden Road (the Bowater/Great Northern Paper Company Road), drive north on the Golden Road. After passing

Ripogenus Dam, bear to the right, following signs to Frost Pond Camps, and drive three miles to the campground. Please remember that you are on a private logging road where heavily laden logging trucks have the right-of-way. Be prepared to stop and pull over for trucks.

Trip notes: Frost Pond Camps is located on a beautiful, remote pond surrounded by hundreds of square miles of uninhabited wildlands. This rustic retreat, featuring isolated sites and classic backcountry cabins, is a classic hunting and fishing camp in the heart of the North Woods of Maine. Fish for brook trout in Frost Pond or venture to Chesuncook Lake, the West Branch of the Penobscot River, or any of the numerous nearby rivers or streams to catch salmon, bass, and other species. The Appalachian Trail is a mere five miles away, and Baxter State Park lies within a 50-minute drive. For more information on the area, see the trip notes for the Allagash Gateway Campsite (campground number 31).

Note: Bicycles, motorcycles, and all-terrain vehicles are not permitted on paper company lands and must be left at the gate.

Open: May 1 to November 30.

---

③① Allagash Gateway Campsite

Location: On the shores of Ripogenus Lake; Northern Maine map page 32, grid c3.

Campsites, facilities: There are 15 sites for tents and RVs, some with electric hookups. Flush toilets, hot showers, picnic tables, fireplaces, a playground, a boat ramp, and docks are provided. Canoes are available for rent, and canoe shuttle service can be arranged. No pets are allowed.

Reservations, fees: Reservations are recommended. A $5 deposit is required. The Bowater/Great Northern Paper Company requires a special permit for single or combined vehicles measuring 44 feet or longer; for a permit call (207) 723-2106 with registration numbers of all vehicles, as well as arrival and departure dates. Sites are $8 to $10 a night.

Contact: Bill and Jan Reeves, Allagash Gateway Campsite, Star Route 76, Box 675, Greenville, ME 04441; no telephone. Off-season: Bill and Jan Reeves, Allagash Gateway Campsite, Box 396, Millinocket, ME 04462; (207) 723-9215.

Directions: There are two routes to Allagash Gateway Campsite. From Greenville, travel north on the Lily Bay Road through Lily Bay and Kokadjo for about 44 miles to the campground, which is right before the Ripogenus Dam. Or, from the junction of Route 11/157 and the Baxter State Park Road in Millinocket, travel 9.75 miles northwest on the Baxter State Park Road. At the junction with the Golden Road (the Bowater/Great Northern Paper Company Road), travel north on the Golden Road for 23.5 miles. Please remember that you are on a private logging road where heavily laden logging trucks have the right-of-way. Be prepared to stop and pull over for trucks.

Trip notes: Few campgrounds offer as much for the outdoor enthusiast as Allagash Gateway. Ripogenus Lake connects with 30-mile-long Chesuncook Lake as well as Black Pond, the West Branch of the Penobscot River, and numerous other rivers and streams. Fish these waters for salmon, trout, and perch. Or take a boat ride to Chesuncook Village, now home to four permanent residents but at one time a bustling logging town until the log drives were halted in the early 1970s. Canoe on the lakes and rivers or arrange a shuttle for an extended journey. Hike on the Appalachian Trail and venture into nearby Baxter State

Park. Take a guided rafting trip down the Cribworks, Big Ambejackmockamus Falls, and other rapids on the West Branch of the Penobscot. In the fall, hunt for moose, deer, and bear.

Note: Bicycles, motorcycles, and all-terrain vehicles are not permitted on paper company lands and must be left at the gate.

Open: Ice-out (around mid-May) through November 30.

---

32 Abol Bridge Campground

Location: West of Millinocket near Baxter State Park; Northern Maine map page 32, grid c4.

Campsites, facilities: There are 37 sites for tents and RVs, all without hookups. Flush toilets, hot showers, picnic tables, fire rings, and a limited store are provided. Campers have access to a beach and rental canoes. The owners restrict the use of generators to between noon and 5 P.M. daily. Leashed pets are permitted.

Reservations, fees: Reservations are recommended and require a deposit of one night's fee. The Bowater/Great Northern Paper Company requires a special permit for single or combined vehicles measuring 44 feet or longer; for a permit call (207) 723-2106 with registration numbers of all vehicles as well as arrival and departure dates. There is a $4 fee to enter the paper company's woodlands, where the campground is located. Sites are $13 a night.

Contact: Art and Linda Belmont, Abol Bridge Campground, P.O. Box 536, Millinocket, ME 04462-0536; no phone.

Directions: From the junction of Route 11/157 and the Baxter State Park Road in Millinocket, travel 9.75 miles northwest on the Baxter State Park Road. At the junction

with the Golden Road (the Bowater/Great Northern Paper Company Road), travel north on the Golden Road for 8.2 miles. Please remember that you are on a private logging road where heavily laden logging trucks have the right-of-way. Be prepared to stop and pull over for trucks.

Trip notes: Abol Bridge Campground is located at the confluence of Abol Stream and the West Branch of the Penobscot River, making this an ideal destination for those who enjoy swimming, fishing, and canoeing. Additionally, the views of mile-high Katahdin—Maine's tallest peak—are simply breathtaking. This area is a haven for outdoorsmen and women. Nearby Baxter State Park offers hiking, rock climbing, fishing, and canoeing. More hiking terrain is available on the 2,158-mile-long Appalachian Trail, which you can access south of Baxter State Park.

Note: Bicycles, motorcycles, and all-terrain vehicles are not permitted on paper company lands and must be left at the gate.

Open: May 15 through September 30.

---

33 Nahmakanta Management Unit

Location: South of Baxter State Park; Northern Maine map page 32, grid d3.

Campsites, facilities: There are nine primitive tent sites and one Appalachian Trail lean-to. Each site has a pit toilet and a fire ring. Pets are permitted.

Reservations, fees: Reservations are not accepted, and the sites are available on a first-come, first-served basis. There is no fee.

Contact: Maine Bureau of Parks and Lands, 22 State House Station, Augusta, ME 04333; (207) 287-3821.

Directions: From Millinocket, drive south on Route 11 for about 15 miles. Turn right on the Jo-Mary Road, a logging road, and continue northwest to access the unit. Or, you can enter by hiking in on the Appalachian Trail.

Trip notes: Encompassing more than 43,000 acres, this is the largest management unit in the state's public lands system. It is crossed by the Appalachian Trail, which hugs the south shore of Nahmakanta Lake. Some 56 lakes and ponds also lie within the unit, many of which support native populations of trout and salmon. Nahmakanta and the nearby Debsconeag Lakes area provide a wonderful challenge for experienced backpackers, cross-country skiers, and snowshoers.

Open: Year-round.

③④ Pine Grove Campground and Cottages

Location: In East Millinocket; Northern Maine map page 32, grid d4.

Campsites, facilities: There are 30 sites for tents and RVs with full, partial, and no hookups. Flush toilets, hot showers, picnic tables, fire rings, a dump station, laundry facilities, a playground, a rec hall, horseshoe pits, basketball, hiking trails, and a store are provided. Canoes and cabins are available for rent. Leashed pets are permitted.

Reservations, fees: Reservations are recommended. A deposit of 50 percent of the total amount due is required. Sites are $14 to $17 a night.

Contact: Judy and Charlie Theriault, Pine Grove Campground and Cottages, HCR 86, Box 107B, Medway, ME 04460; (207) 746-5172. Off-season: Judy and Charlie Theriault, 40 Pine Street B, East Millinocket, ME 04430; (207) 746-5105.

Directions: From Interstate 95 in Medway, take exit 56 and travel west on Route

157 for one mile. Turn right on Route 11 and travel north for four miles.

Trip notes: Situated in low, swampy lands along the East Branch of the Penobscot River, Pine Grove is a moist and shady spot, the kind of place where mosquitoes thrive. On the plus side, the river flowing through here is quite beautiful, and the swimming, canoeing, and fishing (for smallmouth bass) is excellent. Also, Pine Grove is just 20 miles or so from the southern entrance gate to Baxter State Park, and is within a short drive of dozens of lakes, rivers, and streams.

Open: May 15 through Columbus Day.

③⑤ Katahdin Shadows Campground

Location: In Medway; Northern Maine map page 32, grid d4.

Campsites, facilities: There are 125 sites for tents and RVs, 17 with full hookups, 81 with water and electric, and 27 with none. Group tenting areas are available. Wheelchair-accessible rest rooms with flush toilets, free hot showers, picnic tables, fireplaces, a dump station, laundry facilities, and a store are provided. For recreation, there is a playground, a rec room, fields, a heated pool, hiking trails, volleyball, and basketball. There's also canoe rentals, guided fishing trips, and float trips. Ice and firewood are available. Leashed pets are permitted.

Reservations, fees: Reservations are not necessary. Sites are $16 to $20 a night.

Contact: Rick LeVasseur, Katahdin Shadows Campground, Route 157, P.O. Box H, Medway, ME 04460; (207) 746-5267 or (800) 794-5267.

Directions: From Interstate 95 in Medway, take exit 56 and travel west on Route 11/157 for 1.7 miles to the campground.

Trip notes: Providing good access to the Maine Woods, this large, popular campground is set right off the interstate on the road to Millinocket. Baxter State Park is less than 15 miles away, and many of the lakes and rivers that characterize the region are within an easy drive. One distinguishing feature of this campground is the plethora of rabbits. Domestic rabbits are everywhere—hopping along the roads, through the woods, and in the campsites. If you don't like rabbits, head elsewhere.

Open: May 1 through Thanksgiving.

36 Holeb Preserve Management Unit

Location: On the Moose River and Attean Pond near Jackman; Northern Maine map page 32, grid d1.

Campsites, facilities: There are about 26 primitive campsites in this unit and on neighboring lands. All are waterfront sites set along the shores of Attean Pond and the Moose River, and are accessible only by water. The typical site includes a picnic table, fire ring, and pit toilet. Pets are permitted.

Reservations, fees: Registration is not required, and sites are available on a first-come, first-served basis. There is no fee.

Contact: Maine Bureau of Parks and Lands, 22 State House Station, Augusta, ME 04333; (207) 287-3821.

Directions: From the junction of U.S. 201 and Route 6/15 in Jackman, drive west on Attean Pond Road for two miles to the boat launch.

Trip notes: The preserve incorporates the popular Moose River, one of the best streams for multiday canoe trips in the state. Put your paddle to these waters and

you'll float through a region of wild rivers, expansive lakes, dense forests, and rugged mountains. Fishing, swimming, and hiking are popular summer activities, while in winter the area lures snowmobilers, cross-country skiers, snowshoers, and ice-fishing enthusiasts. Be very careful when driving on U.S. 201 at night: this road is known as Moose Alley, and many an unfortunate driver has collided with one of the 1,000-pound beasts.

Open: Year-round.

37 Loon Echo Campground

Location: South of Jackman on Lake Parlin; Northern Maine map page 32, grid d2.

Campsites, facilities: There are 15 tent sites without hookups. Flush toilets, hot showers, picnic tables, fireplaces, and a dump station are provided. For recreation, you'll find a small boat ramp, canoe and fly-fishing equipment rentals, and a playing field. White-water rafting trips in the Kennebec River Gorge can be arranged. Leashed pets are permitted.

Reservations, fees: Reservations are recommended. A 50 percent deposit is required. Sites are $13 a night.

Contact: Bill and Holly Erven, Loon Echo Campground, P.O. Box 711, Jackman, ME 04945; (207) 668-4829.

Directions: From Jackman, drive 12 miles south on U.S. 201 to the campground.

Trip notes: Loon Echo is a very peaceful, quiet campground with spectacular shoreline sites overlooking a large North Woods lake surrounded by hundreds of square miles of uninhabited woodlands, the kind of place where you'll want to settle in for a while. Campers have access to 900 feet of waterfront on Lake Parlin. While you're here, take advantage of Bill Erven's expertise with the fly rod; he offers instruction right on the premises. For more information about the Jackman area, see the trip notes for the Holeb Preserve Management Unit (campground number 36).

Open: May 1 through October 15.

---

38 John's Four Season Accommodations

Location: In Jackman; Northern Maine map page 32, grid d2.

Campsites, facilities: There are 12 sites for tents and RVs, six with electricity and six with no hookups. Flush toilets, hot showers, picnic tables, a dump station, a rec room, and laundry facilities are provided. Leashed pets are permitted.

Reservations, fees: Reservations are not necessary. Tent sites are $8 a night, and RV sites are $10 to $15 a night.

Contact: John Baillargeon, John's Four Season Accommodations, Star Route 64, Box 132, Jackman, ME 04945; (207) 668-7683.

Directions: From the junction of U.S. 201 and Route 6/15 in Jackman, drive half a mile north on U.S. 201 to the campground.

Trip notes: The main attraction at John's isn't the campground itself, which is very nondescript. Rather it's the sense of being at the very edge of civilization that draws people here. This is an outpost in the true sense of the word, an establishment that caters to the sportsmen and women who come to the Jackman region for an unsurpassed wilderness adventure. For more information on the Jackman area, see the trip notes for the Holeb Preserve Management Unit (campground number 36).

Open: Year-round.

39 Jackman Landing Campground

Location: On Wood Pond in the town of Jackman; Northern Maine map page 32, grid d2.

Campsites, facilities: There are 25 sites for tents and RVs, 16 with water and electric hookups and nine without hookups. Flush toilets, hot showers, picnic tables, fireplaces, a dump station, laundry facilities, and cable TV are provided. For recreation, there is a boat launch and dock, canoe rentals, and canoe shuttle service. A floatplane on site will take campers for rides over the Maine Woods. Leashed pets are permitted.

Reservations, fees: Reservations are accepted. Sites are $12 to $16 a night.

Contact: Stephen Coleman, Jackman Landing Campground, P.O. Box 567, Main Street, Jackman, ME 04945; (207) 668-3301.

Directions: From the junction of U.S. 201 and Route 6/15 in Jackman, drive north on U.S. 201 for approximately 1.5 miles to the campground.

Trip notes: Jackman Landing is a great little campground on beautiful Wood Pond, a clean and cold lake that's part of the Moose River system. The campground is located right in the tiny frontier town of Jackman, very close to the Quebec border, and the general store and post office are within convenient walking distance. Don't be surprised to hear French spoken as often as English, for in this border country families who live on both sides of the line are related. For additional information on the Jackman area, see the trip notes for the Holeb Preserve Management Unit (campground number 36).

Open: Year-round.

⓸ Moose River Campground

Location: In Jackman; Northern Maine map page 32, grid d2.

Campsites, facilities: There are 52 sites for tents and RVs, 11 with full hookups, 26 with water and electric, 2 with electric only, and 13 without hookups. Flush toilets, hot showers, picnic tables, fireplaces, a dump station, laundry facilities, and a store with a restaurant are provided. A swimming pool, trout ponds, canoe rentals, a playground, volleyball, badminton, and horseshoes are among the recreational offerings. Leashed pets are permitted.

Reservations, fees: Reservations are accepted. Sites are $12 to $17 a night.

Contact: Francis and Carmen Cousineau, Moose River Campground, P.O. Box 98, Jackman, ME 04945; (207) 668-3341.

Directions: From the junction of U.S. 201 and Route 6/15 in Jackman, drive two miles north on U.S. 201 to Nichols Road, then turn right and drive 1.5 miles east to the campground.

Trip notes: The clean and well-kept Moose River Campground is a great little spot near a tiny border town in a wild corner of the state. It adjoins hundreds of miles of wilderness trails open to camping vehicles in the summer and snowmobiles in the winter. The woods and woodland streams here offer outdoorsmen and women tremendous opportunities for hunting and fishing, and hikers can tackle the trails of nearby Sally and Bald Mountains. For more information on the Jackman area, see the Holeb Preserve Management Unit (campground number 36).

Open: May 5 through October 1.

⓻ The Last Resort Campground and Cabins

Location: On Long Pond near Jackman; Northern Maine map page 32, grid d2.

Campsites, facilities: There are four tent sites and eight rental cabins. Tent sites have picnic tables, fireplaces with grills, and pit toilets, and the resort provides centrally located hot showers. Cabins are fully equipped with gas ranges and refrigerators, wood stoves, kerosene and gas lamps, and the necessary cooking, eating, and bedding supplies. A rustic fishing lodge has board games, books, and videos. Leashed pets are permitted.

Reservations, fees: Reservations are accepted. Cabins are $275 to $400 a week. Tent sites are $5 a night per person.

Contact: Tim and Ellen Casey, The Last Resort Campground and Cabins, P.O. Box 777, Jackman, ME 04945; (207) 668-5091.

Directions: From the center of Jackman, drive six miles east on Moose River Road (four-wheel-drive vehicles are recommended) to the campground.

Trip notes: The Last Resort is a very rustic, remote fishing camp, a private getaway in the Maine Woods. Tent sites are situated along the lakeshore and are spaced far enough apart to allow for maximum privacy. However, if you've ever dreamed of having your own little log cabin beside a wilderness lake in the North Woods, this is the place for you. Each cabin is constructed of hand-hewn logs and is nestled among 70 acres of spruce, cedar, pine, and birch trees along the shores Long Pond, a narrow lake that stretches for 12 miles. Each cabin has a front porch overlooking the lake, with a spectacular view of the mountains across the water.

Open: Year-round.

㊷ Chain of Ponds Management Unit

Location: Along the Dead River, northwest of Flagstaff Lake; Northern Maine map page 32, grid d1.

Campsites, facilities: Some primitive campsites are located on the shores of the ponds. Some are drive-up sites, while others are accessible by boat. Water is available from the rivers and ponds. Boat launches are provided nearby. Pets are permitted.

Reservations, fees: Reservations are not accepted, and sites are available on a first-come, first-served basis. There is no fee.

Contact: Maine Bureau of Parks and Lands, 22 State House Station, Augusta, ME 04333; (207) 287-3821.

Directions: From Eustis, drive approximately 12 miles north on Route 27 to the management unit.

Trip notes: Campers will feel as if they are miles away from civilization when they arrive at this remote retreat. Each secluded lakefront site is like a true backcountry spot. You can fetch drinking water from the ponds or rivers—just be sure to filter or treat it before consumption. The "chain" of ponds includes Nautis, Long, Bag, and Lower Ponds. These wilderness pools are connected by navigable sections of the Dead River, so bring a canoe and explore all the hidden coves and inlets. Anglers should not leave behind their fishing rods. If you have two cars and want to arrange a shuttle, the North Branch of the Dead River makes for an excellent flatwater canoe trip.

Open: Year-round.

㊸ Cathedral Pines Campground

Location: On the west shore of Flagstaff Lake in Eustis; Northern Maine map page 32, grid d1.

Campsites, facilities: There are 115 sites, including two group sites, 98 with water and electric hookups and 17 with no hookups. Flush toilets, hot showers, picnic tables, fireplaces, a dump station, and laundry facilities are provided. For recreation, there is a boat ramp and docking facilities, canoe rentals, a playground, and a rec room. Leashed pets are permitted.

Reservations, fees: Reservations are necessary. A deposit of one night's fee is required. Sites are $13 to $16 a night.

Contact: Cathedral Pines Campground, HC 72, Box 80, Eustis, ME 04936; (207) 246-3491.

Directions: From the intersection of Routes 16 and 27 in Stratton, drive four miles north on Route 27 to the campground.

Trip notes: Just 26 miles from the Canadian border, this campground is set in a magnificent 300-acre grove of towering red pines on the shore of giant Flagstaff Lake. It would be easy to mistake the place for a state or national park campground because the sites are so well spaced and the grounds are impeccably clean. Flagstaff Lake, nestled among some of the most spectacular mountain scenery in Maine, is renowned for supporting a high-quality freshwater sport fishery. Campers will want to cool off at the sandy beach or paddle their canoes around the lake. Hikers should not miss the opportunity to explore the mountains of the Bigelow Range looming over these waters. The Appalachian Trail crosses the range, providing access for day hikes as well as multiday treks. History buffs will be interested to know that the campground stands on the site of one of General Benedict Arnold's stops during his ill-fated march to Quebec in 1775; a monument at the entrance marks his visit.

Open: May 15 through October 1.

④ Dead River Management Unit

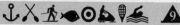

Location: On the north shore of Flagstaff Lake; Northern Maine map page 32, grid d2.

Campsites, facilities: There are several primitive campsites on the north shore of Flagstaff Lake. While some of the sites on the lake are accessible only by water, other sites on the Dead River can be reached by vehicle. Each site has a picnic table, fire ring, and pit toilet. A boat ramp on the lake is located just south of Long Falls. Pets are permitted.

Reservations, fees: Reservations are not accepted, and sites are available on a first-come, first-served basis. Camping is free of charge, but you must pay a paper company road fee (it varies, but is less than $10) to access the management unit.

Contact: Maine Bureau of Parks and Lands, 22 State House Station, Augusta, ME 04333; (207) 287-3821.

Directions: From the crossroads at North New Portland, drive north on the Long Falls Road for about 22 miles to the management unit.

Trip notes: Remote campsites dot the wild and undeveloped shores of both the Dead River and Flagstaff Lake. These sites are spaced far apart, so you definitely won't feel crowded. Anglers should not leave their fishing rods at home, for this is a good place to cast a line. If you're a skilled white-water paddler, the Dead River presents challenging terrain for kayaking and canoeing; just

be sure to assess your skills well beforehand, as this is not a beginner's river. From the campground, you'll gain spectacular views across the lake to the Bigelow Mountains. On the way to or from the management unit, hikers should spend a day (or a week) hiking or traversing this range. For more information, see the trip notes for the Bigelow Preserve Management Unit (campground number 63).

Open: Year-round; contact the Maine Bureau of Parks and Lands in the winter to check on road conditions.

④ Indian Pond Campground

Location: On Indian Pond north of The Forks; Northern Maine map page 32, grid d2.

Campsites, facilities: There are 27 sites, all without hookups; 22 are suitable for tents, trailers, and self-contained units; five are tent platforms. A three-bedroom house is available year-round for rent. Flush toilets, hot showers, tables, fireplaces, a dump station, and laundry facilities are provided. There also a boat launch, a dock, and canoe rentals. Leashed pets are permitted.

Reservations, fees: Reservations are accepted. For stays of up to three days, payment in full is required, and for four or more days, a 50 percent deposit is requested. Refunds are given with seven days' prior notice. Sites are $14 a night.

Contact: Indian Pond Campground, HCR 63, Box 52, The Forks, ME 04985; (800) 371-7774.

Directions: From U.S. 201 in The Forks, turn right and drive five miles east on Moxie Pond Road to Moxie Pond. Turn left on Harris Station Road and drive eight miles north to the Indian Pond Reception Center.

Trip notes: Just downstream of giant Moosehead Lake on the Kennebec River is Indian Pond, a 3,600-acre lake with 35 miles of undeveloped shoreline surrounded by hundreds of square miles of uninhabited woodlands. The pond is known for offering a superlative smallmouth bass fishery as well as for its healthy populations of trout and salmon. In the fall the campground is open to hunters tracking down deer, bear, moose, and birds. This is an off-the-beaten-path destination for those in search of some North Woods adventure.

Open: Mid-April through mid-October.

46 Little Squaw Management Unit

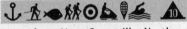

Location: Near Greenville; Northern Maine map page 32, grid d2.

Campsites, facilities: There are five primitive campsites on Big Squaw Pond and Little Squaw Pond. Each site has a pit toilet. Pets are permitted.

Reservations, fees: Reservations are not accepted, and the sites are available on a first-come, first-served basis. There is no fee.

Contact: Maine Bureau of Parks and Lands, 22 State House Station, Augusta, ME 04333; (207) 287-3821.

Directions: To access the unit, hike in from Route 6/15 in Greenville.

Trip notes: This is a spectacular 13,500-acre parcel of land overlooking the southern end of Moosehead Lake, the largest lake set entirely in New England. Within the area are five remote ponds that offer fishing, canoeing, and a few scenic campsites; the Little Squaw Mountains, with their hiking trails and terrific views; and miles of forest open for hunting, fishing, cross-country skiing, and snowmobiling.

Open: Year-round.

47 Old Mill Campground

Location: On Moosehead Lake in Rockwood; Northern Maine map page 32, grid d2.

Campsites, facilities: There are 50 sites for tents and RVs with full and partial hookups. Flush toilets, hot showers, picnic tables, fire rings, a dump station, laundry facilities, a playground, rec room, boat ramp, horseshoe pits, volleyball, badminton, and a store are provided. Cabins are available. The campground also rents motorboats, paddleboats, and canoes and can arrange the services of a fishing guide. Leashed pets are permitted.

Reservations, fees: Reservations are recommended. A deposit of one night's fee is required for stays of less than one week; for stays of a week or more, a deposit of 25 percent is required. Sites are $13 to $15 a night for two people, plus $2 for each additional person.

Contact: Kay and Rick Annunziato, Old Mill Campground, Route 15, Rockwood, ME 04478; (207) 534-7333.

Directions: From Greenville, travel 18 miles north on Route 6/15 to the campground entrance.

Trip notes: Located on the western side of Moosehead Lake, Old Mill Campground offers a spectacular waterfront setting with many sites set right on the shoreline. Surrounded by hundreds of square miles of unpeopled woodlands, this campground is well situated for hunters who venture this way to try for deer, bear, moose, and grouse in the fall months. For more information on the Moosehead Lake area, see the trip notes for Lily Bay State Park (campground number 52).

Open: Mid-May to mid-October; the cabins are open from May to November.

48 Seboomook Wilderness Campground

Location: On Moosehead Lake; Northern Maine map page 32, grid d3.

Campsites, facilities: There are 84 sites for tents and RVs with full, partial, and no hookups. Flush toilets, hot showers, picnic tables, fireplaces, a dump station, and a store are provided. For recreation, there is a boat launch and dock, a sand beach, rental canoes and motorboats, a playing field, volleyball, badminton, and horseshoes. Leashed pets are permitted.

Reservations, fees: Reservations are accepted. Sites are $8 to $12 a night.

Contact: Seboomook Wilderness Campground, HC 85, Box 560, Rockwood, ME 04478; (207) 534-8824.

Directions: From Jackman, travel east on Route 6/15 to Rockwood. At the Moose River Bridge in Rockwood, turn left and head north for approximately 28 miles on logging roads to the campground. You can also boat or take a seaplane from either Rockwood or Greenville.

Trip notes: Seboomook Wilderness Campground is tucked away at the northwest end of Moosehead Lake, a remote and peaceful setting in the heart of the Maine Woods. The place is a bit off the beaten path, as it's accessible by logging road, by boat from Greenville or Rockwood, or by seaplane from either of those towns. Sites are strewn along the waterfront and offer sweeping views over the lake and the surrounding mountains. Bring your fishing gear: the angling for salmon, brook trout—or squaretail, as they are called here—and togue is renowned. In autumn, pack your rifle and warm clothing and stalk the wildlands around you for deer, bear, and grouse. In winter, the campground keeps several heated cabins open and available for snowmobilers, snowshoers, cross-country skiers, and ice fishers.

Open: Year-round.

49 Moosehead Lake Management Unit

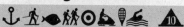

Location: On Moosehead Lake; Northern Maine map page 32, grid d3.

Campsites, facilities: There are 26 primitive tent sites on the shore of Moosehead Lake. Each site has a pit toilet, picnic table, and fire ring. Pets are permitted.

Reservations, fees: Reservations are not accepted, and the sites are available on a first-come, first-served basis. There is no fee.

Contact: Maine Bureau of Parks and Lands, 22 State House Station, Augusta, ME 04333; (207) 287-3821.

Directions: Access to the unit is gained via boat, canoe, foot, cross-country ski, or snowmobile over the surface of the lake. Good points of departure are the towns of Greenville and Rockwood, and Lily Bay State Park. You could also drive in on a labyrinth of logging roads, which would require a detailed map.

Trip notes: At 40 miles long and up to 10 miles wide, Moosehead Lake is the largest lake set entirely within New England. The public landholding incorporates two large islands and extensive acreage on the lake's eastern shore. There are numerous boat-in campsites, as well as trails that ascend the 1,806-foot summit of Mount Kineo, where a fire tower rewards hikers with spectacular views over the sprawling lake. For more information on the Moosehead Lake area, see the trip notes for Lily Bay State Park (campground number 52).

Open: Year-round.

50 Casey's Spencer Bay Camps

Location: On Moosehead Lake; Northern Maine map page 32, grid d3.

Campsites, facilities: There are 65 sites for tents and RVs, 10 with full hookups, 11 with electric only, and 44 with no hookups. Flush toilets, hot showers, picnic tables, fireplaces, laundry facilities, a dump station, and a store are provided. For recreation, there are canoe and motorboat rentals, bike rentals, hiking trails, and horseshoes. Leashed pets are permitted.

Reservations, fees: Reservations are accepted. Sites are $14 to $18 a night.

Contact: Casey's Spencer Bay Camps, P.O. Box 1161, Greenville, ME 04441; (207) 695-2801.

Directions: From the intersection of Route 6/15 and the Lily Bay Road in Greenville, drive 12 miles north on the Lily Bay Road, then turn left and travel six miles west on the campground road.

Trip notes: Casey's Spencer Bay Camps enjoys a great location on a narrow peninsula jutting into Moosehead Lake, the largest lake entirely within New England and an outdoors-lover's paradise since Henry David Thoreau passed through here in the mid-nineteenth century. The fishing in the lake is superb, and miles of secluded coves and undeveloped wooded shoreline are perfect for canoe outings. Views over the water to distant peaks only enhance the scenic beauty of this spot. The campground is reached via several miles of logging roads and is well off the traveled path. Campers can swim and fish right from their site, paddle a canoe around for a few hours, or maybe explore on a bike. If that's not enough, Baxter State Park, with its more than 200,000 acres of woods, waters, and

mountains, is nearby. For more information on the Moosehead Lake area, see Lily Bay State Park (campground number 52).

Open: Mid-May through mid-October.

51 Northern Pride Lodge

Location: On First Roach Pond in Kokadjo; Northern Maine map page 32, grid d3.

Campsites, facilities: There are 24 sites for tents and RVs, all without hookups. Pit toilets, a central water supply, hot showers, picnic tables, fire rings, a boat launch, and docks are provided. Mountain bikes, motorboats, canoes, paddleboats, and an 18-foot pontoon boat are available for rent. A lodge and a restaurant are on the premises. Leashed pets are permitted.

Reservations, fees: Reservations are not necessary. Sites are $16 a night for two people, plus $1 for each additional person. The fee for pets is $2 a night.

Contact: Jeff and Barbara Lucas, Northern Pride Lodge, HC 76, Box 588, Kokadjo, ME 04441; (207) 695-2890.

Directions: From Greenville, travel northeast on the Kokadjo Road for about 20 miles.

Trip notes: Located on First Roach Pond, Northern Pride Lodge is an upscale yet inexpensive place to spend your camping vacation. Just remember to bring the fishing gear. The pond is limited to fly-fishing and spin casting, while the Roach River is limited to catch-and-release fly-fishing. Big brook trout—also known in these parts as squaretail—togue, and large salmon live in these waters in healthy numbers. Seaplane trips to more remote lakes can be arranged through the campground. Swimming, canoeing, and boating on the pond and in the river are other popular pursuits. In the fall, base yourself here for moose, deer, bear, and bird hunting excursions. And note that even though the campground does close for the winter, the lodge is open year-round for cross-country skiing, snowshoeing, and snowmobiling. For additional information about the Moosehead Lake area, see Lily Bay State Park (campground number 52).

Open: May 1 through November 1.

52 Lily Bay State Park

Location: North of Greenville on Moosehead Lake; Northern Maine map page 32, grid d3.

Campsites, facilities: There are 91 sites for tents and RVs, all without hookups. Each site has a pit toilet, picnic table, and fireplace. A dump station, playground, boat launch, beach, and hiking trails are provided. Leashed pets are permitted.

Reservations, fees: Reservations are accepted, and the total amount due must accompany your request. Contact the Maine Bureau of Parks and Lands at the number below. The State of Maine allocates some sites on a first-come, first-served basis. Sites are $11.50 a night for residents of Maine and $15 for nonresidents.

Contact: Lily Bay State Park Ranger, (207) 695-2700. Maine Bureau of Parks and Lands, 22 State House Station, Augusta, ME 04333; (207) 287-3821.

Directions: From Greenville, drive north on the Lily Bay Road for nine miles to the park entrance and the campground.

Trip notes: Lily Bay State Park is tucked into a cove on the shores of giant Moosehead Lake and overlooks this very beautiful expanse of water dotted with dozens of islands. Campers can explore the 40-mile-long, 10-mile-wide lake by boat or canoe, while anglers will be thrilled by the superb fishing for salmon, perch, togue, and trout.

From Greenville, known as the gateway town to the North Woods, campers can secure guide services, rent canoes or boats, arrange for a rafting trip on the West Branch of the Penobscot River, or embark on a scenic seaplane ride. A restored 1914 steamboat, the SS *Katahdin*, takes passengers on three-hour cruises around the lake. A six-hour cruise stops at Mount Kineo, a rocky cliff rising 750 feet above the lake. Paths lead to a fire tower atop the cliff, and a trail along the shore circles the peninsula. The Moosehead Marine Museum, home of the SS *Katahdin*, houses a display chronicling the history of steamboats on the lake since 1836.

Open: May 1 through October 15.

53 Moosehead Family Campground

Location: In Greenville; Northern Maine map page 32, grid d3.

Campsites, facilities: There are 40 sites for tents and RVs, 14 with water and electric and 26 with none. Chemical toilets, hot showers, picnic tables, fire rings, a dump station, a playground, and a rec room are provided. Leashed pets are permitted.

Reservations, fees: Reservations are not necessary. Sites are $12 to $16 a night.

Contact: Bob and Lillian Weingart, Moosehead Family Campground, P.O. Box 1244, Greenville, ME 04441; (207) 695-2210.

Directions: From Greenville, travel a mile south on Route 6/15 to the campground.

Trip notes: Just south of Greenville, this family campground puts you very close to Moosehead Lake, Baxter State Park, and the numerous attractions of the Maine Woods. It's a no-frills place that serves as a launching pad for outdoor adventures throughout the region. For information on activities in the Moosehead Lake region, see Lily Bay State Park (campground number 52). For more on Baxter State Park, see Abol Campground (campground number 27).

Open: May 1 through February 28.

---

54 Balsam Woods Campground

Location: In Abbot Village; Northern Maine map page 32, grid d3.

Campsites, facilities: There are 50 sites for tents and RVs, 39 with water and electric hookups and 11 with no hookups. Flush toilets, hot showers, picnic tables, fire rings, a dump station, laundry facilities, and a store with a snack bar are provided. The campground also offers a playground, rec hall, pavilion, pool, horseshoe pits, basketball, badminton, volleyball, hiking trails, and movies. Leashed pets are permitted.

Reservations, fees: Reservations are recommended. For less than one week, a deposit of one night's fee is required; for a week or more, a deposit of 25 percent of the total cost is required. Sites are $13 to $17 a night.

Contact: Jay and Lynn Eberhard, Balsam Woods Campground, Piper Pond Road, Abbot Village, ME 04406; (207) 876-2731; E-mail: balsmwds@users.pita.org; Web page under Maine Camping: http://www.pits.org/~balsmwds.

Directions: From Dover-Foxcroft, drive west on Route 6/15/16 to the junction with Route 6/15 in Abbot Village. Drive north for one mile on Route 15, then turn left on Piper Pond Road and drive three miles west to the campground.

Trip notes: Off-the-beaten-path Balsam Woods is a peaceful, comfortable campground that is also very well maintained. Close to Moosehead Lake, the Appalachian Trail, Baxter State Park, and white-water rafting on the West Branch of the Penobscot River, the place is well situated for campers who want to venture out on day trips, yet is far enough from the region's attractions to virtually guarantee peace and quiet. If you don't feel like driving half an hour to Moosehead Lake, you'll find a public beach and boat ramp one mile down the road at Piper Pond.

Open: Memorial Day through November 17.

---

55 Peaks-Kenny State Park

Location: In Dover-Foxcroft on Sebec Lake; Northern Maine map page 32, grid d3.

Campsites, facilities: There are 56 sites for tents and RVs, all without hookups. Wheelchair-accessible rest rooms, flush toilets, hot showers, picnic tables, fireplaces and grills, a playground, and a dump station are provided. There's also a beach with a lifeguard and hiking trails. Leashed pets are permitted.

Reservations, fees: Reservations are taken, and the total amount due must accompany your request. Contact the Maine Bureau of Parks and Lands at the number below. The State of Maine allocates some sites on a first-come, first-served basis. Sites are $12 a night for residents of Maine and $16 for nonresidents.

Contact: Peaks-Kenny State Park Ranger, (207) 564-2003. Maine Bureau of Parks and Lands, 22 State House Station, Augusta, ME 04333; (207) 287-3821.

Directions: From Dover-Foxcroft, travel north on Route 153 for six miles. Turn left at the end of the road and continue west for approximately three miles to the park.

Trip notes: Park yourself here to spend some time fishing, boating, swimming, or just soaking up the North Woods beauty. For many, the Sebec Lake region is where the real Maine Woods of lore begin, for there are no paved roads between Sebec Lake and the Canadian border. The lake itself, undeveloped and with little road access, is nestled in the mountains. A public boat launch is available just down the road from the campground, and the surrounding mountains and woodlands await hikers. From Sebec Lake, Moosehead Lake is just an hour away and Baxter State Park is one and a quarter hours away.

Open: Year-round; fully operational May 15 through September 30.

---

56 Appalachian Trail

Location: Along the Appalachian Mountains; Northern Maine map page 32, grid d3.

Campsites, facilities: There are 31 lean-tos, accommodating up to six people each, and six primitive tent campsites along this stretch of the trail. Some sites have fire rings and pit toilets. Pets are permitted.

Reservations, fees: Sites are first come, first served. There is no fee.

Contact: Maine Appalachian Trail Club, P.O. Box 283, Augusta, ME 04330. Appalachian Trail Conference, P.O. Box 807, Harper's Ferry, WV 25425; (304) 535-6331.

Directions: Maine's portion of the Appalachian Trail enters the state at the base of Mount Carlo in the Mahoosuc Range in the White Mountain National Forest, winds north to the base of the Bigelow Range, and continues to just east of Bald Mountain Pond. The final 130-mile section in the northern part of the state ascends the summit of mile-high Katahdin, Maine's tallest mountain and the terminus of the trail.

Trip notes: From Springer Mountain in Georgia to the summit of Katahdin in Maine, the Appalachian Trail traverses the Appalachian Mountain chain on a 2,158-mile continuous, marked footpath. The first 150 miles in Maine cross spectacular mountain ranges, including the Mahoosucs, the Baldpates, the Saddlebacks, and the Bemis. Views of the Rangeley Lakes and the major mountains of New Hampshire and western Maine are stunning. The Mahoosuc Notch, a deep cleft in the mountains filled with house-sized boulders, is considered the toughest stretch of the entire route. While most day-hikers swarm to the nearby Presidential Range in New Hampshire, people who hike this section get to bask in the stunning views, remoteness, and an overall sense of quiet. The most popular hike in this region is the one that ascends 4,180-foot-high Old Speck Mountain. Try your luck at fishing (or just cool off by dunking) in one of the area's many streams, rivers, or ponds.

Moving eastward, the Bigelow Range traverse is among the finest long-distance, high-elevation hikes in Maine, crossing six major peaks and several lesser ones. From these ridgetops, views of the surrounding country—graced by forests and lakes—are expansive. The trail also wanders through the Carry Ponds country, a beautiful lake-filled region that was traversed by General Benedict Arnold and American army troops during a surprise attack on Quebec in 1775. Continuing on toward the summit of Katahdin, a major portion of trail's final 130 miles lies within the so-called 100-Mile Wilderness, an uninhabited stretch of forests, mountains, rivers, and lakes as wild as any region in the lower 48 states. If you plan to hike here, make sure you carry adequate supplies and are well prepared; of the entire 2,100-plus miles of the Appalachian Trail, this portion is the most untame.

Open: Year-round.

57 Jo-Mary Lake Campground

Location: South of Millinocket; Northern Maine map page 32, grid d4.

Campsites, facilities: There are 60 sites for tents and RVs, all without hookups. Flush toilets, hot showers, picnic tables, fireplaces, a dump station, laundry facilities, a playground, a rec room, and a store are provided. You'll also find horseshoe pits, a basketball hoop, a sandy beach, and rental canoes, rowboats, and paddleboats. Leashed pets are permitted.

Reservations, fees: Reservations are recommended. A $10 deposit is required for weekend stays; for a full week a $20 deposit is required. There is a two-night minimum for reservations. Sites are $14 a night.

Contact: Jim and Lauretta Smith, Jo-Mary Lake Campground, P.O. Box 329, Millinocket, ME 04462; (207) 723-8117 or (207) 746-5512.

Directions: From Millinocket, travel south on Route 11 for 15 miles. Turn right on a logging road and travel northwest for about five miles to the campground.

Trip notes: The Katahdin Iron Works/Jo-Mary Multiple Use Management Forest surrounds this campground on the south shore of Upper Jo-Mary Lake. Teeming with salmon, trout, togue, and white perch, the five-mile-long, two-mile-wide lake is a great spot for fishing as well as canoeing, boating, and swimming. For hikers, the Appalachian Trail is just five miles away. A hike to Gulf Hagas, known as the Grand Canyon of the East with its three-mile-long canyon and five major waterfalls, makes a good day outing. The campground is approximately 50 miles away from Baxter State Park.

Open: Mid-May through October 1.

58 Seboeis Management Unit

Location: South of Millinocket; Northern Maine map page 32, grid d4.

Campsites, facilities: There are four primitive campsites. RVers may be able to negotiate the entry roads, but no services are available. Each site has a picnic table, fire ring, and pit toilet. Pets are permitted.

Reservations, fees: Reservations are not accepted, and the sites are available on a first-come, first-served basis. There is no fee.

Contact: Maine Bureau of Parks and Lands, 22 State House Station, Augusta, ME 04333; (207) 287-3821.

Directions: To access the unit, drive south from Millinocket on Route 11 for approximately 12 miles.

Trip notes: Several large lakes are contained within this 13,000-acre public land unit. The land around the shorelines was cut prior to when the state acquired ownership, thus the forest is in a stage of regrowth. Campers and day visitors can enjoy hunting, fishing, and savoring the impressive views of surrounding mountains, including Katahdin. In winter, snowmobilers pass through the unit while traveling between the villages of Milo and Medway. Ice fishing on Seboeis Lake is also popular at that time.

Open: Year-round.

59 Lakeside Camping Area

Location: On Cold Stream Pond in Enfield; Northern Maine map page 32, grid d4.

Campsites, facilities: There are 32 sites for tents and RVs with full and partial hookups. Flush toilets, hot showers, picnic tables, fire rings, a dump station, playground, rec room, and store are provided. Boat rentals are available. Leashed pets are permitted.

Reservations, fees: Reservations are not necessary. Sites are $13 to $18 a night.

Contact: Gene and Candy Libby, Lakeside Camping Area, Enfield, ME 04433; (207) 732-4241. Off-season: Gene and Candy Libby, P.O. Box 38, Lincoln, ME 04457; (207) 732-4241.

Directions: From Interstate 95 in Howland, take exit 55 and drive east on Route 155 for about five mile to the intersection with Route 188 in Enfield. Continue north on Route 155 for approximately 2.5 miles to the campground.

Trip notes: Vehicles and tents are lined up in rows at this campground on the shore of Cold Stream Pond. The pond has a reputation for offering good fishing for togue, salmon, and trout. Additionally, the park is within a short drive of many other lakes and rivers where you can escape for a day of fishing, boating, and rafting. For non-anglers (or anglers needing a refreshing dip), the camp has a sandy beach, perfect for swimming. Canoes, paddleboats, and "splash" boats are available for rent.

Open: May 1 through Columbus Day.

⑥⓪ Mattawamkeag Wilderness Park Campground

Location: Near the town of Mattawamkeag; Northern Maine map page 32, grid d5.

Campsites, facilities: There are 50 sites for tents and RVs, some with electric hookups, plus 11 lean-tos. Flush toilets, hot showers, picnic tables, fireplaces, a recreation building, and a limited store are provided. Pets are permitted.

Reservations, fees: Reservations are not necessary. Sites are $9 to $11 a night.

Contact: Mattawamkeag Wilderness Park Campground, U.S. 2, Box 5, Mattawamkeag, ME 04459; (207) 736-4881.

Directions: From the junction of U.S. 2 and Route 157 in Mattawamkeag, drive approximately half a mile south on U.S. 2. After crossing the Mattawamkeag River, drive about six miles east on a logging road to Mattawamkeag Wilderness Park.

Trip notes: Mattawamkeag Wilderness Park offers superb outdoor recreation opportunities for just about everyone. Hikers can enjoy 15 miles of wilderness trails; anglers will discover good salmon and trout fishing along the Mattawamkeag River; and canoeists have some 60 miles of wilderness to paddle through, including several exciting stretches of white water. There's even a beach for swimmers. You'll have a rustic Maine camping experience in a splendid wilderness setting.

Open: Mid-May to mid-September.

⑥① Maine Wilderness Camps

Location: Between the towns of Topsfield and Springfield; Northern Maine map page 32, grid d5.

Campsites, facilities: There are 19 sites for tents and RVs, four with water and electric hookups and 15 with none. Flush toilets and hot showers are located at the main campground, while the wilderness sites, which are accessible by trail or boat, have pit toilets. Picnic tables and fireplaces are provided, and you'll find a limited store and a lodge at the main campground. There's a sandy beach; a boat dock; motorboat, canoe, and kayak rentals; and horseshoes.

Several housekeeping cabins are available for rent. Leashed pets are permitted.

Reservations, fees: Reservations are recommended. A deposit of one-third of the total cost is required. Sites are $8 to $15 a night.

Contact: Terry and Paula McGrath, Maine Wilderness Camps, RR 1, Box 1085, Springfield, ME 04487; (207) 738-5052 (this is a radio phone; let it ring).

Directions: From Interstate 95 near Lincoln, take exit 55 to U.S. 2 and then Route 6 and drive east for 34 miles until you enter Washington County. Continue 4.5 miles east of the county line on Route 6, then turn right at the sign for Maine Wilderness Camps and follow the very rough logging road for 3.5 miles. If you are unsure about your vehicle's ability to handle deep ruts, washboards, and rocks, call ahead.

Trip notes: Once you make it here you'll appreciate the rough access road you were just cursing, because this camp bordering a wilderness lake is definitely way off the beaten path. For many people, this is as close as they will ever come to a true wilderness experience. The rustic facility at the end of the road is the only sign of humanity on Pleasant Lake, and campers are surrounded by hundreds of square miles of unpopulated woodlands. It's a great spot for those who want to get away from it all, perhaps launching off on an extended canoe trip. A short portage out of Pleasant Lake leads to the Grand Lake Chain and more than 40 miles of wilderness waterways. If you want to begin a long canoe expedition here, Maine Wilderness Camps offers a full outfitting and shuttle service. Anglers and hunters will find full guide services at the campground, too. This is a sportsperson's paradise, where the fishing for landlocked salmon, brook and lake trout, bass, and white perch is excellent. In the fall, make this your base camp for deer,

moose, bear, and game bird hunting. And during winter, explore the dirt roads and lakes (if frozen) by snowmobile or cross-country skis. For those who want their own rustic lakeside retreat, several housekeeping cabins are rented out.

Open: Year-round.

⑥② Greenland Cove Campground

Location: On East Grand Lake near the town of Danforth; Northern Maine map page 32, grid d5.

Campsites, facilities: There are 40 sites for tents and RVs, some with water and electric hookups. Flush toilets, hot showers, a dump station, picnic tables, fire rings, a playground, rec hall, canoe and paddleboat rentals, a boat ramp, horseshoe pits, volleyball, basketball, and a store are provided. Leashed pets are permitted.

Reservations, fees: Reservations are recommended. A deposit of $15 for one night or $30 for two or more nights is required. Sites are $17 to $19 a night.

Contact: Roger and Brenda Habrie, Greenland Cove Campground, Danforth, ME 04424; (207) 448-2863.

Directions: From the intersection of Route 169 and U.S. 1 in Danforth, drive south on U.S. 1 for 2.3 miles. Turn left on Campground Road and drive 2.5 miles east to the campground.

Trip notes: Many sites at Greenland Cove are on the shore of a large, remote lake, while others are perched on a wooded hillside directly overlooking the water. Be sure to bring your rod and reel, for East Grand Lake is one of the best fisheries for landlocked salmon in Maine. Anglers will also find it's an excellent place to try for bass, perch, and togue. As part of the international boundary, the lake provides an unusual opportunity to fish in both American and Canadian waters, and international bass and salmon tournaments are conducted here throughout the season. If you would rather not cast a line, there is a sandy beach for swimming.

Open: Ice-out (usually around mid-May) through October 1.

⑬ Bigelow Preserve Management Unit

Location: On and just south of Flagstaff Lake; Southern Maine map page 33, grid a2.

Campsites, facilities: There are about 16 primitive campsites. Sites for backpackers are located along the ridgeline of the mountain range and typically include a lean-to or tent platform, a fire ring, and a pit toilet. Tent sites with fire rings and pit toilets are set at various points on the lakeshore and are accessed by water or by hiking trail. One group site on the lake can accommodate up to 30 people. Pets are permitted.

Reservations, fees: Registration is not required, and sites are available on a first-come, first-served basis. There is no fee.

Contact: Maine Bureau of Parks and Lands, 22 State House Station, Augusta, ME 04333; (207) 287-3821.

Directions: To access the preserve, follow gravel roads off of Route 16/27 in Carrabassett, or take Long Falls Dam Road north from North New Portland.

Trip notes: The Bigelow Range and 20 miles of the southern shore of Flagstaff Lake are part of this wilderness preserve that encompasses 35,000 acres. Hiking options include many one-day and multiday hikes on the 30 miles of Appalachian Trail that bisect the management unit. The sum-

mits of the Bigelow Range are above tree line and offer sweeping vistas of the surrounding forests, mountains, and lakes. Fishing, boating, canoeing, and swimming are popular pursuits on Flagstaff Lake. Given the wide range of habitat in the preserve, many of the wildlife species indigenous to the state are represented here. In the fall, the backcountry area is open to deer, bear, moose, and grouse hunting. In the winter, snowmobilers travel on more than 20 miles of trails within the preserve, while snowshoers and cross-country skiers head off on hiking trails and unplowed roads. A heated lodge is kept open in the winter as a warming station.

Open: Year-round.

⑭ Cupsuptic Campground

Location: On the north end of Cupsuptic Lake near Rangeley; Southern Maine map page 33, grid a1.

Campsites, facilities: There are 76 sites for tents and RVs, 66 with full hookups and 10 with no hookups. Flush toilets, hot showers, picnic tables, fireplaces, a dump station, and a store are provided. For recreation, there is a boat launch, canoe rentals, a rec room, volleyball, badminton, and horseshoes. Leashed pets are permitted.

Reservations, fees: Reservations are accepted. Sites are $12 to $16 a night.

Contact: Cupsuptic Campground, Rangeley, ME 04970; (207) 864-5249.

Directions: From the junction of Routes 4 and 16 in Oquossoc, drive 4.5 miles northwest on Route 16 to the campground.

Trip notes: Secluded among a mature forest on the northern end of Cupsuptic Lake, these sites provide welcome privacy for campers. And the setting, on a vast freshwater lake connected to several other enormous freshwater lakes—among them Mooselookmeguntic, Rangeley, and Upper and Lower Richardson—couldn't be much more conducive to getting out and exploring. Miles of waterways await adventuresome souls. Bring a canoe or rent one here for days of peaceful paddling. Meanwhile, fishing fans will be busy casting into these freshwater pools. This is wild country, with plenty of woods, water, and wildlife to satisfy hunters in search of deer, duck, moose, and grouse.

Open: May 1 through December 1.

⑥⑤ Aziscoos Valley Camping Area

Location: On the banks of the Magalloway River, northwest of Bethel; Southern Maine map page 33, grid a1.

Campsites, facilities: There are 31 sites for tents and RVs, 16 with water and electric hookups and 15 with no hookups. Flush toilets, hot showers, picnic tables, fireplaces with grills, a dump station, laundry facilities, and a playground are provided. A large tepee is available for rent. Leashed pets are permitted.

Reservations, fees: Reservations are not necessary. Sites are $8 to $11 a night.

Contact: Muriel and Norman Littlehale, Aziscoos Valley Camping Area, HCR 10, Box 302, Wilsons Mills, ME 03579; (207) 486-3271.

Directions: From Errol, New Hampshire, travel north on Route 16 for 14 miles. The campground is on your left.

Trip notes: Situated on a well-maintained lawn that stretches down a hill to the Magalloway River, the Aziscoos campground is especially clean and offers spacious sites. Jumping into the river for a dip

is a popular activity here. The main attraction to the area, however, is the easy access it affords those who want to explore nearby waterways. From the campground, you can launch a canoe into the Magalloway River, which flows into Umbagog Lake and ultimately into the Androscoggin River. In addition to this waterway, campers can use the nearby public boat launches for trips on Aziscohos Lake and Richardson Lake. From these two launching points, a camper can access hundreds of miles of canoeing, boating, and fishing water. Hikers can hit the trails at Aziscohos Mountain, a 3,215-foot peak only a few miles from the campground.

Open: May 15 through October 30.

⑥⑥ Black Brook Cove Campground

Location: On Aziscohos Lake in Oquossoc, west of Rangeley; Southern Maine map page 33, grid a1.

Campsites, facilities: In the central camping area, there are 28 RV sites with water and electric hookups and 6 tent sites. It offers hot showers, flush toilets, a dump station, boat ramp, playground, beach, and store. On the east shore of the lake, there are 20 additional sites for small campers or tents. Finally, there are 16 remote sites on 20-acre Beaver Island, accessible by boat. Sites on the east shore and the island have outhouses. Picnic tables and fire rings are provided at all sites. Leashed pets are permitted.

Reservations, fees: Reservations are recommended and, on summer weekends, are necessary. A deposit of 50 percent is required. Sites are $14 to $16 a night.

Contact: Bob and Cecile Paradis, Black Brook Cove Campground, P.O. Box 319, Oquossoc, ME 04964; (207) 864-2161 (radio phone; let it ring).

Directions: From the junction of Routes 4 and 16 in Oquossoc, travel west on Route 16 for 16 miles. Turn right on Aziscohos Road and drive half a mile north.

Trip notes: Though well maintained, this campground offers a wilderness setting. The sites on the east shore of the lake are spaced 75 to 100 feet apart, allowing for privacy and a greater sense of remoteness. Boat-in sites on Beaver Island are very popular, drawing some campers who return to the same spots each year. Aziscohos is a large, undeveloped lake surrounded by mountains. Evidently it has the best waters in the area for brook trout, but people also try their hand at catching landlocked salmon. If fishing isn't your passion, paddling or cruising around this peaceful lake is a great way to spend a few days. Fishing guides, a seaplane, and a shuttle service are also available. If you get tired of the water, take a hike on the wooded trails or to the summit of nearby Aziscohos Mountain.

Open: April 15 through November 15.

⑥⑦ Stephen Phillips Memorial Preserve

Location: On Mooselookmeguntic Lake near Oquossoc; Southern Maine map page 33, grid a1.

Campsites, facilities: There are 60 tent sites with no hookups. Fireplaces, picnic tables, and non-flush toilets are provided. Leashed pets are permitted.

Reservations, fees: Reservations must be paid in full two weeks prior to arrival. Cancellations must be received a week before arrival for a full refund. Sites are $8 a night, plus $1 a night for dogs.

Contact: Jim and Olive Turner, Stephen Phillips Memorial Preserve, P.O. Box 21, Oquossoc, ME 04964; (207) 864-2003.

Directions: From the junction of Route 4 and Bald Mountain Road in Oquossoc, drive south on Bald Mountain Road for four miles to the campground.

Trip notes: Stephen Phillips Memorial Preserve provides a wilderness camping experience for those who are looking for peace and solitude in a true Maine Woods setting. Most of the sites are on islands or are scattered along the wooded shores of Mooselookmeguntic Lake, a large, wild body of water that stretches for many miles and is renowned as a high-quality freshwater sport fishery. These sites are reached by canoe or boat, while other sites are located on the mainland. The charitable trust that manages the preserve strives to maintain the land in its natural state. Come here for primitive camping in a spectacular mountain, forest, and lake setting.

Open: May 1 through September 30.

⑥⑧ Rangeley Lake State Park

Location: On Rangeley Lake; Southern Maine map page 33, grid a1.

Campsites, facilities: There are 50 sites for tents and RVs, all without hookups. Wheelchair-accessible rest rooms, hot showers, a dump station, a concrete boat launch ramp with floats, a group camping area, a playground, and a swimming area are provided. Leashed pets are permitted.

Reservations, fees: Reservations are accepted, and the total amount due must accompany your request. Contact the Maine Bureau of Parks and Lands at the number below. The State of Maine allocates some sites on a first-come, first-served basis. Fees are $11.50 a night for residents of Maine and $15 for nonresidents.

Contact: Rangeley Lake State Park Ranger, (207) 864-3858. Maine Bureau of Parks and Lands, 22 State House Station, Augusta, ME 04333; (207) 287-3821.

Directions: From Rangeley, drive three miles south on Route 4, then turn right on South Shore Road and go five miles west.

Trip notes: A real gem, Rangeley Lake State Park is situated on a large lake nestled among the mountains of western Maine. Eight large lakes—Aziscohos, Upper and Lower Richardson, Cupsuptic, Mooselookmeguntic, Kennebago, Umbagog, and Rangeley—lie within a 20-mile radius of the village of Rangeley. There are also dozens of ponds and miles of wild streams and rivers, plus tall, fir-covered mountains, making this area one of Maine's prime vacation destinations. You can fish in the big lakes for trout and landlocked salmon, or explore these waters by boat or canoe. Campers can secure guide services, rent canoes or boats, hike trails to the summits of nearby mountains, or find fine dining and shops in the village of Rangeley. In winter, this is paradise for cross-country and downhill skiers: the Saddleback Ski Resort is just north of town.

Open: Year-round; fully operational May 15 through October 1.

---

⑥⑨ Deer Farm Campground

Location: Near the Sugarloaf Resort in Kingfield; Southern Maine map page 33, grid a2.

Campsites, facilities: There are 47 sites for tents and RVs, 45 with water and electric hookups and 2 with no hookups. Flush toilets, hot showers, picnic tables, fireplaces, a standing barbecue grill, a dump station, laundry facilities, and a store are provided. For recreation, there is a play-ground, rec room, volleyball, basketball, and horseshoe pits. A private beach for campers is located nearby. Leashed pets are permitted.

Reservations, fees: Reservations are not necessary. Sites are $14 a night.

Contact: Brenda Finwick, Deer Farm Campground, Tufts Pond Road, Kingfield, ME 04947; (207) 265-4599.

Directions: From Kingfield go about two miles north on Route 27. Turn left on Tufts Farm Road and drive to the campground.

Trip notes: A raw, well-used feeling marks this campground, where the roads and campsites, which are tucked into the woods, have become eroded. Campers can swim and canoe at a private beach across the street and about half a mile down a dirt road from here. The lake is adequate for a dip, but neither the beach nor the views will entice you to remain for hours. While this is not the most appealing campground, the Carrabasset Valley is home to some great hiking routes. Not far away, hikers can head off for day trips or multiday treks to Sugarloaf Mountain, the Bigelow Range, or Mount Abram.

Open: Mid-May through Columbus Day.

---

⑦⓪ Happy Horseshoe Campground

Location: In North New Portland; Southern Maine map page 33, grid a2.

Campsites, facilities: There are 91 sites for tents and RVs with water and electric hookups. Flush toilets, hot showers, picnic tables, fireplaces, a dump station, laundry facilities, and a store are provided. A playground, rec room, volleyball, basketball, shuffleboard, badminton, and horseshoe pits are among the recreational facilities. Leashed pets are permitted.

Reservations, fees: Reservations are required on weekends and you must make a deposit of one night's fee. Sites are $18 a night.

Contact: Judy and Buster Pinkham, Happy Horseshoe Campground, HCR 68, Box 170, North New Portland, ME 04961; (207) 628-3471.

Directions: From the junction of Routes 146 and 16 in North New Portland, drive east on Route 16 for half a mile, then head north on Long Falls Dam Road for 5.25 miles to the campground.

Trip notes: Very clean, nondescript, and unassuming, this campground caters almost exclusively to the local people living within a 50-mile radius who use it for weekend getaways in the summer.

Open: Memorial Day through Labor Day.

⓰ Four Ponds Management Unit

Location: Just east of Mooselookmeguntic Lake in the Rangeley area; Southern Maine map page 33, grid a1.

Campsites, facilities: There is a campsite on Little Swift River Pond and a lean-to on Sabbath Day Pond. Fire rings and a pit toilet are provided, and campers can get water from the ponds. These backcountry sites are accessible by foot only.

Reservations, fees: Reservations are not accepted, and sites are allocated on a first-come, first-served basis. There is no fee.

Contact: Maine Bureau of Parks and Lands, 22 State House Station, Augusta, ME 04333; (207) 287-3821.

Directions: From Houghton, drive north on Route 17 for approximately seven miles to where the Appalachian Trail crosses the road. Park and start hiking northeast on the trail. You'll reach the shelter in about

3.5 miles; the campsite is about five miles farther up the trail.

Trip notes: This area is characterized by mountainous terrain, a thick spruce forest, and six ponds (not four as the name implies). Campers access the lean-to and campsite by hiking on the Appalachian Trail, which crosses the length of this 6,000-acre unit. With the highest elevation just under 3,000 feet, the area offers relatively easy backpacking. You'll find the lean-to nestled between Long and Sabbath Day Ponds, while the campsite lies some five miles farther down the trail on the smaller Little Swift River Pond. Fishing enthusiasts should be aware that all of the ponds contain brook trout. A population of Sunapee trout was introduced in Long Pond in 1977 and remains viable. In addition to trout, Beaver Mountain Lake holds salmon and smelt. After a day or even a few hours of hauling a backpack, you may want to take a dip in the fresh water, a truly inviting prospect. There are some private camps, accessed by private roads, on Beaver Mountain Lake.

Open: Year-round.

⓱ South Arm Campground

Location: On the Richardson Lakes near Andover; Southern Maine map page 33, grid b1.

Campsites, facilities: There are 30 isolated wilderness tent sites on the shores of Upper and Lower Richardson Lakes and on several islands. The main campground at South Arm has an additional 65 wooded sites for tents and RVs, all with water and electric hookups. Most are situated along the waterfront, and each has a picnic table and fire ring. Hot showers, flush toilets, laundry facilities, a store and deli, motorboat and canoe rentals, a dump station, playing field, and boat launch are provided at the main campground. Leashed pets are permitted.

Reservations, fees: Reservations are required. There is a two-night minimum stay on weekends except for Memorial Day, July 4, and Labor Day, when you must reserve at least three nights. Deposits must be received within five days of making reservations by telephone. In the main camping area, beach sites are $21 a night, waterfront sites are $19, and off-water sites are $16. Wilderness tent sites are $12 a night.

Contact: South Arm Campground, P.O. Box 310, Andover, ME 04216; (207) 364-5155 or (207) 784-3566.

Directions: From Andover, drive about 12 miles north on South Arm Road.

Trip notes: One of the country's premier wilderness regions—a land graced with lakes, forests, and mountains—is home to South Arm Campground. From the main camping area, Upper and Lower Richardson Lakes stretch northward for 17 miles and connect with several other equally expansive and undeveloped lakes. Paddlers can put in for multiday wilderness canoe trips from here, and anglers can cast a line for landlocked salmon, trout, and togue in these waters, which are renowned for their excellent fishing. In this truly wild region, you can find that North Woods wilderness experience you've been seeking.

Open: May 20 through September 9.

⑦ Coos Canyon Campground

Location: About halfway between Rumford and Oquossoc, in the Coos Canyon of the Swift River; Southern Maine map page 33, grid b1.

Campsites, facilities: There are 20 primitive sites for tents, pop-ups, truck campers, and small trailers. Each site has a picnic table, a fireplace with grill, and a swinging bench. Water is provided at the entrance, outhouses are available near the campsites, and hot showers are centrally located. There's also a store selling limited supplies. Leashed pets are permitted.

Reservations, fees: Reservations are accepted. A deposit of the first night's fee is required. Sites are $10 to $12 a night.

Contact: Gerry and Rosey Perrier, Coos Canyon Campground, Route 17, HC 62, Box 408, Byron, ME 04275; (207) 364-3880.

Directions: From the town of Mexico, travel 13 miles northwest on Route 17 to the campground.

Trip notes: Quiet time is all the time at this peaceful spot. An off-the-beaten-path find, the simple, well-tended campground is located next to a dramatic gorge. Sites are nestled in the woods and allow for more privacy than you'll find at most campgrounds. A novel addition is the swinging wooden bench that hangs from a tree at each site. Whether you use the bench to read a book, enjoy a cup of tea, or chat with a loved one, you'll agree that every campground should add this special touch.

Coos Canyon is a gorge that was cut into bedrock by the flows of the Swift River, and you'll be surrounded by cliffs as high as 30 feet. Swimming and fishing in the clear water are popular pastimes, as are walking and biking the trails and dirt roads that pass by the canyon. The most unique activity here, however, is panning for gold. From the early years of the eighteenth century, gold panning has been a favorite pursuit in the Swift River. Lessons are available, and the campground will rent or sell you the necessary prospecting equipment.

Open: April 15 through November 30.

74 Dummer's Beach Campground

Location: Next to Webb Lake in the town of Weld; Southern Maine map page 33, grid b1.

Campsites, facilities: There are 200 sites for tents and RVs, nearly all with water and electric hookups. Flush toilets, hot showers, picnic tables, fireplaces, a dump station, laundry facilities, and a store are provided. For recreation, there is a sandy beach, a playground, swings, a rec room, volleyball, basketball, and horseshoe pits. Leashed pets are permitted.

Reservations, fees: Reservations are welcome. Sites are $17 to $21 a night.

Contact: Elizabeth Dummer Shreve, Dummer's Beach Campground, P.O. Box 82, Weld, ME 04285; (207) 585-2200.

Directions: From Weld, at the junction of Routes 142 and 156, follow Bypass Road for less than one mile to Fire Lane 9. Drive southwest on Fire Lane 9 to the camp.

Trip notes: The half-mile-long natural sand beach on clear-water Webb Lake is no doubt the highlight of this campground. Swimming here is a popular activity with youngsters, as the water deepens gradually, while others can launch canoes and boats right from the campground. Hikers may want to trek to any of three nearby peaks: Mount Blue (elevation 3,187 feet), Tumbledown Mountain (3,035 feet), and Little Jackson Mountain (3,535 feet). Bring a fishing rod and frying pan if you choose to head to Tumbledown, for you'll discover a trout lake when you reach the summit. Back at Webb Lake, there is good fishing for trout, bass, pickerel, and white perch. For more information on the area, see Mount Blue State Park (campground number 75).

Open: Memorial Day through Labor Day.

75 Mount Blue State Park

Location: In the western mountains near Weld; Southern Maine map page 33, grid b1.

Campsites, facilities: There are 136 sites for tents and trailers, all without hookups. Fire rings, picnic tables, non-flush toilets, a dump station, playground, and boat ramp are provided. Canoes and rowboats are rented out. Leashed pets are permitted.

Reservations, fees: Campsites may be reserved for stays between June 15 and Labor Day, but otherwise are available on a first-come, first-served basis. Fees are $11.50 a night for residents of Maine and $15 for nonresidents.

Contact: Mount Blue State Park Ranger, (207) 585-2347 in the summer, or (207) 585-2261 in the winter. Maine Bureau of Parks and Lands, 22 State House Station, Augusta, ME 04333; (207) 287-3821.

Directions: From Weld, drive two miles west on Route 142, then turn left in Weld Corner and drive approximately four miles south to the campground.

Trip notes: Mount Blue State Park is effectively split into two parts: the mountain section just north of the town of Weld and the section that lies along the western shore of beautiful Webb Lake. The mountains are laced with miles of hiking, cross-country skiing, mountain biking, and snowmobile trails. Webb Lake, on the other hand, offers superb swimming, fishing, and canoeing opportunities. The state park campground on the shores of the lake is pleasant, spacious, well maintained, and affords expansive views over the water to the mountains beyond. Some trails lead through the forest and to the summits of surrounding peaks.

Open: Year-round; fully operational May 15 through October 15.

76 Mahoosuc Management Unit

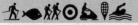 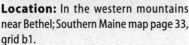

Location: In the western mountains near Bethel; Southern Maine map page 33, grid b1.

Campsites, facilities: There are five hike-in lean-to shelters in or immediately adjacent to the boundaries of the unit. Each site has a fire ring and pit toilet. Leashed pets are permitted.

Reservations, fees: Registration is not required, and the sites are available on a first-come, first-served basis. There is no fee.

Contact: Maine Bureau of Parks and Lands, 22 State House Station, Augusta, ME 04333; (207) 287-3821.

Directions: From Newry, drive approximately 12 miles west on Route 26 to access the unit.

Trip notes: Natural wonders fill this rugged 27,000-acre section of the Mahoosuc Range. The Appalachian Trail traverses the spine of the mountain range, offering excellent hikes along the ridgeline, and it reaches some of the highest summits in the state, affording spectacular views of mountains, forests, and lakes in all directions. Features include the infamous Mahoosuc Notch—considered the toughest leg of the entire 2,158-mile-long Appalachian Trail—Cataract Gorge, and Speck Pond, a glacial lake perched high atop Old Speck Mountain. The unit extends on either side of Grafton Notch State Park.

Open: Year-round.

77 Stony Brook Recreation

Location: Near Hanover; Southern Maine map page 33, grid b1.

Campsites, facilities: There are 30 sites for tents and RVs, some with full hookups, many with water and electric, and some with no hookups. Flush toilets, hot showers, picnic tables, fireplaces, a dump station, laundry facilities, and a store are provided. For recreation, there is a playground, rec room, pool, miniature golf, volleyball, shuffleboard, basketball, and horseshoe pits. Leashed pets are permitted.

Reservations, fees: Reservations are not required. Sites are $14 to $18 a night.

Contact: Bruce and Shirley Powell, Stony Brook Recreation, U.S. 2, HCR 61, Box 130, Hanover, ME 04237; (207) 824-283.

Directions: From the intersection of U.S. 2 and Route 26 in Newry, drive one mile east to the campground.

Trip notes: Stony Brook is a small campground situated on 50 acres of woods and fields near the western mountains of Maine. The sites are well spaced and offer some privacy. Many natural attractions are close at hand, including the White Mountain National Forest, the Appalachian Trail, Grafton Notch State Park, Umbagog Lake National Wildlife Refuge, and the Sunday River Ski Resort. From here you can hike the Appalachian Trail, visit Screw Auger Falls in nearby Grafton Notch State Park, canoe on the Androscoggin River, or fish in nearby rivers and lakes.

Open: Year-round.

78 Littlefield Beaches Lakeside Campground

Location: In the town of Bryant Pond; Southern Maine map page 33, grid b1.

Campsites, facilities: There are 130 sites for tents and RVs, 8 with full hookups, 117 with water and electric, and 5 with no hookups. Flush toilets, hot showers, picnic tables, fireplaces, a dump station, laundry facilities, and a store are provided. For recreation, there is a natural sand beach, a playground, rec room, boat ramp, volleyball and basketball courts, and horseshoe pits. A golf course is six miles away in Bethel. Leashed pets are permitted.

Reservations, fees: Reservations are recommended, especially in July and August. A deposit of $20 is required. Sites are $17 a night, plus $1 for sewage hookups.

Contact: Sue Stevens, Littlefield Beaches Lakeside Campground, RR 2, Box 4300, Bryant Pond, ME 04219; (207) 875-3290.

Directions: From the intersection of U.S. 2 and Route 26 in Bethel, drive six miles southeast on Route 26 to the campground.

Trip notes: Families will enjoy this pleasant campground in the foothills of the White Mountains in western Maine. In addition to the recreation opportunities of the Bethel area, such as hiking in the White Mountains, canoeing the Androscoggin River, and mountain biking on miles of little-traveled back roads, campers can take advantage of the three connecting lakes that virtually surround the campground, providing miles of canoe routes awaiting exploration. Anglers should bring their gear, as these waters are alive with togue and bass.

Open: Memorial Day through October 1.

---

⑦ Honey Run Beach and Campground

Location: On Worthley Pond in Peru; Southern Maine map page 33, grid b2.

Campsites, facilities: There are 90 sites for tents and RVs with full and partial hookups. Flush toilets, hot showers, picnic tables, fireplaces, a dump station, laundry facilities, and a store are provided. For rec-

reation, there is a beach area, playground, large field, and basketball court. Leashed pets are permitted.

Reservations, fees: Reservations are not necessary. Sites are $13 to $17 a night.

Contact: Dennis Thibodeau, Honey Run Beach and Campground, RR 1, Box 1230, Peru, ME 04290; (207) 562-4913.

Directions: From Rumford, travel east on Route 108 for 10 miles. Turn right at the sign for Worthley Pond and drive 3.5 miles south to the campground.

Trip notes: The owners of this very well maintained park pride themselves on offering leisurely family camping at spacious sites in open fields. Across the street from the campground is Worthley Pond, which boasts a sandy beach and a shallow, sloping shore—perfect for swimming with small children. The pond is about 2.5 miles long and is nestled among the woods and low mountains that are characteristic of the area. If you are a racing fan, be sure to head over to nearby South Paris to watch the race cars at the Oxford Plains Speedway.

Open: Memorial Day to Columbus Day.

---

⑧ Riverbend Campground

Location: Near Androscoggin Lake in Leeds; Southern Maine map page 33, grid b2.

Campsites, facilities: There are 80 sites for tents and RVs, 60 with water and electric hookups and 20 with no hookups. Flush toilets, hot showers, picnic tables, fireplaces, a dump station, laundry facilities, and a store are provided. For recreation, there is a playground, rec room, horseshoe pits, a swimming pool, 3,000 feet of river frontage, and canoe and motorboat rentals. Leashed pets are permitted.

Reservations, fees: Reservations are recommended. Sites are $15 to $18 a night.

Contact: The Gomolkas, Riverbend Campground, HCR 70, P.O. Box 50, Route 106, Leeds, ME 04263; (207) 524-5711.

Directions: From the intersection of U.S. 202 and Route 106, drive 7.5 miles north on Route 106 to the campground.

Trip notes: Riverbend is a pleasant campground situated on a slow-moving stream that flows into Androscoggin Lake, a large body of water renowned for its excellent bass fishing. Wildlife and nature enthusiasts will enjoy spending hours exploring the lake, the woods, and the quiet river.

Open: May 1 through September 30.

---

⑧¹ Beaver Brook Campground

Location: On Androscoggin Lake in North Monmouth; Southern Maine map page 33, grid b2.

Campsites, facilities: There are 191 RV sites with water and electric hookups and five tent sites with no hookups. Flush toilets, hot showers, picnic tables, fireplaces, a dump station, laundry facilities, a snack bar, and a store are provided. You'll also find a lake with a sandy beach, a swimming pool, canoe and rowboat rentals, a boat ramp, playground, rec room, volleyball, basketball, shuffleboard, miniature golf, Frisbee golf, badminton, and horseshoe pits. Ice, firewood, and LP gas are available. Leashed pets are permitted.

Reservations, fees: Reservations are recommended. A 50 percent deposit is required. Sites are $16 to $26 a night.

Contact: Jean Parent, Beaver Brook Campground, RFD 1, Box 1835, North Monmouth, ME 04265; (207) 933-2108 or (800) 873-CAMP/2267.

Directions: From Auburn, take U.S. 202 northeast to Monmouth. Turn left on Back Street and head north for three miles to the campground.

Trip notes: Set on the wooded shores of eight-square-mile Androscoggin Lake, which is renowned for its great bass fishing, is Beaver Brook, a family-oriented campground. For a large campground, this place offers some well-spaced sites. The lake hosts four bass tournaments each year, so bring the fishing tackle. Even if you don't fish, you will not run out of things to do here. With a full schedule of children's activities, live entertainment on Saturday nights, a miniature golf course, and a continuing array of other options, campers may never find a moment to rest. The state capital in Augusta is only half an hour away.

Open: May 1 through Columbus Day.

---

⑧² Allen Pond Campground

Location: On a small pond outside of Lewiston-Auburn; Southern Maine map page 33, grid b2.

Campsites, facilities: There are 65 sites for tents and RVs, 55 with water and electric hookups and 10 with no hookups. Flush toilets, hot showers, picnic tables, fire rings, a dump station, and a limited store are provided. For recreation, the campground offers a playground, ball field, boat ramp, swimming area, basketball, and miniature golf. The maximum RV length is 20 feet. Leashed pets are permitted.

Reservations, fees: Reservations are recommended. Sites are $10 to $17.50 a night.

Contact: Gary Yakawonis, Allen Pond Campground, RFD 1, Box 2030, Greene, ME 04236; (207) 946-7439.

Directions: From Lewiston, travel north

on U.S. 202 for about six miles. Turn left on Patten Road and then take the first right onto Quaker Ridge Road. Turn left at the first road, Allen Pond Road, and travel about two miles to the top of the lake. Turn left and follow signs to the campground.

Trip notes: Situated on the side of a hill overlooking Allen Pond, this campground is popular with the locals and attracts many seasonal campers. Swimming, boating, canoeing, and fishing at the waterfront are the main activities, though visitors will also find an old miniature golf course and a worn-out playground. With its eroded land, low-maintenance landscaping, and setting in a dark woods, the campground has a tired appearance. Nearby are the twin cities of Lewiston-Auburn, which offer the usual assortment of restaurants, theaters, and shops.

Open: Mid-May through September 30.

83 Hebron Pines Campground

Location: On Bog Brook in Hebron; Southern Maine map page 33, grid b2.

Campsites, facilities: There are 24 sites for tents and RVs, most with water and electric hookups and the rest with no hookups. Flush toilets, hot showers, picnic tables, fireplaces, a dump station, and a limited store are provided. For recreation, there is a pool, playground, rec room, hiking and mountain biking trails, volleyball, basketball, badminton, and horseshoe pits. Leashed pets are permitted.

Reservations, fees: Reservations are not necessary. Sites are $10 to $14 a night.

Contact: Hebron Pines Campground, RR 1, Box 1955, East Hebron, ME 04238; (207) 966-2179.

Directions: From the junction of Routes

119 and 124 in West Minot, travel 2.5 miles north on Route 124 to the campground.

Trip notes: Hebron Pines is situated on 400 acres in the southern interior portion of the state. There's plenty to do here, so come prepared for lots of activity. A must-do day trip is a hike to the summit of nearby Streaked Mountain, where a fire tower awaits those who make it to the top. Mountain bikers will enjoy hitting the network of dirt roads and wooded trails, while anglers should be sure to bring their gear, for this region is laced with small lakes and streams. Hebron Pines also prides itself on staging an impressive lineup of music festivals throughout the summer, good news for those who like to swing their partners to bluegrass tunes.

Open: Memorial Day to Columbus Day.

84 Crocker Pond Campground

Location: South of Bethel in the White Mountain National Forest; Southern Maine map page 33, grid b1.

Campsites, facilities: There are seven primitive sites. Three are suitable for RVs but have no hookups. Wheelchair-accessible vault toilets, a hand pump for water, picnic tables, and fire rings with grates are provided. Leashed pets are permitted.

Reservations, fees: Reservations are not accepted, and sites are allocated on a first-come, first-served basis. The fee is $10 a night except during winter, when they are free (for hardy souls!).

Contact: White Mountain National Forest, Evans Notch Ranger District, RR 2, Box 2270, Bethel, ME 04217; (207) 824-2134.

Directions: From Bethel, travel south on Route 5 for about five miles. Turn right on Forest Service Road 7 and continue west for approximately four miles, following signs to the campground.

Trip notes: Crocker Pond Campground is a gem tucked away in the mountains on the shore of a small lake. The sites, scattered among hemlock, pine, and hardwood trees, are secluded and peaceful. Hiking trails leave the parking lot and climb to the summit of Albany Mountain. You can spend your days fishing or swimming in nearby Round Pond or Broken Bridge Pond as well as in Crocker Pond; brook trout is the major game fish, and Crocker Pond also is home to horned pout. Not far away is the self-guided Patte Brook auto tour, which shows various aspects of forest management (signs are evident on the way in to campground). Hunting is permitted in season for game that includes grouse, hare, deer, black bear, and migratory birds. Cross-country skiing, snowmobiling, and snowshoeing are popular wintertime pursuits.

Open: Year-round, but the road to the campground may not be plowed in winter. Check with the ranger station.

85 Hastings Campground

Location: In the White Mountain National Forest at Evans Notch; Southern Maine map page 33, grid b1.

Campsites, facilities: There are 24 sites for tents and RVs, all without hookups. Wheelchair-accessible vault toilets, picnic tables, fire rings with grates, and a hand pump for drinking water are provided. Leashed pets are permitted.

Reservations, fees: Reservations are accepted for a maximum of 14 days. Call (800) 280-2267 or (800) 879-4496. Sites are $10 a night.

Contact: White Mountain National Forest, Evans Notch Visitor Center, 18 Mayville Road, Bethel, ME 04217; (207) 824-2134.

Directions: From Bethel, travel approximately nine miles west on U.S. 2 to the junction with Route 113. Turn left and travel south on Route 113 for about three miles to Hastings Campground.

Trip notes: One of the most scenic yet least visited corners of the White Mountain National Forest is the site of this campground. Situated in a stately stand of white spruce trees that were planted by members of the Civilian Conservation Corps in the 1930s, the camping area is close to fishing in the Wild River and hiking in the surrounding mountains. Hikes up the western side of the Carter-Moriah Mountains to the west or in the Caribou–Speckled Mountain Wilderness to the east provide moderate challenges. The vistas from trails on both sides of Route 113 encompass many miles of mountain scenery. Continue down that road into New Hampshire to find a bounty of hiking options in the Royce Mountains, the Baldfaces, and others.

Hunting in the fall for deer, grouse, moose, and bear is popular in season, while the trails and old logging roads are well used in the winter months by snowmobilers, cross-country skiers, and snowshoers. Hastings Campground is one of four U.S. Forest Service campgrounds on Route 113 in this area. See the New Hampshire chapter for information on the Wild River, Basin, and Cold River Campgrounds.

Open: Mid-May through mid-October.

86 Pleasant River Campground

Location: In West Bethel; Southern Maine map page 33, grid b1.

Campsites, facilities: There are 45 sites for tents and RVs, 10 with water and electric hookups and 35 with no hookups. Flush toilets, hot showers, picnic tables, fireplaces, laundry facilities, a dump station, and a swimming pool are provided. Leashed pets are permitted.

Reservations, fees: Reservations are accepted. Sites are $16 a night.

Contact: Barbara Dumont, Pleasant River Campground, P.O. Box 27, Route 2, West Bethel, ME 04286; (207) 836-3575.

Directions: From the junction of U.S. 2 and Route 5 in Bethel, drive 4.5 miles west on U.S. 2 to the campground on the left.

Trip notes: Pleasant River Campground sits in the Androscoggin River Valley in the shadows of the Mahoosuc and Carter-Moriah Mountains near the boundary of the White Mountain National Forest. Here campers have access to a river where they can canoe and fish. Hiking trails radiate from the area in all directions, many of them ascending the summits of nearby peaks. Just to the east is the town of Bethel, which has been a summer and winter resort community since the mid-1800s, when the Portland-to-Montreal railroad began stopping here. Today, Bethel is primarily known as the home of the giant Sunday River Ski Resort. If you love the outdoors, this is a good place to spend some time.

Open: May 15 through October 15.

⑧⑦ Kezar Lake Camping Area

Location: On Kezar Lake in Lovell; Southern Maine map page 33, grid b1.

Campsites, facilities: There are 110 sites for tents and RVs, 104 with water and electric hookups and 6 with no hookups.

Flush toilets, hot showers, picnic tables, fireplaces, a dump station, laundry facilities, and a store are provided. For recreation, there is a playground, rec room, boat ramp, canoe and paddleboat rentals, volleyball, basketball, and horseshoe pits. Leashed pets are permitted.

Reservations, fees: Reservations are welcome. A deposit of 50 percent is required. Sites are $16 to $31 a night.

Contact: Tom Pierce, Kezar Lake Camping Area, RR 1, Box 246, Lovell, ME 04051; (207) 925-1631.

Directions: From the town of Lovell, drive 2.5 miles north on Route 5. Turn left at the Kezar Lake Camping Area sign and drive three miles to the entrance on the right.

Trip notes: A large, popular family campground, the park is located on a crystal-clear lake in Maine's western hills. Kezar Lake offers a wide range of camping accommodations, from waterfront sites along the 400 feet of shoreline, wooded sites set back in the shade trees, or sunny spots in open fields. Anglers should bring their gear to try for landlocked salmon, trout, and large-mouth and smallmouth bass. This is a great place for those who wish to take advantage of all the area's attractions, including hiking in the White Mountains, canoeing the Saco River, or shopping at outlets in nearby North Conway, New Hampshire.

Open: Year-round.

⑧⑧ Papoose Pond Resort and Campground

Location: Northeast of Fryeburg in North Waterford; Southern Maine map page 33, grid b1.

Campsites, facilities: There are 170 sites for RVs, most with full hookups, plus 10 tent sites with no hookups. Cabins, cottages, and trailers are available for rent. Flush toilets, hot showers, picnic tables, fireplaces, a dump station, laundry facilities, and a store are provided. For recreation, there is a playground, rec room, horseshoe pits, a softball field, and courts for volleyball, basketball, tennis, and shuffleboard. Leashed pets are permitted in certain areas.

Reservations, fees: Reservations are required. You must send a deposit of 50 percent. Sites are $18 to $45 a night.

Contact: Papoose Pond Resort and Campground, RR 1, P.O. Box 2480, North Waterford, ME 04267; (207) 583-4470.

Directions: From Fryeburg, drive north on Route 5 to the intersection with Route 35 in Lynchville. Continue straight on Route 35 for one mile, then turn left on Route 118 and drive approximately three miles to the campground on the left.

Trip notes: Papoose Pond is a large, bustling, popular family-oriented campground set beside a small lake in the foothills of Maine's western mountains. The campground is situated on 1,000 acres in the woods alongside a half-mile-long sandy beach. Papoose Pond prides itself on its full schedule of organized activities such as canoe trips, scavenger hunts, T-shirt painting, and sandcastle building. For those who want to get out and explore the surrounding countryside, the campground is within an easy drive of New Hampshire's scenic White Mountain National Forest.

Open: May 10 through Columbus Day.

89 Zen Farm RV Resort

Location: Just north of Fryeburg; Southern Maine map page 33, grid b1.

Campsites, facilities: There are 68 sites for tents and RVs, 40 with water and elec-

tric hookups and 28 with none. Flush toilets, hot showers, picnic tables, fireplaces, a dump station, and a store are provided. There's also a boat launch, swimming pool, canoe rentals, a rec room, volleyball, basketball, badminton, and horseshoe pits. Leashed pets are permitted.

Reservations, fees: Reservations are accepted. Sites are $15 to $25 a night.

Contact: Zen Farm RV Resort, RR 1, Box 97A, Fryeburg, ME 04037; (207) 697-2702.

Directions: From the intersection of U.S. 302 and Route 5 in Fryeburg, drive four miles north on Route 5, then turn left on Fish Street and travel 1.5 miles west to the campground.

Trip notes: You'll find the new campground known as Zen Farm just north of Fryeburg, a small village tucked away in the Saco River Valley at the base of the White Mountains. The surrounding countryside is sprinkled with large freshwater lakes known for their excellent bass and trout fishing. Hikers can head to nearby White Mountain National Forest to hit the trails there, while skiers flock to the region in the winter to test their skills on the area's other trails and slopes. The Saco River is a popular summer destination for canoe trips, and there are several outfitters ready to rent you a canoe and shuttle you to and from the river. Finally, for the more sedentary camper, there is unsurpassed factory outlet shopping just across the state line in North Conway, New Hampshire.

Open: Year-round.

90 Canal Bridge Campground

Location: On the Saco River in Fryeburg; Southern Maine map page 33, grid b1.

Campsites, facilities: There are 52 sites

for tents and RVs, 37 with water and electric hookups and 15 with no hookups. Flush toilets, hot showers, picnic tables, fireplaces, a dump station, and a limited store are provided. For recreation, you'll find a playground, boat ramp, large sandy beach, volleyball, badminton, and horseshoe pits. Canoes are available for rent, and shuttle service may be arranged. Leashed pets are permitted.

Reservations, fees: Reservations are recommended; they are necessary for weekends. A deposit of 50 percent is required. Sites are $14 to $17 a night.

Contact: Dick and Anita Lamby, Canal Bridge Campground, P.O. Box 181, Fryeburg, ME 04037; (207) 935-2286 or (508) 744-2549.

Directions: From the town of Fryeburg, travel north on Route 5 for about four miles to the campground.

Trip notes: Located on the shore of the Saco River in a floodplain forest, Canal Bridge has many waterfront sites to offer. For swimmers, there is a large, sandy beach, but the main attraction here is the canoeing. From Canal Bridge, paddlers can put in for day trips on the river. After trying out those cool waters, they can explore Bog Pond, the Hemlock Covered Bridge area, and Kezar Pond, all easy side trips off of the stream itself. Advanced paddling skills are not needed in this section of river. While the water flows at a moderate pace for most of the way, paddlers will encounter small rapids at Walker's Falls, seven miles from the campground. Note: You should arrange a shuttle before you begin.

Open: May 1 through October 15.

⑨ Bear Mountain Village Cabins and Sites

Location: North of Bridgton on Bear Pond; Southern Maine map page 33, grid b1.

Campsites, facilities: There are 65 sites, all with water and electric hookups, and 20 housekeeping cabins. Flush toilets, hot showers, picnic tables, fireplaces, a dump station, laundry facilities, and a small store are provided. For recreation, there is a playground, rec room, volleyball, basketball, and horseshoe pits. Canoes, rowboats, and paddleboats may be rented. Leashed pets are permitted.

Reservations, fees: Reservations are recommended. A deposit of 50 percent is required. For holiday weekends, there is a minimum three-night stay and full payment must be received in advance. Sites are $18 to $25 a night.

Contact: Bear Mountain Village Cabins and Sites, RR 2, Box 745, Harrison, ME 04040; (207) 583-2541. Off-season: 114 Bennett Avenue, Auburn, ME 04210; (207) 782-2275.

Directions: From Bridgton, travel north on Route 117. Bear left on Route 37 in North Bridgton. After a few miles, bear left onto Bear Pond Road and continue to the campground.

Trip notes: You'll find Bear Mountain Village Cabins and Sites a bit off the beaten path in the Sebago Lake region. It's situated on private Bear Pond, and the waterfront is the center of all the action. Campers can bring their own canoes or they can rent a canoe, rowboat, or even an aqua bike for the day. Many footpaths lead through the woods and near the lake at the 33-acre site. Only three miles to Long Lake and 30 miles to Sebago Lake, Bear Mountain Village is conveniently placed for those who want to take in all the major attractions of this region. For more information on the area, see the trip notes for Sebago Lake State Park (campground number 105).

Open: May 15 through October 15.

❽ Lakeside Pines Campground

Location: Near the Songo Locks in Bridgton; Southern Maine map page 33, grid b1.

Campsites, facilities: There are 185 sites for tents and RVs, 140 with full hookups and 45 with water and electric. Flush toilets, hot showers, picnic tables, fireplaces, a dump station, and laundry facilities are provided. For recreation, there is a swimming beach, a float and diving tower, a dock, playground, rec room, basketball court, and horseshoe pits. Leashed pets are permitted.

Reservations, fees: Reservations are recommended and must be for a minimum of one week in July and August. Sites are $22 to $28 a night.

Contact: The Doucettes, Lakeside Pines Campground, P.O. Box 182, North Bridgton, ME 04057; (207) 647-3935.

Directions: From the junction of U.S. 302 and Route 117 in Bridgton, drive two miles north on Route 117 to the campground.

Trip notes: Lakeside Pines is located on Long Lake, a clear body of water connected to giant Sebago Lake via the Songo Locks. Campsites—situated on 50 acres of woods and streams—are strewn along the shore of the narrow, 15-mile-long lake. The campground is in a stand of tall virgin pine trees, and the terrain is varied, with a pleasant brook meandering through here. For more on the area, see the trip notes for Sebago Lake State Park (campground number 105).

Open: Memorial Day to September 15.

❾ Two Lakes Muskegon Campground

Location: In Oxford; Southern Maine map page 33, grid c2.

Campsites, facilities: There are 113 sites for tents and RVs, 15 with full hookups and 98 with water and electric. Flush toilets, hot showers, picnic tables, fireplaces, a dump station, laundry facilities, and a store are provided. For recreation, there is a playground, rec room, volleyball, basketball, a bocce court, shuffleboard, buggy rides, horseshoe pits, a boat ramp and dock, canoe rentals, and 600 feet of sandy beach. Leashed pets are permitted.

Reservations, fees: Reservations are recommended. Sites are $17 to $27 a night.

Contact: Barbara Varney, Two Lakes Muskegon Campground, P.O. Box 206, Oxford, ME 04270; (207) 539-4001.

Directions: From the intersection of Routes 26 and 121 in Oxford, drive approximately one mile south on Route 26 to the turnoff for the campground.

Trip notes: There is good fishing for largemouth and smallmouth bass here in Hogan and Whitney Lakes. The campground also offers a full range of planned activities, such as a buffet breakfast every Sunday morning, a summer Halloween party, pool table tournaments, and paddleboat races. If you are a racing fan, you may enjoy the stock car races at the nearby Oxford Plains Speedway. An hour's drive will bring you to the White Mountains to the west or the coast of Maine to the south.

Open: May 1 through October 1.

❾❹ Hemlock Camping Area

Location: On Tripp Lake in West Poland; Southern Maine map page 33, grid c2.

Campsites, facilities: There are 60 sites for tents and RVs, some with full hookups and most with water and electric. Flush toilets, hot showers, picnic tables, fireplaces, a dump station, laundry facilities, and a store are provided. For recreation, there is a sandy beach, swimming float, boat launch, playground, rec room, horseshoe pits. Canoes, rowboats, and paddleboats may be rented. Leashed pets are permitted.

Reservations, fees: Reservations are not necessary. Sites are $17 to $20 a night.

Contact: Leo and Cecile Bilodeau, Hemlock Camping Area, 161 Washington Street, Auburn, ME 04210; (207) 998-2384.

Directions: From Mechanic Falls, travel southwest on Route 11 to the intersection with Route 26 and Tenney Road. Turn right on Tenney Road and continue to the end, then turn left on Megouier Hill Road. Follow signs to the campground.

Trip notes: Tripp Lake offers good boating, fishing, and swimming. Filled with bass, brown trout, and pickerel, this three-mile-long lake will keep fishing enthusiasts busy. From West Poland, campers can take day trips to the coast of Maine, Sebago Lake, and the White Mountains. Only a few miles from Lewiston-Auburn, the campground provides easy access to the various restaurants, shops, and theaters in these small cities.

Open: Mid-May through October 1.

95 Poland Spring Campground

Location: In Poland Spring; Southern Maine map page 33, grid c2.

Campsites, facilities: There are 100 sites for tents and RVs, 42 with full hookups, 50 with water and electric, and 8 with none. Wheelchair-accessible flush toilets, metered hot showers, picnic tables, fire rings, a dump station, laundry facilities, and a store are provided. A playground, rec room, volleyball, basketball, and horseshoe

pits are among the recreational offerings. Leashed pets are permitted.

Reservations, fees: Reservations are recommended. Sites are $16 to $20 a night.

Contact: The Wight Family, Poland Spring Campground, P.O. Box 409, Route 26, Poland Spring, ME 04274; (207) 998-2151.

Directions: From the town of Gray, drive 12 miles north on Route 26 to the campground. The entrance sign is half a mile beyond the causeway between Middle and Lower Range Ponds.

Trip notes: Poland Spring Campground is located on Lower Range Pond, a lovely three-mile-long lake that is regularly stocked with brown and rainbow trout. The fishing for largemouth and smallmouth bass and pickerel is also excellent. Best of all, a 9.9 horsepower limit on boat motors ensures that loons and other resident waterfowl—not to mention anglers—are not disturbed, and helps preserve the peaceful setting. The pond has a sandy beach and a gradually sloping sand bottom, perfect for people swimming with small children.

Open: May 1 through October 9.

96 Range Pond Campground

Location: In Poland; Southern Maine map page 33, grid c2.

Campsites, facilities: There are 80 sites for tents and RVs, 62 with full hookups, 13 with water and electric, and 5 with no hookups. Flush toilets, hot showers, picnic tables, fireplaces, a dump station, laundry facilities, and a store are provided. For recreation, there is a playground, rec room, volleyball court, badminton court, horseshoe pits, and a large swimming pool. Leashed pets are permitted.

Reservations, fees: Reservations are

necessary. Payment in full for holidays is required. Sites are $14 to $18 a night.

Contact: Paul and Sheila Vaccaro, Range Pond Campground, RR 3, P.O. Box 635, Poland, ME 04273; (207) 998-2624.

Directions: From the junction of Routes 26 and 122 in Poland Spring, drive east on Route 122 for 1.3 miles, then bear left and drive north on Empire Road for 1.3 miles. Bear left again on Plains Road and drive half a mile to the campground.

Trip notes: The campground is located directly next to Range Ponds State Park on Lower Range Pond. This is a family-oriented facility with planned activities such as horseshoe tournaments, karaoke, a Fourth of July Parade, and Christmas in July, as well as an arts and crafts program for children. The fishing is good in the nearby Range Ponds. Also in the area is the historic Sabbathday Lake Shaker Community and Museum, the last functioning Shaker community in the United States; it's well worth a visit.

Open: April 15 through October 15.

⑰ Woodland Acres Camp 'N' Canoe

Location: In Brownfield; Southern Maine map page 33, grid c1.

Campsites, facilities: There are 58 sites for tents and RVs, 37 with water and electric hookups and 21 with no hookups. Flush toilets, hot showers, picnic tables, fireplaces, a dump station, laundry facilities, and a store are provided. For recreation, there is a playground, rec room, volleyball, basketball, horseshoe pits, canoe rentals, and a sandy beach. Leashed pets are permitted.

Reservations, fees: Reservations are recommended. A deposit of 50 percent must be received within seven days of mak-

ing a reservation. In July and August riverfront sites are available for a minimum of seven nights. Sites are $17 to $25 a night.

Contact: Woodland Acres Camp 'N' Canoe, Route 160, RR 1, Box 445, Brownfield, ME 04010; (207) 935-2529.

Directions: From the intersection of Routes 160 and 5/113 in Brownfield, drive north on Route 160 for one mile. The campground is on the left, just before you reach the bridge over the Saco River.

Trip notes: Woodland Acres offers camping in a wooded setting in the foothills of the White Mountains, but the main draw is its accessibility to the Saco River, a great stream for swimming, canoeing, and fishing for trout and bass. This is a well-maintained, spacious campground with private sites situated directly on the waterfront. It makes an ideal base camp for those interested in paddling a canoe down the cool, clear waters of the Saco River with frequent stops on its sandy beaches.

Open: May 10 through October 15.

⑱ River Run Canoe and Camping

Location: In Brownfield; Southern Maine map page 33, grid c1.

Campsites, facilities: There are 22 sites for tents and RVs, all without hookups. Non-flush toilets, picnic tables, and fireplaces are provided. There are group tenting areas, and many sites are situated directly on the Saco River. Well-behaved, leashed pets are permitted.

Reservations, fees: Reservations are accepted. Sites are $5 a night per person.

Contact: Joyce and Bob Parker, River Run Canoe and Camping, P.O. Box 90, Brownfield, ME 04010; (207) 452-2500.

Directions: From the intersection of

Routes 160 and 5/113 in Brownfield, drive 1.25 miles north on Route 160. Directly after crossing the bridge over the Saco River, turn right into the campground.

Trip notes: A beautiful, primitive campground, River Run lies directly on the shore of the Saco River, a popular canoeing stream that flows down from the White Mountains to the west. Campsites are dispersed over 130 acres of woods, fields, and meadows, and afford a great deal of privacy. The campground maintains a fleet of 100 rental canoes and provides shuttle service to and from the river. Hikers can head to the nearby White Mountain National Forest for trails. If you are looking for a quiet facility to be a base camp for outdoor adventures in the Saco Valley, this is the place.

Open: May 15 through September 30.

99 Granger Pond Camping Area

Location: Just outside the town of Denmark; Southern Maine map page 33, grid c1.

Campsites, facilities: There are 45 sites for tents and RVs; all RV sites have water and electric hookups, and some come with additional sewer connections. Flush toilets, hot showers, picnic tables, fireplaces, and a dump station are provided. For recreation, there is a beach and a floating dock, a playground, and a basketball hoop. Leashed pets are permitted.

Reservations, fees: Reservations are accepted. A deposit of $10 is required. Sites are $15 to $16.75 a night.

Contact: Susan Cody, Granger Pond Camping Area, Bush Row Road, Denmark, ME 04022; (207) 452-2342.

Directions: From Denmark, travel northeast on Route 117. Take the first right onto Bush Row Road and continue 1.5 miles south to the campground.

Trip notes: Granger Pond does steady business with seasonal campers: about half of the sites have permanent residents. The campground is located in the forest on the rise above a small, quiet lake. Canoeing on this calm pond is a pleasant experience, as it's a bit small for many motorboats. From the rise, campers can look west and on many nights experience a colorful sunset. While the town of Denmark itself is small and unremarkable, from here campers can access Sebago Lake, the White Mountains, and the Maine coast in less than an hour.

Open: Memorial Day through Columbus Day.

100 Bridgton Pines Cabins and Campground

Location: In Bridgton; Southern Maine map page 33, grid c1.

Campsites, facilities: There are 30 sites for tents and RVs with water and electric hookups. Fully equipped cabins are also available for rent. Flush toilets, hot showers, picnic tables, fireplaces, a dump station, and a store are provided. For recreation, there is a pool, playground, rec room, and horseshoe pits. Leashed pets are permitted.

Reservations, fees: Reservations are not necessary. Sites are $14 a night.

Contact: Bridgton Pines Cabins and Campground, RR 2, Box 723, Bridgton, ME 04009; (207) 647-8227.

Directions: From the town of Bridgton, travel south on U.S. 302 for about two miles to the campground.

Trip notes: While Bridgton Pines is somewhat close to the White Mountains, the Sebago Lake region, and many of Maine's bigger cities, it is not in the immediate vicinity of any of these attractions. As a result, campers spend most of their time here enjoying the swimming pool, the arcade, and the play area. The "walk-in" pool is popular with young families. Campers also use this site as a base for day trips to the areas mentioned above: mountains, lakes, and cities all lie within an hour's drive.

Open: May 15 through October 15.

101 Colonial Mast Campground

Location: On Long Lake in Naples; Southern Maine map page 33, grid c1.

Campsites, facilities: There are 79 sites for tents and RVs, with either full or partial hookups. Wheelchair-accessible rest rooms with flush toilets and hot showers, picnic tables, fireplaces, a dump station, laundry facilities, and a store selling limited supplies are provided. For recreation, there is a sandy beach, a playground, rec room, pavilion, boat ramp and docks, volleyball, basketball, horseshoe pits, and shuffleboard. A schedule of planned activities for children and teens is offered. Rowboats, paddleboats, and canoes are available for rent. Leashed pets are permitted.

Reservations, fees: Reservations are recommended. Sites are $20 to $24 a night.

Contact: Eileen and Peter Marucci, Colonial Mast Campground, Kansas Road, P.O. Box 95, Naples, ME 04055; (207) 693-6652.

Directions: From Naples, travel north for three miles on U.S. 302. Turn right onto Kansas Road and continue two-tenths of a mile east to the campground.

Trip notes: Tucked into Mast Cove on Long Lake, this campground has a small sandy beach as well as a boat ramp that allows campers to access Long Lake and, through the Songo Locks, neighboring

Sebago Lake. Especially popular are the waterfront sites, where you can head out for an early-morning or late-evening dip from your tiny, private beach. If you bring your own boat, be sure to reserve a slip at the campground, so you can easily access more than 40 miles of water for boating and fishing. The rec room here resembles a rustic lodge, complete with pine floors and comfortable furniture. For more information on Sebago Lake, see the trip notes for Sebago Lake State Park (campground number 105).

Open: Mid-May through late September.

102 Four Seasons Camping Area

Location: On Long Lake in the Sebago–Long Lake Region; Southern Maine map page 33, grid c1.

Campsites, facilities: There are 114 sites for tents and RVs, most with water and electric hookups and a few with no hookups. Groups may also pitch tents in a large field. Flush toilets, hot showers, picnic tables, fireplaces, a dump station, and a store are provided. For recreation, there is a playground, rec room, volleyball, basketball, and horseshoe pits. A field with barbecue grills is available for cookouts and gatherings. There is a sandy beach with a boat ramp and dock, and you can rent canoes, rowboats, paddleboats, or a motorboat. Leashed pets are permitted.

Reservations, fees: Reservations are recommended and are accepted for a minimum of one week. Weekend reservations are not accepted. A deposit of $70 is required. Sites are $19 to $34 a night.

Contact: Bob and Judith Van Dee Zee, Four Seasons Camping Area, P.O. Box 927, Naples, ME 04055; (207) 693-6797.

Directions: From the junction of U.S. 302

and Route 11 in Naples, travel 2.5 miles northwest on U.S. 302 to the campground.

Trip notes: Whether nestled under birch and pine trees, pitched on the hilly terrain, or set right on the shoreline, the sites in this popular campground are all well maintained. A long, sandy beach is the main attraction on most days. The gradually sloping bottom here makes swimming safe for young children, while the sundeck and float are popular destinations for more able swimmers. Many people bring their powerboats and rent a slip for the week. From the campground, more than 40 miles of lake water are accessible. For more peaceful exploration, bring or rent a canoe. The large field with barbecue grills provides a great gathering place for multifamily dinners and impromptu games. For more information on the area, see the trip notes for Sebago Lake State Park (campground number 105).

Open: Mid-May through mid-October.

⑩⑬ K's Family Circle Campground

Location: On Trickey Pond in Naples; Southern Maine map page 33, grid c1.

Campsites, facilities: There are 125 sites for tents and RVs with water and electric hookups. Flush toilets, hot showers, picnic tables, fireplaces, a dump station, laundry facilities, and a store are provided. For recreation, there's a playground, rec room, volleyball, basketball, and horseshoe pits, in addition to a full activities program. On the waterfront you'll find a sandy beach, a boat launch and docks, and rental canoes and boats. Ice and firewood are available. Leashed pets are permitted.

Reservations, fees: Reservations are recommended. Sites are $19 to $23 a night.

Contact: K's Family Circle Campground,

Route 114, Box 557M, Naples, ME 04055; (207) 693-6881.

Directions: From Naples, travel south on U.S. 302, then bear left onto Route 114. The campground is on the left, a couple miles down the road.

Trip notes: Plenty of freshwater fish live in Trickey Pond, a clear spring-fed pool surrounded by a mature forest, and the waterfront at this classic family campground is always bustling with people fishing from docks, children swimming, and canoes and boats launching. In case you get your fill of all this water-based fun, the extensive activities program will keep you and your family busy. While you may not want to leave this delightful pond, campers can easily travel from here to other nearby, bigger lakes—Sebago and Long.

Open: May 15 through September 15.

⑩⑭ Bay of Naples Family Camping

Location: In Naples on the Bay of Naples; Southern Maine map page 33, grid c1.

Campsites, facilities: There are 150 sites for tents and RVs, 61 with full hookups, 60 with water and electric, and 29 with no hookups. Flush toilets, hot showers, picnic tables, fireplaces, a dump station, laundry facilities, and a store are provided. For recreation, there is a playground, two rec halls, volleyball, basketball, badminton, horseshoe pits, a sandy beach, and boat slips. Canoes and rowboats are available for rent. No pets are allowed.

Reservations, fees: Reservations are highly recommended. They may be made for a minimum of three days, and full payment must be received to guarantee the reservation. Sites are $20 to $25 a night.

Contact: The Ruhlins, Bay of Naples Family Camping, Route 114, Box 240, Naples, ME 04055; (207) 693-6429 or (800) 348-9750.

Directions: From Interstate 95 at Portland, take exit 8 and travel north on U.S. 302 for 26 miles to the town of Naples. Turn left onto Route 11/114 and travel another mile to the campground.

Trip notes: This campground is located on the Bay of Naples, a small lake set between Long Lake and the Songo Locks, which lead to Sebago Lake. The sites here are spacious and well maintained. With a large sandy beach at the Bay of Naples, campers have good access to swimming, boating, and fishing right from the campground. The shallow beach is inviting to young bathers, and the older children often swim out to the floating dock. For an additional fee, motorboats can be docked in a waterfront slip. Adjacent to this campground is an 18-hole golf course. For more information on the area, see Sebago Lake State Park (campground number 105).

Open: Memorial Day through Columbus Day.

---

105 Sebago Lake State Park

Location: On Sebago Lake; Southern Maine map page 33, grid c1.

Campsites, facilities: There are 250 sites for tents and RVs, all without hookups. Wheelchair-accessible rest rooms, hot showers, a dump station, boat ramp, sandy beaches, bathhouses, lifeguards, and a group camping area are provided. The maximum RV length is 30 feet. No pets are allowed in the campground or on park beaches, but leashed pets are permitted in the picnic area.

Reservations, fees: Reservations are accepted, and the total amount due must accompany your request. Contact the Maine Bureau of Parks and Lands at the number below. The State of Maine allocates some sites on a first-come, first-served basis. Sites are $11.50 a night for residents of Maine and $15 for nonresidents.

Contact: June 20 through Labor Day—Sebago Lake State Park Ranger, (207) 693-6613. After Labor Day through June 19—Sebago Lake State Park Ranger, (207) 693-6231. Maine Bureau of Parks and Lands, 22 State House Station, Augusta, ME 04333; (207) 287-3821.

Directions: From the intersection of U.S. 302 and Route 11/114 in Naples, drive four miles east on U.S. 302 to the park entrance sign. Follow the entrance road for 2.5 miles to the gate.

Trip notes: Sebago Lake is a spectacular body of water, some 11 miles long by eight miles wide. Ringed by wooded hills, this clear, cool lake is renowned as a high-quality freshwater sport fishery for landlocked salmon and togue. The campsites are sheltered in a mixed pine forest directly adjacent to the water and are bordered by long, sandy beaches. Campers can take advantage of an active interpretive program, an amphitheater, and guided hikes. The lake bottom is sandy and drops off at a gentle angle, perfect for swimming. Many visitors tour the lake on the *Songo River Queen*, a 90-foot-long stern-wheeler. Another way to see the lake is aboard the *Mail Boat*, a pontoon boat that travels on local waterways. If you'd like a bird's-eye view of the region, hike to the summit of Douglas Mountain, a Nature Conservancy preserve; it'll take only about 20 minutes. More hikes are available at nearby Pleasant Mountain. Naples is the primary town in the Sebago Lake region.

Open: Year-round for tenting; fully operational June 20 to Labor Day.

106 Point Sebago Golf and Beach RV Resort

Location: On Sebago Lake; Southern Maine map page 33, grid c1.

Campsites, facilities: There are 500 sites for tents and RVs, 244 with full hookups and 256 with water and electric. Vacation rental units are also available. Facilities include flush toilets, hot showers, picnic tables, fireplaces, a dump station, laundry, and a store. For recreation, there is an 18-hole golf course; miniature golf; motorboat, sailboat, and canoe rentals; a playground; rec room; volleyball, tennis, and basketball courts; horseshoe pits; shuffleboard; and movies. No pets are allowed.

Reservations, fees: Reservations are recommended. A deposit of 50 percent is required within 10 days of making a reservation. Sites are $39 to $46 a night.

Contact: Point Sebago Golf and Beach RV Resort, RR 1, Box 712B, Casco, ME 04015; (800) 655-1232.

Directions: From Interstate 95 at Portland, take exit 8 and drive west on U.S. 302 for 22 miles to the gate.

Trip notes: Point Sebago is a vacation resort destination that happens to be a campground rather than a hotel. Situated on 800 wooded acres on the northeastern shore of beautiful Sebago Lake, Point Sebago provides a host of amenities not normally found at campgrounds, such as a championship 18-hole golf course, a marina, a cruise boat, a nightclub, and a staff of more than 400 people. Golfers will be pampered with putting greens, a sand trap and chip-shot area, a driving range, and a learning center. For those hoping to include a little golf in their camping itinerary, this is the place to do it in style.

Open: May 1 through October 31.

107 Twin Brooks Camping Area

Location: In Gray; Southern Maine map page 33, grid c1.

Campsites, facilities: There are 43 sites for tents and RVs, 10 with full hookups, 28 with water and electric, and 5 with no hookups. Flush toilets, hot showers, picnic tables, fireplaces, and a dump station are provided. For recreation, there is basketball, badminton, horseshoes, volleyball, canoe rentals, and a boat ramp. Leashed pets are permitted.

Reservations, fees: Reservations are accepted. Sites are $13 to $18 a night.

Contact: Geneva and Calvin Austin, Twin Brooks Camping Area, P.O. Box 194, Gray, ME 04039; (207) 428-3832.

Directions: From Route 26 in Gray, drive one mile north on North Raymond Road to where it intersects with Egypt Road. Turn left on Egypt Road and drive approximately one mile to the campground.

Trip notes: Twin Brooks is a small campground located at the northern tip of Little Sebago Lake. The sites are spacious and secluded, and campers have access to a sandy beach for swimming. The campground is only 25 miles from Portland and the many attractions of the Maine coast.

Open: Memorial Day through September 15.

108 Kokatosi Campground

Location: On Crescent Lake in Raymond; Southern Maine map page 33, grid c1.

Campsites, facilities: There are 162 sites for tents and RVs, 71 with full hookups, 82 with water and electric, and 9 with no hookups. Flush toilets, hot showers, picnic tables, fireplaces, a dump station, laundry facilities, and a store are provided. For recreation, there is a sandy beach; canoe, paddleboat, and motorboat rentals; a playground; rec room; volleyball; basketball; and horseshoe pits. Ice, wood, and LP gas are available. Leashed pets are permitted.

Reservations, fees: Reservations are recommended. Sites are $22 to $29 a night.

Contact: Kokatosi Campground, 635 Route 85, Raymond, ME 04071; (207) 627-4642.

Directions: From the intersection of U.S. 302 and Route 85 in Raymond, drive 6.5 miles north on Route 85 to the campground.

Trip notes: Families will enjoy Kokatosi's location on the shores of crystal-clear, five-mile-long Crescent Lake. Take a canoe and paddle a mile and a half on the Tenney River into Panther Pond, another five-mile-long lake with good fishing and plenty of hidden coves and inlets to explore. At Kokatosi's waterfront, enjoy the sandy beach, swimming, and boating. The campground also offers many planned activities, live bands, and special events. Kids will love taking a ride in the campground's restored fire engine.

Open: May 15 through Columbus Day.

109 Highland Lake Park

Location: On Highland Lake in Windham; Southern Maine map page 33, grid c2.

Campsites, facilities: There are 40 sites for tents and RVs, several of which offer full hookups. Facilities include flush toilets, hot showers, picnic tables, fireplaces, and a dump station. You'll also find a lake and a playground. No pets are allowed.

Reservations, fees: Reservations are accepted. Sites are $12 to $18 a night.

Contact: Arthur and Pat McDermott, Highland Lake Park, 19 Roosevelt Trail, Windham, ME 04062; (207) 892-8911.

Directions: From the Maine Turnpike (Interstate 95) near Portland, take exit 8 and drive 4.5 miles north on U.S. 302 to the campground on the right.

Trip notes: Located between Sebago Lake and Portland, this campground is situated within a short drive of woods, lakes, beaches, and the attractions of the city of Portland. Nearby you'll find riding stables, golf courses, and the Windham Covered Bridge. Also within easy reach are the historic Portland Head Lighthouse, Old Orchard Beach, Two Lights State Park, and Crescent Beach State Park.

Open: Year-round.

110 Windsong Campground

Location: In Kezar Falls; Southern Maine map page 33, grid c1.

Campsites, facilities: There are 43 sites for tents and RVs, 28 with water and electric hookups and 15 without hookups. Flush toilets, showers, tables, fireplaces, a dump station, laundry, and a store are provided. There's a playground, rec room, volleyball, basketball, horseshoes, a pool, and a kids' library. Leashed pets are permitted.

Reservations, fee: Reservations are not necessary. Sites are $10 to $15 a night.

Contact: Bruce Frantz, Windsong Campground, P.O. Box 547, Kezar Falls, ME 04047; (207) 625-4389.

Directions: From Kezar Falls, drive south on Elm Street for 1.5 miles. Turn left on Banks Road, which becomes Pendexter Road, and continue one mile east.

Trip notes: Windsong is a small, out-of-the-way place. Situated in the woods in a semirural area, the campground is not near any attractions, but it is within 30 minutes of Sebago Lake, the White Mountain National Forest, and the Saco River. The campground itself is very quiet, and the sites are under tall shade trees. If you are looking for a place where there are very few distractions, this may be a good choice for you.

Open: Year-round.

---

⑪ Locklin Camping Area

Location: On a small lake in Kezar Falls; Southern Maine map page 33, grid c1.

Campsites, facilities: There are 45 sites for tents and RVs, some with water and electric hookups. Flush toilets, hot showers, picnic tables, fireplaces, and a dump station are provided. For recreation, there is good lake swimming, rental canoes, a playing field, volleyball, badminton, softball, and horseshoe pits. Leashed pets are permitted.

Reservations, fees: Reservations are accepted. Sites are $15 to $18 a night.

Contact: Lionel Locklin, Locklin Camping Area, P.O. Box 197, Kezar Falls, ME 04047; (207) 625-8622.

Directions: From the junction of Routes 25 and 160 in Kezar Falls, drive two miles north on Route 160 to the campground.

Trip notes: A small, simple campground, Locklin is situated on a pretty lake in a rural area between giant Sebago Lake to the east, the White Mountains to the west, and the Portland area on the Maine coast to the south. Hike in the White Mountains, take a drive in the scenic Mount Washington Valley, or just relax at your site on the shore of Staley Pond. If you are feeling adventurous, there is good canoeing in the vicinity on the Ossipee River and on the Saco River.

Open: Memorial Day through Labor Day.

⑫ Sebago Lake Resort and Campground

Location: On Sebago Lake; Southern Maine map page 33, grid c1.

Campsites, facilities: There are 100 sites for RVs, 43 with full hookups and 57 with water and electric, plus wilderness tent sites. Flush toilets, hot showers, cable TV, picnic tables, fireplaces with grills, a dump station, laundry facilities, a restaurant, and a store are provided. For recreation, there is a playground, rec room, volleyball, badminton, horseshoe pits, a private sandy beach, paddleboat and canoe rentals, and a boat dock. Leashed pets are permitted.

Reservations, fees: Reservations are recommended. You must send a deposit of 50 percent within seven days of reserving. Sites are $22 to $28 a night.

Contact: Sebago Lake Resort and Campground, RFD 1, Box 9360, Route 114, Sebago Lake, ME 04075; (207) 787-3671.

Directions: From the intersection of Routes 35 and 114 in Sebago Lake, drive seven miles north on Route 114 to the campground.

Trip notes: Spacious, wooded sites on Sebago Lake—a huge and spectacular body of water within an hour of Portland and the Maine coast—are featured at this campground. For more information on the area, see the trip notes for Sebago Lake State Park (campground number 105).

Open: Memorial Day to Columbus Day.

---

⑬ Acres of Wildlife

Location: West of Sebago Lake in the town of Steep Falls; Southern Maine map page 33, grid c1.

Campsites, facilities: There are 200

sites for tents and RVs, 65 with full hook-ups, 102 with water and electric, and 33 with no hookups. In addition, trailers, cabins, houses, and rooms in a rustic inn may be rented. Hot showers, flush toilets, a dump station, laundry facilities, and a store are provided. For recreation, there's a playground, ball field, volleyball, basketball, horseshoes, miniature golf, walking trails, and a daily activities schedule. Campers may rent canoes, kayaks, paddleboats, rowboats, inner tubes, and bikes. Leashed pets are permitted.

Reservations, fees: Reservations are recommended and are accepted for no fewer than two nights. On holiday weekends, a three-night reservation is required. Reservations for less than one week in July and August will only be accepted 30 or more days prior to arrival. Sites are $22 to $32 a night. There is also a $5 fee per dog per night on holiday weekends.

Contact: The Wentworth Family, Acres of Wildlife, P.O. Box 2, Steep Falls, ME 04085; (207) 675-3211.

Directions: From Gorham, travel west on Route 25 for approximately six miles. Bear right onto Route 113 and continue for six miles. Turn right on the campground road and travel another 2.5 miles.

Trip notes: Surrounding two small lakes, this campground is an off-the-beaten-path choice in the Sebago Lake area. Rainbow Lake and Chub Pond are stocked with largemouth bass and rainbow trout. No license is required for anglers who want to try their luck in these waters. For walkers, five miles of trails extend from the campground into the surrounding woods. A daily activities schedule offers a multitude of options for campers including hayrides, scavenger hunts, and family sports challenges. Special themed weeks and weekends—such as Elvis in the Fifties, Halloween Week, and Downeast Days—are planned. In addition

to the many activities at the campground, there are plenty of options for day trips. It's a short distance to Sebago Lake, the ocean beaches are a half hour's drive away, and the city of Portland can be reached in 45 minutes.

Open: April 15 through December 1.

114 Family-N-Friends Campground

Location: Near Sebago Lake; Southern Maine map page 33, grid c1.

Campsites, facilities: There are 39 sites for tents and RVs, 9 with full hookups, 27 with water and electric, and 3 with no hookups. Flush toilets, hot showers, picnic tables, fireplaces, a dump station, laundry facilities, and a store are provided. For recreation, there is a heated pool and hot tub, a playground, rec room, volleyball, basketball, and horseshoe pits. Also available are planned children's activities, dances, and theme weekends held throughout the season. Leashed pets are permitted.

Reservations, fees: Reservations are recommended. Sites are $15 to $21 a night.

Contact: Dick and Sheri Huff, Family-N-Friends Campground, Route 114, Box 9895, Sebago Lake, ME 04075; (207) 642-2200.

Directions: From the intersection of Routes 114 and 35 in Sebago Lake, travel northwest on Route 114 for three-quarters of a mile to the campground.

Trip notes: Just down the road from Sebago Lake, Family-N-Friends Campground offers all the amenities of a big campground in a smaller setting. The large, heated pool and the bubbling Jacuzzi are the main attractions. An exhaustive activities schedule includes karaoke, live bands, children's events, and bonfires. A series of theme weekends begins in May and continues to the end of the season: pig roasts, adults-only weekends, and Yard Sale weekend are among the special events. Only a few miles away is Sebago Lake with its full range of opportunities for boating, fishing, and lake swimming. For more information on the area, see the trip notes for Sebago Lake State Park (campground number 105).

Open: May 1 through November 1.

115 Wassamki Springs Campground

Location: In Westbrook; Southern Maine map page 33, grid c1.

Campsites, facilities: There are 160 sites for tents and RVs with full, partial, and no hookups. Phone hookups are available. Flush toilets, hot showers, picnic tables, fireplaces, a dump station, laundry facilities, and a store are provided. For recreation, there is a lake with a sand beach, a stocked trout pond, boat rentals, playgrounds, a rec room, volleyball, basketball, and horseshoe pits. Leashed pets are permitted.

Reservations, fees: Reservations are required. You must leave a deposit of $10 for every night you plan to stay. Sites are $19 to $24 a night.

Contact: The Hillock Family, Wassamki Springs Campground, 855 Saco Street, Westbrook, ME 04092; (207) 839-4276.

Directions: From the Maine Turnpike (Interstate 95) west of Portland, take exit 7 and drive one mile south on Payne Road, then head 2.5 miles north on Route 114. Turn right on Saco Street and drive half a mile north to the campground.

Trip notes: Both lakefront and wooded sites are available at Wassamki Springs, a large campground with a private 30-acre lake. A mile of sandy beach borders these crystal-clear waters, which are stocked with

trout for fishing. This is the closest campground to downtown Portland and puts campers within minutes of the Old Port area, fine shops and restaurants, historic sites, beaches, lighthouses, and the many attractions of the South and Mid-Coast regions of Maine.

Open: May 1 through October 15.

116 Blackburn's Campground

Location: In Waterboro Center; Southern Maine map page 33, grid c1.

Campsites, facilities: There are 85 sites for tents and RVs, 65 with full hookups and 20 with water and electric hookups. Many sites come with additional cable TV and telephone connections. Flush toilets, hot showers, picnic tables, fireplaces, and a dump station are provided. For recreation, there is access to a private pond, canoe and paddleboat rentals, a dock, volleyball and badminton nets, and horseshoes. Leashed pets are permitted.

Reservations, fees: Reservations are accepted. Sites are $15 a night.

Contact: Blackburn's Campground, Box 369, Ossipee Lake, Waterboro, ME 04030; (207) 247-5875.

Directions: From U.S. 202 north of Waterboro, follow Route 5 west to Waterboro Center. The campground is near the intersection of Route 5 and Buxton Road.

Trip notes: The campground is situated on the shores of scenic Ossipee Lake, where you can play on a sandy beach or plunk in a canoe for a lazy day of paddling. The lake is home to landlocked salmon, togue, brook trout, bass, and pickerel, so come prepared to cast a line. Campsites on the upper level are wooded, and those on the lower level are set along the waterfront. Hiking trails that lead to the summit of Ossipee Mountain begin at the campground.

Open: May 1 through October 1.

⑰ B&B Family Camping

Location: On a roadside in South Lebanon, near the New Hampshire border; Southern Maine map page 33, grid d1.

Campsites, facilities: There are 56 sites for tents and RVs with full, partial, and no hookups. Picnic tables, fireplaces, a dump station, and laundry facilities are provided. The grounds also offer a playground, swimming pool, rec room, volleyball and basketball courts, and horseshoe pits. Leashed pets are permitted.

Reservations, fees: Reservations are not necessary. Sites are $18 to $20 a night for RVs and $14 a night for tents.

Contact: B&B Family Camping, Route 202, South Lebanon, ME 04027; (207) 339-0150.

Directions: From South Lebanon at the Maine–New Hampshire border, drive 1.25 miles east on U.S. 202 to the campground on the right.

Trip notes: B&B is no destination resort. But if you're in the area and need a simple place to stop for the night, this may be a good choice for you. Sites are crowded, and the zooming of passing cars and trucks on busy U.S. 202 will buzz in your ears all night. The campground is an hour from the prime attractions of the area: the White Mountains, the coast, and several large lakes.

Open: May 1 through October 31.

⑱ Kings and Queens Court Vacation Resort

Location: On the Salmon Falls River in South Lebanon; Southern Maine map page 33, grid d1.

Campsites, facilities: There are 450 sites for tents and RVs, 200 with full hookups and 250 with water and electric. Facilities include flush toilets, hot showers, picnic tables, fireplaces, a dump station, laundry, a snack bar, and a store. For recreation, there are two heated swimming pools, a playground, rec room, volleyball, basketball, horseshoe pits, a waterslide, whirlpool, miniature golf course, and a river and pond for swimming and fishing. Some sites come with cable TV hookups. LP gas and RV supplies are available on site. Leashed pets are permitted.

Reservations, fees: Reservations are accepted. A deposit of $40 is required for weekend stays, $65 for three-day holiday weekends, and $125 for a week. Sites are $24 to $25 a night.

Contact: Ralph and Elinor Davis, Kings and Queens Court Vacation Resort, Flat Rock Ridge Road, RFD 1, Box 763, East Lebanon, ME 04027; (207) 339-9465.

Directions: From the Spaulding Turnpike in Rochester, New Hampshire, take exit 16 to Route 16 heading north. Take the second right onto River Road and drive one mile east to the campground.

Trip notes: A Disneyland-type feeling pervades this very large RV park situated on the New Hampshire–Maine border about an hour's drive from the ocean and an hour from the mountains. In fact, there's almost too much going on at Kings and Queens: among the numerous amenities, the park has two heated swimming pools, a giant waterslide, four hot tubs, a pond with a sandy beach, and the Salmon Falls River, where you can cast out a fishing line. Wagon rides and arts and crafts are just some of the many scheduled activities to keep campers busy.

Open: May 17 through September 29.

⑪⑨ Potter's Place Adult Park

Location: In North Lebanon; Southern Maine map page 33, grid d1.

Campsites, facilities: There are 100 sites, all with water and electric hookups. Flush toilets, hot showers, picnic tables, fireplaces, free firewood, and a dump station are provided. For recreation, there is a playground, rec room, pond, and nature trails. Leashed pets are permitted.

Reservations, fees: Reservations are not necessary. Sites are $14 a night for the first five nights, $10 a night thereafter.

Contact: Tom and Barbara Potter, Potter's Place Adult Park, RR 2, Box 490, North Lebanon, ME 04027; (207) 457-1341.

Directions: From the junction of Route 11/109 and U.S. 202 in Sanford, drive west on U.S. 202 for six miles to Depot Road in East Lebanon. Turn right on Depot Road and drive two miles north, then turn right on Baker's Grant Road and continue one mile east to the campground.

Trip notes: Potter's Place provides an especially relaxed, pleasant, and peaceful camping experience in a classic rural New England locale. These spacious sites for adults—no children are permitted—are very well tended and are found in a mix of open and wooded settings. Maintained nature trails, a six-acre spring-fed pond, and floral gardens round out the surroundings. Come prepared to relax: this was one of the most restful campgrounds we visited.

Open: May 1 through October 15.

⑫⓪ Apache Campground

Location: On Estes Lake in Sanford; Southern Maine map page 33, grid d1.

Campsites, facilities: There are 150 sites for tents and RVs, 20 with full hookups and 130 with water and electric. Flush toilets, hot showers, picnic tables, fireplaces, a dump station, laundry facilities, and a store are provided. Recreational offerings include a lake with a sandy beach; a playground; rec room; courts for volleyball, basketball, and bocce ball; and horseshoe pits. Leashed pets are permitted.

Reservations, fees: Reservations are accepted and require a deposit of one night's fee. Sites are $14 to $19 a night.

Contact: Gerard and Rita Bernier, Apache Campground, Bernier Road, Sanford, ME 04073; (207) 324-5652.

Directions: From the junction of Routes 109 and 4 in Sanford, drive two miles north on Route 4, then 1.5 miles east on New Dam Road to Bernier Road. The campground is six-tenths of a mile ahead on the right.

Trip notes: Large wooded sites on the shores of Estes Lake are offered at Apache Campground. Bring your fishing gear, because this part of the state is known as the lakes region of southern Maine. Twenty-five lakes are sprinkled throughout the area. For a change of pace, or if you'd rather cast for bluefish instead of bass, ocean beaches are a mere 20 minutes away.

Open: May 15 through October 15.

⑫① Apple Valley Campground

Location: Near Acton; Southern Maine map page 33, grid d1.

Campsites, facilities: There are 160 sites for RVs with full and partial hookups. Flush toilets, hot showers, picnic tables, fireplaces, a dump station, laundry facilities, and a store are provided. For recreation, there's a pool, playground, rec room, a perfectly round man-made pond for fishing, a miniature golf course, volleyball, basketball, and horseshoe pits. Leashed pets are permitted.

Reservations, fees: Reservations are not necessary. Sites are $18 a night.

Contact: Apple Valley Campground, P.O. Box 92, Route 109, Acton, ME 04001; (207) 636-2285.

Directions: From the junction of Routes 11 and 109 in Emery Mills south of Acton, drive two miles north on Route 109 to the campground.

Trip notes: A lush valley near the foothills of the White Mountains is the setting for this campground. Most of the guests at Apple Valley are seasonal campers who use their RVs as summer vacation homes. Virtually every camper we saw here appeared to own a golf cart for getting around in, and this was the only place where we noticed that kind of traffic. In other words, it's a popular spot for retirees.

Open: May 15 through October 15.

---

⑫ Walnut Grove Campground

Location: In Alfred; Southern Maine map page 33, grid d1.

Campsites, facilities: There are 93 sites for tents and RVs, all with water and electric hookups. Facilities include flush toilets, hot showers, picnic tables, fireplaces, a dump station, laundry, a snack bar, and a store. For recreation, there is a playground, rec room, volleyball and basketball, horseshoe pits, and hiking trails. Leashed pets are permitted.

Reservations, fees: Reservations are recommended and require a deposit of $16.50. Sites are $15.50 to $16.50 a night.

Contact: Arthur and Sandy Roberts, Walnut Grove Campground, Gore Road, Box 260, Alfred, ME 04002; (207) 324-1207.

Directions: From the intersection of U.S. 202 and Routes 4 and 111, drive one mile north on U.S. 202/4. Turn left on Gore Road and drive 2.75 miles northwest to the campground.

Trip notes: Wooded and open sites are available at Walnut Grove. This campground is located in the lakes region of southern Maine, a mostly rural slice of the state that's dotted with 25 lakes, so anglers should bring their fishing gear. The beaches of southern Maine are a half hour's drive away.

Open: May 1 through October 15.

---

⑫ Bunganut Lake Camping Area

Location: On Bunganut Lake in Alfred; Southern Maine map page 33, grid d1.

Campsites, facilities: There are 110 sites for tents and RVs, all with water and electric hookups. Flush toilets, hot showers, picnic tables, fireplaces, a dump station, laundry facilities, and a store are provided. For recreation, there is a playground, rec room, volleyball, basketball, and horseshoe pits. The maximum RV length is 20 feet. Leashed pets are permitted.

Reservations, fees: Reservations are accepted. Sites are $18 to $20 a night.

Contact: Bunganut Lake Camping Area, P.O. Box 141, Alfred, ME 04002; (207) 247-3875.

Directions: From the junction of U.S. 202 and Routes 4 and 111 in Alfred, drive 2.5 miles north on U.S. 4/202. Turn right on Brock Road and drive 1.5 miles east to Williams Road. Turn right on Williams Road and drive one mile south to the campground.

Trip notes: The sites at Bunganut Lake

Camping Area are perched on a steep, sloping wooded hillside above a freshwater lake. The grounds are well maintained, and the campground has a spacious, private feel. The lake is a great place to go for a swim or fish for your supper. Kids may enjoy visiting with the animals in the petting zoo, but we thought the cages looked awfully small.

Open: May 1 through September 31.

124 Scott's Cove Camping Area

Location: On Bunganut Lake in Alfred; Southern Maine map page 33, grid d1.

Campsites, facilities: There are 50 sites for tents and RVs, two with full hookups and 48 with water and electric. Flush toilets, hot showers, picnic tables, fireplaces, a dump station, and a store are provided. Recreational offerings include a lake with a sandy beach; rowboat, canoe, and paddleboat rentals; a playground; basketball and volleyball courts; and horseshoe pits. Firewood is available. No pets are allowed.

Reservations, fees: Reservations are accepted. Sites are $16 to $20 a night.

Contact: Brenda and Stew Stoney, Scott's Cove Camping Area, Alfred, ME 04002; (207) 324-6594.

Directions: From the junction of U.S. 202 and Routes 4 and 111 in Alfred, drive 2.5 miles north on U.S. 202/4. Turn right on Brock Road and drive half a mile east to the campground.

Trip notes: A bustling campground, Scott's Cove Camping Area is situated in woods overlooking a freshwater lake. The place is popular with seasonal campers who enjoy fishing and paddling around in boats, and has a very crowded, urban atmosphere.

Open: May 1 through Columbus Day.

125 Beaver Dam Campground

Location: On a small pond in Berwick; Southern Maine map page 33, grid d1.

Campsites, facilities: There are 60 sites for tents and RVs, 50 with water and electric hookups and 10 with none. Flush toilets, hot showers, picnic tables, fireplaces, a dump station, and a store are provided. Recreational facilities include a brook, fishing pond, sandy beach, playground, rec room, paddleboat and canoe rentals, volleyball, basketball, horseshoe pits, and miniature golf. Leashed pets are permitted.

Reservations, fees: Reservations are accepted. Sites are $17 to $22 a night.

Contact: Larry and Letty Erwin, Beaver Dam Campground, 551 Route 9, Berwick, ME 03901; (207) 698-1985.

Directions: From the junction of Routes 236 and 9 in Berwick, drive five miles east on Route 9 to the campground.

Trip notes: Beaver Dam is a pleasant little campground with sites spread out on 40 partially wooded acres. Kids will enjoy going for a hayride, just one of the camp's planned activities. There is a 20-acre pond for fishing and swimming, and yes, beavers do live in the pond and streams here. Maine's beaches lie just half an hour's drive to the south, while the White Mountains of New Hampshire are only an hour away to the northwest.

Open: May 17 through September 15.

126 Indian Rivers Campground

Location: On the Piscataqua River in Eliot; Southern Maine map page 33, grid d1.

Campsites, facilities: There are 35 sites

for tents and RVs, with full hookups available. Each site has a picnic table and fireplace. Flush toilets, hot showers, and a dump station are provided. For recreation, there is a heated indoor swimming pool, a playground, rec room, horseshoe pits, a sandy beach, canoe rentals, and a swimming float. The maximum length for trailers is 30 feet. Leashed pets are permitted.

Reservations, fees: Reservations are accepted. Sites are $15 to $19 a night, plus 50 cents for pets.

Contact: Lloyd and Philice Burt, Indian Rivers Campground, Route 101, Eliot, ME 03903; (207) 748-0844.

Directions: From Interstate 95 in Kittery, take exit 3 and travel seven miles north on Route 236. Turn left on Route 101 and drive a quarter mile west to the campground.

Trip notes: The campground is set in the woods alongside a tidal stream within a short drive of the beaches of Maine and New Hampshire. Bring your fishing gear and cast for bluefish or striped bass in the Piscataqua and Cocheco Rivers, or swim in the salt water. There's no drop-off, so it's safe for children, and there is a sandy beach for sunbathing.

Open: May 1 through November 1.

⑫⑦ Camp Eaton

Location: Across from Long Sands Beach in York Harbor; Southern Maine map page 33, grid d1.

Campsites, facilities: There are 307 sites for RVs, most with full hookups; cabins and tent sites are available. Flush toilets, hot showers, picnic tables, fireplaces, and a dump station are provided. You'll also find a playground, rec room, volleyball and basketball courts, horseshoe pits, and shuffleboard. Leashed pets are permitted.

Reservations, fees: Reservations are recommended. Sites are $26 a night.

Contact: Peter and Kathy Wagner, Camp Eaton, P.O. Box 626, Route 1A, York Harbor, ME 03911; (207) 363-3424.

Directions: From the Maine Turnpike (Interstate 95) at York Village, take exit 4 (the "Yorks") and drive a quarter mile south on U.S. 1, then get on U.S. 1A and drive three miles northeast to the campground on the left.

Trip notes: Since 1923 this venerable RV park has been a fixture above the sands of York Beach. Perched on a bluff overlooking the surf, the campground is ideally situated for those looking for a site within walking distance of the shops and restaurants in the picture-postcard village of York Harbor, as well as the rides, amusements, and tacky souvenir shops of York Beach. Long Sands Beach, just across U.S. 1A from the campground, extends for two miles. While you're here, be sure to take a short drive to the scenic Nubble Light on Cape Neddick.

Open: May 1 through October 2.

⑫⑧ Libby's Oceanside Camp

Location: Near Long Sands Beach in York Harbor; Southern Maine map page 33, grid d1.

Campsites, facilities: There are 95 sites for tents and RVs with full hookups. Flush toilets, free hot showers, picnic tables, fireplaces, and a rec room are provided. Campers enjoy easy access to long sandy beaches. Leashed pets are permitted.

Reservations, fees: Reservations are accepted for stays of one week or longer. A deposit of $50 per week is required. Sites are $30 to $35 a night.

Contact: Norm and Cindy Davidson,

Libby's Oceanside Camp, P.O. Box 40, U.S. 1A, York Harbor, ME 03911; (207) 363-4171.

Directions: From the Maine Turnpike (Interstate 95) at York Village, take exit 4 (the "Yorks") and drive a quarter mile south on U.S. 1, then get on U.S. 1A and drive three miles northeast to the campground on the right.

Trip notes: Like nearby neighbor Camp Eaton (see campground number 127), this RV spot has overlooked the York Beach sands since 1923 from its blufftop perch above the surf. It is a good choice for those campers who are looking for an oceanside site within walking distance of both the shops and restaurants in the picturesque village of York Harbor and the tacky rides, amusements, and souvenir shops of touristy York Beach.

Open: May 15 through October 15.

129 Flagg's Trailer Park

Location: In the town of York Beach; Southern Maine map page 33, grid d1.

Campsites, facilities: There are 84 sites for RVs up to 35 feet in length, with full and partial hookups. Flush toilets, hot showers, picnic tables, fireplaces, and a playground are provided. Seasonal campers can obtain telephone and cable TV hookups. No pets are allowed.

Reservations, fees: Reservations are recommended. Sites $24 a night.

Contact: Flagg's Trailer Park, Webber Road, Box 232, York Beach, ME 03910; (207) 363-5050.

Directions: From the Maine Turnpike (Interstate 95) at York Village, take exit 4 (the "Yorks") and drive a quarter mile south on U.S. 1, then get on U.S. 1A and drive 3.5 miles northeast to the campground on the left.

Trip notes: Yet another campground within walking distance of the sandy beaches, souvenir shops, and amusements of York Beach, Flagg's is a small trailer park with a family orientation. If you plan on singing around the campfire well into the wee hours, move on to the next spot: Flagg's imposes "quiet hours" from 10 P.M. to 8 A.M. every night.

Open: May 11 through September 30.

130 York Beach Camper Park

Location: On U.S. 1A in York Beach; Southern Maine map page 33, grid d1.

Campsites, facilities: There are 46 sites for tents and RVs, 34 with full hookups, five with water and electric, and seven with none. Flush toilets, hot showers, picnic tables, fireplaces, a dump station, laundry facilities, a store, and a playground are provided. Sandy beaches are within walking distance. Leashed pets are permitted.

Reservations, fees: Reservations are accepted. Sites are $18.50 to $27.50 a night.

Contact: York Beach Camper Park, U.S. 1A, Box 127, York Beach, ME 03910; (207) 363-1343.

Directions: From the Maine Turnpike (Interstate 95) at York Village, take exit 4 (the "Yorks") and drive north on U.S. 1 for 3.3 miles. Turn right on U.S. 1A and travel 1.1 miles east to the campground.

Trip notes: Found near the heart of York Beach's popular attractions, including restaurants, beaches, and York's Wild Kingdom and Amusement Park, the campground is central to all that this resort community has to offer. Also nearby are boat operators offering whale watching and deep-sea fishing excursions.

Open: May 15 through October 1.

131 Cape Neddick Oceanside Campground

Location: On the oceanfront and along the Cape Neddick River; Southern Maine map page 33, grid d1.

Campsites, facilities: There are 80 sites for tents and RVs, 50 with electric hookups and 30 with no hookups. Flush toilets, hot showers, picnic tables, fireplaces, a dump station, and a store are provided. Campers have access to the ocean and saltwater swimming, boating, and fishing. The maximum RV length is 28 feet. No pets are allowed.

Reservations, fees: Reservations are required, and you must make a 20 percent deposit. The reservation must be for at least one week, starting on a Sunday. Sites are $22 to $25 a night.

Contact: Cape Neddick Oceanside Campground, P.O. Box 1, Cape Neddick, ME 03902; (207) 363-4366.

Directions: From the intersection of U.S. 1A and Shore Road, drive 1.25 miles north on Shore Road to the campground.

Trip notes: Tenters and those traveling with small self-contained campers or trailers will find that their needs will be catered to at this campground. Many sites are located directly on the oceanfront and along the Cape Neddick River. Stay here and you'll be within easy walking distance of the various amusements and tourist-trap souvenir shops of York Beach and within a short drive of fine restaurants, playhouses, and nature preserves in the town of York Harbor and in nearby Ogunquit to the north. Needless to add, dozens of miles of sand and surf are also close at hand for beach lovers who want to sunbathe, swim, or toss a Frisbee.

Open: May 15 through October 15.

132 Dixon's Campground

Location: Between Ogunquit and York; Southern Maine map page 33, grid d1.

Campsites, facilities: There are 100 sites for tents and RVs, 22 with water and electric hookups and 78 with no hookups. Flush toilets, metered hot showers, picnic tables, fireplaces, a dump station, store, and playground are provided. Ice is available. Campers have easy access to saltwater swimming, boating, and fishing. The maximum RV length is 30 feet. No pets are allowed.

Reservations, fees: Reservations are accepted for stays of three nights or more. If staying less than one week, the reservation must be paid in full. Sites are $24 to $28 a night.

Contact: Dixon's Campground, 1740 U.S. 1, Cape Neddick, ME 03902; (207) 363-2131.

Directions: From the village of Ogunquit, drive two miles south on U.S. 1 to the campground.

Trip notes: Another medium-sized campground in the York Beach area, this one caters to tenters and people with small campers and trailers. Stay here and you'll be close to beaches, restaurants, nature preserves, and summer theater. Bring your camera to photograph the Nubble Light, a lighthouse built in 1879 on a high rocky island.

Open: Memorial Day through September 15.

133 Pinederosa Camping Area

Location: Near Ogunquit; Southern Maine map page 33, grid d1.

Campsites, facilities: There are 152

sites for tents and RVs, some with full hookups and others with water and electric. Flush toilets, hot showers, picnic tables, fireplaces, a dump station, laundry facilities, a swimming pool, and a store are provided. Sand beaches, natural areas, and deep-sea fishing boats are accessible nearby. Leashed pets are permitted.

Reservations, fees: Reservations are accepted. Sites are $18 to $23 a night.

Contact: Barbara Stevens, Pinederosa Camping Area, RR 1, Box 1330, Wells, ME 04090; (207) 646-2492.

Directions: From Ogunquit, drive one mile north on U.S. 1. Turn left on Captain Thomas Road and drive 1.5 miles west to the campground.

Trip notes: Family-owned Pinederosa is a wooded, riverside campground that enjoys a semirural setting. Private wooded sites are available in addition to those set in open fields. The campground is within a few minutes' drive of ocean beaches, summer theater, fine restaurants, and nature preserves. For more information on attractions in the Wells and Ogunquit area, see Beach Acres (campground number 134).

Open: May 15 through October 1.

⑬④ Beach Acres

Location: On U.S. 1 in Wells; Southern Maine map page 33, grid d1.

Campsites, facilities: There are 300 sites for tents and RVs, most with full hookups and some with no hookups. Flush toilets, hot showers, picnic tables, fireplaces, a dump station, laundry facilities, and a store are provided. For recreation, campers have use of a swimming pool, playground, rec room, shuffleboard, and a basketball hoop. Ice and firewood are available. No pets are allowed.

Reservations, fees: Reservations are recommended. Sites are $20 to $26 a night.

Contact: Marc and Sandy Batchelder, Beach Acres, 563 Post Road, Wells, ME 04090; (207) 646-5612.

Directions: From the Maine Turnpike (Interstate 95) near Wells, take exit 2 and drive 1.5 miles east on Route 9/109. Turn right on U.S. 1 and travel two miles south to Eldridge Road. Turn left on Eldridge Road and drive one block east to the campground.

Trip notes: A large campground, Beach Acres is within walking distance of sandy ocean beaches that stretch for some nine miles. The resort town of Wells, where the campground is located, boasts plenty of antique stores and factory outlets. For those who want to escape the hectic pace of town and nearby U.S. 1, the Rachel Carson National Wildlife Refuge offers peace and quiet. This woodland retreat overlooks a salt marsh, tidal channels, and an estuary, and has a boardwalk that winds throughout the area. The Wells National Estuarine Research Reserve at Laudholm Farm is another great getaway. With seven miles of trails meandering through 1,600 acres of fields, woods, wetlands, and barrier beaches, the reserve is worth a visit.

Open: Memorial Day through Labor Day.

⑬⑤ Ocean Overlook

Location: On U.S. 1 in Wells; Southern Maine map page 33, grid d1.

Campsites, facilities: There are 50 sites for tents and RVs, most with full hookups. Flush toilets, hot showers, picnic tables, fireplaces, and a dump station are provided. Also on the grounds are two pools, a playground, recreation fields, and badminton and volleyball nets. Beaches are nearby. No pets are allowed.

Reservations, fees: Reservations are recommended. Weekly rentals require a deposit of $50. Sites are $25 to $27 a night.

Contact: The Martinez Family, Ocean Overlook, U.S. 1, P.O. Box 309, Wells, ME 04090; (207) 646-3075.

Directions: From the Maine Turnpike (Interstate 95) near Wells, take exit 2 and drive 1.5 miles east on Route 9/109. Turn right on U.S. 1 and travel 1.5 miles south to the campground on the right.

Trip notes: Ocean Overlook is one of several options for those who are looking for a place to set up camp near the popular sand beaches in Wells and Ogunquit. This facility has spacious, grassy sites set back from busy U.S. 1. While in Wells, check out the nearby Rachel Carson National Wildlife Refuge and the Webhannet River Marsh natural area. For more information on the Wells area, see the trip notes for Beach Acres (campground number 134).

Open: May 15 through Columbus Day.

---

136 Wells Beach Resort

Location: On U.S. 1 in Wells; Southern Maine map page 33, grid d1.

Campsites, facilities: There are 212 sites for tents and RVs, 171 with full hookups and 41 with no hookups. Cable TV hookups are available. Flush toilets, hot showers, tables, fireplaces, a dump station, laundry facilities, and a store are provided. For recreation, there is a swimming pool, two playgrounds, a rec room, fitness room, miniature golf, volleyball, basketball, and horseshoe pits. Leashed pets are permitted.

Reservations, fees: Reservations are accepted. A deposit of $50 is required for stays of three days or less, and a deposit of $100 is required for stays of four or more days. Sites are $25.50 to $36 a night.

Contact: Ken and Shirley Griffen, Wells Beach Resort, 1000 Post Road, U.S. 1, Wells, ME 04090; (207) 646-7570 or (800) 640-2267/CAMP.

Directions: From the Maine Turnpike (Interstate 95) near Wells, take exit 2 and drive 1.5 miles east on Route 9/109. Turn right on U.S. 1 and travel 1.25 miles south to the campground on the right.

Trip notes: Wells Beach Resort is a popular commercial campground located on a major highway just one mile from the sandy beaches of Wells. Very clean and well maintained, the park is also close to deepsea fishing and whale watching excursion boats, summer playhouses, factory outlets, amusement parks, and wildlife refuges. For more information on the Wells area, see Beach Acres (campground number 134).

Open: May 15 through October 15.

---

137 Ocean View Cottages and Campground

Location: Near the beach in Wells; Southern Maine map page 33, grid d1.

Campsites, facilities: There are 108 sites for tents and RVs, 60 with full hookups, 35 with water and electric, and 13 with none. Flush toilets, hot showers, picnic tables, fireplaces, a dump station, laundry facilities, and a store are provided. For recreation, campers will find a pool, playground, rec room, shuffleboard, and basketball and tennis courts. Leashed pets are permitted.

Reservations, fees: Reservations are recommended, and must be for at least four nights in July and August. A deposit of $20 is required for stays of under a week; for a week or longer it's $40. Sites are $18 to $25 a night.

Contact: Ocean View Cottages and Campground, P.O. Box 153, 84 Harbor Road, Wells, ME 04090; (207) 646-3308.

Directions: From the junction of U.S. 1 and Route 9 in Wells, drive north on U.S. 1 for one-tenth of a mile. Turn right at the fire station and drive a quarter mile east on Lower Landing Road to the campground.

Trip notes: As the name suggests, this campground, which is situated above the Webhannet River Marsh natural area and two miles from sandy beaches, affords an ocean view. But not all the senses are pampered here, for the place is also just off busy, noisy U.S. 1. For more information on the Wells area, see the trip notes for Beach Acres (campground number 134).

Open: May 1 through Columbus Day.

138 Sea-Vu Campground

Location: Near the beach in Wells; Southern Maine map page 33, grid d1.

Campsites, facilities: There are 220 sites for tents and RVs, 170 with full hookups, 36 with water and electric, and 14 with no hookups. Flush toilets, hot showers, picnic tables, fireplaces, a dump station, laundry facilities, and a store are provided. On the property there's also a pool, playground, sports field, rec room, library, aerobics classes, miniature golf, volleyball and basketball courts, and horseshoe pits. LP gas is available. Leashed pets are permitted.

Reservations, fees: Reservations are recommended. For holidays and stays of less than four days, send the full amount due; for stays of four or more days, send half the total amount. Sites are $26 to $34 a night with advance reservations, and $27 to $35 without a reservation.

Contact: Sea-Vu Campground, U.S. 1, P.O. Box 67, Wells, ME 04090; (207) 646-7732.

Directions: From the Maine Turnpike (Interstate 95) near Wells, take exit 2 and drive 1.5 miles east on Route 9/109. Turn left and drive half a mile north on U.S. 1 to the campground on the right.

Trip notes: Sea-Vu is another large, crowded campground situated to the side of a busy highway in a semi-wooded location close to sand beaches. The campground overlooks the salt marshes of Wells Harbor and is within five miles of Ogunquit and Kennebunkport. Nearby activities include deep-sea fishing and whale watching excursions, hiking or canoeing in wildlife refuges, and strolling through picturesque villages. For more information on the Wells area, see Beach Acres (campground number 134).

Open: May 15 through Columbus Day.

139 Gregoire's Campground

Location: In Wells; Southern Maine map page 33, grid d1.

Campsites, facilities: There are 130 sites, 31 with full hookups, 62 with water and electric, and 37 with none. Flush toilets, hot showers, picnic tables, fireplaces, a dump station, laundry facilities, and a store are provided. There's also a playground and a rec room. Leashed pets are permitted.

Reservations, fees: Reservations are accepted. Sites are $13 to $19 a night.

Contact: Albert and Virginia Gregoire, Gregoire's Campground, Route 109, Wells, ME 04090; (207) 646-3711.

Directions: From the Maine Turnpike (Interstate 95) in Wells, take exit 2 and continue 100 yards north on Route 109 to the campground.

Trip notes: Providing campsites in an open field setting, Gregoire's Campground is located within a short drive of sandy beaches. Also nearby is the Ogunquit Playhouse, one of the country's best summerstock theaters. For more information on the Wells area, see Beach Acres (campground number 134).

Open: May 15 through September 15.

140 Sea Breeze Campground

Location: On U.S. 1 in Wells; Southern Maine map page 33, grid d1.

Campsites, facilities: There are 58 sites for tents and RVs, most with full hookups. Flush toilets, hot showers, picnic tables, fireplaces, a dump station, laundry facilities, and a store are provided. A heated swimming pool, a playground, and rec room are also on the property. Cable TV hookups are available. Leashed pets are permitted.

Reservations, fees: Reservations are recommended. A 50 percent deposit for weeklong stays and a full deposit for shorter stays is required. Sites range from $21 to $27 a night.

Contact: Sea Breeze Campground, 2073 Post Road, Wells, ME 04090; (207) 646-4301 or fax (207) 646-4803.

Directions: From the Maine Turnpike (Interstate 95) near Wells, take exit 2 and drive 1.5 miles east on Route 9/109. Turn left on U.S. 1 and drive 1.3 miles north to the campground.

Trip notes: Sea Breeze is a small campground set in a wooded area off busy U.S. 1 within minutes of sandy beaches, wildlife refuges, summer-stock theaters, deep-sea fishing and whale watching operators, and picturesque villages. For more information on the Wells area, see the trip notes for Beach Acres (campground number 134).

Open: May 15 through Columbus Day.

141 Stadig Campground

Location: Just off the U.S. 1 bypass in Wells; Southern Maine map page 33, grid d1.

Campsites, facilities: There are 139 sites for tents and RVs, 37 with full hookups, 5 with water and electric, and 97 with none. Flush toilets, hot showers, picnic tables, fireplaces, a dump station, laundry facilities, and a store are provided. You'll also find a playground, rec room, volleyball, basketball, shuffleboard, and horseshoe pits. No pets are allowed.

Reservations, fees: Reservations are accepted. Sites are $14 to $20 a night.

Contact: Stadig Campground, RFD 2, Box 850, Wells, ME 04090; (207) 646-2298.

Directions: From the Maine Turnpike (Interstate 95) near Wells, take exit 2 to U.S. 1 and drive two miles north to the intersection with the U.S. 1 bypass. Drive a quarter mile north on the U.S. 1 bypass to the campground.

Trip notes: The campground is nestled in the woods off a busy highway and puts campers within a short drive of sandy beaches, deep-sea fishing and whale watching excursions, summer theater playhouses, shops, and villages.

Open: May 30 through October 1.

142 Kennebunkport Camping

Location: Near the coast in Kennebunkport; Southern Maine map page 33, grid d1.

Campsites, facilities: There are 82 sites for tents and RVs, 33 with full hookups, 26 with water and electric, and 23 with none. Flush toilets, free hot showers, picnic tables, fireplaces, a dump station, and a store are provided. For recreation, there is a play area, horseshoes, badminton, and volleyball. Ice and firewood are available. Leashed pets are permitted.

Reservations, fees: Reservations are accepted and require a deposit of one night's fee. Sites are $14 to $20 a night.

Contact: The Roberge Family, Kennebunkport Camping, 117 Old Cape Road, Kennebunkport, ME 04046; (207) 967-2732 or fax (207) 967-3519.

Directions: From the intersection of Routes 9A/35 and 9, drive two miles east on Route 9, then turn left and drive one-tenth of a mile north on Old Cape Road to the campground.

Trip notes: There's plenty to do when you camp in Kennebunkport. Hit the beach, hop on a boat for a whale watching or deep-sea fishing trip, poke around the picturesque villages of Kennebunkport and Cape Porpoise, and visit natural areas such as the Rachel Carson National Wildlife Refuge in nearby Wells. The campground is located close to President George Bush's summer home, which is visible from a turnout along the road.

Open: May 15 through October 15.

143 Fran-Mort Campground

Location: In Kennebunkport; Southern Maine map page 33, grid d1.

Campsites, facilities: There are 101 sites for tents and RVs, 75 with full hookups and 26 with none. Flush toilets, hot showers, picnic tables, fireplaces, a dump station, laundry facilities, and a playground are provided. Leashed pets are permitted.

Reservations, fees: Reservations are accepted. Sites are $15 a night.

Contact: Morrell Swain, Fran-Mort Campground, Sinnott Road, Kennebunkport, ME 04046; (207) 967-4927.

Directions: From the junction of U.S. 1 and Route 9A/35 in Kennebunk, drive north on U.S. 1 for about 1.25 miles. Turn right on Log Cabin Road and travel approximately one mile to the intersection with Sinnott Road, where you turn right and continue to the campground.

Trip notes: Fran-Mort is a large, open-field campground situated near beaches, picturesque coastal villages, and shops. The curious may opt for a drive along the shore past nearby Walkers Point, site of President George Bush's summer home, which you can glimpse from a scenic turnout on the road.

Open: May 30 through October 12.

144 Salty Acres Campground

Location: Near the ocean in Kennebunkport; Southern Maine map page 33, grid d1.

Campsites, facilities: There are 400 sites for tents and RVs, 70 with full hookups, 90 with water and electric, and 240 with none. Flush toilets, hot showers, picnic tables, fireplaces, laundry facilities, a dump station, and a store are provided on the grounds. For recreation, there is a swimming pool, playground, sports field, volleyball and badminton nets, horseshoes, and access to the ocean and a river for fishing, boating, and swimming. Leashed pets are permitted.

Reservations, fees: Reservations are accepted. Sites are $17 to $22 a night.

Contact: Priscilla Spang, Salty Acres Campground, Route 9, 277 Mills Road, Kennebunkport, ME 04046; (207) 967-2483.

Directions: From the junction of Routes 9A/35 and 9, drive five miles east on Route 9 to the campground.

Trip notes: One of southern Maine's prettiest, and possibly the most overlooked, stretches of coastline is home to Salty Acres, a very large full-service campground. Stay here and you'll be near Walkers Point, the home of George Bush, and within minutes of both downtown Kennebunkport with its shops and restaurants and Kennebunkport Harbor, where you can join fishing charters or go on a boating excursion. There are fine opportunities for ocean swimming, fishing, and boating close by at Goose Rocks Beach and Fortunes Rocks Beach. Bicyclists will find the lightly traveled roads in the area are good for riding.

Open: May 15 through October 15.

145 Yogi Bear's Jellystone Park

Location: Near Sanford; Southern Maine map page 33, grid d1.

Campsites, facilities: There are 132 sites for tents and RVs, 74 with full hookups, 43 with water and electric, and 15 with none. Flush toilets, hot showers, picnic tables, fireplaces, a dump station, laundry facilities, and a store are provided. A swimming pool, playground, rec room, volleyball, basketball, and badminton courts, and horseshoe pits are also on the property. Planned activities include hayrides. The maximum RV length is 35 feet. Leashed pets are permitted.

Reservations, fees: Reservations are accepted. Sites are $16 to $20 a night.

Contact: Yogi Bear's Jellystone Park, 1175 Main Street/Route 109, Sanford, ME 04073; (207) 324-7782.

Directions: From the junction of Routes

4 and 109 in Sanford, drive four miles east on Route 109 to the campground.

Trip notes: The campground is situated on a sandy plain in a nondescript second-growth forest about 20 minutes by car from the nearest attractions of the area. Sites are either wooded or open. Unfortunately, the park has fallen into a state of neglect and disrepair.

Open: May 1 through Columbus Day.

146 Yankeeland Campground

Location: Near Kennebunk; Southern Maine map page 33, grid d1.

Campsites, facilities: There are 200 sites for tents and RVs with full, partial, and no hookups. Flush toilets, hot showers, picnic tables, fireplaces, a dump station, laundry facilities, and a store are provided. For recreation, you'll find a playground, pool, rec room, basketball, and horseshoe pits. Leashed pets are permitted.

Reservations, fees: Reservations are recommended and require a deposit of one day's fee. Sites are $15 to $17 a night.

Contact: The Robinson Family, Yankeeland Campground, P.O. Box 829, Kennebunk, ME 04043; (207) 985-7576 or (800) 832-7059.

Directions: From the Maine Turnpike (Interstate 95) near Kennebunk, take exit 3 and drive 2.7 miles west on the Alfred Road to the campground.

Trip notes: Many permanent summer retirement homes have been established in this large campground set on a flat, sandy plain in an unspectacular second-growth forest. Beaches and the other wonderful area attractions are approximately 20 minutes away by car.

Open: May 1 through Columbus Day.

147 Mousam River Campground

Location: Near Kennebunk; Southern Maine map page 33, grid d1.

Campsites, facilities: There are 115 sites for RVs with full hookups. Flush toilets, hot showers, picnic tables, fireplaces, laundry facilities, a dump station, and a store are provided. A swimming pool, rec room, pavilion, badminton nets, and horseshoes are also on the grounds. Leashed pets are permitted.

Reservations, fees: Reservations are accepted. Sites are $20 a night.

Contact: Mousam River Campground, West Kennebunk, ME 04094; (207) 985-2507.

Directions: From the intersection of U.S. 1 and Route 35, drive two miles north on Route 35 to an overpass on the Maine Turnpike (Interstate 95). At the fork after the overpass, go straight onto the Alfred Road and continue 1.5 miles north to the campground.

Trip notes: A meandering river flows by the large wooded sites here. However, like several other nearby campgrounds, this place is not too attractive, as it's surrounded by a stunted, second-growth forest in a semirural area. Mousam River is also pretty far removed from all the great attractions of the region, some 20 minutes by car from Maine's attractive sand beaches.

Open: May 15 through October 15.

148 Shamrock RV Park

Location: Near Biddeford; Southern Maine map page 33, grid d1.

Campsites, facilities: There are 60 sites for tents and RVs, 25 with full hookups, 19 with water and electric, and 16 with none. Flush toilets, free hot showers, a dump station, picnic tables, and fireplaces are provided. For recreation, there is a swimming pool, playground, rec room, and fishing pond. Leashed pets are permitted.

Reservations, fees: Reservations are recommended. Sites are $15 to $25 a night.

Contact: Irene Lamarche, Shamrock RV Park, 391 West Street, Biddeford, ME 04005; (207) 284-4282.

Directions: From the intersection of Route 111, U.S. 1, and West Street in downtown Biddeford, drive 4.5 miles east on West Street to the campground.

Trip notes: Offering quiet and secluded sites, Shamrock RV Park is a wooded campground situated in a rural area near some of the finest scenery along Maine's South Coast. Be sure to visit Biddeford Pool, Fortunes Rocks Beach, and Goose Rocks Beach, and drive along the shore road to Cape Porpoise and Kennebunkport. In Kennebunkport Harbor, you might want to charter a deep-sea fishing boat or head out to open waters to look for whales.

Open: May 30 through October 1.

149 Saco/Portland South KOA

Location: In Saco; Southern Maine map page 33, grid d2.

Campsites, facilities: There are 124 sites for tents and RVs with full, partial, and no hookups. Flush toilets, free hot showers, picnic tables, fireplaces, a dump station, laundry facilities, and a store are provided, as are a pool, playground, rec room, volleyball, basketball, and horseshoe pits. LP gas is available. Leashed pets are permitted.

Reservations, fees: Reservations are recommended. Sites are $20 to $28 a night.

Contact: Saco/Portland South KOA, 814A Portland Road, Saco, ME 04072; (207) 282-0502 or (800) KOA-1886.

Directions: From the Maine Turnpike (Interstate 95), take exit 5 to Interstate 195. After driving a short distance, take exit 2B and continue north on U.S. 1 for 1.6 miles to the campground on the left.

Trip notes: No surprises here. KOA is a nation-wide chain, just like McDonald's and Wal-Mart, and campers know what they are going to get. The large commercial facility is situated in 30 acres of woods two miles from the sand beaches, amusements, and souvenir shops of Old Orchard Beach.

Open: May 9 through October 17.

⑮⓪ Cascadia Park Campground

Location: In Saco; Southern Maine map page 33, grid d2.

Campsites, facilities: There are 100 sites for tents and RVs, 47 with full hook-ups, 26 with water and electric, and 27 with none. Flush toilets, hot showers, picnic tables, fireplaces, laundry facilities, and a dump station are provided. Volleyball and badminton nets are also available. Leashed pets are permitted.

Reservations, fees: Reservations are accepted. Sites are $15 to $19 a night.

Contact: Cascadia Park Campground, 911 Portland Road, U.S. 1, Saco, ME 04072; (207) 282-1666.

Directions: From the Maine Turnpike (Interstate 95), take exit 5 to Interstate 195. After driving a short distance, take exit 2B and continue north on U.S. 1 for 2.5 miles to the campground.

Trip notes: Although it has an unenviable location along a busy highway, Cascadia is still close to some very worthwhile places

to visit. The Scarborough Marsh Nature Center in Scarborough and the Biddeford Pool tidal basin to the south, as well as several other nature preserves along the southern Maine coast, are all within easy reach. Old Orchard Beach, with its seven-mile-long sandy beachfront and associated shops and amusements, is just minutes away by car.

Open: May 1 through October 30.

⑮① Bayley's Camping Resort

Location: In Scarborough; Southern Maine map page 33, grid d2.

Campsites, facilities: There are 470 sites for tents and RVs, 250 with full hookups, 100 with water and electric, 40 with electric only, and 80 with none. Flush toilets, free hot showers, wheelchair-accessible rest rooms, picnic tables, fireplaces, a dump station, laundry facilities, and a store are provided. For recreation, there's a playground, rec room, three pools, a stocked fishing pond, miniature golf, volleyball, basketball, and horseshoe pits. Ice, firewood, groceries, LP gas, and RV supplies are available. Leashed pets are permitted.

Reservations, fees: Reservations are accepted. A deposit of $150 is required, and reservations for four days and under must be paid in full. Sites are $30 to $39 a night.

Contact: Bayley's Camping Resort, Box T-6, Ross Road, West Scarborough, ME 04074; (207) 883-6043.

Directions: From the Maine Turnpike (Interstate 95) in Scarborough, take exit 6 and drive 1.5 miles south on U.S. 1 to Route 9. Turn left on Route 9 and drive three miles east to Pine Point. In Pine Point follow the signs to the campground.

Trip notes: Bayley's is a very large, private campground that's close to all the attractions of Old Orchard Beach and Maine's southern coast. Although virtually every camper spends much of the time at the seashore, the resort does offer enough activities to keep a family busy for weeks. The wide variety of water-related recreation options includes swimming pools, spas, trout ponds, and paddleboat ponds. An extensive activities program—from fishing derbies and wagon rides to soccer games and bike rodeos—is organized for children and adults alike. When you tire of the crowds, be sure to check out the nearby Scarborough Marsh Nature Center and Prouts Neck Bird Sanctuary.

Open: May 1 through Columbus Day.

⓯ Old Orchard Beach Campground

Location: In Old Orchard Beach; Southern Maine map page 33, grid d2.

Campsites, facilities: There are 400 sites for tents and RVs, many with full hookups. Flush toilets, hot showers, picnic tables, fireplaces, a dump station, and laundry facilities are provided. For recreation, they offer a pool with a waterslide, a playground, rec room, volleyball, basketball, and horseshoe pits. Leashed pets are permitted.

Reservations, fees: Reservations are recommended. Sites are $18 to $22 a night.

Contact: The Daigle Family, Old Orchard Beach Campground, Ocean Park Road, Old Orchard Beach, ME 04064; (207) 934-4477.

Directions: From the Maine Turnpike (Interstate 95) near Saco, take exit 5 and drive east on Interstate 195 for 2.5 miles. Turn left on Route 5 and travel 100 feet east to the campground.

Trip notes: For those who want their fun prepackaged and in large doses, Old Orchard Beach is like heaven on earth. If you fit that description, this campground is bound to please. Take a shuttle bus from the campground and be sure to check out such tourist attractions as Funtown (an amusement park), Aquaboggan (a waterslide), the Maine Mall, harness racing and stock car racing tracks, and hundreds of T-shirt shops. For more information on the Old Orchard Beach area, see the trip notes for Acorn Village (campground number 158).

Open: May 1 through Columbus Day.

⓲ Wagon Wheel Campground and Cabins

Location: In Old Orchard Beach; Southern Maine map page 33, grid d2.

Campsites, facilities: There are 400 sites for tents and RVs, many with full hookups. Flush toilets, hot showers, picnic tables, fireplaces, a dump station, laundry facilities, and a store are provided. Two swimming pools, a playground, rec room, volleyball, basketball, and horseshoe pits are among the recreational offerings. A shuttle bus service runs to the beach. Ice and firewood are available. Leashed pets are permitted.

Reservations, fees: Reservations are accepted. Sites range from $16.50 to $21.50 a night. Weekly and off-season rates also are available.

Contact: Wagon Wheel Campground and Cabins, 3 Old Orchard Road, Old Orchard Beach, ME 04064; (207) 934-2160.

Directions: From the Maine Turnpike (Interstate 95) near Saco, take exit 5 and drive about 2.5 miles east on Interstate 195. Turn left on Route 5 and travel a quarter mile east, then turn right and drive another quarter mile south on Saco Road to the campground entrance.

Trip notes: This large, popular trailer and RV park lies within two miles of the sandy beaches, rides, and amusements of Old Orchard Beach. For more information on the Old Orchard Beach area, see Acorn Village (campground number 158).

Open: May 1 through Columbus Day.

154 Virginia Tent and Trailer Park

Location: Near Old Orchard Beach; Southern Maine map page 33, grid d2.

Campsites, facilities: There are 135 sites for tents and RVs, 48 with full hookups, 50 with water and electric, and 37 with no hookups. Flush toilets, hot showers, picnic tables, fireplaces, a dump station, laundry facilities, and a store are provided. There's also a swimming pool, playground, and shuffleboard courts on the property. Leashed pets are permitted.

Reservations, fees: Reservations are accepted and require a $25 deposit. Sites are $19 to $24 a night.

Contact: Virginia Tent and Trailer Park, P.O. Box 242, Temple Avenue, Old Orchard Beach, ME 04064; (207) 934-4791.

Directions: From the Maine Turnpike (Interstate 95) near Saco, take exit 5 and drive 2.5 miles east on Interstate 195. Turn left on Route 5 and travel half a mile east, then turn right on Temple Avenue and drive half a mile south to the campground.

Trip notes: Yet another option in bustling downtown Old Orchard Beach, this campground offers a quiet, open setting with shaded sites. It's just half a mile from the area's sandy beaches. For more information on the area, see the trip notes for Acorn Village (campground number 158).

Open: Memorial Day through September 24.

155 Wild Acres Family Camping Resort

Location: In Old Orchard Beach; Southern Maine map page 33, grid d2.

Campsites, facilities: There are 400 sites for tents and RVs, half with full hookups, the rest with either water and electric or no hookups. Facilities include flush toilets, hot showers, picnic tables, fireplaces, a dump station, laundry, and a store. For recreation, there are two swimming pools, three whirlpools, a playground, an adult rec room, a game room, tennis, volleyball, basketball, horseshoe pits, a nature trail, and a stocked fishing pond. Leashed pets are permitted.

Reservations, fees: Reservations are accepted. Sites are $22 to $30 a night.

Contact: Dick and Marion Ahearn, Wild Acres Family Camping Resort, 179 Saco Avenue, Old Orchard Beach, ME 04064; (207) 934-2535.

Directions: From the Maine Turnpike (Interstate 95) near Saco, take exit 5 and drive 2.5 miles east on Interstate 195. Turn left on Route 5 and travel three-quarters of a mile east to the campground.

Trip notes: Established in 1929, this is Old Orchard Beach's most venerable trailer park. The campground is located close to miles of sand beaches, amusement park rides, boating and deep-sea fishing excursions, restaurants, and shops. For more information on the Old Orchard Beach area, see Acorn Village (campground number 158).

Open: May 15 through Labor Day.

156 Ne're Beach Family Campground

Location: In Old Orchard Beach; Southern Maine map page 33, grid d2.

Campsites, facilities: There are 60 sites for tents and RVs, 13 with full hookups and 47 with water and electric hookups. Flush toilets, free hot showers, picnic tables, fireplaces, a dump station, laundry facilities, and a store are provided. There's a pool on the property and sandy ocean beaches nearby. Leashed pets are permitted.

Reservations, fees: Reservations are recommended July 1 through Labor Day. A deposit of $20 is required. Sites are $18 to $19 a night.

Contact: Phil and Michelle Boisjoly, Ne're Beach Family Campground, P.O. Box 537, 38 Saco Avenue/Route 5, Old Orchard Beach, ME 04064; (207) 934-7614.

Directions: From the Maine Turnpike (Interstate 95) near Saco, take exit 5 and drive 2.5 miles east on Interstate 195, then turn left on Route 5 and go 1.75 miles east to the campground.

Trip notes: Here's yet another option for those looking to camp near the sandy beaches and amusements of Old Orchard Beach. Sites are grassy and shaded by trees. For more information on the Old Orchard Beach area, see the trip notes for Acorn Village (campground number 158).

Open: May 15 through September 8.

157 Paradise Park Resort Campground

Location: In Old Orchard Beach; Southern Maine map page 33, grid d2.

Campsites, facilities: There are 200 sites for tents and RVs, 50 with full hookups, 100 with water and electric hookups, and 50 with none. Flush toilets, hot showers, picnic tables, fireplaces, a dump station, laundry facilities, and a store are provided. For recreation, there is a swimming pool, playground, rec room, volleyball, basket-

ball, horseshoe pits, paddleboat rentals, and pond and saltwater fishing and swimming. Leashed pets are permitted.

Reservations, fees: Reservations are recommended. Sites range from $18.50 to $26 a night.

Contact: Paradise Park Resort Campground, P.O. Box 4, Adelaide Road, Old Orchard Beach, ME 04064; (207) 934-4633.

Directions: From the Maine Turnpike (Interstate 95) near Saco, take exit 5 and drive 2.5 miles east on Interstate 195. Take Route 5 east for 4.2 miles, then turn left on Adelaide Road and continue a quarter mile north to the campground entrance at the end of the road.

Trip notes: A large spring-fed pond is on the 40-acre grounds of this wooded campground for families (no campers traveling alone are allowed). Park your car and leave it until you are ready to depart: Paradise Park claims to be the area's closest campground to the beach and is only 800 feet from downtown with its boardwalk, pier, amusement park, and other attractions. For more information on the Old Orchard Beach area, see Acorn Village (campground number 158).

Open: Memorial Day through September 15.

158 Acorn Village

Location: In Old Orchard Beach; Southern Maine map page 33, grid d2.

Campsites, facilities: There are 75 sites for tents and RVs with full, partial, and no hookups. Twenty heated cottages are also available. Flush toilets, hot showers, picnic tables, fireplaces, a dump station, laundry facilities, and a pool are provided. No pets are allowed.

Reservations, fees: Reservations are accepted. Sites are $18 to $26 a night.

Contact: Lionel and Cynthia Bisson, Acorn Village, 42 Walnut Street, Old Orchard Beach, ME 04064; (207) 934-4154.

Directions: From the Maine Turnpike (Interstate 95) near Saco, take exit 5 onto Interstate 195 then onto Route 5. Follow Route 5 east into the town of Old Orchard Beach. Make a quick left then a quick right onto Walnut Street and continue to the campground.

Trip notes: While there are nearly 3,500 miles of shoreline in Maine, sandy beach-front covers fewer than 100 miles. Most of these beaches are found south of Portland and are open to the public. The silvery, sandy beaches of the South Coast stretch for miles and are very popular with locals and travelers, as well as French-Canadian visitors. (You are likely to hear French being spoken wherever you go in this area.) Old Orchard Beach is a resort town with a varied assortment of tacky tourist traps and an amusement park. The highlight of the area is the seven-mile-long white sand beach. Acorn Village, located within the town of Old Orchard Beach, is a cottage village and campground within walking distance of the beach, pier, and amusements.

Open: Memorial Day through Labor Day.

⒧⒯ Hid'n Pines Campground

Location: In Old Orchard Beach; Southern Maine map page 33, grid d2.

Campsites, facilities: There are 254 sites for tents and RVs, many with full hookups. Flush toilets, free hot showers, picnic tables, fireplaces, a dump station, laundry facilities, and a store are provided. For recreation, there is a heated pool, a playground, a rec room, and a basketball hoop. Leashed pets are permitted.

Reservations, fees: Reservations are recommended and require a deposit of $30. There is a three-night minimum stay on holidays. Sites are $18 to $22 a night.

Contact: Lary and Lori Owen, Hid'n Pines Campground, 8 Cascade Road, P.O. Box 647, Old Orchard Beach, ME 04064; (207) 934-2352.

Directions: From the Maine Turnpike (Interstate 95) near Saco, take exit 5 and drive 2.5 miles east on Interstate 195, then two miles east on Route 5. From the junction of Routes 5 and 98, drive 1.5 miles north on Route 98 to the campground.

Trip notes: True to its name, Hid'n Pines is located on 25 acres of pine trees and apple orchards and is within easy walking distance of Old Orchard Beach's famous and very popular seven-mile-long sandy ocean beach. For more information on the Old Orchard Beach area, see the trip notes for Acorn Village (campground number 158).

Open: May 15 through September 15.

⒧⒭ Powder Horn Family Camping

Location: In Old Orchard Beach; Southern Maine map page 33, grid d2.

Campsites, facilities: There are 458 sites, 217 with full hookups, 104 with water and electric, and 137 with none. Flush toilets, free hot showers, picnic tables, fireplaces, a dump station, laundry facilities, and a store are provided. For recreation, there are nearby sand beaches, three pools, a hot tub, playground, rec room, volleyball, basketball, badminton, shuffleboard, miniature golf, and horseshoe pits. Leashed pets are permitted.

Reservations, fees: Reservations are recommended on busy weekends. Sites are $22 to $30 a night.

Contact: David and Glenna Ahearn, Powder Horn Family Camping, P.O. Box 366, Route 98, Old Orchard Beach, ME 04064; (207) 934-4733.

Directions: From the Maine Turnpike (Interstate 95) near Saco, take exit 5 to U.S. 1. Drive north on U.S. 1 to Route 98. Turn right and drive 1.8 miles to the campground on the left.

Trip notes: Set on 80 acres of pine groves and open fields, Powder Horn Family Camping is another of the large private campgrounds found near the sandy beaches, amusements, and souvenir shops of Old Orchard Beach. You can cool off in the pool, unwind in the hot tub, or putter around the 18-hole miniature golf course. For more information on the Old Orchard Beach area, see the trip notes for Acorn Village (campground number 158).

Open: Memorial Day through Labor Day.

161 Cedar Haven Campground

Location: In Freeport; Southern Maine map page 33, grid c2.

Campsites, facilities: There are 58 sites for tents and RVs, 4 with full hookups, 44 with water and electric, and 10 with none. Facilities include flush toilets, free hot showers, picnic tables, fireplaces, laundry, a dump station and on-site service, and a store. A swimming pond, miniature golf, a rec room, volleyball, basketball, badminton, and horseshoe pits are among the recreational offerings. Leashed pets are permitted.

Reservations, fees: Reservations are accepted. Sites are $16 to $21 a night. Group and senior discounts are available.

Contact: The Kirby Family, Cedar Haven Campground, 19 Baker Road, Freeport, ME 04032; (207) 865-6254.

Directions: From Interstate 95 in Freeport, take exit 20 and drive half a mile north on Route 125/136, then go half a mile north on Route 125. Turn right and drive a quarter mile northeast on Baker Road to the campground.

Trip notes: Most sites at Cedar Haven are wooded, and the roads are wide enough to accommodate RVs of any length. There's also a separate tenting area with spacious sites. Just inland from the coast and island-speckled Casco Bay, the campground is within a short drive of many Mid-Coast attractions, including downtown Freeport and the giant L.L. Bean store. To escape the crowds in Freeport, head to Wolf Neck Woods State Park, where trails wander through woods along a rocky shoreline. Another nearby option for a quiet walk is the Audubon Society of Maine's Mast Landing Wildlife Sanctuary, where the hiking paths cross wooded ridges, fields, and orchards. Both are pleasant places to walk aimlessly and clear your head. For a swim, Popham Beach State Park is about 30 minutes away by car.

Open: May 1 through October 26.

162 Florida Lake Campground

Location: On a small lake in Freeport; Southern Maine map page 33, grid c2.

Campsites, facilities: There are 40 sites for tents and RVs, some with water and electric hookups. Facilities include flush toilets, hot showers, picnic tables, fireplaces, and a dump station. For recreation, there's a playing field; a 30-acre lake for swimming, boating, and fishing; and a swimming pool. Canoe and paddleboat rentals are available. Leashed pets are permitted.

Reservations, fees: Reservations are recommended and require a deposit of $20 for weekend stays and $40 for weekly reservations. Sites are $12 to $14 a night.

Contact: Alan and Vera Rogers, Florida Lake Campground, 82 Wardtown Road, Freeport, ME 04032; (207) 865-4874.

Directions: From Interstate 95 at Freeport, take exit 20 and drive three miles north on Route 125 to the campground on the right.

Trip notes: The small campground at Florida Lake is within minutes of downtown Freeport, L.L. Bean, and more than 100 factory outlet stores. For more information on the Freeport area, see Cedar Haven Campground (campground number 161).

Open: May 15 through October 15.

---

163 Flying Point Campground

Location: On Casco Bay in Freeport; Southern Maine map page 33, grid c2.

Campsites, facilities: There are 38 sites for tents and RVs, some with water and electric hookups. Facilities include flush toilets, hot showers, picnic tables, fireplaces, and a dump station. For recreation, there is saltwater swimming, fishing, and boating; volleyball and badminton nets, and horseshoes. Leashed pets are permitted.

Reservations, fees: Reservations are recommended and require a deposit of $18 for a weekend or $30 for a week. Sites are $15 to $18 a night.

Contact: Flying Point Campground, Lower Flying Point Road, Freeport, ME 04032; (207) 865-4569.

Directions: From Interstate 95 north of Yarmouth, take exit 19 and drive 1.5 miles south on U.S. 1 into Freeport. At the L.L. Bean store in the center of town, turn south onto Bow Street, which becomes Flying Point Road, and drive 3.75 miles to Lower

Flying Point Road. Turn right and drive less than a quarter mile to the campground.

Trip notes: Flying Point is a side of Freeport that most outlet shoppers never get a chance to explore, a beautiful neck of land jutting into island-strewn Casco Bay. The campsites here are situated directly on the oceanfront. This is the place for people who seek the beauty and tranquillity of the Maine coast, yet want to be near the attractions of downtown Freeport. For more information on the Freeport area, see the trip notes for Cedar Haven Campground (campground number 161).

Open: May 1 through October 15.

---

164 Recompense Shore Campground

Location: On Casco Bay in Freeport; Southern Maine map page 33, grid c2.

Campsites, facilities: There are 103 sites for tents and RVs, eight with partial hookups and 95 with no hookups. Facilities include flush toilets, hot showers, picnic tables, fireplaces, a dump station, and a store. For recreation, there is saltwater swimming, fishing, and boating; volleyball and badminton nets; and horseshoes. Leashed pets are permitted.

Reservations, fees: Reservations are accepted. Sites are $12 to $18 a night.

Contact: Recompense Shore Campground, 10 Burnett Road, Freeport, ME 04032; (207) 865-9307.

Directions: From Interstate 95 north of Yarmouth, take exit 19 and drive 1.5 miles south on U.S. 1 into Freeport. At the L.L. Bean store in the center of town, turn south onto Bow Street, which becomes Flying Point Road, and drive 2.25 miles east. Turn south on Wolf Neck Road and go 2.4 miles to the campground.

Trip notes: Recompense Shore is owned and operated by the University of Southern Maine, which employs the land as a demonstration of sustainable natural and recreational resource management. The campground claims a great location on the shore of island-filled Casco Bay, and sites are either situated on or near the shore, tucked away in and among towering pines, or bordering the fields of the campground's 600-acre farm. Next door is Wolf Neck Woods State Park, offering miles of hiking trails that meander through the woods and along the water. Also nearby is the Audubon Society of Maine's Mast Landing Wildlife Sanctuary. The lightly traveled roads in the area are great for biking. And for shoppers, the campground is only minutes from L.L. Bean in downtown Freeport. For more information on the Freeport area, see the trip notes for Cedar Haven Campground (campground number 161).

Open: Mid-May through mid-October.

⒖ Desert of Maine Campground

Location: In Freeport; Southern Maine map page 33, grid c2.

Campsites, facilities: There are 50 sites for tents and RVs, four with full hookups, 37 with water and electric hookups, and 9 with none. Flush toilets, hot showers, picnic tables, fireplaces, a dump station, laundry facilities, and a store are provided. Leashed pets are permitted.

Reservations, fees: Reservations are recommended. Sites are $16 to $20 a night.

Contact: The Dobson Family, Desert of Maine Campground, Desert Road, Freeport, ME 04032; (207) 865-6962.

Directions: From Interstate 95 in Freeport, take exit 19 and drive two miles west on Desert Road to the campground.

Trip notes: Offering a thought-provoking lesson on what can happen when people abuse land, the Desert of Maine is a 40-acre plot of sand that was once a prosperous farm. After being intensively cultivated, the land was heavily logged. Eventually, the topsoil blew away, leaving nothing but sand. Campers are given free admission to the Desert of Maine Visitor Center, where they'll find nature trails and narrated coach tours. The campground is within a short drive of downtown Freeport and its centerpiece attraction: the famous L.L. Bean store that never closes. From the campground you can catch a shuttle to downtown Freeport. For more information on the Freeport area, see Cedar Haven Campground (campground number 161).

Open: May 5 through October 15.

⒗ Blueberry Pond Campground

Location: West of Freeport in Pownal; Southern Maine map page 33, grid c2.

Campsites, facilities: There are 40 sites for tents and RVs, some with water and electric hookups. Flush toilets, free hot showers, picnic tables, fireplaces, and a dump station are provided. For recreation, there is a playground, hiking trails, a swimming pool, and horseshoe pits. Leashed pets are permitted.

Reservations, fees: Reservations are accepted. Sites are $14.50 to $17.50 a night.

Contact: Donald and Patricia Searfoss, Blueberry Pond Campground, 218 Poland Range Road, Pownal, ME 04069; (207) 688-4421.

Directions: From Interstate 95 at Freeport, take exit 20 and drive 2.5 miles north on Route 136 to Pownal Road. Turn left on Pownal Road and drive 1.5 miles west to the campground.

Trip notes: Blueberry Pond is a small, peaceful campground situated in a rural, wooded setting within an easy drive of Portland, Freeport, and Maine's coastal beaches and islands. Each site covers half an acre, providing plenty of privacy. Nature trails for strolling and bird-watching wind through the property. For more serious hiking, head to nearby Bradbury Mountain State Park (campground number 167).

Open: May 15 through October 15.

167 Bradbury Mountain State Park

Location: In Pownal; Southern Maine map page 33, grid c2.

Campsites, facilities: There are 41 sites for tents and trailers, all without hookups. Picnic tables, fireplaces, piped water, and pit toilets are provided. Hiking trails and a playing field are found within the park. Leashed pets are permitted.

Reservations, fees: Reservations are accepted, and the total amount due must accompany your request. Contact the Maine Bureau of Parks and Lands at the number below. Note that the State of Maine allocates some sites on a first-come, first-served basis. Sites are $8 a night for residents of Maine and $10 for nonresidents.

Contact: Bradbury Mountain State Park Ranger, (207) 688-4712. Maine Bureau of Parks and Lands, 22 State House Station, Augusta, ME 04333; (207) 287-3821.

Directions: From the center of Pownal, drive one mile east on Route 9 to the park. The campsites are located near the park entrance.

Trip notes: Bradbury Mountain is a lovely wooded ridge topped with a 460-foot peak that affords splendid views of Casco Bay, New Hampshire's White Mountains, and the surrounding countryside. The summit of the "mountain"—actually more of a low-lying ridge—is easily accessible via hiking trails that depart from the picnic area. Situated within six miles of downtown Freeport and the coast, the 297-acre parkland is within easy reach of Mid-Coast Maine's many attractions.

Open: Year-round.

168 Big Skye Acres Campground

Location: Near Bradbury Mountain State Park in Durham; Southern Maine map page 33, grid c2.

Campsites, facilities: There are 153 sites, 80 with full hookups and 73 with water and electric hookups. Facilities include flush toilets, hot showers, picnic tables, fireplaces, laundry, a dump station, and a store. For recreation, there is a pavilion, swimming pool, rec room, hiking trails, volleyball and badminton nets, and horseshoes. Leashed pets are permitted.

Reservations, fees: Reservations are accepted. Sites are $12 to $20 a night.

Contact: Big Skye Acres Campground, 1430 Hallowell Road, Durham, ME 04222; (207) 688-4147.

Directions: From Interstate 95 at Freeport, take exit 20 heading west toward Pownal Center and follow the signs to Bradbury Mountain State Park. When you reach the park entrance, drive 2.5 miles east on Route 9 to the campground.

Trip notes: Though it's just inland from the ocean and only minutes from the factory outlet stores in downtown Freeport, this campground feels as if it could be a hundred miles away from those popular tourist destinations and all their crowds. That's because it's surrounded by rural, rolling farm country. Nearby is Bradbury Mountain State Park, which provides visitors with views of the White Mountains which rise up to the west, and the ocean to the east. For more information on the area, see the trip notes for Bradbury Mountain State Park (campground number 167).

Open: May 15 through October 15.

⑯⑨ Durham Leisure Center and Campground

Location: In Durham; Southern Maine map page 33, grid c2.

Campsites, facilities: There are 38 sites for tents and RVs, several with full hookups. Flush toilets, hot showers, picnic tables, fireplaces, a dump station, laundry facilities, and a store are provided. You'll also find an indoor heated pool and a spa with private hot tubs and a sauna, as well as a playground, basketball court, and horseshoe pits. Leashed pets are permitted.

Reservations, fees: Reservations are required for holiday weekends. Sites are $17 to $20 a night.

Contact: Harold and Lorraine Cochrane, Durham Leisure Center and Campground, Route 136, Durham, ME 04222; (207) 353-4353.

Directions: From Interstate 95 at Freeport, take exit 20 and drive about 5.5 miles north on Route 136 to the campground on the right.

Trip notes: Bring your bathing suit and robe and get ready to relax, for the owners claim that this is Maine's only campground with an indoor heated pool and spa. The facility is located in a rural setting within minutes of Freeport, L.L. Bean, and the Maine coast.

Open: Year-round.

⑰⓪ Pinewood Family Farm

Location: In Sangerville; Southern Maine map page 33, grid a3.

Campsites, facilities: There are 20 sites for tents and RVs with water and electric hookups. Flush toilets, hot showers, picnic tables, fireplaces, a dump station, laundry facilities, a playground, and a store are provided. Leashed pets are permitted.

Reservations, fees: Reservations are accepted. Sites are $10 to $12 a night.

Contact: Gene and Myrna Johnson, Pinewood Family Farm, RFD 1, Box 576, Sangerville, ME 04479; (207) 876-4161.

Directions: From Dexter, travel north on Route 7 for four miles. Turn left on Silvers Mills Road and continue west for 4.1 miles. Turn at the sign for the Pinewood Family Farm and drive one mile to the campground.

Trip notes: This campground is in the process of being expanded. When complete, it may have a petting zoo, horseback riding facilities, a driving range, boat rentals, bike rentals, and nature trails—but as of this writing those amenities remain in the planning stage. The park is located on Center Pond, a fine spot for swimming, fishing, and boating. Moosehead Lake and Baxter State Park can be reached by car in about an hour and 15 minutes.

Open: May 15 through October 1.

⑰① Two Rivers Campground

Location: On the Kennebec River near Skowhegan; Southern Maine map page 33, grid a2.

Campsites, facilities: There are 65 sites

for tents and RVs, 40 with full hookups, 12 with water and electric, and 13 without hookups. Flush toilets, hot showers, picnic tables, fireplaces, cable TV, a dump station, laundry facilities, and a store are provided. For recreation there is a playground, horseshoe pits, a volleyball court, canoe rentals, and 1,300 feet of waterfront for swimming, fishing, and boating. A state-run boat ramp is nearby. Leashed pets are permitted.

Reservations, fees: Reservations are recommended. Sites are $15 to $18 a night.

Contact: The Beauregard Family, Two Rivers Campground, HCR 71, Box 14, Skowhegan, ME 04976; (207) 474-6482.

Directions: From the intersection of U.S. 2 and U.S. 201 in Skowhegan, drive 2.5 miles east on U.S. 2 to the campground.

Trip notes: A peninsula at the confluence of the Kennebec River and Wesserunsett Stream is the site of this campground. Sites are either in open fields or under cool shade trees along the waterfront. The campground is spacious and well maintained, and there is ample access to the shore for fishing, boating, and swimming.

Open: May 1 to October 31.

172 Skowhegan/ Canaan KOA

Location: West of Skowhegan in Canaan; Southern Maine map page 33, grid a2.

Campsites, facilities: There are 120 sites for tents and RVs, 59 with full hookups, 43 with water and electric, and 18 without hookups. Flush toilets, hot showers, picnic tables, fireplaces, a dump station, laundry facilities, an adult lounge, and cable TV are provided. For recreation, there is a playground, video game room, swimming pool, volleyball, basketball, and badminton. LP gas is available. Leashed pets are permitted.

Reservations, fees: Reservations are accepted. Sites are $16 to $24 a night.

Contact: The Kennedy Family, Skowhegan/Canaan KOA, P.O. Box 87, Route 2, Canaan, ME 04924; (207) 474-2858 or (800) 291-3514.

Directions: From Interstate 95 near Fairfield, take exit 36 and head north on U.S. 201 toward Skowhegan. Turn right onto Route 23 and travel north for eight miles to Canaan. Turn right onto U.S. 2 and drive east for 1.5 miles to the campground.

Trip notes: You'll find no surprises here, for every KOA looks pretty much the same whether it's in Kansas or Maine. This is a full-service campground with all the usual options. The Skowhegan/Canaan KOA is located on a grassy hillside above a major east-west highway.

Open: May 1 through December 1.

173 Sandy Beach Lakeside Camping

Location: On Wesserunsett Lake in Madison; Southern Maine map page 33, grid a2.

Campsites, facilities: There are 103 sites for tents and RVs with partial hookups. Flush toilets, picnic tables, fireplaces, a dump station, and laundry facilities are provided. For recreation, there is a boat ramp, canoe rentals, volleyball, horseshoes, basketball, and, of course, a sandy beach. Leashed pets are permitted.

Reservations, fees: Reservations are recommended. A 50 percent deposit is required; on holiday weekends, you must deposit 100 percent of the total fee. Sites are $16.50 a night.

Contact: Norma Fulton, Sandy Beach Lakeside Camping, Route 201, Box 729, Madison, ME 04950; (207) 474-5975.

Directions: From the intersection of U.S.

2 and U.S. 201 in Skowhegan, drive seven miles north on U.S. 201 to the campground.

Trip notes: Sandy Beach has wooded sites on the shores of Wesserunsett Lake, a four-mile-long lake just north of Skowhegan. The gently sloping, sandy beach here is great for swimming with little children. Bring your fishing rod and try for bass, perch, and pickerel. There is a full list of scheduled activities, including weekly square dances, so bring your hat and boots and come prepared to swing your partner. Popular with locals from Skowhegan and its environs, the campground attracts many seasonal campers.

Open: Memorial Day through October 1.

174 Abnaki Camping Center

Location: On Wesserunsett Lake in Madison; Southern Maine map page 33, grid a2.

Campsites, facilities: There are 96 sites for tents and RVs with partial hookups. Flush toilets, hot showers, picnic tables, fireplaces, a dump station, and a store are provided. For recreation, there is a sandy beach, a playground, rec room, volleyball, horseshoe pits, and canoe and bicycle rentals. Leashed pets are permitted.

Reservations, fees: Reservations are recommended. A deposit of 25 percent is required. Wooded sites are $18 a night, and waterfront sites are $20 a night.

Contact: Dot Labonte, Abnaki Camping Center, RR 2, Box 1500, Madison, ME 04950; (207) 474-2070.

Directions: From the intersection of U.S. 201 and Madison Avenue in Skowhegan, drive six miles north on Madison Avenue.

Trip notes: This venerable old campground offers well-spaced sites set amid pine trees on the shores of Wesserunsett

Lake. The pretty, sandy beach has no drop-off, making this is a good place to swim with small children. Bring your fishing gear if you'd like to catch dinner while the others swim. Like many campgrounds in central Maine, Abnaki caters to locals, in this case the weekend crowd from Skowhegan.

Open: Memorial Day through Labor Day.

175 Maine Roads Camping

Location: On a busy highway near Norridgewock; Southern Maine map page 33, grid a2.

Campsites, facilities: There are 44 sites for tents and RVs, 26 with full hookups and 18 with none. Flush toilets, hot showers, tables, and fireplaces are provided. A playground, volleyball nets, horseshoes, and a swimming pool are also on the grounds. Leashed pets are permitted.

Reservations, fees: Reservations are accepted. Sites are $12 to $16 a night.

Contact: Bob Waites and Karen Bailey, Maine Roads Camping, RFD 2, Box 3440, Norridgewock, ME 04957; (207) 634-4952.

Directions: From the intersection of U.S. 201A/8 and U.S. 2 in Norridgewock, drive four miles west on U.S. 2.

Trip notes: Just off a busy east-west highway, the campground is in a flat, grassy field. Maine Roads is convenient if you find yourself traveling along U.S. 2 and need a place to stay for the night.

Open: May 15 through October 31.

176 Great Pond Campground

Location: On a lake near Belgrade Lakes; Southern Maine map page 33, grid b2.

Campsites, facilities: There are 45 sites for tents and RVs, 30 with full hookups and 15 with water and electric. Flush toilets, hot showers, picnic tables, fireplaces, a dump station, laundry facilities, and a store are provided. Seasonal campers can get cable TV. For recreation, there is a sandy beach; a boat launch and boathouse; paddleboat, motorboat, and canoe rentals; a playground; rec room; and swimming pool. Leashed pets are permitted.

Reservations, fees: Reservations are recommended. A deposit of 25 percent is required. Sites are $17 to $20 a night.

Contact: Doris Bilodeau, Great Pond Campground, RFD 1, Box 913, Belgrade, ME 04917; (207) 495-2116.

Directions: From the Belgrade Lakes town center, drive half a mile south on Route 27 to the campground.

Trip notes: Great Pond Campground surrounds a large body of water in the Belgrade Lakes chain, a string of lakes renowned as great fishing spots for northern pike, landlocked salmon, bass, trout, perch, and pickerel. This lake covers 8,300 acres and is bordered by a sandy beach with boat docks. The nearby small town of Belgrade Lakes is an attractive village situated at the junction of two lakes. The campground is small and pleasant, but some sites are backed up too close to Route 27 and are occasionally hit with traffic noise.

Open: May 1 through September 30.

⓱⓱ Pleasant Point Campground

Location: North of Augusta in Oakland; Southern Maine map page 33, grid b2.

Campsites, facilities: There are 47 sites for tents and RVs with full, partial, and no hookups. Flush toilets, hot showers, picnic tables, fireplaces, and a dump station are provided. For recreation, there is a lake with a boat launch, volleyball, badminton, and horseshoes. Leashed pets are permitted.

Reservations, fees: Reservations are accepted Sites are $15 a night.

Contact: Pleasant Point Campground, RFD 2, Box 705, Oakland, ME 04963; (207) 465-7265.

Directions: From Interstate 95 at Oakland, take exit 33 and drive 4.5 miles west on Route 137. Turn left on McGrath Pond Road and continue south for a quarter mile to the campground.

Trip notes: Pleasant Point has lakeside sites on the shores of McGrath Pond, a long pool of freshwater in the Belgrade Lakes region. This entire area is very popular with family vacationers, as it offers plenty of opportunities for boating, windsurfing, and fishing for native trout and landlocked salmon. Just south of here and within easy driving distance is Augusta, the state capital where, among other things, you'll find historical museums and displays.

Open: Memorial Day through Labor Day.

⓱⓼ Green Valley Campground

Location: On Webber Pond in Vassalboro; Southern Maine map page 33, grid b3.

Campsites, facilities: There are 90 sites for tents and RVs, half with full hookups, some with water and electric, and nine without hookups. Flush toilets, hot showers, picnic tables, fireplaces, a dump station, laundry facilities, and a store are provided. For recreation, there is a boat launch, a large swimming float, canoe and boat rentals, a playground, rec room, volleyball, bocce court, basketball, and horseshoes. Leashed pets are permitted.

Reservations, fees: Reservations are not necessary. Sites are $18 to $20 a night.

Contact: Sybil and Fred Saucier, Green Valley Campground, Vassalboro, ME 04989; (207) 923-3000.

Directions: From the junction of U.S. 201 and Webber Pond Road north of Augusta, drive north on Webber Pond Road for 4.5 miles, following signs to the campground.

Trip notes: Green Valley is aptly named, for this is a very pleasant, quiet campground in a fertile, pastoral region of rolling hills and farms. Its centerpiece, the 1,254-acre Webber Pond, has warm water and a gently sloping, sandy bottom, making this a terrific choice for people who enjoy swimming and bass fishing.

Open: May 1 through September 30.

179 Augusta West Lakeside Resort Kampground

Location: On Annabessacook Lake in Winthrop; Southern Maine map page 33, grid b2.

Campsites, facilities: There are 81 sites for tents and RVs, some with partial hookups and others without hookups. Flush toilets, hot showers, picnic tables, fireplaces, a dump station, and a laundry facility are provided. For recreation, there is a boat launch and dock; a swimming pool; a lake with a sandy beach; canoe, paddleboat, and motorboat rentals; badminton and volleyball; and horseshoes. LP gas is available. Leashed pets are permitted.

Reservations, fees: Reservations are accepted. A 30 percent deposit is required. Sites are $15 to $33 a night.

Contact: Augusta West Lakeside Resort Kampground, Box 232, Winthrop, ME 04364; (207) 468-6930.

Directions: From the intersection of U.S. 202 and Route 41 in Winthrop, drive three-quarters of a mile east on U.S. 202. Turn right on Highland Avenue and drive one mile south, then go three-quarters of a mile west to the campground.

Trip notes: Augusta West is located in rolling, rural countryside just eight miles from the state capital in Augusta. A shallow, sandy beach here is perfect for swimming with young children, and the fishing in the lake for smallmouth bass, perch, and pickerel is great. Moreover, the campground offers an unsurpassed array of mechanized rides for all to enjoy. If riding in a seaplane, Jet Skiing, or waterskiing is your idea of summer fun, Augusta West won't disappoint, for plenty of very loud, gas-guzzling, motorized vehicles cover the surface of Annabessacook Lake.

Open: May 15 through October 15.

180 Augusta/ Gardiner KOA

Location: In Richmond; Southern Maine map page 33, grid b2.

Campsites, facilities: There are 85 sites for tents and RVs, 28 with full hookups, 46 with water and electric, and 11 with no hookups. Flush toilets, hot showers, picnic tables, fireplaces, laundry facilities, a dump station, and a store are provided. For recreation, there is a swimming pool, canoe and rowboat rentals, a rec room, volleyball, basketball, badminton, and horseshoes. Leashed pets are permitted.

Reservations, fees: Reservations are accepted. Sites are $17.50 to $23 a night.

Contact: Augusta/Gardiner KOA, Route 1, Box 2410, Richmond, ME 04357; (207) 582-5086.

Directions: From Interstate 95 near Gardiner, take exit 27 and drive 2.25 miles south on U.S. 201 to the campground.

Trip notes: KOA is a national chain, so you will find no surprises here. The campground is situated on Pleasant Pond, actually a wide part of Cobbosseecontee Stream. This part of Maine features pretty, rolling farm and forest country dotted with lakes, and lies within easy driving distance of the coast. The campground is just minutes from the state capital at Augusta and the historic Kennebec River town of Hallowell, where you'll find shops, restaurants, and a bustling nineteenth-century waterfront.

Open: May 20 through October 15.

⑱ Hermit Island Campground

Location: On Hermit Island in Casco Bay; Southern Maine map page 33, grid c2.

Campsites, facilities: There are 275 tent sites, all without hookups. Trailers and RVs are not allowed, but pickup trucks and small campers are permitted. Flush toilets, hot showers, picnic tables, and fireplaces are provided. For recreation, there is a boat launch, canoe and rowboat rentals, a rec room, pavilion, volleyball, basketball, badminton, and horseshoes. Leashed pets are permitted.

Reservations, fees: Reservations are accepted with full payment. Sites are $23.75 to $33.75 a night.

Contact: Hermit Island Campground, 42 Front Street, Bath, ME 04530; (207) 443-2101.

Directions: From Bath, head south on Route 209. When you reach the junction of Routes 209 and 216, continue south for four miles on Route 216 to Hermit Island and the campground.

Trip notes: You'll find the campground on a 255-acre private island, where each site has been designed with maximum privacy in mind. Sites have been placed in the woods, in open fields, and directly on the shore of Casco Bay. This is the perfect setting for sailors, boaters, and especially sea kayakers, who can set up a base camp for long journeys among the plentiful islands strewn along this portion of the Maine coast. And don't forget to bring your fishing gear: the campground owns a 50-foot deep-sea fishing boat that sails daily from the on-site wharf in search of cod and giant bluefin tuna. For landlubbers, hiking trails extend through the green forest, along sandy beaches, and across rocky ocean bluffs.

Open: May 15 through Columbus Day.

⑱ Ocean View Park Campground

Location: Near Popham Beach in Phippsburg; Southern Maine map page 33, grid c2.

Campsites, facilities: There are 48 sites for tents and RVs, 11 with full hookups, 31 with water and electric, three with electric only, and three with none. Flush toilets, hot showers, picnic tables, fireplaces, a dump station, and a store are provided. Leashed pets are permitted.

Reservations, fees: Reservations are recommended. Sites are $18 to $21 a night.

Contact: Bernadette and Charlie Konzelman, Ocean View Park Campground, Route 209, Phippsburg, ME 04562; (207) 389-2564 or (207) 443-1000.

Directions: From the junction of U.S. 1 and Route 209 in Bath, drive 13 miles south on Route 209 to the campground.

Trip notes: As they say in the real estate business, location is everything, and can you imagine a better location than this?

Ocean View Park sits at the very end of the Phippsburg Peninsula, where the land gives way to the open Atlantic, and is situated right next to Popham Beach State Park, widely considered the most attractive sandy beach in Maine. From your campsite you can soon be swimming in the ocean or fishing for mackerel, bluefish, and striped bass. The campground is close to wildlife refuges, historic forts, and miles of scenic ocean drives. Need we say more?

Open: May 10 through September 23.

183 Orrs Island Campground

Location: On Orrs Island; Southern Maine map page 33, grid c2.

Campsites, facilities: There are 70 sites for tents and RVs, 35 with full hookups, 18 with water and electric, and 17 without hookups. Flush toilets, hot showers, picnic tables, fireplaces, laundry facilities, a dump station, and a store are provided. For recreation, there are canoe rentals, a floating dock, a boat mooring, hiking trails, volleyball, badminton, and horseshoes. Leashed pets are permitted.

Reservations, fees: Reservations are accepted for stays of two or more days. A $30 deposit is required. Sites are $18 to $24 a night.

Contact: Orrs Island Campground, RR 1, P.O. Box 650, Orrs Island, ME 04066; (207) 833-5595.

Directions: From the junction of U.S. 1 and Route 24 west of Bath, drive 11 miles south on Route 24 to the campground.

Trip notes: Catering to families, this campground is perched on a 42-acre bluff overlooking Harpswell Sound, one of the most scenic long reaches of salt water on Maine's Mid-Coast. The 70 sites are both open and wooded, and many sit high above the water on a rocky bluff where visitors enjoy unbroken views over the sound. Saltwater swimming and fishing are within easy reach. And it's just a short drive to the town of Brunswick, home of Bowdoin College, and Bath, where guided missile cruisers are built at the venerable Bath Iron Works, one of the oldest shipbuilders in the country. Just off the southern tip of Bailey Island (which is connected to Orrs Island by a bridge) is Eagle Island, where Admiral Robert Peary, discoverer of the North Pole, used to live.

Open: Memorial Day through September 15.

184 Camp Seguin Ocean Camping

Location: On Georgetown Island; Southern Maine map page 33, grid c2.

Campsites, facilities: There are 30 sites for tents and RVs, some with water and electric hookups. Flush toilets, hot showers, picnic tables, fireplaces, a dump station, and a limited store are provided. Ice and firewood are available. There's also a rec room and a playground. The maximum RV length is 22 feet. Leashed pets are permitted.

Reservations, fees: Reservations are accepted for stays of two or more nights. A 50 percent deposit is required. Sites are $17 to $24 a night.

Contact: Camp Seguin Ocean Camping, Reid State Park Road, Georgetown, ME 04548; (207) 371-2777.

Directions: From the intersection of Route 127 and U.S. 1 in Bath, drive 10 miles south on Route 127. Bear right on Reid State Park Road and drive two miles south to the campground.

Trip notes: Camp Seguin has a very attractive location: a stretch of rocky shoreline overlooking Sheepscot Bay and the open Atlantic Ocean. The sites are well spaced among evergreen trees, giving the campground a peaceful, natural feel. Adjacent is Reid State Park, with its 1.5 miles of open sandy beach, tide pools, freshwater ponds, and thick undeveloped woods. For sea kayakers, fishing enthusiasts, and sunbathers, this is the place. From the shore, you can cast out a line for mackerel and bluefish, among other species.

Open: Memorial Day through Columbus Day.

185 Gray Homestead Ocean Front

Location: On the island of Southport; Southern Maine map page 33, grid c2.

Campsites, facilities: There are 40 sites for tents and RVs, some with water and electric hookups. Flush toilets, hot showers, picnic tables, fireplaces, laundry facilities, a dump station, volleyball, basketball, and horseshoes are provided. Campers have access to the ocean and a sandy beach. Leashed pets are permitted.

Reservations, fees: Reservations are recommended June through August. Sites are $15 to $22 a night.

Contact: Suzanne and Stephen Gray, Gray Homestead Ocean Front, HC 66, Box 334, Southport, ME 04576; (207) 633-4612.

Directions: From U.S. 1 east of Wiscasset, drive south on Route 27 to Southport. Take Route 238 south for two more miles to the campground.

Trip notes: Like several other campgrounds mentioned in this guide, a place like Gray Homestead could only be found in New England. Here, along the rockbound coast on your perch above the crashing

swells, the salt tang of the sea blends with the scent of evergreens—and you know without a doubt that you are in Maine. Suzanne and Stephen Gray make you feel at home in New England, too, offering to order fresh Maine seafood for you to cook on your fire. And if you want to sample someone else's cooking, there are plenty of fine restaurants and other attractions in nearby Boothbay Harbor.

Open: May 1 through October 10.

186 Meadowbrook Camping Area

Location: On the road to Popham Beach in Bath; Southern Maine map page 33, grid c2.

Campsites, facilities: There are 100 sites for tents and RVs, 55 with full hookups and 45 with water and electric. Flush toilets, free hot showers, picnic tables, fireplaces, laundry facilities, a dump station, and a store are provided. For recreation, there is a mile-long trail and a nature preserve, a swimming pool, miniature golf, a rec room, volleyball, basketball, badminton, and horseshoes. LP gas is available. Leashed pets are permitted.

Reservations, fees: Reservations are required in winter. Sites range from $17 to $23 a night.

Contact: Cathy and Gary Bilodeau, Meadowbrook Camping Area, HCR 32, Box 280B, Bath, ME 04530; (207) 443-4967 or (800) 370-CAMP/2267.

Directions: From the junction of U.S. 1 and Route 209 in Bath, drive 2.5 miles south on Route 209, then turn right and drive three miles southwest on Meadowbrook Road to the campground.

Trip notes: Like several others in this area, Meadowbrook Camping Area is set on an arm of the Atlantic Ocean that reaches up into the Mid-Coast of Maine. This region is filled with islands and bays, wildlife-rich estuaries, and long peninsulas stretching out from the coast like fingers. The campground, with its large open and forested sites, is well situated to offer access to this unique part of the country. While you are here, enjoy a Meadowbrook specialty: the "Downeast" lobster and clam bake. Staying here puts you close to Popham Beach State Park, Reid State Park, L.L. Bean, and the Maine Maritime Museum, where the state's seafaring legacy is brought to life.

Open: May 1 through October 15 for vehicles requiring hookups; year-round for tents and self-contained RVs.

⑱⑦ Thomas Point Beach and Campground

Location: On the shore in Brunswick; Southern Maine map page 33, grid c2.

Campsites, facilities: There are 75 sites for tents and RVs, some with water and electric hookups. Flush toilets, hot showers, picnic tables, fireplaces, a dump station, and a store are provided. There's also a sandy beach, a rec room, an ice cream shop, and a playing field. Ice and firewood are available. No pets are allowed.

Reservations, fees: Reservations are accepted. Sites are $16 a night.

Contact: Patricia Crooker, Thomas Point Beach and Campground, 29 Meadow Road, Brunswick, ME 04011; (207) 725-6009.

Directions: From the intersection of U.S. 1 and Route 24 at Cooks Corner, drive 100 yards south on Route 24, then go approximately 2.5 miles east on Thomas Point Road to the campground.

Trip notes: Thomas Point Beach is a popular waterfront gathering place for lo-

cal people who use it as a town park for reunions, company picnics, and other functions. There are campsites situated in the tall pines near the shore, and the clean, sandy beach is watched over by a lifeguard. Note, however, that the campground is near a very busy intersection, that consumption of alcohol is not allowed in the park, and that pets are not permitted. Also be aware that this place has one of the earliest closing dates of any campground in the state.

Open: Memorial Day through August 24.

⑱⑧ White's Beach and Campground

Location: In Brunswick; Southern Maine map page 33, grid c2.

Campsites, facilities: There are 45 sites for tents and RVs, some with water and electric hookups. Flush toilets, hot showers, picnic tables, fireplaces, a dump station, and a store are provided. For recreation, there is freshwater swimming, a playground, volleyball, basketball, and hiking trails. Leashed pets are permitted.

Reservations, fees: Reservations are accepted. Sites are $13 to $16 a night.

Contact: White's Beach and Campground, Durham Road, Brunswick, ME 04011; (207) 729-0415.

Directions: From the intersection of U.S. 1 and Durham Road in Brunswick, drive 2.2 miles north on Durham Road to the campground.

Trip notes: White's Beach is a tidy little campground set on a small freshwater lake. There is a spacious sandy beach with a lifeguard on duty, quiet wooded sites, and hiking trails that meander throughout the premises. An added attraction is that the campground is convenient to downtown

Freeport, with its shops, restaurants, and the main attraction, L.L. Bean.

Open: May 15 through October 15.

189 Sherwood Forest Campsite

Location: On the ocean in New Harbor; Southern Maine map page 33, grid c3.

Campsites, facilities: There are 80 sites for tents and RVs, 64 with water and electric hookups and 16 without hookups. Flush toilets, hot showers, picnic tables, fireplaces, laundry facilities, a dump station, and a store are provided. You'll also find a swimming pool, canoe rentals, a rec room, volleyball, basketball, badminton, and horseshoes. Ice and firewood are available. Leashed pets are permitted.

Reservations, fees: Reservations are accepted. Sites are $16 to $18 a night.

Contact: Sherwood Forest Campsite, Pemaquid Trail, P.O. Box 189, New Harbor, ME 04554; (207) 677-3642.

Directions: From Damariscotta, travel south on Route 130. When you reach the intersection of Routes 130 and 32 in New Harbor, continue a quarter mile south on Route 130, then head west on Pemaquid Beach Road for three-quarters of a mile. Go south from there on Pemaquid Trail for a quarter mile to the campground.

Trip notes: Pemaquid Point is a long, rural peninsula pointing like an arrowhead into the Atlantic Ocean. Sherwood Forest Campsite, which lies on this peninsula, is an attractive campground with an enviable water location. From here you have access to great saltwater fishing, sea kayaking, birding in the nearby Rachel Carson Salt Pond Preserve, puffin viewing trips out to Egg Rock, excursions to Monhegan Island—where the Wyeth family paints—

bicycling on the lightly traveled roads that ring the peninsula, and much more.

Open: May 15 through October 1.

190 Chewonki Campgrounds

Location: In Wiscasset; Southern Maine map page 33, grid c3.

Campsites, facilities: There are 47 sites for tents and RVs, 8 with full hookups, 30 with water and electric hookups, and 9 with no hookups. Flush toilets, hot showers, picnic tables, fireplaces, a dump station, and a store are provided. For recreation, there is a boat launch, swimming pool, tennis court, canoe rentals, a rec room, volleyball, basketball, badminton, and horseshoes. Leashed pets are permitted.

Reservations, fees: Reservations are accepted. For stays of three days or less, a $20 deposit is required; for four or more days, there is a $50 deposit. Sites are $18 to $25 a night.

Contact: Pamela Brackett and Ann Brackett Beck, Chewonki Campgrounds, Box 261, Wiscasset, ME 04578; (207) 882-7426 or (800) 465-7747.

Directions: From the junction of U.S. 1 and Route 144 in Wiscasset, drive a quarter mile south on Route 144, then one mile southwest to the campground.

Trip notes: Wiscasset calls itself the "prettiest" village in Maine, and this seaport town where the Sheepscot River empties into the Atlantic Ocean is indeed picturesque. The campground is located on Chewonki Neck, one of numerous fingers of land jutting out into the ocean in this part of the state, and has great access to the water, tidal rivers, salt marshes, and estuaries of the region. Be warned, however, that the Maine Yankee nuclear power plant shares this splendid natural setting with the campground.

Open: Mid-May through mid-October.

191 Shore Hills Campground

Location: On the Cross River near Boothbay Harbor; Southern Maine map page 33, grid c3.

Campsites, facilities: There are 150 sites for tents and RVs, 83 with full hookups, 52 with water and electric hookups, and 15 with no hookups. Flush toilets, hot showers, picnic tables, fireplaces, laundry facilities, a dump station, and a store are provided. For recreation, there is saltwater fishing and swimming, boating and sea kayaking, a rec room, volleyball, basketball, badminton, and horseshoes. Leashed pets are permitted.

Reservations, fees: Reservations are recommended. A $15 deposit is required. Sites are $14 to $21 a night.

Contact: Milon and Peggy Fuller, Shore Hills Campground, Route 27, Box 448, Boothbay, ME 04537; (207) 633-4782.

Directions: From the junction of U.S. 1 and Route 27 in Edgecomb, drive eight miles south on Route 27 to the campground.

Trip notes: Shore Hills Campground is located on the Cross River, a pretty tidal stream that empties into the Atlantic Ocean. Waterfront sites, fishing rocks, and direct access to the water are just some of the perks. From here it is a short distance to the shops and restaurants of Boothbay Harbor. And the park is within easy reach of other Mid-Coast attractions, such as boating and deep-sea fishing excursions, sandy beaches, wildlife refuges, and picturesque seaside villages. A shuttle bus to Boothbay Harbor is provided. Note that

Shore Hills has one of the earliest opening dates of any campground in Maine. So if you want to brave the last of winter's icy winds, come on up. Brrr.

Open: April 19 through Columbus Day.

192 Little Ponderosa Campground

Location: In Boothbay; Southern Maine map page 33, grid c3.

Campsites, facilities: There are 93 sites for tents and RVs, 37 with full hookups, 53 with water and electric, and 3 with no hookups. Wheelchair-accessible rest room facilities, flush toilets, hot showers, cable TV, picnic tables, fireplaces, laundry facilities, a dump station, and a store are provided. You will find canoe and rowboat rentals, a rec room, miniature golf, volleyball, basketball, badminton, and horseshoes. LP gas and RV supplies are available. Leashed pets are permitted.

Reservations, fees: Reservations are recommended. Sites are $16 to $21 a night.

Contact: The Roberts Family, Little Ponderosa Campground, Boothbay, ME 04537; (207) 633-2700.

Directions: From the junction of U.S. 1 and Route 27 in Edgecomb, drive five miles south on Route 27 to the campground.

Trip notes: Little Ponderosa is located on the Cross River, a tidal inlet in Maine's Mid-Coast region. This is a spectacular land- and seascape of maritime spruce-fir forests, peninsulas jutting into the ocean, and mazes of interconnected waterways. The area is rich in natural beauty and wildlife, and you could easily spend months trying to see it all. Little Ponderosa would be a good place to start. The sites are nestled among tall pine trees, and 30 of them have been placed along the shore. Weekend activities are scheduled in July and August, including a gospel concert on Saturday night and mini-church services on Sunday. The campground provides a shuttle bus to Boothbay Harbor.

Open: May 15 through October 15.

193 Sherman Lake View Campground

Location: In North Edgecomb; Southern Maine map page 33, grid c3.

Campsites, facilities: There are 30 sites for tents and RVs, 8 with full hookups, 10 with water and electric, and 12 with no hookups. Flush toilets, hot showers, picnic tables, fireplaces, laundry facilities, a swimming pool, and a dump station are provided. Leashed pets are permitted.

Reservations, fees: Reservations are accepted. Sites are $17 to $22 a night.

Contact: Norm and Ann Benner, Sherman Lake View Campground, RR 1, P.O. Box 1150, North Edgecomb, ME 04556; (207) 563-3239.

Directions: From the intersection of U.S. 1 and Route 27 in Edgecomb, drive approximately 3.5 miles north on U.S. 1 to the campground.

Trip notes: Sherman Lake View does indeed afford a fine view over Sherman Lake from the top of a hill; however, the campground is situated directly across busy U.S. 1 from the lake. As a base camp from which to venture forth and explore the area, it's only minutes away from the towns of Bath, Wiscasset, and Damariscotta as well as within easy reach of the ocean. This is a convenient place to spend the night if you are on your way to Downeast Maine or to the Canadian Maritime Provinces.

Open: Memorial Day through Columbus Day.

194 Down East Family Camping

Location: In Wiscasset; Southern Maine map page 33, grid c3.

Campsites, facilities: There are 40 sites for tents and RVs, 2 with water and electric hookups, 6 with electric only, and 32 with no hookups. Flush toilets, free hot showers, picnic tables, fireplaces, and a store are provided. For recreation, there is a boat launch, canoe and rowboat rentals, a rec room, volleyball, badminton, and horseshoes. Leashed pets are permitted.

Reservations, fees: Reservations are accepted. A deposit of one night's fee is required. Sites are $15 to $20 a night.

Contact: Bob and B. J. Nesbitt, Down East Family Camping, RR 3, Box 223, Wiscasset, ME 04578; (207) 882-5431.

Directions: From the intersection of U.S. 1 and Route 27 in Wiscasset, drive four miles north on Route 27 to the campground.

Trip notes: Down East Family Camping is designed for tent campers. The sites are large, private, and wooded, and the campground boasts more than 6,000 feet of waterfront on a spring-fed lake. The swimming, boating, canoeing, and fishing are all great, and a feeling of peaceful relaxation pervades this wild setting.

Open: May 25 through September 15.

195 Town Line Campsites

Location: On Damariscotta Lake in North Nobleboro; Southern Maine map page 33, grid c3.

Campsites, facilities: There are 55 sites for tents and RVs, some with partial hookups. Flush toilets, hot showers, picnic tables, fireplaces, laundry facilities, a dump station, and a store are provided. There are also two sandy beaches with floats, canoe and rowboat rentals, a rec room, volleyball, basketball, badminton, and horseshoes. Leashed pets are permitted.

Reservations, fees: Reservations are accepted. Payment in full is required for reservations of one week or less; send one week's fee for stays lasting longer than a week. Sites are $10 to $20 a night.

Contact: Louise Newbert, Town Line Campsites, RR 1, P.O. Box 820, Jefferson, ME 04348; (207) 832-7055.

Directions: From the intersection of Route 32 and East Pond Road in Jefferson, drive three miles south on East Pond Road to the campground.

Trip notes: Town Line Campsites offers 160 acres of shorefront on 14-mile-long Damariscotta Lake, which has a reputation for good salmon, trout, bass, pickerel, and perch fishing. The campground is tucked away in pine trees surrounded by rural countryside and rolling hills and is very quiet and peaceful. Town Line prides itself on its noncommercial atmosphere, so if you are looking for a place to kick back and relax, this may be the one.

Open: Memorial Day through Labor Day.

196 Lake Pemaquid Campground

Location: On Lake Pemaquid in Damariscotta; Southern Maine map page 33, grid c3.

Campsites, facilities: There are 250 sites for tents and RVs, 120 with full hookups and 130 with water and electric. Flush toilets, metered hot showers, picnic tables, fireplaces, laundry facilities, a dump station, and a store are provided. There's also a boat launch, swimming pool, canoe rentals, a rec room, volleyball, basketball, badminton, and horseshoes. Ice, firewood, and LP gas are available. Leashed pets are permitted.

Reservations, fees: Reservations are accepted. For stays of fewer than seven days, payment in full is required; for stays of over a week, send a 50 percent deposit. Sites are $22 to $37 a night.

Contact: Lake Pemaquid Campground, Box 967, Damariscotta, ME 04543; (207) 563-5202.

Directions: From the intersection of Business U.S. 1 and Biscay Road in Damariscotta, drive two miles on Biscay Road, then follow signs for three-quarters of a mile to the campground.

Trip notes: The campground is located on a large (seven miles long) freshwater lake that boasts excellent bass, perch, pickerel, and brown trout fishing. The interconnected waterways actually provide access to more than 15 miles of lakes and streams for exploration. If you don't have your own boat, you can rent a motorboat, canoe, paddleboat, sailboat, or even an aqua bike from the campground. Some of the sites are situated directly along the shore, while others are tucked back in the woods of pine, white birch, and oak trees. For those who come to Maine for the seafood, lobsters and clams are sold in the campground store.

Open: May 15 through Columbus Day.

197 Duck Puddle Campground

Location: On Lake Pemaquid in Nobleboro; Southern Maine map page 33, grid c3.

Campsites, facilities: There are 95 sites for tents and RVs, 35 with full hookups, 55 with water and electric, and five with no hookups. Flush toilets, hot showers, picnic tables, fireplaces, laundry facilities, a dump station, and a store are provided. For recreation, there is a boat launch; swimming pool; canoe, paddleboat, and motorboat rentals; a rec room; volleyball; basketball; badminton; and horseshoes. Leashed pets are permitted.

Reservations, fees: Reservations are accepted. Sites are $17 to $26 a night.

Contact: Sue and Jim Ferrier, Duck Puddle Campground, Duck Puddle Road, P.O. Box 176, Nobleboro, ME 04555; (207) 563-5608.

Directions: From the intersection of U.S. 1 and Duck Puddle Road in Nobleboro, drive 1.5 miles on Duck Puddle Road to the campground.

Trip notes: Duck Puddle is a family campground situated on a seven-mile-long freshwater lake. While all of the sites are well maintained, those on the waterfront have wonderful views of Lake Pemaquid. The open and wooded sites are spacious. Much of the activity takes place at the shore, where there is a small swimming beach and good trout, bass, and pickerel fishing. Families can rent canoes, paddleboats, and motorboats. If you bring your own boat, be sure to reserve a dock space. This is a clean, well-tended campground within easy reach of Mid-Coast Maine's attractions.

Open: May 1 through October 31.

⑲⑧ Loon's Cry Campground

Location: On North Pond in Warren; Southern Maine map page 33, grid c3.

Campsites, facilities: There are 45 sites for tents and RVs, 4 with full hookups, 15 with water and electric, and 26 with no hookups. Flush toilets, hot showers, picnic tables, fireplaces, laundry facilities, a dump station, and a store are provided. For recreation, there are canoe and paddleboat rent-

als, a playground, hiking trails, and horseshoes. Leashed pets are permitted.

Reservations, fees: Reservations are accepted. A $10 deposit is required. Sites are $17 to $20 a night.

Contact: The Goff Family, Loon's Cry Campground, Route 1, Warren, ME 04864; (207) 273-2324 or (800) 493-2324.

Directions: From the intersection of U.S. 1 and Route 90, drive a mile south on U.S. 1 to the campground.

Trip notes: Loon's Cry offers large, spacious sites in open fields, in the woods, and along the shores of North Pond, a spring-fed freshwater lake. The campground owns 1,500 feet of shoreline with a boat launch and a sandy beach. Loon's Cry is a clean, attractive facility that's well situated in the heart of the Mid-Coast region and within easy reach of the nearby villages and attractions of Camden, Rockland, Rockport, and Penobscot Bay.

Open: May 1 through October 15.

⑲⑨ Saltwater Farm Campground

Location: On the St. George River in Thomaston; Southern Maine map page 33, grid c3.

Campsites, facilities: There are 30 sites for tents and RVs, some with full hookups. Flush toilets, hot showers, picnic tables, fireplaces, laundry facilities, a dump station, and a store are provided. For recreation, there is a swimming pool, a rec room, volleyball, and horseshoes. Leashed pets are permitted.

Reservations, fees: Reservations are recommended. Sites are $17 to $22 a night.

Contact: Linda and Bruce Jennings, Saltwater Farm Campground, P.O. Box 165, Thomaston, ME 04861; (207) 354-6735.

Directions: From the intersection of U.S. 1 and Wadsworth Street in Thomaston, drive 1.5 miles southeast on Wadsworth Street to the campground.

Trip notes: Saltwater Farm is an attractive campground set on a high, open meadow above the mouth of the St. George River where it flows into the Atlantic Ocean. This is a lovely, scenic spot with wide-open views to the east and south. The campground has 500 feet of frontage on the St. George River, offering excellent saltwater fishing and sea kayaking access.

Open: May 15 through October 15.

200 Lobster Buoy Campsite

Location: On Penobscot Bay in South Thomaston; Southern Maine map page 33, grid c3.

Campsites, facilities: There are 40 sites for tents and RVs, with full, partial, and no hookups. Flush toilets, hot showers, picnic tables, fireplaces, a dump station, and a store are provided. Leashed pets are permitted.

Reservations, fees: Reservations are recommended. A deposit of one night's fee is required. Sites are $12 to $23 a night.

Contact: Mabel Batty and Eleanor Carpenter, Lobster Buoy Campsite, CR 33, Box 625, South Thomaston, ME 04858; (207) 594-7546.

Directions: From the junction of U.S. 1 and Route 73 in Rockland, drive seven miles south on Route 73 to the campground.

Trip notes: Here is the campground for those who want little more than direct and easy access to the ocean. Lobster Buoy is situated right where the waters of Penobscot Bay empty into the wide Atlantic Ocean, separated from the open sea by

Muscle Ridge, a line of rock-rimmed, spruce-covered granite islands jutting up from the cold depths. The campground has 400 feet of ocean frontage. Understandably, this is paradise for sea kayakers and sailors. But if seafaring isn't for you, don't forget to bring your fishing gear to try for various saltwater species. No campsite is more than 150 yards from the water, and all have expansive ocean views.

Open: May 15 through October 15.

201 Mic Mac Cove Campground

Location: On Crawford Pond in Union; Southern Maine map page 33, grid b3.

Campsites, facilities: There are 82 sites for tents and RVs, some with water and electric hookups. Flush toilets, hot showers, picnic tables, fireplaces, a dump station, and a store are provided. For recreation, there is a boat launch, canoe and rowboat rentals, a sandy beach, a rec room, a sauna, volleyball, and horseshoes. Leashed pets are permitted.

Reservations, fees: Reservations are accepted. A deposit of 50 percent is required. Sites are $16 to $18 a night.

Contact: Howard Brinckenhoff, Mic Mac Cove Campground, Route 17, Union, ME 04862; (207) 785-4100.

Directions: From the intersection of Route 17 and Route 131 in Union, drive one mile east on Route 17 to the campground.

Trip notes: Located midway between the state capital at Augusta and the coastal towns of Camden and Rockport, Mic Mac Cove is a pleasant, spacious, shaded campground on a hillside that slopes down to the shores of Crawford Pond, a large spring-fed lake.

Open: May 1 through October 5.

202 Robert's Roost Campground

Location: In West Rockport; Southern Maine map page 33, grid b3.

Campsites, facilities: There are 53 sites for RVs, all with full hookups and 12 of them with cable TV. A wilderness tenting area is also available. Flush toilets, hot showers, picnic tables, fireplaces, laundry facilities, a dump station, and a store are provided. You'll also find volleyball, badminton, and horseshoes. Leashed pets are permitted.

Reservations, fees: Reservations are recommended. Sites are $18 to $24 a night.

Contact: David and Kathi Southworth, Robert's Roost Campground, Box F, West Rockport, ME 04865; (207) 236-2498.

Directions: From the junction of Route 17 and Route 90 near Rockport, drive one mile east on Route 90 to the campground.

Trip notes: Robert's Roost is a clean little campground set amid pine trees not far from the attractive villages of Camden and Rockport. As the campground is only minutes from the coast and mountains of the Camden area, this is a good bet if you are planning to stay in the vicinity and Camden Hills State Park is full. For more information on the area, see the trip notes for Camden Hills State Park (campground number 208).

Open: May 1 through October 1.

203 Megunticook Campground by the Sea

Location: In Rockport; Southern Maine map page 33, grid b3.

Campsites, facilities: There are 71 sites for tents and RVs, 10 with full hookups, 41 with water and electric, and 20 with none. Flush toilets, hot showers, tables, fireplaces, cable TV, laundry facilities, a dump station, and a store are provided. A heated swimming pool, kayak and bicycle rentals, a deck overlooking the ocean, a rec room, playing field, badminton, and horseshoes are also available. Leashed pets are permitted.

Reservations, fees: Reservations are recommended. A deposit of one night's fee is required. Sites are $18 to $21 a night.

Contact: John Alexander, Megunticook Campground by the Sea, U.S. 1, Rockport, ME 04856; (207) 594-2428 or (800) 884-2428 or fax (207) 594-0549; E-mail: mebythesea@midcoast.com.

Directions: From the junction of U.S. 1 and Route 90 in Rockport, drive two miles south on U.S. 1 to the campground.

Trip notes: Unfortunately, this place is too close to busy U.S. 1. Megunticook Campground by the Sea is nonetheless an exceptionally attractive and well-run facility set among tall shade trees next to the shores of Penobscot Bay. But the real lure is the surrounding area, which offers almost too much to even contemplate doing. No matter what your preference, you will probably find it nearby: hiking in Camden Hills State Park; shopping, restaurants, and movies in Camden; strolling through the picturesque village of Rockport; enjoying a schooner cruise on Penobscot Bay; sea kayaking among the many offshore islands; deep-sea fishing and whale watching—the list goes on. . . .

Open: May 15 through October 15.

204 Sennebec Lake Campground

Location: On Sennebec Lake in Appleton; Southern Maine map page 33, grid b3.

Campsites, facilities: There are 65 sites for tents and RVs with full, partial, and no hookups. Flush toilets, hot showers, tables, fireplaces, laundry facilities, a dump station, and a store are provided. There is a large freshwater lake with a beach, a boat launch and dock, canoe and rowboat rentals, a rec room, volleyball, badminton, and horseshoes. Leashed pets are permitted.

Reservations, fees: Reservations are accepted. A deposit of one night's fee is required. Sites are $16 to $22 a night.

Contact: Pat and John Blennerhasset, Sennebec Lake Campground, Route 31, Box 602, Appleton, ME 04862; (207) 785-4250.

Directions: From the junction of Route 131 and Route 17 in Union, drive three miles north on Route 131 to the campground.

Trip notes: Sennebec Lake is actually the point where the St. George River widens to fill a scenic, rural valley between rolling, forested hills. Located just inland from the coast near Camden, Sennebec Lake and environs feel like a place apart, a Currier & Ives vision of New England where at the dawn of the twenty-first century, the twentieth has yet to arrive. The campground is spacious, with several discreet areas and a long shorefront that holds some hidden coves. This is a relaxed, well-kept place near the coastal attractions of Camden and Rockport, yet with its own considerable attributes as well. Potluck dinners are held every Friday night, and there's live entertainment on Saturday night.

Open: Early May through mid-October.

205 Aldus Shores Lakeside Campground

Location: On Quantibacook Lake in Searsmont; Southern Maine map page 33, grid b3.

Campsites, facilities: There are 150 sites for tents and RVs, 148 with partial hookups and two with no hookups. Facilities include flush toilets, hot showers, picnic tables, fireplaces, laundry, a dump station, and a store. For recreation, there is a boat launch, canoe rentals, a rec room, playing field, volleyball, badminton, and horseshoes. Leashed pets are permitted.

Reservations, fees: Reservations are recommended. Payment in full is required for stays of up to three nights; for four or more nights, a deposit of $30 is required. Sites are $17 to $19 a night for RVs; tent sites are $3 a night, plus $3 per person.

Contact: John and Phyllis McEvoy, Aldus Shores Lakeside Campground, Route 131, P.O. Box 38, Searsmont, ME 04973; (207) 342-5618.

Directions: From the junction of Route 3 and U.S. 1 in Belfast, drive six miles west on Route 3. Turn left on Route 131 and drive 2.5 miles south. Make a right turn at the campground sign and drive half a mile west to the campground.

Trip notes: You'll find Aldus Shores in the rolling, rural countryside just inland from the coast and Penobscot Bay. The campground is situated on Quantibacook Lake, which offers excellent fishing for bass, perch, and pickerel. The spacious campsites are either directly on the lakeshore or set back under shade trees. This pleasant spot is within easy reach of Mid-Coast Maine's plentiful attractions.

Open: May 15 through October 15.

206 Lake St. George State Park

Location: On Lake St. George in Liberty; Southern Maine map page 33, grid b3.

Campsites, facilities: There are 38 sites

for tents and RVs, all without hookups. Facilities include hot showers, a dump station, boat rentals, a concrete boat ramp, group camping area, playground, and swimming area. Leashed pets are permitted.

Reservations, fees: Reservations are accepted, and the total amount due must accompany your request. Contact the Maine Bureau of Parks and Lands at the number below. The State of Maine allocates some sites on a first-come, first-served basis. Sites are $12 for residents of Maine and $16 for nonresidents.

Contact: Lake St. George State Park Ranger, (207) 589-4255. Maine Bureau of Parks and Lands, 22 State House Station, Augusta, ME 04333; (207) 287-3821.

Directions: From Belfast, drive west on Route 3 to Liberty. Continue one mile east on Route 3 to the park entrance.

Trip notes: Midway between the state capital at Augusta and the coast at Belfast, Lake St. George State Park makes the perfect stopover point for travelers who want to cool off with a refreshing swim as well as those searching for a great place to spend the night. The park incorporates part of the shoreline of a clear, spring-fed lake. There is a swimming area with lifeguards and a bathhouse, and boat and canoe rentals are available. For landlubbers, eight miles of hiking trails wind through the park. In winter, a snowmobile trail connecting the park with the Frye Mountain Game Management Area is maintained.

Open: Year-round; fully operational May 15 through September 30.

207 Pine Ridge Campground and Cottages

Location: Near Lake St. George State Park

in Liberty; Southern Maine map page 33, grid b3.

Campsites, facilities: There are 35 sites for tents and RVs, 9 with full hookups, 8 with water and electric, and 18 with no hookups. Flush toilets, hot showers, picnic tables, fireplaces, laundry facilities, a dump station, and a store are provided. For recreation, there is a heated swimming pool, canoe rentals, hiking trails, a rec room, volleyball, badminton, and horseshoes. Leashed pets are permitted.

Reservations, fees: Reservations are accepted. Sites are $18 to $24 a night.

Contact: Randy and Rachel Gardner, Pine Ridge Campground and Cottages, P.O. Box 7, Liberty, ME 04949; (207) 589-4352.

Directions: From the intersection of Route 3 and Route 220 in the town of Liberty, drive 1.5 miles east on Route 3 to the campground.

Trip notes: Not only is Pine Ridge conveniently located between the state capital of Augusta and the coastal town of Belfast, it is also close to Lake St. George State Park, a great destination for anglers and boaters. This campground is open year-round, with cozy cabins available for rent in the summer and winter. In addition, it's set along the International Trail System, so snowmobilers can ride from here all the way to Canada. For more information on the area, see the trip notes for Lake St. George State Park (campground number 206).

Open: Year-round.

208 Camden Hills State Park

Location: Just north of the town of Camden; Southern Maine map page 33, grid b4.

Campsites, facilities: There are 112 sites for tents and RVs, all without hookups. Facilities include wheelchair-accessible flush toilets, hot showers, a dump station, a group camping area, and a playground. The maximum RV length is 31 feet. Leashed pets are permitted.

Reservations, fees: Reservations are taken, and the total amount due must accompany your request. Contact the Maine Bureau of Parks and Lands at the number below. The State of Maine allocates some sites on a first-come, first-served basis. Sites are $11.50 for residents of Maine and $15 for nonresidents.

Contact: Camden Hills State Park Ranger, (207) 236-3109. Maine Bureau of Parks and Lands, 22 State House Station, Augusta, ME 04333; (207) 287-3821.

Directions: From the junction of Route 105 and U.S. 1 in Camden, drive two miles north on U.S. 1 to the park entrance.

Trip notes: The coastal village of Camden is widely considered one of the prettiest in the entire country. With its quaint clapboard houses, white church steeples, and schooner-dotted harbor, it certainly appears to be the quintessential New England village. Camden Hills State Park is set amid all this splendid scenery, encompassing much of the Megunticook Mountain Range, which rises up directly behind the town in a stunning backdrop.

From the summit of Mount Battie, the views of Camden, Camden Harbor, and Penobscot Bay are absolutely breathtaking. Similar to Acadia National Park, Camden Hills State Park has something to please almost everyone: mountains, ocean, forests, freshwater lakes, hiking trails, and easy access to the shops and restaurants in town. One trail near the campsites traces the shore of Penobscot Bay.

Open: Year-round; fully operational May 15 through October 15.

209 Old Massachusetts Homestead Campground

Location: North of Camden at Lincolnville Beach; Southern Maine map page 33, grid b4.

Campsites, facilities: There are 68 sites for tents and RVs, 10 with full hookups, 33 with water and electric, and 25 with no hookups. Flush toilets, hot showers, picnic tables, fireplaces, laundry facilities, a dump station, and a store selling limited supplies are provided. You'll also find a swimming pool, rec room, volleyball, horseshoes, and hiking trails. Leashed pets are permitted.

Reservations, fees: Reservations are accepted with Visa or MasterCard. Sites are $19 to $22 a night.

Contact: Dwight Wass, Old Massachusetts Homestead Campground, P.O. Box 5, Lincolnville, ME 04849; (207) 789-5135 or (800) 213-8142.

Directions: From the junction of U.S. 1 and Route 173 in Lincolnville, drive two miles north on U.S. 1 to the campground entrance.

Trip notes: When all was said and done, the Old Massachusetts Homestead emerged as one of our favorites. Perhaps we were won over by the location among great tall pines, or the clean, well-kept facilities, or the private, wooded sites tucked away in a mature forest. It might be due to the way the campground loops are laid out discreetly through the woods, or the fact that the place has obviously been so well cared for over the years. Regardless, this little campground, whose main building dates back to 1718, is a special destination within easy access of the Mid-Coast region's many attractions.

Open: May 1 through November 1.

Warren Island State Park

Location: On Warren Island in Lincolnville; Southern Maine map page 33, grid b4.

Campsites, facilities: There are 10 tent sites and two Adirondack lean-tos with no hookups. Pit toilets, fire rings, drinking water, and docking and mooring facilities are provided on the property. Leashed pets are permitted.

Reservations, fees: Reservations are accepted, and the total amount due must accompany your request. Contact the Maine Bureau of Parks and Lands at the number below. The State of Maine allocates some sites on a first-come, first-served basis. Sites are $11.50 a night for residents of Maine and $15 for nonresidents.

Contact: Warren Island State Park, c/o Camden Hills State Park Ranger, (207) 236-0849. Maine Bureau of Parks and Lands, 22 State House Station, Augusta, ME 04333; (207) 287-3821.

Directions: To reach these campsites on Warren Island, launch a boat at any of the public docks along the coast. Lincolnville is the closest.

Trip notes: This spruce-covered island lies just offshore from Lincolnville and adjacent to the much larger Islesboro Island in Penobscot Bay, considered by many to be the most beautiful body of water in the entire state of Maine. The park was designed to serve the needs of small-boat travelers and is accessible only by boat or sea kayak. There is no public transportation to the island. If you have the means to get here, camping on Warren Island is a great way to literally leave it all behind. You can spend time swimming, fishing, and relaxing.

Open: May 1 through October 15.

 Northport Travel Park Campground

Location: North of Camden in Belfast; Southern Maine map page 33, grid b4.

Campsites, facilities: There are 75 sites for tents and RVs with full, partial, and no hookups. Flush toilets, hot showers, picnic tables, fireplaces, laundry facilities, a dump station, and a store are provided. There's also a pool, a stocked trout pond, hiking trails, a rec room, volleyball, badminton, and horseshoes. Leashed pets are permitted.

Reservations, fees: Reservations are recommended. Sites are $11 to $16 a night.

Contact: Charles Knight, Northport Travel Park Campground, U.S. 1, Northport, ME 04849; (207) 338-2077.

Directions: From the junction of U.S. 1 and Route 3 in Belfast, drive six miles south on Route 3 to the campground.

Trip notes: Both open and shaded sites are offered at Northport. Located just off busy U.S. 1, five miles south of Belfast and 10 miles north of Camden, the campground lies right across the highway from Penobscot Bay. From here, you have easy access to Camden Hills State Park, restaurants, shops, boat excursions, sea kayaking, and saltwater fishing, as well as the picturesque seacoast towns of Belfast, Searsport, and Camden. Sites are at the edge of a wooded area surrounding the stocked trout pond. Those desiring more privacy can request one of the secluded sites in the woods.

Open: May 15 through October 15.

The Moorings Oceanfront Campground

Location: On Penobscot Bay in Belfast; Southern Maine map page 33, grid b4.

Campsites, facilities: There are 39 sites for tents and RVs, some with partial hookups. Flush toilets, hot showers, picnic tables, fireplaces, laundry facilities, and a dump station are provided. You'll also find a sandy beach, a rec room, volleyball, tetherball, badminton, and horseshoes. Leashed pets are permitted.

Reservations, fees: Reservations are recommended. A 25 percent deposit is required. Sites are $20 to $21 a night.

Contact: Ben Hill, The Moorings Oceanfront Campground, RR 1, P.O. Box 69, Searsport Avenue, Belfast, ME 04915; (207) 338-6860.

Directions: From the intersection of U.S. 1 and the Belfast Harbor Bridge, drive 2.1 miles north on U.S. 1 to the campground.

Trip notes: The Moorings lies directly off U.S. 1 where the highway parallels the ocean between the villages of Belfast and Searsport. All sites have ocean views over the wide expanse of Penobscot Bay, and campers enjoy easy access to saltwater fishing and swimming. The campground is new—having opened in 1993—and faces south, with great exposure to the sun and to cool ocean breezes. Both Belfast and Searsport are classic Maine villages where you'll find shops, museums, restaurants, and boat-excursion operators.

Open: May 15 through October 15.

㉑ Searsport Shores Campground

Location: On Penobscot Bay in Searsport; Southern Maine map page 33, grid b4.

Campsites, facilities: There are 125 sites for tents and RVs, 100 with water and electric hookups and 25 with no hookups. Chemical non-flush toilets, wheelchair-accessible rest room facilities, hot showers, picnic tables, fireplaces, laundry facilities, a dump station, and a store are provided. For recreation, there is a playground, rec room, hiking trails, volleyball, basketball, and horseshoes. A nearby town wharf can be used for boat launching. Leashed pets are permitted.

Reservations, fees: Reservations are accepted. Sites are $15 to $26.50 a night.

Contact: Asthig Koltookian Tangway, Searsport Shores Campground, 216 West Main Street, Searsport, ME 04974; (207) 584-6059.

Directions: From the center of Searsport, drive one mile south on U.S. 1 to the campground.

Trip notes: This clean, attractive campground is located right on the shore of Penobscot Bay. The spacious RV sites are scattered among shade trees, while the tent sites are separated by a small brook in a wild seaside setting. There are sandy beaches for swimmers and sunbathers, hiking trails, and plenty of places to launch a sea kayak. A unique touch is the fax and word processing service available for those who want to mix a little work in with their play.

Open: May 15 through Columbus Day.

㉑ Duck Lake Management Unit

Location: East of Burlington; Southern Maine map page 33, grid a4.

Campsites, facilities: There are six primitive tent sites on the shores of Duck Lake, Gassabias Lake, and Upper and Lower Unknown Lake. Pit toilets, picnic tables, and fire rings are provided. Pets are permitted.

Reservations, fees: Sites are first come, first served. There is no fee.

Contact: Maine Bureau of Parks and Lands, 22 State House Station, Augusta, ME 04333; (207) 287-3821.

Directions: From the village of Burlington northeast of Bangor, follow rough logging roads east for several miles to access the unit.

Trip notes: Duck Lake is a 25,000-acre preserve in the remote and sparsely populated eastern woodlands of Maine. In addition to the namesake pond, several other small lakes with sand beaches—including Gassabias Lake, the Unknown Lakes, and Fourth Machias Lake—are contained in the unit's boundaries. Duck Lake is more popular with campers than the others, and thus more crowded. Renowned for its excellent cold-water fishing for landlocked salmon and brook trout, Duck Lake lures many visitors who arrive armed with fishing rods. Equally good warm-water fishing is available on the other lakes. For a pleasant canoe trip in which you'll float through a variety of wildlife habitats, put your canoe and paddles into Gassabias Stream.

Open: Year-round.

215 Villa Vaughn Campground

Location: On Pushaw Lake near Orono; Southern Maine map page 33, grid a4.

Campsites, facilities: There are 75 sites for tents and RVs, some with full hookups and some with water and electric. Flush toilets, hot showers, picnic tables, fireplaces, laundry facilities, a dump station, and a store are provided. There's also a boat launch, canoe and rowboat rentals, a rec room, and horseshoes. Leashed pets are permitted.

Reservations, fees: Reservations are required for lakefront sites. Sites are $14 to $18 a night.

Contact: Villa Vaughn Campground, RFD 5, Box 205, Bangor, ME 04401; (207) 945-6796.

Directions: From Interstate 95 near Orono, take exit 51 and drive one mile south on Stillwater Avenue. Turn right and go three miles west on Forest Avenue to the campground.

Trip notes: The sites at Villa Vaughn are set beneath shade trees and beside the shore of Pushaw Lake, a nine-mile-long body of water offering some excellent bass, perch, and pickerel fishing and calm water for canoeing. It's an open, airy place with a shallow, sandy beach that's safe for swimming. Nearby Orono is home to the University of Maine.

Open: May 15 through October 15.

216 Stetson Shores Campground

Location: On Pleasant Lake in Stetson; Southern Maine map page 33, grid a4.

Campsites, facilities: There are 43 sites for tents and RVs, 40 with water and electric hookups and three with no hookups. Facilities include flush toilets, hot showers, picnic tables, fireplaces, laundry, a dump station, and a store. For recreation, there is a boat launch; canoe, kayak, and paddleboat rentals; lake fishing; volleyball; badminton; and horseshoes. Leashed pets are permitted.

Reservations, fees: Reservations are accepted. Sites are $17 to $19 a night.

Contact: The Adams Family, Stetson Shores Campground, Route 143, P.O. Box 86B, Stetson, ME 04488; (207) 296-2041.

Directions: From Interstate 95 west of Hampden, take exit 43 and drive six miles north on Route 143 until you reach the campground entrance.

Trip notes: Rural and woodsy, this campground is set on 32 acres beside the shores of a large spring-fed lake known for its excellent bass, perch, and pickerel fishing. For campers the main attraction is the lake. If you bring your own boat, you can use the on-site boat launch. Otherwise, rent a kayak, paddleboat, or canoe for a lazy day on the water. Sites are available in the woods, in an open field, or right on the lakefront. This is a no-frills kind of place, where improvements have been kept to a minimum.

Open: May 15 through October 15.

217 Christie's Campground

Location: On Sebasticook Lake in Newport; Southern Maine map page 33, grid a4.

Campsites, facilities: There are 50 sites, 9 with full hookups, 27 with water and electric, and 14 without hookups. Flush toilets, hot showers, picnic tables, fireplaces, a dump station, laundry facilities, and a store are provided. For recreation, there is a boat launch, canoe and boat rentals, a beach, playground, rec room, volleyball, basketball, badminton, and horseshoe pits. Leashed pets are permitted.

Reservations, fees: Reservations are recommended. Sites are $12.50 to $18.50 a night.

Contact: Bruce and Patti Newhall, Christie's Campground, Route 2, Box 565, Newport, ME 04953; (207) 368-4645 or (800) 688-5141.

Directions: From the junction of Interstate 95 and U.S. 2 at Newport, drive three miles east on U.S. 2 to the campground.

Trip notes: Offering quiet shorefront sites on Sebasticook Lake, Christie's Campground is a shady, comfortable facility with an established feel and a relaxed pace. This pleasant park is well situated for campers who want to take day trips to the mountains that lie to the north or the coast to the south. Bring your fishing tackle and frying pan, because Sebasticook Lake is renowned for its smallmouth bass, perch, and pickerel fishing.

Open: May 1 through October 30.

218 Tent Village Travel Trailer Park

Location: On Sebasticook Lake in Newport; Southern Maine map page 33, grid a4.

Campsites, facilities: There are 50 sites for tents and RVs with full, partial, and no hookups. Flush toilets, hot showers, picnic tables with rooftops, fireplaces, metered LP gas, a dump station, and a store are provided. For recreation, there is a swimming pool; boat launch; canoe, paddleboat, and motorboat rentals; a rec room; volleyball, basketball, badminton, and horseshoes. Leashed pets are permitted.

Reservations, fees: Reservations are accepted and require a deposit of one night's fee. Sites are $12.50 to $18.50 a night.

Contact: Vern and Joan Holyokes, Tent Village Travel Trailer Park, RR 2, Box 580, Newport, ME 04953; (207) 368-5047 or (800) 319-9333.

Directions: From the junction of Interstate 95 and U.S. 2 at Newport, drive two miles east on U.S. 2 until you reach the campground entrance.

Trip notes: Tent Village is a clean, well-maintained, and established campground on the shores of Sebasticook Lake. The 50 wooded or sunny sites are spread out over 50 acres, giving visitors a sense of open space and privacy. Though it's near no major attractions, the place does make you feel right at home. People looking for a lakeside camp, or those who are just passing through the area, may find it worthwhile to stop at Tent Village.

Open: May 15 through October 15.

㉑⑨ Shady Acres Campground

Location: In Carmel, a few miles west of Bangor; Southern Maine map page 33, grid a4.

Campsites, facilities: There are 50 sites for tents and RVs, some with full hookups and others with water and electric. Flush toilets, hot showers, picnic tables, fireplaces, laundry facilities, a dump station, and a store are provided. For recreation, there is a fishing pond, swimming pool, rec room, volleyball, badminton, and horseshoes. Leashed pets are permitted.

Reservations, fees: Reservations are accepted with a $5 deposit. Sites are $14 to $18 a night.

Contact: Mike and Elsie Hamel, Shady Acres Campground, RR 2, Box 7890, Carmel, ME 04419; (207) 848-5515.

Directions: From the intersection of Interstate 95 and Route 69 south of Carmel, drive 2.5 miles west on Route 69 to the campground.

Trip notes: Here is yet another small campground located close to Bangor. Although there are few attractions in the immediate area, you will not be too far from the coast, the North Woods, and the Canadian border. As the name suggests, the campsites at Shady Acres are set amid trees, giving the park a peaceful, pretty quality and providing cooling shade in the summer. Best of all for anglers, the trout fishing in the pond is reputed to be excellent.

Open: May 15 through October 15.

㉒⓪ Pleasant Hill Campground

Location: In Bangor; Southern Maine map page 33, grid a4.

Campsites, facilities: There are 105 sites for tents and RVs, 33 with full hookups, 52 with water and electric, and 20 with none. Flush toilets, free hot showers, picnic tables, fireplaces, laundry facilities, a dump station, cable TV, and a store are provided. For recreation, there is a heated swimming pool, miniature golf, a rec room, volleyball, basketball, badminton, and horseshoes. Leashed pets are permitted.

Reservations, fees: Reservations are recommended. For stays of up to three days, send a deposit of one night's fee; for four or more days, send a $40 deposit. Sites are $13 to $24.50 a night.

Contact: Bev and Frank Montford, Pleasant Hill Campground, RFD 3, P.O. Box 180, Bangor, ME 04401; (207) 848-5127.

Directions: From the intersection of Interstate 95 and Union Street near exit 47 in Bangor, drive five miles west on Union Street to the campground.

Trip notes: The aptly named Pleasant Hill Campground is spread out over rolling, shaded hills that catch cooling breezes and make for a quiet, relaxing retreat. Someone obviously had children in mind when they designed this place: in addition to two playgrounds, a good-sized swimming pool, and a miniature golf course, the park boasts children's trout fishing in a private stocked pond and a private frog pond.

Located within the city limits of Bangor, the crossroads of the state, Pleasant Hill Campground is convenient to the downtown area, the airport, and the University of Maine, as well as within easy reach of Acadia National Park, the Canadian

Maritime Provinces, and the wild regions of northern Maine.

Open: May 1 through Columbus Day.

㉑ Wheeler Stream Camping Area

Location: In Bangor; Southern Maine map page 33, grid a4.

Campsites, facilities: There are 23 sites for tents and RVs, all with partial hookups. Flush toilets, free hot showers, picnic tables, fireplaces, laundry facilities, a dump station, and whirlpool are provided. Leashed pets are permitted.

Reservations, fees: Reservations are recommended. Sites are $13 to $15 a night.

Contact: David and Marybeth Archdeacon, Wheeler Stream Camping Area, RR 2, Box 2800, Bangor, ME 04401; (207) 848-3713.

Directions: From Interstate 95 at Bangor, take exit 44 and drive 2.5 miles west on Cold Brook Road to the intersection with U.S. 2. The campground is 300 feet ahead on U.S. 2.

Trip notes: Wheeler Stream is a small, open campground in the middle of a residential/business section of Bangor and was not designed to be a vacation spot for visitors to the area. Many of those who stay here are out-of-state contractors and construction workers who prefer to live at the campground in their own RVs instead of at a motel.

Open: May 15 through October 15.

㉒ Paul Bunyan Campground

Location: Just off Interstate 95 in Bangor; Southern Maine map page 33, grid a4.

Campsites, facilities: There are 52 sites for tents and RVs, 12 with full hookups and 40 with water and electric. Facilities include flush toilets, hot showers, picnic tables, fireplaces, a dump station, and a store. For recreation, there's a heated swimming pool, a rec room, a fishing pond, volleyball, basketball, badminton, and horseshoes. Leashed pets are permitted.

Reservations, fees: Reservations are recommended. For stays of up to three days, send one night's fee as a deposit; for four or more days, send a $40 deposit. Sites are $12.50 to $23.75 a night.

Contact: Dennis and Shirley Hachey, Paul Bunyan Campground, 1862 Union Street, Bangor, ME 04401; (207) 941-1177.

Directions: From the intersection of Interstate 95 and Union Street near exit 47 in Bangor, drive 2.5 miles west on Union Street to the campground.

Trip notes: For a campground located within the limits of Bangor—one of Maine's largest cities—Paul Bunyan is surprisingly peaceful and relaxing. Nestled in rolling countryside near the middle of the state, this is an ideal place to stop for those traveling to Acadia National Park, the Canadian Maritime Provinces, or the wild northern reaches of the state.

Open: Year-round.

㉓ Greenwood Acres

Location: Near Brewer; Southern Maine map page 33, grid a4.

Campsites, facilities: There are 40 sites for tents and RVs with full, partial, and no hookups. Flush toilets, hot showers, picnic tables, fireplaces, a dump station, laundry facilities, and a store are provided. You'll also find a swimming pool, playground, rec room, volleyball, basketball, and horseshoe pits. Leashed pets are permitted.

Reservations, fees: Reservations are recommended. Sites are $12 to $17 a night.

Contact: Tom and Donna Foster, Greenwood Acres, RFD 2, Box 210, Brewer, ME 04412; (207) 989-8898.

Directions: From the junction of U.S. 1A and Route 9 in Brewer, drive 4.5 miles east on Route 9, then one mile north on Route 178 to the campground.

Trip notes: Greenwood Acres is situated just off busy Route 178 on a 50-acre parcel of land covered with pine trees and open fields very near the twin cities of Bangor and Brewer. Most of the activity here takes place at the on-site playground and swimming pool. The Penobscot River, which happens to be a very good stream for salmon fishing, is directly across the highway from the campground and within easy walking distance. If you want to bask in the natural beauty of Maine, this isn't your best choice. It is, however, a convenient stop on the way to or from the various highlights of the state.

Open: Year-round.

❷❷❹ Red Barn RV Park

Location: In Holden; Southern Maine map page 33, grid a4.

Campsites, facilities: There are 100 sites for RVs, some with full hookups and others with water and electric. Flush toilets, hot showers, picnic tables, fireplaces, laundry facilities, a dump station, and a store are provided. A swimming pool, rec room, volleyball, basketball, badminton, and horseshoes are among the recreational offerings. Leashed pets are permitted.

Reservations, fees: Reservations are recommended July through Labor Day and require a $10 deposit. Sites are $14 to $17 a night.

Contact: Phil and Belinda Robinson, Red

Barn RV Park, U.S. 1A, Holden, ME 04429; (207) 843-6011.

Directions: From the intersection of Interstate 395 and U.S. 1A near Bangor, drive three miles east on U.S. 1A to the campground.

Trip notes: The campground is set in a grassy field just off a major highway. Convenient to downtown Bangor, known as the crossroads of Maine, this is a good place to stop if you are heading east to the Canadian Maritime Provinces, south to the coast, or north to the Maine Woods. Though not a destination campground for most vacationers, it does provide a clean, pleasant place to spend a day or two while traveling.

Open: May 15 through October 15.

❷❷❺ Branch Lake Camping Area

Location: On Branch Lake in Ellsworth; Southern Maine map page 33, grid b4.

Campsites, facilities: There are 55 sites for tents and RVs with full and partial hookups. Flush toilets, hot showers, picnic tables, fireplaces, a dump station, and a store are provided. For recreation, there is a large freshwater lake with a sandy beach, a boat launch, boat rentals, and a playground. Leashed pets are permitted.

Reservations, fees: Reservations are recommended. Sites are $12 to $20 a night.

Contact: Dick and Brenda Graves, Branch Lake Camping Area, RFD 5, Box 473, Ellsworth, ME 04605; (207) 667-5174.

Directions: From the junction of Route 46 and U.S. 1A in Holden, drive south on U.S. 1A for approximately six miles. Turn right and head west on Winkumpaugh Road, then go south on Landing Road and follow signs to the campground.

Trip notes: Branch Lake is a breezy,

shaded campground set in rolling forested countryside on a large freshwater lake. The usual array of waterfront activities is available. Cool off in Branch Lake, launch a motorboat or canoe, or grab your fishing rod to catch that night's supper. The campground is located midway between the city of Bangor and Acadia National Park.

Open: May 1 through October 15.

---

226 Masthead Campground

Location: On Hancock Pond in Bucksport; Southern Maine map page 33, grid b4.

Campsites, facilities: There are 38 sites for tents and RVs, all with partial hookups. Flush toilets, hot showers, picnic tables, fireplaces, a dump station, laundry facilities and a store are provided. For recreation, there are two beaches, canoe rentals, a pavilion, a playground, volleyball and badminton nets, and horseshoe pits. Leashed pets are permitted.

Reservations, fees: Reservations are recommended. Sites are $14 to $15 a night.

Contact: Annette and Bob Valenotte, Masthead Campground, P.O. Box 418, Bucksport, ME 04416; (207) 469-3482.

Directions: From the intersection of Route 15 and U.S. 1 in Bucksport, drive two miles east on U.S. 1, then 5.5 miles north on Route 46. Turn right on Mast Hill Road and go three-quarters of a mile east to the campground.

Trip notes: Masthead is one of those quiet, established, rather small campgrounds that makes visitors feel right at home as soon as they enter. The entire grounds are very well tended, the sites are spacious and private, and the mix of open fields, tall trees, and sparkling waters creates a feeling of remoteness and seclusion.

Two beaches on Hancock Pond are the star attractions, and a day at the waterfront is made even more pleasant by the prohibition of motorboats. The rule prevents buzzing engines from disturbing those who simply want to cast out a fishing line or read a book on the shore. Canoes and kayaks are always welcome. This splendid campground is near picturesque fishing villages and Acadia National Park.

Open: Memorial Day through September 15.

---

227 Flying Dutchman

Location: On the banks of the Penobscot River in Bucksport; Southern Maine map page 33, grid b4.

Campsites, facilities: There are 35 sites for tents and RVs, 12 with full hookups, 13 with water and electric, and 10 with none. Flush toilets, hot showers, a whirlpool, picnic tables, fireplaces, a dump station, laundry facilities, and a store are provided. For recreation, there is a heated swimming pool, a boat launch, saltwater fishing, a rec room, playground, volleyball, basketball, badminton, and horseshoe pits. Leashed pets are permitted.

Reservations, fees: Reservations are recommended. For stays of up to three days, send one night's fee as a deposit; for four or more days, a $40 deposit is required. Sites are $15 to $18 a night.

Contact: Hans and Glee Honders, Flying Dutchman, P.O. Box 549, Bucksport, ME 04416; (207) 469-3256.

Directions: From the junction of U.S. 1 and Route 15 in Bucksport, drive one mile south on U.S. 1 to the campground.

Trip notes: Flying Dutchman is a small, well-kept campground located directly on the banks of the Penobscot River just downstream of Fort Knox, an impressive stone fort built during the Civil War era. A sandy beach and boat launch are available across the street at Fort Knox State Park. The heated pool and hot tub at the campground offer welcome warmth after a day in the chilly ocean waters of Maine. From Flying Dutchman, you can take day trips to the beautiful Penobscot Bay area and several nearby seaside communities and attractions, including historic Castine, Blue Hill, and Deer Isle. Acadia National Park is a short drive away.

Open: May 1 through Columbus Day.

228 Shady Oaks Campground

Location: In Orland; Southern Maine map page 33, grid b4.

Campsites, facilities: There are 50 sites for tents and RVs, 28 with full hookups and 22 with water and electric. Flush toilets, free hot showers, picnic tables, fireplaces, laundry facilities, a dump station, and a store are provided. There's also a swimming pool, rec room, volleyball, basketball, badminton, and horseshoes. No dogs are allowed.

Reservations, fees: Reservations are recommended. Sites are $14 to $16 a night.

Contact: Joyce and Don Nelson, Shady Oaks Campground, RR 1, P.O. Box 1874, Orland, ME 04472; (207) 469-7739.

Directions: From the junction of U.S. 1 and Route 15 in Bucksport, drive two miles east on U.S. 1 to the campground.

Trip notes: Small, clean, and not at all noisy, the Shady Oaks Campground is within easy driving distance of many Mid-Coast attractions, including Fort Knox—a Civil War–era fort guarding the Penobscot River—the Deer Isle and Blue Hill areas

with their coastal scenery and pretty fishing villages, and Acadia National Park. The campground offers many amenities to families including a swimming pool, a nature trail, and a schedule of planned activities.

Open: May 1 through October 1.

229 Whispering Pines Campground

Location: On Toddy Pond in the township of East Orland; Southern Maine map page 33, grid b4.

Campsites, facilities: There are 50 sites for tents and RVs, 40 with full hookups, six with water and electric, and four with none. Facilities include flush toilets, hot showers, picnic tables, fireplaces, and a dump station. For recreation, there is a large lake with a sandy beach, a boat launch, free use of canoes and rowboats, a rec room, volleyball, badminton, and horseshoes. Leashed pets are permitted.

Reservations, fees: Reservations are accepted. Sites are $18 to $22 a night.

Contact: Dwight and Sandy Gates, Whispering Pines Campground, East Orland, ME 04431; (207) 469-3443.

Directions: From the junction of U.S. 1 and Route 15 in Bucksport, drive 7.5 miles east on U.S. 1 to the campground.

Trip notes: Whispering Pines is a quiet, well-maintained, spacious campground set among stately mature white pines and hemlocks. The campground is situated along the shores of Toddy Pond, a wild and undeveloped 10-mile-long lake. Two other lakes lie within walking distance, and all three waters offer superb trout, salmon, and bass fishing. Campers are granted free use of rowboats and canoes, allowing children plenty of time to learn how to row or paddle. The sandy beach, with its swimming floats and gradually sloping bottom, is a safe place for children to swim and play. This is an exceptional facility located within easy reach of Mid-Coast Maine's finest attractions.

Open: May 20 through September 30.

❷❸⓿ Balsam Cove Campground

Location: On Toddy Pond in the township of East Orland; Southern Maine map page 33, grid b4.

Campsites, facilities: There are 60 sites for tents and RVs, 30 with water and electric hookups, 20 with electric only, and 10 with no hookups. Flush toilets, hot showers, picnic tables, fireplaces, a dump station, laundry facilities, and a store are provided. For recreation, there is a large lake with a sandy beach, a playground, rec room, volleyball, basketball, and horseshoe pits. Leashed pets are permitted.

Reservations, fees: Reservations are recommended. Sites are $14.75 to $19.75 a night.

Contact: Sharon and Charlie, Balsam Cove Campground, P.O. Box C, East Orland, ME 04431; (207) 469-7771.

Directions: From the intersection of U.S. 1 and Route 15 in Bucksport, drive south on Route 15 for one mile, then turn left on a dirt road and follow the signs to the campground.

Trip notes: With plenty of space between sites, this rustic campground offers welcome peace and privacy for families. The large waterfront sites are very popular. The swimming area, complete with a float and slide, provides access to 10-mile-long Toddy Pond. Bring your canoe and launch it from the beach or reserve dock space for your motorboat. When you tire of freshwater swimming, drive the short distance

to the ocean for a day of swimming, boating, and fishing in salt water. Spectacular Acadia National Park is not too far from here. Note: Be sure to check out the expansive blueberry fields on the drive in to the campground.

Open: May 24 through September 30.

❷❸❶ Patten Pond Camping Resort

Location: On Lower Patten Pond in Ellsworth; Southern Maine map page 33, grid b4.

Campsites, facilities: There are 145 sites for tents and RVs, 105 with partial hookups and 40 with no hookups. Flush toilets, hot showers, picnic tables, fireplaces, laundry facilities, a dump station, and a store are provided. Recreational facilities include a boat launch, canoe rentals, a playground and sports field, hiking trails, a rec room, volleyball, basketball, badminton, and horseshoes. Leashed pets are permitted.

Reservations, fees: Reservations are accepted. Sites are $12 to $19 a night.

Contact: Patten Pond Camping Resort, Ellsworth, ME 04605; (207) 667-5745.

Directions: From the junction of U.S. 1 and U.S. 1A in Ellsworth, drive 7.5 miles west on U.S. 1 to the campground.

Trip notes: The campground is located on the shores of Lower Patten Pond, a freshwater lake within easy driving distance of the coast. This is a good base camp for day trips to Acadia National Park, but don't overlook other attractions in the immediate area. Here you're just north of the village of Blue Hill, with its attractive colonial town center and picturesque harbor, and Castine, home of the Maine Maritime Academy and the scene of naval battles that were waged in the American Revolution and the Civil War.

Open: Mid-May through mid-October.

232 The Gatherings Family Campground

Location: On Weymouth Point in the village of Surry; Southern Maine map page 33, grid b4.

Campsites, facilities: There are 110 sites for tents and RVs, five with full hookups and 105 with water and electric hookups. Flush toilets, hot showers, picnic tables, fireplaces, a dump station, laundry facilities, and a store are provided. There's also a boat launch, a beach, saltwater swimming and fishing, boat and canoe rentals, a playground, rec room, volleyball, basketball, and horseshoe pits. Leashed pets are permitted.

Reservations, fees: Reservations are recommended. Full payment is required for stays of up to three days; for up to 13 days, send three days' fee as a deposit, and for two weeks or more, send 25 percent of the total fee. Sites are $13 to $25 a night.

Contact: Ralph and Ann Jacobsen, The Gatherings Family Campground, RFD 3, Box 69, Ellsworth, ME 04605; (207) 667-8826.

Directions: From the junction of U.S. 1 and Route 172 in Ellsworth, drive four miles south on Route 172 to the campground.

Trip notes: Aside from boasting a spectacular setting on the tip of Weymouth Point at the northern end of Blue Hill Bay, this spacious campground offers fairly secluded waterfront sites with expansive views over the ocean. With more than a quarter mile of ocean frontage on Patten Bay accessible from this campground, it's difficult to think of a reason to leave. But after staring at Cadillac Mountain and the

other peaks of Acadia National Park from your site here, you'll be tempted to head to the nearby park to explore its other natural wonders, including lakes, streams, cliffs, tide pools, and forests. Hiking trails and carriage roads for hiking and biking weave throughout the park. This is a peaceful place with remarkably easy access to the coastal gems of Maine.

Open: May 1 through October 15.

233 Lamoine State Park

Location: On Frenchman Bay in Ellsworth; Southern Maine map page 33, grid b4.

Campsites, facilities: There are 61 sites for tents and RVs up to 20 feet long, all without hookups. Picnic tables, fire rings, rest rooms, a dump station, boat ramp, group camping area, playground, and swimming area are provided. Leashed pets are permitted.

Reservations, fees: Reservations are accepted, and the total amount due must accompany your request. Contact the Maine Bureau of Parks and Lands at the number below. The State of Maine allocates some sites on a first-come, first-served basis. Sites are $11.50 a night for residents of Maine and $15 for nonresidents.

Contact: Lamoine State Park Ranger, (207) 667-4778. Maine Bureau of Parks and Lands, 22 State House Station, Augusta, ME 04333; (207) 287-3821.

Directions: From the junction of U.S. 1 and Route 184 in Ellsworth, drive 10 miles south on Route 184 to the park entrance.

Trip notes: Found on a beautiful peninsula that juts out into Frenchman Bay, Lamoine State Park is the perfect alternative to Acadia National Park for those who wish to enjoy the same stunning scenery and ocean access but also want to get away from the summer crowds. Some sites are right next to the water and, as with other state parks in Maine, all sites afford a good measure of privacy. The day-use area, which stretches along the shoreline, has a large picnic area as well as many hibachi-style grills for barbecues. If you are looking for a splendid campground with easy access to the water, this is the place. Acadia National Park and Bar Harbor are less than an hour away by car.

Open: May 15 through October 15.

---

234 Narrows Too Camping Resort

Location: Near Bar Harbor in Trenton; Southern Maine map page 33, grid b4.

Campsites, facilities: There are 120 sites for tents and RVs, 50 with full hookups, 60 with water and electric hookups, and 10 with none. Flush toilets, hot showers, picnic tables, fireplaces, laundry facilities, a dump station, and a store selling groceries and RV supplies are provided. For recreation, there is a boat launch, a heated swimming pool, canoe rentals, a rec room, miniature golf, volleyball, basketball, badminton, and horseshoes. Ice, firewood, and LP gas are available. Leashed pets are permitted.

Reservations, fees: Reservations are recommended for July and August. A $45 deposit is required for stays of up to three days; for four or more days, send a $90 deposit. Sites are $15 to $33 a night.

Contact: Narrows Too Camping Resort, RR 1, Box 193, Trenton, ME 04605; (207) 667-4300.

Directions: From the junction of Route 3 and Route 230 in Ellsworth, drive a quarter mile south on Route 3 to the campground.

Trip notes: Like its sister resort across the

water, Mount Desert Narrows (see campground number 236), Narrows Too guards the ocean narrows separating Mount Desert Island from the mainland. And as at Mount Desert Narrows, there's something for everyone here, from well-developed RV sites to spacious sites along the water's edge. Though it is large, the park feels spacious, with lots of open space and room to roam. This is a good base camp for outings to Bar Harbor and Acadia National Park.

Open: Memorial Day through Columbus Day.

---

235 Barcadia Campground

Location: On Western Bay, north of Bar Harbor; Southern Maine map page 33, grid b4.

Campsites, facilities: There are 200 sites for tents and RVs, 25 with full hookups, 150 with water and electric hookups, and 25 with none. Flush toilets, hot showers, picnic tables, fireplaces, a dump station, laundry facilities, and a store are provided. There's also a boat launch, a private beach, a playground, rec room, volleyball, basketball, and horseshoe pits. Ice, firewood, and LP gas are available. Leashed pets are permitted.

Reservations, fees: Reservations are recommended and require a deposit of two day's fee. Sites are $16 to $29 a night for four people. Pets are $2 a day.

Contact: Pete and Lynn Desroches, Barcadia Campground, RR 1, Box 2165, Bar Harbor, ME 04609; (207) 288-3520.

Directions: From Ellsworth, drive south on Route 3 onto Mount Desert Island. The campground is at the intersection of Routes 3 and 102/198 at the northern tip of the island.

Trip notes: Barcadia bills itself as the

"gateway to Acadia National Park" and there is some truth to the claim, as this is the first campground you'll encounter after crossing the bridge to Mount Desert Island from the mainland. This is a large park with open and wooded sites, many set directly along the shore of Western Bay. A waterfront site on the private beach is worth the extra fee, given the panoramic views of the bay you'll gain. A shuttle bus provides regular service to Bar Harbor.

Open: May 17 through October 15.

236 Mount Desert Narrows Camping Resort

Location: In Bar Harbor near the bridge to Mount Desert Island; Southern Maine map page 33, grid b4.

Campsites, facilities: There are 239 sites for tents and RVs, 50 with full hookups, 136 with water and electric hookups, and 53 with none. Flush toilets, hot showers, picnic tables, fireplaces, laundry facilities, a dump station, and a store selling groceries and RV supplies are provided. For recreation, there is a heated swimming pool, saltwater swimming and fishing, miniature golf, canoe rentals, volleyball, basketball, badminton, and horseshoes. Ice, firewood, and LP gas are available. Leashed pets are permitted.

Reservations, fees: Reservations are recommended. A $45 deposit is required for stays of up to three days; for four or more days, it's a $90 deposit. Sites are $20 to $36 a night.

Contact: Mount Desert Narrows Camping Resort, Route 3/Bar Harbor Road, RR 1, Box 2045, Bar Harbor, ME 04609; (207) 288-4782.

Directions: From Ellsworth, drive south on Route 3 onto Mount Desert Island. After you reach the intersection of Routes 3 and 102/198, drive another 1.5 miles east on Route 3 to the campground.

Trip notes: Situated directly on the ocean narrows separating Mount Desert Island from the mainland, this large campground has something for everyone. The park offers distinct RV and "wilderness" tenting areas, a full range of amenities and amusements, and oceanfront and oceanview sites on an expansive shoreline. It's a quick drive to the center of Bar Harbor and the entrance to Acadia National Park.

Open: May 1 through October 25.

237 Spruce Valley Campground

Location: In Bar Harbor; Southern Maine map page 33, grid b4.

Campsites, facilities: There are 100 sites for tents and RVs, 10 with full hookups, 30 with water and electric hookups, and 60 with none. Flush toilets, hot showers, picnic tables, fireplaces, laundry facilities, a dump station, and a camp store are provided. For recreation, there is a heated swimming pool with a slide, a rec room, volleyball, basketball, and horseshoes. Leashed pets are permitted.

Reservations, fees: Reservations are recommended in July and August. A deposit of two night's fee is required. Sites are $16 to $21 a night.

Contact: Harry and Paula Luhrs, Spruce Valley Campground, Route 102, Box 2420, Bar Harbor, ME 04609; (207) 288-5139.

Directions: From Ellsworth, drive south on Route 3 onto Mount Desert Island. At the intersection of Routes 3 and 102/198, follow Route 102/198 south for 1.5 miles to the campground on the left.

Trip notes: Spruce Valley is a clean, quiet family campground centrally located near Bar Harbor and Acadia National Park. Although there are no water views or oceanfront sites, this is an attractive park within easy reach of hiking, biking, sea kayaking, whale watching, and other Mount Desert Island attractions. Children will love the heated swimming pool with slide as well as the cedar playground.

Open: May 10 through October 31.

238 Hadley's Point Campground

Location: In Bar Harbor; Southern Maine map page 33, grid b4.

Campsites, facilities: There are 180 sites for tents and RVs, 15 with full hookups, 117 with water and electric hookups, and 48 with none. Flush toilets, hot showers, picnic tables, fireplaces, a dump station, laundry facilities, a store, and Sunday church services are provided. The property also has a playground, swimming pool, shuffleboard, basketball, and horseshoe pits. Leashed pets are permitted.

Reservations, fees: Reservations are recommended. Sites are $16 to $20 a night.

Contact: The Baker Family, Hadley's Point Campground, Hadley's Point Road, Box 1790, Bar Harbor, ME 04609; (207) 288-4808.

Directions: From Ellsworth, drive south on Route 3 onto Mount Desert Island. After you reach the intersection of Routes 3 and 102/198, drive another three miles east on Route 3 to the campground on the left.

Trip notes: Just four miles from the entrance to Acadia National Park, Hadley's is well situated for those who want to take advantage of the scenic and recreational opportunities of Mount Desert Island. The sites are set in open fields and woods near,

but not on, the waterfront. A public saltwater beach is just a five-minute stroll from the campground. If chilly salt water doesn't appeal to you, take a dip in the campground's pool. Shuttle service from Hadley's to Bar Harbor runs daily from late June to Labor Day. Religious campers will appreciate that church services are held every Sunday at the campground.

Open: May 15 through October 15.

239 Bar Harbor Campground

Location: Just outside the town of Bar Harbor; Southern Maine map page 33, grid b4.

Campsites, facilities: There are 300 sites for tents and RVs, 60 with full hookups, 100 with water and electric hookups, and 140 with none. Flush toilets, hot showers, picnic tables, fireplaces, a dump station, laundry facilities, and a store are provided. For recreation, there is a swimming pool, playground, rec room, shuffleboard, basketball, and horseshoe pits. Leashed pets are permitted.

Reservations, fees: Reservations are not accepted. Sites are $17 to $24 a night.

Contact: Craig Robbins, Bar Harbor Campground, RFD 1, Box 1125, Bar Harbor, ME 04609; (207) 288-5185.

Directions: From Ellsworth, drive south on Route 3 onto Mount Desert Island. After you reach the intersection of Routes 3 and 102/198, drive another five miles east on Route 3 to the campground on the left.

Trip notes: The designers of this very large campground have managed to create sites in a maritime spruce-fir forest that offer plenty of privacy yet have a spacious feel. Located just north of the village of Bar Harbor and close to the Nova Scotia ferry terminal, the campground is well placed for folks who seek quick access to all that the region has to offer, including the wondrous features of Acadia National Park—among them its forests, beaches, mountains, cliffs, wildlife, lakes, and offshore islands. By walking a short distance from here, campers can soon be exploring the town of Bar Harbor and sampling the food at the wonderful restaurants there. A lobster pound, just across the street from Bar Harbor Campground, is a great place to shop for a Downeast dinner.

Open: Memorial Day through Columbus Day.

⓶⓸⓪ Blackwoods Campground

Location: In Acadia National Park; Southern Maine map page 33, grid b4.

Campsites, facilities: There are 306 sites for tents and RVs, all without hookups. Facilities include wheelchair-accessible flush toilets, picnic tables, fireplaces, and a dump station. Hiking trails and bike paths leave from the campground. Leashed pets are permitted.

Reservations, fees: Reservations are strongly recommended. Contact Ticketron or Acadia National Park at the numbers below. Sites are $14 a night.

Contact: Ticketron, (800) 365-2267. Acadia National Park, P.O. Box 177, Bar Harbor, ME 04609; (207) 288-3338.

Directions: From Ellsworth, drive south on Route 3 to the town of Bar Harbor on Mount Desert Island. After you reach the intersection of Routes 3 and 233, continue another five miles south on Route 3 to the campground.

Trip notes: Blackwoods Campground

bears an appropriate name, as it is situated in a thick maritime forest of dark spruce and fir trees. This place definitely has a northern feel, and even on the hottest summer days the air is cool and fresh. As with virtually every public campground in Maine, whether run by state or federal authorities, the sites at Blackwoods are very well spaced and afford a remarkable amount of privacy. Staying here puts you on the east side of Mount Desert Island, and from the campground you can hop on the long, gentle trail that leads to the summit of Cadillac Mountain, which rises 1,530 feet above the sea.

Open: Year-round.

⓶⓸① Mount Desert Campground

Location: At the tip of Somes Sound on Mount Desert Island; Southern Maine map page 33, grid b4.

Campsites, facilities: There are 150 sites for tents and RVs, some with water and electric hookups and some without. Flush toilets, hot showers, picnic tables, fireplaces, and a store are provided. For recreation, there is a boat launch, canoe rentals, and saltwater swimming. The maximum RV length is 20 feet. Dogs are not permitted during July and August.

Reservations, fees: Reservations are accepted for stays of three or more days from Memorial Day through Labor Day. There is a $30 reservation fee. Waterfront sites must be reserved for a week or more and require a $50 reservation fee. Sites are $20 to $27 a night.

Contact: Owen and Barbara Craighead, Mount Desert Campground, Route 198, Mount Desert, ME 04660; (207) 244-3710.

Directions: From Ellsworth, drive south on Route 3 onto Mount Desert Island. Follow Route 102/198 south, then drive three-quarters of a mile south on Route 198 to the campground.

Trip notes: It is not possible to be more centrally located on Mount Desert Island than right here at Mount Desert Campground. Located at the very tip of Somes Sound—the only fjord on the East Coast—the campground is within minutes of the villages of Bar Harbor, Northeast Harbor, and Southwest Harbor in addition to being close to the natural and scenic attractions of Acadia National Park, including hiking and biking trails, freshwater lakes, sand beaches, and ocean cliffs. The sites are well spaced and set beneath tall trees, offering a tremendous sense of privacy and seclusion.

Open: May 15 through October 1.

242 Somes Sound View Campground

Location: On Somes Sound in Mount Desert; Southern Maine map page 33, grid b4.

Campsites, facilities: There are 60 sites for tents and RVs, 20 with partial hookups and 40 without hookups. Flush toilets, hot showers, picnic tables, fireplaces, and a dump station are provided. A boat launch is available, and sailboats and canoes can be rented. The maximum RV length is 16 feet. Leashed pets are permitted.

Reservations, fees: Reservations are accepted and require a $20 deposit. Sites are $18 to $21 a night.

Contact: Sharon Musetti, Somes Sound View Campground, Hall Quarry Road, Mount Desert, ME 04660; (207) 244-3890.

Directions: From Ellsworth, drive south on Route 3 onto Mount Desert Island. Follow Route 102/198 south, then follow Route 102 south for two more miles. Turn left on Hall Quarry Road and continue

three-quarters of a mile east to the campground entrance.

Trip notes: The campground is perched on a rocky hill directly above Somes Sound, a deep arm of the Atlantic Ocean that reaches into the very center of Mount Desert Island and is the only fjord on the East Coast. The road down to the campground is steep, with several narrow turns, and is not suitable for large campers or RVs. Kayakers, canoeists, and sailors will be in their element here, for the water access is unsurpassed in this area. If you left your canoe or sailboat at home, rent one at the campground and explore the nooks and crannies of Somes Sound.

Open: Memorial Day through Columbus Day.

243 Smuggler's Den Campground

Location: In Southwest Harbor on Mount Desert Island; Southern Maine map page 33, grid b4.

Campsites, facilities: There are 100 sites for tents and RVs, 22 with full hookups, 43 with water and electric hookups, and 35 with none. Flush toilets, hot showers, picnic tables, fireplaces, laundry facilities, a dump station, and a store are provided. For recreation, there is a heated swimming pool, volleyball, badminton, and horseshoes. Leashed pets are permitted.

Reservations, fees: Reservations are recommended and require a $30 deposit. Sites are $18 to $25 a night.

Contact: Jean Conroy, Smuggler's Den Campground, P.O. Box 787, Southwest Harbor, ME 04679; (207) 244-3944.

Directions: From Ellsworth, drive south on Route 3 onto Mount Desert Island. Follow Route 102/198 south, then follow

Route 102 south for five more miles to the campground.

Trip notes: Smuggler's Den is a spacious, attractive campground lying at the foothills of some of Mount Desert Island's mountains. Campsites, which are set in the woods bordering a large open field, afford a feeling of openness and privacy. The campground claims an ideal location about halfway down the western, or "quiet," side of the island, very near freshwater lakes, hiking trails, ocean access points, and the pretty villages of Somesville and Southwest Harbor.

Open: Memorial Day through Columbus Day.

244 Seawall Campground

Location: In Acadia National Park near Southwest Harbor; Southern Maine map page 33, grid b4.

Campsites, facilities: There are 212 sites for tents and RVs, all without hookups. A group camping area is also available. Facilities include wheelchair-accessible flush toilets, picnic tables, and fireplaces. A self-guided nature trail leaves from the campground, and a picnic area is located across the street at the beach. Leashed pets are permitted.

Reservations, fees: Sites are available on a first-come, first-served basis. The fee is $14 a night.

Contact: Acadia National Park, P.O. Box 177, Bar Harbor, ME 04609; (207) 288-3338.

Directions: From Ellsworth, drive south on Route 3 onto Mount Desert Island. Follow Route 102/198 to Southwest Harbor and continue south on Route 102. At the fork, bear left onto Route 102A (Manset Road) and continue approximately five miles to the campground, on your right.

Trip notes: While most of Acadia National Park is on the eastern peninsula of Mount Desert Island, a few of its gems dot the western peninsula. Here on the "quiet" side of the island, separated from the hustle and bustle of Bar Harbor and the park's main attractions, Seawall is the kind of place where you can relax and enjoy all that the coast of Maine has to offer. As you look out across the street, you will soon realize how the campground got its name: a natural seawall, formed by the piling up of rocks and boulders set loose by winter storms, stretches along the coastline in the vicinity. The beach across the road is perfect for picnics, photography, beachcombing, kayaking, windsurfing, and—for hardy souls—swimming. The campsites are spacious, well maintained, and afford a good deal of privacy. And an extensive array of programs that will interest both adults and children take place on summer evenings at the campground's amphitheater. In a short drive you can be back on the eastern side of the park, hiking Cadillac Mountain, biking or horseback riding on the carriage trails, canoeing in Somes Sound, or simply driving the loop road. Be sure to stop at the charming town of Southwest Harbor.

Open: Late May through late September.

245 Bass Harbor Campground

Location: In Bass Harbor, on the western side of Mount Desert Island; Southern Maine map page 33, grid b4.

Campsites, facilities: There are 130 sites for tents and RVs, 56 with water and electric hookups and 74 without hookups. Flush toilets, free hot showers, picnic tables, fireplaces, a dump station, laundry facilities, and a store are provided. Cable TV is available. You'll find a heated swimming pool, a playground, rec room, miniature golf, shuffleboard, basketball, and horseshoe pits on the grounds. No pets are allowed.

Reservations, fees: Reservations are recommended. Sites are $19 to $24 a night.

Contact: The McAfee Family, Bass Harbor Campground, P.O. Box 122, Route 102A, Bass Harbor, ME 04653; (207) 244-5857.

Directions: From Ellsworth, drive south on Route 3 onto Mount Desert Island. Follow Route 102/198 south, then continue south on Route 102. From the intersection with Route 102A in Southwest Harbor, drive five miles south on Route 102A.

Trip notes: The western, or "quiet," side of Mount Desert Island is home to this attractive campground located near many of Acadia National Park's finest natural jewels, including mountains, beaches, and the pounding surf of the Atlantic Ocean. Also nearby are the picturesque Bass Harbor Head Lighthouse, the scenic fishing village of Bernard, and hiking trails that trace the oceanside at Ship Harbor. While you are close to the hustle and bustle of the national park, you're not in the center of the action, a plus for those who want to get away from the crowds. The park's Seawall section is a short drive away. A long, sandy beach nearby makes the perfect spot for an evening picnic when you return to the campground after a day of exploring.

Open: Memorial Day through September 30.

246 Quietside Campground

🚴 ⚓ 🐟 🏃 🛶 🏊 　 RV 🔺7

Location: On the western side of Mount Desert Island in West Tremont; Southern Maine map page 33, grid b5.

Campsites, facilities: There are 30 sites, six for RVs with partial hookups and 24 tent

sites with no hookups. Flush toilets, hot showers, picnic tables, fireplaces, laundry facilities, a playground, and a dump station are provided. The maximum RV length is 22 feet. Leashed pets are permitted.

Reservations, fees: Reservations are recommended, and you must send a 50 percent deposit. Sites are $16 to $19 a night. Pets are $5 a night.

Contact: Hugh and Susan McIsaac, Quietside Campground, Route 102, P.O. Box 8, West Tremont, ME 04690; (207) 244-5992.

Directions: From Ellsworth, drive south on Route 3 onto Mount Desert Island. Follow Route 102/198 south, then go south on Route 102. From the intersection with Route 102A in Southwest Harbor, drive 3.25 miles south on Route 102 to the campground.

Trip notes: The name refers to the fact that this small, peaceful campground is located on the far edge of the western side of Mount Desert Island, known as the "quiet" side. Most of the sites are tucked into the woods, affording a good deal of privacy. Fresh Maine food is available nearby: check out the wild blueberry fields to see if the delicious fruit is in season (you can buy berries from roadside stands or pick wild ones yourself) and travel to one of the working harbor towns for fresh fish or lobster. Still within a short drive of the action in touristy Bar Harbor village and the natural and scenic splendors of Acadia National Park, the campground is a haven of relaxation after a day pursuing the myriad activities available to visitors on Mount Desert Island.

Open: June 15 through Columbus Day.

247 Sunshine Campground

🚴 ⚓ 🐟 🍴 🏊 　 RV 🔺9

Location: On Deer Isle; Southern Maine map page 33, grid b4.

Campsites, facilities: There are 22 sites for tents and RVs, 15 with partial hookups and seven with no hookups. Facilities include flush toilets, hot showers, picnic tables, fireplaces, laundry, a dump station, and a limited store. For recreation, there is a rec room, access to the water, and horseshoes. Leashed pets are permitted.

Reservations, fees: Reservations are accepted. Sites are $12 to $15 a night.

Contact: Barbara and Marshall Rice, Sunshine Campground, RR 1, Box 521D, Deer Isle, ME 04627; (207) 248-6681.

Directions: From U.S. 1 in Bucksport, follow Route 175 all the way south to Deer Isle. Take Route 15 south, then turn left on Sunshine County Road and drive 5.75 miles east to the campground.

Trip notes: Small and intimate Sunshine Campground sits at the end of a long, narrow peninsula jutting into Blue Hill Bay, one of the prettiest bodies of water anywhere on the Maine coast. The campground is set in a thick maritime forest on several bumpy knolls, and none offer water views or oceanfront locales. Instead, you must access the water across the road from the campground. This is a clean, well-kept facility, perfect for those looking to literally get away from it all by heading to land's end. As a point of departure for sea kayakers, Sunshine Campground would be hard to beat: after pushing off from this spot, kayakers are soon surrounded by dozens of islands.

Open: Memorial Day through October 15.

248 Greenlaw's Mobile and RV Park

Location: In the small fishing village of Stonington on Deer Isle; Southern Maine map page 33, grid b4.

Campsites, facilities: There are 50 sites for tents and RVs, 15 with full hookups, 17 with water and electric hookups, and 18 with none. Flush toilets, hot showers, picnic tables, fireplaces, and a dump station are provided. You'll also find hiking trails, badminton nets, and horseshoes. Leashed pets are permitted.

Reservations, fees: Reservations are accepted. Sites are $10 to $16 a night.

Contact: Greenlaw's Mobile and RV Park, Airport Road, Box 72, Stonington, ME 04681; (207) 367-5049.

Directions: From U.S. 1 in Bucksport, follow Route 175 all the way south to Deer Isle. Take Route 15 south for 10.75 miles to Stonington, then go 1.5 miles west on County Road to the campground.

Trip notes: Stonington is truly a place that has been untouched by time, a little fishing village at the very tip of Deer Isle overlooking Merchant Row, a cluster of dozens of islands floating in Penobscot Bay. Those islands, along with miles of secluded bays, coves, and inlets, are part of why this area is considered the finest sailing and sea kayaking territory on the East Coast—and possibly in all of North America. So, if you want to get down to the sea, check out this campground with wooded sites at land's end.

Open: Early December through early April.

249 Isle au Haut Campground

Location: On Isle au Haut in Acadia National Park; Southern Maine map page 33, grid c4.

Campsites, facilities: There are five lean-tos accommodating up to six people each. Pit toilets, picnic tables, and fireplaces are provided. Hiking trails leave from the campground. Leashed pets are permitted.

Reservations, fees: Reservations are required. Sites are $25 a night per lean-to.

Contact: Acadia National Park, P.O. Box 177, Bar Harbor, ME 04609; (207) 288-3338.

Directions: The campground is accessible by boat only. From U.S. 1 in Bucksport, follow Route 175 all the way south to Deer Isle. Take Route 15 south to Stonington, then catch the mail boat to Duck Harbor Landing on Isle au Haut. Or paddle your own canoe or sea kayak through the islands of Merchant Row to the campground.

Trip notes: French Explorer Samuel de Champlain dubbed this place Isle au Haut, or the High Island, in 1603 because of the way its rocky summit looms more than 500 feet above the ocean swells. Footpaths and hiking trails crisscross the island, tracing the shore of its bays and inlets, traversing thick maritime forests, and climbing some of the higher points. This is a wild and serene place at the edge of the open ocean, and memories of a stay here will not soon be forgotten. For sea kayakers, it's a very popular destination.

Open: Mid-May through mid-October.

---

250 Donnell Pond Management Unit

Location: East of Ellsworth; Southern Maine map page 33, grid b5.

Campsites, facilities: Several primitive campsites for tents are available. They are currently undeveloped and have no facilities. Pets are permitted.

Reservations, fees: Sites are available on a first-come, first-served basis. There is no fee.

Contact: Maine Bureau of Parks and Lands, 22 State House Station, Augusta, ME 04333; (207) 287-3821.

Directions: From Ellsworth, drive 12 miles east on Route 182 or Route 183 to access the management unit.

Trip notes: Donnell Pond is an extremely scenic parcel of land that displays a great diversity of natural attractions, all of it open to campers who are willing to hike or boat to one of the preserve's primitive campsites. Located just a few miles from the ocean, the unit includes miles of undeveloped shoreline on several wilderness lakes. A private boat ramp, which at this time the public can use, is located just outside the management unit at the Card Mill site in Franklin. While there is no prohibition on high-powered boats, this is a remote area that attracts wildlife and many species of birds, making a smaller boat or canoe the preferred method of travel. The preserve also encompasses Schoodic, Black, and Caribou Mountains. A hiking trail system accesses the Black Mountain area, while other trails climb Schoodic Mountain from Schoodic Beach. In addition to these routes, some old roads and former trails offer plenty of opportunities to explore the unit on foot, mountain bike, snowshoes, or cross-country skis.

Open: Year-round.

---

251 Mountainview Campground

Location: On Frenchman Bay in East Sullivan; Southern Maine map page 33, grid b5.

Campsites, facilities: There are 50 sites for tents and RVs, four with full hookups and 46 with water and electric hookups. Flush toilets, hot showers, picnic tables, fireplaces, a dump station, and a store are provided. For recreation, there is a beach, a playground, horseshoe pits, and miniature golf. Leashed pets are permitted.

Reservations, fees: Reservations are

not necessary. Sites are $12 to $14.50 a night.

Contact: Mountainview Campground, U.S. 1, East Sullivan, ME 04607; (207) 422-6215.

Directions: From the junction of U.S. 1 and Route 185 in Sullivan, drive one mile east on U.S. 1 to the campground.

Trip notes: As the name would suggest, the views of the mountains in Acadia National Park across Frenchman Bay are exceptional from this campground. If you have traveled this far east along the Maine coast, by now you probably realize that you've left the crowds, and the modern world, behind. From here to the New Brunswick border the roads are emptier, the little towns smaller, and the scenery more spectacular than what you'll encounter to the west. Mountainview Campground is just what you might expect in this part of Maine, a rather worn and somewhat weather beaten, no-frills place right on the water.

Open: Memorial Day through October 1.

❷❺❷ Mainayr Campground

Location: On Joy Cove near Steuben; Southern Maine map page 33, grid b5.

Campsites, facilities: There are 30 sites for tents and RVs, 5 with full hookups, 5 with water and electric, 7 with electric only, and 13 with none. Flush toilets, hot showers, picnic tables, fireplaces, a dump station, laundry facilities, and a store are provided. For recreation, there is a beach, playground, rec room, volleyball and badminton nets, and horseshoe pits. Leashed pets are permitted.

Reservations, fees: Reservations are recommended. Sites are $15 to $18 a night.

Contact: David and Kathy Ayers, Mainayr

Campground, RR 1, P.O. Box 69, Steuben, ME 04680; (207) 546-2690.

Directions: From the intersection of U.S. 1 and Steuben Road in Steuben, drive half a mile east on Steuben Road to the campground.

Trip notes: Mainayr is situated on a tidal cove emptying into the open Atlantic Ocean. The feeling here is one of wildness, woods and waters, and fresh sea breezes. Wildlife abounds in the estuary, in the salt marshes, and in the forested uplands that surround campers. This is a real retreat, an off-the-beaten-path refuge that provides peace and quiet in an unspoiled Maine coast setting.

Open: Memorial Day through Columbus Day.

❷❺❸ Ocean Wood Campground

Location: On the Schoodic Peninsula in Birch Harbor; Southern Maine map page 33, grid b5.

Campsites, facilities: There are 70 sites for tents and RVs, 20 with partial hookups and 50 with no hookups. Flush toilets, hot showers, picnic tables, and fireplaces are provided. Leashed pets are permitted.

Reservations, fees: Reservations are accepted. Sites are $14 to $24 a night.

Contact: The Brunton Family, Ocean Wood Campground, P.O. Box 111, Birch Harbor, ME 04613; (207) 963-7194.

Directions: From Ellsworth, drive east on U.S. 1, then turn right on Route 186 heading south toward Schoodic Point. At the intersection of Route 186 and Birch Harbor Road in Birch Harbor, turn south on Birch Harbor Road and drive half a mile to the campground.

Trip notes: One section of Acadia National Park that most people never see is the Schoodic Peninsula, which lies across Frenchman Bay from Bar Harbor and Mount Desert Island. This lovely, windswept point juts out into the frothy Atlantic, a rocky, pine-covered headland far from the summer crowds you'll see elsewhere. Just one mile from the park boundary in Birch Harbor, Ocean Wood Campground caters to those who can't wait to get off the beaten path. The spacious sites cover more than a quarter acre on average, and many are located right on the waterfront. This is definitely a place for someone looking to get away from it all.

Open: May 1 through October 31.

㉕㊃ Bayview Campground

Location: In the town of Milbridge on Narraguagus Bay; Southern Maine map page 33, grid b5.

Campsites, facilities: There are 24 sites for tents and RVs, 14 with water and electric hookups and 10 with no hookups. Flush toilets, hot showers, picnic tables, fireplaces, a recreation pavilion, and a dump station are provided. Leashed pets are permitted.

Reservations, fees: Reservations are accepted. Sites are $12 to $15 a night.

Contact: Bayview Campground, Box 243, Milbridge, ME 04658; (207) 546-2946.

Directions: From the intersection of U.S. 1 and U.S. 1A in Milbridge, drive a quarter mile north on U.S. 1A, then turn right and go half a mile east on Bayview Street to the campground.

Trip notes: The campground has open sites overlooking the sparkling waters of Narraguagus Bay, a long reach of the Atlantic Ocean where the Narraguagus River flows into the sea. Enjoy a view over the

dark blue swells, watch lobstermen ply their trade, or launch your sea kayak and explore this unspoiled slice of the Maine coast. And if you think Maine's coastal communities are all chock-full of tourist traps and lobster pounds, Milbridge will be a pleasant surprise. This is truly a "Downeast" Maine town, home to one of the region's last surviving sardine canneries as well as a Christmas wreath factory, two examples of the state's traditional industries. While in the area be sure to visit the Petit Manan National Wildlife Refuge, where a five-mile hiking path clings to the shoreline. Bicyclists will find lots of little-traveled roads and logging routes in the vicinity of the campground.

Open: May 15 through October 15.

㉕㊄ Pleasant Lake Campground

Location: Near the crossroads of Alexander, west of Calais; Southern Maine map page 33, grid a6.

Campsites, facilities: There are 120 sites for tents and RVs with full, partial, and no hookups. Facilities include flush toilets, hot showers, picnic tables, fireplaces, a dump station, laundry, a playground, rec room, boat ramp, horseshoe pits, basketball, hiking trails, and a store. There's also a sandy beach and lake for swimming, fishing, and canoeing. Leashed pets are permitted.

Reservations, fees: Reservations are accepted. Sites are $12 to $18 a night.

Contact: Jim Davis, Pleasant Lake Campground, Alexander, ME 04694; (207) 454-7467.

Directions: From Calais, travel west on Route 9 for approximately 16 miles. Turn left at the sign for the campground and drive south for two miles.

Trip notes: Nearly always full with trailers that aren't about to go anywhere, this campground attracts seasonal campers from nearby New Brunswick. The park is located on a large freshwater lake, only 16 miles from the Canadian border. Ironically, despite the fact that it is well off the beaten path in a little-traveled area, the place has an urban feel.

Open: Mid-May to mid-October.

256 Rocky Lake Management Unit

Location: North of East Machias; Southern Maine map page 33, grid a6.

Campsites, facilities: There are six primitive campsites. Four are reachable by water only, while two are vehicle-accessible. Pit toilets, picnic tables, and fire rings are provided. Pets are permitted.

Reservations, fees: Registration is not required, and sites are available on a first-come, first-served basis. There is no fee.

Contact: Maine Bureau of Parks and Lands, 22 State House Station, Augusta, ME 04333; (207) 287-3821.

Directions: From East Machias, drive six miles north on Route 191 to access the management unit.

Trip notes: The Rocky Lake Management Unit is an 11,000-acre wildland typical of this portion of eastern Maine. A glacial landscape dotted with rocky, jagged-edged lakes and with watersheds divided by low ridges, the unit is laced by meandering streams bordered by abundant natural wetlands. The preserve incorporates Rocky Lake, a beautiful and remote body of water with numerous coves, inlets, and islands that offer excellent fishing. Also within the boundaries of the unit are stretches of the East Branch of the Machias River, a stream

renowned as a great canoeing and fishing destination.

Open: Year-round.

257 Keene's Lake Campground

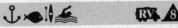

Location: In Calais; Southern Maine map page 33, grid a6.

Campsites, facilities: There are 151 sites for tents and RVs, 142 with water and electric hookups and nine with no hookups. Flush toilets, hot showers, picnic tables, fireplaces, laundry facilities, a dump station, and a store are provided. A boat launch, canoe rentals, a rec room, volleyball, basketball, miniature golf, and horseshoes are among the recreational offerings. Leashed pets are permitted.

Reservations, fees: Reservations are recommended. Sites are $14 a night.

Contact: Keene's Lake Campground, Shattuck Road, RR 1, Box 179, Calais, ME 04619; (207) 454-8557.

Directions: From Calais, drive eight miles south on U.S. 1. Turn right on Shattuck Road and drive one mile west.

Trip notes: The campground is located on a wilderness lake with sheltered inlets and coves surrounded by miles of woodlands. Fish in the lake or in nearby Passamaquoddy Bay, launch a canoe from the campground or a kayak from the town landing in Robbinston, or spend a day helping the U.S. Fish and Wildlife Service band woodcocks at nearby Moosehorn National Wildlife Refuge. Be sure to visit Quoddy Head State Park and check out Campobello Island, the summer home of President Franklin Delano Roosevelt. For more information on the area, see Cobscook Bay State Park (campground number 262).

Open: May 15 through October 1.

258 Hilltop Campground

Location: Near the hamlet of Robbinston; Southern Maine map page 33, grid a6.

Campsites, facilities: There are 117 sites for tents and RVs, 34 with full hookups, 69 with water and electric, and 14 tent platforms. Flush toilets, wheelchair-accessible rest rooms, hot showers, picnic tables, fire rings, a dump station, laundry facilities, a playground, rec hall, swimming pool, horseshoe pits, basketball, volleyball, and a store are provided. Leashed pets are permitted.

Reservations, fees: Reservations are recommended. A deposit of 50 percent of the total fee is required. One-night reservations are not accepted for weekends in July or August unless approved by management. Sites are $12 to $18 a night.

Contact: Harold and Pamela Brooks, Hilltop Campground, RR 1, Box 298, Robbinston, ME 04671; (207) 454-3985.

Directions: From the intersection of U.S. 1 and Ridge Road in Robbinston, drive one mile west on Ridge Road to the campground.

Trip notes: This place is popular with seasonal campers from Canada who flock to the United States in the summer months and stay long enough to legally buy American merchandise duty-free. The campground sits high atop an open ridge overlooking the broad reaches of Passamaquoddy Bay and the New Brunswick shore off in the distance across the water. Don't forget to bring your fishing tackle so you can catch your dinner. Or bring a sea kayak to launch at the town dock in Robbinston. For more information on the area, see the trip notes for Cobscook Bay State Park (campground number 262).

Open: Mid-May to late September.

259 Knowlton's Seashore Campground

Location: Near the tiny hamlet of Perry; Southern Maine map page 33, grid a6.

Campsites, facilities: There are 80 sites for tents and RVs, 50 with full hookups, 10 with water and electric, and 20 without hookups. Flush toilets, hot showers, picnic tables, fire rings, a dump station, and a playground are provided. Leashed pets are permitted.

Reservations, fees: Reservations are recommended. A $5 deposit is required. Sites are $9 to $14 a night.

Contact: Mr. and Mrs. Lloyd Knowlton, Knowlton's Seashore Campground, U.S. 1, Perry, ME 04667; (207) 726-4756.

Directions: From Calais, drive south on U.S. 1 to Perry. After you reach the junction with Route 190 in town, continue three miles south on U.S. 1 to the campground.

Trip notes: From its prime location on a narrow peninsula jutting out into the water, Knowlton's Seashore Campground offers splendid views up and down Cobscook Bay. Campsites are strung along the shore in a grassy, open field, giving you a sensation of being out at sea. Fish, canoe, kayak, and swim right from the campground if you wish, or explore the broad expanses and hidden coves, islands, and inlets of Cobscook and Passamaquoddy Bays. For more information on the area, see Cobscook Bay State Park (campground number 262).

Open: May 21 to mid-October.

260 The Seaview

Location: In Eastport; Southern Maine map page 33, grid a6.

Campsites, facilities: There are 74 sites

for RVs with full hookups, plus some tent sites and cabins. Flush toilets, hot showers, picnic tables, fire rings, a dump station, laundry facilities, cable TV hookups, a playground, rec room, boat ramp, horseshoe pits, and a store are provided. Leashed pets are permitted.

Reservations, fees: Reservations are recommended. Sites range from $11 to $19.50 a night.

Contact: The Seaview, 16 Norwood Road, Eastport, ME 04631; (207) 853-4471.

Directions: From Calais, drive south on U.S. 1 to Perry. At the junction of U.S. 1 and Route 190, bear left and drive five miles south on Route 190, then turn left on Norwood Road and go a quarter mile east to the campground.

Trip notes: Located on a slight hill overlooking the broad blue reaches of Passamaquoddy Bay, The Seaview has sites in an open field sloping toward the water. The campground does afford great views, but because the park is tucked away on a long, narrow strip of waterfront property, there is a lack of open space and the trailers, rental houses, and cabins are packed quite close together. With its good boating access, the waterfront is the recreational focal point for campers. If you like shellfish, try digging for clams in the flats of Passamaquoddy Bay at low tide. For more information on the area, see Cobscook Bay State Park (campground number 262).

Open: May 15 to October 15.

261 Sunset Point Trailer Park

Location: On a peninsula jutting into Cobscook Bay in Lubec; Southern Maine map page 33, grid a6.

Campsites, facilities: There are 25 sites

for tents and RVs with water and electric hookups. Facilities include flush toilets, hot showers, picnic tables, fire rings, a dump station, laundry, cable TV hookups, horseshoe pits, and badminton nets. Leashed pets are permitted.

Reservations, fees: Reservations are accepted. Sites are $11 to $16 a night.

Contact: Jane Hallett, Sunset Point Trailer Park, Route 189, Lubec, ME 04652; (207) 733-2150.

Directions: From East Machias, follow U.S. 1 northeast to Whiting. Bear right onto Route 189 and travel nine miles east to the campground.

Trip notes: Sunset Point is a small campground sitting on a peninsula in Cobscook Bay. Open and airy with gorgeous views over the pine- and spruce-rimmed bay, this quiet place enjoys a setting of stunning natural beauty. Campers get good water access and can easily swim, fish, canoe, or kayak in the ocean from here. Anglers will also find a small freshwater pond for fishing. The tiny town of Lubec is the gateway to Campobello Island, site of Roosevelt-Campobello International Park. And just down the road from the campground is Quoddy Head State Park. For more information on the area, see Cobscook Bay State Park (campground number 262).

Open: Memorial Day through Columbus Day.

262 Cobscook Bay State Park

Location: South of Dennysville on Cobscook Bay; Southern Maine map page 33, grid a6.

Campsites, facilities: There are 125 sites for tents and RVs, all without hookups. Each site has a picnic table and fire ring. Pit toilets, hot showers, a dump station, boat launch, nature trails, and a playground are also provided. Leashed pets are permitted.

Reservations, fees: Reservations are accepted. Contact the Maine Bureau of Parks and Lands at the number below. The State of Maine allocates some sites on a first-come, first-served basis. Sites are $11.50 a night for residents of Maine and $15 for nonresidents.

Contact: Cobscook Bay State Park Ranger, (207) 726-4412. Maine Bureau of Parks and Lands, 22 State House Station, Augusta, ME 04333; (207) 287-3821.

Directions: From the junction of Route 86 and U.S. 1 in Dennysville, drive south on U.S. 1 for six miles to the park.

Trip notes: Twenty-four-foot tides—the highest in the state—and the famous Reversing Falls near Pembroke make this one of the most scenic and dramatic natural areas in the country. And this park, located in undeveloped "Downeast" Maine, is a real gem. Camping spots are perched above the water as well as in the maritime boreal forest of thick spruce and fir. Launch your boat, canoe, or kayak on the bay, or hike one of the nature trails that leave right from the campground. Additionally, be sure to take a day trip to Quoddy Head State Park, the easternmost point in the United States and the first place in the country to be struck by the sun's rays every morning. Also a short drive away are Roosevelt-Campobello International Park, where President Franklin Delano Roosevelt and his family spent their summers, and Moosehorn National Wildlife Refuge. To the southwest is Roque Bluffs State Park, which boasts sugary sand beaches and both saltwater and freshwa-ter swimming. The campground is a delectable spot to stay while traveling to or from Canada's Maritime Provinces.

Open: May 15 through October 15.

263 Cutler Coast Management Unit

Location: Near the village of Cutler and the ocean; Southern Maine map page 33, grid b6.

Campsites, facilities: There are three primitive tent sites accessible by foot only. Each site has a pit toilet, picnic table, and fire ring. Pets are permitted.

Reservations, fees: Registration is not required, and sites are available on a first-come, first-served basis. There is no fee.

Contact: Maine Bureau of Parks and Lands, 22 State House Station, Augusta, ME 04333; (207) 287-3821.

Directions: From Cutler, drive approximately three miles north on Route 191 to access the management unit.

Trip notes: Located on "Downeast" Maine's Bold Coast—the easternmost region in the United States—this unit encompasses almost five miles of undeveloped ocean shoreline. A trail network traces along the shore, providing access to remote hike-in campsites that allow intrepid souls to have a wild maritime camping experience. After you break camp, return via the trail as it crosses overland through the thick forests and open meadows of the interior to gain a full perspective on all that the area has to offer.

Open: Year-round.

New Hampshire

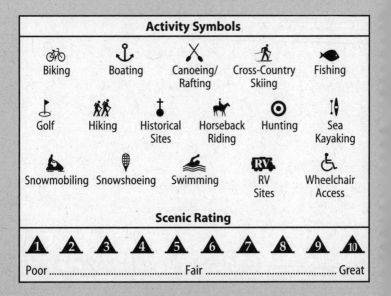

Activity Symbols

Biking	Boating	Canoeing/ Rafting	Cross-Country Skiing	Fishing
Golf	Hiking	Historical Sites	Horseback Riding	Hunting	Sea Kayaking
Snowmobiling	Snowshoeing	Swimming	RV Sites	Wheelchair Access

Scenic Rating

Poor .... Fair .... Great

Northern New Hampshire

Adjoining Maps: East: Southern Maine .... *page 33*
West: Vermont .... *pages 280–281*
South: Southern New Hampshire ...... *page 169*

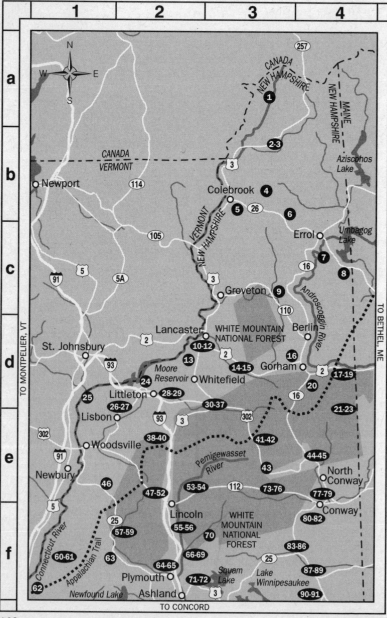

Southern New Hampshire

Adjoining Maps: North: Northern New Hampshire ..... *page* 168
East: Southern Maine .... *page* 33
West: Vermont .... *pages* 280–281
South: Massachusetts .... *pages* 354–355

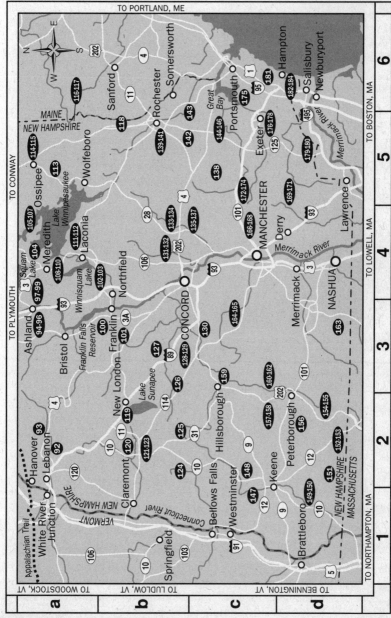

TO PORTLAND, ME

TO CONWAY

TO PLYMOUTH

MAINE
NEW HAMPSHIRE

Somersworth

Sanford

Rochester

Hampton

Salisbury

Newburyport

Portsmouth

Great
Bay

Exeter

Wolfeboro

Ossipee

Meredith

Squam
Lake

Lake
Winnipesaukee

Laconia

Winnisquam
Lake

Franklin Falls
Reservoir

Ashland

Bristol

Northfield

Franklin

New London

Lake
Sunapee

Claremont

Manchester

Derry

Lawrence

Merrimack River

Merrimack

NASHUA

CONCORD

Hillsborough

Keene

Peterborough

Westminster

Bellows Falls

Brattleboro

Springfield

Appalachian Trail

Hanover

Lebanon

White River
Junction

VERMONT
NEW HAMPSHIRE

Connecticut River

NEW HAMPSHIRE
MASSACHUSETTS

TO BOSTON, MA

TO LOWELL, MA

TO NORTHAMPTON, MA

TO WOODSTOCK, VT

TO LUDLOW, VT

TO BENNINGTON, VT

a **b** **c** **d**

❶ Deer Mountain Campground

Location: North of the Second Connecticut Lake; Northern New Hampshire map page 168, grid a3.

Campsites, facilities: There are 20 sites for tents and RVs, all without hookups. Piped water and primitive toilets are provided. Water is not available after mid-October. Leashed pets are permitted.

Reservations, fees: For reservations, call the New Hampshire Division of Parks and Recreation at (see phone number below) on weekdays between 8:30 A.M. and 3:30 P.M. from January through August. Sites are $12 a night.

Contact: Deer Mountain Campground, Connecticut Lakes State Forest, U.S. Route 3, Pittsburg, NH 03592; (603) 538-6965. New Hampshire Division of Parks and Recreation, (603) 271-3628.

Directions: From Pittsburg, travel north on U.S. 3 for 20 miles to the campground entrance.

Trip notes: These primitive wooded sites are found along the Connecticut River between the First and Second Connecticut Lakes. Hiking trails leave from the campground and explore Moose Falls, a small and lovely waterfall. Fishing in the river and the lakes is allowed; be sure to check on regulations before you cast a line, though, as some areas are restricted to fly-fishing and catch-and-release, and you can keep only one salmon and one lake trout from the lakes. Moose viewing is a popular pastime in this area just south of the Canadian border. The rangy beasts usually come out for a bite to eat around dusk. In late August, the North Country holds a Moose Festival with parades, mock moose stew, and dancing in the street. For many years, this portion of the northern forest was heavily logged. Today the abandoned logging roads make good mountain biking trails.

Open: Mid-May through mid-December.

❷ Hidden Acres Campground

Location: North of Pittsburg; Northern New Hampshire map page 168, grid b3.

Campsites, facilities: There are 60 sites

for tents and RVs, some with water and electric hookups. A dump station, rest rooms, and hot showers are provided. Ice and firewood are sold on the property. Leashed pets are permitted.

Reservations, fees: Reservations are accepted. Sites start at $13 a night for two people. Seasonal rates are available.

Contact: Hidden Acres Campground, P.O. Box 94, Pittsburg, NH 03592; (603) 538-6919.

Directions: From Pittsburg, travel two miles north on U.S. 3. The campground entrance is on the right (east) side of the road.

Trip notes: Here's the best option for RVers in the Connecticut Lakes region. Public boat launches are provided on all four of the Connecticut Lakes. This campground lies on the stretch of road known as Moose Alley. Dusk is the best time to spot the largest member of the deer family. Don't approach these beasts on foot, however, since they are unpredictable and can be dangerous. The 300 square miles of land known as Pittsburg, New Hampshire—a township larger in acreage than the entire state of Rhode Island—once belonged to Native Americans. Most of the land is now owned by the Champion Paper Company.

Open: May 1 through early October.

---

❸ Lake Francis State Park

Location: On the northwest tip of Lake Francis; Northern New Hampshire map page 168, grid b3.

Campsites, facilities: There are 41 sites for tents and RVs, all without hookups. A dump station, rest rooms, and tables are provided. Services and supplies are available in Pittsburg. Water is not available after mid-October. Leashed pets are permitted.

Reservations, fees: For reservations, call the New Hampshire Division of Parks and Recreation (see phone number below) on weekdays between 8:30 A.M. and 3:30 P.M. from January through August. Sites are $12 to $16 a night.

Contact: Lake Francis State Park, Connecticut Lakes State Forest, 37B River Road, Pittsburg, NH 03592; (603) 538-6965. New Hampshire Division of Parks and Recreation, (603) 271-3628.

Directions: From Pittsburg, travel north on U.S. 3 for seven miles to the campground sign. Turn right on River Road and continue south to the campground entrance.

Trip notes: Water, water everywhere. Lake Francis is one pristine, undeveloped tall drink of water. These sites are scattered along an odd arm that juts north from the eastern end of the main body of the lake. Five of the 41 sites are "hike-ins," set about a two-minute walk from the parking lot; these sites are near the Connecticut River and have tent platforms. A boat launch is located at the day-use area south of the campground. The shoreline is heavily wooded, and boaters should be watchful of high winds when out on the water. Trout and salmon are the primary game fish. This 2,051-acre body of water is the last in the chain of lakes that forms the headwaters of the Connecticut River. Fittingly, the lake was named for Saint Francis, the patron saint of wildlife: some of the many creatures who call the area home include beavers, hawks, eagles, osprey, herons, otters, fisher cats, and moose.

Open: Mid-May through mid-December.

---

❹ Coleman State Park

Location: Northeast of Colebrook; Northern New Hampshire map page 168, grid b3.

Campsites, facilities: There are 30 sites for tents and self-contained RVs, all without hookups. Pit toilets, piped water, a dump station, and a playground are provided. Water is not available after mid-October. The maximum RV length is 35 feet. Leashed pets are permitted.

Reservations, fees: Sites are available on a first-come, first-served basis. The fee is $12 a night per family.

Contact: Coleman State Park, RFD 1, Box 183, Colebrook, NH 03576; (603) 237-4520.

Directions: From Colebrook, travel east on Route 26 for seven miles. Turn left on Diamond Pond Road and head north for five miles to the campground.

Trip notes: Anglers are the primary customers at these backcountry campsites. Self-contained RVs up to 35 feet in length can make it into the wooded area near Little Diamond Pond. That loch is noted for its excellent trout fishing, home to both rainbows and browns. Diamond Pond and Little Diamond Pond were named for Isaac Diamond, who shot a bull moose in the area in 1778. Man and beast had a good scrap in which Isaac lost all his clothing before the moose went down. These campsites make a good jumping-off point for hunting trips into the surrounding heavily timbered wilderness. The state snowmobile corridor crosses the park and continues through spruce-fir country to the Canadian border. Roads as we know them don't exist up here; instead you'll find mostly old skidder routes cut through the hills and dales.

Open: Mid-May through mid-December.

---

❺ Mohawk Valley Camping Area

Location: East of Colebrook; Northern New Hampshire map page 168, grid b3.

Campsites, facilities: There are 100 sites for tents and RVs, 36 with water and electric hookups and 64 with none. Each site comes with a picnic table, fire ring, and grill. A dump station, rest rooms, hot showers, a swimming pool, horseshoe pits, and a playground are provided. A camp store on the property carries ice and firewood. Leashed pets are permitted.

Reservations, fees: Reservations are accepted. Sites are $12 to $17 a night per family.

Contact: Mohawk Valley Camping Area, 3 Bridge Street, Colebrook, NH 03576; (603) 237-5756.

Directions: From Colebrook, head east on Route 26 for five miles. Turn right at the campground sign, which you'll see on the left side of the road.

Trip notes: As they say up here in the northern reaches of New Hampshire, you don't need to go to heaven to get to God's Country. With bugs and moose for company, you can enjoy mountain vistas and trout fishing in solitude at these grassy meadow sites strewn along the banks of the Mohawk River. To the east lies Dixville Notch State Park, a spectacular landholding encompassing a two-mile-long gap featuring rocky outcrops and cascades; the five-mile Dixville Notch Heritage Trail hits all the highlights. The Balsams Wilderness, the last of New Hampshire's grand resort hotels, is also to the east of here, just in case you're in need of some civility, four-star restaurant style. The hotel operates a public golf course where you can tee off while enjoying splendid mountain views. For supplies, head into the frontierlike town of Colebrook. If you're road touring, a scenic picnic spot lies north of Colebrook on Route 145, where Beaver Brook Falls cascades over 75-foot-high rocks and ledges.

Open: Late May through early October.

➏ Log Haven Campground

Location: West of Errol; Northern New Hampshire map page 168, grid b3.

Campsites, facilities: There are 88 sites for tents and RVs, some with full hookups. Each site has a picnic table and fire ring. A dump station, rest rooms, hot showers, laundry facilities, a lounge, a pool, and a playground are provided. A camp store on the grounds carries ice and firewood. Leashed pets are permitted.

Reservations, fees: Reservations are accepted. Tent sites are $12 a night and RV sites with full hookups are $22 a night per family.

Contact: Log Haven Campground, P.O. Box 239, Errol, NH 03579; (603) 482-3249.

Directions: From Errol, travel west on Route 26 for 5.5 miles to the campground on the right (north) side of the road.

Trip notes: Smack in the middle of the North Country, Log Haven offers sites set beside Clear Stream. You can fish for trout at the campground, but anglers may want to try Akers Pond to the east for some serious pickerel wrangling. The pond has a beach and boat launch and is just west of the town of Errol. Log Haven lies at the foot of Dixville Notch State Park, where the Heritage Trail leads hikers past such highlights as cascades, outlooks, and the craggy profiles of Martha Washington and Daniel Webster; though lesser known than their cousin in Franconia, the Old Man of the Mountain, these countenances are nonetheless spectacular. The campground is studded with tall pine trees that provide shade for these mostly grassy sites. A restaurant and lounge with live entertainment are also operated on the property.

Open: Year-round.

➐ Mollidgewock State Park

Location: South of Errol; Northern New Hampshire map page 168, grid c4.

Campsites, facilities: There are 42 sites for tents and RVs up to 30 feet in length, all without hookups. Piped water and pit toilets are provided. Ice and wood are sold at a grocery store. Supplies and services can be found in Errol. Leashed pets are permitted.

Reservations, fees: For reservations, call the New Hampshire Division of Parks and Recreation (see phone number below) on weekdays between 8:30 A.M. and 3:30 P.M. from January through August. Sites are $14 a night per family.

Contact: Mollidgewock State Park, P.O. Box 29, Errol, NH 03579; (603) 482-3373. New Hampshire Division of Parks and Recreation, (603) 271-3628.

Directions: From Errol, travel three miles south on Route 16 to the campground.

Trip notes: Located in the Thirteen Mile Woods Scenic Area south of Errol, these primitive wooded sites are on the bank of the mighty Androscoggin River. Additional remote sites are accessible by either canoe or car. Once used to float logs from out of the north woods to paper mills in Berlin, the Androscoggin is now a white-water playground. From Errol to Berlin, the river offers 30 miles of excellent paddling or kayaking, with dependable Class III white water, three stretches of rapids, and views of the Presidential Range to the south. The Thirteen Mile Woods is also known for the many moose that venture out to the road to watch the passing cars. A small natural beach is available at the campground, and anglers will find many spots where they can cast for trout and salmon.

Open: Mid-May through mid-October.

❽ Umbagog Lake Campground

Location: At the south shore of Umbagog Lake; Northern New Hampshire map page 168, grid c4.

Campsites, facilities: There are 59 sites for tents and RVs, 30 with water and electric hookups. Each site has a picnic table and fire ring. A dump station, rest rooms, hot showers, and laundry facilities are provided. A small grocery store sells ice. Rental boats are available at the campground. Pets with rabies vaccination certification are allowed on a leash.

Reservations, fees: Reservations are recommended. Per family, fees range from $18 a night for wilderness tent sites to $22 a night for waterfront sites with hookups.

Contact: Umbagog Lake Campground, Box 181, Errol, NH 03579; (603) 482-7795.

Directions: From Errol, travel eight miles southeast on Route 26 to the campground.

Trip notes: Umbagog Lake straddles the Maine–New Hampshire border east of the town of Errol, and these campsites put you at its southern end. Nearly 8,000 acres of water are available for wildlife viewing, canoeing, boating, fishing, and swimming. Four tent sites and 30 RV sites with hookups are located on the shore of the lake at base camp. Another 25 wilderness tent sites on secluded shores and islands are accessible only by boat. If you don't bring your own canoe or rowboat, you can rent one at the campground or use the camp's shuttle service.

Most of the New Hampshire shoreline is protected by the Umbagog Lake National Wildlife Refuge and conservation easements stipulating that the land remains as it is. Most of the Maine shoreline is privately owned but remains virtually undeveloped.

The landscape consists of rolling hills with a distant backdrop of mountains, all blanketed in thick pine forest. There's fair to good fishing on the lake for landlocked salmon, trout, perch, and pickerel. The Androscoggin River, which flows out of the lake on the northwest shore, is open to fly-fishing; it's one of two area waterways that support salmon. The lake is known for its pair of nesting bald eagles and the more than 15 pairs of loons. Osprey, ducks, herons, moose, and deer are other common wildlife. Be aware that winds can come up instantly on this large lake and create treacherous boating conditions. There are numerous inlets and islands to explore via canoe, including the Androscoggin River.

Open: Late May through mid-September.

❾ Nay Pond Campground

Location: North of Berlin; Northern New Hampshire map page 168, grid c3.

Campsites, facilities: There are 50 sites for tents and RVs up to 30 feet long, some with full hookups. Use of air conditioners and heaters is allowed. A dump station, rest rooms, hot showers, laundry facilities, and a playground are provided. Ice and firewood are available. Leashed pets are permitted.

Reservations, fees: Reservations are accepted. For two people, tent or walk-in sites are $10 a night and sites with full hookups are $15 a night.

Contact: Nay Pond Campground, RR 3, Box 3193, West Milan, NH 03570; (603) 449-2122.

Directions: From the junction of Routes 16 and 110 in Berlin, travel nine miles northwest on Route 110 to the campground.

Trip notes: Set in a mix of hard and softwood trees on 62-acre Nay Pond, these sites are secluded and quiet. A beach, boat ramp, and picnic grove are available to campers. The warm-water pond is open to motorized boating and supports rock bass, small-mouth bass, black crappie, pickerel, and horned pout. From the park, the northern reaches of the White Mountain National Forest are visible including the Mahoosuc and Kilkenney Ranges. For a short scenic hike, head northwest of the campground to the South Pond Recreation Area off Route 110. There, the Devils Hopyard Trail is a moderate 2.6-mile hike that passes by a mossy, boulder-strewn gorge and cascade.

Open: June 1 through October 1.

⑩ Beaver Trails Campground

Location: On the Connecticut River in Lancaster; Northern New Hampshire map page 168, grid d2.

Campsites, facilities: There are 46 sites for tents and RVs, 40 with full hookups. Each site has a picnic table and fire ring. Use of air conditioners and heaters is allowed. A dump station, rest rooms, hot showers, laundry facilities, a pool, and a playground are provided. Courts for volleyball and horseshoes are available. A general store sells LP gas, gasoline, ice, and firewood. Leashed pets are permitted.

Reservations, fees: Reservations are recommended. Sites start at $20 a night. Seasonal rates are available on request.

Contact: Beaver Trails Campground, RR 2, Box 315, Lancaster, NH 03584; (603) 788-3815.

Directions: From the junction of U.S. 3 and U.S. 2 in Lancaster, travel west on U.S. 2 for three-quarters of a mile to the campground entrance.

Trip notes: The Connecticut River flows by these sites in a grassy meadow, so campers can cool off in natural water in addition to the campground pool. Bring your own boat or rent a canoe and paddle the Connecticut through pastoral farmland with panoramic mountain views. Don't forget to drop in a line while you're at it—trout, bass, and many other species live in the river. A few miles north of the campground on U.S. 3 is the Lancaster Fairgrounds, which hosts an agricultural fair usually on Labor Day weekend. To the east of the campground lies the northern reaches of the White Mountain National Forest, including the Pliny and Pilot mountain ranges, with extensive and little-used hiking trails for day or overnight trips into the backcountry.

Open: May 1 through October 31.

⑪ Roger's Campground and Motel

Location: Southeast of Lancaster; Northern New Hampshire map page 168, grid d2.

Campsites, facilities: There are 404 sites for tents and RVs, 304 with full hookups, 40 with water and electric, and 60 with none. Each site has a table, fire ring, and grill. Use of air conditioners and heaters is allowed, and phone hookups are available. A dump station, rest rooms, hot showers, laundry facilities, a rec hall, pools, and a playground are provided. Off-season RV storage and a group rally site for tents and RVs are located on the property. Courts for basketball, tennis, badminton, shuffleboard, volleyball, and horseshoes are available. A store carries LP gas, ice, and firewood. Entry is controlled by a traffic gate. Leashed pets are permitted.

Reservations, fees: Reservations are recommended July 1 through Labor Day and require a prepaid deposit. For two people, tent sites start at $17 a night and RV sites with full hookups start at $20 a night.

Contact: Roger's Campground and Motel, RFD 2, Box 474, Lancaster, NH 03584; (603) 788-4885 in the summer, or (941) 368-6741 in the winter.

Directions: From Lancaster, travel southeast on U.S. 2 for about two miles to the campground entrance.

Trip notes: Rumpled mountain ridges surround this 300-acre campground and motel resort. Most sites are pull-throughs that can accommodate any size RV. Sites are grassy and open and don't afford much privacy, but this isn't a good choice for wilderness campers anyway. On the grounds are a waterslide, a miniature golf course, and a large arcade area. Group RV caravans are welcome to stay in a field equipped with hookups and portable grills. Two on-site function halls can accommodate groups of up to 200 and 1,000 people, respectively. To the immediate southwest is Weeks State Park, the former estate of John Wingate Weeks. This mountaintop park commemorates the onetime secretary of war and U.S. congressman who introduced legislation that established the White Mountain National Forest. From atop Prospect Mountain's fire tower in the park you can gaze for miles in every direction. About four miles south of the campground on U.S. 2 is Santa's Village, a Christmas-theme amusement park with rides, live reindeer, shows, and the jolly red-suited man himself.

Open: Late April through late October.

⑫ Lantern Motor Inn and Campground

Location: Northwest of Jefferson; Northern New Hampshire map page 168, grid d3.

Campsites, facilities: There are 64 sites for tents and RVs, 23 with full hookups, 30 with water and electric, and 11 with none. Each site has a picnic table, fire ring, and

grill. A dump station, rest rooms, hot showers, laundry facilities, a rec hall, pool, and playground are provided. Courts for badminton, volleyball, and horseshoes are available. A camp store carries ice and firewood. Leashed pets are permitted.

Reservations, fees: Reservations are accepted with prepaid deposits. Sites are $13 to $20 a night per family of four.

Contact: Lantern Motor Inn and Campground, P.O. Box 97, Jefferson, NH 03583; (603) 586-7151.

Directions: From the junction of U.S. 2 and Route 115 south of Jefferson, travel 4.5 miles northwest on U.S. 2 to the campground entrance.

Trip notes: You're in big-view country now: Lantern Motor Inn and Campground is set on a grassy plain with a view of the surrounding White Mountains. The facility is located between the public Waumbek Golf Course and Santa's Village. The latter is a Christmas-theme amusement park operated under the guise of Mr. Claus' summer residence. There are trained tropical birds, a roller coaster, shows, and the Skyway Sleigh Monorail. For more natural recreation, head into the northern reaches of the White Mountain National Forest east of the campground.

Open: May 15 through October 15.

⑬ Mountain Lake Campground

Location: On Blood Pond south of Lancaster; Northern New Hampshire map page 168, grid d2.

Campsites, facilities: There are 97 sites for tents and RVs, 28 with full hookups and 69 with water and electric. Each site has a picnic table and fire ring. Use of air conditioners and heaters is allowed, and cable TV is available. A dump station, rest rooms, hot showers, laundry facilities, a rec hall, heated pool, and a playground are provided. Courts for basketball, badminton, volleyball, and horseshoes are available. A grocery store carries LP gas, RV supplies, tackle, ice cream, ice, and firewood. Log cabins and tepees are also for rent. Leashed pets are permitted.

Reservations, fees: Reservations are recommended and require a nonrefundable deposit. Sites are $15 to $20 a night, with surcharges for air conditioners, heaters, and guests. Lakefront and prime sites cost extra. Seasonal rates are available.

Contact: Mountain Lake Campground, P.O. Box 475, Lancaster, NH 03584; (603) 788-4509.

Directions: From Lancaster, travel four miles south on U.S. 3 to the campground.

Trip notes: Mountains surround Blood Pond and provide the dominant scenery for these wooded and open sites on and near the shore. Canoe, rowboat, and paddleboat rentals are available at the campground, and a dock is provided for campers with boats. The pond supports a variety of warm-water fish species. You can swim at the campground beach, but on colder days you'll probably opt for the heated pool. To sample some of the local produce, check out the farmer's market in Lancaster, held on most weekends during the summer. About three miles south off U.S. 3, the Mountain View Golf Course has nine scenic holes open to the public.

Open: May 1 through October 31.

⓮ Israel River Campground

Location: In the Jefferson Meadows; Northern New Hampshire map page 168, grid d3.

Campsites, facilities: There are 120 sites for tents and RVs, some with full hookups and most with water and electric. Each site has a picnic table and fire ring. A dump station, rest rooms, hot showers, laundry facilities, a rec hall, pool, horseshoe pits, and a playground are provided. Courts for volleyball, basketball, horseshoes, and croquet are also on the property. A camp store carries ice and firewood. Leashed pets are permitted.

Reservations, fees: Reservations are recommended. Sites range from $14 a night with just water to $18 a night with full hookups for two people. Weekly rates are available.

Contact: Israel River Campground, Box 179A, Jefferson, NH 03583; (603) 586-7977.

Directions: From the junction of Route 115A and U.S. 2 in Jefferson, travel southwest on Routes 115A and 115B for 2.5 miles to the campground.

Trip notes: Here in graceful meadowlands the peaks of the Presidential Range rise into full view. Campers swim in the pool, while trout swim in the Israel River, which flows through the grounds. You can hike on rugged forest trails or take easy swings on 18 public holes at the Waumbek Golf Course in Jefferson. Six Gun City and Santa's Village, two theme amusement parks, are within a few miles.

Open: May 1 through October 15.

⓯ Jefferson Campground

Location: In Jefferson; Northern New Hampshire map page 168, grid d3.

Campsites, facilities: There are 100 sites for tents and RVs, 32 with full hookups, 25 with water and electric, and 43 with none. Each site has a picnic table, fire ring, and grill. Use of air conditioners and heaters is allowed. A dump station, rest rooms, hot showers, laundry facilities, a pool, and a playground are provided. Courts for basketball, badminton, volleyball, and horseshoes are available. A small grocery store carries RV supplies, LP gas, ice, and firewood. Leashed pets are permitted.

Reservations, fees: Reservations are accepted. Per family, sites without hookups are $12 a night; sites with full hookups are $14 a night.

Contact: Jefferson Campground, Box 112A, Jefferson, NH 03583; (603) 586-4510.

Directions: From the junction of U.S. 2 and Route 115 south of Jefferson, travel half a mile northwest on U.S. 2 to the campground entrance.

Trip notes: Frustrated cowboys will think they've died and gone to heaven when they arrive at these campsites next to Six Gun City. The campground boasts mountain views and is just off U.S. 2, but the main attraction is the Wild West theme park next door. Six Gun City features a fort, an Indian camp, ranch animals, cowboy skits, a frontier show, and burro rides. If that's not enough excitement, a few miles to the northwest is Santa's summer home; Santa's Village is a Christmas theme park with sleigh rides, live tropical birds, elves, and reindeer. In addition to the campground, the owners operate an RV sales office and service garage. One drawback is that the sites are small—only about 20 feet wide—and lack privacy.

Open: Memorial Day through Labor Day.

16 Moose Brook State Park

Location: South of Berlin; Northern New Hampshire map page 168, grid d4.

Campsites, facilities: There are 56 sites for tents and RVs up to 35 feet long, all without hookups. Each site has a picnic table and fire ring. Rest rooms, metered hot showers, and horseshoe pits are provided, as are courts for badminton, volleyball, and basketball. A camp store carries ice and firewood. Leashed pets are permitted.

Reservations, fees: Individual sites are available on a first-come, first-served basis. Groups of 10 or more people may make reservations. Sites are $14 a night per family.

Contact: Moose Brook State Park, RFD 1, 30 Jimtown Road, Gorham, NH 03581; (603) 466-3860.

Directions: From the junction of Route 16 and U.S. 2 in Gorham, head west for two miles on U.S. 2 to the park on the right (north) side of the road.

Trip notes: Moose Brook and Perkins Brook flow through this wooded campground, and anglers can pull trout from either one. The sites are a good base camp for those who want to make treks into the White Mountain National Forest, but there are also miles of multiuse trails in the park itself. Mountain bikers will find plenty of challenging terrain. A pool on Moose Brook serves as a swimming area.

Open: Mid-May through mid-October.

17 White Birches Camping Park

Location: East of Gorham in the White Mountain National Forest; Northern New Hampshire map page 168, grid d4.

Campsites, facilities: There are 102 sites for tents and RVs, 30 with full hookups, 25 with water and electric, and 47 with none. Each site has a picnic table and fire ring. Use of air conditioners and heaters is allowed. A dump station, rest rooms, hot showers, laundry facilities, a rec hall, pool, and playground are provided. Group sites are available for tents and RVs. Courts for basketball, badminton, volleyball, and horseshoes are on the property. A camp store carries RV supplies, LP gas, ice, and firewood. Leashed pets are permitted.

Reservations, fees: Reservations are recommended and require a prepaid deposit. Sites are $14 to $18 a night for two people.

Contact: White Birches Camping Park, 218 U.S. 2, Shelburne, NH 03581; (603) 466-2022.

Directions: From the junction of U.S. 2 and Route 16 in Gorham, travel east for 2.5 miles on U.S. 2 to the campground.

Trip notes: The campground is divided into three sections: The village area has full hookups and grassy pull-through sites for RVs. The rendezvous sites are wooded, set in the high meadow of a birch and hemlock forest. And the "topknot" area has wilderness sites in the foothills of Mount Moriah—the most private spots in the whole park. There is a short hiking and biking trail on the property, but just a short drive from here miles of trails await on the lands of the White Mountain National Forest. Not only is this the only campground offering RV hookups in winter, it's also right on a state-maintained snowmobile trail. The Wildcat Ski Area is 10 miles south of here, and Maine's Sunday River Ski Resort is 30 miles to the east.

Open: Year-round.

⑱ Timberland Camping Area

Location: West of Shelburne; Northern New Hampshire map page 168, grid d4.

Campsites, facilities: There are 133

sites for tents and RVs, 41 with full hookups, 37 with water and electric, and 55 with none. Each site has a picnic table, fire ring, and grill. Use of air conditioners and heaters is allowed, and full-hookup sites also have satellite TV. A dump station, rest rooms, hot showers, laundry facilities, a rec hall, pool, and playground are provided. Courts for basketball, badminton, croquet, volleyball, and horseshoes are available. A general store carries ice and firewood. Supplies are available in Gorham, four miles west. Leashed pets are permitted.

Reservations, fees: Reservations are recommended and require a prepaid deposit. Sites are $15 to $20 for two people. Weekly and monthly rates are available.

Contact: Timberland Camping Area, P.O. Box 303, Gorham, NH 03581; (603) 466-3872.

Directions: From Gorham, travel five miles east on U.S. 2 to the campground entrance.

Trip notes: You'll find large wooded sites with mountain views at Timberland. Equally suited to tents and RVs, these spots look out over the Androscoggin River before it heads into Maine. The Androscoggin Valley Country Club west of the campground is open to the public with 18 holes on a grassy riverside meadow. The Appalachian Trail crosses U.S. 2 near the campground and offers good day hikes or longer treks into the White Mountain National Forest.

Open: May 1 through late October.

⑲ Appalachian Trail

Location: From the New Hampshire–Vermont border, the trail crosses central New Hampshire on a northeast tack, meeting the Maine border at Success in the Mahoosuc Range; Northern New Hampshire map page 168, grid d4.

Campsites, facilities: Numerous lean-tos, tent platforms, cabins, and huts are located along the New Hampshire section of the Appalachian Trail. Most of this portion lies within the White Mountain National Forest, and backcountry camping is permitted below tree line away from trails and streams. Primitive toilets and an untreated water source are provided at most formal sites; topographic maps and published guides indicate sites where water may not be available. Leashed pets are permitted.

Reservations, fees: Most tent and lean-to sites are available free of charge on a first-come, first-served basis. Huts and shelters operated by the Appalachian Mountain Club (AMC) and some of the national forest cabins have caretakers and charge an overnight fee; some also require reservations (see AMC Huts and Lodges, campground number 48).

Contact: Appalachian Trail Conference, P.O. Box 807, Harper's Ferry, WV 25425; (304) 535-6331. (This nonprofit group publishes 10 sectional guides, which are accompanied by topographic maps.) The Appalachian Mountain Club, 5 Joy Street, Boston, MA 02108; for reservations, contact P.O. Box 298, Gorham, NH 03581; (603) 466-2727. White Mountain National Forest, P.O. Box 638, Laconia, NH 03274; (603) 528-8721.

Directions: The Appalachian Trail comes into New Hampshire from Norwich, Vermont, at Hanover on a small bridge over the Connecticut River near the Dartmouth College boathouses. The trail crosses into Maine from New Hampshire on the ridge of the wild, rugged Mahoosuc Range at a shallow notch between Mounts Carlo and Success, in Maine and New Hampshire respectively. The 31-mile section of the Appalachian Trail in the Mahoosucs is unbroken by roads. This portion is accessible at its crossing of U.S. 2 and the Androscoggin River near Shelburne.

Trip notes: From Springer Mountain in Georgia to Mount Katahdin in Maine, the Appalachian Trail traverses the Appalachian Mountain chain on a 2,158-mile continuous, marked footpath. The trail and its adjacent lands—about 270,000 acres—link more than 75 parks and forests in 14 states, including eight units of the national forest system and six units of the national park system. Countless wild, scenic, historic, and pastoral settings are enjoyed along the footpath by "through-hikers"—those who typically start in Georgia and make a six-month trek to Maine—day hikers, and overnight backpackers. On average, fewer than 200 through-hikers complete the 2,000-mile journey each year.

From the Vermont–New Hampshire line at the Connecticut River, the trail is surrounded by farms, roads, and houses, traverses cleared fields, and passes through some wilderness before entering the White Mountain National Forest in Warren. The first major peak encountered from this direction is Mount Moosilauke, after which the trail crosses Route 112 and heads into Kinsman Notch. From here, the trail continues northeast through Franconia Notch, the Pemigewasset Wilderness, and Crawford Notch before running over the tallest peak on the entire trail, Mount Washington at 6,288 feet. For the next 10 or so miles, the trail doesn't descend below 5,000 feet and thus is one of the most treacherous portions of the trail. After crossing Mount Madison at the north end of the Presidential Range, the trail veers south to Pinkham Notch. Shortly after crossing Route 16, it heads northeast again through the Carter and Mahoosuc Ranges to the Maine border.

The New Hampshire section of the trail offers an exercise in polar extremes: some of the wildest sections of the entire route are in this state, including the alpine garden on Mount Washington, a rare Arctic ecosystem.

But summiting Washington can be a bit of a disappointment, for once on top you'll find a snack bar, a visitors center, and hordes of tourists who drive up the auto road each year or take the Cog Railway. Because it has become so developed, some locals call the summit the "slummit" and refer to the railway as the "Smog Railway." However, once you turn your back to the commercialization, the views in all directions are breathtaking.

Open: Year-round.

⑳ Dolly Copp Campground

Location: In Pinkham Notch in the White Mountain National Forest; Northern New Hampshire map page 168, grid d4.

Campsites, facilities: There are 176 sites surrounding the historic Dolly Copp homestead. Picnic tables, fire rings, vault toilets, and piped water are provided. Coin-operated hot showers, topographic maps, and camping supplies are available at the AMC Pinkham Notch Visitor Center to the south. Leashed pets are permitted.

Reservations, fees: Reservations are necessary from June through September for some sites. Call the National Forest Reservation Center at (800) 280-2267. For each reservation, an $8 fee is charged. Sites are $12 a night.

Contact: White Mountain National Forest, Androscoggin Ranger District, 80 Glen Road, Gorham, NH 03581; (603) 466-2713.

Directions: From Gorham, travel six miles south on Route 16 to the campground.

Trip notes: Large wooded sites are separated into several areas at this campground along the Peabody River, a stream that is stocked with rainbow, brook, and brown trout. This is one of the largest camp-grounds in the entire national forest system, and as many as 1,000 people may be camped here at any time on busy summer weekends. The campground is named for a member of the colorful Copp family who lived here during the 1800s. Remnants of the Copp homestead still exist. Dolly and Hayes Copp were married for five decades, toiling as innkeepers and farming the land. On their 50th anniversary, Dolly decided enough was enough and the two parted possessions and ways. The Forest Service provides ample information about the history of the region. Other nearby attractions include the Mount Washington Auto Road, Tuckerman's Ravine, Crystal Cascade, and hiking trails in the Presidential and Carter Ranges. Interpretive programs are offered at the campground in summer. The Barnes Field group camping area is nearby, and sites there can be reserved through the Androscoggin Ranger District office.

Open: Mid-May through mid-October.

㉑ Wild River

Location: On the Wild River in Beans Purchase in the White Mountain National Forest; Northern New Hampshire map page 168, grid e4.

Campsites, facilities: There are 12 sites, three suitable for RVs, but no hookups. One site has a lean-to. Picnic tables, fire rings, vault toilets, and piped water are provided. Leashed pets are permitted.

Reservations, fees: Sites are available on a first-come, first-served basis. The fee is $10 a night.

Contact: White Mountain National Forest, Evans Notch Ranger District, RFD 2, Box 2270, Bethel, ME 04217; (207) 824-2134.

Directions: From the junction of U.S. 2 and Route 113 in Gilead, Maine, follow

Route 113 southwest for three miles. Turn right onto a dirt Forest Service road and continue five miles west to the campground.

Trip notes: You'll find plenty of peace, quiet, and privacy at these wilderness sites tucked away in the woods along the Wild River. Brook and rainbow trout dwell in the river, so you can try to catch something for an evening fish fry on your campfire. From here, several trails lead deep into the Wild River Valley and remote wilderness areas of Beans Purchase.

Open: Mid-May through mid-October.

22 Basin Campground

Location: North of Fryeburg, Maine, in the White Mountain National Forest; Northern New Hampshire map page 168, grid e4.

Campsites, facilities: There are 21 sites for tents and RVs, all without hookups. Picnic tables, fire rings, flush toilets, and piped water are provided. Leashed pets are permitted.

Reservations, fees: Reservations are accepted for some sites for June through September. Call the National Forest Reservation Center at (800) 280-2267. For each reservation, an $8 fee is charged. Campsites are $12 a night.

Contact: White Mountain National Forest, Evans Notch Ranger District, RFD 2, Box 2270, Bethel, ME 04217; (207) 824-2134.

Directions: From Fryeburg, Maine, travel 15 miles north on Route 113. Following the signs, turn left and continue to the campground entrance.

Trip notes: Sites here are nestled in the woods on Basin Pond, which has a boat ramp and a wheelchair-accessible fishing dock. Nonmotorized boating is allowed on this 23-acre impoundment. Anglers will find brook trout in Basin Pond, the Cold

River, and other small streams. Just east of the campground, Brickett Place is a 175-year-old brick building constructed by one of the first settlers in this area.

Open: Mid-May through mid-October.

23 Cold River

Location: In White Mountain National Forest near the Maine border in North Chatham; Northern New Hampshire map page 168, grid e4.

Campsites, facilities: There are 14 sites, 12 suitable for RVs, but none with hookups. Picnic tables, fire rings, flush toilets, and piped water are provided. You'll also find an open grassy area for sports and a picnic shelter for small groups. Leashed pets are permitted.

Reservations, fees: Reservations are accepted for some sites for June through September. Call the National Forest Reservation Center at (800) 280-2267. For each reservation, an $8 fee is charged. Campsites are $10 a night.

Contact: White Mountain National Forest, Evans Notch Ranger District, RFD 2, Box 2270, Bethel, ME 04217; (207) 824-2134.

Directions: From Fryeburg, Maine, travel 15 miles north on Route 113 to the campground on the left.

Trip notes: Located at the foot of Evans Notch in North Chatham, these open and wooded campsites are close to excellent hiking terrain, offering campers plenty of day-hiking options. Trails lead to the summits of Mount Meader and Ragged Jacket from Basin Pond. Trout fishing is good in both the Cold River and Basin Pond; the latter has a boat ramp and is open to nonmotorized boating. Cold River is one of the first Forest Service campgrounds to become snow-free each year, making it a favorite destination of early season fishing enthusiasts. A small picnic shelter is provided at the campground.

Open: Mid-May through mid-October.

㉔ Crazy Horse Campground

Location: On Moore Reservoir west of Littleton; Northern New Hampshire map page 168, grid d2.

Campsites, facilities: There are 150 sites for tents and RVs, 17 with full hookups, 83 with water and electric, and 50 with none. Each site has a picnic table, fire ring, and grill. Use of air conditioners and heaters is allowed, and phone hookups are available. A dump station, rest rooms, hot showers, laundry facilities, a rec hall, sports field, pool, pavilion, and playground are provided. Courts for badminton, volleyball, and horseshoes are available. A camp store carries LP gas, RV supplies, ice, and firewood. Tepees and RVs may also be rented. Leashed pets are permitted.

Reservations, fees: Reservations are accepted. Per family, tent sites start at $16 a night and RV sites with full hookups are $20 a night. Weekly, monthly, and seasonal rates are available on request.

Contact: Crazy Horse Campground, 788 Hilltop Road, Littleton, NH 03561; (603) 444-2204.

Directions: From Interstate 93 west of Littleton, take exit 43. Head east then southwest on Route 135 for 1.5 miles. Take a right onto Hilltop Road and continue 1.25 miles to the campground.

Trip notes: Moore Reservoir is a 12-mile lake on the Connecticut River open to powerboating, fishing, and swimming. These sites are set back from the lake in a rural, grassy area, and many of them are partially shaded. The campground, which is crisscrossed by paved roads, has a pool and patio, canoe rentals, and, a quarter mile away, a boat launch. When you get out on the lake, bass, trout, and other warm-water species are fair game. Nature trails on the property are open to snowmobiling and skiing in season, and the state corridor of snowmobile trails is accessible nearby in Littleton. Franconia Notch State Park is a short ride south of here, and paddlers may want to consider embarking on longer trips down the Connecticut River from this home base. Littleton is a large city where campers can obtain all goods and services.

Open: Year-round.

㉕ Connecticut River Canoe Sites

Location: Along the Connecticut River; Northern New Hampshire map page 168, grid d1.

Campsites, facilities: There are 17 primitive sites on the river from East Ryegate, Vermont, south to the Massachusetts border. Most sites have pit or chemical toilets and fire rings. At several sites, supplies can be obtained by walking a short distance into nearby towns. Sites are designated by a blue-on-yellow sign with a tent and river symbol. Pets are allowed.

Reservations, fees: Sites are available on a first-come, first-served basis. A fee is charged at Wilgus State Park.

Contact: Upper Valley Land Trust, 19 Buck Road, Hanover, NH 03755; (603) 643-6626. New England Power Company, 407 Miracle Mile, Lebanon, NH 03766; (603) 448-2200. Toll-free river line: (888) FLO-FONE/356-3663.

Directions: Sites are located on either bank of the Connecticut River, which forms the boundary between Vermont and New Hampshire.

Trip notes: The valley where the Connecticut River forms the border between New Hampshire and Vermont is a place of beauty and history. Once a through-way for log drives headed to sawmills in Massachusetts, this section of the 410-mile-long liquid highway is New England's largest renewable energy system. Except for a few well-marked breached dams and one set of rapids below White River Junction, the river is an easy to moderate journey in canoe, kayak, or small motorboat.

Though the river begins in the Fourth Connecticut Lake on the New Hampshire–Quebec border in Pittsburg, most canoe trips start below the dam in Canaan, Vermont. From here to the Massachusetts border, 17 canoe campsites are maintained on a 278-mile stretch of the river by different groups including the Upper Valley Land Trust, the New England Power Company, and the Student Conservation Association. From north to south they are:

Dodge Falls (Ryegate Dam, Monroe, New Hampshire): Two shelters and a chemical toilet are provided at this campsite.

Horse Meadow (North Haverhill, New Hampshire): After passing Horse Meadow, look for a small island. The campsite is high on the New Hampshire riverbank behind the island.

Vaughan Meadow (South Newbury, Vermont): The site is located about one mile south of the Bedell Bridge abutment. Look for a broad wooded riverbank above a curving beach.

Bugbee Landing (Bradford, Vermont): Behind the Bugbee campsite the commercial district of Bradford is visible across a golf course. This camping facility is large enough to accommodate groups and is also accessible by car.

Underhill Campsite (Piermont, New Hampshire): Look for the site immediately above Eastman Brook; the town of Piermont is high above on a hill.

Birch Meadow (Fairlee, Vermont): This site is set above marshland at the outlet of Lake Morey.

Thetford Canoe Campsite (Thetford, Vermont): The site lies on a straight stretch of wooded shoreline several hundred meters beyond a white frame house on the New Hampshire side. Watch out for poison ivy here. No open fires are allowed.

Loveland Point Campsite (in Vermont just north of Hanover, New Hampshire): You'll find this campsite on a piney point on the west shore just south of the mouth of the Ompompanoosuc River in Norwich, Vermont.

Gilman Island Campsites (on Gilman Island): The site is on the south end of the island about a mile below Ledyard Bridge. The section of the river to the north gets a lot of use by crew teams and powerboaters in addition to being the site of Dartmouth College's Ledyard Canoe Club. The Ledyard Bridge is also where the Appalachian Trail crosses from Vermont into New Hampshire.

Burnap's Island Campsite (south of White River Junction in Plainfield, New Hampshire): Just below the campsite—located at the mouth of the Ottauquechee River—there are huge boulders in the river known as "Chicken and Hens." The Sumner Falls/Hartland rapids are just ahead.

Burnham Meadow (Windsor, Vermont): You'll get a good view of Mount Ascutney to the west from this site. Three miles south of here there's a covered bridge and the village of Windsor.

Wilgus State Park (Weathersfield, Vermont): The state park campground is located on the west bank, about a mile below the Ascutney bridge. A fee is charged.

Student Conservation Association Canoe Camp (Charleston, New Hampshire): Two small, separate campsites are located approximately two miles below Hubbard Island.

Lower Meadow Campsite (South Charleston, New Hampshire): This site is in a thicket of small trees near the lower end of a series of hayfields. It is isolated from the mainland by a backwater marsh.

Windyhurst Farm (Putney, Vermont): The red barns of Windyhurst Farm are set on a hill above this campsite, which is located in low woods downstream from a large tilled field.

Wantastiquet Campsite (Hinsdale, New Hampshire): A large lumberyard stands opposite this site about one mile below the girder railroad bridge, which angles across the river just below downtown Brattleboro.

Stebbins Island Campsite (in Hinsdale, New Hampshire, just north of the Ashuelot River outlet): Two sites are on this large island one mile below the Vernon dam. A one-mile paddle up the Ashuelot River brings you to the town of Hinsdale.

Experienced paddlers can cover up to 30 miles a day. Plan on significantly less mileage if you want to stop frequently or make side trips to some of the interesting and accessible towns and natural or historic sites along the river valley. The water is clean but must be treated for consumption. Swim wherever you please using good judgment. The only time you might not want to swim is following heavy rains when some of the agricultural agents used at riverside farms get washed into the river. Many species of fish live in this waterway, including bass, trout, walleye, and northern pike. Check New Hampshire and Vermont state laws regarding fishing on the river: you will need a license.

Open: Year-round as weather and river conditions permit.

㉖ Littleton KOA Kampground

Location: On the Ammonoosuc River southwest of Littleton; Northern New Hampshire map page 168, grid d2.

Campsites, facilities: There are 60 sites for tents and RVs, 12 with full hookups, 29 with water and electric, and 19 without hookups. Each site comes with a picnic table, fire ring, and grill. A dump station, rest rooms, hot showers, laundry facilities, a rec room, a heated swimming pool, and a playground are provided. Cable TV is available. Courts for badminton, horseshoes, and volleyball are provided on the property. A grocery store carries LP gas, ice, and firewood. Leashed pets are permitted.

Reservations, fees: Reservations are accepted with prepaid deposits. For two people, sites start at $23 a night without hookups and $27 a night for full hookups. Cable TV costs $2 a day.

Contact: Littleton KOA Kampground, 2154 U.S. 302, Littleton, NH 03561; (603) 838-5525 or (800) 562-5836 (for reservations).

Directions: From Interstate 93 at Littleton, take exit 42. Travel southwest for five miles on U.S. 302 to the campground.

Trip notes: RVers and families especially will appreciate these meadowland campsites scattered along the Ammonoosuc River. At the campground you can enjoy a heated swimming pool, a hot tub, and full amenities, including meal service if you want dinner catered at your site. From here, scenic drives explore Franconia Notch State Park or the various attractions of Vermont across the Connecticut River.

Open: Early May through mid-October.

㉗ Mink Brook Family Campground

Location: North of Lisbon; Northern New Hampshire map page 168, grid d2.

Campsites, facilities: There are 54 sites for tents and RVs, 26 with water and electric hookups and 28 without hookups. Each site has a picnic table, fire ring, and grill. A dump station, rest rooms, hot showers, a rec hall, swimming pool, playground, horseshoe pits, and a court for volleyball and badminton are provided. A camp store sells groceries, ice, and firewood. Leashed pets are permitted.

Reservations, fees: Reservations are recommended. Sites are $17 to $20 a night for two people.

Contact: Mink Brook Family Campground, U.S. Route 302, Lisbon, NH 03585; (603) 838-6658.

Directions: From the junction of Route 117 and U.S. 302 in Lisbon, travel 1.25 miles southwest on U.S. 302 to the campground on the left.

Trip notes: With the White Mountains at their back, these open and shaded campsites for tenters and RVers claim a rural location yet are close to many North Country attractions. The small campground has a swimming pool on the grounds, but the Ammonoosuc River is just across the road if you want to try for trout or take a dip in natural water. To the south in Bath the river is spanned by a 376-foot-long bridge built back in 1832. For a breathtaking drive through this peaceful countryside, head north to Sugar Hill and take Route 117 east to Franconia. You'll pass old inns, mountain vistas, and the Sugar Hill Historical Museum before descending into the valley and Franconia.

Open: Early May through mid-October.

㉘ Snowy Mountain Campground and Motel

Location: West of Bethlehem; Northern New Hampshire map page 168, grid d2.

Campsites, facilities: There are 40 sites for tents and RVs, 16 with water and electric hookups. Each site has a picnic table, fire ring, and grill. A dump station, rest rooms, hot showers, a rec hall, pool, and playground are provided. Courts for badminton, volleyball, and horseshoes are available. A small grocery store carries ice and firewood; additional supplies and services are available in Bethlehem or Littleton. Leashed pets are permitted.

Reservations, fees: Reservations are recommended. Sites are $14 to $16 a night per family.

Contact: Snowy Mountain Campground and Motel, RFD 1, Box 692, Bethlehem, NH 03574; (603) 869-2600.

Directions: From Interstate 93 at exit 40 in Bethlehem, travel one mile east on U.S. 302 to the campground entrance.

Trip notes: Operated in conjunction with a small motel, these landscaped and wooded sites just off the interstate can accommodate any size RV. Southwest of the motel and campground is a protected property known as The Rocks. This former estate is owned by the Society for the Protection of New Hampshire Forests. In summer, the public may use picnic areas and three miles of self-guided educational nature trails. The Rocks is also a working Christmas tree farm with more than 50,000 trees in the ground. Special programs include the Wildflower Festival, held in early June, and the Shakespeare Festival, which hits the boards in July. Bethlehem is a good jumping-off point for excursions into the White Mountain

National Forest. Stop in at the Ammonoosuc Ranger Station off U.S. 3 for free maps and information.

Open: May 1 through October 31.

㉙ Apple Hill Campground

Location: North of Bethlehem; Northern New Hampshire map page 168, grid d2.

Campsites, facilities: There are 65 sites for tents and RVs, 20 with full hookups. Each site has a picnic table and fire ring. A dump station, rest rooms, hot showers, laundry facilities, a rec room, and a playground are provided. Courts for badminton, volleyball, and horseshoes are available. A small grocery store carries ice and firewood. Leashed pets are permitted.

Reservations, fees: A nonrefundable deposit is required with all reservations. Tent sites are $16 a night per family and sites with full hookups are $19 a night.

Contact: Apple Hill Campground, P.O. Box 388, Bethlehem, NH 03574; (603) 869-2238 or (800) 284-2238.

Directions: From Interstate 93 in Bethlehem, take exit 40 and travel east on U.S. 302 for three miles. Turn left when you see the campground sign and head north for one mile to the campground entrance.

Trip notes: This rural, wooded campground in the town of Bethlehem offers level sites and provides separate areas for tents and RVs. From here, several North Country attractions are within a short drive including the western theme amusement park Six Gun City in Jefferson. A small pond on the property can be used for swimming (or skating in winter), and nature trails weave through the woods. For a lakeside picnic in birch groves, head north to Forest Lake State Park in Dalton where you'll also find a swimming beach and good warm-water fishing.

In Bethlehem, two golf courses are open to the public. The downtown area has several junk and antique shops, funky restaurants, and an art deco movie theater. A number of historic oddities exist in town, such as a 160-year-old patched pine tree (reinforced with steel retaining rods) at the Bretzfelder Memorial Park off Main Street and The Rocks, an estate that now serves as a working Christmas tree farm. Self-guided nature trails at The Rocks double as ski trails in the winter. Both The Rocks and Bretzfelder are owned by the Society for the Protection of New Hampshire Forests. Apple Hill Campground is open year-round, and snowmobilers and skiers will find trails at the campground in addition to many more in the surrounding mountains and valley. Perhaps inspired by its name, Bethlehem puts on an old-time Christmas celebration each year with tours of decorated homes, sleigh rides at The Rocks, and ice skating parties.

Open: Year-round.

㉚ Twin Mountain KOA Kampground

Location: North of Twin Mountain; Northern New Hampshire map page 168, grid d3.

Campsites, facilities: There are 65 sites for tents and RVs, 8 with full hookups, 35 with water and electric, and 22 with none. Each site has a picnic table and fire ring. A dump station, rest rooms, hot showers, a rec hall, amphitheater, pool, laundry facilities, and a playground are provided. Courts for badminton, volleyball, and horseshoes are available. A camp store carries ice and firewood. Leashed pets are permitted.

Reservations, fees: A deposit of one night's fee is required for reservations. Sites start at $20 a night for two people.

Contact: Twin Mountain KOA Kampground, P.O. Box 148, Twin Mountain, NH 03595; (603) 846-5559.

Directions: From the intersection of U.S. 3 and U.S. 302 in Twin Mountain, travel north for two miles on U.S. 3. Turn right on Route 115 and head northeast for three-quarters of a mile to the campground entrance.

Trip notes: Cherry Mountain rises to an elevation of 3,050 feet behind these level campsites in the woods. Part of the national KOA chain, this campground caters to families with a well-stocked store, sturdy playground equipment, and a game room. The pool and patio offer a view of the surrounding peaks. On weekends, campers gather in the amphitheater for sing-a-longs and bonfires, or at the rec hall for pancake breakfasts. Head into the mountains for day hikes, take a drive along scenic byways dotted with many picnic spots and pull-offs, or visit nearby commercial attractions such as the Mount Washington Cog Railway off U.S. 302 or Six Gun City, a western amusement park with roller coasters, waterslides, and a miniature horse show just north of here in Jefferson.

Open: Mid-May through mid-October.

---

31 Beech Hill Campground and Cabins

Location: West of Twin Mountain; Northern New Hampshire map page 168, grid d3.

Campsites, facilities: There are 87 sites for tents and RVs, 15 with full hookups, 33 with water and electric, and 39 with none. Each site has a picnic table and fire ring. A dump station, rest rooms, hot showers, a rec hall, laundry facilities, a pool, and a playground are provided. Courts for badminton, volleyball, and horseshoes are available. A camp store carries ice and firewood. Several cabins are also available for rent. Leashed pets are permitted.

Reservations, fees: Reservations are recommended. Sites start at $18 a night per family. Seasonal rates are available.

Contact: Beech Hill Campground and Cabins, P.O. Box 129, Twin Mountain, NH 03595; (603) 846-5521.

Directions: From the intersection of U.S. 3 and U.S. 302 in Twin Mountain, travel west on U.S. 302 for two miles to the campground entrance on the right (north) side of the road.

Trip notes: Surrounded by deep piney woods and mountain vistas, these campsites are available year-round. Twin Mountain is on the state's maintained snowmobile corridor—from here you can drive your sled to the Canadian border and almost as far south as Massachusetts, as long as there's snow. Wilderness and day hiking is available in the White Mountain National Forest to the southeast of the campground, while country comforts are served up a short drive to the west in the funky little town of Bethlehem, known as the poetry capital of New Hampshire, probably because it gives an annual stipend to its "poet laureate." Several good restaurants, antique and junk shops, and a summer movie theater line the main street.

Open: Year-round.

---

32 Tarry-Ho Campground and Cottages

Location: West of Twin Mountain; Northern New Hampshire map page 168, grid d3.

Campsites, facilities: There are 67 sites for tents and RVs, 9 with full hookups and 53 with water and electric. Each site has a picnic table, fire ring, and grill. A dump station, rest rooms, hot showers, a rec hall, pool, and playground are provided. Courts for badminton, volleyball, and horseshoes are also available. A camp store carries ice and firewood. Leashed pets are permitted.

Reservations, fees: Reservations are recommended. Sites start at $16 a night.

Contact: Tarry-Ho Campground and Cottages, P.O. Box 369, Twin Mountain, NH 03595; (603) 846-5577.

Directions: From the intersection of U.S. 3 and U.S. 302 in Twin Mountain, travel west on U.S. 302 for three-quarters of a mile to the campground entrance on the left (south) side of the road.

Trip notes: Cottages and campsites share the mountain views from this grassy meadow flanking the Ammonoosuc River, where you can fish for trout from your own site. With hundreds of miles of backcountry trails, the nearby White Mountain National Forest is an ideal destination for outdoorspeople, from mountain bikers to backpackers. And a few miles west on U.S. 302 is Bretton Woods, a four-season recreation center. In summer, visitors can ride to the top of Rosebrook Mountain on a chairlift for a lunch in the clouds then bike back down. The mountaintop restaurant also serves dinner on weekends; its outdoor deck and bank of windows look out across the valley to the Mount Washington Hotel, which resembles a fairy-tale castle in the rosy light of evening alpenglow. In winter, Bretton Woods is a Nordic and alpine ski center with a large number of wide, intermediate trails.

Open: Year-round.

33 Twin Mountain Motor Court and RV Park

Location: Near the junction of U.S. 302 and U.S. 3 in Twin Mountain; Northern New Hampshire map page 168, grid d3.

Campsites, facilities: There are 18 sites for RVs, and only full-hookup units are welcome. Each site has a picnic table and fire ring. Rest rooms, hot showers, a rec hall, pool, and laundry facilities are provided. You'll also find courts for basketball, badminton, shuffleboard, volleyball, and horseshoes. A camp store carries ice and firewood. Leashed pets are permitted.

Reservations, fees: Reservations are strongly recommended. Sites are $25 a night for two people.

Contact: Twin Mountain Motor Court and RV Park, P.O. Box 104, Twin Mountain, NH 03595; (603) 846-5574 or (800) 332-TWIN/8946.

Directions: From the intersection of U.S. 3 and U.S. 302 in Twin Mountain, travel south on U.S. 3 for one mile to the campground entrance.

Trip notes: For RVers only, this motor court is on the way to many North Country attractions. The Ammonoosuc River flows by the property and is open to trout fishing for anglers with licenses. Clients of the hotel and RV sites share a pool. Twin Mountain has a small municipal airport that offers scenic rides—a real feast of color during the fall foliage display in early October. This is moose and bear country, so keep a watchful eye on the roads at dusk and make sure your food and garbage are tightly sealed.

Open: May 15 through October 15.

34 Ammonoosuc Campground

Location: In Twin Mountain; Northern New Hampshire map page 168, grid d3.

Campsites, facilities: There are 112 sites for tents and RVs, 75 with full hookups, 13 with water and electric, and 24 with none. Each site has a picnic table, fire ring and grill. Use of air conditioners and heaters is allowed. A dump station, rest rooms, hot showers, a rec hall, laundry facilities, a pool, and a playground are provided. Courts for badminton, volleyball, and horseshoes are also available. A general store is located a quarter mile north of the campground. Leashed pets are permitted.

Reservations, fees: Reservations are encouraged and may be made by phone or by mail. They must be accompanied by a nonrefundable $10 deposit, and fees are payable in full upon arrival. Tent sites are $18 a night and RV sites with full hookups are $21 a night per family.

Contact: Ammonoosuc Campground, P.O. Box 178N, Twin Mountain, NH 03595; (603) 846-5527.

Directions: From the intersection of U.S. 3 and U.S. 302 in Twin Mountain, head south on U.S. 3 for just a quarter mile to the campground on the left (east) side of the road.

Trip notes: Ammonoosuc Campground is located at the crossroads of U.S. 3 and U.S. 302 in Twin Mountain. The bulk of the White Mountain National Forest lies south and east of these campsites; from here you can see the foothills of Mount Hale, the Twin Mountains, and the Sugarloafs. Some sites are in the woods, while others are more open and grassy providing several camping habitats for RVers and tenters. Go for a dip in the swimming pool or take a short walk north to the Ammonoosuc River for a more natural way to cool off. Any number of day and overnight hikes are accessible within a short drive. The campground is also open in winter and is situated directly on a state-maintained snowmobile corridor—in fact, Twin Mountain is known as the snowmobile capital of New Hampshire. If you need a warm meal after running around all day, a pizza restaurant is operated on the property.

Open: Year-round.

35 Living Water Campground

Location: On the Ammonoosuc River in Twin Mountain; Northern New Hampshire map page 168, grid d3.

Campsites, facilities: There are 86 sites for tents and RVs, 13 with full hookups, 29 with water and electric, and 44 with none. Each site has a picnic table and fire ring. A dump station, rest rooms, hot showers, laundry facilities, a rec hall, pool, and playground are provided. Courts for basketball, badminton, volleyball, and horseshoes are also available. A grocery store carries camping supplies, ice, and firewood. No pets are allowed.

Reservations, fees: An advance deposit of $20 is required with all reservations. Tent sites without hookups are $20 a night for two people, and RV sites with full hookups are $24 for two people. Riverfront sites cost $2 extra. Visitors are not permitted during holiday weekends.

Contact: Living Water Campground, P.O. Box 158, Twin Mountain, NH 03595; (603) 846-5513 or (800) 257-0708.

Directions: From the intersection of U.S. 3 and U.S. 302 in Twin Mountain, travel east on U.S. 302 for 1,000 feet to the campground entrance on the right (south) side of the road.

Trip notes: Mountain views and grassy, riverside sites greet campers at Living Water, a quiet family campground with clean, safe facilities. The Ammonoosuc River, a healthy trout stream, runs along the property. Alas, this isn't a good place to swim as there are no pools and it's shallow, but wading in the mountain waters is a great way to cool off. A motel is operated in conjunction with the campground, and there are no seasonally-rented campsites. Numerous

White Mountain attractions, both natural and man-made, are within a short drive. To the east, the Mount Washington Cog Railway chugs up to the summit of the tallest peak in the northeast (elevation 6,288 feet). A scenic drive heads southeast through Crawford Notch with great views throughout the gap. Much of the land on either side of the byway is part of Crawford Notch State Park, and several pull-offs offer hikes to gushing falls or other points of interest.

Open: Memorial Day through Columbus Day weekend.

36 Zealand Campground

Location: East of Twin Mountain in the White Mountain National Forest; Northern New Hampshire map page 168, grid d3.

Campsites, facilities: There are 11 sites along the Ammonoosuc River with picnic tables, fire rings, vault toilets, and piped water. No pets are allowed.

Reservations, fees: Sites are available on a first-come, first-served basis. The fee is $10 a night.

Contact: White Mountain National Forest, Ammonoosuc Ranger District, Box 230, Bethlehem, NH 03574; (603) 869-2626.

Directions: From the intersection of U.S. 302 and U.S. 3 in Twin Mountain, travel east for two miles on U.S. 302. The campground is on the right (south) side of the road.

Trip notes: Shaded, grassy sites are located directly on scenic byway U.S. 302, making this is a good place to catch moose in action. The large beasts are frequently observed feeding near lakes and streams at dusk. Zealand is open through December and serves as a good base camp for early winter trips into the Pemigewasset Wilderness. With reservations you can also get overnight accommodations at the

Zealand Falls Appalachian Mountain Club hut. The sites are close to the Cog Railway and Mount Washington, New Hampshire's highest peak at 6,288 feet. Also nearby, the Mount Washington Hotel and Resort offers golf, tennis, gourmet dining, and nightlife in the summer.

Open: May through mid-December.

37 Sugarloaf Campgrounds I and II

Location: East of Twin Mountain in the White Mountain National Forest; Northern New Hampshire map page 168, grid d3.

Campsites, facilities: There are 29 sites at Sugarloaf I and 32 sites at Sugarloaf II for tents and RVs. Each site has a picnic table and fire ring. Wheelchair-accessible vault toilets are provided at Sugarloaf II, and flush toilets are provided at Sugarloaf I. Piped water is available at both campgrounds. No pets are allowed.

Reservations, fees: Reservations are accepted for some sites for May through October. Call the National Forest Reservation Center at (800) 280-2267. For each reservation, an $8 fee is charged. Sites are $12 a night.

Contact: White Mountain National Forest, Ammonoosuc Ranger District, Box 230, Bethlehem, NH 03574; (603) 869-2626.

Directions: From the intersection of U.S. 302 and U.S. 3 in Twin Mountain, travel east for two miles on U.S. 302. Turn right on Zealand Road and continue half a mile to the campgrounds.

Trip notes: These wooded sites make good base camps for treks into the Pemigewasset Wilderness; with reservations you can also get overnight accommodations at the Zealand Notch Appalachian Mountain Club hut. The sites are close to the Cog Railway and Mount Washington (New Hampshire's highest peak) as well as the Mount Washington Hotel and Resort, where golf, tennis, gourmet meals, and nightlife are available in summer. The Sugarloaf peak trails are short, moderate hikes, and both rocky summits afford views of the wilderness area and the Franconia Ridge to the southwest.

Open: Sugarloaf I is open from mid-May through mid-October, and Sugarloaf II stays open through mid-December.

---

38 Fransted Family Campground

Location: On Meadow Brook in Franconia; Northern New Hampshire map page 168, grid e2.

Campsites, facilities: There are 96 sites for tents and RVs, 26 with full hookups. Use of air conditioners and heaters is allowed. A dump station, rest rooms, hot showers, laundry facilities, and a playground are provided. A miniature golf course, horseshoe pits, and a court for badminton and volleyball are located on the property. A small grocery store sells bait, ice, and firewood. Leashed pets are permitted.

Reservations, fees: Reservations are accepted with prepaid deposits. Sites are $15 to $18 a night for two people. Groups are welcome, but in July and August they may consist of no more than 12 people.

Contact: The Hultgren Family, Fransted Family Campground, P.O. Box 155, Route 18, Franconia, NH 03580; (603) 823-5675.

Directions: From Interstate 93 at Franconia, take exit 38. Travel 50 feet west, then head south on Route 18 for one mile to the campground.

Trip notes: From their setting in a riverside meadow these grassy sites offer a front-row view of the Franconia Range from the north. Meadow Brook babbles through the campground, allowing campers access to prime trout habitat. The stream feeds into the spirited Gale River just north of the campground. A moderate 8.5-mile paddle with Class II rapids on the Gale starts below the bridge in Franconia and passes through undeveloped land as it flows toward Twin Mountain, affording views of the Kinsman Ridge along the way. By far the most spectacular scenery is in Franconia Notch to the south. Land on either side of this gap is protected by the state. A good way to take it all in is on an eight-mile-long bike path extending from the Cannon Mountain tram to The Flume, a scenic gorge north of Lincoln. Bike rentals are available in Franconia. Winter sites are open to seasonal campers; there are numerous cross-country skiing trails in the immediate area, and the Cannon Mountain alpine ski center a few miles south has the biggest vertical drop—2,146 feet—of any lift-served area in the state. In summer, the state maintains a swimming beach nearby on Echo Lake.

Open: Tent sites are available May 1 through Columbus Day, but seasonal RV campers are welcome year-round.

---

39 Cannon Mountain

Location: North of Echo Lake in Franconia Notch State Park; Northern New Hampshire map page 168, grid e2.

Campsites, facilities: There are seven sites for RVs, and only full-hookup units are accepted. Tables and a public phone are provided. No pets are allowed.

Reservations, fees: For reservations, call the New Hampshire Division of Parks and Recreation (see phone number below) on weekdays between 8:30 A.M. and 3:30 P.M. from January through August. Sites are $24 a night.

Contact: Cannon Mountain, c/o Lafayette Campground, Route 3, Franconia, NH 03580; (603) 823-9513. New Hampshire Division of Parks and Recreation, (603) 271-3628.

Directions: From the Franconia Notch Parkway (Interstate 93) south of Franconia, take exit 3 heading toward Echo Lake. Travel west for about a quarter mile to the campground entrance.

Trip notes: From fly-fishing on Profile Pond to hiking high in the mountains, campers can experience Franconia Notch State Park to the utmost when they stay in one of these sites. The sites themselves aren't anything special; they're at the edge of a big dirt parking lot, but mountains stand in full view in every direction and there's a pristine swimming lake, boat ramp, and fly-fishing pond a short walk from your RV door. Echo Lake is next to these sites and has a swimming beach, snack bar, boat rentals, and good trout fishing; there's also a boat ramp on its southern end.

A short walk south, Profile Pond is set beneath one of the White Mountains' most recognizable attractions, the Old Man of the Mountain. For an easy high, take the five-minute ride on the Cannon Mountain aerial tram, which you'll find at state park headquarters. It ascends more than 2,000 vertical feet. On top of the mountain, you can take a short walk to an observation tower. To explore the eight-mile-long notch, try the paved bike path running north to south with many points of interest along the way. In winter, these RV sites are staked out by skiers as Cannon Mountain is one of two state-owned alpine ski centers. The bike path doubles as a cross-country skiing trail in winter.

Open: Year-round.

40 Lafayette Campground

Location: In Franconia Notch State Park; Northern New Hampshire map page 168, grid e2.

Campsites, facilities: There are 97 sites for tents and RVs, all without hookups. Each site has a picnic table, fire ring, and grill. Rest rooms, hot showers, and a playground are provided. A small grocery store carries ice and firewood. No pets are allowed.

Reservations, fees: For reservations, call the New Hampshire Division of Parks and Recreation (see phone number below) on weekdays between 8:30 A.M. and 3:30 P.M. from January through August. Sites are $14 a night.

Contact: Lafayette Campground, U.S. 3, Franconia, NH 03580; (603) 823-9513. New Hampshire Division of Parks and Recreation, (603) 271-3628.

Directions: Take the Tramway exit (exit 2) off the Franconia Notch Parkway (Interstate 93). Reverse your direction and head south on the parkway for 2.5 miles to the Lafayette Place/Campground exit.

Trip notes: Stunning mountain views await at this location at the bottom of the notch on the Pemigewasset River. Sites are sandy and tucked into the woods at the base of the Cannon Balls, two massive rolling summits. The walls of the notch rise more than 4,000 feet on either side of Interstate 93, with Mount Lafayette the tallest peak on the east side of the gap at 5,260 feet. This eight-mile-long state park receives a lot of traffic due to its many pulloffs and points of interest. The Old Man of the Mountain is a rocky ledge that takes on a stern male countenance when viewed from the north. At the south end of the park there's The Flume, a dramatic, skinny gorge with footpaths and boardwalks. The Basin, just south of the campground, is a deep glacial pothole spanning nearly 30 feet across.

Several good day hikes leave from the campground including a short hike to Lonesome Lake, where you'll find an Appalachian Mountain Club hut, and the longer Falling Waters/Bridle Path loop on the east side of the notch, which crosses the summits of Little Haystack, Lincoln, and Lafayette on the narrow, rocky Franconia Ridge. Campers may swim and boat in Echo Lake at the north end of the notch by showing their campground pass. The lake has a lifeguard, boat ramp, sandy beach, and snack bar.

Open: Mid-May through mid-December.

④① Dry River Campground

Location: In Crawford Notch State Park; Northern New Hampshire map page 168, grid e3.

Campsites, facilities: There are 30 sites for tents and RVs, all without hookups. Pit toilets, piped water, and picnic tables are provided. Leashed pets are permitted.

Reservations, fees: Sites are available on a first-come, first-served basis. The fee is $12 a night.

Contact: Dry River Campground, Crawford Notch State Park, P.O. Box 177, Twin Mountain, NH 03595; (603) 374-2272.

Directions: From the junction of U.S. 302 and Route 16 in Glen, travel northwest on U.S. 302 for 16 miles. The campground is on the right (east) side of the highway.

Trip notes: Primitive wooded sites are strung along the Dry River, a tempting trout stream. Crawford Notch State Park serves as a centrally located base camp for excursions into the Presidential Range and surrounding national forestlands. From here,

the summit of Mount Washington is 16 miles northeast. Close by, Arethusa Falls—at more than 200 feet high the tallest falls in the state—are accessible on a moderate three-mile loop trail that starts half a mile south of the campground near the site of the Willey House. This site was once the home of an early settler, Samuel Willey Jr., who moved his family here in 1825. The family died in a great storm and slide the following year. They had left the house to find safety, and ironically, the house was the only untouched object in the valley.

Open: Mid-May through mid-December.

④② Crawford Notch General Store and Campground

Location: In Crawford Notch State Park; Northern New Hampshire map page 168, grid e3.

Campsites, facilities: There are 75 sites for tents and RVs up to 35 feet long, 23 with electric hookups. Each site has a table, fire ring, and grill. Chemical toilets, piped water, dish-washing stations, hot showers, and a public phone are provided. A general store carries groceries, ice, and firewood. Leashed pets are permitted.

Reservations, fees: Reservations are recommended. Sites start at $18 a night for four people.

Contact: Crawford Notch General Store and Campground, U.S. 302, Harts Location, NH 03812; (603) 374-2779.

Directions: From the junction of Route 16 and U.S. 302 in Glen, travel northwest on U.S. 302 for 14.5 miles to the campground.

Trip notes: Here at the only privately owned campground in Crawford Notch State Park, 75 secluded and roomy sites are set either beside or near the Saco River. Fish and swim in the river at the campground, or take one of the many nearby hiking trails into the mountains. Numerous other trails and forest roads in the area are open to mountain biking.

Open: May 1 through October 31.

---

⑬ Silver Springs Campground

Location: West of Bartlett on the Saco River; Northern New Hampshire map page 168, grid e3.

Campsites, facilities: There are 58 sites for tents and RVs, 24 with water and electric hookups. Each site has a picnic table, fire ring, and grill. A dump station, rest rooms, hot showers, and a playground are provided. Courts for badminton, volleyball, and horseshoes are available. A camp store carries groceries, live bait, ice, and firewood. Well-behaved, leashed pets are permitted.

Reservations, fees: Reservations are recommended. There is a minimum stay requirement during holiday weekends. Sites are $16 a night for two adults with surcharges for hookups and guests.

Contact: Silver Springs Campground, P.O. Box 38, Bartlett, NH 03812; (603) 374-2221.

Directions: From the junction of Route 16 and U.S. 302 in Glen, travel northwest on U.S. 302 for eight miles to the campground on the right side of the road.

Trip notes: Many of these shaded and open sites are right on the Saco River. On hot days, campers head for the campground swimming hole, which features a 100-foot natural waterslide down river rocks. Mountain vistas can be had in every direction. A short drive north on U.S. 302 leads to numerous pull-offs and trailheads. One scenic jaunt is two miles east of the camp: take Bear Notch Road south from

Bartlett and enjoy nine miles of overlooks on the way to the Kancamagus Highway (Route 112). From Bartlett, the Saco River is canoeable for 20 miles to Center Conway and offers views of the Presidentials. You'll encounter Class II and III rapids.

Open: Mid-May through mid-October.

---

⑭ Green Meadow Camping Area

Location: North of Glen; Northern New Hampshire map page 168, grid e4.

Campsites, facilities: There are 93 sites for tents and RVs, 31 with full hookups, 32 with water and electric, and 30 with none. Each site has a picnic table, fire ring, and grill. Cable TV is available. A dump station, rest rooms, hot showers, a basketball hoop, a volleyball and badminton court, horseshoe pits, and a pool are provided. A camp store carries RV supplies, ice, and firewood. Leashed pets are permitted.

Reservations, fees: Reservations are recommended during the summer months. Sites are $15 to $20 a night per family.

Contact: Green Meadow Camping Area, P.O. Box 246, Glen, NH 03838; (603) 383-6801.

Directions: From the junction of Route 16 and U.S. 302 in Glen, travel a quarter mile north on Route 16, then turn right and go another quarter mile east to the campground entrance.

Trip notes: The craggy contours of New Hampshire's White Mountains are in full view of these meadow sites. Of the two campgrounds in the immediate Glen area, this one is probably better suited to adults, though there are some sports courts and a swimming pool to keep campers with children happy. It's also the only year-round option for RVs. While hiking, biking, and canoeing are popular summer pursuits, in winter the valley comes to life in a different way. To the north in Jackson, there are miles of maintained cross-country ski trails in and out of town, challenging backcountry skiing in Pinkham Notch, and alpine ski areas in Conway and Pinkham Notch. This campground is next door to Story Land, a theme park with rides and costumed characters based on favorite tales including Humpty Dumpty and the Old Woman in the Shoe.

Open: Year-round.

④⑤ Glen-Ellis Family Campground

Location: South of Glen; Northern New Hampshire map page 168, grid e4.

Campsites, facilities: There are 182 sites for tents and RVs, 99 with water and electric hookups. Each site has a picnic table, fire ring, and grill. Use of air conditioners and heaters is allowed. A dump station, rest rooms, hot showers, a rec hall, pool, pavilion, sports field, and playground are provided. Courts for basketball, badminton, shuffleboard, tennis, volleyball, and horseshoes are available, as are group tent sites. A grocery store carries RV supplies, ice, and firewood. There's a traffic control gate at the entrance. Leashed pets are permitted.

Reservations, fees: Reservations are accepted. Per family, tent sites are $18 night and sites with hookups are $20 a night. Add $2 for waterfront sites. Seasonal rates are available on request.

Contact: Glen-Ellis Family Campground, P.O. Box 397, Glen, NH 03838; (603) 383-4567.

Directions: From the junction of Route 16 and U.S. 302 in Glen, travel a quarter mile west on U.S. 302 to the campground.

Trip notes: This campground is at an important crossroads in the White Mountains. To the north lie the resort town of Jackson and, beyond that, Pinkham Notch. To the northwest lie Crawford Notch and the Presidential Range. And to the south lies the town of North Conway, known for its outlet shopping, restaurants, and hotels. Glen-Ellis is on a mountain meadow nestled between the Ellis and Saco Rivers and offers many waterfront sites. A wilderness tent area (sites 101 through 110) is right on the Saco, which is open to fishing and canoeing. Large play areas, a gazebo, pool, and patio make this campground both attractive and practical for families. Just north are two commercial attractions: the Heritage New Hampshire museum retraces the state's history from the colonial voyage from England to America in 1634; Story Land is a theme park with rides that bring such tales as Cinderella and Humpty Dumpty to life.

Open: Late May through mid-October.

④⑥ Oliverian Valley Campground

Location: West of Glencliff; Northern New Hampshire map page 168, grid e1.

Campsites, facilities: There are 24 sites for tents and self-contained RVs, all without hookups. Each site has a picnic table, privy, and fire ring or grill. Rest rooms, hot showers, a volleyball court, horseshoe pits, and a rec hall are provided. Leashed pets are permitted.

Reservations, fees: Reservations are accepted with a 25 percent deposit. Sites start at $20 a night per family.

Contact: Oliverian Valley Campground, P.O. Box 91, East Haverhill, NH 03765; (603) 989-3207.

Directions: From the junction of Routes 10 and 25 in Haverhill, travel east on Route

25 for approximately eight miles to the campground entrance.

Trip notes: These wooded sites set in a 2,000-acre preserve are strictly for the privacy-conscious. The preserve surrounds a working farm, maple sugaring operation, and organic garden. A self-guided nature trail on the property was developed with the Department of Fish and Game to create wildlife habitat demonstration areas. Guided tours and trail lunches are available on request. More than 10 miles of trails traverse marsh, stream, field, and forest and present views of the Connecticut River Valley, Mount Moosilauke, and other scenic spots along the way. On weekends, the sugar shack serves breakfast and a cabin one mile into the woods serves refreshments in the evening while campers swap stories and stoke a communal fire.

Open: May 15 through October 15.

㊼ Wildwood Campground

Location: West of North Woodstock in the White Mountain National Forest; Northern New Hampshire map page 168, grid e2.

Campsites, facilities: There are 26 sites for tents and RVs, all without hookups. Picnic tables, fire rings, vault toilets, and piped water are provided. Leashed pets are permitted.

Reservations, fees: Sites are available on a first-come, first-served basis. The fee is $10 a night.

Contact: White Mountain National Forest, Ammonoosuc Ranger District, Box 230, Bethlehem, NH 03574; (603) 869-2626.

Directions: From Lincoln, travel west on Route 112 for seven miles to the campground entrance.

Trip notes: Set in Kinsman Notch across the road from the Ammonoosuc River, these sites are wooded and offer good mountain views. Try to catch a trout for dinner in the river, and when you're ready for a hike, head three miles south to where the Appalachian Trail crosses Route 112. From there, the challenging Beaver Brook Trail ascends Mount Moosilauke. An easier trek to the north ascends Mount Wolf via the Kinsman Ridge Trail.

Open: Mid-May through mid-December.

㊽ AMC Huts and Lodges

Location: In the White Mountain National Forest and Franconia Notch State Park; Northern New Hampshire map page 168, grid e2.

Campsites, facilities: There are eight huts, one hostel, and one lodge. Bunk beds, wool blankets, pillows, and cold running water are provided. Self-service huts have fully equipped kitchens, partially heated common rooms, and unheated bunk rooms. Some huts have pit or flush toilets. Full-service stays include hot meals at dinner and breakfast. Lights and appliances are solar-powered or run on propane gas. Other facilities differ from hut to hut. Pets are not allowed in any AMC facility.

Reservations, fees: Reservations are strongly recommended. Prepayment is encouraged, and is required for package plans. Prepaid deposits must be received within seven days of reserving by phone. For adults, full-service rates range from $50 a night for members to $57 for nonmembers. Self-service rates (no meals) are $10 a night for members and $15 for nonmembers. Discounted rates apply for package stays and children. Stays during weekends in August are slightly more expensive.

Contact: The Appalachian Mountain Club, 5 Joy Street, Boston, MA 02108; for reservations, contact P.O. Box 298, Gorham, NH 03581; (603) 466-2727. White Mountain National Forest, P.O. Box 638, Laconia, NH 03274; (603) 528-8721.

Directions: The AMC huts and lodges are strung along 56 miles of the Appalachian Trail. Trailheads are accessible on Interstate 93, Routes 112 and 16, U.S. 302, and U.S. 2 in the White Mountains region of the state.

Trip notes: More than a century ago, the Appalachian Mountain Club (AMC) opened its first hut in the White Mountains with the aim of providing comfortable accommodations for hikers much like the alpine huts of Europe. Back then, a night's stay at the Madison Springs cabin cost 50 cents and you had to bring your own food. Today, hikers can carry little more than a light backpack and lunches for an extended hiking tour of the White Mountains, and accommodations can cost more than $50 a night. Trail and ecology information is available at all huts, as the AMC has a dual mission of education and responsible recreation. Accommodations include shared bunk rooms, common rooms, and hot meals. Suppers include homemade bread, salad, vegetables, and dessert in addition to a main dish of chicken, fish, beef, turkey, or lasagna. A hiker shuttle operates June through October between Crawford and Pinkham Notch, stopping at numerous points in between.

From west to east, AMC accommodations include:

Lonesome Lake hut (on Lonesome Lake in Franconia Notch State Park): This is the most popular destination for families since the hike in is short and easy.

Greenleaf hut (below the summit of Mount Lafayette): Greenleaf is located at tree line and offers spectacular sunsets.

Galehead hut (on the north edge of the Pemigewasset Wilderness): The most remote hut in the system, Greenleaf offers views of the Pemigewasset Wilderness.

Zealand Falls hut (near the Pemigewasset Wilderness): The easy hike to the hut in summer makes it a favorite with families. It's open year-round and is a popular destination for backcountry skiers.

Crawford Hostel (off U.S. 302 north of Crawford Notch): The facility is open year-round and offers bunk rooms, showers, and a self-service kitchen.

Mizpah Spring hut (on Mount Clinton): Moderate hiking leads to this scenic outlook over Crawford Notch—a great fall foliage destination.

Lakes of the Clouds hut (on the southern shoulder of Mount Washington): This is the AMC's highest, largest, and most popular hut. It sleeps 90.

Madison Springs hut (above the sheer walls of Madison Gulf): After a strenuous trek in to this hut, hikers are rewarded with sunsets over the Presidentials.

Pinkham Notch Visitors Center Lodge (off Route 16 in the Mount Washington Valley): Bunk rooms, hot showers, hot meals, a trading post (selling books and outdoor gear), and an information desk are available at this year-round facility.

Carter Notch hut (below the summit of Wildcat Mountain): Open year-round, this is a good base for exploring nearby mountains and ponds.

Open: Most huts are open May through October; the Zealand and Carter huts are open year-round, as are the Crawford Hostel and Pinkham Notch Lodge.

㊾ Country Bumpkins Campground and Cottages

Location: In North Woodstock on U.S. 3; Northern New Hampshire map page 168, grid e2.

Campsites, facilities: There are 46 sites for tents and RVs, some with full hookups. Each site has a picnic table and fireplace. A dump station, rest rooms, hot showers, laundry facilities, a game room, horseshoe pits, and a playground are provided. A camp store carries ice and firewood. Leashed pets are permitted.

Reservations, fees: Reservations are accepted. Sites are $16 to $20 a night per family of four. Weekly, monthly, and seasonal rates are available.

Contact: Country Bumpkins Campground and Cottages, RR 1, Box 83, U.S. 3, Lincoln, NH 03251; (603) 745-8837.

Directions: From Interstate 93, take exit 33 for Lincoln. Travel south on U.S. 3 for half a mile to the entrance.

Trip notes: The busy interstate and the Pemigewasset River border these wooded sites. There's a small pond in the center of the campground. From here, wild and contrived attractions abound, from the Whale's Tale water park—complete with games, rides, and shows—to The Flume, an 800-foot-long gorge with walls up to 90 feet high and in places only 12 feet wide; both are north of the campground on U.S. 3. The Flume is about three miles north and lies at the south end of Franconia Notch State Park, a spectacular eight-mile-long mountain pass.

Open: Year-round.

50 Cold Spring Campground

Location: On the Pemigewasset River in Lincoln; Northern New Hampshire map page 168, grid e2.

Campsites, facilities: There are 37 sites for tents and RVs, 5 with full hookups, 12 with water and electric, and 20 with none.

Rest rooms, hot showers, picnic tables, fire rings, and grills are provided. Leashed pets are permitted.

Reservations, fees: Reservations are accepted. Sites range from $10 a night for one person to $18 a night for two people with full hookups. Seasonal rates are available.

Contact: Cold Spring Campground, RFD 3, Box 84, Lincoln, NH, 03251; (603) 745-8351.

Directions: From Interstate 93, take exit 33 for Lincoln. Travel south on U.S. 3 for half a mile to the entrance.

Trip notes: If it's the middle of July and all the other campgrounds around here are full, try Cold Spring. The small family campground has seasonal campsites and a few primitive spots for overnighters. The Pemigewasset River flows by the property, should you be in the mood to fish. The towns of North Woodstock and Lincoln are within a short car or bike ride.

Open: April 15 through October 15.

51 Maple Haven Camping, Cottages, and Lodge

Location: West of North Woodstock; Northern New Hampshire map page 168, grid e2.

Campsites, facilities: There are 36 sites for tents and RVs, 22 with water and electric hookups. Each site has a picnic table and fire ring. A dump station, rest rooms, hot showers, a rec area, and courts for badminton, volleyball, and horseshoes are provided. A camp store carries ice and firewood. No pets are allowed.

Reservations, fees: Reservations are recommended. For two people, tent sites are $18 a night; RV sites with hookups are $26 a night. Weekly, monthly, and seasonal rates are available.

Contact: Maple Haven Camping, Cottages, and Lodge, RFD 1, Box 54, North Woodstock, NH 03262; (603) 745-3350 or (800) 221-3350.

Directions: From Interstate 93 at North Woodstock, take exit 32. Turn right and head west on Route 112 for one mile to the campground entrance. You'll pass through a stoplight in North Woodstock on the way.

Trip notes: Moosilauke Brook, also known as the Lost River, passes by this campground as does Route 112. Operated in conjunction with cabins and a lodge, these sites are set in wooded areas and several of them offer mountain views. While Route 112 can get busy in the summer, campers here remain off the beaten paths of Lincoln and North Woodstock. Another plus is that you can fish for trout from your campsite. Five minutes away are natural points of interest including Loon Mountain and Lost River Reservation, a series of caves on Moosilauke Brook. All supplies and services are available in North Woodstock, about half a mile away.

Open: April 15 through October 31.

---

52 Lost River Valley Campground

Location: West of Woodstock at the confluence of the Lost River and Walker Brook; Northern New Hampshire map page 168, grid e2.

Campsites, facilities: There are 130 sites for tents and RVs, 8 with full hookups, 51 with water and electric, and 71 with none. Each site has a picnic table and fire ring. Use of air conditioners and heaters is allowed. A dump station, rest rooms, hot showers, laundry facilities, a rec hall, sports field, and playground are provided. Courts for tennis, basketball, badminton, shuffleboard, volleyball, and horseshoes are located on the property. A grocery store carries ice and firewood. An entry gate controls traffic. Leashed pets are permitted.

Reservations, fees: Reservations are accepted for stays of three or more days with prepaid deposits. Overnight sites are available on a first-come, first-served basis. Sites are $20 to $27 a night for two people. Weekly stays are subject to a 10 percent discount.

Contact: Lost River Valley Campground, 951 Lost River Road, North Woodstock, NH 03262; (603) 745-8321 in the summer, or (407) 286-1825 in the winter.

Directions: From Interstate 93 at North Woodstock, take exit 32. Turn right and head west on Route 112 for four miles to the campground entrance. You'll pass through a stoplight in North Woodstock on the way.

Trip notes: Not one but two mountain streams are at your disposal when you bed down at Lost River Valley Campground. Walker Brook flows to one side, and the namesake Lost River is on the other; there's also a swimming pond and a sandy beach for additional aquatic recreation. Private wooded sites line this peninsula. Sites 107 through 116 and the mid-50s are the most remote. With the woods and mountain views to yourself, it's hard to believe you're only half a mile from one of the White Mountains' most popular family attractions: West of the campground, Lost River Reservation features a chaotic jumble of glacially sculpted boulders on Moosilauke Brook. For a nominal fee, you can follow the river through a series of boardwalks and caves including the so-called Lemon Squeezer. West of Lost River, the Appalachian Trail crosses Route 112; a challenging day hike leads up some steep and rocky steps on the Beaver Brook Trail to the summit of Mount Moosilauke.

Open: Mid-May through Columbus Day weekend.

⑤ Hancock Campground

Location: East of Lincoln on the Kancamagus Highway in the White Mountain National Forest; Northern New Hampshire map page 168, grid e2.

Campsites, facilities: There are 56 sites, all without hookups; 35 offer easy access for trailers. Fire grills, picnic tables, vault toilets, and piped water are provided. Leashed pets are permitted.

Reservations, fees: Sites are available on a first-come, first-served basis. The fee is $12 a night.

Contact: White Mountain National Forest, Pemigewasset Ranger District, RFD 3, Box 15, Plymouth, NH 03264; (603) 536-1310.

Directions: From Interstate 93 at Lincoln, take exit 32 and travel east on the Kancamagus Highway (Route 112) for four miles to the campground.

Trip notes: A grove of hardwood trees shades these sites situated near the Pemigewasset River, which is open to fishing. A five-minute walk from the campground leads to Upper Lady's Bath, a secluded swimming hole. This calm pool of water has a rocky ledge bottom. Just a few miles east of Interstate 93, Hancock Campground is close to many White Mountain attractions including the natural rock formations of Indian Head and the Old Man of the Mountain. In winter, nearby Loon Mountain offers all levels of downhill skiing while the Lincoln Woods Visitor Center, across Route 112 from the campground, maintains eight miles of cross-country ski trails. From the center, multiuse trails lead to several points of interest, among them Black Pond with its panoramic views of the mountains, Franconia Falls, and beaver ponds.

Open: Year-round. The roads are plowed in winter.

⑤ Big Rock Campground

Location: East of Lincoln on the Kancamagus Highway in the White Mountain National Forest; Northern New Hampshire map page 168, grid e2.

Campsites, facilities: There are 28 sites for tents and RVs, all without hookups. Fire grills, picnic tables, vault toilets, and piped water are provided. Leashed pets are permitted.

Reservations, fees: Sites are available on a first-come, first-served basis. Fees are $12 a night in spring, summer, and fall, and $6 a night in winter.

Contact: White Mountain National Forest, Pemigewasset Ranger District, RFD 3, Box 15, Plymouth, NH 03264; (603) 536-1310.

Directions: From Interstate 93 at Lincoln, take exit 32 and travel east on the Kancamagus Highway (Route 112) for six miles to the campground.

Trip notes: Glacial erratics, or large boulders, were sprinkled here during the last ice age and inspired the name of this campground. Tiers of campsites are set in a hardwood forest and can serve as convenient base camps for winter and summer forays into the Whites. Big Rock is two miles east of the Lincoln Woods Visitor Center, a haven of homey hospitality, especially during the cold winter months. Eight miles of maintained cross-country ski trails start at the center, where a wood stove cranks out warmth and heats up water for hot chocolate. From the center, multiuse trails lead to several natural points of interest including Black Pond, which affords a panoramic view of the mountains, Franconia Falls, and beaver ponds housing busy or hibernating inhabitants, depending on the season.

Open: Year-round, but the roads are not plowed in the winter.

55 Russell Pond

Location: In Woodstock in the White Mountain National Forest; Northern New Hampshire map page 168, grid f2.

Campsites, facilities: There are 86 sites for tents and RVs, all without hookups. Piped water, flush toilets, metered hot showers, picnic tables, and fire rings are provided. Leashed pets are permitted.

Reservations, fees: Reservations are accepted for some sites for May through October with an $8 fee. Call the National Forest Reservation Center at (800) 280-2267. Sites are $12 a night.

Contact: White Mountain National Forest, Pemigewasset Ranger District, RFD 3, Box 15, Plymouth, NH 03264; (603) 536-1310.

Directions: From Interstate 93 north of Woodstock, take exit 31. Head east on Tri-poli Road for 1.5 miles. Turn left at Russell Pond Road and continue about two miles.

Trip notes: Russell Pond is a spring-fed pool stocked with brook and brown trout. There's a beach area for swimmers, and paddlers will have enough room to drop in a canoe. Some short trails explore the immediate area surrounding the wooded campsites, but for great hiking you should continue east on Tripoli Road to check out a bowl formed by Mounts Tripyramid, Tecumseh, and Osceola. The Mount Osceola Trail is a challenging 6.4-mile trek that climbs 2,000 vertical feet to the summit of that peak at 4,340 feet.

Open: Mid-May through mid-October.

Campsites, facilities: There are 130 sites for tents and RVs, 15 with full hookups and 70 with water and electric. Each has a table and fire ring. A dump station, rest rooms, hot showers, laundry facilities, a rec hall, pool, pavilion, and playground are provided. Courts for badminton, volleyball, and horse-shoes are available. A store sells LP gas, ice, and wood. Leashed pets are permitted.

Reservations, fees: Reservations are accepted. Sites start at $21 a night for two people. There are surcharges for hookups, air conditioners, heaters, extra campers, and guests. Seasonal rates are available.

Contact: Broken Branch Koa Kampground, P.O. Box 6, Woodstock, NH 03293; (603) 745-8008.

Directions: From Interstate 91 at exit 31 at Woodstock, travel south on Route 175 for two miles to the campground.

Trip notes: Pull up a lawn chair and look out over the Pemigewasset River from these plateau sites with mountain views. The rocky river is accessible from the campground for fishing and inner tubing. Clean modern facilities, a safe pool, and a miniature golf course cater to families with young kids. The campground is right off the highway, and both Interstate 93 and U.S. 3 lead north to North Woodstock and Lincoln, where man-made attractions are as plentiful as the surrounding wilderness of the White Mountain National Forest. In North Woodstock, Clark's Trading Post features the only trained bears in New England. In Lincoln, the Whale's Tale water park has rides, games, shows, and a petting zoo.

Open: May 1 through mid-October.

56 Broken Branch KOA Kampground

Location: South of Woodstock; Northern New Hampshire map page 168, grid f2.

57 Moose Hillock Campground

Location: North of Warren; Northern New Hampshire map page 168, grid f2.

Campsites, facilities: There are 151 sites for tents and RVs, 31 with full hook-ups, 72 with water and electric, and 48 with none. Each site has a picnic table and fire ring. Use of air conditioners and heaters is allowed. A dump station, rest rooms, hot showers, laundry facilities, a rec hall, sports field, swimming pools, and playground are provided. Courts for basketball, badminton, volleyball, and horseshoes are available. A camp store carries RV supplies, LP gas, ice, and firewood. Leashed pets are permitted.

Reservations, fees: Reservations are recommended. Sites are $23 to $26 a night per family.

Contact: Moose Hillock Campground, Route 118, Warren, NH 03279; (603) 764-5294.

Directions: From Interstate 93 at Plymouth, take exit 26. Travel northwest on Route 25 for 20 miles through the towns of Rumney, Wentworth, and Warren. Take a right onto Route 118 and continue north for one mile to the campground entrance.

Trip notes: Mount Moosilauke, the state's tenth highest peak at elevation 4,810 feet, is visible through a break in the trees on the campground duck pond, which is shaped like the United States. Sites at Moose Hillock are exceptionally private and wooded, each with their own driveway and yard area. Some spots are on the water, and the most remote sites are reserved for tenters. Batchelder Brook tumbles over rocks and forms pools on its way through the property. There's fishing and swimming in the brook, but the campground also has three swimming pools, including one with a natural rock slide, cave, and waterfall. A 200-year-old post and beam barn serves as the rec hall. Planned events abound for parents and kids including visits from the costumed character Bruce the Moose and dancing to cover bands in the barn. Trailheads for Moosilauke are within a short drive. Miles of logging roads and dirt roads offer challenging mountain biking. And yes, this is moose country, so keep your eyes peeled for the large gangly beasts.

Open: Mid-May through mid-October.

58 Scenic View Campground

Location: In Warren on the Baker River and Patch Brook; Northern New Hampshire map page 168, grid f2.

Campsites, facilities: There are 106 sites for tents and RVs, 44 with full hookups, 48 with water and electric, and 14 with none. Each site has a picnic table and fire ring. Use of air conditioners and heaters is allowed, and cable TV is available. A dump station, rest rooms, hot showers, laundry facilities, a rec hall, pool, sports field, and playground are provided. Courts for basketball, badminton, volleyball, and horseshoes are available. A camp store carries LP gas, ice, and firewood. Leashed pets are permitted.

Reservations, fees: Reservations are accepted with a prepaid deposit. Holiday weekend stays require full prepayment. Sites are $20 to $23 a night per family.

Contact: Scenic View Campground, 193AA South Main Street, Warren, NH 03279; (603) 764-9380.

Directions: From Interstate 93 at Plymouth, take exit 26. Travel northwest on Route 25 for 18 miles to the campground, just south of the Warren town center.

Trip notes: Choose from grassy, sunny sites with hookups along the brook or wilderness tent sites in the woods along the trout stream. Scenic View is in Warren, a sleepy town on the west side of the White Mountain National Forest. A mix of seasonal and vacation campers gathers here for nature programs, fishing derbies, campfires, and tournaments in the shadow of the mountains. Down the road is the Warren Fish Hatchery, which has some interpretive programs and a self-guided science center. The hatchery land is also open to hunting, and the local wildlife includes deer, fox, and coyote. Mount Moosilauke rises to the north of town, a bald, broad 4,000-footer offering sweeping views of the Whites.

Open: May 1 through October 15.

59 Swain Brook Campground

Location: On Swain Brook north of Wentworth; Northern New Hampshire map page 168, grid f 2.

Campsites, facilities: There are 75 sites for tents and RVs, some with full hookups. Each site has a picnic table and fire ring. A dump station, rest rooms, hot showers, a rec hall, pool, horseshoe pits, tetherball, a TV room, and a playground are provided. A camp store carries groceries, sporting goods, ice, and firewood. Group sites are available for tents and RVs. Leashed pets are permitted.

Reservations, fees: Reservations are recommended and require prepaid deposits. Sites are $16 to $25 a night per family.

Contact: Swain Brook Campground, P.O. Box 157, Beech Hill Road, Wentworth, NH 03282; (603) 764-5537.

Directions: From the junction of Routes 25 and 25A in Wentworth, travel north on Route 25 for half a mile to Beech Hill Road. Take a left and continue north for three-quarters of a mile to the campground entrance.

Trip notes: Swain Brook runs through this 417-acre privately owned nature preserve. Sites are natural and wooded and set near a small fishing hole, Downing Pond. In all

there are five mountain brooks on the property and over a mile of hiking trails leading to cascades, potholes, and trout habitat. Wild apple trees, berry patches, blue herons, and deer are common sights. More extensive day hikes are a few miles west of the campground on the Appalachian Trail.

Open: Early May through early November.

60 The Pastures Campground

Location: On the Connecticut River in South Orford; Northern New Hampshire map page 168, grid f1.

Campsites, facilities: There are 58 sites for tents and RVs, all with water and electric hookups. Each site has a picnic table and fire ring. A dump station, rest rooms, and hot showers are provided. You'll also find courts for basketball and horseshoes. Firewood is sold on the property. Leashed pets are permitted.

Reservations, fees: Reservations are recommended. Sites are $15 a night per family. Weekly, monthly, and seasonal rates are available.

Contact: The Pastures Campground, RR 1, Box 58, South Orford, NH 03777; (603) 353-4579.

Directions: From Interstate 91 north of White River Junction in Vermont, take exit 15 for Fairlee-Orford. Turn left onto U.S. 5 and head north for three-quarters of a mile to Route 25A. Turn right onto the green bridge, cross the Connecticut River, then turn right and head south on Route 10 for one mile to the campground.

Trip notes: Throughout the summer, campers here gather to enjoy community meals. Then they bed down for the night at campsites that line the grassy banks of the Connecticut River, which forms the boundary between Vermont and New Hampshire. Docks are provided, so campers will have a place to tie up their own boats or sit for a few hours of fishing. The river is home to numerous species of warm-water and cold-water fish; just be sure to obtain a fishing license before dropping in a line. You can't swim right at the campground, but once you get out on the water, you're free to jump in. From here, the river is navigable via canoe for 20 miles in either direction. Goods and services are available nearby in Orford.

Open: Mid-May through mid-October.

⑥ Jacobs Brook Campground

Location: On the Vermont–New Hampshire border along Jacobs Brook; Northern New Hampshire map page 168, grid f1.

Campsites, facilities: There are 75 sites for tents and RVs, 15 with full hookups, 35 with water and electric, and 25 with none. Each site has a picnic table and fireplace. Use of air conditioners and heaters is allowed. On-site facilities include a dump station, laundry, rest rooms, hot showers, a pool, and a playground. A camp store sells ice and firewood. Courts for basketball, badminton, and horseshoes are located on the property as are a sports field and hiking trails. The maximum RV length is 36 feet. Leashed pets are permitted.

Reservations, fees: Reservations are recommended. Tent sites are $16 a night, sites with water and electricity are $20, and sites with full hookups are $23 a night. Weekly, monthly, and seasonal rates are available.

Contact: Jacobs Brook Campground, P.O. Box 167, High Bridge Road, Orford, NH 03777; (603) 353-9210.

Directions: From Interstate 91 north of White River Junction in Vermont, take exit 15 for Fairlee-Orford. Turn left onto U.S. 5 and head north for three-quarters of a mile to Route 25A. Turn right onto the green bridge, cross the Connecticut River, then turn left onto Route 10 and travel north for one mile. Turn right on Archertown Road and head east for one mile to the campground entrance.

Trip notes: Shady campsites are set along Jacobs Brook, which feeds into the Connecticut River about a mile to the west, making this a good jumping-off point for those who want to embark on longer canoe and fishing outings on the river. The brook itself features several waterfalls and natural pools that make ideal swimming spots. Orford is largely an agricultural community, and the town's many farms indirectly support a sizable wild turkey population. If you come during May, don't be surprised by the hordes of turkey hunters you're likely to encounter around town. A few miles to the east the Appalachian Trail intersects Route 25. From this trailhead, Mount Cube to the south is a good destination for a day hike.

Open: May 15 through October 15.

⑥ Storrs Pond Campground

Location: North of Hanover; Northern New Hampshire map page 168, grid f1.

Campsites, facilities: There are 33 sites for tents and RVs, 15 with water and electric hookups. Each site has a picnic table, fire ring, and grill. Use of air conditioners and heaters is allowed. A dump station, laundry facilities, rest rooms, hot showers, a pool, a pavilion, and a playground are provided. Courts for basketball, badminton, tennis, volleyball, and horseshoes are on the property. Firewood can be purchased on site. Leashed pets are permitted.

Reservations, fees: Reservations are recommended between Memorial Day and Labor Day and require a nonrefundable deposit. Sites range from $7 a night (midweek, for backpackers and cyclists) to $22 a night (during weekends, for sites with water and electric hookups) in season. Off-season rates apply before Memorial Day and after Labor Day.

Contact: Storrs Pond Campground, P.O. Box 106, Hanover, NH 03755; (603) 643-2134.

Directions: From the intersection of Interstates 91 and 89 at White River Junction, Vermont, go five miles north on Interstate 91 to exit 13. Cross the Connecticut River and drive one mile east on Wheelock Street. Take a left and head north on Route 10. Turn right on Reservoir Street and head east for one mile to the campground.

Trip notes: This small but well-equipped campground operates in conjunction with a recreation center on Storrs Pond. A swimming beach is located on part of the shoreline, and fishing and nonmotorized boating are permitted outside of the swimming area. Athletic facilities, including four tennis courts, are provided on the grounds. There's also a snack bar serving ice cream, pizza, and sandwiches. Campsites are secluded, set in a mix of wooded and grassy terrain that's near the town of Hanover and just a few miles east of the Appalachian Trail. Like so much of New Hampshire, the entire area is very popular with cyclists. The state's oldest educational institution, Dartmouth College, is located in Hanover; it was chartered in 1769 by King George III. Dartmouth's art galleries, pastoral campus, and performing arts center are open to the public.

Open: Mid-May through mid-October.

63 Pine Haven Campground

Location: On the Baker River west of Rumney; Northern New Hampshire map page 168, grid f1.

Campsites, facilities: There are 88 sites for tents and RVs, 19 with full hookups, 44 with water and electric, and 25 with none. Each site has a picnic table, fire ring, and grill. Air conditioners are allowed, but heaters are prohibited. A dump station, rest rooms, hot showers, laundry facilities, a rec hall, pool, and playground are provided. Courts for basketball, badminton, shuffleboard, volleyball, and horseshoes are available. A grocery store carries LP gas, RV supplies, ice, and firewood. Leashed pets are permitted.

Reservations, fees: Reservations are accepted. Sites start at $18 a night per family. Bicycle groups receive special rates. Weekly, monthly, and seasonal rates are available on request.

Contact: Pine Haven Campground, P.O. Box 43N, Wentworth, NH 03282; (603) 786-9942, or for reservations only (800) 370-PINE/7463.

Directions: From Interstate 93 at Plymouth, take exit 26 and travel west on Route 25 toward Wentworth for 12 miles. The campground is on the left side of the road, about three-quarters of a mile north of the junction of Routes 25 and 118.

Trip notes: A pine forest envelops these sites on the Baker River. Some sites are occupied by seasonal campers who gather for group events including tournaments and dinners. Canoes may be rented at the campground for an easy to moderate paddle on the Saco River from West Rumney to Plymouth. One of the region's prettiest lakes lies northeast of the campground. Stinson Lake is ringed by perky mountains and has a public boat launch at its southern end. The Stinson Mountain Trail is an old logging road that leaves from south of the lake to a 2,900-foot summit affording views of the region.

Open: May 15 through October 15.

64 Baker River Campground

Location: On the Baker River in Rumney; Northern New Hampshire map page 168, grid f2.

Campsites, facilities: There are 40 sites for tents and RVs, some with full hookups. Each site has a picnic table and fire ring. A dump station, rest rooms, hot showers, a rec hall, and a playground are provided. Ice and firewood are sold on the property. Leashed pets are permitted.

Reservations, fees: Reservations are accepted. Sites start at $14 a night per family. Weekly, monthly, and seasonal rates are available on request.

Contact: Baker River Campground, 56 Campground Road, Rumney, NH 03266; May through October 14: (603) 786-9707, October 15 through April: (813) 755-5222.

Directions: From Interstate 93 at Plymouth, take exit 26 and head west on Route 25 for about three miles to Smith Bridge Road. Cross the Baker River on the Smith Bridge, then turn left on Quincy Road. The campground is two miles ahead on the left.

Trip notes: Forty large wooded sites are strung along the shoreline of the Baker River. Fish for trout, paddle Class II rapids, float downriver in an inner tube, or cool off at the sandy beach on this clear mountain stream. For canoeists, a put-in is located in West Rumney below the bridge. Canoes and inner tubes may be rented at the campground. A 14-mile paddle to Plymouth

passes under a covered bridge and gives you a view of Stinson Mountain. The campground lies across the river from Polar Caves Park, a series of granite caves and passages formed 50,000 years ago when blocks of granite cracked and loosened from Hawks Cliff during a glacial thaw; there is an admission charge to take the self-guided tour of the caves. Ducks and fallow deer are just some of the local wildlife you might see in this area.

Open: Mid-May through Labor Day.

65 Plymouth Sands Campground

Location: On the Baker River in Plymouth; Northern New Hampshire map page 168, grid f2.

Campsites, facilities: There are 75 sites for tents and RVs, some with full hookups. Each site has a picnic table and fire ring. A dump station, rest rooms, hot showers, and a playground are provided, and a camp store sells ice, firewood, and snacks. The maximum RV length is 26 feet. Leashed pets are permitted.

Reservations, fees: Reservations are accepted. Sites are $13 to $16 a night per family. Weekly and seasonal rates are available on request.

Contact: Plymouth Sands Campground, RR 1, Box 3172, Plymouth, NH 03264; (603) 536-2605 in the summer, or (603) 352-1856 in the winter.

Directions: From Interstate 93 at Plymouth, take exit 26 and head west on Route 25 for a short distance, then follow U.S. 3 north for one-tenth mile to Fairground Road. Turn left and head west on Fairground for three miles to the campground entrance on the left (south) side, just past the junction with Smith Bridge Road.

Trip notes: A sandy beach on the Baker River is the center of action at this campground. You just need an inner tube to take advantage of the cooling currents. This clear mountain stream also provides healthy habitat for trout. All but beginner canoeists can enjoy Class II paddling on the Baker River between West Rumney and Plymouth. The waterway offers mountain views and passes beneath a covered bridge just before you reach Plymouth. To get the lay of the land, head up Plymouth Mountain. From the trailhead located to the south of here off Route 25 in Hebron, the Plymouth Mountain Trail ascends the 2,187-foot summit on a moderate six-mile walk through protected wilderness.

Open: Memorial Day through Labor Day.

⑥⑥ Pemi River Campground

Location: On the Pemigewasset River in Campton; Northern New Hampshire map page 168, grid f2.

Campsites, facilities: There are 60 sites for tents and RVs, 34 with water and electric hookups. Each site has a table and fireplace. A dump station, rest rooms, hot showers, a game room, and a playground are provided. Sports facilities include a soccer field, a court for badminton and volleyball, horseshoe pits, and inner tube and kayak rentals. A small store carries ice and firewood. Leashed pets are permitted.

Reservations, fees: Reservations are accepted. Sites start at $16 a night per family. Weekly, monthly, and seasonal rates are available.

Contact: Pemi River Campground, RFD 1, Box 926, Campton, NH 03223; (603) 726-7015 in the summer, or (603) 625-2879 in the winter.

Directions: From Interstate 93 at exit 29

for Campton-Thornton, head north on U.S. 3 for several yards to the campground entrance on the right side of the road.

Trip notes: Tenters will find wooded sites on the Pemigewasset River while RVers are accommodated in grassy, shaded pull-throughs. The "Pemi" is the main attraction here, and the campground rents kayaks, canoes, and inner tubes to suit any camper's preferred style of exploration. The White Mountain National Forest lies to the north, east, and west of the campground with endless options for short, long, and overnight hikes.

Open: May 15 through October 15.

⑥⑦ Branch Brook Four Season Campground

Location: On the Pemigewasset River in West Campton; Northern New Hampshire map page 168, grid f2.

Campsites, facilities: There are 150 sites for tents and RVs, 46 with full hookups, 59 with water and electric, and 45 with none. Each site has a picnic table and fire ring. A dump station, rest rooms, hot showers, laundry facilities, a rec hall, and a playground are provided. Courts for basketball, badminton, volleyball, and horseshoes are available. A small grocery store carries LP gas, RV supplies, ice, and firewood. RV storage and rental RVs are available. Leashed pets are permitted.

Reservations, fees: Reservations are recommended Memorial Day through Labor Day and require a prepaid deposit. Holiday weekend reservations must be prepaid in full. Sites are $18 to $22 a night per family. Weekly, monthly, and seasonal rates are available.

Contact: Branch Brook Four Season Campground, P.O. Box 390, Campton, NH 03223; (603) 726-7001.

Directions: From Interstate 93 in Campton at exit 28, travel west on Route 49 for half a mile to the campground.

Trip notes: On a typical hot day, the Pemigewasset River is full of campers floating on inner tubes to keep cool. Branch Brook intersects the campground, and a small five-acre pond on the brook is open to fishing. Full-hookup RV sites are set in a pine-forested area accessible via a road or on a pretty footpath that crosses the brook on a covered bridge. A second area offers grassy meadow sites on the brook, while yet another section is in the woods near the shores of the "Pemi."

There's a swimming beach on the river, and canoes may be rented at the campground for those who want to explore the waterway. The White Mountain National Forest lies to the north, east, and west of the campground offering myriad options for short, long, and overnight hikes.

Open: May 1 through late October, but seasonal sites are open year-round.

⑥⑧ Campton Campground

Location: In the White Mountain National Forest north of Campton Pond; Northern New Hampshire map page 168, grid f2.

Campsites, facilities: There are 58 sites for tents and RVs up to 30 feet long, all without hookups. Piped water, metered hot showers, fire rings, tables, and a playing field are provided. A small store sells ice and firewood. Across Route 49 there are three group sites. Leashed pets are permitted.

Reservations, fees: Reservations are recommended. Call the National Forest Reservation Center at (800) 280-2267. Sites are $14 a night per family. Group rates range from $15 to $80 for up to 100 people.

Contact: White Mountain National Forest, Pemigewasset Ranger District, RFD 3, Box 15, Plymouth, NH 03264; (603) 536-1310.

Directions: From Interstate 93 at Campton, take exit 28 and travel two miles east on Route 49 to the campground entrance.

Trip notes: Towering white pines dominate this heavily wooded campground at the westerly edge of the White Mountain National Forest. Interpretive programs are offered on Saturday evenings in the summer, and a playing field provides room for a variety of team sports. Stores and restaurants are close by in Waterville Valley and Campton. The Mad River flows through the campground and is open to fishing, swimming, and boating. Many hiking trails can be accessed in the vicinity, including the wilderness areas of the Sandwich Range to the east. A short loop is just northeast of the campground off Mad River Road. Dickey and Welch Mountains are accessible on this moderate 4.4-mile round-trip hike; there's a parking area on Orris Road.

Open: Mid-May through early September, but the group sites are open year-round.

⑥⑨ Goose Hollow Campground

Location: East of Campton; Northern New Hampshire map page 168, grid f2.

Campsites, facilities: There are 165 sites for tents and RVs, 48 with full hookups, 17 with water and electric, and 100 with none. Each site has a picnic table and fire ring. Use of air conditioners and heaters is allowed. A dump station, rest rooms, hot showers, a pool, and a rec hall are provided. Courts for basketball, volleyball, and horseshoes are also on the property. Ice is available at the campground. Leashed pets are permitted.

Reservations, fees: Reservations are recommended. Sites are $10 to $19 a night for two people.

Contact: Goose Hollow Campground, P.O. Box 292, Route 149, Waterville Valley, NH 03215; (603) 726-2000.

Directions: From Interstate 93 at Campton, take exit 28 and travel 3.5 miles east on Route 49 to the campground entrance.

Trip notes: Brook and rainbow trout are your neighbors at these campsites near and on the state-stocked Mad River. Most sites are set in an open grassy meadow by the river. Trees line the edge of the campground. A swim in the campground pool will feel especially good after a day spent exploring the mountainous countryside. One scenic drive is just to the east of the campground: Sandwich Notch Road passes through Sandwich Notch. Near the top of the notch are trailheads for hikes to Guinea Pond and Black Mountain. The road continues southeast to Center Sandwich and the northern reaches of the Lakes Region.

Open: Year-round.

⑦⓪ Waterville Campground

Location: South of Waterville Valley in the White Mountain National Forest; Northern New Hampshire map page 168, grid f3.

Campsites, facilities: There are 27 sites for tents and RVs up to 22 feet long, all without hookups. Fire grills, picnic tables, piped water, and vault toilets are provided. The campground is across the street from a convenience store and a gas station. Leashed pets are permitted.

Reservations, fees: Most sites are available on a first-come, first-served basis, but reservations are accepted for a few sites. Call the National Forest Reservation Center at (800) 280-2267. Campsites are $12 a night per family.

Contact: White Mountain National Forest, Pemigewasset Ranger District, RFD 3, Box 15, Plymouth, NH 03264; (603) 536-1310.

Location: From Interstate 93 at Campton, take exit 28 and travel northeast on Route 49 for nine miles. Turn left on Forest Service Road 30 and continue a quarter mile to the campground.

Trip notes: A scenic bowl formed by Mounts Tecumseh, Osceola, Kancamagus, Tripyramid, and Sandwich Dome cradles these wooded campsites near the town of Waterville Valley and the ski resort of the same name. The Mad River flows by the campground and is open to fishing and boating. Multiuse trails for biking, hiking, cross-country skiing, and horseback riding cut through the valley. In spring, summer, and fall, the biggest attraction is the miles of hiking trails that traverse the Sandwich Range Wilderness, all accessible within a quarter mile of here. One 1.2-mile hike starts across the road from the campground entrance and leads to Fletcher's Cascades, a beautiful waterfall. Nearby are golf courses, shopping, and the Waterville Valley Alpine Ski Center. These sites are open in the winter, but campers must hike in when the roads are not cleared of snow.

Open: Year-round, but roads are not plowed in winter.

⑦① Bethel Woods Campground

Location: Near Little Squam Lake; Northern New Hampshire map page 168, grid f2.

Campsites, facilities: There are 95 sites for tents and RVs, 50 with water and electric hookups. Each site has a picnic table and fire ring. Use of air conditioners and heaters is allowed. A dump station, laundry facilities, rest rooms, hot showers, a rec hall, pool, and playground are provided. A small grocery store sells RV supplies, LP gas, ice, and firewood. Courts for basketball, badminton, volleyball, and horseshoes are located on the property. A gate controls traffic at the campground entrance. The maximum RV length is 35 feet. Leashed pets are permitted.

Reservations, fees: Reservations are recommended at all times. Sites start at $18 a night for two people.

Contact: Bethel Woods Campground, P.O. Box 201, Holderness, NH 03245; (603) 279-6266.

Directions: From Interstate 93 at Ashland, take exit 24. Travel east on U.S. 3/Route 25 for four miles to the campground entrance on the left (north) side of the road.

Trip notes: Though many seasonal campers have claimed these natural wooded sites close to the recreational offerings of the Lakes Region, Bethel Woods does have room for overnight campers; just be sure to call ahead. Squam Lake and Little Squam Lake provide access to powerboating, fishing, and canoeing within a mile or two radius, but it's also possible to have water-based fun right at the campground. A pool, sauna, and whirlpool complex is complemented by a spacious sundeck. Your vehicle can get in on the wet action with Bethel Woods' RV steam wash, part of a full-service RV repair shop next to the campground.

Putters will find a campground green where they can practice their shots before teeing off at the White Mountain Country Club, an 18-hole public golf course to the north in Ashland. Church services are another on-site amenity. For an educational family day trip, try the Science Center of New Hampshire in Holderness. Using hands-on exhibits, games, and puzzles, staff members teach visitors about native New Hampshire plants and animals. It includes a 200-acre wildlife sanctuary and a short walking trail that leads past black bear, white-tailed deer, owls, foxes, otters, and bald eagles living in natural enclosures. The facility hosts field trips, courses, and lectures as well as a regularly scheduled natural history cruise on Squam Lake.

Open: May 15 through October 15.

72 Squam Lakes Camp Resort

Location: On Little Squam Lake; Northern New Hampshire map page 168, grid f3.

Campsites, facilities: There are 119 sites for tents and RVs, 66 with full hookups, 41 with water and electric, and 12 with none. Each site has a picnic table, fire ring, and grill. A dump station, laundry facilities, rest rooms, hot showers, a rec hall, pool, and playground are provided. Leashed pets are permitted.

Reservations, fees: Reservations are recommended and require a deposit. Sites are $18 to $26 a night for two people.

Contact: Squam Lakes Camp Resort, RFD 1, Box 42, Ashland, NH 03217; (603) 968-7227.

Directions: From the junction of Routes 113 and U.S. 3/Route 25 in Holderness, travel half a mile southeast on U.S. 3/Route 25 to the campground entrance.

Trip notes: Squam Lakes Camp Resort is located at Lakeside Farm on Little Squam Lake. In addition to shaded campsites on a hill above the shore, the facility includes a restaurant, ice cream shop, and full-service marina. Bring your own boat or use one of the rental canoes, motorboats, or pontoon boats to explore public islands, secluded coves, and sandy beaches. This is a four-season resort, and amenities include a heated pool, an outdoor Jacuzzi with a sprawling sundeck, and a lodge with an exercise room, an indoor Jacuzzi, a billiard room, and a big-screen TV. To the northeast lies Squam Lake, the state's second largest body of water; it's famous as the setting for the Hollywood film *On Golden Pond*. Loons are the unofficial mascot of the Squam Lakes, and visitors are asked to take special care not to disturb nests or young families. For a spectacular view of the entire Lakes Region, head north from Holderness on Route 113 for about four miles to the Old Bridle Path Trailhead. From there, an easy 1.8-mile hike ascends 1,260-foot West Rattlesnake Mountain.

Open: Year-round.

⑦ Passaconaway Campground

Location: On the Kancamagus Highway in the White Mountain National Forest; Northern New Hampshire map page 168, grid e3.

Campsites, facilities: There are 33 sites for tents or trailers with no hookups. Fire grills, tables, vault toilets, and piped water are provided. Leashed pets are permitted.

Reservations, fees: Sites are available on a first-come, first-served basis. The fee is $12 a night.

Contact: White Mountain National Forest, Saco Ranger Station, 33 Kancamagus Highway, Conway, NH 03818; (603) 447-5448.

Directions: From the junction of Routes 16 and 112 in Conway, travel 16 miles west on the Kancamagus Highway (Route 112).

Trip notes: Directly across the Kancamagus Highway from the Potash Mountain Trail, Passaconaway Campground offers access to some of the best hiking terrain in the southern reaches of the White Mountain National Forest. A covered picnic pavilion at the site is surrounded by balsam and white pine trees.

Open: May through October.

⑦ Jigger Johnson Campground

Location: On the Kancamagus Highway in the White Mountain National Forest; Northern New Hampshire map page 168, grid e3.

Campsites, facilities: There are 75 sites for tents or trailers with no hookups. Fire grills, tables, flush toilets, and piped water are provided. Leashed pets are permitted.

Reservations, fees: Sites are available on a first-come, first-served basis. The fee is $12 a night.

Contact: White Mountain National Forest, Saco Ranger Station, 33 Kancamagus Highway, Conway, NH 03818; (603) 447-5448.

Directions: From the junction of Routes 16 and 112 in Conway, travel 12.5 miles west on the Kancamagus Highway (Route 112).

Trip notes: Named for an old logging boss, Jigger Johnson is set in a dense white pine forest near the historic Russell-Colbath House, a restored homestead from 1830. Interpretive talks are offered during the summer months.

Open: May through October.

⑦ Covered Bridge Campground

Location: West of Conway in the White Mountain National Forest; Northern New Hampshire map page 168, grid e3.

Campsites, facilities: There are 49 sites for tents or small trailers with no hookups.

Fire grills, picnic tables, vault toilets, and piped water are provided. Leashed pets are permitted.

Reservations, fees: Reservations are necessary for 20 sites located directly on the Swift River. Call the National Forest Reservation Center at (800) 280-2267. For each reservation, an $8 fee is charged. Sites are $12 a night.

Contact: White Mountain National Forest, Saco Ranger Station, 33 Kancamagus Highway, Conway, NH 03818; (603) 447-5448.

Directions: From the junction of Routes 16 and 112 in Conway, travel six miles west on the Kancamagus Highway (Route 112). Signs will lead you over a bridge across the Swift River and into the campground.

Trip notes: To reach the campground, you must drive over the 1858 Albany Covered Bridge, hence the name. Sites are set in a white pine forest nestled between the base of a granite cliff and the aptly named Swift River, a good trout stream. You'll find a fishing pier within a short walk of here. The campground is located off a Forest Service road, which makes a challenging mountain biking route up to and over Bear Notch and into Bartlett.

Open: May through October.

76 Blackberry Crossing

Location: On the Kancamagus Highway west of Conway in the White Mountain National Forest; Northern New Hampshire map page 168, grid e3.

Campsites, facilities: There are 26 sites for tents or trailers with no hookups. Fire grills, tables, and vault toilets are provided. Piped water is available in spring, summer, and fall. Leashed pets are permitted.

Reservations, fees: Sites are available on a first-come, first-served basis. The fee

is $12 a night from May through October; there is no fee in winter, when there are no services.

Contact: White Mountain National Forest, Saco Ranger Station, 33 Kancamagus Highway, Conway, NH 03818; (603) 447-5448.

Directions: From the junction of Routes 16 and 112 in Conway, travel six miles west on the Kancamagus Highway (Route 112) to the campground entrance on the left (south) side of the road.

Trip notes: These wooded sites are large and private. Located at the southwest edge of the White Mountain National Forest, Blackberry Crossing is close to wilderness hiking and biking as well as scenic byways to the north and south. Members of Franklin Roosevelt's Civilian Conservation Corps "Tree Army" originally settled this site. In 1941, 200 men lived here in military camp fashion while they worked on various projects in the White Mountains. Two immense stone chimneys remain from the headquarters and rec hall buildings; now they serve campers as grand outdoor fireplaces.

Open: Year-round, with limited service after mid-October.

77 Saco River Camping Area

Location: On the Saco River north of Conway; Northern New Hampshire map page 168, grid e4.

Campsites, facilities: There are 140 sites for tents and RVs, 71 with full hookups and 67 with water and electric. Each site has a picnic table, fire ring, and grill. Use of air conditioners is allowed. A dump station, rest rooms, hot showers, laundry facilities, a rec hall, sports field, and playground are provided. Courts for basketball, badminton, shuffleboard, volleyball, and horseshoes are available. Group sites are available for tents and RVs. A camp store carries LP gas, RV supplies, ice, and firewood. A guarded gate controls traffic at the campground entrance. Leashed pets are permitted.

Reservations, fees: Reservations are recommended May through October. A prepaid nonrefundable deposit equal to one night's stay is required for a reservation. Sites are $17 to $21 a night per family depending on services and proximity to the river.

Contact: Saco River Camping Area, P.O. Box 546N, Route 16, North Conway, NH 03860; (603) 356-3360.

Directions: From the southern junction of Route 16 and U.S. 302 north of Conway, travel a quarter mile south on Route 16/302 to the campground entrance on the right (west) side of the road.

Trip notes: Set in the thick of the North Conway factory outlet shopping district, these campsites allow consumers to enjoy mountain views while they spend. Route 16 is commercially developed here with many hotels, restaurants, and strip malls. Dense stands of trees buffer the campsites from the busy road. Sites 29 through 56 are right on the Saco River, a good trout stream, though sites 29 through 31 abut the sandy beach that's open to all campers. Most spots are roomy and shaded and can handle any size RV. From here you can walk to eateries, grocery stores, a movie theater, and shops. On weekends and holidays, a staff recreation director organizes bonfires, games, and theme events. Two miles north, the North Conway Country Club has a public golf course; there's also a racquet club nearby.

Canoes may be rented at the campground, and from here the Saco River offers 12 miles of quiet water to paddle to the Maine border. In North Conway, the Conway Scenic Railroad conducts one-hour rides through Crawford Notch and the Conway-Bartlett

Valley. For lake swimming in breathtaking surroundings, head north to Echo Lake State Park in North Conway. With White Horse Ledge in the background, you can swim in the clear lake and use the beach for a nominal fee. Hiking trails lead to the top of the cliff; White Horse and neighboring Cathedral Ledge are heavily used rock climbing routes.

Open: May 1 through October 15.

⑦⑧ The Beach Camping Area

Location: On the Saco River north of Conway; Northern New Hampshire map page 168, grid e4.

Campsites, facilities: There are 120 sites for tents and RVs, 87 with full hookups, 21 with water and electric, and 12 with none. Each site has a picnic table, fire ring, and grill. Use of air conditioners and heaters is allowed. A dump station, rest rooms, hot showers, laundry facilities, a rec hall, pavilion, and playground are provided. Courts for basketball, badminton, shuffleboard, volleyball, and horseshoes are available. A camp store carries RV supplies, ice, and firewood. Leashed pets are permitted.

Reservations, fees: Reservations are recommended July through Columbus Day and are accepted after April 1. All reservations must be accompanied by a $30 deposit per weekend. Per family, tent sites with water and electricity are $18 a night, and RV sites with full hookups are $21 a night. Waterfront sites cost $2 extra.

Contact: The Beach Camping Area, P.O. Box 1007, Conway, NH 03818; (603) 447-2723.

Directions: From Conway, travel north on Route 16 for 1.5 miles to the campground entrance on the left (west) side of the road.

Trip notes: Aptly named, this campground on the eastern edge of the White Mountain National Forest has a gigantic sandy beach on the Saco River. About a third of the sites are right beside the water, and many have mountain views. The Saco is clean and refreshing, a great place to swim or fish for trout. Trees, a mix of hardwoods and softwoods, provide shade. The best way to explore the Saco is via canoe. You may bring your own or rent one nearby. It's a quiet-water paddle from here to Maine, and you'll pass under two covered bridges just south of the campground in Conway Village. On weekends, organized activities at the campground range from square dances to bonfires. Numerous day hikes are accessible a short drive west in the national forest.

Open: Mid-May through mid-October.

---

⑦⑨ Eastern Slope Camping Area

Location: On the Saco River in Conway; Northern New Hampshire map page 168, grid e4.

Campsites, facilities: There are 260 sites for tents and RVs, 32 with full hookups and 228 with water and electric. Each site has a sheltered picnic table and fire ring. A dump station, rest rooms, hot showers, a rec hall, and a playground are provided. Courts for badminton, volleyball, and horseshoes are available. A grocery store carries ice and firewood. Pets are allowed after Labor Day.

Reservations, fees: Reservations are recommended and require a nonrefundable deposit. Sites start at $20 a night per family. Seasonal rates are available on request.

Contact: Eastern Slope Camping Area, P.O. Box 1127, Conway, NH 03818; (603) 447-5092.

Directions: From Conway travel one mile

north on Route 16 to the campground entrance on the left (west) side of the road.

Trip notes: The Saco River loops around this campground full of wooded sites—many set right beside the river—with mountain views. Each site has a sheltered picnic table. Two large beaches are available for swimming and sunbathing, and canoeists can take long and short paddles on the Saco River; it's quiet water from this point into Maine. Two covered bridges are just south of the campground: the Saco River bridge, which was built in 1890, and the Swift River bridge, which dates back just as far and was completely restored in 1991. From Conway, drive west on the Kancamagus Highway, New England's only national forest scenic byway. The paved road rises to 3,000 feet and overlooks falls, notches, and valleys. Numerous day hikes and picnic areas are marked along the roadway. At the junction of Route 112 (the "Kanc") and Route 16, the Saco Ranger Station has all the information you need to take advantage of the national forest, and most of it is free.

Open: Late May through mid-October.

---

⑧⓪ Pine Knoll Campground and RV Resort

Location: On the north shore of Iona Lake in Albany; Northern New Hampshire map page 168, grid f4.

Campsites, facilities: There are 175 sites for tents and RVs, 40 with full hookups and 135 with water and electric. Each site has a picnic table and fire ring. Use of air conditioners and heaters is allowed, and phone hookups are available. A dump station, rest rooms, hot showers, laundry facilities, a rec hall, sports field, and playground are provided. Courts for basketball, badminton, volleyball, and horseshoes are available. A camp store carries ice and firewood. A guarded gate controls traffic at the entrance. Leashed pets are permitted.

Reservations, fees: Reservations are accepted. Per family, tent sites are $14 a night; sites with full hookups are $18 a night. There are surcharges for air conditioners, extra kids, and extra tents.

Contact: Pine Knoll Campground and RV Resort, Route 16, Conway, NH 03818; (603) 447-3131.

Directions: From the village of Conway, travel four miles south on Route 16 to the campground entrance on the left.

Trip notes: Iona Lake is surrounded by oak and pine trees and is a haven for smallmouth bass, pickerel, horned pout, and trout. Some of these large wooded sites are right on the lake, while others are set back a bit from the water on grassy, more open plots. Swimmers have a huge sandy beach at their disposal, and nonmotorized boats can be launched at the campground. Canoes and rowboats are available for rent. To the southeast at Madison Boulder Natural Area the largest known glacial erratic in North America stands 23 feet high and 83 feet long. The granite enormity has an estimated weight of 7,650 tons. To the north, the Kancamagus Highway links Conway and Lincoln on a 34.5-mile route featuring dramatic vistas from 3,000 feet. Make the return trip on a loop via U.S. 302 to the north through more gaps and valleys, but watch for moose if you're driving at night.

Open: Year-round.

⑧ White Ledge

Location: South of Conway in the White Mountain National Forest; Northern New Hampshire map page 168, grid f4.

Campsites, facilities: There are 28 sites for tents or trailers with no hookups. Fire grills, tables, vault toilets, and piped water are provided. Leashed pets are permitted.

Reservations, fees: Certain sites may be reserved from May through October. Call the National Forest Reservation Center at (800) 280-2267. For each reservation, an $8 fee is charged. Sites are $10 a night.

Contact: White Mountain National Forest, Saco Ranger Station, 33 Kancamagus Highway, Conway, NH 03818; (603) 447-5448.

Directions: From Conway, travel five miles south on Route 16. The campground entrance is on the right (west) side of the road.

Trip notes: Though these campsites are wooded, there isn't much of a buffer between busy Route 16 and the campground. Still, this is a popular base camp for hikers who come to make overnight treks into the White Mountains, as several trails lead from here into the Mount Chocorua Scenic Area.

Open: Mid-May through mid-October.

⑧ Cove Camping Area

Location: On the west shore of Conway Lake; Northern New Hampshire map page 168, grid f4.

Campsites, facilities: There are 83 sites for tents and RVs up to 30 feet long, 5 with full hookups, 38 with water and electric, and 40 with none. Each site has a picnic table and fire ring. A dump station, rest rooms, hot showers, laundry facilities, a rec hall, pavilion, horseshoe pits, two boat ramps, and a playground are provided. A camp store carries ice and firewood. Rental tents are available. Dogs are allowed after Labor Day.

Reservations, fees: Reservations require a prepaid deposit. Sites are $19 to $31 a night for two adults with surcharges for children, guests, air conditioners, heaters, and dock space.

Contact: Cove Camping Area, P.O. Box 778, Conway, NH 03818; (603) 447-6734.

Directions: From the junction of Routes 16 and 113 in Conway, travel one mile east on Route 113. Turn right on Stark Road and head south for 1.75 miles. Make a left onto Cove Road and continue one mile to the campground.

Trip notes: Laughing loons may rouse you in the morning at these heavily wooded lakeside sites. Set on 1,300-acre Conway Lake, this campground is well away from the hustle and bustle of commercial North Conway. Mountain views, abundant wildlife, and great fishing are the spoils at this location. Canoeing is the best way to explore the lake's islands, marshy inlets, and wooded shoreline. Winds can get ornery on this large body of water, so be aware weather-wise. Piscine residents include rainbow trout, salmon, pickerel, horned pout, and smallmouth bass. There are two boat ramps and a dock in case you bring your own vessel; if not, canoes and rowboats are for rent at the campground.

Open: Late May through mid-October.

83 Chocorua Camping Village

Location: On Moores Pond in Chocorua; Northern New Hampshire map page 168, grid f4.

Campsites, facilities: There are 45 sites for tents and RVs, most with water and electric hookups. Each site has a picnic table and fire ring. A dump station, laundry facilities, rest rooms, hot showers, a rec hall, and a playground are provided. A camp store sells LP gas, ice, and firewood. Leashed pets are permitted.

Reservations, fees: Reservations are recommended. Sites start at $20 a night per family for stays of less than three days; for stays of three or more days, sites start at $16 a night per family.

Contact: Chocorua Camping Village, P.O. Box 118N, West Ossipee, NH 03890; (603) 323-8563 or (800) 462-2426.

Directions: From the northern junction of Routes 16 and 25 in West Ossipee, travel three miles north on Route 16 to the campground entrance on the right (east) side of the road.

Trip notes: Two hundred wooded acres on the north shore of Moores Pond provide a scenic backdrop to Chocorua Camping Village. Sites are spacious, private, and set either beside or near the pond. Boats and canoes are available for rent at the campground, and there's a designated swimming area with a sandy beach. Walkers will find little-used nature trails in the surrounding woodlands. For good cold-water fishing, try the Chocorua River north of the campground or White Lake State Park across Route 16 to the south. Not only does White Lake have a boat launch, it's also the site of a National Natural Landmark: a stand of mature pitch pine covers 72 acres, some trees with diameters measuring up to two feet. Such an uncut area is a rare occurrence in the northeast.

Open: Year-round.

84 Foothills Campground

Location: North of White Lake State Park; Northern New Hampshire map page 168, grid f4.

Campsites, facilities: There are 65 sites for tents and RVs, 53 with water and electric hookups. Each site has a picnic table and fire ring. A dump station, rest rooms, hot showers, a pavilion, pool, horseshoe pits, a basketball court, and a playground are provided. A small grocery store sells ice, LP gas, and firewood. The maximum RV length is 33 feet. Leashed pets are permitted.

Reservations, fees: Reservations are accepted. Sites range from $16 to $18 a night per family.

Contact: Foothills Campground, P.O. Box 128, Tamworth, NH 03886; (603) 323-8322.

Directions: From the northern junction of Routes 16 and 25 in West Ossipee, travel 1.5 miles north on Route 16 to the campground on the left (west) side of the road.

Trip notes: Here's another camping option right off busy Route 16. Tall pines tower over these sites located north of White Lake State Park. A small pond on the property is open to fishing, but more adventuresome anglers will want to check out White Lake to the south. There's a pool on site for those who want to cool off on hot summer days as well as many lakes and rivers for natural swimming. Several trails explore the surrounding pine forest; for longer treks, head north to Hemenway State Forest and hike through groves of white pines. A 125-acre section of the forest that holds 150-year-old conifers is protected as the Big Pines Natural Area. In nearby Tamworth you'll find the state's oldest summer theater, the Barnstormers. They stage a different comedy, musical, or mystery every week in July and August.

Open: Mid-May through mid-October.

85 Tamworth Camping Area

Location: On the Swift River in Tamworth; Northern New Hampshire map page 168, grid f4.

Campsites, facilities: There are 100 sites for tents and RVs, 46 with full hookups, 36 with water and electric, and 18 with none. Each site has a picnic table, fire ring, and grill. Use of air conditioners and heaters is allowed. A dump station, laundry facilities, rest rooms, hot showers, a rec hall, and a playground are provided. A small grocery store sells LP gas, RV supplies, ice, and firewood. Off-season RV storage is available. Courts for basketball, shuffleboard, badminton, volleyball, and horseshoes are located on the property. Traffic is controlled by an entry gate. Leashed pets are permitted.

Reservations, fees: Reservations are recommended, especially during holiday weekends and in July and August. A 50 percent deposit is required for all reservations, and full prepayment is required on three-day holiday weekends. Riverfront sites start at $26 a night per family, and off-river sites range from $16 a night for no hookups to $23 a night for full hookups.

Contact: Tamworth Camping Area, P.O. Box 99, Tamworth, NH 03886; (603) 323-8031.

Directions: From the northern junction of Routes 16 and 25 in West Ossipee, go north on Route 16 for three-quarters of a mile. Turn left on Depot Road and head west for three miles to the campground entrance.

Trip notes: Private campsites are set in a woodsy meadow on or near the Swift River. A sandy beach is available for swimming, but many riverside sites come with their own individual small beaches. Popular pursuits include trout fishing and tubing on the river. Kids can feed and visit with sheep, lambs, and goats at the campground's petting zoo. There are open areas for group camping. Numerous sites are rented by seasonal campers who join together on weekends for parades, dances, pig roasts, and tournaments. In the winter, snowmobilers and cross-country skiers can head to nearby White Lake State Park; the state snowmobile corridor (running parallel to Route 16) is also not too far to the east.

Open: Year-round.

86 White Lake State Park

Location: On White Lake in West Ossipee; Northern New Hampshire map page 168, grid f4.

Campsites, facilities: There are 200 sites for tents and RVs, all without hookups. Each site has a picnic table, and some are also equipped with fire rings. Rest rooms and a playground are provided. A camp store sells ice and firewood. The maximum RV length is 30 feet. No pets are allowed.

Reservations, fees: For reservations, call the New Hampshire Division of Parks and Recreation (see phone number below) on weekdays between 8:30 A.M. and 3:30 P.M. from January through August. Sites are $14 to $20 a night per family.

Contact: White Lake State Park, P.O. Box 41, West Ossipee, NH 03890; (603) 323-7350. New Hampshire Division of Parks and Recreation, (603) 271-3628.

Directions: From the northern junction of Routes 16 and 25 in West Ossipee, travel north on Route 16 for one mile to the campground entrance on the left (west) side of the road.

Trip notes: The wooded sites here in the foothills of the White Mountains are linked by dirt and paved roads. Many campsites are right on the shore of pristine White Lake. Trolling motors are allowed on the water, and canoes may be rented at the park. Swimming, however, is the main attraction—the park maintains a clean, sandy beach. There's also good trout fishing in these waters. Hiking trails explore the surrounding forest and the White Lake Pitch Pine Area, a National Natural Landmark;

this stand of native pine covers 72 acres and includes several trees with trunk diameters of nearly two feet. White Lake is one of the most popular state park campgrounds; to snag a waterfront site you must reserve very early in the year.

Open: Mid-May through mid-October.

87 Bearcamp River Campground

Location: On the Bearcamp River; Northern New Hampshire map page 168, grid f4.

Campsites, facilities: There are 68 sites for tents and RVs, most with water and electric hookups. Each site has a picnic table and fire ring. A dump station, rest rooms, hot showers, a rec hall, and a playground are provided. Courts for basketball, badminton, volleyball, and horseshoes are also on the property. Supplies can be purchased in West Ossipee and Center Ossipee. Leashed pets are permitted.

Reservations, fees: Reservations are accepted. Tent sites away from the water start at $15 a night per family, and waterfront tent sites start at $17 a night. Waterfront sites with RV hookups are $19 a night per family. Seasonal rates are available.

Contact: Bearcamp River Campground, P.O. Box 104, West Ossipee, NH 03890; (603) 539-4898.

Directions: From the southern junction of Routes 16 and 25 at Center Ossipee, travel northwest on Route 16 for 3.5 miles to Newman Drew Road. Turn left (west) and enter the campground on the right. It's next to Gitchee Gumee Campground.

Trip notes: Nearly half of these large sites are located on the Bearcamp River, a clear mountain stream. Towering hemlocks, pines, and spruce trees shade the campground. An easy two-hour paddle downriver brings canoeists to Ossipee Lake to the south; boats may be rented at the campground. Trout inhabit the Bearcamp River, and many ponds and lakes in the area offer remote spots for warm-water and cold-water fishing. All are easily explored in a cartop boat. The Mount Whittier Waterslide—where you can hop into a bumper boat if that's your preference—is located near the campground. For hiking, the Mount Whittier summit lies just to the west of here and can be reached in an easy to moderate hike. Many seasonal campers roost at Bearcamp, thus reservations are strongly suggested.

Open: Year-round, but winter sites are available for seasonal campers only.

88 Gitchee Gumee Campground

Location: On the Bearcamp River in West Ossipee; Northern New Hampshire map page 168, grid f4.

Campsites, facilities: There are 144 sites for tents and RVs, most with water and electric hookups. Each site has a table and fire ring. A dump station, laundry facilities, rest rooms, hot showers, a rec hall, playground, snack bar, and game room are provided. Firewood, LP gas, and ice are sold on site. Leashed pets are permitted.

Reservations, fees: Reservations are accepted. Sites are $16 to $20 a night.

Contact: Gitchee Gumee Campground, P.O. Box 146, Newman Drew Road, West Ossipee, NH 03890; (603) 539-6060.

Directions: From the southern junction of Routes 16 and 25 at Center Ossipee, travel northwest on Route 16 for 3.5 miles to Newman Drew Road. Turn left (west) and continue to the campground entrance on the right. It's next to Bearcamp River Campground.

Trip notes: The Bearcamp River flows by these wooded, spacious sites shaded by hemlock, pine, and spruce trees. An easy two-hour paddle on this clear mountain stream brings canoeists to Ossipee Lake to the south. Gitchee Gumee Campground offers rental boats and maintains a large sandy beach on the Bearcamp River. If you like fishing, bring your gear, as this is a good trout stream. Winter sites are available to seasonal campers who want to take advantage of the vast network of snowmobile trails accessible from the campground. The area's many ponds and lakes offer unlimited ice fishing opportunities.

Open: Year-round.

89 Westward Shores Campground

Location: On the northwest shore of Ossipee Lake; Northern New Hampshire map page 168, grid f4.

Campsites, facilities: There are 248 sites for tents and RVs, 49 with full hookups and 199 with water and electric. Each site has a picnic table and fire ring. Air conditioners and heaters are allowed, and cable TV hookups are available. A dump station, laundry facilities, rest rooms, hot showers, a rec hall, pavilion, and a playground are provided, and a camp store sells ice and firewood. Courts for basketball, badminton, volleyball, and horseshoes are located on the property. Off-season RV storage is available. Traffic is controlled by an entry gate. Leashed pets are permitted.

Reservations, fees: All reservations must be accompanied by a 33 percent deposit. A minimum three-day stay is required during holiday weekends. Sites are $20 to $25 a night per family. Boat slips are $10 a day. Seasonal rates are available.

Contact: Westward Shores Campground, P.O. Box 308, West Ossipee, NH 03890; (603) 539-6445.

Directions: From the northern junction of Routes 16 and 25 in West Ossipee, travel 3.5 miles south on Route 16. Turn left on Nichols Road and head east for a short distance to the campground entrance.

Trip notes: Birch trees provide welcome shade for these sites near the shore of Ossipee Lake. A small marina, an expansive sandy beach, and boat rentals give campers several different ways to enjoy the open water. Fishing enthusiasts will find bass, horned pout, perch, pickerel, salmon, and trout in the lake, while fly-fishers will want to head south to the Lovell River for some of the state's best trout fishing; the Lovell feeds into the lake just near a road bearing the same name. Also to the south, the Indian Mound Golf Club is open to the public; it was built on an old Ossipee Indian burial ground. The southeast shore of the lake, called Heath Pond Bog, is a protected area. This National Natural Landmark is fragile and undeveloped: a floating mat of peat is covered with moss and provides habitat for a unique plant community including orchids and insectivorous plants. A nature trail explores the bog and the surrounding forest of spruce and tamarack. Seasonal renters may use sites in the winter months, maybe as a base camp for excursions on the area's extensive snowmobiling and cross-country skiing trails, or to enjoy ice fishing and skating on the lake.

Open: Year-round.

---

⑨⓪ Terrace Pines Campground

Location: Between Big and Little Dan Holes in Center Ossipee; Northern New Hampshire map page 168, grid f4.

Campsites, facilities: There are 183 sites for tents and RVs, 178 with full hookups and five with water and electric. Cabins and A-frame shelters are also for rent. Each site has a picnic table and fire ring. Phone hookups are available. Use of air conditioners and heaters is allowed. A dump station, laundry facilities, rest rooms, hot showers, a rec hall, and a playground are provided, and a camp grocery store sells LP gas, ice, and firewood. Courts for basketball, badminton, volleyball, and horseshoes are located on the property. The maximum RV length is 29 feet. Leashed pets are permitted.

Reservations, fees: A 50 percent prepaid deposit is required with all reservations except for those on holiday weekends, which must be prepaid in full. Sites are $22 to $25 a night per family. Seasonal rates are available on request.

Contact: Terrace Pines Campground, P.O. Box 98, Center Ossipee, NH 03814; (603) 529-6210.

Directions: From the village of Center Ossipee near the southern junction of Routes 16 and 25, travel 1.5 miles southwest on Moultonville Road. Stay left at the fork and continue southeast for 1.75 miles on Valley Road. Bear left on Bents Road and continue half a mile to the campground entrance.

Trip notes: Lake lovers can have the best of both worlds at Terrace Pines. The campground offers sites in hilly wooded areas beside and near both Big and Little Dan Hole ponds. The bigger lake is open to powerboating and waterskiing, while only nonmotorized boating is allowed on Little Dan Hole. There are three beach areas for swimming as well as a boat launch and dock. Anglers can try for lake trout and salmon in Big Dan Hole. North of the campground, a short footpath leads to the summit of Sentinel Mountain.

Open: Mid-May through mid-October.

91 Deer Cap Campground

Location: South of Center Ossipee; Northern New Hampshire map page 168, grid f4.

Campsites, facilities: There are 75 sites for tents and RVs, some with full hookups. Each site comes with a picnic table and fire ring. A dump station, rest rooms, hot showers, a rec hall, a heated swimming pool, and a playground are provided, as are courts for volleyball and horseshoes. Ice and firewood are sold on the grounds. Leashed pets are permitted.

Reservations, fees: Reservations are accepted. Sites start at $15 a night for two people.

Contact: Deer Cap Campground, P.O. Box 332, Center Ossipee, NH 03814; (603) 539-6030.

Directions: From the junction of Routes 16 and 28 in Ossipee, travel north for approximately 3.5 miles on Route 16 to the campground entrance on the left (west) side of the road.

Trip notes: Deer Cap Campground doubles as a cross-country ski center and camping facility. Note that winter sites are available for seasonal campers only, however. Sites are roomy and shaded by tall pine trees beside the Beech River, a small trout-filled stream. In winter, campers can ski on miles of groomed trails that leave from the campground and afterward soak in Deer Cap's heated outdoor pool. For summer recreation, Ossipee Lake to the north is open to powerboating, fishing, and swimming and has a public boat launch on Deer Cove. The Indian Mound Golf Club offers 18 holes beside the lake and is open to the public.

Open: Year-round, but winter sites are available for seasonal campers only.

92 Mascoma Lake Campground

Location: In Enfield on the western shore of Mascoma Lake; Southern New Hampshire map page 169, grid a2.

Campsites, facilities: There are 96 sites for tents and RVs, 46 with full hookups, 26 with water and electric, and 24 with none. Each site has a picnic table and fireplace. Use of air conditioners and heaters is allowed. A rec hall, dump station, laundry facilities, rest rooms, hot showers, and a playground are provided. A camp store sells ice and firewood. Courts for basketball, volleyball, and horseshoes are located on the property. Leashed pets are permitted.

Reservations, fees: Reservations are recommended and must be accompanied by one night's fee. Holiday stays must be prepaid in full. Per family, sites are $16 a night in the wilderness tent area, $18 to $20 a night for sites with water and electric hookups, and $22 a night for sites with full hookups. Weekly, monthly, and seasonal rates are available.

Contact: Mascoma Lake Campground, RR 2, Box 331, Enfield, NH 03748; (603) 448-5076 or (800) 769-7861.

Directions: From Interstate 89 at Lebanon, take exit 17 and travel east on U.S. 4 for approximately two miles to Route 4A. Turn right onto Route 4A and head south for seven-tenths of a mile to the campground entrance on the left side of the road.

Trip notes: The campsites here are set in tiers on the side of a mountain, allowing each one to have a view of Mascoma Lake. Water sports, including swimming, boating, and paddling around in a canoe, are the focus of summertime activities, and boat owners may dock their craft at the campground for $2 a day. Mascoma Lake is home to smallmouth and largemouth bass, rock bass, and trout. Nature hikes on the mountain leave from the campground. For those who like to stay close to home, group activities such as crafts and community dinners are organized for adults and children from May through September.

Open: Mid-May through early October.

---

⑨³ Crescent Campsites

Location: On Canaan Street Lake in Canaan; Southern New Hampshire map page 169, grid a2.

Campsites, facilities: There are 82 sites for tents and RVs, 72 with water and electric hookups. Each site has a table and fireplace. A dump station, laundry facilities, rest rooms, metered hot showers, a sports field, boat ramp, and a playground are provided. There's also a rec room with video games, a jukebox, and a pool table. A small grocery store sells ice and firewood. Courts for basketball and horseshoes are located on site. Leashed pets are permitted.

Reservations, fees: Reservations are recommended. Tenters may stay for up to two weeks, and one tent per site is allowed. Sites with water and electricity are $19 a night per family, and sites with no hookups are $17 a night. Weekly, monthly, and seasonal rates are available.

Contact: Jean-Paul and Barbara Soucy, Crescent Campsites, P.O. Box 238, Canaan, NH 03741; (603) 523-9910.

Directions: From Interstate 89 at Lebanon, take exit 17 and travel 12 miles east on U.S. 4 to Canaan. At the blinking yellow light in the center of town, turn left on Canaan Street, just west of the junction of U.S. 4 and Route 118. Head north for one-eighth mile on Fernwood Street, then bear right at the fork in the road and continue about a mile to the campground.

Trip notes: Grassy, wooded campsites beside Canaan Street Lake offer easy access for boaters. The waterway is open to powerboating, waterskiing, and canoeing, and a sandy swimming beach is also provided. Anglers can try to catch their dinner here, as bass, pickerel, and perch inhabit the lake. Summer weekends are filled with organized meals and dances for campers. Excellent hiking routes are found a short drive to the east in Mount Cardigan State Park. Moderate and easy trails for hikers of all ages and abilities include a 3,121-foot summit hike on the West Ridge Trail. Panoramic views of the Lakes Region can be had from the fire tower atop the mountain. Another popular family attraction is Ruggles Mine, located south of Canaan off U.S. 4. Nearly 200 years old, this open pit mine contains more than 150 minerals including mica, amethyst, and garnet. Giant rooms and tunnels in the mine are open for exploration, and visitors are welcome to collect minerals.

Open: Mid-May through mid-October.

---

⑨⁴ Ames Brook Campground

Location: Southeast of Ashland on Ames Brook; Southern New Hampshire map page 169, grid a3.

Campsites, facilities: There are 52 sites for tents and RVs, 25 with full hookups, 17 with water and electric, and 10 with none. Each site has a picnic table and fire ring. Cable TV hookups are available. A dump station, rest rooms, laundry facilities, hot showers, a rec hall, pool, and playground are provided. A camp store sells LP gas, ice, and firewood. Courts for badminton, volleyball, and horseshoes are located on the property. Leashed pets are permitted.

Reservations, fees: Reservations are

accepted. For two people, tent sites start at $21 a night and sites with full hookups start at $25 a night. Off-season, weekly, monthly, and seasonal rates are available.

Contact: Ames Brook Campground, RFD 1, Box 102, Ashland, NH 03217; (603) 968-7998 or (800) 234-7998.

Directions: From Interstate 93 at Ashland, take exit 24 and travel three-quarters of a mile south on U.S. 3. Continue south for another quarter mile on Route 132, then turn left on Winona Road and head east. The campground is half a mile ahead on the south side of the road.

Trip notes: Ames Brook tumbles by wooded campsites, some of which are set right beside the water. A separate tent area has larger, more private campsites underneath the trees. On weekends, campers awake to the smell of bacon and eggs, for a small restaurant on the property serves breakfast. Organized activities on the weekends include haywagon rides, water aerobics in the pool, sundae festivals, and candy bar bingo. Ames Brook is open to fishing, but for more lively waters try Little Squam Lake to the north; there's a public boat launch in Holderness, and the lake supports both warm-water and cold-water species. Ashland is a sweet old mill town: there's still a five-and-dime on Main Street that sells penny candy. Just a few miles off Interstate 93, this campground makes a good jumping-off point for day trips to the White Mountains and to the various attractions of the Lakes Region.

Open: Late April through late October.

⑳ Yogi Bear's Jellystone Park Camp Resort

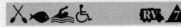

Location: On the Pemigewasset River south of Ashland; Southern New Hampshire map page 169, grid a3.

Campsites, facilities: There are 228 sites for tents and RVs, 19 with full hookups, 204 with water and electric, and the rest with none. RVs and cabins are also available for rent. Each site has a picnic table and fire ring. Use of air conditioners and heaters is allowed. A dump station, laundry facilities, rest rooms, hot showers, a rec hall, pool, game room, and playground are provided. A store sells groceries, ice, LP gas, RV supplies, and firewood. You'll also find courts for basketball, shuffleboard, badminton, volleyball, and horseshoes. Roads are paved within the park and a guard controls the front entrance. Leashed pets are permitted.

Reservations, fees: Reservations are recommended Memorial Day through Labor Day. Sites are $31 to $38 a night per family.

Contact: Yogi Bear's Jellystone Park Camp Resort, RR 1, Box 396, Ashland, NH 03217; (603) 968-9000.

Directions: From Interstate 93 south of Ashland, take exit 23 for the Lakes Region. Travel east on Route 104 for 500 yards, then head north for four miles on Route 132. The campground entrance will be on the left (west) side of the road.

Trip notes: Yogi Bear's is a family camping theme park. The resort is located on the Pemigewasset River, which is open to canoeing, swimming, and fishing; you can rent boats at the campground. Sites are small and mostly open, though some offer shade trees. A full slate of organized activities includes visits from Yogi Bear every day, movies and cartoons, dances, outdoor concerts, bingo marathons, and ceramics. In addition to the services listed above, baby-sitting is available. There's a restaurant on site as well as a 19-hole miniature golf course. Many sites are rented by seasonal campers. The campground caters to families who want to stay busy from dawn to dusk.

Open: Late May through mid-October.

⑨⑥ Davidson's Country-side Campground

Location: On the Pemigewasset River; Southern New Hampshire map page 169, grid a3.

Campsites, facilities: There are 130 sites for tents and RVs, 5 with full hookups, 110 with water and electric, and 15 with none. Each site has a picnic table and fire ring. A dump station, rest rooms, hot showers, a rec hall, pool, and playground are provided. A small grocery store sells snacks, ice, RV supplies, and firewood. Courts for basketball, badminton, volleyball, and horseshoes are located on the property. Leashed pets are permitted.

Reservations, fees: Reservations are accepted. Sites start at $21 a night per family. Monthly and seasonal rates are available on request. Off-season RV storage is $2 per day.

Contact: Davidson's Countryside Campground, RFD 2, Box 485, Schofield Road, Bristol, NH 03222; (603) 744-2403.

Directions: From Interstate 93 south of Ashland, take exit 23 heading toward Bristol and travel west on Route 104 for two miles. Take a right onto River Road and travel north to the campground entrance a half mile ahead.

Trip notes: All full-hookup sites at Davidson's are occupied by seasonal campers, but about 30 sites with water and electricity are reserved for overnighters and vacation travelers. Three of the overnight sites (54, 54A, and 55) are on the shoreline of the Pemigewasset River. Campers will find a variety of settings here, from open and grassy to wooded and riverfront. Swift-flowing and clear, the "Pemi" winds south to Franklin, where it meets the Merrimack River. Fish for trout from the shoreline or float for hours in an inner tube. From the campground you can paddle on Class II and III rapids to Franklin just before the falls; canoes and one rowboat are available for rent at the campground. Northwest of the campground lies Newfound Lake, a 4,000-acre waterway renowned for its trout fishing. Wellington State Park is on the west shore and offers a swimming beach and a birding trail. One other perk: Davidson's owners make and sell maple syrup at the campground.

Open: May 24 through October 14.

⑨⑦ Twin Tamarack Family Camping and RV Resort

Location: On Pemigewasset Lake; Southern New Hampshire map page 169, grid a4.

Campsites, facilities: There are 259 sites for tents and RVs, 40 with full hookups and 219 with water and electric. Each site has a picnic table and fire ring. Air conditioners are allowed, but heaters are prohibited. A dump station, laundry facilities, rest rooms, hot showers, a pool, sports field, rec hall, and playground are provided. A small grocery store sells RV supplies, ice, and firewood. You'll also find courts for basketball, badminton, volleyball, and horseshoes on the property. Off-season RV storage is available. Leashed pets are permitted.

Reservations, fees: Prepaid deposits of $75 a week are required for all reservations except for stays of three days or less, which require full prepayment. Sites are $26 a night per family.

Contact: Gene and Bev Sands, Twin Tamarack Family Camping and RV Resort, Route 104, Box 121, New Hampton, NH 03256; (603) 279-4387.

Directions: From Interstate 93 at New Hampton, take exit 23 and travel east for 2.5 miles on Route 104 to the campground.

Trip notes: Pine-shaded sites in the woods across Route 104 from Pemigewasset Lake are private and roomy. Twin Tamarack maintains a boat launch, beach, and dock area for campers on the lakeshore. Sites are fully equipped to handle RVs of any size, yet the dirt roads and natural landscaping maintain a rustic appearance. Paddleboats, canoes, and rowboats may be rented at the campground. RV rallies are welcome to pull in at a spacious group area and can contact the campground owners on CB channel 14. The pool and rec hall complex includes a hot tub and game room. Seasonal campers occupy most of the full-hookup sites during the summer.

Open: Mid-May through mid-October.

---

98 Clearwater Campground

Location: On the north shore of Pemigewasset Lake; Southern New Hampshire map page 169, grid a4.

Campsites, facilities: There are 153 sites for tents and RVs, 144 with water and electric hookups and some with full hookups, including cable TV. Each site has a picnic table and fire ring. Use of air conditioners and heaters is allowed. A dump station, laundry facilities, rest rooms, hot showers, a sports field, pavilion, rec hall, and playground are provided. A grocery store sells ice, firewood, and RV supplies. Courts for basketball, shuffleboard, badminton, volleyball, and horseshoes are located on the property. Leashed pets are permitted.

Reservations, fees: Reservations for stays of a week or longer require a $75 deposit per week. For stays of three nights or less and on holidays, full prepayment is required. Sites are $28 to $29 a night per family. A limited number of sites offer sewer and cable TV connections for $3 extra. Weekly

and seasonal rates are available. In the spring and fall, off-season rates start at $20 a night. The boat docking fee is $4 a night.

Contact: Clearwater Campground, 26 Campground Road, Meredith, NH 03253; (603) 279-7761.

Directions: From Interstate 93 at New Hampton, take exit 23 and travel east on Route 104 for three miles to the campground entrance on the right (south) side of the road.

Trip notes: Rolling mountains are in full view of the campground's large sandy beach on Pemigewasset Lake. The beach is well suited for waterskiing and is also the site of group campfires and activities. Sites are tightly settled (about 25 feet wide) in the woods by the lake, and campers have access to a boat launch and a 36-slip dock. This location is ideal for families who want to take day trips north to the White Mountains or to the boardwalk beach scene at Weirs Beach on Lake Winnipesaukee. Conveniences and courtesies at the campground include dust control on the facility's dirt roads, mosquito control, and a night manager at the gated entrance.

Open: Mid-May through mid-October.

---

99 Meredith Woods Four Season Camping Area

Location: Near the north shore of Pemigewasset Lake; Southern New Hampshire map page 169, grid a4.

Campsites, facilities: There are 64 sites for tents and RVs, all with full hookups. Each site has a picnic table and fire ring. Use of air conditioners and heaters is allowed, and cable TV and telephone hookups are available. A dump station, laundry facilities, rest rooms, hot showers, a pavilion, rec hall, pool, and playground are provided. A camp store sells ice and firewood. Courts for basketball, shuffleboard, badminton, volleyball, and horseshoes are located on the property. There's a traffic control gate at the campground entrance. Leashed pets are permitted.

Reservations, fees: Reservations for stays of a week or longer require a $75 deposit per week. For stays shorter than a week, or for weekends, full prepayment is required. Per family, sites are $32 a night in summer and $28 a night in winter. Weekly and seasonal rates are available.

Contact: Meredith Woods Four Season Camping Area, 26 Campground Road, Meredith, NH 03253; (603) 279-5449.

Directions: From Interstate 93 at New Hampton, take exit 23 and travel east on Route 104 for three miles to the campground entrance on the left.

Trip notes: Four seasons of recreation await visitors to this campground in the Lakes Region. Most sites are rented seasonally, so call ahead to see if they have space. The facility is co-owned with Clearwater Campground across the street (see campground number 98), thus Meredith Woods' campers have full use of the large sandy beach on Pemigewasset Lake. Boats may be docked across the street at Clearwater Campground for $4 a night. Sandy, wooded sites are tightly settled, averaging about 25 feet wide. The owners take measures to control dust and mosquitoes in the park. Though tent spaces are available, the campground is dominated by RVers. For winter users, Meredith Woods offers an indoor heated pool and spa. Snowmobilers can get on the state's trail corridor from the campground, and cross-country skiers will find bountiful tracks through the surrounding pine forest. Pemigewasset Lake is a hotbed of ice fishing from January through March.

Open: Year-round.

Pine Grove Campground

Location: West of the Pemigewasset River and north of Franklin; Southern New Hampshire map page 169, grid b3.

Campsites, facilities: There are 29 sites for tents and RVs, seven with full hookups and 11 with water and electric. Each site has a table and fire ring. A dump station, laundry facilities, rest rooms, hot showers, a pavilion, and a playground are provided. A camp store sells ice and wood. Courts for badminton, volleyball, and horseshoes are located on site. Leashed pets are permitted.

Reservations, fees: Reservations are accepted, and weekly, monthly, and seasonal rates are available for sites with hookups. Sites start at $14 a night for two people.

Contact: Pine Grove Campground, 14 Timberlane Drive, Franklin, NH 03235; (603) 934-4582.

Directions: From Franklin, travel five miles north on Route 3A to the campground entrance on the left.

Trip notes: Quiet, peaceful camping in an open grassy area is offered at Pine Grove. Swim in the campground's pool or head east to the Pemigewasset River for a day of tubing, canoeing, fishing, or swimming. Part of the Franklin Falls Dam Project, the river is enveloped in protected lands and provides habitat for horned pout, bass, pickerel, and perch.

Open: May 15 through October 15.

Thousand Acres Family Campground

Location: South of Franklin on Shaw Brook; Southern New Hampshire map page 169, grid b3.

Campsites, facilities: There are 150 sites for tents and RVs, 47 with full hookups, 74 with water and electric, and 29 with none. Each site has a table and stone fireplace. Use of air conditioners and heaters is allowed. A dump station, rest rooms, hot showers, a rec hall, and playground are provided. A grocery store sells ice and wood. Group camping areas for tents and RVs are available. Courts for basketball, badminton, volleyball, and horseshoes are located on the property. Leashed pets are permitted.

Reservations, fees: Reservations are recommended July 1 through Labor Day. Per family, sites range from $20 a night with no hookups to $24 with full hookups. Weekly and seasonal rates are available.

Contact: Thousand Acres Family Campground, Route 3, Franklin, NH 03235; (603) 934-4440.

Directions: From Interstate 93 at Penacook, take exit 17. Travel north on U.S. 3 toward Franklin for 10 miles to the campground entrance on the left.

Trip notes: Family fun and games are the main attraction at Thousand Acres. Campsites are set amid the trees and have sandy driveways. Weekend events at the campground include free hayrides, ice cream socials, ceramics, movies, bingo for all ages, a golf league, and sporting competitions. A small pond on Shaw Brook is privately owned, so you can fish there without a license. There's a sandy swimming beach on the pond and canoes for rent.

Open: May 15 through October 1.

102 Winnisquam Beach Resort

Location: On the southwest shore of Winnisquam Lake; Southern New Hampshire map page 169, grid a4.

Campsites, facilities: There are 146 sites for tents and RVs, some with full hookups. Each site has a picnic table and fire ring. A dump station, laundry facilities, rest rooms, hot showers, and a playground are provided. No pets are allowed.

Reservations, fees: Reservations are accepted. Sites are $20 a night per family. Seasonal rates are provided on request.

Contact: Winnisquam Beach Resort, P.O. Box 67, Lochmere, NH 03252; (603) 524-0021.

Directions: From Interstate 93 near Tilton, take exit 20 and head north on U.S. 3 for two miles to Grey Rock Road. Turn right and look for the campground just ahead.

Trip notes: Here's another lakeside campground with shady sites near the water. A boat launch, beach, and dock space are available for campers. Winnisquam Lake has both cold-water and warm-water piscine habitats supporting bass, salmon, trout, and several other species.

Open: Year-round, but winter sites are available to seasonal campers only.

103 Silver Lake Park Campground

Location: On the east shore of Silver Lake south of Laconia; Southern New Hampshire map page 169, grid a4.

Campsites, facilities: There are 77 sites for tents and RVs, 70 with full hookups, 5 with water and electric, and 2 with none. Each site has a table and fire ring. Use of air conditioners and heaters is allowed, and cable TV hookups are available. A dump station, laundry facilities, rest rooms, hot showers, a rec hall, and a playground are provided. A store sells ice and wood. Courts for badminton, volleyball, and horseshoes are located on site. Dogs are not allowed.

Reservations, fees: Reservations are recommended July 1 through Labor Day weekend and must be accompanied by a nonrefundable deposit. For two people, tent sites start at $18 a night, sites with water and electricity start at $22, and sites with full hookups start at $24. There are surcharges for air conditioners, cable TV, and boat ramps. Seasonal rates are available.

Contact: Silver Lake Park Campground, P.O. Box 7, 64 Jamestown Road, Lochmere, NH 03252; (603) 524-6289.

Directions: From Interstate 93 near Tilton, take exit 20 and travel north on U.S. 3 for two miles. Turn right on Silver Lake Road and travel one mile south to the campground entrance.

Trip notes: Shrubs, lawns, and flower gardens punctuate many of the seasonal sites on a hillside overlooking the campground's sandy beach on Silver Lake. The warm-water loch supports smallmouth and largemouth bass and is big enough for good waterskiing. A quiet-water canoe excursion leads south out of the lake on the Winnipesaukee River. To the north, the Lakeview Golf Club is open to the public and offers nine holes overlooking Winnisquam Lake. If you're feeling lucky, take a short drive south to the Lakes Region Greyhound Park and place a bet on your favorite canine.

Open: Early May through mid-October.

104 Harbor Hill Camping Area

Location: North of Meredith; Southern New Hampshire map page 169, grid a4.

Campsites, facilities: There are 140 sites for tents and RVs, 81 with full hookups, 26 with water and electric, and 33 with none. Each site has a picnic table and fire ring. Air conditioners are allowed, but heaters are prohibited. Phone hookups are available. A dump station, laundry facilities, rest rooms, hot showers, a rec hall, pool, and playground are provided. A grocery store sells LP gas, ice, and firewood. Courts for basketball, shuffleboard, badminton, volleyball, and horseshoes are located on the property, and the entrance has a traffic control gate. The maximum RV length is 35 feet. Leashed pets with rabies vaccination certification are permitted.

Reservations, fees: A 50 percent deposit is required for all reservations. Per family, tent sites are $18 a night, sites with water and electric hookups are $22 a night, and full hookups are $24 a night. Cabins are available for $40 a night. There are fees for guests and use of air conditioners.

Contact: Harbor Hill Camping Area, 189 Route 25, Meredith, NH 03253; (603) 279-6910.

Directions: From the junction of Route 25 and U.S. 3 in Meredith, travel two miles east on Route 25 to the campground.

Trip notes: Dirt roads wind through a mixed hardwood forest of beech, birch, and oak trees, accessing these small but private campsites. Most are fully equipped for RVs up to 35 feet long, but tenters are offered spots in a wilderness hilltop area. A public boat launch is available just north of the campground at Leavitt Park on Lake Winnipesaukee, and you are free to explore the more than 44,500 acres of freshwater and islands via powerboat (with a license), kayak, or canoe. Numerous marinas rent every kind of waterborne mode of transport, from sailboards and sailboats to Jet Skis and powerboats with cuddy cabins. Harbor Hill is within easy driving distance of several Lakes Region attractions including bustling Weirs Beach and the Castle in the Clouds (a stone mansion built in the early 1900s and now open for tours, with panoramic views of Lake Winnipesaukee), yet it is far enough away that you won't be bothered by the crowds.

Open: Mid-May through mid-October.

Camp Iroquois Campground

Location: On Moultonborough Neck on Lake Winnipesaukee; Southern New Hampshire map page 169, grid a4.

Campsites, facilities: There are 90 sites for tents and RVs, all with water and electric hookups. Each site has a picnic table and fire ring. A dump station, rest rooms, warm showers, and a pavilion are provided. Some provisions including firewood are sold on site. Courts for basketball, tennis, and horseshoes are located on the property. The maximum RV length is 35 feet. Leashed pets are permitted.

Reservations, fees: Reservations are only accepted for stays of a week or longer and must be accompanied by a $40 deposit. For stays shorter than a week, or for weekends, sites are available on a first-come, first-served basis. Sites start at $18 a night per family.

Contact: Camp Iroquois Campground, P.O. Box 150, Center Harbor, NH 03226; (603) 253-4287.

Directions: From Center Harbor, travel 1.5 miles northeast on Route 25. Turn right on Moultonborough Neck Road and continue 1.5 miles southeast to the campground entrance on the right side of the road.

Trip notes: Pine trees shade these campsites scattered along the northern shore of giant Lake Winnipesaukee on Ash Cove on Moultonborough Neck. A boat ramp and a swimming beach are provided for campers. Casting from shore is prohibited, but once you're out on the state's largest body of water you'll find excellent fishing for many

species including salmon, bass, and trout. The lake's 44,586 acres are open to every kind of boating as well as Jet Skiing in certain areas. A marina close to the campground sells boat licenses and provides rule booklets. Just south of the campground is the Kona Wildlife Management Area, which is open to hunting in season. Supplies and services are available in the village of Center Harbor.

Open: Mid-May through October 1.

Provident Winnipesaukee

Location: On Moultonborough Neck on Lake Winnipesaukee; Southern New Hampshire map page 169, grid a4.

Campsites, facilities: There are 92 sites for tents and RVs, 80 with water and electric hookups and 12 with none. Each site has a picnic table and fire ring. A dump station, laundry facilities, rest rooms, hot showers, a rec hall, pool, and playground are provided. A camp store sells ice and firewood. Courts for shuffleboard, badminton, volleyball, and horseshoes are located on the property. Leashed pets are permitted.

Reservations, fees: Reservations are recommended. Sites are $17 to $20 a night for two people.

Contact: Provident Winnipesaukee, HCR 62, Box 182B, Center Harbor, NH 03226; (603) 253-6251.

Directions: From Center Harbor, travel 1.5 miles northeast on Route 25. Turn right on Moultonborough Neck Road and continue four miles southeast to the campground entrance.

Trip notes: Tucked into the woods, these small, quiet sites are a short distance from the shore of giant Lake Winnipesaukee, at 44,586 acres the state's largest body of water. Campers have access to an on-site pool and recreation area, or they can opt to swim in the lake at several nearby public access points. The campground's lands are adjacent to the Kona Wildlife Management Area, where hunting is permitted for big and small game, fur-bearing animals, and game birds.

Open: May 1 through October 31.

107 Long Island Bridge Campground

Location: On Long Island on Lake Winnipesaukee; Southern New Hampshire map page 169, grid a4.

Campsites, facilities: There are 112 sites for tents and RVs, 76 with full hookups, 23 with water and electric, and 12 with none. Each site has a picnic table and fire ring. Use of air conditioners and heaters is allowed. A dump station, laundry facilities, rest rooms, hot showers, and a playground are provided. A camp store sells ice and firewood. Courts for basketball, volleyball, and horseshoes are located on the property. The maximum RV length is 32 feet. Leashed pets are permitted.

Reservations, fees: Reservations are accepted. Sites are $16 to $22 a night per family.

Contact: Long Island Bridge Campground, HCR 62, Box 455, Center Harbor, NH 03226; (603) 253-6053.

Directions: From Center Harbor, travel 1.5 miles northeast on Route 25. Turn right on Moultonborough Neck Road and travel southeast for 6.5 miles to the campground.

Trip notes: Pine trees protect the open and shaded sites on Long Island, one of the largest islands on Lake Winnipesaukee. On either side of Long Island are numerous smaller islands, making this a favorite area among kayakers. At the campground, a boat ramp, dock, and swimming beach are provided for campers. Out on the lake, there's excellent fishing for many species including salmon, bass, and trout. Lake Winnipesaukee is the state's largest, and its 44,586 acres are open to every kind of boating including Jet Skis in certain areas. Be sure to check the rules and regulations before you head out; booklets are available at any marina on the lake. The Kona Wildlife Management Area just south of the campground is open to hunting in season. Supplies and services are available in the village of Center Harbor.

Open: May 1 through October 1.

108 Hack-Ma-Tack Family Campground

Location: North of Weirs Beach; Southern New Hampshire map page 169, grid a4.

Campsites, facilities: There are 76 sites for tents and RVs, 2 with full hookups, 68 with water and electric, and 6 with none. Each site has a picnic table and fire ring. A dump station, rest rooms, hot showers, a rec hall, pool, and a playground are provided. A small grocery store sells RV supplies, ice, charcoal, and firewood. Courts for shuffleboard, basketball, and horseshoes are located on the property. Leashed pets are permitted.

Reservations, fees: Reservations require a $25 deposit for stays of fewer than seven days and $50 per full week. Full prepayment is required on holiday weekends. Sites are $20 to $23 a night for two people with discounted rates after three days. There are surcharges for guests and sewer connections. Refunds are given within one hour of registration if you are unhappy with your site.

Contact: Hack-Ma-Tack Family Campground, Route 3, Box 90, Laconia, NH 03246; (603) 366-5977.

Directions: From the junction of U.S. 3 and Route 104 in Meredith, travel 2.5 miles south on U.S. 3 to the campground entrance on the left (east) side of the road.

Trip notes: These roomy wooded sites are right in the thick of the Lakes Region's booming commercial district. Arcades, entertainment centers, a beach boardwalk, shops, restaurants, and boat cruises are available less than two miles south in bustling Weirs Beach, a resort area on the shore of giant Lake Winnipesaukee. Less developed resort towns to the north and south of the campground are not as rough around the edges as Weirs Beach and offer lake access.

Open: May 10 through Columbus Day.

---

109 Weirs Beach Tent and Trailer Park

Location: Just north of Weirs Beach; Southern New Hampshire map page 169, grid a4.

Campsites, facilities: There are 168 sites for tents and RVs, 70 with full hookups, 70 with water and electric, and 28 with none. Each site has a picnic table and fire ring. A dump station, horseshoe pits, rest rooms, and hot showers are provided. The maximum RV length is 31 feet. Leashed pets are permitted.

Reservations, fees: Reservations require the sum of one night's fee as a nonrefundable deposit. For two people, primitive sites are $16 a night, sites with water and electric hookups are $18 a night, and those with full hookups are $20 a night. The boat parking fee is $5 a night. Seasonal rates are available.

Contact: Weirs Beach Tent and Trailer

Park, RFD 3, Box 98, Laconia, NH 03246; (603) 366-4747.

Directions: From the junction of U.S. 3 and Route 104 in Meredith, travel four miles south on U.S. 3 to the campground.

Trip notes: Small sites are organized in rows separated by birch, oak, maple, pine, and beech trees amid the melee of the Weirs Beach commercial resort district. Arcades, entertainment centers, a beach boardwalk, shops, restaurants, and boat cruises are a short walk south of here on the shore of Lake Winnipesaukee. These campsites offer few amenities since all goods and services can be obtained nearby in Weirs Beach. Swimming areas and marinas are close by.

Open: May 15 through September 15; self-contained units can stay from September 15 through Columbus Day.

---

110 Paugus Bay Campground

Location: On Paugus Bay in Lake Winnipesaukee; Southern New Hampshire map page 169, grid a4.

Campsites, facilities: There are 127 sites for tents and RVs, 102 with full hookups and 25 with water and electric. Each site has a picnic table and fire ring. A dump station, laundry facilities, rest rooms, hot showers, a rec hall, pavilion, horseshoe pits, and a playground are provided. A small grocery store sells ice and firewood. Leashed pets are permitted.

Reservations, fees: A $50 deposit is required with all reservations. In July and August, sites must be reserved for a minimum of seven days. Sites are $26 to $28 a night per family. Weekly, monthly, and seasonal rates are available. After Labor Day, sites start at $20 a night.

Contact: Paugus Bay Campground, Hilliard Road, Laconia, NH 03246; (603) 366-4757.

Directions: From the junction of U.S. 3 and Route 104 in Meredith, head southeast on U.S. 3 toward Weirs Beach for four miles. Turn right on Hilliard Road and continue two-tenths of a mile to the campground.

Trip notes: Sites here are staggered on a hillside beside Paugus Bay and most of the ones with full hookups are occupied by seasonal campers, so be sure to call ahead. All the attractions at Weirs Beach—waterslides, arcades, a beach boardwalk, and go-carts—are a short walk away. Boaters can dock their craft at the campground, and others may explore the bay and Lake Winnipesaukee in rental canoes. This is the state's largest lake with more than 44,500 freshwater acres open to fishing, boating, and swimming. Check rules and regulations on boating and fishing before setting out; booklets are available at all marinas.

Open: May 15 through October 15.

111 Ellacoya State RV Park

Location: On the southwest shore of Lake Winnipesaukee; Southern New Hampshire map page 169, grid a4.

Campsites, facilities: There are 38 sites for RVs only, all with full hookups. Each site has a picnic table. Laundry facilities, rest rooms, hot showers, and a community fire pit are provided. A camp store sells ice and firewood. Pets, tents, and tent trailers are not allowed.

Reservations, fees: For reservations, call the New Hampshire Division of Parks and Recreation (see phone number below) on weekdays between 8:30 A.M. and 3:30 P.M. from January through August. Sites are $30 a night per family.

Contact: Ellacoya State RV Park, P.O. Box 7277 Gilford, NH 03246; (603) 293-7821. New Hampshire Division of Parks and Recreation, (603) 271-3628.

Directions: From the junction of Route 11 and U.S. 3 at Weirs Beach, travel five miles south on Route 11.

Trip notes: These RV sites look out on the Ossipee and Sandwich Mountains across Lake Winnipesaukee. Only vehicles with full hookups are allowed. There is a swimming beach, a boat launch for cartop vessels, and a picnic area at the campground. To launch larger boats, head north to Sanders Bay, which has a public boat ramp. Once out on the state's largest lake, you'll find that these 44,000-plus acres offer anglers both warm-water and cold-water habitat, supporting numerous fish species. On good weather weekends, the lake is crowded with power-boats, Jet Skis, and sailors. Before you head out, find out about rules and regulations at any of the many local marinas.

Open: Mid-May through mid-October.

112 Gunstock Campground

Location: At the base of Gunstock Mountain in Gilford; Southern New Hampshire map page 169, grid a4.

Campsites, facilities: There are 300 sites for tents and RVS, 113 with water and electric hookups. Each site has a picnic table, fire ring, and grill. Air conditioners are allowed, but heaters are prohibited. A dump station, rest rooms, hot showers, a rec hall, pavilion, pool, sports field, and playground are provided. A grocery store sells RV supplies, LP gas, ice, and firewood. Group sites for tents and RVs are available. You'll also find courts for basketball, badminton, volleyball, and horseshoes. A traffic control gate and security guard are posted at the entrance. Leashed pets with rabies vaccination certification are permitted.

Reservations, fees: A nonrefundable deposit must accompany all reservations. For two adults or a family, sites start at $19 a night without hookups and $23 a night with water and electricity.

Contact: Gunstock Campground, P.O. Box 1307, Gilford, NH 03247; (800) GUNSTOCK/486-7862, extension 191. Web page: http:\\www.gunstock.com.

Directions: From the north edge of town in Gilford, travel east on Route 11A for 3.5 miles to the campground.

Trip notes: Gunstock Mountain rises from the south shore of Lake Winnipesaukee, the state's largest body of water, providing a dramatic backdrop to these campsites. They are located in the woods at the mountain's base, which is also home to a four-season recreational facility. In winter, the mountain offers alpine and Nordic skiing at two different centers. In spring and summer, mountain bikers take to the ski trails, earning verdant views of Lake Winnipesaukee after a rugged ride to the top. Motorcyclists participate in a Hill Climb in June during Motorcycle Week when the entire Lakes Region is overrun with two-wheeled enthusiasts. At the campground, a pool and a small pond can be used for swimming, fishing, boating, and canoeing. Boats are for rent on site. In the fall, visitors climb Gunstock Mountain to get colorful views of the region dressed in its bright foliage hues. This campground can feel crowded because all the facilities are also open for day use. To escape the throngs, hike up the Red Trail to Belknap Mountain south of Gunstock Mountain. It's a moderate 1.5-mile trek to a summit fire tower.

Open: Mid-May through mid-October, then mid-December through ski season.

113 Wolfeboro Campground

RV 7

Location: North of Lake Wentworth; Southern New Hampshire map page 169, grid a5.

Campsites, facilities: There are 50 sites for tents and RVs, 40 with water and electric hookups and 10 with none. Each site has a table, fire ring, and grill. A dump station, rest rooms, hot showers, a rec hall, and a playground are provided. A store sells LP gas, ice, and firewood. Courts for badminton, volleyball, and horseshoes are located on the property. The maximum RV length is 40 feet. Leashed pets are permitted.

Reservations, fees: Reservations are recommended. Sites are $16 a night per family, plus charges for whatever electricity is used. Weekly, monthly, and seasonal rates are available.

Contact: Wolfeboro Campground, 61 Haines Hill Road, Wolfeboro, NH 03894; (603) 569-9881.

Directions: From Wolfeboro, travel north for 4.5 miles on Route 28 to Haines Hill Road. Bear right heading uphill and the campground will be 1,000 feet ahead.

Trip notes: Secluded and rural, these sites are enveloped in stands of tall pine trees. This is the ideal spot for RVers who want to tour the Lakes Region but desire a quiet, private place to return to at the end of the day. To the south, Wentworth State Park is a small state-owned parcel of land on Lake Wentworth. A picnic area and swimming beach there are open to the public. World War II buffs should pay a visit to the Wright Museum of American Enterprise in Wolfeboro, where scenes of American life are recreated using authentic uniforms, vehicles, periodicals, and memorabilia.

Open: May 15 through October 15.

114 Beaver Hollow Campground

Location: Northeast of Ossipee; Southern New Hampshire map page 169, grid a5.

Campsites, facilities: There are 131 sites for tents and RVs, all with water and electric hookups. Each site has a picnic table, fire ring, and grill. Use of air conditioners and heaters is allowed. A dump station, laundry facilities, rest rooms, hot showers, a rec hall, pool, a picnic pavilion, and a playground are provided. A small grocery store sells RV supplies, ice, and firewood. Courts for basketball, shuffleboard, badminton, volleyball, bocce ball, and horseshoes are located on the property. Leashed pets are permitted.

Reservations, fees: Reservations are recommended Memorial Day through Labor Day and require a nonrefundable deposit. Sites are $18 a night per family, with a $2 surcharge for heaters and air conditioners. Weekly, monthly, and seasonal rates are available.

Contact: Beaver Hollow Campground, P.O. Box 437, Ossipee, NH 03864; (603) 539-4800 or (800) 226-2557.

Directions: From the junction of Routes 16 and 28 in Ossipee, travel south for one mile on Route 16 to the campground entrance on the left (east) side of the road.

Trip notes: Busy Route 16, a major thoroughfare for travelers headed to the White Mountains, borders this campground. Campsites are set far enough back in the woods so road noise isn't a nuisance, but you should be prepared to deal with traffic, especially on weekends, once you leave the campground. Frenchman's Brook runs through the grounds, with sites 70 through 77 set right on the shore. You can fish in the stream, but you'll find two really good cold-water ponds just north and east of here: White Pond and Duncan Lake are stocked with brook and rainbow trout. Pine River State Forest is northeast of the campground and has some multiuse trails. State-maintained snowmobile trails are also accessible from the campground. On weekends, organized activities include live entertainment and group dinners.

Open: Year-round; fully operational May 1 through Columbus Day.

115 Beachwood Shores Campground

Location: On the southwest shore of Province Lake; Southern New Hampshire map page 169, grid a5.

Campsites, facilities: There are 87 sites for tents and RVs, all with full hookups. Each site has a picnic table, fire ring, and grill. A dump station, laundry facilities, rest rooms, hot showers, a rec hall, and a playground are provided. A camp store sells RV supplies, limited groceries, LP gas, ice, and firewood. Courts for basketball, badminton, volleyball, and horseshoes are located on the property. Leashed pets are permitted.

Reservations, fees: Reservations are accepted. Sites start at $18 a night per family. Seasonal rates are available on request.

Contact: Beachwood Shores Campground, HC Box 228, East Wakefield, NH 03830; (603) 539-4272 or (800) 371-4282.

Directions: From north of Union at the junction of Route 16 and Route 153 (which turns into Mountain Laurel Road), travel north for 12 miles on Route 153. Turn left on Bonnyman Road and head west for two miles to the campground entrance.

Trip notes: Choose from lakefront, lakeview, wooded, and riverfront sites at Beachwood Shores Campground. All sites are large and sandy, shaded by tall pine trees beside Province Lake. The lake is open to warm-water fishing, powerboating, and swimming. Boats are available for rent at the campground, and there's a ramp near the beach. Hiking trails lead into Pine River State Forest to the west. The Pine River flows through that parcel of land and is canoeable over a 20-mile stretch during high water; it's also favored by local trout fishermen. To the east of the campground on the Maine border is the Province Lake Country Club, with its public golf course and tennis courts.

Open: Mid-May through mid-October.

116 Lake Ivanhoe Campground

Location: On the north shore of Lake Ivanhoe near the Maine border; Southern New Hampshire map page 169, grid a5.

Campsites, facilities: There are 75 sites for tents and RVs, 49 with full hookups, 18 with water and electric, and 8 with none. Each site has a picnic table and fire ring. Use of air conditioners and heaters is allowed. A dump station, laundry facilities, rest rooms, hot showers, a rec hall, and a playground are provided. Also on the property are an 18-hole miniature golf course and courts for basketball, shuffleboard, badminton, volleyball, and horseshoes. A camp store carries LP gas, RV supplies, ice, and firewood. Leashed pets are permitted.

Reservations, fees: Reservations are recommended in July and August and require a 50 percent deposit. Sites are $19 to $28 a night for two people. Weekly, monthly, and seasonal rates are available.

Contact: Lake Ivanhoe Campground, 631 Acton Ridge Road, East Wakefield, NH 03830; (603) 522-8824.

Directions: From north of Union at the junction of Route 16 and Mountain Laurel Road, travel half a mile east on Mountain Laurel Road. Turn left and travel north for 2.5 miles on Route 153. Turn right on Acton Ridge Road and travel 1.2 miles east to the campground entrance.

Trip notes: Pine trees tower above these large sites near the north shore of Lake Ivanhoe. Campers can get out on the 100-acre spring-fed lake via rental rowboats, canoes, or paddleboats. A large sandy swimming beach is a short walk from the campsites. Group activities at Lake Ivanhoe Campground include haywagon rides, sports tournaments, and adult bingo. Wakefield has several bicycle routes for visitors to explore the town's 11 lakes, passing by rivers, rolling pastures, and forests; maps are available at the campground office. One rainy day option is a visit to the Museum of Childhood in Wakefield. The collection includes 3,000 dolls, dollhouses, teddy bears, puppets, and music boxes.

Open: Mid-May through mid-October.

117 Lake Forest Resort

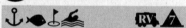

Location: On Great East Lake near the Maine border; Southern New Hampshire map page 169, grid a5.

Campsites, facilities: There are 160 sites for RVs only, 130 with full hookups and a group area containing 30 sites with water and electric hookups. Each site has a picnic table and fire ring. A dump station, laundry facilities, rest rooms, hot showers, and a rec hall are provided. Leashed pets are permitted.

Reservations, fees: Reservations are recommended. Sites are $23 a night for two people. Seasonal rates are available.

Contact: Lake Forest Resort, HC 66, Box 115A, East Wakefield, NH 03830; (603) 522-

3306 in the summer, or (603) 569-6186 in the winter.

Directions: From north of Union at the junction of Route 16 and Mountain Laurel Road, travel half a mile east on Mountain Laurel Road. Turn left and travel north for 2.5 miles on Route 153. Turn right on Acton Ridge Road and travel east for 1.6 miles to Dearborn Road. Turn right and follow signs to the campground entrance.

Trip notes: Lake Forest's sites are nestled in the woods on Great East Lake, a seven-mile-long body of clear water with a sandy bottom straddling the New Hampshire–Maine border. Adult seasonal campers are the predominant clientele; no tents or pop-up trailers are allowed, and only family members are welcome as guests. A short golf course on site is a good place to warm up for action on any of the six 18-hole courses in the greater Wakefield area. There's also a post and beam clubhouse (much like an old-style barn) that's used for pancake breakfasts, bingo tournaments, suppers, and dances. At the shore a long wooden dock and deck makes a comfy place to look out upon the lake and, in the distance, the rolling hills. The lake is open to swimming, fishing, and all types of boating.

Open: May 10 through October 14.

118 Mi-Te-Jo Campground

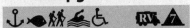

Location: On Milton Pond in Milton; Southern New Hampshire map page 169, grid b5.

Campsites, facilities: There are 179 sites for tents and RVs, 46 with full hookups and 133 with water and electric. Each site has a picnic table and fire ring. Use of air conditioners and heaters is allowed. A dump station, rest rooms, hot showers, a rec hall, sports field, and playground are provided. A camp store sells LP gas, RV supplies, ice, and firewood. Courts for basketball, shuffleboard, badminton, volleyball, and horseshoes are located on the property. Leashed pets are permitted.

Reservations, fees: Reservations are recommended June through September. Sites are $21 to $25 a night per family.

Contact: Mi-Te-Jo Campground, P.O. Box 830, Milton, NH 03851; (603) 652-9022.

Directions: From the Spaulding Turnpike (Route 16) in Milton, take exit 17 and travel east on Route 75 for three-quarters of a mile. Take a left onto Route 125 and head north for 3.25 miles to Townhouse Road. Turn right and head east for one mile to the campground entrance on the left.

Trip notes: Mi-Te-Jo is an out-of-the-way lakeside campground with wooded sites. Milton Pond is open to fishing, swimming, and boating; a ramp and dock are provided at the campground. There are also a few canoes and rowboats for rent. Hiking trails explore the streams and forests in the area including land across the border in Maine. Milton is famous as the site of the New Hampshire Farm Museum, located off the Spaulding Turnpike at exit 18. This National Historic Site has guided tours of connected farm buildings, blacksmith and cobbler shops, a country store, animals, and a nature trail. On weekends, visitors can learn old-time farm skills and crafts at demonstrations and workshops.

Open: May 10 through October 15.

119 Otter Lake Campground

Location: On the west side of Otter Lake near Georges Mills; Southern New Hampshire map page 169, grid b2.

Campsites, facilities: There are 28 sites for tents and RVs, 12 with water and electric hookups. Each site has a picnic table and fireplace. A dump station, rec hall, rest rooms, hot showers, horseshoe pits, rental boats, and a playground are provided. Ice and firewood are sold on site. The maximum RV length is 30 feet. Leashed pets are permitted.

Reservations, fees: Reservations are accepted. Campsites start at $17 a night per family.

Contact: Steve and Judy Belden, Otter Lake Campground, 55 Otterville Road, New London, NH 03257; (603) 763-5600.

Directions: From Interstate 89 south of Lebanon, take exit 12 for New London. Head west for one mile on Route 11. Turn right on Otterville Road and proceed a short distance to the campground.

Trip notes: Both open and wooded sites are offered at this campground set near Otter Lake. There's a sandy beach for sunning and swimming, and campers may rent rowboats, canoes, and paddleboats here. Nature trails explore Phillips Memorial Preserve, which lies adjacent to the campground. Just south of the campground is Sunapee Lake with its three working lighthouses and numerous hidden coves. Several outfitters rent powerboats, canoes, sailboats, and sailboards for day-use on the water. Head to Mount Sunapee State Park at the south end of that lake to take advantage of hiking trails and a scenic chairlift ride. At the same end of the lake, an easy hike leads into the John Hay National Wildlife Refuge, a preserve for upland birds. Besides great bird-watching, the preserve—once a summer retreat for former Secretary of State John Hay—features gardens and a marvelous view of Mount Sunapee.

Open: Mid-May through mid-October.

⑫⓪ Loon Lake Campground

Location: On a man-made pond north of Newport; Southern New Hampshire map page 169, grid b2.

Campsites, facilities: There are 102 sites for tents and RVs, 88 with full hookups and the rest with either water and electricity or no hookups. Each site has a picnic table and fireplace. Use of air conditioners is allowed. Facilities include a dump station, rest rooms, hot showers, and a playground. A camp store sells fishing licenses, ice, and firewood. Courts for basketball, volleyball, and horseshoes are located on the property. A rec hall, library, and large screened pavilion are also on the grounds. Leashed pets are permitted.

Reservations, fees: Reservations are recommended. Rates range from $17 a night per family for sites without hookups to $21 and $23 for limited and full hookup sites, respectively. Weekly, monthly, and seasonal rates are available. Deposits are required for a security gate pass and pets.

Contact: Bev and Phil Gerety, Loon Lake Campground, P.O. Box 345, Newport, NH 03773; (603) 863-8176.

Directions: From the intersection of Routes 10 and 11/103 in Newport, travel a few miles east on Route 103. Turn left (north) on Reed's Mill Road and stay to the right for the next two miles until you reach the campground entrance.

Trip notes: One-hundred-acre man-made Loon Lake is the hub of activity for campers here, offering fishing enthusiasts a place to try for smallmouth and largemouth bass, horned pout, brook trout, and rainbow trout. Swimmers and sunbathers have access to a sandy beach. And for those who want to get out on the water, there are four small islands and many inlets to explore via nonmotorized boats. All campsites have views of the lake, and a separate primitive area is reserved for tents. In season, campers gather for potluck dinners and dances. Miles of trails lacing the surrounding woodlands provide forested terrain for hikers and mountain bikers to explore. Seven miles to the southeast, Mount Sunapee State Park is the northern terminus of the Monadnock-Sunapee Greenway, a 51-mile trail connecting two of southern New Hampshire's most notable peaks. Campers can take a scenic chairlift ride to the top of the mountain, do some hiking, or hop aboard a boat for a cruise on 4,085-acre Sunapee Lake at the foot of the mountain.

Open: Mid-May through mid-October.

121 Crow's Nest Campground

Location: On the Sugar River in Newport; Southern New Hampshire map page 169, grid b2.

Campsites, facilities: There are 94 sites for tents and RVs, 27 with full hookups, 47 with water and electric, and 20 with none. Each site has a picnic table and fireplace. Air conditioners are allowed, but heaters are prohibited. A dump station, laundry facilities, rest rooms, hot showers, a pool, a wading pool, and a playground are on the grounds. There's also a rec hall with coin games and a small camp store selling ice and firewood. Volleyball courts, horseshoe pits, a sports field, and a miniature golf course are located on the property. Leashed pets are permitted.

Reservations, fees: Reservations are recommended from Memorial Day through Labor Day. Sites start at $15 a night for two

people. Weekly, monthly, and seasonal rates are available.

Contact: Crow's Nest Campground, 529 South Main Street, Newport, NH 03773; (603) 863-6170 or (800) 424-0900.

Directions: From the intersection of Routes 10 and 11/103 in Newport, travel two miles south on Route 10. The campground is on the right (west) side of the road.

Trip notes: Riverside and grassy, these wooded sites are accessible to an extensive multiuse trail system available year-round for such activities as snowmobiling and cross-country skiing. You won't suffer from frostbitten digits at Crow's Nest Campground, because winter campers can get a break from the cold by sitting around the fireplace in the warm-up lodge. In the summer, free concerts are performed every Sunday evening on the town common. There's good fishing for brown, lake, and rainbow trout on the Sugar River and 18 holes and greens nearby at the John H. Cain Golf Club in Newport.

Open: Year-round.

122 Northstar Campground

Location: In South Newport on Coon Brook and the Sugar River; Southern New Hampshire map page 169, grid b2.

Campsites, facilities: There are 56 sites for tents and RVs, 31 with water and electric hookups. Each site has a picnic table and fireplace. A dump station, rest rooms, hot showers, a pavilion, and a playground are provided. Courts for badminton, volleyball, tetherball, and horseshoes are located on the property, as are a softball field and a croquet lawn. Ice and firewood are available. Leashed pets are permitted.

Reservations, fees: Reservations are accepted. Sites are $14 a night for up to four people. Water and electric hookups are $2 extra. Seasonal and club rates are available.

Contact: The Nemeth Family, Northstar Campground, 43 Coon Brook Road, Newport, NH 03773; (603) 863-4001.

Directions: From the intersection of Routes 10 and 11/103 in Newport, travel 3.5 miles south on Route 10. Turn right on Coon Brook Road and head west for a quarter mile to the campground entrance on the right side of the road.

Trip notes: Roomy, private campsites are set either in a grassy meadow or in the woods alongside Coon Brook or the Sugar River. There's excellent trout fishing in the river and freshwater for swimming in a spring-fed pond that was formed when part of the brook was "cordoned off." Live entertainment is featured at such events as the annual pig roast, held each September. Other organized activities include theme weekends, cookouts, and a fishing derby in October. Foot trails lead into the woods surrounding the campground; you'll discover more challenging hikes if you drive 15 minutes southeast at Mount Sunapee State Park. In early August, the park hosts one of the largest crafts fairs in New England.

Open: Mid-May through mid-October.

---

⑫③ Rand Pond Campground

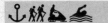

Location: On the south shore of Rand Pond in Goshen; Southern New Hampshire map page 169, grid b2.

Campsites, facilities: There are 100 sites for tents and RVs, 21 with full hookups and 79 with water and electric. Each site has a table, fire ring, and grill. A dump station, laundry facilities, rest rooms, hot showers, a rec hall, sports field, and a playground are provided. A store sells ice and

wood. Courts for badminton, shuffleboard, volleyball, and horseshoes are located on site. Leashed pets are permitted.

Reservations, fees: Reservations are recommended for stays on weekends and holidays and require a deposit equal to one night's fee. Sites are $17 to $20 a night for two people. Seasonal rates are available on request.

Contact: Rand Pond Campground, P.O. Box 10, Brook Road, Goshen, NH 03752; (603) 863-3350.

Directions: From the intersection of Routes 10 and 11/103 in Newport, follow Route 10 south for five miles to Goshen. Turn left on Brook Road and head east for 2.5 miles to the campground.

Trip notes: Campers can choose from open, wooded, and shoreline sites beside Rand Pond. A boat ramp, a dock, and a sandy swimming beach are maintained at the water's edge. There's good trout fishing in these waters, and rental boats are available at the campground. Winter sites attract snowmobilers, for the state snowmobile corridor (a network of groomed trails) is accessible right from the campground. Once the pond is frozen over in the winter, it is cleared for skating. Four miles north of here, Mount Sunapee State Park has hiking trails and a scenic chairlift that runs in the summer. In winter, the mountain's alpine ski center is known for its abundant intermediate trails, but there are also a few challenging chutes for the expert skier.

Open: Year-round; fully operational April 30 through October 15.

---

⑫④ Tamarack Trails Camping Park

Location: On Dodge Brook in East Lempster; Southern New Hampshire map page 169, grid b2.

Campsites, facilities: There are 20 sites for tents and RVs, 15 with water and electric hookups. Each site has a picnic table and fire ring. A dump station, laundry facilities, rest rooms, hot showers, a rec area, and a playground are provided. Firewood is sold at the office. Leashed pets are permitted.

Reservations, fees: Reservations are recommended. Sites start at $12 a night per family. Water and electric hookups are $3 extra. Weekly, monthly, and seasonal rates are available.

Contact: Tamarack Trails Camping Park, P.O. Box 24, East Lempster, NH 03605; (603) 863-6443.

Directions: From the junction of Routes 123 and 10 in Marlow, travel 5.5 miles north on Route 10 and turn left on Dodge Brook Road. The campground is four-tenths of a mile ahead.

Trip notes: Fifteen sites for RVs and five tent sites are surrounded by an 83-acre tree farm on Dodge Brook. Except for three of the RV sites in an open grassy field, all of the spaces are shaded by tall pine trees. Trails explore the tree farm and nearby Dodge Brook State Forest, where black bear, moose, coyotes, bobcats, and beavers have been sighted. There's good trout fishing in Dodge Brook, and nearby Dodge Pond and Long Pond are open to fishing, swimming, and boating.

Open: Mid-May through mid-October.

125 Pillsbury State Park

Location: Northwest of Hillsborough; Southern New Hampshire map page 169, grid b2.

Campsites, facilities: There are 38 sites for tents and RVs, all without hookups. Pit toilets, piped water, tables, and fire rings are provided. Firewood is available. The maxi-

mum RV length is 30 feet. Leashed pets are permitted.

Reservations, fees: Sites are available on a first-come, first-served basis. The fee is $12 a night.

Contact: Pillsbury State Park, P.O. Box 83, Hillsborough, NH 03244; (603) 547-3373 or (603) 863-2860.

Directions: From Hillsborough, travel northwest on Route 31 to Washington, then continue another 17 miles on the same road to the park entrance on the right (east) side.

Trip notes: Wooded, primitive sites are located beside May Pond and three of them are accessible only by canoe, providing a quiet retreat for campers who want to get away from it all. This 2,400-acre parcel of land was deeded to the state by a former sawmill owner and a founder of the Society for the Protection of New Hampshire Forests, and much of it remains undeveloped. In the 1930s the Civilian Conservation Corps cleared and restored ponds that were once clogged with sawdust. Several of the ponds are open to nonmotorized boating and support populations of largemouth bass, horned pout, perch, and pickerel. The 51-mile Monadnock-Sunapee Greenway hiking trail passes through the park's boundaries.

Open: Early May through mid-October.

126 Lake Massasecum Campground

Location: On the southwest shore of Lake Massasecum; Southern New Hampshire map page 169, grid b3.

Campsites, facilities: There are 50 sites for tents and RVs, 35 with water and electric hookups. Each site has a picnic table, fire ring, and grill. There are also six cabins for rent. Facilities include a dump station, rest rooms, hot showers, and a rec room. A small camp store sells ice and firewood. Horseshoe pits and a play area are located on the property. Leashed pets are permitted.

Reservations, fees: Reservations are recommended. Sites are $19 to $21 a night per family for stays of three or fewer days, and $17 to $19 a night for four or more days. Seasonal rates are available.

Contact: Bob and Jane Laurendeau, Lake Massasecum Park and Campground, Lake Massasecum Road, RR 1, Box 499, Bradford, NH 03221; (603) 938-2571.

Directions: From the intersection of U.S. 202 and Route 114 in Henniker, travel six miles north on Route 114 to Bradford. Turn right on Massasecum Road and travel east for half a mile. The campground entrance is on the left.

Trip notes: Partially wooded sites allow for easy access to the shores of Lake Massasecum, known for its fabulous mountain views across the water. Campers and locals alike are welcome to use the sandy swimming beach, so it can get pretty crowded here, especially on weekends when the weather is good. Massasecum's 402 acres of warm-water habitat support horned pout and largemouth and smallmouth bass. Plunk a canoe into the water and you might catch something for an evening fish fry at your campsite grill. To the northwest, a short hiking trail at Harriman Chandler State Forest leads to the summit of Stewarts Peak.

Open: Mid-May through mid-September.

⑫ Cold Brook Campground

Location: South of Webster; Southern New Hampshire map page 169, grid b3.

Campsites, facilities: There are 60 sites for tents and RVs, 28 with full hookups and 32 with water and electric. Each site has a picnic table and fire ring. Use of air conditioners is allowed. A dump station, laundry facilities, rest rooms, hot showers, and a playground are provided. You'll also find basketball and shuffleboard courts and horseshoe pits. Firewood is sold on site. Leashed pets are permitted.

Reservations, fees: Reservations are recommended. Sites are $12 to $14 a night per family. Weekly and seasonal rates are available.

Contact: Denny and Kathy Stevens, Cold Brook Campground, Route 127, Webster, NH 03303; (603) 529-2528.

Directions: From Interstate 89 at Davisville, take exit 7 and travel three-quarters of a mile east on Route 103, then go three miles north on Route 127. The campground entrance is on the left (west) side of the road.

Trip notes: Roomy sites with plenty of shade line the banks of the Blackwater River. From here, canoeists can venture north to Lake Winnepocket on quiet water. Rent a boat at the campground or bring your own; no motors are allowed. Swimmers have a private beach on the Blackwater, which is also open to fishing.

Open: May 1 through October 1.

⑫⑧ Mile-Away Campground

Location: North of U.S. 202 in Henniker; Southern New Hampshire map page 169, grid b3.

Campsites, facilities: There are 190 sites for tents and RVs, 53 with full hookups, 131 with water and electric, and 6 with none. Each site has a picnic table and fire ring. Use of air conditioners and heaters is allowed, and phone hookups are available. Tent and RV groups can be accommodated. A dump station, laundry facilities, rest rooms, hot showers, a rec hall, pavilion, and playground are provided. A small grocery store carries LP gas, sandwiches, ice, and firewood. Courts for volleyball, basketball, badminton, shuffleboard, and horseshoes are located on the property, as is a miniature golf course. Leashed pets are permitted.

Reservations, fees: A 50 percent deposit is required with all reservations, which should be made as far in advance as possible. Stays during holiday weekends must be prepaid in full. Sites start at $20 to $27 a night for a family of four. Winter rates are $165 a month with a three-month minimum stay.

Contact: Mile-Away Campground, 41 Old West Hopkinton Road, Henniker, NH 03242; (603) 428-7617 or (800) 787-4679.

Directions: From Interstate 89 west of Concord, take exit 5 and travel west on Route 9/U.S. 202 for about five miles. At the intersection with Route 114, turn right on Old West Hopkinton Road and travel northeast for one mile to the campground entrance.

Trip notes: Mile-Away Campground has an old-fashioned air. The lounge in the main lodge comes complete with a large stone fireplace, a player piano, and a Yamaha organ, and weekend activities include wine and cheese parties and square dancing. There's a swimming beach on French Pond, which is also stocked with trout. Boats may be rented here or you can bring your own; motors up to six horsepower are allowed. In winter, skaters take to the ice while snowmobilers and cross-country skiers journey through the surrounding country woods on miles of trails. All sites are heavily wooded, and some are set on the shore of the pond.

Open: Year-round.

129 Sandy Beach Family Campground

Location: On Rolf Pond in Hopkinton; Southern New Hampshire map page 169, grid b3.

Campsites, facilities: There are 180 sites for tents and RVs with water and electric hookups. Each site has a picnic table and fire ring. A dump station, rec hall, rest rooms, hot showers, an arcade, and a playground are provided. A camp store carries RV supplies, LP gas, ice, and firewood. RV parts and service are also available. Leashed pets are permitted.

Reservations, fees: Reservations are accepted with prepaid deposits. Sites start at $20 a night per family. Seasonal rates are available on request.

Contact: Sandy Beach Family Campground, 677 Clement Hill Road, Contoocook, NH 03229; (603) 746-3591.

Directions: From the junction of U.S. 202/ Route 9 and Route 127 in Contoocook, travel north on Route 127 for about four miles into the village. Go past the fire station and turn left on Pine Street. Travel west for two miles to Clement Hill Road. Take another left and travel south about half a mile to the campground entrance.

Trip notes: Crystal-clear Rolf Pond sees most of the action at Sandy Beach Family Campground, where wooded sites set 'neath tall pines are close to the water's edge. Contoocook is a small country village where you can find supplies and services. The river bearing the same name runs just south of the campground; it passes by the Hopkinton–Everett Lake Project, a national landholding surrounding Hopkinton Lake. The waterways are open to all types of boating, swimming, and fishing. Duston

Country Club, also a few miles south of here, offers nine holes of laid-back greens.

Open: May 1 through Columbus Day.

---

⑬⓪ Keyser Pond Campground

Location: South of U.S. 202 in Henniker; Southern New Hampshire map page 169, grid c3.

Campsites, facilities: There are 116 sites for tents and RVs, 107 with water and electric hookups and nine with none. Each site has a picnic table and fire ring. Use of air conditioners and heaters is allowed, and phone hookups are available. A dump station, laundry facilities, rest rooms, hot showers, a rec hall, pool, miniature golf course, and playground are provided. A small grocery store carries LP gas, ice, and firewood. Courts for volleyball, basketball, badminton, shuffleboard, and horseshoes are located on the property. Leashed pets are permitted.

Reservations, fees: Nonrefundable deposits are required for all reservations. Sites start at $18 to $20 a night per family. Seasonal rates are available.

Contact: Keyser Pond Campground, 47 Old Concord Road, Henniker, NH 03242; (603) 428-7741.

Directions: From Concord, take Interstate 89 north to exit 5. Travel west on U.S. 202/Route 9 to the intersection with Route 127. Take a left (there's a blinking yellow light); the campground will be just ahead.

Trip notes: A wooded hillside above Keyser Pond is terraced with roomy sites for all types of campers. Recreation is centered around the freshwater pond; electric motors are allowed, and canoes, rowboats, and paddleboats are available for rent at the campground. You can also play a round or

two of miniature golf on the grounds. Many sites are rented by seasonal campers. Small pockets of land are protected in the immediate area: Ames, Contoocook, and Craney Hill State Forests offer some short hikes.

Open: May 15 through October 15.

---

⑬① Cascade Park Camping Area

Location: Just west of Chichester; Southern New Hampshire map page 169, grid b4.

Campsites, facilities: There are 191 sites for tents and RVs, all with full hookups. Each site has a picnic table and fire ring. A dump station, rest rooms, hot showers, a rec hall, dance pavilion, and playground are provided. A camp store carries LP gas, ice, and firewood. Courts for shuffleboard and horseshoes are located on the property. Leashed pets are permitted.

Reservations, fees: Reservations are accepted. Sites start at $17 a night per family. Seasonal rates are available.

Contact: Cascade Park Camping Area, 379 Route 106, South Loudon, NH 03301; (603) 224-3212.

Directions: From Interstate 93 at Concord, take exit 14 and travel east on Route 393/U.S. 4 to Route 106. Turn left and continue north for two miles. The campground is just ahead on the right side of the road.

Trip notes: These shaded sites are located near the shore of the Soucook River, where anglers can try for rainbow, brook, and brown trout. A swimming hole at the campground has a small sandy beach. Many campers at Cascade Park are race fans; a few miles north of here in Loudon the New Hampshire International Speedway revs up crowds all summer long with an international lineup of auto and motorcycle racers.

Open: Mid-May through October 1.

132 Hillcrest Campground

Location: West of Epsom Four Corners; Southern New Hampshire map page 169, grid b4.

Campsites, facilities: There are 123 sites for tents and RVs, 70 with full hookups, 44 with water and electric, and 9 with none. Each site has a picnic table and fire ring. Use of air conditioners and heaters is allowed. Cable TV and phone hookups are available. A dump station, laundry facilities, rest rooms, hot showers, a rec hall, pavilion, pool, and playground are provided. A small grocery store carries RV supplies, LP gas, ice, and firewood. There's a traffic control gate at the entrance. Courts for volleyball, basketball, badminton, shuffleboard, and horseshoes are located on the property. Leashed pets are permitted.

Reservations, fees: Prepaid deposits are required for all reservations. Sites start at $21 a night per family with no hookups; a site with full hookups including cable TV is $26 a night. There are surcharges for guests, air conditioners, and heaters. Weekly, monthly, and seasonal rates are available.

Contact: Hillcrest Campground, 78 Dover Road, Chichester, NH 03234; (603) 798-5124; for information and reservations outside of New Hampshire, call (800) 338-9488.

Directions: From Interstate 93 at Concord, take exit 14 and travel east on Route 393/U.S. 4 for six miles to the campground entrance on the left (north) side of the road.

Trip notes: Hillcrest Campground is located right off U.S. 4, a busy thruway from central New Hampshire to the seacoast. Trees buffer the campsites from much of the noise, but campers have to contend with traffic, especially on weekends, once they leave the campground. The swimming pool, some rental cabins, and group areas are close to the highway, but sites 58 through 68 and those in the 20s and low 30s are set far back from the road near Marsh Brook and Great Meadow Pond. Canoes, rowboats, and paddleboats are available for rent at the campground for people who want to explore the quiet waters of the pond. Every weekend the campground organizes activities with a family theme such as Christmas in July or Lobster Boil Weekend. Concord, the state capital, is a short drive west of here and has several educational family attractions including the Christa McAuliffe Planetarium and the Canterbury Shaker Village. The latter is a living history museum just north of Concord and features 24 historic buildings built by Shakers. Programs, events, and meals help visitors interpret Shaker culture. Candlelight dinners and tours are also offered.

Open: May 1 through October 15.

133 Lazy River Campground

Location: North of Route 9 in Epsom; Southern New Hampshire map page 169, grid b4.

Campsites, facilities: There are 112 sites for tents and RVs, 45 with full hookups and 67 with water and electric. Each site has a picnic table, fireplace, and grill. Air conditioners are allowed, but electric heaters are prohibited. A dump station, rest rooms, hot showers, a rec hall, pool tables, two playgrounds, and a swimming pool are provided. Courts for volleyball, badminton, and horseshoes are located on the property. The campground sells ice and firewood. Leashed pets are permitted.

Reservations, fees: Reservations are accepted. Per family, sites are $22 a night with water and electricity and $25 a night with full hookups. Weekly, monthly, and seasonal rates are available.

Contact: The Blomstrom Family, Lazy River Campground, RR 2, Box 173, Epsom, NH 03234; (603) 798-5900 or (800) 972-4873.

Directions: From Interstate 93 at Concord, take exit 14 and travel east on Route 393/U.S. 4. At the Epsom traffic circle head north on Route 28 for two miles to Depot Road. Take a right and head east for half a mile to the campground entrance.

Trip notes: Piney woods surround both shaded and open sites, which are scattered along the banks of the Suncook River. Canoeists can explore the river and its many tributaries in search of brook, brown, and rainbow trout. Many seasonal and overnight campers are drawn to Lazy River Campground for its proximity to the New Hampshire International Speedway about 12 miles north in Loudon. For hiking and biking trails, head south to Bear Brook State Park (see campground number 137); although the park's day-use areas can get quite crowded in summer, the paths that weave through hilly forests, bogs, and marshlands are little-used.

Open: May 1 through October 1.

---

⑬ Epsom Valley Campground

Location: North of Route 9 in Epsom; Southern New Hampshire map page 169, grid b4.

Campsites, facilities: There are 65 sites for tents and RVs, 60 with water and electric hookups. Each site has a picnic table, fire ring, and grill. Use of air conditioners and heaters is allowed. A dump station, rest rooms, metered hot showers, a miniature golf course, and a playground are provided.

Courts for basketball, volleyball, badminton, and horseshoes are located on the property. Ice and firewood are sold on site. A gate controls traffic at the entrance. Leashed pets are permitted.

Reservations, fees: Reservations are recommended in the summer. Sites are $17 to $19 a night per family. Weekly, monthly, and seasonal rates are available.

Contact: John and Dwyna Arvanitis, Epsom Valley Campground, RFD 2, Box 132, Epsom, NH 03234; (603) 736-9758 in the summer, or (508) 658-4396 in the winter.

Directions: From Interstate 93 at Concord, take exit 14 and travel east on Route 393/U.S. 4. At the Epsom traffic circle head north on Route 28 for 1,500 feet to the campground entrance on the right side of the road.

Trip notes: Lofty pine trees shade these grassy sites lining the bank of the Suncook River. Canoeists can explore the river and its numerous tributaries in this valley south of the Lakes Region. Brook, brown, and rainbow trout are fair game for anglers in these waters. Boat rentals and a beach are available at the campground. Among the many seasonal campers at Epsom Valley are loyal race fans: the New Hampshire International Speedway is about 12 miles north of here in Loudon. Bear Brook State Park to the south offers a network of trails for mountain biking, horseback riding, and hiking across hilly forests, bogs, and marshland.

Open: Memorial Day through October 12.

---

⑬ Circle 9 Ranch Campground

Location: At Epsom Four Corners; Southern New Hampshire map page 169, grid c4.

Campsites, facilities: There are 145 sites for tents and RVs, 60 with full hookups and 85 with water and electric hookups. Each site comes with a picnic table and fire ring. Use of air conditioners and heaters is allowed. A dump station, laundry facilities, rest rooms, metered hot showers, a rec hall, dance hall, swimming pool, and playground are provided. A camp store carries LP gas, ice, and firewood. Courts for volleyball, basketball, and horseshoes are located on the property. Leashed pets are permitted.

Reservations, fees: Reservations are recommended. Sites are $20 a night for tents and pop-ups, $23 a night for trailers and RVs. Weekly, monthly, and seasonal rates are available.

Contact: Circle 9 Ranch Campground, Windymere Drive, P.O. Box 282, Epsom, NH 03234; (603) 736-9656.

Directions: From Interstate 93 at Concord, take exit 14 and travel east on Route 393/U.S. 4. At the Epsom traffic circle head south on Route 28 for a quarter mile. The campground will be on the right (west) side of the road on Windymere Drive.

Trip notes: If you're a country music fan, Circle 9 Campground just might be your kind of place. Choose from a mix of open, grassy, and shaded campsites, all located behind a full-scale dance hall. The dance hall is open to the public for country two-stepping every weekend, and guests should bring their own beverages. Located off a main thruway to the White Mountains, the campground is near a commercial district, but a grove of pine trees does provide something of a buffer zone to shield visitors from the traffic noise. Year-round organized activities will appeal to campers of every age group; there are live bands, dancing, dinners, and ice skating in winter. Young anglers are welcome to try their luck on two small campground ponds where they can drop in a fishing line.

Open: Year-round.

136 Blake's Brook Family Campground

Location: East of Concord; Southern New Hampshire map page 169, grid c4.

Campsites, facilities: There are 50 sites for tents and RVs, 33 with full hookups, 12 with water and electric, and 5 with none. Each site has a picnic table and fire ring. Use of air conditioners is allowed. A dump station, rest rooms, metered hot showers, a rec hall, swimming pool, and playground are provided. Ice and firewood are available. Courts for volleyball, basketball, and horseshoes as well as a small game room are located on the property. Leashed pets are permitted.

Reservations, fees: A 50 percent deposit is required for all reservations. Sites are $18 to $20 a night per family. There are surcharges for guests and air conditioners. Weekly, monthly, and seasonal rates are available.

Contact: Blake's Brook Family Campground, 76 Mountain Road, Epsom, NH 03234; (603) 736-4793.

Directions: From Interstate 93 at Concord, take exit 14 and drive east on Route 393/U.S. 4 to the Epsom traffic circle. Travel halfway around the circle, staying on U.S. 4/202 east. Two miles east of the circle turn right at the campground sign. Continue south for 1.5 miles, then head west for another quarter mile, following signs to the campground entrance.

Trip notes: Thickly settled brookside sites are scattered among the trees at this campground. Campers can cool off in the swimming pool or head a short distance south to Bear Brook State Park to take a refreshing dip in natural water. Swimming and picnicking draw crowds to the park in the summer, and families can enjoy a host of nature programs. Boat rentals are also available. The park has an extensive trail system for mountain biking, horseback riding, and moderate hikes through bogs and marshes. Most visitors stick to the day-use areas, so even in summer you'll likely have these trails to yourself.

Open: Mid-May through mid-October.

⒔ Bear Brook State Park

Location: Southeast of Concord; Southern New Hampshire map page 169, grid c4.

Campsites, facilities: There are 93 sites for tents and RVs, all without hookups. Each site has a picnic table and fire ring. A dump station, laundry facilities, rest rooms, and hot showers are provided. Some facilities are wheelchair accessible. Within the park you'll find picnic areas, ball fields, and play areas. A small grocery store carries ice and firewood. Leashed pets are permitted.

Reservations, fees: For reservations, call the New Hampshire Division of Parks and Recreation (see phone number below) on weekdays between 8:30 A.M. and 3:30 P.M. from January through August. Sites are $14 a night per family. Extra adults must pay $7 each.

Contact: Bear Brook State Park, RFD 1, Box 507, Allenstown, NH 03275; (603) 845-9869. New Hampshire Division of Parks and Recreation, (603) 271-3628.

Directions: From the northern junction of Route 28 and U.S. 3 in Suncook, travel eight miles northeast on Route 28 to the campground entrance.

Trip notes: Wooded campsites at Bear Brook State Park are located on Beaver Pond. The park encompasses 10,000 acres and is traversed by an extensive multiuse trail system open to hikers, mountain bikers, and horseback riders. Summits, bogs, marshlands, and ponds are accessed by these paths. Visitors can rent canoes at Beaver and Catamount Ponds, and rowboats are also available at the campground. The New Hampshire Department of Fish and Game maintains two public archery ranges at Bear Brook, the only two in the state. A museum complex at the park includes a 4-H Nature Center with exhibits on the park's natural history, the New Hampshire Antique Snowmobile Museum, a Museum of Family Camping, and a Civilian Conservation Corps Museum; all are housed in historic CCC buildings.

Open: Mid-May through mid-October.

⒕ Pawtuckaway State Park

Location: On Pawtuckaway Lake in Raymond; Southern New Hampshire map page 169, grid c5.

Campsites, facilities: There are 193 sites at three locations for tents. Each site has a picnic table and fire ring. Rest rooms, metered hot showers, and boat rentals are provided. Within the park you'll find picnic areas, ball fields, and play areas. A small grocery store carries ice and firewood. No pets are allowed.

Reservations, fees: For reservations, call the New Hampshire Division of Parks and Recreation (see phone number below) on weekdays between 8:30 A.M. and 3:30 P.M. from January through August. Inland sites on Big Island are $14 a night; waterfront sites on Big Island and sites on Horse's Island and Neals Cove are $20 a night. All rates are for families. Each additional adult pays half a site fee. Campers 65 and older are offered a $2 discount per site from Sunday through Thursday.

Contact: Pawtuckaway State Park, 128 Mountain Road, Nottingham, NH 03290; (603) 895-3031. New Hampshire Division of Parks and Recreation, (603) 271-3628.

Directions: From the junction of Routes 101 and 156 in Raymond, travel 3.5 miles north on Route 156 to Mountain Road. Turn left and follow the road into the park.

Trip notes: Most of the woodsy, private sites at this state park are set along the shores of Pawtuckaway Lake. Campers may not swim at their sites, but there is a beach area for those who want to jump in. Canoes and paddleboats are available for rent at the campground, and a boat launch is provided; motors are permitted. Pawtuckaway Lake has many small islands and is home to small-mouth and largemouth bass, so fishing enthusiasts should bring their gear. Mountain bikers and hikers can explore the 6,500-acre state park on several loop trails. The Pawtuckaway Mountains, especially the south peak, which has a fire tower, offer sweeping views over this otherwise flat part of the state.

Open: Mid-May through mid-October.

---

139 Grand View Camping Area

Location: On Baxter Lake west of Rochester; Southern New Hampshire map page 169, grid b5.

Campsites, facilities: There are 100 sites for tents and RVs, most with water and electric hookups. Each site has a picnic table and fire ring. A dump station, rest rooms, hot showers, a rec hall, and a playground are provided. A camp store sells ice and firewood. Leashed pets are permitted.

Reservations, fees: Reservations are accepted. Sites are $20 a night per family. Seasonal and yearly rates are available.

Contact: Grand View Camping Area, 51 Four Rod Road, Rochester, NH 03867; (603) 332-1263.

Directions: From the Spaulding Turnpike (Route 16) in Rochester, take exit 14 to Ten Rod Road and travel south for 1.5 miles. Take a right on Four Rod Road; the campground entrance will be a half mile ahead on the west side of the road.

Trip notes: Wooded sites are set on the shore of Baxter Lake, looking out across the water and to the mountains in the distance. Baxter is a warm-water habitat that supports several species of bass as well as pickerel and perch. Boats are available for rent at the campground. The prominent feature on the horizon to the west is Blue Job Mountain. An easy hike starts at First Crown Point Road and ascends the 1,356-foot peak, where a fire tower on top affords views of the ocean on a clear day.

Open: Mid-May through October 1.

---

140 Crown Point Campground

Location: West of the Rochester Reservoir; Southern New Hampshire map page 169, grid b5.

Campsites, facilities: There are 135 sites for tents and RVs, 100 with full hookups and 35 with water and electric. Each site has a picnic table and fire ring. A dump station, rest rooms, hot showers, a rec hall, and a playground are provided. A camp store sells LP gas, limited groceries, ice, and firewood. Courts for badminton, volleyball, and horseshoes are located on the property. Leashed pets are permitted.

Reservations, fees: Reservations are recommended and require a nonrefundable deposit. For a family of five, tent sites are $16 a night, pop-up sites are $18 a night, and RV sites are $20 a night. Seasonal rates are available.

Contact: Crown Point Campground, 44 First Crown Point Road, Rochester, NH 03867; (603) 332-0405.

Directions: From the junction of the Spaulding Turnpike (Route 16) and Ten Rod Road in Rochester at exit 14, travel two-tenths of a mile south on Route 11, then two-tenths of a mile west on Twombley Street, then four miles southwest on Route 202A. Take a right onto First Crown Point Road and the campground entrance will be just ahead on the left.

Trip notes: A clear 6.5-acre pond on Berrys Brook is the center of activity for campers at Crown Point. The privately owned pond is flanked by woods and grass, and anglers may pull fish from its waters without a license. While away a few hours on the pond by paddling or pedaling in a rental boat or join in a game of beach volleyball. At night, campers gather for dances, bonfires, and barbecues. There's a snack bar on the premises, and breakfast is available on weekends. If you're looking for a low-key family camping experience in undeveloped countryside, this is a good choice.

Open: Mid-May through mid-October.

⓲① Ayers Lake Farm Campground

Location: Southwest of Rochester on Ayers Lake; Southern New Hampshire map page 169, grid b5.

Campsites, facilities: There are 50 sites for tents and RVs up to 32 feet long, 44 with water and electric hookups. Each site has a picnic table and fire ring. A dump station, rest rooms, hot showers, and a playground are provided. Ice and firewood are available. Leashed pets are permitted.

Reservations, fees: Reservations are accepted. Sites are $15 to $24 a night per family. Seasonal rates are available.

Contact: Ayers Lake Farm Campground, U.S. Route 202, Barrington, NH 03825; (603) 332-5940.

Directions: From the junction of U.S. 202 and the Spaulding Turnpike (Route 16) in Rochester, travel five miles southwest on U.S. 202 to the campground entrance.

Trip notes: Fifteen acres of forest, field, and shoreline envelop these sites set in a grove of pine trees near and next to Ayers Lake. Anglers can pull perch, horned pout, and pickerel from the pond if they have a New Hampshire license. To get out on the lake, rent a canoe at the campground or launch your own; a public boat ramp is available just to the south of the campground. Many sites are right beside the water, and four "island" sites are found on a private wooded peninsula. A rambling New England farmhouse holds the campground headquarters. The Nippo Lake Golf Course, located a bit farther down U.S. 202, has nine holes for casual chippers.

Open: Late May through late September.

⓲② Barrington Shores Camping Area

Location: On Swains Lake in Barrington; Southern New Hampshire map page 169, grid b5.

Campsites, facilities: There are 140 sites for tents and RVs, 70 with full hookups and 70 with water and electric. Each site has a picnic table and fire ring. Use of air conditioners and heaters is allowed. A dump station, laundry facilities, rest rooms, hot showers, a rec hall, boat rentals, and a playground are provided. A camp store sells LP gas, ice, and firewood. Courts for volleyball, basketball, badminton, and horseshoes are located on the property. Leashed pets are permitted.

Reservations, fees: For reservations during holiday weekends and for stays of fewer than three days, full prepayment is required. Longer stays require a 50 percent deposit. Sites are $20 to $24 a night per family.

Contact: Barrington Shores Camping Area, 70 Hall Road, Barrington, NH 03825; (603) 664-9333.

Directions: From the intersection of U.S. 4 and Route 125 in Lee, travel three miles north on Route 125, then turn left on Beauty Hill Road and go one mile west. Take another left onto Hall Road and travel one mile south to the campground.

Trip notes: Gentle hills covered with a mixed forest of white pine, oak, and maple trees above Swains Lake are terraced with roomy campsites for tents and RVs at Barrington Shores Camping Area. Clubs and organizations can stay in a group area with hookups. Three-mile Swains Lake is a haven for powerboaters; slips, boat rentals, and a boat launch are provided at the campground. There are two beaches for swimming and sunbathing, and great bass fishing in the lake's many shadowy nooks and crannies. Ocean beaches and coastal attractions are about a half-hour's drive to the east.

Open: Early May through late September.

⒁ Old Stage Campground

Location: West of Dover; Southern New Hampshire map page 169, grid b5.

Campsites, facilities: There are 127 sites for tents and RVs, 81 with full hookups and 46 with water and electric. Each site has a picnic table and fire ring. Use of air conditioners and heaters is allowed. A dump station, laundry facilities, rest rooms, metered hot showers, a rec hall, pool, sports field, and playground are provided. A small grocery store carries RV supplies, ice, and firewood. Courts for volleyball, basketball, badminton, shuffleboard, and horseshoes are located on the property. Group sites for tents and RVs are available. Traffic is controlled by a gate at the entrance. Leashed pets are permitted.

Reservations, fees: Reservations are recommended in July and August and must be accompanied by a prepaid deposit. Sites start at $22 a night per family.

Contact: Old Stage Campground, 46 Old Stage Road, Dover, NH 03820; (603) 742-4050.

Directions: From the Spaulding Turnpike (Route 16) in Dover, take exit 8W and travel northwest on Route 9 for approximately 1.5 miles. Turn left on Old Stage Road and continue to the campground entrance a half mile ahead.

Trip notes: The tent and RV campsites in this rural and quiet area on the outskirts of Dover are wooded and offer welcome privacy. In addition to a pool, the grounds hold a small pond for fishing and swimming. A recreation director plans group activities in the summer months. The city of Dover to the east has several historical buildings along the Cocheco River and offers all manner of goods and services. Portsmouth, the hub of cultural activity on the seacoast, lies just a short drive to the east; earthy shops and eateries line that city's small streets, some of which are cobblestoned. At night those streets are filled with pub crawlers and theatergoers, and young crowds from a host of coffeehouses encroach on the sidewalks.

Open: Mid-May through mid-October.

144 Forest Glen Campground

Location: On Wheelright Pond in Lee; Southern New Hampshire map page 169, grid c5.

Campsites, facilities: There are 130 sites for tents and RVs with water and electric hookups. Each site has a table and fire ring. A dump station, laundry facilities, rest rooms, metered hot showers, a rec hall, and a playground are provided. LP gas, ice, and wood are sold on site. You'll also find courts for volleyball, basketball, badminton, and horseshoes. Leashed pets are permitted.

Reservations, fees: Reservations are recommended in the summer. Sites are $18 to $22 a night per family. Weekly and seasonal rates are available on request.

Contact: Forest Glen Campground, P.O. Box 676, Durham, NH 03824; (603) 659-3416.

Directions: From the center of Lee on Route 155, travel one mile north to the campground entrance on the left.

Trip notes: Wheelright Pond is a fishing refuge carved into a pine forest. Warm waters support bass, white perch, pickerel, and horned pout. Campers can launch and dock their boats at the campground if they pay a surcharge and are staying for more than a few days. The town of Durham to the east is home to the University of New Hampshire, where summer cultural offerings include nationally booked musical acts.

Open: May 15 through September 15.

145 Ferndale Acres Campground

Location: Near the center of Lee; Southern New Hampshire map page 169, grid c5.

Campsites, facilities: There are 130 sites for tents and RVs, 50 with full hookups and 80 with water and electric. Each site has a picnic table and fire ring. A dump station, laundry facilities, rest rooms, hot showers, a rec hall, pool, and playground are provided. A small grocery store carries LP gas, ice, and firewood. Courts for volleyball, basketball, badminton, and horseshoes are located on the property. Leashed pets are permitted.

Reservations, fees: Reservations require a nonrefundable deposit. Sites start at $17 a night for two people. Weekly, monthly, and seasonal rates are available on request.

Contact: Ferndale Acres Campground, 132 Wednesday Hill Road, Lee, NH 03824; (603) 659-5082.

Directions: From the intersection of U.S. 4 and Route 155 north of Lee, travel 2.5 miles south on Route 155, then turn left on Wednesday Hill Road and go 1.5 miles east of the center of town. Turn right on the campground road at the sign and continue south for three-quarters of a mile to the campground.

Trip notes: A pine tree canopy provides cooling shade at these campsites found here in the boondocks of Lee. The Little River flows right by the retreat, offering trout fishing and easy flows for paddling lazily in a canoe. Swimmers can cool off in the campground pool or in the river itself. Just to the east in Durham, the Wiswall Dam and Packers Falls flank a pretty swimming hole complete with sunbathing rocks. For four-wheeled entertainment, take the entire family to the New England Speedway to the south in Epping. Special events there include the Funny Car Nationals and Corvette Day. Campers can also find fun closer to home on the weekends when the campground hosts organized activities.

Open: May 15 through September 15.

⒕⒍ Lamprey River Campground

Location: West of the town of New-market; Southern New Hampshire map page 169, grid c5.

Campsites, facilities: There are 99 sites for tents and RVs, 89 with water and electric hookups and 10 with none. Each site has a picnic table and fire ring. A dump station, laundry facilities, rest rooms, metered hot showers, a rec hall, sports field, pool, and playground are provided. A camp store carries LP gas, ice, and firewood. Courts for volleyball and badminton and horseshoe pits are located on the property. Leashed pets are permitted.

Reservations, fees: Reservations are recommended. Sites are $18 to $20 a night per family. Weekly, monthly, and seasonal rates are provided on request.

Contact: Lamprey River Campground, 16 Campground Road, Lee, NH 03824; (603) 659-3852.

Directions: From the junction of Routes 125 and 152 in South Lee, travel just under two miles east on Route 152. At the campground road, take a right and head south to the campground entrance less than a quarter mile ahead.

Trip notes: Lamprey River Campground features a primitive tenting area and tent sites set beside the river in addition to many fully equipped RV sites. The Lamprey—a stream that is known in these parts for its good trout fishing—follows a roundabout course but eventually veers southeast and enters Great Bay. For paddlers, there is an easy canoe route that starts at Newmarket and ends on the bay, passing through urban and undeveloped areas on the shallow estuary.

Open: May 15 through October 15.

⒕⒎ Surry Mountain Camping Area

Location: On Surry Mountain Lake; Southern New Hampshire map page 169, grid c1.

Campsites, facilities: There are 43 sites for tents and RVs, 38 with water and electric hookups. Each site has a picnic table, fire ring, and grill. A portable dump service, flush toilets, and hot showers are provided. Ice and firewood are sold on site. Horseshoe pits and a volleyball court are located on the property. Leashed pets are permitted.

Reservations, fees: Reservations are recommended. Sites are $17 to $19 a night per family.

Contact: Surry Mountain Camping Area, East Shore Road, Keene, NH 03431; (603) 352-9880.

Directions: From the junction of Routes 12 and 12A north of Keene, head north on Route 12A for four miles. Take a right turn onto the entrance road and head southeast for a quarter mile to the campground.

Trip notes: Spacious and wooded sites offer maximum privacy and access to almost 2,000 acres of protected land in the neighboring Surry Mountain Lake Project, a holding of the U.S. Army Corps of Engineers. Good warm-water fishing for largemouth bass, pickerel, horned pout, and yellow perch is offered on the 265-acre lake. If trout is your preferred game, head south of the dam and wade into the spirited Ashuelot River. Motors up to 10 horsepower are welcome on Surry Mountain Lake, and you'll find a maintained beach and picnic area on project land. Several hiking trails traverse the protected area. For golfers, less than two miles south of here on Route 12A, the 27-hole Bretwood Golf Course is open to the public.

Open: May 15 through October 15.

⓵⓸⓼ Hilltop Campground and Adventure Games

Location: South of Sullivan; Southern New Hampshire map page 169, grid c2.

Campsites, facilities: There are 39 sites for tents and RVs, 32 with water and electric hookups and the rest with none. Each site has a picnic table and fire ring. Facilities include a dump station, rest rooms, hot showers, a pavilion, pool, and playground. A store sells ice and firewood. Courts for volleyball, badminton, and horseshoes are provided. Services and supplies are available in Sullivan, a few miles north of the campground. Leashed pets are permitted.

Reservations, fees: Reservations are recommended. Sites without hookups start at $15 a night per family, and sites with hookups start at $18 a night.

Contact: Hilltop Campground and Adventure Games, HCR 33, Box 186, Keene, NH 03431; (603) 847-3351.

Directions: From the northern junction of Routes 9 and 10 north of Keene, travel one mile east on Route 9, then turn left and drive another two miles northeast on Sullivan Road. The campground is on the east side of the road.

Trip notes: Mountain views and a choice of open and shaded sites are just some of the features of this campground located in a rural, rolling countryside setting. Ferry Brook runs through the property and is open to fishing, but better fishing can be found by driving a short distance northeast to Otter Brook, a healthy trout stream near East Sullivan. Just south of the campground is the Otter Brook Lake Project and dam; the lake is open to nonmotorized boating, and has a swimming beach and a ball field near the shore. Hilltop Campground also oper-

ates a paintball adventure game company on the grounds. Campers can rent "guns" in the pro shop and play a souped-up version of capture the flag. Staff members are well trained and use radio communication to ensure that games run safely and smoothly.

Open: May 1 through October 1.

⓵⓸⓽ Swanzey Lake Camping Area

Location: On Swanzey Lake; Southern New Hampshire map page 169, grid d1.

Campsites, facilities: There are 75 sites for tents and RVs, 30 with full hookups, 10 with water and electric, and 35 with none. A dump station, pit toilets, a rec hall, metered hot showers, tables, and fire rings are provided. Also on the grounds are a ball field and a volleyball court. Ice and firewood are sold on site. The maximum RV length is 35 feet. Pets are allowed before Memorial Day and after Labor Day.

Reservations, fees: Reservations are recommended. Sites are $15 to $21 a night for two people.

Contact: Swanzey Lake Camping Area, East Shore Road, Keene, NH 03431; (603) 352-9880.

Directions: From the intersection of Routes 10 and 12 in Keene, travel south on Route 12 for one mile. Bear right on Route 32 and continue south for five more miles. Take a right onto Lake Road and head southwest for two miles. Take another right onto East Shore Road and head north to the campground on the left side of the road at number 88.

Trip notes: Gentle green hills surround spring-fed Swanzey Lake, which is home to trout and bass. Wooded sites are set near and on the shoreline. Sink your toes into cool sand, dive into the crystal-clear water, or ply the surface for a few hours in a rented boat. A number of dirt roads to the north of the lake are good routes for mountain bike excursions; three nearby covered bridges can be reached on a 10-mile loop. For more extensive rides, head west to Pisgah State Park, once known as the Pisgah Wilderness. With more than 30 miles of old logging roads, summits, valleys, marshes, and ponds, it makes a great day-trip destination.

Open: Mid-May through mid-October.

---

⑮⓪ Forest Lake Campground

Location: On the north shore of Forest Lake in Winchester; Southern New Hampshire map page 169, grid d2.

Campsites, facilities: There are 150 sites for tents and RVs, 85 with full hookups, 55 with water and electric, and 10 with none. Each site has a picnic table, fire ring, and grill. Air conditioners are allowed, and phone hookups are available. A dump station, rest rooms, hot showers, a pool, ball field, rec hall, and playground are provided. There are also courts for basketball, shuffleboard, and horseshoes. A store sells ice, LP gas, and firewood. Supplies and services can be obtained 1.5 miles south in Winchester. The maximum RV length is 35 feet. Leashed pets are permitted.

Reservations, fees: Reservations are recommended in July and August and are accepted with a nonrefundable deposit of two days' fees. Sites start at $17 a night and $102 a week for a family of four. Monthly and seasonal rates are available.

Contact: Forest Lake Campground, 331 Keene Road, Winchester, NH 03470; (603) 239-4267.

Directions: From the junction of Routes 10 and 9 in Keene, travel south for 10 miles on Route 10 to the campground entrance on the left (east) side of the road.

Trip notes: Boat rentals, a boat launch, and a big beach on Forest Lake center the action here at water's edge. Roomy wooded sites are set back from the shoreline, and some even boast mountain views. This warm-water lake near the Massachusetts border is home to pickerel, smallmouth bass, and horned pout. Just west of the campground on the other side of Route 10 lies Pisgah State Park, formerly called the Pisgah Wilderness. Twenty square miles of low ridges, dividing valleys, and ponds, streams, and marshes are accessed by more than 30 miles of old logging roads perfect for moderate mountain bike rides.

Open: May 1 through October 1.

---

⑮① Shir-Roy Camping Area

Location: On Cass Pond in Richmond; Southern New Hampshire map page 169, grid d2.

Campsites, facilities: There are 110 sites for tents and RVs, 107 with water and electric hookups and three with none. Each site has a picnic table, fire ring, and grill. Air conditioners are allowed, but heaters are prohibited. A dump station, laundry facilities, rest rooms, hot showers, and a playground are provided. You'll also find courts for volleyball, badminton, and horseshoes and a camp store selling groceries, RV supplies, ice, and firewood. Tent cottages and tent trailers are also for rent. Off-season RV storage is available. Leashed pets are permitted.

Reservations, fees: Reservations are recommended Memorial Day through Labor Day and require a 50 percent deposit. There is a three-day minimum stay during holiday weekends. Sites without hookups start at $17 a night per family. With hookups, sites start at $20 a night per family.

Contact: Shir-Roy Camping Area, 100 Athol Road, Richmond, NH 03470; (603) 239-4768.

Directions: From the center of Richmond at the intersection of Routes 32 and 119, travel one mile south on Route 32 to the campground entrance on the left (east) side of the road.

Trip notes: You'll find lakeside campsites under pine trees at Shir-Roy, where fishing, boating, and swimming on Cass Pond are the main activities. Anglers can try for largemouth bass, pickerel, horned pout, and perch; fishing licenses are for sale at the campground. A sandy beach welcomes swimmers and sunbathers at the water's edge. Canoes, rowboats, and paddleboats may be rented by the hour or the half-day, and for a small fee you may dock your own vessel on site. To the northeast of Shir-Roy lies Rhododendron State Park and Little Monadnock Mountain. Nature trails weave through more than 16 acres of wild rhododendrons, and a one-mile hike leads to the summit of Little Monadnock Mountain; this peak offers a view of Mount Monadnock and the smaller peaks in the area from the south.

Open: Late May through early October.

⓲ Laurel Lake Campground

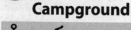

Location: South of Fitzwilliam near the Massachusetts border; Southern New Hampshire map page 169, grid d2.

Campsites, facilities: There are 65 sites for tents and RVs, 54 with water and electric hookups and the rest with none. Each site has a table and fire ring. Use of air conditioners and heaters is not allowed. A dump station, laundry facilities, rest rooms, hot showers, and a playground are provided. There are also courts for basketball, volleyball, and horseshoes. A snack bar and a store are nearby. The maximum RV length is 32 feet. Leashed pets are permitted.

Reservations, fees: Reservations are recommended July 1 through Labor Day. Sites start at $19 a night per family.

Contact: Laurel Lake Campground, P.O. Box 114, Fitzwilliam, NH 03447; (603) 585-3304.

Directions: From the intersection of Routes 12 and 119 in Fitzwilliam (at the blinking light), travel 1.5 miles west on Route 119, then turn left on East Lake Road and go 1.5 miles south to the campground.

Trip notes: Cottages, homes, and a girls' camp dot the wooded shoreline of crystal-line Laurel Lake. This spring-fed beauty is small enough to be private yet large enough for waterskiing. You'll be competing with lots of local fishermen for the resident brown and rainbow trout, smallmouth bass, pickerel, and horned pout. Campsites are tucked into the woods behind a grassy area on the lake. A dock is provided, and there's also a group area for tents. Fitzwilliam is a classic New England town with a hospitable inn and several churches on its picturesque common. It's also home to Rhododendron State Park, a National Natural Landmark; a walking path there explores more than 16 acres of wild rhododendrons that are usually in full bloom by mid-July.

Open: May 15 through October 15.

⓳ Hunter's State Line Campground

Location: On Sip Pond near the Massachusetts border; Southern New Hampshire map page 169, grid d2.

Campsites, facilities: There are 100 sites for tents and RVs, some with full hookups. Each site has a picnic table and fire ring. A dump station, laundry facilities, rest rooms, hot showers, a snack bar, and a playground are provided. A store sells ice, firewood, and bait. Leashed pets are permitted.

Reservations, fees: Reservations are recommended. Sites start at $18 a night per family. Weekly, monthly, and seasonal rates are available.

Contact: Hunter's State Line Campground, Route 12, Box 132, Fitzwilliam, NH 03447; (603) 585-7726.

Directions: From Fitzwilliam, travel four miles south on Route 12 to the campground.

Trip notes: Year-round camping in the sticks beside Sip Pond is what's offered at Hunter's State Line. In the summer months, campers enjoy the swimming beach, dock, and rental paddleboats on this undeveloped lake. Many species of warm-water fish lurk in the shallow waters. In fall and spring, hunters can comb miles of woods and marshland in search of deer and hare. Then in winter, ice fishers try for pickerel and perch. An easy family day hike is located west of the campground at Rhododendron State Park. The park itself is in full bloom in mid- to late July. A trail on the north side of the park leads into Little Monadnock State Park, where a one-mile hike through a hardwood forest over moderate terrain brings you to the 1,833-foot summit of Little Monadnock Mountain for an outstanding view of Mount Monadnock from the south.

Open: Year-round.

154 Woodmore Campground

Location: On the southwest shore of Contoocook Lake in Rindge; Southern New Hampshire map page 169, grid d2.

Campsites, facilities: There are 130 sites for tents and RVs, 90 with full hookups, 20 with water and electric, and 20 with none. Each site has a table, fire ring, and grill. Air conditioners are allowed, but heaters are prohibited. A dump station, laundry facilities, rest rooms, hot showers, a pool, and a playground are provided. A grocery store sells RV supplies, LP gas, ice, and firewood. RV storage is available as are group tent and RV sites. Courts for basketball, volleyball, badminton, shuffleboard, and horseshoes are provided. Leashed pets are permitted.

Reservations, fees: Reservations are recommended Memorial Day through Labor Day. Sites without hookups start at $14 a night per family, and sites with hookups start at $19 a night. Weekly, monthly, and seasonal rates are available.

Contact: Woodmore Campground, P.O. Box 830, Rindge, NH 03461; (603) 899-3326.

Directions: From the intersection of U.S. 202 and Route 119 in Rindge, travel north for one mile on U.S. 202 then turn right on Davis Crossing Road. After a quarter mile, turn left on Woodbound Road and continue half a mile to the campground entrance.

Trip notes: Sun-dappled sites are set near and along the shore of Contoocook Lake in rural Rindge. Boats are rented at the campground, and a dock is provided in case you bring your own boat (motors up to 35 horsepower are allowed on the lake). The cove in front of the campground is prime habitat for bass and horned pout; the best time to fish for the latter species is late at night. On weekends, potluck dinners and tournaments bring Woodmore's campers together. Mount Monadnock to the northwest is the most striking feature in this area; you can see it from the northeast end of Contoocook Lake. Monadnock is also one of the most-hiked mountains in the world. The state park entrance and hiking trails are located off Route 124 in Jaffrey.

Open: May 15 through September 20, then weekends only through Columbus Day.

⓺ Emerald Acres Campground

Location: On Cheshire Pond in Jaffrey; Southern New Hampshire map page 169, grid d2.

Campsites, facilities: There are 52 sites for tents and RVs, 44 with full hookups and the rest with none. Each site has a picnic table and fire ring. A dump station, laundry facilities, rest rooms, hot showers, a rec hall, and a playground are provided. Supplies can be obtained less than a mile away in Jaffrey. Leashed pets are permitted.

Reservations, fees: Reservations are recommended. Sites start at $10 a night for two people, with surcharges for all services. Seasonal rates are available.

Contact: Emerald Acres Campground, 39 Ridgecrest Road, Jaffrey, NH 03452; (603) 532-8838.

Directions: From the intersection of U.S. 202 and Route 124 in Jaffrey, travel north on U.S. 202 for three-quarters of a mile to Ridgecrest Road. Turn left and continue to the campground at the end of the street.

Trip notes: These pondside sites set in the shade of pine trees are favored by seasonal campers, so be sure to call ahead and find out if there are any openings. Campers can take a dip in the pond or set out in a canoe. Paddleboats and canoes are rented at the campground. Better swimming and fishing can be found at any of the nearby lakes. Downtown Jaffrey is nearby and offers all the necessary services and supplies. The town is also home to Mount Monadnock, one of the most-hiked peaks in the world. Named for a Native American word meaning "stands alone," this isolated peak affords

views of all six New England states on a clear day. In summer, Jaffrey hosts several cultural events including a bandstand concert series, a lecture forum, and the largest fireworks show on the northeast coast.

Open: May 1 through October 14.

⓺ Monadnock State Park

Location: At the base of Mount Monadnock in Jaffrey; Southern New Hampshire map page 169, grid d2.

Campsites, facilities: There are 21 individual sites for tents and several group camping areas. RVs are not allowed, and there are no hookups. Each site has a picnic table and fire ring. Pit toilets, flush toilets, and piped water are provided in summer, and pit toilets only are maintained in winter. A small camp store sells ice, firewood, and limited supplies. No pets are allowed.

Reservations, fees: Sites are available on a first-come, first-served basis at a fee of $12 a night for up to four people. Youth group sites must be reserved in advance through the campground office.

Contact: Monadnock State Park, P.O. Box 181, Jaffrey, NH 03452; (603) 532-8862.

Directions: From the intersection of U.S. 202 and Route 124 in Jaffrey, travel four miles west on Route 124 to Slade Road. Turn right and head north, following signs to the state park and the campground.

Trip notes: Mount Monadnock has the dubious distinction of being one of the most-hiked mountains in the world. Summit trails here are challenging though relatively short. Since the mountain is a solitary peak (or a monadnock), unobstructed long-distance views are attainable from the summit. In fact, on a clear day you can see points in all six New England states. Fire and deforestation have left behind a bare, rocky top. Heavily used trails leave from the campground, but for less-traveled routes you need only drive a short distance west to either Dublin or Marlborough. These campsites are set in the woods near the state park headquarters. In winter, 14 miles of challenging trails are open to cross-country skiing in the lower elevations.

Open: Year-round.

---

157 Seven Maples Camping Area

Location: North of Hancock on Norway Pond; Southern New Hampshire map page 169, grid c2.

Campsites, facilities: There are 100 sites for tents and RVs, 80 with water and electric hookups. Each site has a picnic table, fire ring, and grill. A dump station, rec hall, rest rooms, hot showers, a pool, and a playground are provided. A store sells LP gas, ice, and firewood. The grounds also have courts for volleyball, badminton, shuffleboard, and horseshoes. Leashed pets are permitted.

Reservations, fees: Reservations are accepted and require a nonrefundable deposit. Sites start at $21 a night per family. Weekly, monthly, and seasonal rates are available.

Contact: Seven Maples Camping Area, 24 Longview Road, Hancock, NH 03449; (603) 525-3321.

Directions: From the intersection of Routes 137 and 123 in Hancock, travel north for half a mile on Route 137 to Longview Road. Turn left and head northwest for a short distance to the campground entrance.

Trip notes: Seasonal campers are the main customers at these tightly clustered sites tucked into the woods near Norway Pond. If you're looking to join an established camping community in a rural setting, this is a good choice. A swimming pool, tennis courts, and hiking trails are right on the property. Moose Brook flows through the campground before emptying into Norway Pond. Brook trout live in the stream, while the pond is home to warm-water species including bass and perch; both waters are open to fishing. A short drive to the west gets you to a prime powerboating destination: Nubanusit Lake, which you can access by using a public boat launch. Prize rainbow trout have been pulled from that lake, so bring your fishing gear.

Open: Early May through mid-October.

---

158 Field 'N' Forest Recreation Area

Location: South of Hancock near Beaver Pond; Southern New Hampshire map page 169, grid c2.

Campsites, facilities: There are 40 sites for tents and RVs, eight with water and electric hookups and the rest with none. Each site has a picnic table, fire ring, and grill. A dump station, sports field, rest rooms, and hot showers are provided. Ice and firewood are sold on site. You'll also find volleyball and badminton courts and horseshoe pits. Leashed pets are permitted.

Reservations, fees: Reservations are accepted and require a nonrefundable deposit. Sites start at $18 a night per family. Weekly, monthly, and seasonal rates are available.

Contact: Field 'N' Forest Recreation Area, Route 137, Hancock, NH 03449; (603) 525-3568.

Directions: From the intersection of Routes 137 and 123 in Hancock, travel south for three miles on Route 137 to the campground entrance on the left (east) side of the road.

Trip notes: Tranquillity and privacy reign at this small rural campground. Campers can select from open, wooded, or grassy sites. Whichever you choose, you will be near Beaver Pond, which is open to swimming and fishing. Nature trails meander into a mixed forest abutting the pond and head south into protected lands around the Edward MacDowell Lake Project. Operated by the U.S. Army Corps of Engineers, MacDowell Dam is the site of nature and interpretive programs held in the summer months, including story programs for kids.

Open: Memorial Day through Labor Day.

159 Oxbow Campground

Location: Near Hillsborough; Southern New Hampshire map page 169, grid c3.

Campsites, facilities: There are 74 sites for tents and RVs, 60 with full hookups and 14 with none. Each site has a picnic table, fire ring, and grill. Air conditioners are allowed, but heaters are prohibited. Cable TV and telephone hookups are available. Facilities include a dump station, laundry, rest rooms, hot showers, a rec hall, pavilion, and playground. A store sells ice, firewood, and snacks. Courts for basketball, volleyball, badminton, shuffleboard, and horseshoes are provided. Leashed pets are permitted.

Reservations, fees: Reservations are accepted. Sites without hookups start at $16 a night per family, and sites with full hookups start at $21 a night. Weekly, monthly, and seasonal rates are available.

Contact: Oxbow Campground, RFD 1, Box 11, Hillsborough, NH 03244; (603) 464-5952.

Directions: From the junction of U.S. 202

and Route 149 in Hillsborough, travel three-quarters of a mile south on Route 149 to the campground entrance.

Trip notes: A mix of lawns and thick woodlands surrounds the roomy sites at Oxbow, where campers can choose from open or shaded settings. A spring-fed swimming pond on the property is flanked by a sandy beach, and more than 100 acres of forestland here are traversed by trails for hiking and cross-country skiing; one favorite destination is a giant red oak tree. For longer hikes and excellent birding, head north to Fox State Forest in Hillsborough. More than 20 miles of foot trails explore the moderate hills of this 1,432-acre sanctuary studded with hardwoods and orchards. The north-flowing Contoocook River runs through downtown Hillsborough just to the north of Oxbow Campground and offers challenging and technical white-water canoeing above the bridge; it's also a good place to fish for trout. South of town on U.S. 202, the Angus Lea nine-hole golf course is open to the public. Hillsborough is a quiet country town for the most part, but in late September when the neighboring community of Deerfield hosts the annual Deerfield Fair, both towns swell with visitors who attend agricultural events including tractor pulls, mutant and prize vegetable exhibits, harness racing, and horse, sheep, and cow shows.

Open: Fully operational May 15 through October 15 and open for winter camping November 15 through April 15; closed two months of the year.

160 Greenfield State Park

Location: On Otter Lake in Greenfield; Southern New Hampshire map page 169, grid c3.

Campsites, facilities: There are 252

sites for tents and RVs, all without hookups. Each site has a picnic table and fire ring. Facilities include a dump station, rest rooms, hot showers, and a playground. A store sells ice, firewood, and limited supplies. Youth group camping and day-use areas are available by reservation. Leashed pets are permitted in designated areas.

Reservations, fees: For reservations, call the New Hampshire Division of Parks and Recreation (see phone number below) on weekdays between 8:30 A.M. and 3:30 P.M. from January through August. Sites are $14 a night for up to four people.

Contact: Greenfield State Park, P.O. Box 203, Greenfield, NH 03047; (603) 547-3497. New Hampshire Division of Parks and Recreation, (603) 271-3628.

Directions: From the center of Greenfield, travel one mile west on Route 31 to the state park entrance.

Trip notes: Natural campsites are set in the woods near Otter Lake. Canoes and rowboats are rented out at the campground, and you may launch your own boat at Greenfield State Park's public ramp. Many youth groups organize overnight outings here, so be forewarned that the park is often overrun with young campers during the summer months. Hiking trails explore the surrounding woods and marshlands. Otter Brook supports several warm-water species of fish and attracts anglers who come to cast out a line.

To get a bird's-eye view of the area, drive to the Crotched Mountain Rehabilitation Center via the road across from the park entrance. Leave your car at the crest of the hill and follow a trail to the summit of Crotched Mountain. You will see old ski trails on the hillside, and, on clear days, Franconia Notch in the White Mountains will be visible to the north.

Open: Mid-May through Columbus Day.

161 Friendly Beaver Campground

Location: Northwest of New Boston; Southern New Hampshire map page 169, grid c3.

Campsites, facilities: There are 172 sites for tents and RVs, 131 with full hookups and 41 with water and electric. Each site has a picnic table and fire ring. Group sites are available. Use of air conditioners is allowed. A dump station, laundry facilities, rest rooms, hot showers, a rec hall, patio area, four pools, and a playground are provided. A small camp store carries groceries, LP gas, ice, and firewood. Courts for basketball, badminton, and horseshoes are located on the property. There's also a sports field and a recreation director. Leashed pets are permitted.

Reservations, fees: Prepaid deposits are required for all reservations, and holiday weekend reservations must be prepaid in full. Sites are $23 to $28 a night per family. Weekly, monthly, and year-round seasonal rates are available.

Contact: Friendly Beaver Campground, Old Coach Road, New Boston, NH 03070; (603) 487-5570.

Directions: From the junction of Routes 77, 136, and 13 (known as the Southwest Corner in New Boston), travel two miles west on Old Coach Road, following signs to the campground entrance on the right.

Trip notes: Closely settled campsites at Friendly Beaver are tucked in under the trees, providing adequate privacy. Numerous sites are occupied by seasonal campers who use the facility year-round. An aquatic compound featuring an open-air deck with umbrellas and tables is the center of action in both winter and summer, offering three outdoor pools for sports, wading, and swimming and an indoor heated pool and a Jacuzzi. Miles of multiuse trails leave from the campground; in winter they are popular with snowmobilers who rejuvenate in the whirlpool after a day out in the elements. The playground is surrounded by a chain-link fence and features natural wood play structures such as Noah's Ark, airplanes, castles, and trucks. Families can choose from a long list of organized activities including sing-a-longs, carnivals, dances, parades, and competitions. Ceramics classes are conducted at an on-site studio.

Open: Year-round.

⓲ Wildwood Campground

Location: Southwest of New Boston; Southern New Hampshire map page 169, grid c3.

Campsites, facilities: There are 100 sites for tents and RVs, 35 with full hookups, 62 with water and electric, and 3 with none. Each site has a picnic table, fire ring, and grill. Use of air conditioners and heaters is allowed. A dump station, laundry facilities, rest rooms, metered hot showers, a rec room, pool, and playground are provided. A grocery store carries LP gas, ice, and firewood. Courts for volleyball, badminton, and horseshoes are located on the property. Leashed pets are permitted.

Reservations, fees: Advance reservations are accepted with a 50 percent prepaid deposit. Tent sites are $18 a night and full-hookup sites are $22 a night for a family of four. In winter, all sites start at $22 a night. Weekly, monthly, seasonal, and group rates are available.

Contact: Wildwood Campground, 540 Old Coach Road, New Boston, NH 03070; (603) 487-3300.

Directions: From the junction of Routes 77, 136, and 13 (known as the Southwest Corner in New Boston), travel 3.5 miles southwest on Old Coach Road to the campground entrance on the left.

Trip notes: Camping in the southern New Hampshire sticks is what you'll find at Wildwood. Tall pine trees shade densely settled campsites in the backwoods of New Boston. Kids can fish in a small pond on the property, but grown-ups will have to head to other nearby brooks and rivers to cast a line. There's a swimming pool on the grounds. The resident country band Pony Express plays regularly for campers, and bonfires, hayrides, and bingo games round out the planned activities schedule. Sites are open for overnight and seasonal camping in winter.

Open: Year-round; fully operational May 1 through October 15.

⓳ Field and Stream Park

Location: Near Pontanipo Pond in Brookline; Southern New Hampshire map page 169, grid d3.

Campsites, facilities: There are 54 sites for tents and RVs, 19 with full hookups and 35 with water and electric. Each site has a picnic table and fire ring. Use of air conditioners and heaters is allowed. A dump station, laundry facilities, rest rooms, metered hot showers, a rec hall, pavilion, pool, and playground are provided. A camp store sells LP gas, ice, and firewood. Courts for volleyball, basketball, badminton, and horseshoes are located on the property. A gate controls traffic at the entrance. Leashed pets are permitted.

Reservations, fees: Reservations are required from November through April and accepted at other times. Sites start $17 a night per family.

Contact: Field and Stream Park, 5 Dupaw Gould Road, Brookline, NH 03033; (603) 673-4677.

Directions: From the intersection of Routes 13 and 130 in Brookline, travel one mile west on Route 130 (Mason Road) to Dupaw Gould Road. Turn right and travel a quarter mile north to the campground entrance.

Trip notes: Any size RV can be accommodated at Field and Stream. The campground is aptly named, as most of the sites are on grassy plots in a lightly wooded area along Gould Mill Brook, which is stocked with trout. Canoeists can put in at the campground and paddle a short distance southwest to Pontanipo Pond, a warm-water habitat supporting bass and horned pout. A few miles from the Massachusetts border, this campground is located in a small town but is close to Nashua, New Hampshire's second largest city. Winter sites are open to seasonal campers only.

Open: Year-round; fully-operational May 1 through October 31.

164 Autumn Hills Campground

Location: South of Weare Center; Southern New Hampshire map page 169, grid c3.

Campsites, facilities: There are 97 sites for tents and RVs, 76 with full hookups and 21 with water and electric. Each site has a picnic table, grill, and fire ring. A dump station, rest rooms, metered hot showers, a rec hall, pavilion, pool, and playground are provided. A camp store carries LP gas, ice, and firewood. Courts for volleyball, basketball, badminton, and horseshoes are located on the property. Leashed pets are permitted.

Reservations, fees: Prepaid deposits must accompany reservations. Sites start at

$18 a night per family. Weekly, monthly, and seasonal rates are available.

Contact: Autumn Hills Campground, 285 South Stark Highway, South Weare, NH 03281; (603)-529-2425.

Directions: From the junction of Routes 114 and 149 in South Weare, travel 2.5 miles east on Route 149 to the campground entrance on the left (north) side of the road.

Trip notes: Rolling woodlands of tall oak and pine trees shade the sites at this full-service RV park near Horace Lake and Clough State Park. Huse Brook forms a small pond on the property and is open to fishing. A few miles to the north, Clough State Park is situated on a river pool that is stocked with trout. Sandy beaches for swimming are available at the state park and also at larger Horace Lake to the west. A public boat launch and wide, clear waters at Horace Lake attract powerboaters and water-skiers, especially on weekends. The community of seasonal campers at Autumn Hills takes part in dancing, dinners, and theme weekends. They also crown an annual winner in a male beauty contest.

Open: Late April through late September.

165 Cold Springs Campground

Location: West of Goffstown; Southern New Hampshire map page 169, grid c3.

Campsites, facilities: There are 250 sites for tents and RVs, 150 with full hookups and 90 with water and electric. Each site has a table and fire ring. A dump station, laundry facilities, rest rooms, hot showers, a rec hall, pavilion, two heated pools, and a playground are provided. A camp store carries LP gas, ice, and wood. Courts for volleyball and horseshoes are located on the property. Leashed pets are permitted.

Reservations, fees: Nonrefundable deposits are required for all reservations. Sites start at $15 a night for two people. Seasonal rates are available on request.

Contact: Cold Springs Campground, 22 Wildlife Drive, Weare, NH 03281; (603) 529-2528.

Directions: From the junction of Routes 101 and 114 in Bedford, travel north on Route 114 through Goffstown. Five miles north of Goffstown Center take the first right after the Cold Springs RV Sales Center onto Barnard Hill Road. Signs will lead to the campground entrance.

Trip notes: Operated in conjunction with a full-blown RV sales office, Cold Springs draws hordes of people in motor homes. The campground is well forested, and the sites are scattered beside the shore of a pond. Pull-through sites and paved roads are designed to handle vehicles of any size. Once you park, you'll find a wide array of recreational offerings from tennis courts (you can rent equipment) and two heated pools to a sundeck and a whirlpool. Regularly organized events include live entertainment, bingo tournaments, scavenger hunts, and special meals. There is also a family restaurant on the property.

Open: Mid-April through Columbus Day.

166 Calef Lake Camping Area

Location: East of Massabesic Lake in Auburn; Southern New Hampshire map page 169, grid c4.

Campsites, facilities: There are 130 sites for tents and RVs up to 29 feet long, 121 with water and electric hookups. Each site has a picnic table, fire ring, and grill. A dump station, laundry facilities, rest rooms, metered hot showers, and a pavilion are provided. A small camp store carries LP gas, ice, and firewood. Courts for basketball, badminton, volleyball, and horseshoes are located on the property. Leashed pets are permitted.

Reservations, fees: Reservations are recommended. Sites are $17 to $20 a night per family. Weekly and seasonal rates are available.

Contact: Bill Cooper, Calef Lake Camping Area, 556 Chester Road, Auburn, NH 03032; (603) 483-8282.

Directions: From the junction of Bypass Route 28 and Route 121 near Auburn, travel 5.5 miles south on Route 121. The campground is on the left (east) side of the road.

Trip notes: Primarily occupied by seasonal campers, the sites at Calef Lake are set in thick woods near and on a privately owned lake. Because the lake belongs to the campground, you are welcome to fish without a license. Canoes, paddleboats, and rowboats may be rented on site; only electric motors are allowed on the water. Wildlife flourish in these quiet environs, so you will see everything from small mammals to songbirds. Beavers have built lodges on another small pond on the property. Several miles of old logging roads are a good pick for short hikes and mountain bike rides.

Open: May through October.

167 Silver Sands Campground

Location: On North Pond east of Derry; Southern New Hampshire map page 169, grid c4.

Campsites, facilities: There are 100 sites for tents and RVs, 50 with full hookups, 20 with water and electric, and 30 with none. Each site has a picnic table and fire ring. A dump station, laundry facilities, rest rooms, metered hot showers, a rec hall, pavilion, pool, and playground are provided. A camp store carries LP gas, ice, and firewood. Courts for volleyball, basketball, badminton, and horseshoes as well as a ball field are located on the property. Leashed pets are permitted.

Reservations, fees: Reservations are recommended. Sites start at $18 a night.

Contact: Silver Sands Campground, 603 Raymond Road, Chester, NH 03036; (603) 887-3638.

Directions: From Interstate 93 in Derry, take exit 4 and travel east for 10 miles on Route 102 to North Pond Road. The campground entrance is just ahead.

Trip notes: North Pond is a privately owned bass pond on the grounds at Silver Sands, so campers can hook their dinner without having to obtain a license. Most of the clientele are seasonal family campers from the region who retreat to the pond's sandy beach on hot weekends. Sites are both open and wooded, and all are close to the water. Whether paddling the calm surface waters or gathering for a Silver Sands barbecue, campers here kick back in the company of tall trees—and little else—for miles around.

Open: May 1 through October 1.

---

168 Hidden Valley RV and Golf Park

Location: Northeast of Derry; Southern New Hampshire map page 169, grid c4.

Campsites, facilities: There are 280 sites for tents and RVs, 250 with full hookups, 10 with water and electric, and 20 with none. Each site has a picnic table and fire ring. Use of air conditioners and heaters is allowed. A dump station, laundry facilities, rest rooms, metered hot showers, a rec hall, game room,

and playground are provided. A camp store carries LP gas, RV supplies, ice, and firewood. Courts for volleyball, basketball, badminton, shuffleboard, and horseshoes are located on the property. The entrance has a traffic control gate. Leashed pets are permitted.

Reservations, fees: Reservations are accepted. Sites are $20 to $24 a night.

Contact: Hidden Valley RV and Golf Park, 81 Damren Road, Derry, NH 03038; (603) 887-3736 in the summer, or (904) 423-3170 in the winter.

Directions: From Interstate 93 in Derry, take exit 4 and travel two miles east on Route 102. Continue east for 4.5 miles on East Derry Road. Turn left on Damren Road and head north for one mile.

Trip notes: Golfers will appreciate these RV sites set beside a pond and bordering a nine-hole par-3 golf course. Rolling woods on a country lane provide the scenery. A beach is provided for campers, and the pond is open to fishing and boating—but only electric motors are allowed. Church services are offered on the premises every Sunday. Fans of Robert Frost should pay a visit to the poet's farm just east of the campground in Derry Village. This simple, white clapboard two-story house was Frost's home from 1900 to 1909. Guides conduct tours in season, but you can also head out on your own on the nature-poetry interpretive trail through fields and woodlands and get a sense of Frost's rural muse.

Open: May 1 through October 15.

---

169 Sanborn Shore Acres Campground

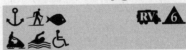

Location: On Island Pond in Hampstead; Southern New Hampshire map page 169, grid d5.

Campsites, facilities: There are 140 sites for RVs, most with full hookups and a limited number of transient sites available with water and electric hookups. Tents are allowed. Each site has a picnic table and fire ring. A dump station, rest rooms, hot showers, a rec hall, game room, and playground are provided. Ice and firewood are sold on site. Courts for volleyball, basketball, badminton, shuffleboard, and horseshoes are located on the property. Leashed pets are permitted.

Reservations, fees: Reservations are accepted. Sites start at $22 a night per family. Weekly, monthly, and seasonal rates are available.

Contact: Sanborn Shore Acres Campground, P.O. Box 626, Main Street, Hampstead, NH 03841; (603) 329-5247.

Directions: From Interstate 93 near the town of Salem, take exit 3 and travel east for eight miles on Route 111, then turn left and head two miles north on Route 121 to the campground entrance on the left (west) side of the road.

Trip notes: Shady sites on Island Pond are primarily occupied by seasonal campers. A few spots, however, are available for overnight stays, but be sure to call ahead to see if there's room. All campers may fish, swim, and boat in the lake, and seasonals may rent dock space for the summer. Organized activities include pizza parties, horseshoe tournaments, and dancing to tunes spun by a DJ. A snack bar and ice cream stand operated at the campground serves three meals a day. Canobie Lake Park, the state's only major amusement park, is located just 15 minutes away by car. In winter, the frozen lake teems with ice skaters, snowmobilers, ice fishers in search of pickerel, and cross-country skiers.

Open: April 15 through October 15 and November 15 through March 15.

170 Angle Pond Grove Camping Area

Location: On Angle Pond in Sandown; Southern New Hampshire map page 169, grid d5.

Campsites, facilities: There are 140 sites for RVs, all with full hookups. Each site has a picnic table and fire ring. Use of air conditioners is allowed. Laundry facilities, rest rooms, metered hot showers, a rec hall, ball field, and playground are provided. A small grocery store carries LP gas, ice, and firewood. Courts for volleyball, bocce ball, basketball, badminton, shuffleboard, and horseshoes are located on the property. A gate controls traffic at the campground entrance. No pets are allowed.

Reservations, fees: A 50 percent deposit must accompany all reservations. Sites are $16 a night for two people. Weekly and seasonal rates are available.

Contact: Angle Pond Grove Camping Area, P.O. Box 173, East Hampstead, NH 03826; (603) 887-4434.

Directions: From Interstate 495 near Plaistow, take exit 51 and head north on Route 125 for 1.5 miles, then continue north on Route 121A to East Hampstead. Stay on this road for another six-tenths of a mile, passing through the intersection with Route 111. Turn left on Pillsbury Road and look for the campground just ahead.

Trip notes: Small wooded sites are either near or right beside Angle Pond, a developed lake set in southern New Hampshire. This warm-water habitat supports horned pout and pickerel, fair game for anglers. Private homes line the shore of the 150-acre pond, which is open to all kinds of boating. The campground has a roped-off swimming area and a sloping sandy beach but no boat launch. If you're not a fan of tents or pets, this is the place for you, as neither are welcome at Angle Pond Grove.

Open: May 15 through October 15.

171 Sunset Park Campground

Location: On Wash Pond in Hampstead; Southern New Hampshire map page 169, grid d5.

Campsites, facilities: There are 145 sites with water and electric hookups occupied largely by seasonal campers; five sites for tents or RVs are available for overnight stays. Each has a table and fire ring. A dump station, laundry facilities, rest rooms, hot showers, a rec hall, and a playground are provided, as are volleyball and basketball courts, a softball field, and horseshoe pits. Leashed pets are permitted.

Reservations, fees: Reservations are recommended. Sites are $15 for two people.

Contact: Sunset Park Campground, P.O. Box 16N, 104 Emerson Road, Hampstead, NH 03841; (603) 329-6941.

Directions: From Interstate 93 near Salem, take exit 3 and travel east for eight miles on Route 111, then go one mile north on Route 121. Turn right on Emerson Road and head a quarter mile east.

Trip notes: The roomy, shaded sites next to Wash Pond are occupied mostly by seasonal campers. For a fee you can bring your own canoe, rowboat, or powerboat to use on the pond, and large powerboats are admitted with permission from the owners. A 400-foot swimming beach is provided. To the southwest in North Salem is an interesting natural attraction, America's Stonehenge; considered by many the oldest stone-constructed site in North America, it can still be used to determine solar and lunar events. Ongoing research is being conducted to determine whether the structure was built by Native Americans or a migrant European population.

Open: May 24 through October 14.

172 Exeter River Camping Area

Location: Near Fremont Station; Southern New Hampshire map page 169, grid c5.

Campsites, facilities: There are 50 sites for tents and RVs, some with hookups. Each site has a table and fire ring. A dump station, rest rooms, hot showers, a rec hall, and playground are provided. Ice and firewood are sold on site. Leashed pets are permitted.

Reservations, fees: Reservations are recommended. Sites start at $16 and $18 a night per family. Weekly, monthly, and seasonal rates are available on request.

Contact: Exeter River Camping Area, 13 South Road, Fremont, NH 03044; (603) 895-3448.

Directions: From the northern junction of Routes 111A and 107 in Fremont, travel south on Route 111A for one mile to the campground entrance on the right (west) side of the road at the sign for Clough Road.

Trip notes: Here near the origin of the Exeter River, campers can vie for brown, brook, and rainbow trout from these wooded sites set along the riverbank. The New Hampshire seacoast is about a 30-minute drive to the east.

Open: May 15 through October 1.

173 Pine Acres Family Campground

Location: On Dead Pond in Raymond; Southern New Hampshire map page 169, grid c5.

Campsites, facilities: There are 350 sites for tents and RVs, 330 with water and electric hookups and 20 with none. Each site has a picnic table and fire ring. A dump station, laundry facilities, rest rooms, metered hot showers, a rec hall, pavilion, pool, sports field, and playground are provided. A grocery store carries LP gas, ice, and firewood. Courts for volleyball, badminton, and horseshoes are located on the property. There is a guard at the front gate. Leashed pets are permitted.

Reservations, fees: Reservations are recommended July 1 through Labor Day. Holiday reservations must be paid in full within a week of making a reservation. Deposits are required for all other reservations, and there is a $10 service charge for cancellations with 30 days' notice. Sites start at $24 a night without hookups and $28 a night with hookups; all prices are per family. Seasonal rates are available.

Contact: Pine Acres Family Campground, 74 Freetown Road, Raymond, NH 03077; (603) 895-2519.

Directions: From Route 101 in Raymond, take exit 5. Head south on Route 107 for three-quarters of a mile to the campground entrance on the left.

Trip notes: Tall pine trees cloak this large campground in cool shade beside Dead Pond, which is anything but what its name suggests. Action-oriented campers can choose from a long list of organized activities, from mountain bike rides and arm-wrestling tournaments to candlelight parades and hog calling competitions. Most folks take to the water for bass fishing, swimming, or boating (motorized cruising up to seven miles per hour is allowed). There are separate docks for fishing and boating as well as canoes, rowboats, and paddleboats for rent. A 19-hole miniature golf course is located on the property, and several miles of old railroad beds near the campground double as mountain bike trails; yes, Pine Acres also rents bikes. A giant waterslide was recently added to the recreational lineup. About half the sites are occupied by seasonal campers, and a separate area near a small pond is reserved for tents. Adult-oriented events include live bands and DJ dancing.

Open: April 15 through November 15.

---

174 Three Ponds Campground

Location: South of Epping; Southern New Hampshire map page 169, grid c5.

Campsites, facilities: There are 135 sites for tents and RVs with full hookups. Each site has a picnic table and fire ring. A dump station, laundry facilities, rest rooms, hot showers, a pavilion, rec hall, gazebo, ball field, and playground are provided. A camp store carries ice cream, ice, and firewood. Courts for volleyball, bocce ball, basketball, badminton, and horseshoes are located on the property. Leashed pets are permitted.

Reservations, fees: Reservations are accepted. Sites start at $20 a night for a family of four. Seasonal rates are provided on request.

Contact: Three Ponds Campground, 146 North Road, Brentwood, NH 03833; (603) 679-5350.

Directions: From Exeter, travel five miles west on Route 101. At the Rockingham County Complex sign, turn left onto North Road. The campground entrance will be just ahead on the right.

Trip notes: Acres of green lawns surround the three small, clear ponds here. Gravel roads lead to roomy sites, some of which have shade trees. The largest pond offers a swimming beach and is stocked with largemouth bass. One of the smaller ponds is also open to fishing. Boats are available for rent at the campground. Campers can take part in bonfires, tugs-of-war, and bocce ball tournaments, relax in the golf-course-like landscape, or explore the surrounding countryside on nature trails.

Open: May 15 through October 15.

175 Great Bay Camping Village

Location: Near Great Bay in Newfields; Southern New Hampshire map page 169, grid c6.

Campsites, facilities: There are 115 sites for tents and RVs, 69 with full hookups, 18 with water and electric, and 28 with none. Each site has a picnic table and fire ring. Use of air conditioners and heaters is allowed. A dump station, laundry facilities, rest rooms, metered hot showers, a rec hall, pool, pavilion, and playground are provided. A convenience store carries LP gas, gasoline, groceries, ice, and firewood. Also on the property are courts for volleyball, basketball, badminton, and horseshoes. One leashed pet per site is allowed.

Reservations, fees: Reservations are accepted. Per family, rates start at $15 a night for tent sites and $19 a night for sites with full hookups.

Contact: Great Bay Camping Village, P.O. Box 331, Newfields, NH 03856; (603) 778-0226.

Directions: From Interstate 95 at exit 2 in Hampton, travel 7.5 miles west on Route 101. At the intersection with Route 108, exit and travel north on Route 108 for four miles. Take the road directly behind the Citgo gas station and head into the campground.

Trip notes: Tall oaks and pines shade these sites located either right beside or

near the Squamscott River. A special area has been set aside for seasonal campers, and natural tent sites are nearer to the water. Bluefish and striped bass are among the tasty saltwater game fish that thrive in the Squamscott, and the tidal flats at the campground are prime for oyster digging. Campers have use of a boat launch and dock on the property. One of the best methods of exploring the river and Great Bay is via kayak. You'll encounter protected lands, large marinas, and, finally, the open ocean. The town center of Newfields is postcard perfect with its white clapboard church and stone bridge, but you'll have to go into Exeter to obtain most goods and services.

Open: May 15 through October 15.

176 The Green Gate Camping Area

Location: On the Exeter River; Southern New Hampshire map page 169, grid c5.

Campsites, facilities: There are 118 sites for tents and RVs, 96 with full hookups and 22 with water and electric. Each site has a picnic table and fire ring. A dump station, laundry facilities, rest rooms, hot showers, a rec hall, a pool, canoe rentals, and a playground are provided. A camp store carries ice and firewood. Courts for volleyball, badminton, shuffleboard, and horseshoes are located on the property. No pets are allowed.

Reservations, fees: Nonrefundable deposits are required for all reservations. Sites start at $19 a night per family. Seasonal rates are provided on request.

Contact: The Green Gate Camping Area, P.O. Box 185, Exeter, NH 03833; (603) 772-2100.

Directions: From the junction of Routes 111 and 108 in Exeter, travel 1.5 miles south on Route 108 to the campground entrance on the right (west) side of the road.

Trip notes: Here's another family campground on one of the region's major rivers, the Exeter. Sites, many of which are occupied by seasonal campers, are well shaded. Swimmers can choose from taking a dip in the river or in the swimming pool. You can cast a line for trout right from the campground. For cross-country running trails or short mountain bike rides, head north on Route 108 for about a mile to Phillips Exeter Academy. Take Gilman Street to the school's stadium; behind the facility are miles of dirt roads and trails along the river.

Open: May 1 through October 1.

⑰ Exeter Elms Campground

Location: On the Exeter River; Southern New Hampshire map page 169, grid c5.

Campsites, facilities: There are 200 sites for tents and RVs, 81 with full hookups, 52 with water and electric, and 67 with none. Each site has a picnic table and fire ring. Use of air conditioners and heaters is allowed. A dump station, laundry facilities, rest rooms, hot showers, a rec hall, pavilion, pool, boat rentals, and a playground are provided. A camp store carries RV supplies, ice, and firewood. Courts for volleyball, basketball, badminton, shuffleboard, and horseshoes are located on the property. There's also a security guard on duty. Leashed pets are permitted.

Reservations, fees: Reservations are recommended, and a prepaid 50 percent deposit must accompany all reservations. Three-day minimum stays during holiday weekends must be prepaid in full. Per family, sites range from $16 a night for tents to $26 a night for full hookups, with surcharges

for dogs, preferred and waterfront sites, and visitors. Seasonal rates are available.

Contact: Exeter Elms Campground, 188 Court Street, Exeter, NH 03833; (603) 778-7631.

Directions: From the junction of Routes 111 and 108 in Exeter, travel 1.5 miles south on Route 108 to the campground entrance on the left (east) side of the road.

Trip notes: Family fun and big wooded sites along the Exeter River put the Elms in high demand by both seasonal and vacation campers. If you are at one of the many waterfront sites, you can pull up your canoe or rowboat right on shore. A recreation director coordinates dances, live entertainment, tournaments, canoe races, and puppet shows as part of a full schedule of activities. Other amenities include a wide-screen TV in the clubhouse, an insect control system, and a Ping-Pong table. No motors are allowed on the river here, but paddling is the best way to explore the Exeter anyway. For a classic excursion, put in your canoe below the bridge in town, where public parking is available. Then paddle to the Squamscott River and head out toward Great Bay, a largely undeveloped, shallow estuary. Be sure to check the tide charts lest you risk getting beached on a mudflat.

Open: May 15 through September 15.

⑱ Wakeda Campground

Location: East of Exeter; Southern New Hampshire map page 169, grid c5.

Campsites, facilities: There are 320 sites for tents and RVs, 225 with water and electric hookups and 95 with none. Each site has a picnic table, fire ring, and grill. Use of air conditioners and heaters is allowed. A dump station, laundry facilities, rest rooms, hot showers, a rec hall, pavilion, miniature golf course, and playground are provided. In the off-season, RVs may be stored on site. Rental RVs are available. A small grocery store carries ice and firewood. Courts for volleyball, basketball, badminton, shuffleboard, and horseshoes are located on the property. The entrance has a guarded gatehouse. Leashed pets are permitted.

Reservations, fees: Reservations are recommended in July and August and require a nonrefundable prepaid deposit. Tent sites start at $14 a night per family, and sites with full hookups start at $24 a night per family. Seasonal rates are available.

Contact: Wakeda Campground, 294 Exeter Road, Hampton Falls, NH 03844; (603) 772-5274.

Directions: From the junction of Routes 88 and 101 in Exeter, travel 2.6 miles south on Route 88 to the campground.

Trip notes: Wakeda Campground displays a unique rustic charm—all of the buildings and picnic tables here were fashioned by the owners' hands from cathedral pines grown and milled on site. As you enter the campground you are greeted by a colorful totem pole and a flower bed of annuals. A seasonal camper carved the pole, also made from a Wakeda pine. Don't worry though, plenty of trees have been left untouched to tower over the roomy campsites. The majority of sites are suitable for trailers up to 40 feet long, plus there are a few primitive sites near a beaver pond and a special tent area.

The campground was named for a Native American word meaning one who hunts. If you are wakeda, hunting grounds are located just to the east in the Saltmarsh Wildlife Management Area. Check on state laws before you set out; possible game includes deer, otter, hare, and ducks. Ocean beaches are eight miles to the east. At Hampton Beach State Park you'll find a boat launch (there's a fee), a fishing pier, and miles of sandy beach. From the commercial pier many boats offer deep-sea fishing excursions. In the town of Hampton Beach, a lively boardwalk features restaurants, shops, arcades, and Wednesday night fireworks in the summertime.

Open: May 15 through October 1.

⑰⑨ Country Shore Camping Area

Location: On Country Pond in Kingston; Southern New Hampshire map page 169, grid d5.

Campsites, facilities: There are 100 sites for RVs, all with full hookups. Each site has a picnic table and fire ring. A dump station, rest rooms, metered hot showers, a rec hall, and a playground are provided. Courts for volleyball, basketball, softball, badminton, shuffleboard, and horseshoes are located on the property. One leashed pet per site is allowed.

Reservations, fees: A $200 deposit must be paid by May 1 to reserve seasonal sites. Other reservations require a 50 percent deposit. Sites are $20 a night per family, plus $3 a day for guests. Per season, dock space is $100 for boats without motors and between $110 and $120 for powerboats. Weekly and seasonal rates are available.

Contact: Country Shore Camping Area, P.O. Box 559, Plaistow, NH 03865; (603) 642-5072.

Directions: From the junction of Routes 125 and 111 in Kingston, travel southwest on Route 125 for about four miles to the campground entrance on the left.

Trip notes: This seasonal RV camping destination in the woods beside Country Pond is designed especially for boaters. You can keep your vessel at the campground dock and head out on the water to fish, water-ski, or simply explore. There's also a separate fishing dock at the water's edge. Bake Park, a wildlife and natural area on the north shore of the lake, is home to numerous species of birds and small and large mammals. For hiking or mountain biking, an old railroad grade crosses the wildlife area then continues into some surrounding undeveloped land.

Open: Memorial Day through October 1.

---

⑱⓪ Tuxbury Pond Camping Area

Location: On Tuxbury Pond east of Kingston; Southern New Hampshire map page 169, grid d5.

Campsites, facilities: There are 208 sites for tents and RVs, 149 with full hookups and 59 with water and electric. Each site has a picnic table and fire ring. Use of air conditioners is allowed. A dump station, laundry facilities, rest rooms, metered hot showers, a rec hall, pavilion, and playground are provided. A small grocery store carries LP gas, ice, and firewood. Courts for volleyball, basketball, badminton, shuffleboard, and horseshoes are located on the property. A traffic control gate is at the entrance, and personnel conduct night patrols. Leashed pets are permitted.

Reservations, fees: Reservations are recommended Memorial Day through Labor Day and require a nonrefundable deposit. Sites start at $21 a night for four people.

Contact: Tuxbury Pond Camping Area, 88 Whitehall Road, South Hampton, NH 03827; (603) 394-7660.

Directions: From the junction of Interstate 495 and Route 150 in Amesbury, Massachusetts, take exit 54 and head north on Route 150. In three-quarters of a mile, turn

left at the blinking yellow light onto Highland Street and travel northwest for a quarter mile to Lions Mouth Road. Turn left again and head west for a little over a mile to Newton Road. Turn right and travel north for one mile, then follow signs into the campground.

Trip notes: Lanky pine trees shelter waterside sites at Tuxbury Pond Camping Area, which draws a mix of seasonal and vacation campers. They're all after the same thing: swimming, fishing, and quiet boating on a spring-fed pond. Some open, grassy sites are set right beside the water, and there's even a separate "adult community" section of the park that's free of children. Canoes and rowboats may be rented near the beach.

Open: Mid-May through mid-October.

---

⑱① Shel-Al Family Campground

Location: Near Hampton Beach; Southern New Hampshire map page 169, grid c6.

Campsites, facilities: There are 200 sites for tents and RVs up to 31 feet long, 68 with full hookups, 66 with water and electric, and 66 with none. Each site has a picnic table, all but the full-hookup sites have fireplaces, and some have grills. Rest rooms, metered hot showers, and a playground are provided. A small grocery store carries ice and firewood. Courts for basketball, shuffleboard, and horseshoes are located on the property. Leashed pets are permitted.

Reservations, fees: A nonrefundable deposit is required with all reservations. No one-night reservations are accepted. Sites are $12 to $18 a night for two people.

Contact: Shel-Al Family Campground, Route 1, Hampton, NH 03842; (603) 964-5730.

Directions: From the junction of Route 111 and U.S. 1 in Hampton, travel north for half a mile on U.S. 1 to the campground.

Trip notes: Grassy, level sites are located right off busy U.S. 1 about three miles from the seacoast. They are densely settled in a grove of young trees. Head out Route 111 to North Hampton State Beach to enjoy a day of sun and surf. For a floral detour, take a walk through Fuller Gardens in North Hampton. One of the few remaining early twentieth-century estate gardens in the country, it features award-winning annuals and 1,500 rose bushes that are usually in their grandeur in mid- to late June.

Open: May 15 through October 1.

182 Tidewater Campground

Location: Near Hampton Beach; Southern New Hampshire map page 169, grid d6.

Campsites, facilities: There are 225 sites for tents and RVs, 175 with water and electric hookups and 50 with none. Each site has a picnic table and fire ring. Use of air conditioners and heaters is not allowed. A dump station, rest rooms, metered hot showers, a rec hall, pool, and playground are provided. A small grocery store carries RV supplies, ice, and firewood. Basketball courts and horseshoe pits are located on the property. Traffic is controlled by a gate at the entrance. No pets are allowed.

Reservations, fees: Reservations are accepted for stays of three or more nights and must be accompanied by a nonrefundable deposit. Sites are $22 to $24 a night per family. Seasonal rates are provided on request.

Contact: Tidewater Campground, 160 Lafayette Road, Hampton, NH 03842; (603) 926-5474.

Directions: From the junction of Route

101 and U.S. 1 in Hampton, head south on U.S. 1 for a quarter mile to the campground entrance on the right (west) side of the road.

Trip notes: Yet another RV park near the beach, Tidewater Campground puts you close to all that the seaside has to offer. Just two miles to the east is Hampton Beach State Park, a sunbather's mecca all summer long. Spread out blankets in the sand dunes or on the beach; if you prefer to fish, head south to the Hampton State Pier just before the Seabrook Bridge. For a fee you can park and launch your vessel or drop a line from the 350-foot fishing pier. Many deep-sea fishing charters leave from this dock.

Open: May 15 through October 15.

183 Hampton Beach State RV Park

Location: On the Atlantic Ocean near the Massachusetts border; Southern New Hampshire map page 169, grid d6.

Campsites, facilities: There are 20 sites for RVs; only units with full hookups are allowed. A park store carries some supplies including ice. Groceries and services can be obtained in Hampton Beach. Campfires, tents, trailers, and pets are not allowed.

Reservations, fees: Reservations are accepted. Call the park on Monday through Friday between 10 A.M. and 3 P.M. from January through April; from May through October, the office accepts calls from 9 A.M. to 9 P.M. The minimum stay is two nights, and on holiday weekends is three nights; the maximum allowable stay is 14 days. A nonrefundable deposit is required with all reservations. Sites are $30 a night.

Contact: Hampton Beach State RV Park, P.O. Box 606, Rye Beach, NH 03871; (603) 926-8990.

Directions: From Interstate 95 at Hampton, take exit 2 and head south on Route 101 for three miles. Take a right onto Route 1A, then travel one mile south to the park.

Trip notes: Miles of sandy beach for saltwater fishing and swimming are directly accessible from these open sites on the Atlantic Ocean. It's a short walk, bike, or skate up to the hub of beachdom along the Hampton Beach boardwalk. Sunbathers parade the commercial strip in colorful and skimpy attire, hawkers sell fried dough and cotton candy, lights flash from pinball arcades, machines twist and pull saltwater taffy in storefront windows, and limousines deliver big-name musical acts to the Casino Ballroom, a 1,800-seat nightclub. In the summer, public concerts are staged at the seashell on various evenings and fireworks displays light up the sky every Wednesday night and on holidays.

Open: Mid-May through mid-October.

⑱ New Hampshire Seacoast Campground

Location: A mile inland from Seabrook Beach; Southern New Hampshire map page 169, grid d6.

Campsites, facilities: There are 100 sites for tents and RVs up to 35 feet long, 80 with full hookups and 20 with none. Each site has a picnic table and fire ring. A dump station, rest rooms, hot showers, a rec hall, horseshoe pits, and a playground are provided. A camp store carries ice and firewood. There's also shuttle service

between the campground and ocean beaches. Leashed pets are permitted.

Reservations, fees: Reservations are recommended and must be accompanied by a nonrefundable deposit. Sites start at $18 a night per family.

Contact: New Hampshire Seacoast Campground, P.O. Box 235, Seabrook, NH 03874; (603) 474-9813 or (800) 313-6306.

Directions: From Interstate 95 at exit 60 near the Massachusetts border, head east on Route 286. At the second stoplight, turn left into the campground entrance.

Trip notes: A mile-long bike, drive, or shuttle bus ride on a busy road brings campers from these level, wooded sites to Seabrook Beach on the ocean. The sandy beach is open to the public, and a boat launch is located just north of the Hampton River on Route 1A. Fish for stripers and bluefish right from the shore or head out on the open water. Seabrook is commercially developed along the beach road where you'll find some eateries and shops, but it's not as oppressive as Hampton with its honky-tonk strip, nightclubs, surf shops, and arcades. Seabrook is famous for two things: the Seabrook Nuclear Power Plant, which has sparked several decades of debate, and the Seabrook Greyhound Park on Route 107, which features live dog races and simulcast horse races. To learn more about nuclear power and New Hampshire's seacoast, pay a visit to the Science and Nature Center at Seabrook Station. Exhibits, aquariums, self-guided trails, and a guided tour through a control room simulator are some of the educational highlights.

Open: May 15 through September 15.

Vermont

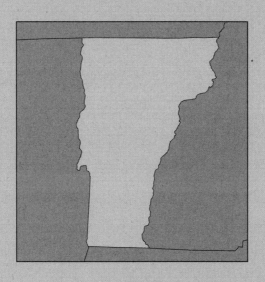

Activity Symbols

Biking	Boating	Canoeing/ Rafting	Cross-Country Skiing	Fishing
Golf	Hiking	Historical Sites	Horseback Riding	Hunting	Sea Kayaking
Snowmobiling	Snowshoeing	Swimming	RV Sites	Wheelchair Access

Scenic Rating

1 2 3 4 5 6 7 8 9 10

Poor .... Fair .... Great

Northern Vermont

Adjoining Maps: East: New Hampshire .... *pages* 168-169
South: Southern Vermont .... *page* 281

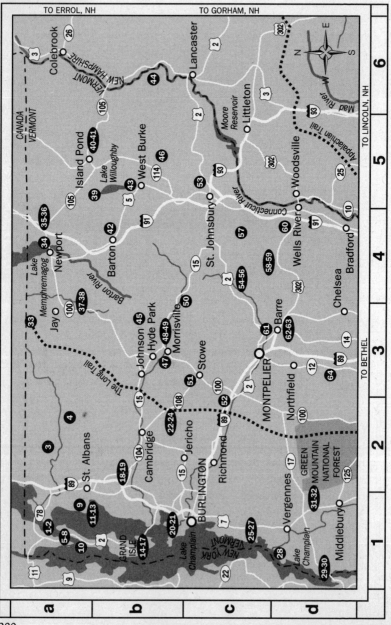

TO ERROL, NH

TO GORHAM, NH

TO LINCOLN, NH

TO BETHEL

CANADA
VERMONT

NEW HAMPSHIRE
VERMONT

Colebrook
26
3
105
Island Pond
40-41
West Burke
105
Lake Willoughby
39
43
5
114
46
Barton
42
91
35-36
Newport
34
Lake Memphremagog
Barton River
37-38
100
Jay
33
Johnson
45
Hyde Park
50
48-49
Morrisville
47
Stowe
51
The Long Trail
15
108
22-24
52
100
89
Cambridge
104
Jericho
15
18-19
BURLINGTON
20-21
14-17
7
GRAND ISLE
2
10
St. Albans
4
3
89
9
11-13
78
1-2
5-8
11
9

Lancaster
2
302
N E S W
Moore Reservoir
44
2
Littleton
3
93
302
Woodsville
93
5
302
Connecticut River
53
St. Johnsbury
57
15
2
54-56
58-59
60
Wells River
91
10
Bradford
302
Chelsea
Barre
61
62-63
14
12
89
64
MONTPELIER
Northfield
100
2
89
Richmond
Vergennes
17
GREEN MOUNTAIN NATIONAL FOREST
31-32
125
28
Lake Champlain
29-30
Middlebury
22

NEW YORK
VERMONT
Lake Champlain
25-27

Mad River
Appalachian Trail
25

a   b   c   d

1   2   3   4   5   6

Southern Vermont

Adjoining Maps: North: Northern Vermont .... page 280
East: New Hampshire .... pages 168-169
South: Western Massachusetts .... page 354

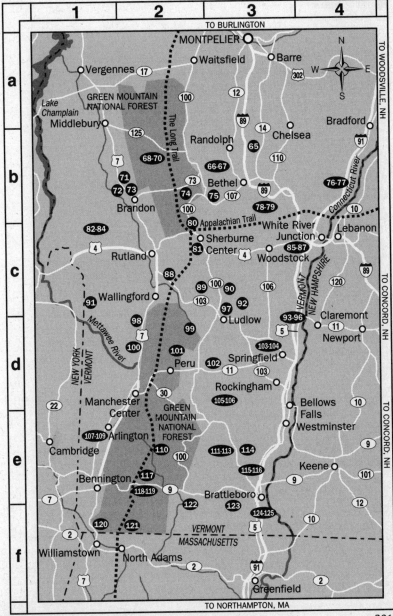

TO BURLINGTON

MONTPELIER

Waitsfield · Barre

Vergennes 17

302

W — N — E

12

GREEN MOUNTAIN
NATIONAL FOREST

100

89

Lake
Champlain

14 · Chelsea

Bradford

Middlebury

125

Randolph

65

91

The Long Trail

7

68-70

110

71

66-67

73

72 · 73

Brandon

73

74

Bethel

75 · 107

89

76-77

100

78-79

Connecticut River

10

80 · Appalachian Trail

White River
Junction · Lebanon

82-84

Sherburne
Center

85-87

4 · Rutland

81

4 · Woodstock

89

Wallingford

88

89 · 100 · 90

106

120

91

98

103

97 · 92

93-96

Claremont

7

99

Ludlow

5

11 · Newport

100

101

103-104

VERMONT / NEW HAMPSHIRE

Mettawee River

Peru

102

Springfield

NEW YORK / VERMONT

11

103

Rockingham

22

30

105-106

Bellows
Falls

10

Manchester
Center

GREEN
MOUNTAIN
NATIONAL
FOREST

Westminster

107-109 · Arlington

Cambridge

110

111-113 · 114

9

100

115-116

Keene

101

Bennington

117

9

12

118-119 · 9

Brattleboro

122

123

124-125

10

120 · 121

5

VERMONT
MASSACHUSETTS

7

2

Williamstown · North Adams

2

91

2

TO NORTHAMPTON, MA

Greenfield

TO WOODSVILLE, NH

TO CONCORD, NH

281

Vermont features:

Vermont State Parks

The state of Vermont operates nearly 40 campgrounds for public use. Most are open from mid-May through early September or October, though a few offer year-round sites where noted. Reservations are encouraged, especially in summer and during the fall foliage season in early October. You may reserve through the mail or by phoning the appropriate regional office; telephone reservations are only accepted on Tuesday and Thursday from 9 A.M. to 4 P.M. from the first Tuesday in January through May 14. Requests made through the mail must be postmarked no earlier than January 1. All parks will accept reservation requests for specific sites for stays of four or more consecutive nights. Most parks (except Branbury, Burton Island, Lake St. Catherine, and Silver Lake) will accept requests for fewer than four nights beginning May 15 but may not guarantee a specific site.

Mailed reservations are accepted in order of receipt of a completed application with full payment at the appropriate regional office or at a particular park after May 15. A $3 nonrefundable processing fee must accompany each request. Refunds are issued in the form of credit cheques for unused days, but a $10 charge is assessed on all refunds.

The following regional office addresses and phone numbers should be used when reserving between the first Tuesday in January through May 14 (after that, contact the park directly). Northwest: Ranger Supervisor, 111 West Street, Essex Junction, VT 05452; (802) 879-5674. Northeast: Ranger Supervisor, 324 North Main Street, Barre, VT 05641; (802) 479-4280. Southwest: Ranger Supervisor, RR 2, Box 2161, Pittsford, VT 05763; (802) 483-2001. Southeast: Ranger Supervisor, RR 1, Box 33, North Springfield, VT 05150; (802) 886-2434.

For additional information or reservation applications, contact the Vermont Department of Forests, Parks, and Recreation, 103 South Main Street, Waterbury, VT 05671-0601; (802) 241-3655. A Web site with general Vermont information can be reached at http://www.state.vt.us/anr/fpr/parks.

❶ Alburg RV Resort

Location: On Lake Champlain near the Canadian border; Northern Vermont map page 280, grid a1.

Campsites, facilities: There are 185 sites for tents and RVs, 150 with full hookups, 25 with water and electric, and 10 with none. Each site has a picnic table and fire ring. Air conditioners are allowed, but heaters are not. RV storage, dump stations, hot showers, laundry facilities, a grocery store, playground, pool, rec hall, sports courts, an athletic field, and horseshoe pits are provided. RV supplies, an RV sales office, LP gas, ice, and firewood are available. Leashed pets are permitted.

Reservations, fees: Reservations are recommended July 1 through Labor Day and must be accompanied by a nonrefundable deposit of 10 percent of the total fee, with a $20 minimum. Sites are $20 to $22 a night for two people, with surcharges for additional campers and services. Weekly, monthly, and seasonal rates are available.

Contact: Alburg Travel Trailer Park Company, Inc., RR 2, Box 50, Alburg, VT 05440; (802) 796-3733.

Directions: From the junction of U.S. 2 and Route 78 in Alburg Center, travel east for two miles on Route 78. Turn right and drive half a mile south on Blue Rock Road.

Trip notes: Shoreline is plentiful at Alburg, a well-manicured camping resort set on the northern shore of Lake Champlain. The grassy, tidy sites are tucked in the trees just offshore, and many are occupied by seasonal campers, some with large permanent trailers. A nearby boat ramp provides lake access to larger craft, but windsurfers, kayakers, and canoeists can launch right from the campground's 1,500-foot sandy beach. Alburg's protected location on Lake Champlain makes it a popular spot for all types of sailing. On a clear day, you'll enjoy views of the Green Mountains from the beach. Tent sites are available, but the soft-roof set might want to camp at less-developed sites in North Hero State Park (see campground number 6) on Grand Isle to the south. Camping in the Champlain Islands can prove to be a cultural experience, as many Canadians venture south during the summer months.

Open: May 1 through October 1.

❷ Lakewood Campground

Location: On Lake Champlain in Swanton; Northern Vermont map page 280, grid a1.

Campsites, facilities: There are 262 sites for tents and RVs, some with hookups. A dump station, rec hall, pool, rest rooms, hot showers, baseball field, and laundry facilities are provided. A small grocery store carries LP gas, ice, and firewood. On the grounds are a playground and tennis courts. Leashed pets are permitted.

Reservations, fees: Reservations are recommended. Campsites start at $14 and $18 a night.

Contact: Colette R. Levesque, Lakewood Campground, Tabor Road, Swanton, VT 05488; (802) 868-7270.

Directions: From Swanton, travel eight miles west on Route 78. Turn left on Tabor Road and head south to the campground entrance.

Trip notes: Yet another RV park in the heart of Lake Champlain country, this one is landscaped with perennials and hardwood trees—with at least one per site to provide campers with cooling shade. Paved roads lead through a grid of pull-through sites near the lakeshore; only Tabor Road comes between the campground and the lake. For water-lovers there's a swimming pool with a waterslide and a lakeside boat dock and swimming beach.

Just to the northeast of here is the Missisquoi National Wildlife Refuge, which protects the delta of the Missisquoi River with the goal of enhancing feeding and nesting areas for migratory waterfowl. The refuge consists primarily of marshy, wooded swampland traversed by numerous creeks that are ideal for bird-watching via canoe in spring and fall (the bird population is slim at the height of summer). A nature trail loops beside two of the creeks.

Open: May 1 through October 1.

❸ Lake Carmi State Park

Location: Northwest of Enosburg Falls on Lake Carmi; Northern Vermont map page 280, grid a2.

Campsites, facilities: There are 178 sites for tents and RVs including 35 lean-tos, all without hookups. Each site has a table and fire ring. Facilities include a dump station, playground, beach, boat ramp, boat rentals, snack bar, metered hot showers, and flush toilets. Leashed pets with rabies vaccination certification are permitted, but not in day-use areas.

Reservations, fees: Reservations are recommended. Tent sites are $12 a night and lean-tos are $16 a night for four people. Each additional person four years and older will be charged $3 at a tent site and $4 at a lean-to. The maximum allowable number of people at a site is eight, and there must be at least one person 18 years of age or older with each camping party. Two cabins are rented for $32 a night. See also page 284.

Contact: Lake Carmi State Park, RR 1, Box 1710, Enosburg Falls, VT 05450; (802) 933-8383.

Directions: From Enosburg Falls, travel three miles west on Route 105. Turn right on Route 236 and head north for three more miles to the campground.

Trip notes: Families with a penchant for water sports flock to Lake Carmi in the summertime. Big, wooded sites set back from the lake and easy water access draw campers to this spot just shy of the Canadian border. If you are interested in exploring the Missisquoi River via canoe, the state park is a good jumping-off point, as there's a popular put-in at Enosburg Falls. Be sure to bring your mountain bike—the main roads here are sparsely traveled, and many "secondary" roads are scenic dirt byways.

Open: Mid-May through Labor Day.

❹ Brookside Campground North

Location: On Bogue Brook south of Enosburg Center; Northern Vermont map page 280, grid a2.

Campsites, facilities: There are 26 sites for tents and RVs, five with full hookups and 21 with water and electric. Each site has a table and fire ring. A dump station, horseshoe pits, laundry facilities, a group area, and a playground are provided, and ice and firewood are available. Leashed pets are permitted.

Reservations, fees: Reservations are recommended. Sites are $10 to $14 a night. Seasonal rates are available.

Contact: Douglas and Wanda Snider, Brookside Campground North, RR 2, Box 3300, Enosburg Falls, VT 05450; (802) 626-1204.

Directions: From Enosburg Falls, travel three miles east on Route 105 to Boston Post Road. Turn right and head south for six miles to the campground entrance.

Trip notes: Grassy, level plots are carved out beside Bogue Brook, where campers select either open, sunny sites or ones that are shaded and more private. You can cast a fishing line in the brook or explore some of the surrounding hardwood forest on a nature trail. This is the closest campground to the town of Richford on the Canadian border, a popular put-in location for canoe trips on the lower Missisquoi River to Lake Champlain.

Open: May 1 through October 1. Hunters, however, may reserve sites into late fall.

❺ Goose Point Campground

Location: In South Alburg; Northern Vermont map page 280, grid a1.

Campsites, facilities: There are 140 sites for tents and RVs, 50 with full hookups, 46 with water and electric, and 44 with none. Each site has a table and fire ring. Air conditioners are not allowed. A dump station, rec hall, flush toilets, hot showers, a camp store, laundry facilities, and a playground are on the grounds. A small store carries bait, tackle, ice, and firewood. For recreation there's a pool, shuffleboard, horseshoe pits, and badminton and volleyball courts. The owners speak French. Leashed pets are permitted.

Reservations, fees: Reservations are recommended and require a 50 percent deposit. Sites start at $16 a night for four people; beach sites start at $18.

Contact: Gordon and Pauline Beyor, Goose Point Campground, RR 1, Box 76A, South Alburg, VT 05440; (802) 796-3711.

Directions: From the junction of U.S. 2 and Route 78 in Alburg Center, travel three miles southeast on U.S. 2.

Trip notes: Goose Point is a 117-acre outcrop of land facing north toward Missisquoi Bay. Sites are varied, from sunny and parklike to lakefront; tent spaces are in a separate, well-shaded area. Sailing is especially popular in these northern reaches of Lake Champlain, and Missisquoi Bay to the north is a destination for serious anglers in search of northern pike, walleye, and lake trout. Take a dip in the campground pool or the invigorating waters of Lake Champlain. There are some walking trails at the campground, as well as a boat launch. If you're tenting and get rained out, you can escape to the bed-and-breakfast on the premises.

Open: May through November.

⑥ North Hero State Park

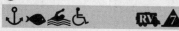

Location: On the Lake Champlain Islands; Northern Vermont map page 280, grid a1.

Campsites, facilities: There are 117 sites for tents and RVs including 18 lean-tos, all without hookups. Each site has a table and fire ring. A dump station is provided. Facilities include a playground, beach, boat ramp, metered hot showers, and flush toilets. Ice, firewood, and boat rentals are available. Leashed pets with rabies vaccination certification are permitted, but not in day-use areas.

Reservations, fees: Reservations are recommended. Tent sites are $12 a night and lean-tos are $16 a night for four people. Each additional person four years and older will be charged $3 at a tent site and $4 at a lean-to. The maximum allowable number of people at a site is eight, and there must be at least one person 18 years of age or older with each camping party. See also page 284.

Contact: North Hero State Park, RR 1, Box 259, North Hero, VT 05474; (802) 372-8727.

Directions: From North Hero, travel four miles north on U.S. 2. Bear left on Town Road and continue northeast for four more miles to the park.

Trip notes: Though it does fill up in the summer, this state park is less of a mob scene than Grand Isle. Sites are set in a lowland forest near a beach on Lake Champlain. If you have a boat or wish to rent one, consider spending a day island-hopping to the other state-owned properties of Knight, Woods, and Burton Islands.

Open: Mid-May through Labor Day.

⑦ King's Bay Campground

Location: In North Hero on the east shore of Lake Champlain; Northern Vermont map page 280, grid a1.

Campsites, facilities: There are 40 sites for tents and RVs with full hookups. Hot showers, a dump station, and flush toilets are provided. Leashed pets are permitted.

Reservations, fees: Seasonal reservations require a $100 deposit. Sites start at $12 to $15 a night for two people. Weekly and seasonal rates are available.

Contact: Bud Knapp, King's Bay Campground, P.O. Box 169, North Hero, VT 05474; (802) 372-3735.

Directions: From North Hero, travel north on U.S. 2 for 3.3 miles to Lakeview Drive. Continue one more mile north on Lakeview Drive to the campground entrance.

Trip notes: Lakeside and shaded, these sites are occupied mostly by seasonal campers, so call ahead if you want to stay here. King's Bay offers more than 1,000 feet of shoreline, and some boat docks, on the Champlain Islands. To the east are views of the Cold Hollow Mountains; this chain extends into Canada and is called by many the Northern Green Mountains. Canadians and Americans aren't the only ones who take time off in the islands: the Royal Lipizzan Stallions of Austria have a summer home on North Hero. These horses perform a hoofed ballet on summer weekends.

Open: May 15 through September 15.

⑧ Summer Place Campground and Cabins

Location: On Isle La Motte; Northern Vermont map page 280, grid a1.

Campsites, facilities: There are 70 sites for tents and RVs, most with water and electric hookups. Each site has a table and fire ring. A dump station, laundry facilities, a playground, rest rooms, hot showers, and a rec hall are provided. A store sells ice and firewood. Leashed pets are permitted.

Reservations, fees: Reservations are recommended July 1 through Labor Day. Sites start at $16 a night for four people.

Contact: Mark and Aimee Grimes, Summer Place Campground and Cabins, P.O. Box 30, Isle La Motte, VT 05463; (802) 928-3300.

Directions: From U.S. 2 in Alburg, drive south to Route 129. Take Route 129 west to the island, staying on the road to its end. Continue straight for two miles, then take a left at the stone building and go to the end of the pavement. The campground entrance is just ahead on the right.

Trip notes: Shaded sites look west toward New York with the Adirondack peaks in the distance. A special grassy area with water and electricity has been set aside for tenters. Campers have full access to swimming, boating, and fishing on Lake Champlain at the campground's pier and marina facility. The island area of the lake is especially popular with canoeists and kayakers who seek quiet water. On the premises, the owners also operate a small petting zoo. A few miles north of the campground, St. Anne's Shrine draws visitors to the island; the shrine was erected on the site of Fort St. Anne, the first settlement in Vermont, dating to 1666.

Open: May 15 through October 1.

❾ Champlain Valley Campground

Location: On Lake Champlain south of Swanton; Northern Vermont map page 280, grid a1.

Campsites, facilities: There are 79 sites for RVs up to 32 feet in length, 40 with full hookups and 39 with water and electric. A dump station, rec hall, rest rooms, free hot showers, and a playground are provided. LP gas and firewood are available. Leashed pets are permitted.

Reservations, fees: Reservations are recommended. Sites start at $15 a night.

Contact: Marcel and Jienette Gagne, Champlain Valley Campground, RR 1, Box 4225, Swanton, VT 05488; (802) 524-5146.

Directions: From Swanton, travel four miles south on Route 36 to the campground entrance.

Trip notes: Ideal RV sites are strung along the shore of Lake Champlain, all with hookups. Views of Grand Isle and some of the smaller islands to the south are at your front door, and campers have use of a boat launch. This RV park is dominated by seasonal campers; tenters will want to try for a spot at one of the state parks to the south. To learn more about the Civil War history of this region, visit the Historical Society Museum in St. Albans. The northernmost military action of the war was the St. Albans raid.

Open: Mid-May through mid-October.

❿ Carry Bay Campground

Location: North of North Hero; Northern Vermont map page 280, grid a1.

Campsites, facilities: There are 68 sites for tents and RVs, eight with full hookups and 50 with water and electric, plus some group sites. Each site has a picnic table and fire ring. Use of air conditioners and heaters is allowed. Facilities include a pool and patio, horseshoe pits, a playground, boat rentals, sports courts, and a boat ramp. Ice, wood, and limited groceries are available.

Employees speak French. Leashed pets are permitted.

Reservations, fees: Reservations require a nonrefundable 50 percent deposit. Sites with hookups are $16 to $20 a night for a family of four. Tent sites without electricity are $12 a night. There are surcharges for guests, air conditioners, and heaters. Weekly, monthly, and seasonal rates are available.

Contact: Lonnie and Claire Bushway, Carry Bay Campground, P.O. Box 207, Route 2, North Hero, VT 05474; (802) 372-8233.

Directions: From the North Hero Post Office on U.S. 2, travel north for 1.75 miles to the campground entrance on the left (west) side of the road.

Trip notes: Campsites and cottages speckle this strip of land between North Hero and Grand Isle. Most are grassy and open, and all are densely settled on the shore. Dockage is available for campers with boats; those without can rent 14-foot aluminum boats with 6- and 10-horse-power motors by the hour or the day. You can swim in the brisk waters of 120-mile-long Lake Champlain or splash in the campground's pool surrounded by a wide sundeck. Out on the lake, water-skiers churn up wakes, sailors jibe to their hearts' content, and anglers ply the water for land-locked salmon, smelt, northern pike, and many other species.

Open: Mid-May through mid-October.

⑪ Woods Island State Park

Location: East of North Hero; Northern Vermont map page 280, grid a1.

Campsites, facilities: There are five primitive tent sites and no facilities. Fires are prohibited. Leashed pets with rabies

vaccination certification are permitted, but not in day-use areas.

Reservations, fees: Camping is by permit only on designated sites, and setting up camp prior to permit acquisition is not allowed. Obtain permits at Burton Island State Park. Sites are $10 a night for up to eight people. See also page 284.

Contact: Woods Island State Park, c/o Burton Island State Park, P.O. Box 123, St. Albans Bay, VT 05481; (802) 524-6353.

Directions: From St. Albans Bay, travel southwest on Route 36 and then Point Road to Kill Kare State Park. Parking spaces and a boat ramp are provided. There is no ferry service to the island; you must take your own boat.

Trip notes: Endangered plant species are protected on Woods Island, so no fires are allowed. Five open, primitive campsites offer ultimate privacy on the formerly farmed mile-long preserve. A trail follows the perimeter of Woods Island and crosses over its center where a former owner attempted to build a landing strip. Vestiges of the runway are still visible. Human waste must be buried in cat-holes dug in the top six inches of soil at least 100 feet from shore. Day-users are welcome at a picnic area on the island but must leave before sundown.

Open: Mid-May through Labor Day.

⑫ Knight Island State Park

Location: East of North Hero; Northern Vermont map page 280, grid a1.

Campsites, facilities: There are seven primitive tent sites with fire rings but no other facilities. Firewood is available on the island. Leashed pets with rabies vaccination certification are permitted, but not in day-use areas.

Reservations, fees: Camping is by permit only on designated sites, and setting up camp prior to permit acquisition is not allowed. Obtain permits at the caretaker's residence. Reservations are handled through Burton Island State Park. The minimum stay is three nights and the maximum stay is 14 nights. Sites are $12 to $32 a night for up to eight people. See also page 284.

Contact: Knight Island State Park, c/o Burton Island State Park, P.O. Box 123, St. Albans Bay, VT 05481; (802) 524-6353.

Directions: From St. Albans Bay, travel southwest on Route 36 and then Point Road to Kill Kare State Park. Parking spaces and a boat ramp are provided. Take your own boat over to Knight Island or catch the passenger ferry (no vehicles) that runs to the island once a day, twice on weekends and holidays.

Trip notes: Knight Island is one mile long and nearly half a mile wide. It was farmed long ago, then remained uninhabited for many years. Before being purchased by the state in 1990, the island was operated privately as a primitive campground. Ten acres on the southern tip of the island are still privately owned. Campsites dot the isolated shoreline, and each has a private access path. Dead and down wood is available for campfires. Human waste must be buried in cat-holes dug in the top six inches of soil at least 100 feet from shore. Day-users are welcome at a picnic area on the island but must leave before sundown. There are some marked trails on the island for short hikes.

Open: Mid-May through Labor Day.

⑬ Burton Island State Park

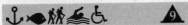

Location: Near St. Albans Bay on Lake Champlain; Northern Vermont map page 280, grid a1.

Campsites, facilities: There are 17 tent sites, 26 lean-to sites, 15 boat moorings, and a 100-slip marina with dockside electricity, fuel service, and a dump station for boats with septic tanks. All tent and lean-to sites have fireplaces and picnic tables. Rest rooms, metered hot showers, a snack bar, playground, and rowboat and canoe rentals are provided on the island. A park store sells firewood and staples. Leashed pets with rabies vaccination certification are permitted, but not in day-use areas.

Reservations, fees: Reservations are recommended. Tent sites are $12 a night for four people, and other sites start at $16 a night. Each additional person four years and older will be charged $3 at a tent site and $4 at a lean-to. The maximum allowable number of people at a site is eight, and there must be at least one person 18 years of age or older with each camping party. See also page 284.

Contact: Burton Island State Park, P.O. Box 123, St. Albans Bay, VT 05481; (802) 524-6353.

Directions: From St. Albans Bay, travel southwest on Route 36 and then Point Road to Kill Kare State Park. Parking spaces and a boat ramp are provided. Take your own boat over to Burton Island or catch the passenger ferry (no vehicles) that runs from 8:30 A.M. to 6:30 P.M. at two-hour intervals.

Trip notes: Cows, pigs, and chickens used to roam 253-acre Burton Island in the early 1900s when it served as pastureland. Now the state-owned island is a unique camping spot offering both a full-service marina and natural tent and lean-to sites along the mostly open northern shore. The island is home to an abundant bird population as well as deer and small mammals. In addition to boat rentals, a swimming beach, and other water-oriented offerings, the island has a resident naturalist who hosts interpretive programs and a network of nature trails that allows visitors to explore the island. Remnants of Burton Island's agricultural past are evident in the woods, from rusted farm implements to an old barn foundation. Because of the marina, the island is a popular stopover for big-boat enthusiasts. Don't worry, the tent and lean-to sites are set apart from the busy recreation area.

Open: Mid-May through Labor Day.

⑭ Champlain Adult Campground

Location: North of Keeler Bay in Grand Isle; Northern Vermont map page 280, grid b1.

Campsites, facilities: There are 100 sites for tents and RVs, some with full hookups. Each site has a table and fireplace. A dump station, rest rooms, hot showers, and a rec hall are provided. Firewood is available. The owners speak French. Leashed pets are permitted.

Reservations, fees: Reservations are recommended. Sites are $15 to $20 a night. Veterans of WW II camp for free, and the owners will pay WW I veterans the daily rate to camp here.

Contact: Emma and Jean Claude Guillon, Champlain Adult Campground, 3 Silent Cedars Circle, Grand Isle, VT 05458; (802) 372-5938.

Directions: From Interstate 89 north of Burlington, take exit 17 and follow U.S. 2 to the Lake Champlain Islands and the intersection with Route 314. Bear left and follow Route 314 north for 2.5 miles to the campground entrance.

Trip notes: Flanked by the ferry to the south and a public golf course to the north, these campsites are set on and back from the shore of 120-mile-long Lake Champlain. A grove of cedars and an old orchard

provide shade and privacy. The campground caters to retired people and adults; you must be 18 or older to stay here. A beach and dock provide front row seats for watching salmon-colored sunsets as the sun disappears behind the Adirondack Mountains. Keep your eyes peeled for Champ, the elusive lake monster and probable cousin of Scotland's Nessie.

Open: Mid-May through mid-October.

⑮ Grand Isle State Park

Location: On the Lake Champlain Islands; Northern Vermont map page 280, grid b1.

Campsites, facilities: There are 155 sites for tents and RVs including 34 lean-tos, all without hookups. Each site has a table and fire ring. A dump station is provided. A playground, beach, boat ramp, boat rentals, a rec hall, metered hot showers, and flush toilets are provided. Ice and firewood are available. Leashed pets with rabies vaccination certification are permitted, but not in day-use areas.

Reservations, fees: Reservations are recommended. Tent sites are $12 a night and lean-to sites are $16 a night for four people. Each additional person four years and older will be charged $3 at a tent site and $4 at a lean-to. The maximum allowable number of people at a site is eight, and there must be at least one person 18 years of age or older with each camping party. A cabin is available for $32 a night. See also page 284.

Contact: Grand Isle State Park, 36 East Shore South, Grand Isle, VT 05458; (802) 372-4300.

Directions: From the town of Grand Isle, travel one mile south on U.S. 2 to the park entrance on the left.

Trip notes: Grand Isle is one of the most developed state parks in Vermont. Campsites line the east shore and are close to the main attraction, a lake beach where swimming, fishing, and boating are the favored activities. This is Vermont's only state park with a recreation hall used for group events. Exercise nuts can work out on the fitness trail that winds through the 226-acre park. One of the isle's more interesting tourist attractions is found north of the park on the east shore: Hyde Log Cabin is believed to be the oldest log cabin in the United States.

Open: Mid-May through mid-October.

16 Apple Tree Bay Resort

Location: On the southern end of Grand Isle; Northern Vermont map page 280, grid b1.

Campsites, facilities: There are 300 sites for tents and RVs, 220 with full hookups and 80 with water and electric. Each site has a picnic table, fire ring, and grill. Air conditioners are allowed. Facilities include RV storage, dump stations, hot showers, laundry, a grocery store, playground, heated pool, rec hall, sports courts, an athletic field, and horseshoe pits. Group sites for tents and RVs, RV supplies, LP gas, gasoline, ice, and firewood are available. An on-site marina has a dock, a ramp, gas, and boat rentals. Leashed pets are permitted.

Reservations, fees: Reservations are recommended Memorial Day through Labor Day. Sites start at $22 a night per family. Weekly, monthly, and seasonal rates are available.

Contact: Paul and Rick Abare, Apple Tree Bay Resort, P.O. Box 183, South Hero, VT 05486; (802) 372-5398.

Directions: From Interstate 89 north of Burlington, take exit 17 toward South Hero and travel six miles west on U.S. 2 to the resort on the right (north) side of the road.

Trip notes: Mountain views and magnificent Lake Champlain greet campers at Apple Tree. This full-service RV park caters to boaters with an on-site marina, dock, ramp, and boat supply store as well as a place to gas up. A nine-hole golf course and a clubhouse are also located on the 188-acre resort. Take a dip in the brisk lake or opt for the resort's heated pool. The northern end of the lake is shared by powerboaters, kayakers, and canoeists. Fishing guides are available for hire at the marina for campers who want to penetrate the deep waters of the 120-mile-long lake and perhaps take home a cooler full of lake trout, landlocked salmon, walleye, smelt, northern pike, or any of several other species. Throughout the summer, bingo, dancing, special dinners, and other group activities are organized.

Open: May 1 through October 20.

17 Camp Skyland on Lake Champlain

Location: On the southern tip of land in Grand Isle County on Lake Champlain; Northern Vermont map page 280, grid b1.

Campsites, facilities: There are 31 sites for tents and RVs, 11 with full hookups and nine with water and electric. Each site has a picnic table and fireplace. A rec hall, flush toilets, hot showers, laundry facilities, boat rentals, and a playground are provided, but there is no dump station. Cabins can be rented. Leashed pets are permitted.

Reservations, fees: Reservations are recommended and require a nonrefundable deposit of $15 ($50 for cabins). Sites start at $16 a night per family of four. There are surcharges for services and guests.

Contact: May through October—Camp Skyland on Lake Champlain, 398 South Street, South Hero, VT 05486; (802) 372-

4200. November through April—Jack and Priscilla Arnold, Box 134, South Royalton, VT 05068; (802) 763-7320.

Directions: From Interstate 89 north of Burlington, take exit 17, head west on U.S. 2, and cross the Sandbar Bridge. In South Hero, turn left on South Street and drive 3.5 miles to the campground.

Trip notes: Unspoiled views are in the offing at Camp Skyland on the southernmost peninsula of Grand Isle. The panoramic vistas of Malletts Bay, Lake Champlain, and the mountains beyond are seemingly infinite. A boat launch for small vessels and canoes is provided at the campground for those who wish to explore the peaceful horizon. On the lakeshore there's a swimming area, a dock, and boat rentals. This is one of the most pastoral places in all of Vermont. Revolutionary War hero Ethan Allen's cousin, Ebenezer, homesteaded the island of South Hero in 1783, and farms, orchards, and hamlets still abound.

Open: Mid-June through late September.

⓲ Homestead Campground

Location: At the north end of Arrowhead Mountain Lake in Milton; Northern Vermont map page 280, grid b2.

Campsites, facilities: There are 150 sites for tents and RVs, all with water and electric hookups. Each site has a picnic table and fire ring. Air conditioners are allowed, but heaters are not. Cable TV hookups are available. Facilities include a dump station, laundry, hot showers, rest rooms, a rec hall, an arcade, two pools, sports courts, horseshoe pits, and a playground. Also available are group sites for tents and RVs, RV rentals, and RV storage. A small grocery store sells RV supplies, LP gas, ice, and firewood. Leashed pets are permitted.

Reservations, fees: Reservations are recommended. Sites start at $20 a night per family.

Contact: Joe and Sue Monty, Homestead Campground, RR 3, Box 3454, Milton, VT 05468; (802) 524-2356.

Directions: From Interstate 89 north of Burlington, take exit 18 and travel a quarter mile south on U.S. 7 to the campground entrance.

Trip notes: Family-oriented camping is found right off the highway at Homestead. Level grassy sites are close together under a canopy of trees. Myriad activities are available on weekends; planned events include flea markets, wagon rides, bingo, and visits from Barney the purple dinosaur. Sports courts, pools, athletic fields, and an on-site arcade keep campers of all ages entertained. Across the street is a driving range and a miniature golf plaza with a snack bar and go-carts. Though tenters are welcome, RVs and seasonal mobile homes dominate the park. The campground is conveniently located near many of northwest Vermont's bigger attractions, such as Lake Champlain, Burlington, and the Green Mountains.

Open: May 1 through mid-October.

⓳ Maple Grove Campground

Location: North of Fairfax; Northern Vermont map page 280, grid b2.

Campsites, facilities: There are 24 sites for tents and RVs, 12 with full hookups and 12 with water and electric. Each site has a fire ring and table. Air conditioners, but not heaters, are allowed. Facilities include a dump station, laundry, a basketball hoop, a playground, badminton and volleyball courts, and horseshoe pits. Limited groceries, RV supplies, ice, and wood are available. Leashed pets are permitted.

Reservations, fees: Reservations are recommended. Sites start at $12 to $17 a night per family.

Contact: BJ and Brenda Harvey Jr., Maple Grove Campground, 1627 Main Street, Fairfax, VT 05454; (802) 849-6439.

Directions: From Interstate 89 north of Burlington, take exit 18 and drive five miles east on Route 104A. Turn left on Route 104 and head north for less than a mile to the campground entrance on the right (east) side of the road.

Trip notes: Though it boasts only 24 sites, Maple Grove is fully equipped for RV camping. RV sites are shaded and level, and there are even some grassy spaces for tents under maple trees. Just to the south, the Lamoille River flows through Fairfax on its way to Malletts Bay. Canoeists can put in at Fairfax Falls for either day trips or full-scale excursions to Lake Champlain. The Lamoille is also open to trout fishing.

Open: May 1 through October 15.

20 Lone Pine Campsites

Location: Near Malletts Bay; Northern Vermont map page 280, grid b1.

Campsites, facilities: There are 260 sites for tents and RVs, 165 with full hookups and 95 with water and electric. Each site has a picnic table, grill, and fire ring. Air conditioners are allowed and phone hookups are available. Facilities include dump stations, rest rooms, hot showers, laundry, a rec room, pavilion, two pools, miniature golf, sports courts, athletic fields, and horseshoe pits. LP gas, RV rentals, RV storage, RV supplies, ice, and firewood are available. Two pets per site are allowed.

Reservations, fees: Reservations are recommended July 1 through Labor Day and are accepted through the mail or over the phone. Sites are $22 to $27 a night for four people.

Contact: Lone Pine Campsites, 104 Bay Road, Colchester, VT 05446; (802) 878-5447.

Directions: From Interstate 89 north of Burlington, take exit 16 and travel north on U.S. 2/7 for 3.5 miles. Turn left on Bay Road and continue one mile north to the campground entrance.

Trip notes: Paved roads and campsites are laid out in a grid fashion with one shade tree per lot. Campsites are level and grassy, and a thick row of trees buffers the facility from Interstate 89. A short drive to the southwest brings you to the shore of Lake Champlain, where boating and fishing opportunities are limited only by your resources and imagination. Organized activities for the whole family are scheduled daily from May through September. Typical planned functions include fire engine rides on Friday and Saturday, line dancing instruction, and cribbage tournaments with cash prizes. A counselor-directed day camp for kids ages six through 15 is open on summer weekdays and features workshops in drama, arts and crafts, and nature exploration. The city of Burlington to the south is home to University Mall, Vermont's largest enclosed shopping center. In summer, the University of Vermont hosts the Champlain Shakespeare Festival at the Royall Tyler Theatre; Tyler, a native Vermonter, was America's first professional playwright.

Open: May 1 through October 15.

21 Malletts Bay Campground

Location: On Malletts Bay; Northern Vermont map page 280, grid b1.

Campsites, facilities: There are 112 sites for tents and RVs, 78 with full hookups and

34 with water and electric. Each site has a table and fire ring. Cable TV hookups are available. Facilities include a dump station, rest rooms, hot showers, laundry, a rec hall, playground, horseshoe pits, and basketball courts. A camp store sells LP gas, ice, and firewood. Leashed pets are permitted.

Reservations, fees: Reservations are recommended. Sites are $20 to $25 a night per family. Weekly, monthly, and seasonal rates are available.

Contact: Salamin and Mountaha Handy, Malletts Bay Campground, 209 Lakeshore Drive, Colchester, VT 05446; (802) 863-6980.

Directions: From Interstate 89 north of Burlington, take exit 16 to U.S. 7. Travel two miles north, then turn left and continue north on Route 127 for three miles to the campground entrance.

Trip notes: Both open and wooded spots are offered at this full-service RV park laid out in a tight grid of sites and streets across a street from Lake Champlain. Waterview sites look out across the bay and boat moorings to the Champlain Islands and New York state. Tent campers can stay on grassy lawns around the RV lots. The campground is bordered to the north by Bayside Park, which has a public beach and boat launch. The surrounding area is developed, offering access to nearby golf courses, shopping centers, ferries, and churches. Malletts Bay Campground is especially popular with seasonal campers.

Open: May 1 through mid-October.

㉒ Smugglers Notch State Park

Location: Northwest of Stowe; Northern Vermont map page 280, grid b2.

Campsites, facilities: There are 38 sites for tents and RVs including 14 lean-tos, all without hookups. A dump station, hot showers, flush toilets, a playground, fireplaces, and picnic tables are provided. Ice and firewood are available. Leashed pets with rabies vaccination certification are permitted, but not in day-use areas.

Reservations, fees: Reservations are recommended. Sites are $11 to $15 a night for four people. Each additional person four years and older will be charged $3 at a tent site and $4 at a lean-to. The maximum allowable number of people at a site is eight, and there must be at least one person 18 years of age or older with each camping party. See also page 284.

Contact: Smugglers Notch State Park, 7248 Mountain Road, Stowe, VT 05672; (802) 253-4014.

Directions: From the village of Stowe, head northwest on Route 108 for eight miles to the park entrance on the right.

Trip notes: The rocky walls of Mount Mansfield and Spruce Peak are separated by a skinny path that makes for a dramatic entrance to the park. These wooded sites lie at the north end of the notch and are the perfect jumping-off point for any number of day and overnight treks in the Green Mountains, as the Long Trail and its many side trails are accessible from the park. According to local lore, bootleggers cached contraband goods during the War of 1812 in a set of rocks known as the Smugglers Caves behind the information booth at Smugglers Notch. Note: High winds often whip through the notch and campground.

Open: Mid-May through early October.

㉓ South Hill Riverside Campground

Location: West of Mount Mansfield; Northern Vermont map page 280, grid b2.

Campsites, facilities: There are 50 sites for tents and RVs up to 32 feet long, 42 with full hookups. Each site has a fire ring and picnic table. Laundry facilities, rest rooms, showers, a playground, and dump station are provided. Ice and firewood are available. Leashed pets are permitted.

Reservations, fees: Reservations are recommended. Tent sites are $17 a night per family; RV sites start at $18 a night.

Contact: Grace Mills, South Hill Riverside Campground, RR 2, Box 287, Underhill, VT 05489; (802) 899-2232.

Directions: From the junction of Routes 15 and 128 in Essex Junction, travel six miles east on Route 15 to the campground entrance on the right.

Trip notes: These campsites beside the Brown River are level, grassy, and naturally shaded. Space is a little tight—sites are only about 25 feet wide—but the panoramic view of Mount Mansfield (at 4,393 feet, Vermont's tallest peak) and a rustic covered bridge make up for it. You can throw a line in the river and try for trout, or take a short drive to Underhill State Park for some of the state's best hiking on the west slope of Mount Mansfield. Less industrious peakbaggers can circle around to the north and hop on the toll road or the gondola to the summit. Whatever means you use to get there, the trip yields the same reward: sweeping views of the Green Mountains, Lake Champlain, and rolling farmland.

Open: May 15 through October 15.

㉔ Underhill State Park

Location: To the southeast of Mount Mansfield; Northern Vermont map page 280, grid b2.

Campsites, facilities: There are 25 sites for tents including 15 lean-tos and a group camping area. Flush toilets, piped water, fireplaces, and picnic tables are provided. Down and dead wood in the state forest can be used for campfires. Supplies are sold in Underhill Center, and more extensive goods and services can be obtained in Jeffersonville. Leashed pets with rabies vaccination certification are permitted, but not in day-use areas.

Reservations, fees: Reservations are recommended. Tent sites are $11 a night and lean-to sites are $15 a night for four people. Each additional person four years and older will be charged $3 at a tent site and $4 at a lean-to. The maximum allowable number of people at a site is eight, and there must be at least one person 18 years of age or older with each camping party. See also page 284.

Contact: Underhill State Park, P.O. Box 249, Underhill Center, VT 05490; (802) 899-3022.

Directions: From Route 15 in Underhill Center, travel four miles east on Town Road. When the pavement turns to gravel, continue east for another four miles on the same road to the state park.

Trip notes: The steep entry road into the campground makes this a poor choice for those with trailers or RVs. Campsites are in a wooded glen on the lower slopes of Mount Mansfield. Nine large lean-to sites set above the other spaces are reserved for use by organized groups. The state park, located at the headwaters of the trout-infested Brown River, is part of 34,000-acre Mount Mansfield State Forest. Four popular trails lead from the campground to the summit ridge of Mount Mansfield, Vermont's tallest peak at 4,393 feet; they branch off above the group camping area. The Sunset Ridge Trail is the most popular and scenic, offering views for much of the way. Vermont's Long Trail crosses the summit, and a network of trails on the other side makes many hiking loops possible. The harsh summit-ridge climate has fostered rare Arctic vegetation; once you summit, you'll see the Stowe Ski Area on the west side of the mountain. The campground includes a day-use area and a large log picnic shelter built by the Civilian Conservation Corps in the late 1930s.

Open: Mid-May through mid-October.

㉕ Shelburne Camping Area

Location: North of Shelburne Village; Northern Vermont map page 280, grid c1.

Campsites, facilities: There are 78 sites for tents and RVs, 28 with full hookups, 40 with water and electric, and 10 with none. Each site has a picnic table and fire ring. Use of air conditioners and heaters is allowed. Laundry facilities, a dump station, rec room, two pools, a basketball hoop, badminton and volleyball courts, and horseshoe pits are provided. Cable TV and phone hookups are available. A small grocery store sells LP gas, ice, and firewood. Leashed pets are permitted.

Reservations, fees: Reservations are recommended July 1 through Labor Day. Sites start at $20 a night for two people.

Contact: The Bissonette Family, Shelburne Camping Area, 2056 Shelburne Road, Shelburne, VT 05482; (802) 985-2540.

Directions: From Shelburne Village, travel one mile north on U.S. 7.

Trip notes: It's hard to miss the entrance—just look out for the Dutch-style windmill. The campground is owned and operated by the proprietors of the Dutch Mill motel and family restaurant, and large, grassy sites with shade trees line up behind the facility in RV park fashion. Seasonal campers tend to favor this place for its prox-imity to Lake Champlain and Burlington and the fact that lake beaches are a short drive away. The nearby town of Shelburne is known for the Shelburne Museum. Founder Electra Havermayer Webb was an eccentric heiress who traveled all over the country in the early part of this century, snapping up canoes, toys, furniture, paintings, quilts, decoys, scrimshaw, weather vanes, and many other folk art items. More than 80,000 pieces are contained in three galleries and seven furnished historic houses on 45 country acres.

Open: May 1 through November 1.

㉖ Old Lantern Campground

Location: In Charlotte; Northern Vermont map page 280, grid c1.

Campsites, facilities: There are 95 sites for tents and RVs, 28 with full hookups, 47 with water and electric, and 20 with none. Each site has a table, fire ring, and grill. Use of air conditioners and heaters is allowed. A dump station, laundry facilities, a rec hall, rest rooms, hot showers, a pool, badminton and volleyball courts, and horseshoe pits are provided. A small store sells LP gas, ice, and firewood. Group sites and phone hookups are available. Leashed pets are permitted.

Reservations, fees: Reservations are recommended. Tent sites are $15 and RV sites start at $20 a night for four people.

Contact: Old Lantern Campground, P.O. Box 221, Charlotte, VT 05445; (802) 425-2120.

Directions: From the junction of Route 5 and U.S. 7 in Charlotte, travel half a mile west on Route 5. Turn left on Greenbush Road and drive south to the campground entrance half a mile ahead.

Trip notes: Snuggled between the interstate and Lake Champlain, these sites are in a private, rural area with views of the Green Mountains to the east and Lake Champlain to the west. Both open and wooded spots are available on rolling hillsides. Lake access and a marina are three miles away, while a short hiking trail is maintained on the property. Ferries to New York sail every half hour from the quaint town of Charlotte, one of the most scenic places to cross the lake. Two miles south of the campground the Vermont Wildflower Farm boasts six acres of wildflower gardens where visitors can take self-guided tours.

Open: May 1 through October 15.

㉗ Mount Philo State Park

Location: Near Lake Champlain in North Ferrisburgh; Northern Vermont map page 280, grid c1.

Campsites, facilities: There are 16 sites for tents and RVs including three lean-tos, all without hookups. Each site has a table and fireplace. No dump station is available. Metered hot showers, flush toilets, recycling bins, a picnic shelter, and a playground are provided. Firewood is available. Leashed pets with rabies vaccination certification are permitted, but not in day-use areas.

Reservations, fees: Reservations are recommended. Sites are $10 to $14 a night for four people. Each additional person four years and older will be charged $3 at a tent site and $4 at a lean-to. The maximum allowable number of people at a site is eight, and there must be at least one person 18 years of age or older with each camping party. See also page 284.

Contact: Mount Philo State Park, RR 1, Box 1049, North Ferrisburgh, VT 05473; (802) 425-2390.

Directions: From North Ferrisburgh, travel one mile north on U.S. 7. Turn right on the town road and drive one mile east to the park entrance, following the signs.

Trip notes: These campsites are set near the top of Mount Philo. And though the summit elevation is only 980 feet, the mountain's proximity to the shores of Lake Champlain make it an ideal lookout for panoramic views to the west of the Adirondack Mountains in New York state. Note that a steep roadway leads into the park, prohibiting access to camping vehicles more than 30 feet in length.

Open: Early May through early October.

㉘ Button Bay State Park

Location: On Lake Champlain west of Vergennes; Northern Vermont map page 280, grid d1.

Campsites, facilities: There are 72 sites for tents and RVs including 13 lean-tos, all without hookups. Each site has a picnic table and fireplace. Metered hot showers, flush toilets, recycling bins, a dump station, picnic shelter, snack bar, a pool, and playground are provided. Leashed pets with rabies vaccination certification are permitted, but not in day-use areas.

Reservations, fees: Reservations are recommended. Sites are $12 to $16 a night for four people. Each additional person four years and older will be charged $3 at a tent site and $4 at a lean-to. The maximum allowable number of people at a site is eight, and there must be at least one person 18 years of age or older with each camping party. See also page 284.

Contact: Button Bay State Park, RR 3, Box 4570, Vergennes, VT 05491; (802) 475-2377.

Directions: From Vergennes, travel half a mile south on Route 22A. Turn right and head west for six miles to the campground, following the signs.

Trip notes: Located on the south shore of Lake Champlain, these campsites offer stunning views of the Adirondack Mountains across the water in New York. Water-skiers and powerboaters sometimes clog the park's boat ramp and dock on summer weekends. Most visitors are drawn to Button Bay for the views and the water sports, while the resident naturalist, nature center, and interesting geography and history only add to the campground's popularity. A footpath at the Button Bay Natural Area leads through a small but impressive oak-hickory woodland with vistas of the lake. The bedrock here is limestone, formed about 450 million years ago. Some of the oldest fossilized coral in the world, as well as the remains of other marine organisms, are found here. "Buttons" were clay deposits, left by retreating glaciers some 10,000 years ago, that cemented into circular shapes with holes in the middle. A collection of these now rare formations is on display at the nature center. Button Bay is where General Benedict Arnold sank America's first naval fleet; British soldiers named the sheltered, strategic location for the buttonlike clay formations.

Open: Mid-May to Columbus Day.

㉙ D.A.R. State Park

Location: On Lake Champlain north of the Chimney Point Bridge; Northern Vermont map page 280, grid d1.

Campsites, facilities: There are 71 sites for tents and RVs, all without hookups. Dump stations, tables, fire rings, and a playground are provided, and ice can be purchased nearby. Firewood is available on site. Leashed pets with rabies vaccination certification are permitted, but not in day-use areas.

Reservations, fees: Reservations are recommended. Sites are $11 to $15 a night for four people. Each additional person four years and older will be charged $3 at a tent site and $4 at a lean-to. The maximum allowable number of people at a site is eight, and there must be at least one person 18 years of age or older with each camping party. See also page 284.

Contact: D.A.R. State Park, RR 3, Box 3493, Vergennes, VT 05491; (802) 759-2345.

Directions: From the junction of Routes 22A and 17 in Addison, travel seven miles southwest on Route 17 to Lake Champlain. The campground borders the water.

Trip notes: D.A.R. State Park is on the shore of Lake Champlain. Campers can launch boats from the campground onto the 120-mile-long lake, as well as go swimming and fishing. Sites are partly shaded and roomy and are in high demand in midsummer, so be sure to reserve.

Open: Mid-May through Labor Day.

㉚ Ten Acre Camping

Location: Near the Chimney Point Bridge; Northern Vermont map page 280, grid d1.

Campsites, facilities: There are 78 RV sites with water and electric hookups and 12 tent sites including two lean-tos. Each site has a picnic table and fire ring. Hot showers, laundry facilities, a heated pool, a pavilion, game room, horseshoe pits, shuffleboard, and miniature golf are provided. LP gas, ice, and firewood are available. Leashed pets are permitted.

Reservations, fees: Reservations are recommended. Sites are $10 to $16 a night for two people.

Contact: Leo and Mary Ann Griffin, Ten Acre Camping, RR 1, Box 3560, Addison, VT 05491; (802) 672-5043.

Directions: From the Chimney Point Bridge, which crosses Lake Champlain, travel one mile south on Route 125 to the campground entrance across the street from the lake.

Trip notes: Set in a wooded niche surrounded by rolling, cleared farmland, this campground is just across the road from 120-mile-long Lake Champlain. Both open and shaded spots are available, and all sites are grassy. A small, stocked fishing pond on the grounds will please the kids, while grown-ups will want to get out on the big lake. Docks are located across the road from the campground, and all types of boats are welcome. Sailing and powerboating are the most popular activities.

Open: May 1 through mid-October.

---

31 Rivers Bend Campground

Location: At the confluence of Otter Creek and the New Haven River; Northern Vermont map page 280, grid d1.

Campsites, facilities: There are 57 sites for tents and RVs, most with water and electric hookups. Each site has a fire ring and table. Air conditioners are allowed. Facilities include a dump station, rest rooms with hot showers, laundry, a pavilion, playground, horseshoe pits, and volleyball. Ice and firewood are available. Leashed pets are permitted.

Reservations, fees: Reservations are recommended. Sites are $18 a night.

Contact: Rivers Bend Campground, P.O. Box 9, New Haven, VT 05472; (802) 388-9092.

Directions: From the junction of Route 125 and U.S. 7 at Middlebury, travel four miles north on U.S. 7. Turn left on Dog Team Road and drive a mile to the entrance.

Trip notes: About half the sites at this campground, located at the confluence of Otter Creek and the New Haven River, are right on the water and are grassy and partially shaded. The campground owns about 4,000 feet of river frontage on waters that are ripe for swimming, fishing, tubing, and canoeing. Otter Creek, which flows north to Lake Champlain, is especially known for its pace, easy enough for paddlers of all levels to handle. Rivers Bend also maintains a sandy beach. Two nature trails explore the hills around the river valley. The Morgan Horse Farm, operated by the University of Vermont, is nearby. Established in the 1870s, the farm is devoted to breeding Morgan horses, the first American breed. Guided tours are given through the stately and historic main barn.

Open: May 1 through mid-October.

---

32 Elephant Mountain Camping Area

Location: South of Bristol in the Green Mountain National Forest; Northern Vermont map page 280, grid d1.

Campsites, facilities: There are 50 sites, most for RVs and a few for tents; all have electric hookups, and some have full hookups. Each site has a fireplace and picnic table. Heaters and air conditioners are not allowed, and motor-driven cycles are prohibited. A pavilion, playground, pool, trails, sports courts, athletic fields, and horseshoe pits are provided. Ice and firewood are available. Leashed pets are permitted.

Reservations, fees: Reservations are recommended and require a $10 deposit. Sites are $11 to $16 a night.

Contact: Elephant Mountain Camping Area, RR 3, Box 850, Bristol, VT 05443; (802) 453-3123.

Directions: From Bristol, drive about three miles south on Route 116. The campground entrance is on the left (east) side of the highway.

Trip notes: Old-fashioned family camping is the gist of Elephant Mountain. Set in the Green Mountain National Forest, the sites are well shaded and have ample natural buffer for privacy. A small brook runs through the property, but most campers swim in the pool. Only a few sites are suitable for tents; they are equipped with tent pads, which must be used. Hiking trails are accessible from the campground. In fact, one of the most striking stretches of the Long Trail lies just to the east of Elephant Mountain: the ridge from Lincoln Gap to Appalachian Gap is as precipitous as it is beautiful, a skinny catwalk that offers sweeping views in every direction.

Open: May 1 through October 30.

㉝ The Long Trail

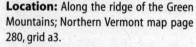

Location: Along the ridge of the Green Mountains; Northern Vermont map page 280, grid a3.

Campsites, facilities: There are 70 campsites along the 270-mile footpath. Some have lodges with wood stoves, many have Adirondack-style lean-tos, and others are wooded tent sites. Primitive toilets are provided at most of them. Group camping is allowed by permit; many campgrounds can accommodate small groups. All sites offer some kind of water source, but not all are reliable or pure. Off-trail camping is allowed in the Green Mountain National Forest and on state-owned lands under an elevation of 2,500 feet. Leashed pets are permitted.

Reservations, fees: All sites are available on a first-come, first-served basis. Use of any overnight facility operated by the Green Mountain Club is limited to three consecutive nights. In the summer months, some of the more heavily used sites are manned by caretakers and charge fees of $3 a night for Green Mountain Club members and $4 for nonmembers. Some of the sites on Green Mountain National Forest property charge a nightly fee and offer no discounts for GMC members.

Contact: The Green Mountain Club, Route 100, RR 1, Box 650, Waterbury Center, VT 05677; (802) 244-7037.

Directions: The southern starting point of the trail can be reached via the Appalachian Trail (AT) or the Pine Cobble Trail. To reach the AT trailhead: From the junction of U.S. 7 and Route 2 at the traffic circle in Williamstown, Massachusetts, travel three miles east to a traffic light at Phelps Avenue. There is no parking at the trailhead; parking is available with permission at the Greylock Community Club one-tenth mile east of the trail or at the Holy Family Catholic Church adjacent to the AT. To reach the Pine Cobble Trailhead: From the junction of U.S. 7 and Route 2 at the traffic circle in Williamstown, Massachusetts, follow Route 2 east for six-tenths of a mile to Cole Avenue. Turn left and travel north for eight-tenths of a mile to where Cole Avenue ends at North Hoosac Road. Turn right, proceed one-third mile, then turn on Pine Cobble Road and continue two-tenths of a mile to the trailhead; parking is available.

Trip notes: Known as the "Footpath in the Wilderness," Vermont's Long Trail is the oldest long-distance hiking trail in America. The 270-mile track follows the main ridge of the Green Mountains north from the Massachusetts-Vermont state line to the Canadian border. This backwoods path crosses rugged summits, follows clear streams, traverses alpine bogs, and cuts through deep rolling woodlands. An end-to-end hike on the Long Trail usually takes a month or less to complete. Many people hike the trail in its entirety, but certain sections are heavily used by day hikers and overnight backpackers, as the route crosses most of the state's highest peaks and penetrates its most remote wilderness reaches. The Green Mountain Club blazed the trail between 1910 and 1930, inspiring the construction of the Appalachian Trail in the process. The two trails converge at the Massachusetts border and work their way north on a single footpath for 100 miles. At Sherburne Pass near Pico Peak, they diverge at Maine Junction, with the Appalachian Trail veering east and the Long Trail continuing north.

Open: The Long Trail is open in summer, fall, and winter. Travel is discouraged during mud season, usually between late March and early May.

---

34 Prouty Beach Campground

Location: On Lake Memphremagog in Newport; Northern Vermont map page 280, grid a4.

Campsites, facilities: There are 50 sites for tents and RVs, 18 with full hookups and 28 with water and electric. Each site has a fire ring, grill, and picnic table. Facilities include a dump station, laundry, boat rentals, a playground, tennis courts, a sports field, horseshoe pits, volleyball courts, and shuffleboard. Ice and firewood are available. Leashed pets are permitted.

Reservations, fees: Reservations are recommended. Sites start at $20 a night for two people. Seasonal rates are available.

Contact: Prouty Beach Campground, Newport City Recreation Department, Newport, VT 05855; (802) 334-7951.

Directions: From Interstate 91 at Derby Center (east of Lake Memphremagog), take exit 27 and travel three miles northwest on Route 191 into Newport. Turn left and head west on Freeman Street, then take another left on Veterans Avenue and drive south to the park.

Trip notes: Thirty-two-mile Lake Memphremagog was a travel route and fishing ground for Native Americans long before settlers arrived. Today, the lake's trout and landlocked salmon populations still attract anglers, while boaters of every sort traverse the northern waters. The city owns and operates sandy Prouty Beach and the campground in addition to maintaining tennis courts and picnic areas for all to enjoy. In July the beach is the site of the annual Summer Fest, a seasonal celebration with family events. Several hundred yards west of the beach is a city-run dock and launching area, complete with boat supplies and slips. The Gateway Center at the dock has a snack bar and open-air deck beside the lake. The main body of the lake and South Bay offer excellent conditions for windsurfing, and a group of islands off Eagle Point to the north is a kayaker's playground. Canada and Vermont share the lake as well as the local legend of Memphre, a large serpentlike creature occasionally spotted out on the water.

Open: Mid-May through mid-October.

---

35 Fireside Campground

Location: East of Lake Memphremagog in Derby; Northern Vermont map page 280, grid a4.

Campsites, facilities: There are 35 sites for tents and RVs, 10 with full hookups and 14 with water and electric. Flush toilets, a dump station, and hot showers are provided. Firewood is available. Leashed pets are permitted.

Reservations, fees: Reservations are recommended. Sites start at $10 a night.

Contact: Skip and Bessie Hastings, Fireside Campground, Newport Road, Derby, VT 05829; (802) 766-5109.

Directions: From Interstate 91 near Derby, take exit 28 and drive north on U.S. 5 for one mile to the campground.

Trip notes: Ten sites at Fireside are set aside for tents, and the rest are level pull-throughs for RVs. The campground accommodates trailers up to 40 feet in length. Though not a booming metropolis, downtown Derby does have restaurants, stores, bowling lanes, and tennis courts, all within walking distance of the campground. Lake Derby nearby is open for swimming and boating. To the north in the town of Derby Line, the world's only international opera house and library straddles the Canadian border: the Haskell Free Library and Opera House has seats on U.S. soil and a stage in Rock Island, Quebec.

Open: Mid-May through October 1.

③⑥ Char-Bo Campground

Location: East of Derby overlooking Lake Salem; Northern Vermont map page 280, grid a4.

Campsites, facilities: There are 45 sites for tents and RVs, 18 with full hookups and 15 with water and electric. Each site has a table, fire ring, and grill. Use of air conditioners is permitted. Facilities include laundry, a dump station, rest rooms, hot showers, a game room, horseshoe pits, a basketball hoop, playground, and pool. RV rentals, RV storage, RV supplies, limited groceries, ice, and firewood are available. Leashed pets are permitted.

Reservations, fees: Reservations are recommended. Sites start at $16 and $18 a night per family of four. Weekly, monthly, and seasonal rates are available.

Contact: Bob and Charlotte Knowles, Char-Bo Campground, P.O. Box 54, Derby, VT 05829; (802) 766-8807.

Directions: From Interstate 91 at Derby, take exit 28 and travel four miles east on Route 105, then turn left and head north on Haywood Road to the campground.

Trip notes: From this hilltop perch campers have panoramic views of Lake Salem and Mounts Pisgah and Hor towering above Lake Willoughby. Grassy sites are divvied up according to camper type: RV sites are open while tent sites have shade trees and more privacy. The campground rents boats for use on the lake, and a path leads down the hill to a swimming beach. In Derby, the Cow Town Elk Ranch is the only elk farm in the state. These animals roamed freely in Vermont in the early 1800s until settlement pushed them north; a good time to visit the ranch is during the 4 P.M. feeding.

Open: Mid-May through October 1.

③⑦ Mill Brook Campground

Location: In the village of Westfield; Northern Vermont map page 280, grid a3.

Campsites, facilities: There are 30 sites for tents and RVs, 16 with full hookups, 12 with water and electric, and 2 with none. Each site has a fireplace and picnic table. Free hot showers, a play area, dump station, rest rooms, and sports courts are provided. Ice and firewood are available. There's also a general store next to the campground. Leashed pets are permitted.

Reservations, fees: Reservations are recommended. Tent sites start at $12 a night for two people, and sites with full hookups start at $14 a night. Seasonal rates are available.

Contact: Ernest Paxman, Mill Brook

Campground, Route 100, P.O. Box 133, Westfield, VT 05874; (802) 744-6673.

Directions: From Interstate 91 at Orleans, take exit 26 to U.S. 5. North of Coventry, turn left and head north on Route 14 to Route 100. Follow Route 100 as it leads south to Westfield. The campground is in the middle of the village.

Trip notes: Grassy, spacious sites for RVs are set along Mill Brook, which is open to trout fishing. Tenters are offered more secluded, wooded sites. A short wade or stroll upstream leads to a waterfall and gorge. Road biking is at its best in this part of the state, where highways are both scenic and lightly traveled. Easy bike routes explore nearby Newport on Lake Memphremagog, Jay Peak, and the verdant farmland of the Northeast Kingdom (the northern reaches of Vermont that lie east of the Green Mountains). For long hikes, hop on the Long Trail and scamper up Jay Peak, the last big rise before the trail's end at the Canadian border.

Open: Mid-May through mid-September.

---

38 Barrewood Campground

Location: South of Jay Peak; Northern Vermont map page 280, grid a4.

Campsites, facilities: There are 45 sites for tents and RVs, six with full hookups and 39 with water and electric. Each site has a picnic table and fire ring. Laundry facilities, hot showers, a rec hall, pavilion, playground, group camping areas, and a dump station are provided. There's also horseshoe pits, a volleyball court, and a badminton net. LP gas, ice, and firewood are for sale. The owners speak French. Leashed pets are permitted.

Reservations, fees: Reservations are recommended. Sites are $10 to $17 a night per family. Seasonal rates are available.

Contact: The Davis Family, Barrewood Campground, Route 100, HCR 13, Westfield, VT 05874; (802) 796-3733 or (802) 744-2068.

Directions: From the intersection of Routes 58 and 100 in Lowell, travel four miles north on Route 100 to the campground entrance on the left (west) side of the road.

Trip notes: Bilingual hospitality is offered at this campground only 10 miles from the Canadian border. Sites are open and grassy. A fishing stream runs through the property, and there's also a swimming pool for cooling off after hiking in the hills to the west. Nature trails leave from here and pass a triple-decker waterfall. The northernmost reaches of the Long Trail are just to the west of the campground. This section crosses over the summit of Jay Peak and continues on to the trail's end at the Canadian border, making for a challenging day hike. You can also drive to Jay Peak, park at the bottom, make your ascent, and take the tram back to the parking lot or hike down the ski trails.

Open: May 1 through mid-October.

---

39 Will-O-Wood Campground

Location: North of Lake Willoughby; Northern Vermont map page 280, grid a5.

Campsites, facilities: There are 117 sites for tents and RVs, 60 with full hookups and 24 with water and electric. Each site has a picnic table, fire ring, and grill. Use of air conditioners and heaters is allowed. The camp provides a rec hall, dump stations, laundry facilities, a pool, playground, sports courts, and horseshoe pits. A camp store sells groceries, LP gas, ice, and firewood. RV rentals are available. Leashed pets are permitted.

Reservations, fees: Nonrefundable deposits are required for reservations. Tent sites are $15 a night per family, and sites with full hookups start at $19. Weekly, monthly, and seasonal rates are available.

Contact: Will-O-Wood Campground, RR 2, Box 316, Orleans, VT 05860; (802) 525-3575.

Directions: From Interstate 91 at Orleans, take exit 26 and travel 6.25 miles east on Route 58. Turn right on Route 5A and drive south for half a mile to the campground.

Trip notes: Roomy sites are perched on a grassy hill overlooking Lake Willoughby a half mile to the south. Mounts Pisgah and Hor rise steeply from opposite ends of the lake, creating a fjordlike vista. Open fields and woodlands at Will-O-Wood provide ample room to relax. Willoughby Beach on the north shore of the lake is a short walk or drive away. Five miles long and 300 feet deep in some spots, the lake attracts windsurfers, powerboaters, anglers, and swimmers. A group called the Westmore Association maintains many miles of hiking trails in the woods and on the five peaks in the immediate area; trail maps are available at the campground. Bald Mountain, the highest summit at 3,315 feet, is accessible by the Long Pond and Mad Brook Trails. A fire tower atop the peak provides 360-degree views of the Green and White Mountains and Lake Memphremagog to the north.

Open: May 1 through October 15.

⑩ Lakeside Campground

Location: On the north side of Island Pond; Northern Vermont map page 280, grid a5.

Campsites, facilities: There are 200 sites for tents and RVs, many with full hookups. A dump station, playground, hot showers, rec hall, game room, laundry facilities, and boat rentals are provided. A grocery store sells LP gas, ice, and firewood. Leashed pets are permitted.

Reservations, fees: Reservations are recommended. Sites start at $14 and $18 a night. Seasonal rates are available.

Contact: Lakeside Campground, RR 1, Box 194, Island Pond, VT 05846; (802) 723-6649.

Directions: From the town of Island Pond, travel two miles east on Route 105 to the campground entrance on the left.

Trip notes: Offering both wooded and open sites on Island Pond, Lakeside Campground focuses on water-based recreation. The campground rents boats and maintains a long, sandy beach for swimming. Cruises are regularly scheduled. The lake is somewhat developed near the town of Island Pond, but miles of wilderness lie just east of the lake, where seemingly endless old logging roads provide entertainment for mountain bikers and, in season, are fruitful hunting grounds. Check in at Mahoney's General Store in Island Pond for bait, ammo, licenses, and maps.

Open: Mid-May through mid-September.

④ Brighton State Park

Location: Between Island and Spectacle Ponds in Brighton; Northern Vermont map page 280, grid a5.

Campsites, facilities: There are 63 tent and RV sites including 21 lean-tos, all without hookups. Each site has a picnic table and fireplace. Facilities include a dump station, flush toilets, hot showers, a playground, and horseshoe pits. Firewood is available. There's a snack bar half a mile away at the day-use area, and supplies can be purchased in the town of Island Pond, two miles to the west. Leashed pets with rabies vaccination certification are permitted, but not in day-use areas.

Reservations, fees: Reservations are recommended. Sites are $12 to $16 a night for four people. Each additional person four years and older will be charged $3 at a tent site and $4 at a lean-to. The maximum allowable number of people at a site is eight, and there must be at least one person 18 years of age or older with each camping party. See also page 284.

Contact: Brighton State Park, P.O. Box 413, Island Pond, VT 05846; (802) 723-4360.

Directions: From the junction of Routes 111 and 105 in Island Pond, travel two miles east on Route 105, then turn left and drive less than a mile to the campground, following the signs.

Trip notes: Wilderness surrounds the campground at Brighton State Park. Land to the east is virtually devoid of streets and towns, and logging roads access wooded mountains and deep, quiet valleys; in winter, snowmobilers flock to the area. Campsites hug the woods at the edge of Spectacle Pond, an excellent fishing hole. Campers may use a small beach and plunk a canoe into the water, but no motors are allowed. Nature trails, a natural history museum, and a garage theater are located at park headquarters. A half mile south of the campground, the park operates a day-use area on Island Pond, which is open to all boating and has a snack bar and boat rentals. The town of Island Pond used to be a major crossroads of rail commerce; it was the site of the first international railroad junction in the United States. A historic district there features a grand two-story railway station.

Open: Mid-May through Columbus Day.

㊷ Belview Campground

Location: On the north end of Crystal Lake; Northern Vermont map page 280, grid b4.

Campsites, facilities: There are 50 sites for tents and RVs, some with full hookups, as well as on-site rental units. Some sites have cable TV hookups. Metered hot showers, a dump station, rest rooms, and a playground are provided. Firewood and ice are available. Leashed pets are permitted.

Reservations, fees: Reservations are recommended and require a 50 percent deposit. Sites are $14 to $19 a night.

Contact: Bob and Joyce Morse, Belview Campground, P.O. Box 222, Barton, VT 05822; (802) 525-3242.

Directions: From Interstate 91, take exit 25 toward Barton. Travel north for one mile on Route 16 to the village of Barton. Turn right onto U.S. 5 and head south for half a mile, then turn right and follow Route 16 east over the railroad tracks to the campground entrance half a mile ahead.

Trip notes: Overlooking Crystal Lake, these sites are set back from the water in the woods. The lake is flanked by rolling hills to the east and flatter farmland to the west. Just west of Belview, Crystal Lake State Park has two sandy beaches, picnic areas, and a boat launch. The lake is open to powerboating as well as fishing; for more of a wilderness experience, explore May Pond and May Pond Mountain just to the east of the campground. Some of Vermont's elusive moose have been spotted here. If you're camping at Belview in August, be sure to check out the Barton Fair, an old-fashioned country event held at the village's extensive fairgrounds.

Open: Mid-May through mid-October.

43 White Caps Campground

Location: On the southern tip of Lake Willoughby; Northern Vermont map page 280, grid b5.

Campsites, facilities: There are 50 sites for tents and RVs, 25 with full hookups and seven with water and electric. Each site has a picnic table and fire ring. Hot showers, flush toilets, a dump station, laundry facilities, and a playground are provided. A camp store carries ice and firewood. Leashed pets are permitted.

Reservations, fees: Reservations are accepted. Sites with water and electric hookups are $14 a night, full hookups are $16, and tent sites are $13 for four people.

Contact: Ralph and Jackie Willemain, White Caps Campground, RR 2, Box 626, Orleans, VT 05860; (802) 467-3345.

Directions: From Interstate 91 north of St. Johnsbury, take exit 23 and head north on U.S. 5 to West Burke, about 10 miles. From the junction of U.S. 5 and Route 5A, travel north for six more miles on Route 5A to the campground entrance on the right (east) side of the road.

Trip notes: Lake Willoughby is sandwiched dramatically between glacially sculpted mountains. White Caps Campground lies at the southern end of the five-mile-long lake, and most sites have superb views. Some of the trailer sites are small, only 20 feet wide, while others can accommodate RVs up to 40 feet in length. White birch trees shade much of the grounds. Across U.S. 5 there's a sandy beach and a boat launch owned by the campground. The Lake Willoughby area is an outdoorsperson's playground: there are craggy cliffs for rock climbing, 300-foot lake depths for scuba diving, five miles of open water for waterskiing and sailing, and miles of quiet country roads for biking. In 1996 a 29-pound lake trout was hooked at Willoughby, setting the world record for ice fishing. The water in this spring-fed lake is clean enough to drink sans treatment.

Open: May 15 through October 15.

44 Maidstone State Park

Location: On Maidstone Lake northeast of St. Johnsbury; Northern Vermont map page 280, grid b6.

Campsites, facilities: There are 83 sites for tents and RVs including 37 lean-tos, all without hookups. Each site has a picnic table and fireplace. A dump station, boat rentals, a group camping area, and a playground are provided. Firewood can be purchased at the park. Leashed pets with rabies vaccination certification are permitted, but not in day-use areas.

Reservations, fees: Reservations are recommended. Tent sites are $12 a night and lean-to sites are $16 a night for four people. Each additional person four years and older will be charged $3 at a tent site and $4 at a lean-to. The maximum allowable number of people at a site is eight, and there must be at least one person 18 years of age or older with each camping party. See also page 284.

Contact: Maidstone State Park, RD Box 455, Guildhall, VT 05905; (802) 676-3930.

Directions: From Guildhall, travel north on Route 102 for 11 miles. Turn left and head southwest on State Forest Highway for five miles to the park entrance.

Trip notes: Covering almost 800 acres, Maidstone Lake offers the full gamut of water sports from trout and perch fishing to sailing and powerboating. Campsites are near the shore; besides the park, much of the shoreline is occupied by seasonal camps. Boat rentals and a public ramp are provided. If you tire of the busy lake, head into the surrounding wilderness. There are no roads in the woods to the west, save for old logging roads that are suitable for mountain bikes and hiking boots. Beaver flowages and ponds, wetlands, and 2,000-foot hills are inhabited by deer, black bear, moose, fisher cat, and other mammals and birds.

Open: Mid-May through Labor Day.

⑤ Lake View Camping Area

Location: On Lake Eden; Northern Vermont map page 280, grid b3.

Campsites, facilities: There are 68 sites for tents and RVs up to 30 feet in length, all with water and electric hookups. Each site has a garbage can, fire ring, grill, and picnic table. Facilities include a dump station, rest rooms, hot showers, a limited grocery store, shuffleboard, badminton courts, and horseshoe pits. Ice, firewood, and bait are available. Leashed pets are permitted but not in the beach area.

Reservations, fees: Reservations require a $25 deposit, which must be received within 14 days of your request. Sites are $16 a night per family (two adults and two children under 12). There are surcharges for air conditioners, heaters, refrigerators, and visitors. Weekly and monthly rates are available. Bicyclists camp for $4 a night.

Contact: Hugh and Elsie Godin, Lake View Camping Area, HCR Box 5, Route 100, Eden Mills, VT 05653; (802) 635-2255; after September 15 call (802) 524-4554.

Directions: From Interstate 89 at Colbyville, take exit 10 and travel north on Route 100. When you reach the junction with Route 118, continue two miles north on Route 100 to the campground entrance.

Trip notes: Route 100 intersects this campground on Lake Eden. Grassy, open field-type sites are set either beside the lake or across the street in a slightly more wooded area. Most have a view of Lake Eden, but the parking lot setup precludes privacy. On the lake there are sandy beaches, a large play area, and a small gift shop and grocery store. The campground gives mountain bikers a price break: if you're touring on two wheels, you can set up camp for $4 a person. For a challenging day hike and a great view, the Long Trail is just five miles to the west. Take the Asbestos Mine Road out of Eden Mills to the Frank Post Trailhead. In two miles, this route meets the Long Trail. Head south to Belvedere Mountain then take the Forester's Trail back to your car. It's seven miles round-trip.

Open: May 15 through September 15.

⑥ Burke Mountain Campground

Location: Northeast of St. Johnsbury near Burke Mountain; Northern Vermont map page 280, grid b5.

Campsites, facilities: There are 25 sites for tents and RVs up to 24 feet in length, including eight lean-tos, all without hookups. Rest rooms, hot showers, horseshoe pits, fireplaces, and picnic tables are provided. Leashed pets are permitted.

Reservations, fees: Reservations are recommended. Sites start at $10 a night.

Contact: Brian Keon, Burke Mountain Campground, East Burke, VT 05832; (802) 626-1204.

Directions: From Interstate 91, take exit 23 toward Lyndonville. Travel three miles north on U.S. 5, then continue east on Route 114 for six miles to East Burke. Turn right on Mountain Road and follow signs to the campground entrance.

Trip notes: Boasting a prime location near the base of Burke Mountain, this campground is a haven for cyclists who like to test their skills and rattle their brains on mountain trails. The hike to the summit is lovely, and wheel-borne tourists can motor to the top on an auto road ($3 for cars, a buck for motorcycles). Gorgeous views reward every style of peakbagger: Lake Willoughby to the north is sandwiched between Mount Pisgah and Mount Hor while the White Mountains show their perky tips to the east. Area lakes and rivers provide ample places to fish and swim. In charming East Burke, Bailey's Country Store carries the best of the new and old, from penny candy to gourmet coffee by the cup.

Open: Memorial Day through Columbus Day.

47 Common Ground Camping Resort

Location: In Hyde Park; Northern Vermont map page 280, grid b3.

Campsites, facilities: There are 20 RV sites with hookups. A dump station, rec hall, miniature golf, volleyball, horseshoes, shuffleboard, and a swimming pool are provided. Ice is available, and firewood is sold nearby. Leashed pets are permitted.

Reservations, fees: Reservations are recommended. Sites start at $17 a night.

Contact: Common Ground Camping Resort, Route 1, Box 1780, Hyde Park, VT 05655; (802) 888-5210.

Directions: From the junction of Routes 15 and 100 north of Morrisville, travel 1.7 miles north on Route 100 to the park entrance on the left.

Trip notes: Kids will love Common Ground, for it's more of an amusement park than a campground. Twenty RV sites flank a recreation complex with bumper boats, go-carts, miniature golf, and a swimming pool. For more natural amusements, the Long Trail is located just to the west, offering day hikes up Mount Mansfield and the surrounding peaks, while Elmore State Park to the southwest has a boat ramp and swimming beach. The glitziest town in Vermont's north country lies just to the south: Stowe's streets are lined with expensive shops and gourmet restaurants.

Open: May 1 through October 1.

48 Mountain View Campground and Cottages

Location: In Morrisville on the Lamoille River; Northern Vermont map page 280, grid b3.

Campsites, facilities: There are 60 sites for tents and RVs, 8 with full hookups, 27 with water and electric, and 25 with none. Each site has a fire ring and table. Use of air conditioners, but not heaters, is allowed. Phone hookups are available. Facilities include a dump station, laundry, heated rest rooms, hot showers, two pools (one heated), a whirlpool, miniature golf, a playground, badminton and volleyball courts, a rec hall, a camp store, and horseshoe pits. Seven cabins are rented out. Leashed pets are permitted.

Reservations, fees: Reservations are recommended; there are no cash refunds for early departures. Tent sites are $15 to $18 a night per family, and RV sites are $18 to $20 a night per family. There are surcharges for air conditioners and visitors. Seasonal rates are available.

Contact: Pauline Allrutz, Mountain View Campground and Cottages, RR 1, Box 6820, Morrisville, VT 05661; (802) 888-2178.

Directions: From Interstate 89 north of

Montpelier, take exit 10 and travel north on Route 100 through Stowe and Morrisville. At the junction with Route 15, take a right and travel east for three miles to the campground entrance.

Trip notes: Bordered by the Lamoille River and Bugbee Brook, these campsites offer mountain views and full amenities in the country. Tent sites line the river, where rainbow trout and smallmouth bass are often hooked, and RV sites with shade trees lie between the river and Route 15. The facilities are spotless and upscale, including a Jacuzzi, one heated pool, and a nine-hole miniature golf course. Canoeing on the Lamoille is easy enough for paddlers of any skill level; the river flows through miles of pastoral farmland west of Morrisville. Just to the south Stowe offers more commercial attractions such as the Mount Mansfield alpine slide and a new outdoor amphitheater for summer concerts on the mountain. A good way to explore the country around Morrisville is via bicycle on little-traveled secondary roads. Though family oriented, Mountain View has rules that are less restrictive than those at many private campgrounds: motorcycles are allowed to travel into and out of the park, and campfires can burn until 1 A.M.

Open: May 1 through October 15.

---

49 Elmore State Park

Location: On the north shore of Lake Elmore; Northern Vermont map page 280, grid b3.

Campsites, facilities: There are 60 sites for tents and RVs including 15 lean-tos, all without hookups. Each site has a table and fire ring. A dump station is provided. Facilities include a playground, beach, boat ramp, boat rentals, a snack bar, metered hot showers, and flush toilets. Ice is available

at the park. Leashed pets with rabies vaccination certification are permitted, but not in day-use areas.

Reservations, fees: Reservations are recommended. Tent sites are $12 a night and lean-to sites are $16 a night for four people. Each additional person four years and older will be charged $3 at a tent site and $4 at a lean-to. The maximum allowable number of people at a site is eight, and there must be at least one person 18 years of age or older with each camping party. See also page 284.

Contact: Elmore State Park, P.O. Box 93, Lake Elmore, VT 05657; (802) 888-2982.

Directions: From Interstate 89 north of Montpelier, take exit 10 and travel north on Route 100 to Morrisville. Follow Route 12 south for five miles.

Trip notes: Surrounded by forested hills and mountains, Lake Elmore is open to all types of water-based sports. Sites are set in the woods just above the north shore, and the park offers a public boat ramp as well as rowboat and canoe rentals. Most of the lake's shoreline is privately owned and developed. A hiking trail leaves from the campground and ascends 2,608-foot Mount Elmore to the southeast. Given the campground's location in the central section of northern Vermont, it provides a scenic base camp for day-trip explorations of the Green Mountains and the northeastern reaches of the state.

Open: Mid-May through mid-October.

---

50 Idle Hours Camping Area

Location: Near Mackville Pond in Hardwick; Northern Vermont map page 280, grid b3.

Campsites, facilities: There are 22 sites

for tents and RVs, nine with full hookups and 13 with water and electric. A dump station, laundry facilities, a playground, pool, hot showers, and flush toilets are provided. Ice and firewood are available. Leashed pets are permitted.

Reservations, fees: Reservations are recommended. Sites start at $13 a night.

Contact: Idle Hours Camping Area, P.O. Box 1053, Hardwick, VT 05843; (802) 472-6732.

Directions: From the junction of Routes 14 and 15 in Hardwick, travel south on Route 15 for about half a mile to Mackville Pond Road. Turn left and go east for one mile. From the camping sign, continue another three-quarters of a mile to the pond, then turn left.

Trip notes: Secluded, wooded sites at Idle Hours are popular with seasonal campers, so call ahead to find out if space is available. There's a pool on the grounds for swimming, but if you seek true peace and quiet, spend an afternoon canoeing on Mackville Pond. Should you desire a little culture, Hardwick hosts a group of local chamber musicians at the town hall every Thursday night in July and August. Anglers can cast flies on the Lamoille River, which flows through downtown, for smallmouth bass, brown trout, and rainbow trout. This waterway eventually empties into Lake Champlain.

Open: June 1 through mid-September.

---

51 Gold Brook Campground

Location: South of Stowe; Northern Vermont map page 280, grid c3.

Campsites, facilities: There are 79 sites for tents and RVs, 26 with full hookups, 24 with water and electric, and 29 with none. Each site has a table, fireplace, and grill.

Facilities include a dump station, free hot showers, laundry, a rec room, pool, playground, shuffleboard, badminton and volleyball courts, and horseshoe pits. Cable TV and telephone connections are available. LP gas, ice, and firewood are for sale on site. Leashed pets are permitted.

Reservations, fees: Reservations are recommended and must be accompanied by a one-day deposit. Tent sites start at $14 a night and RV sites start at $18 a night for a family of four. Weekly, seasonal, and ski-season rates are available.

Contact: Kay and John Nichols, Gold Brook Campground, P.O. Box 1028, Stowe, VT 05672; (802) 253-7683 or (800) 483-7683.

Directions: From Interstate 89 at Waterbury, take exit 10 and head north on Route 100 for 7.5 miles to the campground entrance on the left (west) side of the road.

Trip notes: Gold Brook and the Little River, two waterways that are teeming with trout, skirt the campground property. Most sites have frontage on either stream as well as shade trees around the edge of a large grassy lawn that begs for a game of ultimate Frisbee. There's a small pool at the campground, but swimming is also permitted in Gold Brook and the Little River. Operated in conjunction with Nichols Lodge, the facility offers a breakfast plan during the winter by reservation and runs an ice cream stand during the summer. In snowy months, the winter sports office at the lodge rents out snowmobiles for use on the miles of trails that are accessible from the campground. Several alpine and Nordic ski centers operate in the area, and to the immediate west, the Long Trail ascends the state's tallest peak, Mount Mansfield. Stowe, just two miles north of here, is one of the state's oldest and most posh resort towns, known for its expensive hotels, shops, and fine restaurants.

Open: Year-round.

52 Little River State Park

Location: Northwest of Montpelier on the Waterbury Reservoir; Northern Vermont map page 280, grid c2.

Campsites, facilities: There are 101 sites for tents and RVs including 20 lean-tos, all without hookups. Each site has a picnic table and fireplace. A dump station, metered hot showers, rest rooms, boat rentals, a boat ramp, playground, and beach are provided. The contact station sells ice and firewood. Leashed pets with rabies vaccination certification are permitted at sites, but not in day-use areas.

Reservations, fees: Reservations are recommended. Tent sites are $12 a night and lean-to sites are $16 a night for four people. Each additional person four years and older will be charged $3 at a tent site and $4 at a lean-to. The maximum allowable number of people at a site is eight, and there must be at least one person 18 years of age or older with each camping party. See also page 284.

Contact: Little River State Park, RR 1, Box 1150, Waterbury, VT 05676; (802) 244-7103.

Directions: From Waterbury, travel west on U.S. 2 for half a mile, then turn right on Little River Road. Drive 3.5 miles north to the campground entrance.

Trip notes: The Waterbury Reservoir was created when a dam was placed on the Little River. This campground is located across the cove from the day-use area and has its own beach and boat launch. Some of the northern sites are on remote stretches of shoreline, while the majority are well shaded and roomy, set in the hilly forest on steep banks above the water. The park is part of Mount Mansfield State Forest and is a good jumping-off point for day hikes or overnight backpacking trips on the Long

Trail. A maintained nature trail explores Stevenson Brook, which flows from the west into the reservoir. If you are screaming for ice cream, the Ben and Jerry's Ice Cream Factory churns out its world-famous treats to the south in Waterbury. Tours of the facility include free samples.

Open: Mid-May through Columbus Day.

53 Moose River Campground

Location: East of St. Johnsbury on the Moose River; Northern Vermont map page 280, grid c5.

Campsites, facilities: There are 50 sites for tents and RVs, 20 with full hookups and 20 with water and electric. Each site has a table and fire ring. Phone hookups are available. A dump station, metered hot showers, a badminton court, and horseshoe pits are provided. Ice and firewood are available. Supplies and services are found in St. Johnsbury. Campers need permission before displaying items for sale on their sites. Leashed pets are permitted.

Reservations, fees: Reservations are recommended. Tent sites are $14 a night for two people and RV sites start at $18 a night for two people.

Contact: Clem and Julie Potvin, Moose River Campground, RR 3, Box 197, St. Johnsbury, VT 05819; (802) 748-4334 in the summer or (802) 748-8619 in the winter.

Directions: From Interstate 91, take exit 19 and head south on Interstate 93 for two miles. At exit 1, take Route 18 north for about a third of a mile to U.S. 2. Turn left and continue to the campground entrance 200 feet ahead on the left.

Trip notes: These sites are set on a grassy bend in the Moose River on the outskirts of working-class St. Johnsbury. They are popular with seasonal campers who enjoy the location between the White Mountains of New Hampshire and the Green Mountains, and the proximity to the Connecticut River. (Busy U.S. 2 does detract from the scenery, however.) You can fish on the Moose River. Moore Reservoir a few miles southeast in New Hampshire has a public launch and offers excellent powerboating and swimming; it is often a wild, rowdy scene on weekends. The Fairbanks Museum and Planetarium on Main Street in St. Johnsbury is a bit of a paradox: You step back in time upon entry into the historic building, but the state-of-the-art exhibits include collections from around the world, a weather center, and Vermont's only public planetarium; it's open daily all summer long.

Open: May 1 through October 15.

54 Onion River Campground

Location: East of Montpelier; Northern Vermont map page 280, grid c4.

Campsites, facilities: There are 33 sites, 6 with full hookups, 11 with water and electric, and 16 with none. A dump station, hot showers, laundry facilities, a small store, tables, fire rings, and grills are provided. Recreational facilities include horseshoe pits, hiking trails, and badminton and volleyball courts. LP gas, ice, and firewood are available. Leashed pets are permitted.

Reservations, fees: Reservations are recommended. Sites are $10 to $16 a night.

Contact: Onion River Campground, RR 1, Box 1205, Plainfield, VT 05667; (802) 426-3232.

Directions: From the junction of U.S. 2 and Route 14 east of Montpelier, travel 5.25 miles east on U.S. 2 to the campground entrance on the right (south) side of the road.

Trip notes: Smallmouth bass and trout are the sought-after prey in the Winooski River, which you can cast into from your campsite at Onion River. Here, small and grassy sites are set at the water's edge. Groton State Forest is adjacent to the campground, and multiuse trails for hiking and mountain biking lead through the surrounding hills. In addition to having some glorious swimming holes, the Winooski is also open to paddlers; most people put in at Montpelier and head west to Lake Champlain.

Open: April 1 through November 30.

55 Groton Forest Road Campground

Location: North of Groton State Forest; Northern Vermont map page 280, grid c4.

Campsites, facilities: There are 35 sites for tents and RVs with water and electric hookups. A dump station, metered hot showers, flush toilets, picnic tables, fire rings, free firewood, a playground, a pool, horseshoe pits, and courts for volleyball, badminton, and croquet are provided. Leashed pets are permitted.

Reservations, fees: Reservations are recommended. Sites are $14 a night, $70 a week, or $600 for the season per family.

Contact: Jim and Wanda McDonald, Groton Forest Road Campground, RR 1, Box 402, Marshfield, VT 05658; (407) 894-4899 in the winter, or (802) 426-4122 in the summer.

Directions: From the junction of U.S. 2 and Route 232 in Marshfield, travel three miles south on Route 232 to the campground entrance on the right.

Trip notes: Set on nine acres just outside Groton State Forest, half of these sites are open and grassy while the rest are tucked in the woods. The small and clean campground is a good choice for RVers who need hookups (the state forest campgrounds only have dump stations) and want to enjoy the many lakes, ponds, streams, and trails in the 25,000-acre forest. Various wildlife species inhabit the state's second largest contiguous landholding, including moose, black bear, deer, loons, mink, and grouse. The ponds are open to fishing and swimming. A good rainy day side trip for cheese lovers is just to the north in Cabot, where the Cabot Creamery churns out a line of dairy products; you can tour the factory and watch cheese being made, then sample your way through the gift shop (for information, call 800/242-2740).

Open: May through October, weather permitting. Sites are available during the fall deer hunting season by reservation.

56 New Discovery State Park

Location: In Groton State Forest; Northern Vermont map page 280, grid c4.

Campsites, facilities: There are 61 sites for tents and RVs including 14 lean-tos, all without hookups. Each site has a picnic table and fireplace. Metered hot showers, flush toilets, recycling bins, a dump station, picnic shelter, and playground are provided. Firewood is available. Leashed pets with rabies vaccination certification are permitted, but not in day-use areas.

Reservations, fees: Reservations are recommended. Sites are $10 to $14 a night for four people. Each additional person four years and older will be charged $3 at a tent site and $4 at a lean-to. The maximum allowable number of people at a site is eight, and there must be at least one person 18

years of age or older with each camping party. See also page 284.

Contact: New Discovery State Park, Groton State Forest, RR 600, Marshfield, VT 05658; (802) 584-3820.

Directions: From Marshfield, travel one mile east on Route 232, then bear right and continue south on the same road for 5.5 miles to the campground entrance on the left (east) side of the road.

Trip notes: Of the three campgrounds within the state forest, this is the only one not on a swimming lake and thus is the last to fill up. All three make good jumping-off points for those who want to explore this 25,000-acre tract of land dominated by rolling and steep hills. Open year-round, a network of multiuse trails traverses summits, bogs, and streams. From the campground, the Osmore Pond Trail travels downhill through a stand of spruce and fir and an old logging area to the pond. From here, you can ascend Little or Big Deer Mountains. Warm-water fish can be caught in the park's ponds, while the streams are stocked with trout. The camping fee includes a day-use charge that allows you to visit any of the other state parks here during your stay. (See also campgrounds number 58 and 59.)

Open: Mid-May through Labor Day.

57 Harveys Lake Cabins and Campground

Location: On the north end of Harveys Lake in Barnet; Northern Vermont map page 280, grid c4.

Campsites, facilities: There are 53 sites for tents and RVs up to 30 feet in length, 15 with full hookups, 26 with water and electric, and 12 with none. Each site has a fire pit, table, and grill. A dump station, hot showers, flush toilets, video games, a rec hall, pool and Ping-Pong tables, a basketball court, and horseshoe pit are provided. Eight cabins are for rent. Leashed pets are permitted.

Reservations, fees: Reservations are recommended and require a 50 percent deposit. Sites start at $16 a night per family. Seasonal rates are available.

Contact: Marybeth Vereline, Harveys Lake Cabins and Campground, RR 1, Box 26E, West Barnet, VT 05821; (802) 633-2213.

Directions: From Interstate 91 at Barnet, take exit 18 and travel five miles west. In West Barnet, turn left at the white church, cross a small bridge, and then turn right on the first dirt road at the orange "narrow road" sign.

Trip notes: Harveys Lake is Vermont's oldest private campground. In addition to sites for tents and RVs, eight furnished cabins are also available for rent. Most of the cabins are set in the woods above the beach area on Harveys Lake, and campsites 8 through 13 also have water frontage. Several others are next to a river channel. These small sites (about 20 feet wide) are buffered by large pine trees. The big draw is Harveys Lake, a quiet 350-acre pool that's more than 100 feet deep in places and is perfect for fishing and swimming. Guarded by hills and forest, the lake has no public access and is not overdeveloped, so it's peaceful even in the summer. Recently, someone pulled a 17-pound lake trout out of these waters. The atmosphere at Harveys is low-key, and there are never any planned activities.

Open: May 15 through October 15.

⑤⑧ Stillwater State Park

Location: In Groton State Forest; Northern Vermont map page 280, grid c4.

Campsites, facilities: There are 79 sites for tents and RVs including 17 lean-tos, all without hookups. Each site has a picnic table and fireplace. Metered hot showers, flush toilets, recycling bins, a dump station, picnic shelter, boat rentals, a boat ramp, snack bar, and playground are provided. Firewood is available. You'll find general stores in Marshfield and Groton; more extensive services are offered in Montpelier and Barre. Leashed pets with rabies vaccination certification are permitted, but not in day-use areas.

Reservations, fees: Reservations are recommended. Sites are $12 to $16 a night for four people. Each additional person four years and older will be charged $3 at a tent site and $4 at a lean-to. The maximum allowable number of people at a site is eight, and there must be at least one person 18 years of age or older with each camping party. See also page 284.

Contact: Stillwater State Park, Groton State Forest, RR 2, Box 332, Groton, VT 05046; (802) 584-3822.

Directions: From Groton, travel two miles west on U.S. 302. Take a right onto Route 232 and head north for six miles. Turn right on Boulder Beach Road and head east for half a mile to the campground.

Trip notes: These wooded sites are extremely popular in summertime with campers who want to swim and boat on Lake Groton, the largest body of water in the state forest. Flanked by hills and acres of forestland, this clear gem offers the chance to canoe in a spectacular setting. Sites are set in the woods on or near the lake, and there is a sandy beach at the campground. More than 40 miles of multiuse trails traverse the park. From the nature center at the northern tip of Lake Groton, the Peacham Bog Trail leads to one of Vermont's largest natural bogs.

Open: Mid-May through Labor Day.

59 Ricker Pond State Park

Location: In Groton State Forest; Northern Vermont map page 280, grid c4.

Campsites, facilities: There are 55 sites for tents and RVs including 23 lean-tos, all without hookups. Each site has a picnic table and fireplace. Metered hot showers, flush toilets, recycling bins, a dump station, picnic shelter, boat rentals, a boat ramp, and playground are provided. Firewood is available. Leashed pets with rabies vaccination certification are permitted, but not in day-use areas.

Reservations, fees: Reservations are recommended. Sites are $12 to $16 a night for four people. Each additional person four years and older will be charged $3 at a tent site and $4 at a lean-to. The maximum allowable number of people at a site is eight, and there must be at least one person 18 years of age or older with each camping party. See also page 284.

Contact: Ricker Pond State Park, Groton State Forest, 526 State Forest Road, Groton, VT 05046; (802) 584-3821.

Directions: From Groton, travel two miles west on U.S. 302. Take a right onto Route 232 and drive north for 2.5 miles to the park entrance on the right (east) side of the road.

Trip notes: The sites at this campground, one of three in the state forest, are located on the south side of Ricker Pond, where boat rentals and a ramp are available. Campers also have access to several hiking and multiuse trails. The trailhead for the nearby Silver Ledge Trail is across the road from the camp. Starting out level, it then climbs steeply to a lookout over Lake Groton and Beaver Meadows.

Open: Mid-May through Labor Day.

60 Pleasant Valley Campground

Location: On the north end of Ticklenaked Pond; Northern Vermont map page 280, grid d4.

Campsites, facilities: There are 50 sites for tents and RVs, 17 with water and electric hookups. Each has a table and fireplace. A dump station, laundry facilities, a playground, rec hall, hot showers, rest rooms, paddleboat rentals, a volleyball court, and horseshoe pits are provided. A store sells ice and firewood. Leashed pets are permitted.

Reservations, fees: Reservations are recommended. Sites are $12 to $19 a night; seasonal rates are available.

Contact: Harry and Sandra Cushing, Pleasant Valley Campground, P.O. Box 129C, Wells River, VT 05081; (802) 584-3884.

Directions: From Interstate 91 north of Wells River, take exit 17 and travel one mile west on U.S. 302. Turn right on Ryegate Center Road and continue north for 1.5 miles to the campground entrance.

Trip notes: Open to boating, swimming, and fishing, Ticklenaked Pond is as fun as its name sounds. Sites are set on 100 wooded acres next to the lake, and many are occupied by seasonal campers. You can rent paddleboats at the campground. For a livelier boating experience, trek a short distance east to the Connecticut River. Here in the northern reaches the river is less developed and flows through lush farm country.

Open: Mid-May through mid-October.

61 Green Valley Campground

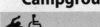

Location: Northeast of Montpelier; Northern Vermont map page 280, grid c3.

Campsites, facilities: There are 45 sites for tents and RVs, 23 with full hookups and 12 with water and electric. Cable TV hookups are available. Use of air conditioners and heaters is allowed. A dump station, laundry facilities, a playground, pool, hot showers, horseshoe pits, a grocery store with limited supplies, and tables are provided. There's also a community fireplace and a rec hall. Ice and LP gas are available. Leashed pets are permitted.

Reservations, fees: Reservations are recommended. Sites with hookups are $20 a night for two people; tent sites are $12 a night for two people. There are surcharges for electric heaters, air conditioners, cable TV, and additional campers.

Contact: The Gosselins, Green Valley Campground, Route 2, P.O. Box 21, East Montpelier, VT 05651; (802) 223-6271.

Directions: From the junction of Interstate 89 and U.S. 2 in Montpelier (exit 8), travel northeast on U.S. 2 for six miles to the campground entrance on the right.

Trip notes: For people traveling north or south on Interstate 89, this is the perfect place to stop for the night. A green hill rises behind the campground, and sites are grassy, wide open, and snug—only about 30 feet wide. Some sites have a shade tree. To the south is the state capital of Montpelier, which has the smallest population of any capital city in the country. To the immediate south in Barre, the Rock of Ages company conducts free tours of their granite quarry, the largest in the world.

Open: May 1 through October 31.

62 Lazy Lions Campground

Location: South of Barre; Northern Vermont map page 280, grid d3.

Campsites, facilities: There are 35 sites, 21 with full hookups and 14 with none. Each site has a table and fire ring. The campground offers a dump station, metered hot showers, rest rooms, laundry facilities, a cafe, and a playground. Ice and firewood are available. Leashed pets are permitted.

Reservations, fees: Reservations are recommended in the summer. Sites with full hookups are $20 a night for two people, and tent sites are $14.

Contact: Ernest Huston, Lazy Lions Campground, P.O. Box 56, Middle Road, Graniteville, VT 05654; (802) 479-2823.

Directions: From Interstate 89 south of Montpelier, take exit 6 and travel east on Route 63. Approximately four miles later, you'll arrive at a stop signal at the junction with Route 14. Continue east for exactly one mile to the campground entrance on the left.

Trip notes: Wooded, grassy sites are divided into two separate areas for tents and RVs. Between the campsites and Route 63 the owners operate the Lazy Lions Cafe, so if you are feeling a little lackadaisical, let them cook breakfast for you. Just south of the campground is the world's largest granite quarry, Rock of Ages. Take a free self-guided tour of the quarry or, for a small fee, a narrated shuttle tour. An observation deck over the Craftsman Center lets visitors watch master stonecutters at work.

Open: May 15 through November 1.

63 Limehurst Lake Campground

Location: South of Williamstown; Northern Vermont map page 280, grid d3.

Campsites, facilities: There are 92 sites for tents and RVs, 25 with full hookups, 51 with water and electric, and 16 with none.

Each site has a fire ring and table. Cable TV and telephone connections are available. Use of air conditioners and heaters is allowed. On site you'll find a camp store, snack bar, laundry facilities, rest rooms, hot showers, LP gas, picnic and safari areas, a rec room, pavilion, sports courts, and horseshoe pits. Trailers are rented out. Leashed pets are permitted.

Reservations, fees: Reservations are recommended July through mid-October. Sites are $17 to $22 a night per family.

Contact: Don and Maggie Dexter, Limehurst Lake Campground, RR 1, Box 462, Williamstown, VT 05679; (802) 433-6662.

Directions: From Interstate 89 south of Barre, take exit 6 and drive east on Route 63 for four miles to Route 14. Turn right (south) on Route 14 and continue six miles to Limehurst Lake and the campground entrance.

Trip notes: Campers at Limehurst Lake can use the 250-foot waterslide next to the campground's sandy beach. Swimming and fishing are popular pursuits here, and no fishing licenses are required at the privately owned facility. The sites, most of which are shaded by trees, are level, grassy, and set back from the 10-acre lake. You can rent rowboats, canoes, and paddleboats at the beach, or play around on the swimming raft and diving board. From the campground, several trails lead into the surrounding Green Mountains.

Open: April 1 through November 15.

64 Allis State Park

Location: In Brookfield on Bear Mountain; Northern Vermont map page 280, grid d3.

Campsites, facilities: There are 27 sites for tents and RVs including eight lean-tos, all without hookups. Each site has a picnic table and a stone or brick fireplace. Metered hot showers, flush toilets, recycling bins, a dump station, a picnic shelter, and a playground are provided. Supplies are available in Randolph and Brookfield. Leashed pets with rabies vaccination certification are permitted, but not in day-use areas.

Reservations, fees: Reservations are recommended. Sites are $10 a night and lean-tos are $14 a night for four people. Each additional person four years and older will be charged $3 at a tent site and $4 at a lean-to. The maximum allowable number of people at a site is eight, and there must be at least one person 18 years of age or older with each camping party. See also page 284.

Contact: Allis State Park, RR 2, Box 192, Randolph, VT 05060; (802) 276-3175.

Directions: From Interstate 89 south of Brookfield, take exit 4 and travel two miles west on Route 66. Turn and drive north on Route 12 for 12 miles to Route 65. Turn right and head east on Route 65 for 1.5 miles to the park entrance on the right (south) side of the road. A park road leads to the top of the mountain.

Trip notes: Families who want to introduce the little ones to hiking will find these mountaintop sites are the ideal place to camp. Originally a farm, Bear Mountain (elevation 2,020 feet) is now adorned with a fire tower that affords views of Mount Mansfield and Camel's Hump to the north, Killington and Ascutney Mountains to the south, and the White Mountains to the east. The campground is small and quiet, set in the woods just off the summit near the fire tower. Two moderate loop trails, Bear Hill and Little Spruce, explore hardwood and softwood forests. Bear Hill passes a limestone outcrop and a shallow cave that once served as a bear den and now makes an interesting pit stop for hikers walking with kids. At the base of Bear Mountain are several lakes open to fishing, boating, and swimming.

Open: Mid-May through Labor Day.

65 Lake Champagne Campground

Location: East of Randolph; Southern Vermont map page 281, grid b3.

Campsites, facilities: There 131 sites for tents and RVs, 68 with full hookups and 44 with water and electric. Each site has a picnic table and fire ring. Hot showers, flush toilets, a dump station, playground, laundry facilities, a rec hall, pavilion, shuffleboard, volleyball courts, and horseshoe pits are provided. LP gas, firewood, and ice are available. Leashed pets are permitted.

Reservations, fees: Reservations are recommended. A deposit of one day's fee will hold a site for a weekend; two day's fee holds one for a week. Sites start at $16 a night per family. There are surcharges for additional adults. Weekly and monthly rates are available.

Contact: Pierre and Elizabeth LaFrance, Lake Champagne Campground, Box C, Randolph Center, VT 05061; (802) 728-5293.

Directions: From Interstate 89 south of Montpelier, take exit 4 and drive a mile east on Route 66 to the campground entrance.

Trip notes: Terraced sites adorn a hillside above secluded Lake Champagne, where campers can use a small sandy beach for swimming and sunning. Most of the slopes around the lake are open and grassy, but tall hardwood trees provide shade for the majority of the campsites. Rustic fencing helps the campground maintain a natural appearance. The upper sites afford good views of the Green Mountains. The Second Branch of the White River, which flows through East Randolph, is a popular fly-

fishing waterway. Also worth a visit is the Floating Bridge at Sunset Lake in nearby Brookfield. First built in 1820, it's been replaced six times and is the most heavily used bridge of its type in the country; it's also where the locals go to swim.

Open: Late May through mid-October.

66 Mobile Acres Campground

Location: On the Third Branch of the White River in Randolph; Southern Vermont map page 281, grid b3.

Campsites, facilities: There are 93 sites for RVs, 78 with full hookups and 15 with water and electric. Each site has a picnic table and fire ring. Dump stations, laundry facilities, a pool, two playgrounds, rest rooms, hot showers, a pavilion, sports field, and horseshoe pits are located on the grounds. LP gas, ice, firewood, and free RV storage are available. Leashed pets are permitted.

Reservations, fees: Reservations are recommended. Sites with full hookups start at $18 a night. Seasonal and monthly rates are available.

Contact: Mobile Acres Campground, RR 1, Box 373-6F, Randolph, VT 05060; (802) 728-5548.

Directions: From Interstate 89, take exit 4 onto Route 66 and drive 2.5 miles west. When you reach Route 12A, continue west for another 2.5 miles to the campground entrance on the left (south) side of the road.

Trip notes: Tents are welcome at Mobile Acres. But unless they don't mind camping in the thick of mobile homes and RVs, tenters will want to head north to Allis State Park (see campground number 64) for wilder, more natural environs. Many of these sites are rented seasonally, and organized activities—including specialty potlucks, ice cream socials, and theme weekends—keep campers busy. This dual mobile home park and RV campground is located on the Third Branch of the White River, offering direct access to boating, fishing, and freshwater swimming.

Open: May 15 through October 15.

⑥⑦ Mountain Trails

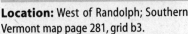

Location: West of Randolph; Southern Vermont map page 281, grid b3.

Campsites, facilities: There are 27 sites for tents and RVs, 5 with full hookups, 10 with water and electric, and 12 with none. A dump station, hot showers, flush toilets, picnic tables, fireplaces, a sandbox and swings, horseshoe pits, and a badminton court are provided. Firewood is available. Leashed pets are permitted.

Reservations, fees: All fees must be paid in advance. Tent sites start at $12 a night, and RV sites start at $15 a night. Prices are per family (two parents, three kids), with surcharges for extra campers.

Contact: Mountain Trails, c/o the Settlers, Quarry Road, RR 1, Box 72, Rochester, VT 05767; (802) 767-3352.

Directions: From Interstate 91 near White River Junction, head northwest on Interstate 89. At exit 3, drive west on Route 107 through Bethel and up to Rochester (at the junction of Routes 12 and 107 north of Bethel, be sure to take a left to stay on Route 107). Head north from Rochester on Route 100 for 2.75 miles. Turn right on Quarry Road and continue east for 1.5 miles to the campground.

Trip notes: When the sun goes down, campers at Mountain Trails can stargaze and enjoy the natural glow of their campfires—just remember to bring a flashlight because there are no lights here. This unsophisticated campground is small and clean. There is no water access on site, but the White River boasts excellent swimming holes nearby. Fifteen sites are for tents and are set in a stand of spruce and maple trees. RV sites are more open, but they do have shade trees. A hiking trail leads from the campground to the rocky summit of Mount Cushman (elevation 2,750 feet).

Open: May 1 to November 30; facilities are limited after archery season, a special deer hunting season in early fall.

⑥⑧ Lake Dunmore Kampersville

Location: North of Lake Dunmore; Southern Vermont map page 281, grid b2.

Campsites, facilities: There are 210 sites for tents and RVs, 119 with full hookups, 67 with water and electric, and 24 with none. Use of air conditioners and heaters is allowed. Cable TV and telephone connections are available. Facilities include laundry, picnic tables, fire rings, grills, a rec hall, snack bar, rest rooms, free hot showers, a pavilion, and a playground. For recreation there are pools, boat rentals, planned group activities, movies, sports courts, athletic fields, and miniature golf. RV storage, RV supplies, ice, firewood, LP gas, and groceries are available. Recycling is mandatory. Leashed pets with rabies vaccination certification are permitted.

Reservations, fees: Reservations are recommended July through Labor Day. Sites are $17 to $26 a night per family, and as much as $33 a night on holidays.

Contact: Lake Dunmore Kampersville, P.O. Box 214, Middlebury, VT; (802) 352-4501.

Directions: From the junction of U.S. 7

and Routes 125 and 30 in Middlebury, travel six miles south on U.S. 7. Turn left on Route 53 and head south for 1.5 miles to the campground entrance on the left.

Trip notes: Lake Dunmore and the surrounding green hills provide the setting for this full-service, family-oriented campground. Sparkling clean sites and facilities, most of them wooded, are located across the street from the lake. In summer, colorful beds of annuals punctuate the grounds. Campers have access to beaches and docks where a host of organized activities takes place, from guided pontoon boat rides to fishing and waterskiing. The lake is fed by a spring and supports landlocked salmon and trout. Most mornings in the summer, the owner of the campground gives guided tours of Kampersville, while recreation personnel lead frequent nature walks to nearby scenic destinations such as secluded Silver Lake and Cascade Falls, both of which are open to swimming. There are tournaments both for kids and adults, from shuffleboard and horseshoes to whist and Ping-Pong, as well as craft classes and yo-yo lessons. Theme weekends are organized throughout the summer. As you've probably guessed, this is a high-energy, high-activity campground.

Open: Year-round; the pools are open Memorial Day through Labor Day.

69 Mount Moosalamoo Campground

Location: East of Lake Dunmore in the Green Mountain National Forest; Southern Vermont map page 281, grid b2.

Campsites, facilities: There are an undetermined number of primitive sites. An outhouse and piped water are provided. No pets are allowed.

Reservations, fees: Sites are offered on a first-come, first-served basis. There is no fee, but donations are accepted.

Contact: Green Mountain National Forest, Middlebury Ranger District, RR 4, Box 1260, Middlebury, VT 05753; (802) 388-4362.

Directions: From U.S. 7 south of Middlebury, travel six miles east on Route 125, passing through Ripton. Turn left on Road 32 and follow the signs to the campground.

Trip notes: These primitive backcountry sites are a hiker's playground. Many miles of trails can be accessed from the campground, including routes to secluded Silver Lake and up Mount Moosalamoo (elevation 2,640 feet). Sugar maple, beach, and birch trees grow in the surrounding woods, while the limestone-rich earth supports many varieties of wildflowers as well as wild ginger and low-bush blueberries. Watch for the animals that feed on this flora; you might spot black bears, moose, deer, rabbits, hawks, and the endangered Peregrine falcon. This camp makes a great jumping-off point for overnight treks on the Long Trail in the surrounding Green Mountains. By the way, the area is named for the Abenaki word for "the moose departs."

Open: Mid-May through October.

70 Falls of Lana

Location: East of Lake Dunmore; Southern Vermont map page 281, grid b2.

Campsites, facilities: There are an undetermined number of primitive sites. An outhouse and piped water are provided. No pets are allowed.

Reservations, fees: Sites are offered on a first-come, first-served basis. There is no fee, but donations are accepted.

Contact: Green Mountain National Forest, Middlebury Ranger District, RR 4, Box 1260, Middlebury, VT 05753; (802) 388-4362.

Directions: From U.S. 7 south of Middlebury, travel six miles east on Route 125, passing through Ripton. Turn left on Road 32, drive past the Moosalamoo parking area, and continue south past the Blueberry Hill Ski Touring Center to Route 27. Take a right and travel northwest to the campground parking area.

Trip notes: These hike-in sites are set just south of a day-use picnic area and state-maintained campground on Silver Lake, where campers can fish and swim. Wooded and private, they are near the starting point of several hiking trails. From the campground, the Leicester Hollow Trail heads south and is open to mountain bikers as well as hikers.

Open: Mid-May through October.

⑦ Branbury State Park

Location: On the south end of Lake Dunmore; Southern Vermont map page 281, grid b2.

Campsites, facilities: There are 39 sites for tents and RVs including six lean-tos, all without hookups. Each site has a picnic table and fireplace. Metered hot showers, flush toilets, recycling bins, a dump station, picnic shelter, snack bar, small store, and playground are provided. Leashed pets with rabies vaccination certification are permitted, but not in day-use areas.

Reservations, fees: Reservations are recommended. Sites are $12 to $16 a night for four people. Each additional person four years and older will be charged $3 at a tent site and $4 at a lean-to. The maximum allowable number of people at a site is eight, and there must be at least one person 18 years of age or older with each camping party. See also page 284.

Contact: Branbury State Park, RR 2, Box 2421, Brandon, VT 05733; (802) 247-5925.

Directions: From the junction of U.S. 7 and Route 73 in Brandon, travel north for four miles on U.S. 7 to the park entrance on the right (east) side of the road.

Trip notes: About half the campsites, including the lean-tos, are tucked into the woods west of Route 53 and are accessible to hiking trails. Another 17 sites are set in an open grassy area near Lake Dunmore. This spring-fed lake holds landlocked salmon and trout, and offers a sandy beach and a large, protected swimming area well away from the boating action. You can launch or beach your boat at the campground, or rent one of the canoes, rowboats, or paddleboats. For easy hiking, try a self-guided half-mile nature trail or the route to the Falls of Lana (see campground number 70). For more of a challenge, head up to the summit of Mount Moosalamoo (2,640 feet) past Rattlesnake Point; the trail is studded with waterfalls and caves. Another hike leads to secluded Silver Lake in the mountains.

Open: Mid-May to Columbus Day.

⑦ Country Village Campground

Location: North of Brandon; Southern Vermont map page 281, grid b1.

Campsites, facilities: There are 44 sites for tents and RVs, 37 with water and electric hookups. A dump station, fire rings, grills, and tables are provided. Use of air conditioners and heaters is allowed. Facilities include a solar-heated pool, miniature golf, sports courts, horseshoe pits, a playground, and metered hot showers. Limited groceries, ice, and firewood are available. Leashed pets are permitted.

Reservations, fees: Reservations are recommended in the summer. Seasonal camping registration deadlines are in June and July. Sites start at $14 a night per family with surcharges for heaters, air conditioners, and guests. Weekly, monthly, and seasonal rates are available.

Contact: Barb and Joe Ceccoli, Country Village Campground, RR 2, Box 2235, Brandon, VT 05733; (802) 247-3333.

Directions: From the junction of U.S. 7 and Route 73 in Brandon, travel three miles north on U.S. 7 to the campground entrance on the left (west) side of the road.

Trip notes: As its name implies, Country Village has a rural flavor. With open meadows and wooded sites, the campground caters to RVers who want to stay awhile. Many seasonal campers return to these cozy sites because of their proximity to several natural attractions. Lake Dunmore, about four miles away, is open to boating, fishing, and canoeing. About the same distance to the west is slow-moving Otter Creek, which can be paddled by canoeists of all skill levels. A popular auto tour is the drive on Route 73 between Rochester and Brandon; the road passes over Brandon Gap and overlooks Mount Horrid and Lake Champlain.

Open: Mid-May through mid-October.

⑦ Smoke Rise Family Campground

Location: North of Brandon; Southern Vermont map page 281, grid b2.

Campsites, facilities: There are 50 sites for tents and RVs, 21 with full hookups and 29 with water and electric. A dump station, pavilion, laundry facilities, fire rings, tables, a pool, an athletic field, and sports courts are provided. LP gas, ice, and firewood are available. Leashed pets are permitted.

Reservations, fees: Reservations are recommended. Sites start at $10 a night.

Contact: Mel and Bea Cousino, Smoke Rise Family Campground, Route 7, Brandon, VT 05733; (802) 247-6472.

Directions: From the town of Brandon, travel two miles north on U.S. 7. The campground entrance is on the right.

Trip notes: Cleared, grassy farmland is open to campers in this rural locale. Developed sites are for RVs, while unlimited tent camping, ideal for large groups, is available in a separate, rolling field. If you're not in the mood to light a campfire, the Smoke Rise Restaurant across the street serves a mean breakfast. Nearby Lake Dunmore to the north is open to boating, fishing, and canoeing, while slow-moving Otter Creek to the west can be paddled by even novice canoeists.

Open: May 15 through October 15.

⑦ Chittendon Brook Recreation Area

Location: North of Rutland on the Long Trail in Green Mountain National Forest; Southern Vermont map page 281, grid b2.

Campsites, facilities: There are 17 tent sites. Tent pads, tables, fire grates, garbage and recycling bins, outhouses, and water pumps are provided. No pets are allowed.

Reservations, fees: Sites are available on a first-come, first-served basis. The fee is $4 a night.

Contact: Green Mountain National Forest, Rochester Ranger District, Route 100, Rochester, VT 05767; (802) 767-4261.

Directions: From Brandon, travel east on Route 73 for 12 miles. Turn right on Route 45 and drive two miles to the recreation area and campground.

Trip notes: Secluded, wooded sites are set along cascading Chittendon Brook, named for Vermont's first governor, Thomas

Chittendon. A wetland area across the brook from the campground offers a chance to view beavers, tree swallows, and the occasional moose. Several hikes leave from the campground; the Chittendon Brook Trail cuts through a spruce and fir forest to the Long Trail about three miles away.

Open: Mid-May through mid-November.

⑦⑤ White River Valley Camping

Location: On the White River in Gaysville; Southern Vermont map page 281, grid b3.

Campsites, facilities: There are 102 sites, 19 with full hookups, 39 with water and electric, and 44 with none. Use of air conditioners and heaters is allowed. Laundry facilities, a dump station, hot showers, rest rooms, a whirlpool spa, rec hall, playground, gaming equipment and courts, and horseshoe pits are provided. Leashed pets are permitted.

Reservations, fees: Reservations are recommended in the summer. Sites are $17 to $22 a night for two people. Weekly, monthly, and seasonal rates are available.

Contact: The Harringtons, White River Valley Camping, P.O. Box 106, Route 107, Gaysville, VT 05746; (802) 234-9115.

Directions: From Interstate 89, take exit 3 and follow Route 107 west for 8.3 miles. Turn right and proceed to the campground entrance on the right.

Trip notes: The frequently held special events at White River Valley Camping are pretty creative, including free pig roasts, bonfires, special meals, and ice cream socials. But then there's the so-called Peanuts from Heaven, in which pilot Dan, one of the owners, flies overhead and drops peanut shells that contain prizes. The White River flows through the campground, and tub-

ing here is a major family attraction. These waters are renowned for their trout fishing, but anglers might also like to visit the Bethel National Fish Hatchery in Gaysville, which releases a million salmon smelts into the Connecticut River annually.

Open: May 1 through October 15.

⑦⑥ Rest 'N' Nest Campground

Location: Near the Connecticut River in Thetford; Southern Vermont map page 281, grid b4.

Campsites, facilities: There are 90 sites, 46 with full hookups, 29 with water and electric, and 15 with none. Each site has a picnic table and fire grill. Use of air conditioners and heaters is allowed. Facilities include laundry, metered hot showers, rest rooms, a rec hall, playground, badminton and basketball courts, and horseshoe pits. RV storage, group sites for tents and RVs, limited groceries, ice, and firewood are available. Leashed pets are permitted.

Reservations, fees: Reservations are recommended the second week in August and require a nonrefundable deposit. Sites are $20 a night per family.

Contact: Ramona Jacobs, Rest 'N' Nest Campground, P.O. Box 258, Thetford Center, VT 05075; (802) 785-2997.

Directions: From Interstate 91 north of White River Junction, take exit 14 and head east on Route 113 for approximately 200 feet. Turn left (north) on Latham Road; the campground entrance is less than a quarter mile ahead.

Trip notes: Tall pines keep campers cool during the summer months at Rest 'N' Nest. The spacious sites are separated into different sections for seasonal campers, RVers, and, in more heavily wooded areas, tenters.

A small spring-fed, man-made pond on the grounds is open for swimming. Great fishing can be had by traveling a mile in either direction: the Ompompanoosuc River and West Brook are about a mile to the west, and the Connecticut River lies to the east. On the Ompompanoosuc, Union Village Dam is operated by the U.S. Army Corps of Engineers and more than six miles of water are stocked with brown and rainbow trout.

Open: April 1 through November 1.

⑦ Thetford Hill State Park

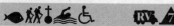

Location: North of White River Junction; Southern Vermont map page 281, grid b4.

Campsites, facilities: There are 16 sites for tents and RVs including two lean-tos, all without hookups. Each site has a picnic table and fireplace. Metered hot showers, flush toilets, recycling bins, a dump station, picnic shelter, and playground are provided. Firewood is available. Leashed pets with rabies vaccination certification are permitted, but not in day-use areas.

Reservations, fees: Reservations are recommended. Sites are $10 to $14 a night for four people. Each additional person four years and older will be charged $3 at a tent site and $4 at a lean-to. The maximum allowable number of people at a site is eight, and there must be at least one person 18 years of age or older with each camping party. See also page 284.

Contact: Thetford Hill State Park, P.O. Box 132, Thetford, VT 05074; (802) 785-2266.

Directions: From Interstate 91, take exit 14 and drive west on Route 113 to Thetford Hill. In the center of town, turn south on Academy Road and travel one mile to the park entrance.

Trip notes: Open, grassy sites flanked by

woods are located near the Thetford Hill District, a historic section of town where most of the buildings predate the Civil War. Some trails lead through the park, but one of the main reasons campers stay here is to fish in the West River. Just down the road to the south, the Union Village Dam Recreation Area is open to swimming and fishing in a six-mile stretch of water that is stocked with brown and rainbow trout and supports a resident population of natural brook trout.

Open: Mid-May through Labor Day.

⑦⑧ Silver Lake State Park

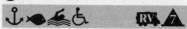

Location: North of Woodstock on the east side of Silver Lake; Southern Vermont map page 281, grid b3.

Campsites, facilities: There are 47 sites for tents and RV including seven lean-tos, all without hookups. A dump station, metered hot showers, flush toilets, fireplaces, a playground, snack bar, picnic shelter, and boat rentals are provided. Firewood is sold on site. Leashed pets with rabies vaccination certification are permitted, but not in day-use areas.

Reservations, fees: Reservations are recommended. Sites are $12 to $16 a night for four people. Each additional person four years and older will be charged $3 at a tent site and $4 at a lean-to. The maximum allowable number of people at a site is eight, and there must be at least one person 18 years of age or older with each camping party. See also page 284.

Contact: Silver Lake State Park, Town Road, Barnard, VT 05031; (802) 234-9451.

Directions: From Interstate 89 northwest of White River Junction, take exit 3 for South Royalton. Travel 3.5 miles west on Route 107 to the junction with Route 12, then head south through the town of

Barnard. From the town center, drive north on Town Road for a quarter mile to the campground and state park entrance.

Trip notes: Silver Lake is for swimmers. Flanked by Vermont's quintessential rolling green hills, this sparkling loch is open to nonmotorized boating only. A beach, diving board, boat rentals, and day-use picnic area are provided, and kids can catch sunfish and perch all day long right from shore. Campsites are in the woods near the lake. To learn about the people who live in these rural hills, visit the Billings Farm and Museum and the Sugarbush Cheese and Maple Syrup Farm to the south in Woodstock. The former has a restored farmhouse and holds many family events highlighting Vermont's agricultural history. Sugarbush demonstrates the modern family farm in action; visitors can watch cheese being hand cut and learn the process of maple sugaring.

Open: Mid-May through Labor Day.

79 Silver Lake Family Campground

Location: North of Woodstock on Silver Lake; Southern Vermont map page 281, grid b3.

Campsites, facilities: There are 67 sites for tents and RVs, 26 with full hookups, 12 with water and electric, and 29 with none. Air conditioners are allowed, but heaters are not. A dump station, rec hall, boat rentals, fire rings, grills, and tables are provided. Firewood and ice are available. For recreation there are volleyball and badminton courts and horseshoe pits. Leashed pets are permitted.

Reservations, fees: Reservations are recommended and require a nonrefundable deposit. Sites are $20 a night.

Contact: Don and Diane Cappuccino,

Silver Lake Family Campground, P.O. Box 111, Barnard, VT 05031; (802) 234-9974.

Directions: From Interstate 89 northwest of White River Junction, take exit 3 for South Royalton. Travel 3.5 miles west on Route 107 to the junction with Route 12, then head south through the town of Barnard. At the general store, turn left on Stage Road; the campground entrance is a quarter mile ahead, across from the post office.

Trip notes: Sending postcards is no problem here because a post office is right across the road. Seasonal campers stake out their plots year to year to take advantage of Silver Lake's peaceful waters. Only nonmotorized boats are allowed, which suits casual perch anglers just fine. Sites are wooded and densely settled—only about 20 feet wide—and some are right on the water. Farmland surrounds the lake, and if you'd like to learn more about Vermont's agricultural economy, the Billings Farm and Museum and the Sugarbush Cheese and Maple Syrup Farm are located in Woodstock to the south.

Open: Mid-May through mid-October.

80 Gifford Woods State Park

Location: Northeast of Rutland; Southern Vermont map page 281, grid b2.

Campsites, facilities: There are 48 sites for tents and RVs including 21 lean-tos, all without hookups. Each site has a picnic table and fireplace. Metered hot showers, flush toilets, recycling bins, a dump station, picnic shelter, and playground are provided. Firewood is available. Leashed pets with rabies vaccination certification are permitted, but not in day-use areas.

Reservations, fees: Reservations are

recommended. Sites are $10 to $14 a night for four people. Each additional person four years and older will be charged $3 at a tent site and $4 at a lean-to. The maximum allowable number of people at a site is eight, and there must be at least one person 18 years of age or older with each camping party. See also page 284.

Contact: Gifford Woods State Park, Route 100, Killington, VT 05751; (802) 775-5354.

Directions: From the junction of U.S. 4 and Route 100 west of Sherburne Center, travel half a mile north on Route 100 to the state park entrance on the right (east) side of the road.

Trip notes: No-frills Gifford Woods is a centrally located, wooded campground with sites near Kent Pond, which is open to bass and trout fishing. Short trails lead throughout the woods, but hikers are also conveniently close to trailheads for the Long and Appalachian Trails; the two footpaths diverge nearby at Sherburne Pass. In summer, this camp is popular with mountain bikers who ride at the Killington Ski and Summer Resort and in the surrounding Green Mountains.

Open: Mid-May to Columbus Day.

⑧⑴ Killington Campground at Alpenhof Lodge

Location: Near the Killington Ski and Summer Resort; Southern Vermont map page 281, grid c2.

Campsites, facilities: There are 10 sites for tents and RVs, five with water and electric hookups. Air conditioners are allowed. Facilities include laundry, hot showers, a bike repair room, hot tubs, fire rings, and tables. Firewood and cable TV hookups are available. Leashed pets are permitted.

Reservations, fees: Reservations are recommended. Sites are $16 to $20 a night for two people.

Contact: Killington Campground at Alpenhof Lodge, Killington Road, RR 1, Box 2880, Killington, VT 05751; (802) 422-9787.

Directions: From Mendon (northeast of Rutland), travel about seven miles east on U.S. 4 to Killington Road. Turn right and look for the campground entrance at Alpenhof Lodge, 2.5 miles ahead on the right.

Trip notes: These sites are located behind a ski lodge one mile from the Killington Ski and Summer Resort. In summer, the resort provides a tennis school, golf course, complete mountain bike center, and more than 50 miles of multiuse trails open to hiking, biking, and horseback riding across six peaks. Campers may use an equipped bike repair room at Alpenhof Lodge. And all year long, the Killington chairlift whisks passengers to the highest point reached by aerial lift in New England, providing an effortless way to view the Green Mountain State.

Open: May 1 through mid-October.

⑧② Lake Bomoseen Campground

Location: On the north end of Lake Bomoseen; Southern Vermont map page 281, grid c1.

Campsites, facilities: There are 131 sites for tents and RVs, 40 with full hookups, 34 with water and electric, and 57 with none. Each site has a picnic table and fire ring. Use of air conditioners and heaters is allowed. Cable and satellite TV hookups are available. Facilities include a dump station, laundry, rest rooms, hot showers, a traffic control gate, rec hall, game room, miniature golf, a swimming pool, sports courts, an athletic field, and horseshoe pits. LP gas, ice, firewood, RV storage, RV supplies, and boat supplies are available on site. There's also a grocery store nearby. Leashed pets are permitted.

Reservations, fees: Reservations are recommended and can be made through the mail or by telephone; a deposit is required. Sites range from $17 to $24 a night per family. There is a three-day minimum stay and a $10 surcharge on holiday weekends. Pets are $1 extra per day; boat launch/dock permits cost $5 and are good for your entire stay.

Contact: Dan and Estelle Adams, Lake Bomoseen Campground, Marine and RV Sales, Service, and Rentals, Route 30, Lake Bomoseen, VT 05732; (802) 273-2061.

Directions: From the junction of U.S. 4 and Route 30 near Castleton, travel five miles north on Route 30 to the campground entrance on the left.

Trip notes: Bomoseen is the state's largest lake, and this campground is set back from the water in the woods at its northern end. A separate tenting area and roomy RV sites are spread out on 33 acres. Boaters and RVers will feel right at home because a marina and RV sales office are operated in conjunction with the campground. Dock space and a boat launch are available. Campers are also welcome to rent boats—pontoon boats, bass boats, fishing boats, rowboats, paddleboats, and canoes are available by the day or half-day.

There is no beach for swimming here, as weeds grow profusely at this corner of the lake, but once you're out on the water you'll want to jump right in. Or take a dip in the campground's 100,000-gallon swimming pool. Fishing is one of the main attractions; the lake is home to rainbow, brown, brook, and lake trout, black bass, northern pike, perch, pickerel, bluegill, and bullhead.

Open: Late April through mid-October.

83 Half Moon State Park

Location: On Half Moon Pond northwest of Lake Bomoseen; Southern Vermont map page 281, grid c1.

Campsites, facilities: There are 69 sites for tents and RVs including 10 lean-tos, all without hookups. Each site has a picnic table and fireplace. Metered hot showers, flush toilets, recycling bins, a dump station, picnic shelter, and playground are provided. You can rent boats at the campground. Leashed pets with rabies vaccination certification are permitted at sites, but not in day-use areas.

Reservations, fees: Reservations are recommended. Sites are $12 to $16 a night for four people. Each additional person four years and older will be charged $3 at a tent site and $4 at a lean-to. The maximum allowable number of people at a site is eight, and there must be at least one person 18 years of age or older with each camping party. See also page 284.

Contact: Half Moon State Park, RR 1, Box 2730, Fair Haven, VT 05473; (802) 273-2848.

Directions: From Rutland, take U.S. 4 west to Route 30. At the intersection, turn and drive south on Route 30 to Route 4A, then go west on Route 4A for one mile. Turn right on Town Road and travel north for seven miles, past Bomoseen State Park, to the Half Moon State Park entrance.

Trip notes: Though this tucked-away campground does attract crowds on summer weekends, you'll find it's a peaceful place during the week. Campsites are set near the shore of three-acre Half Moon Pond, which is open to canoeing, swimming, and fishing. Don't be surprised if you hear a gobble in these woods, because this is prime wild turkey country. Anglers will find trout, bass, and pike in the pond. If you want to head deeper into the hills, take a short hike from the park to High Pond.

Open: Mid-May through Labor Day.

84 Bomoseen State Park

Location: On the west side of Lake Bomoseen; Southern Vermont map page 281, grid c1.

Campsites, facilities: There are 66 sites for tents and RVs including 10 lean-tos, all without hookups. Each site has a picnic table and fireplace. Metered hot showers, flush toilets, recycling bins, a dump station, picnic shelter, snack bar, and playground are provided. Boats can be rented at the campground. Leashed pets with rabies vaccination certification are permitted, but not in day-use areas.

Reservations, fees: Reservations are recommended. Sites are $12 to $16 a night for four people. Each additional person four years and older will be charged $3 at a tent site and $4 at a lean-to. The maximum allowable number of people at a site is eight, and there must be at least one person 18 years of age or older with each camping party. See also page 284.

Contact: Bomoseen State Park, RR 1, Box 2620, Fair Haven, VT 05743; (802) 265-4242.

Directions: From Rutland, take U.S. 4 west to the intersection with Route 30. Turn and drive south on Route 30 to Route 4A, then go west on Route 4A for one mile. Turn right and travel north to the park entrance.

Trip notes: Many privately owned cabins dot the shoreline of large, developed Lake Bomoseen. Campsites are secluded, set well back from the shore. Because of its size, Bomoseen is popular with power-boaters and sees a lot of action on summer weekends. There's a ramp at the state park where you can launch your own boat. Fish-

ing is a big attraction: the lake is home to rainbow, brown, brook, and lake trout, black bass, northern pike, perch, pickerel, bluegill, and bullhead. Roughly 10 miles of trails can be hiked at the state park; the Slate History Trail visits former slate quarries that were active in the 1800s.

Open: Mid-May through Labor Day.

85 Pine Valley RV Resort

Location: In White River Junction; Southern Vermont map page 281, grid c3.

Campsites, facilities: There are 72 sites, 49 with full hookups and 23 with water and electric. Each site has a fire ring and picnic table. Use of air conditioners and heaters is allowed. Recycling bins, dump stations, rest rooms, hot showers, laundry facilities, a rec hall, pool, and playground are provided. Cable TV hookups, limited groceries, rental boats, LP gas, ice, and firewood are available. Leashed pets are permitted.

Reservations, fees: A $25 deposit is required for reservations. Sites are $18 to $24 a night.

Contact: Peter and Margie Robes, Pine Valley RV Resort, 400 Woodstock Road, White River Junction, VT 05001; (802) 296-6711 in the summer or (802) 295-6076 in the winter.

Directions: From Interstate 89 in White River Junction, take exit 1 and drive a quarter mile west on U.S. 4 to the campground entrance on the left (south) side of the road.

Trip notes: Pine trees buffer these sites from the noise of nearby Interstate 89 and U.S. 4. A small pond here is open to fishing, swimming, and boating, and the campground rents out paddleboats and canoes. The pond is stocked with trout—you can keep any fish you catch for 50 cents an inch—and is circumnavigable on a short nature walk. Though tents are welcome, these sites are more suited to RVs—any size can be accommodated—and the campground owners say they cater to overnight travelers. A few miles to the west is Quechee Gorge, a mile-long chasm on the Ottauquechee River. You can hike and walk along the trails, or picnic overlooking waterfalls. The Vermont Raptor Center in nearby Woodstock is home to nonreleasable owls, hawks, eagles, and falcons; visitors are welcome.

Open: May 1 through October 15.

86 Maple Leaf Motel and Campground

Location: In White River Junction; Southern Vermont map page 281, grid c3.

Campsites, facilities: There are 20 sites for tents and RVs, 4 with full hookups, 10 with water and electric, and 6 with none. Some RV sites have cable TV hookups. Hot showers, a dump station, tables, and fire rings are provided. There's also a playground, a badminton court, and horseshoe pits. Ice and firewood are available. Leashed pets are permitted.

Reservations, fees: Reservations are recommended. Sites are $13 to $19 a night per family.

Contact: Bernhard and Maria Poschmann, Maple Leaf Motel and Campground, 406 North Hartland Road, White River Junction, VT 05001-3815; (802) 295-2817.

Directions: From the interchange of Interstates 91 and 89 in White River Junction, travel 2.5 miles south on U.S. 5 to the motel and campground driveway.

Trip notes: Partially shaded and grassy, these sites are located next to a motel on a busy road. While a few sites are suitable for tents, RVers will feel the most comfortable in this exposed campground. If you're look-

ing for a place to pull off the interstate for the night, it is a convenient option. White River Junction hosts a gala celebration of railroading every September. Also in town is the Catamount Brewing Company, which conducts tours and tastings throughout the year.

Open: Mid-May through late October.

87 Quechee Gorge State Park

Location: Near Quechee Gorge in White River Junction; Southern Vermont map page 281, grid c4.

Campsites, facilities: There are 54 sites for tents and RVs including six lean-tos, all without hookups. Each site has a picnic table and fireplace. Metered hot showers, flush toilets, recycling bins, a dump station, picnic shelter, and playground are provided. Firewood is available. Leashed pets with rabies vaccination certification are permitted, but not in day-use areas.

Reservations, fees: Reservations are recommended. Sites are $11 to $15 a night for four people. Each additional person four years and older will be charged $3 at a tent site and $4 at a lean-to. The maximum allowable number of people at a site is eight, and there must be at least one person 18 years of age or older with each camping party. See also page 284.

Contact: Quechee Gorge State Park, 190 Dewey Mills Road, White River Junction, VT 05001; (802) 295-2990.

Directions: From Interstate 89 in White River Junction, take exit 1 and head west on U.S. 4 for three miles to the park entrance on the left (south) side of the road.

Trip notes: Located next to the geological phenomenon of Quechee Gorge on the Ottauquechee River, the sites at this campground are set in a northern hardwood forest interspersed with conifers. A one-mile loop trail provides views of the gorge from the river and the rim. You can cast a line in the river for brook, rainbow, and brown trout, or head to the north end of the gorge to try out a swimming hole. North Hartland Lake Recreation Area is a stone's throw to the southeast; maintained by the U.S. Army Corps of Engineers, the lake there has a developed swimming and recreation area that includes ball fields and a boat ramp.

Open: Early May through early October.

88 Iroquois Land Family Camping

Location: Southeast of Rutland; Southern Vermont map page 281, grid c2.

Campsites, facilities: There are 50 sites for tents and RVs, 12 with full hookups and 38 with water and electric. Rest rooms, hot showers, a dump station, a pool, rec room, sports courts, a playing field, and horseshoe pits are provided. Also available are a camp store, ice, firewood, and RV parts and supplies. Leashed pets with rabies vaccination certification are permitted.

Reservations, fees: Reservations are recommended. Send $20 by check or money order and be sure to note your arrival date, type of camper, hookups needed, and length of stay; reservations are confirmed by return mail. Sites are $18 to $20 a night for two people, with surcharges for extra adults, 30 amp electricity, and children. Weekly and monthly rates are available.

Contact: Karl and Carol Anderson, Iroquois Land Family Camping, East Road, North Clarendon, VT 05759; (802) 773-2832.

Directions: From the southern junction of U.S. 4 and U.S. 7 near Rutland, travel half a mile south on U.S. 7. At the stoplight, turn

left on North Shrewsbury Road and head east for one mile. Turn right on East Road and continue to the campground entrance three-quarters of a mile ahead on the left.

Trip notes: A variety of sites is offered at Iroquois, some set amid pine trees, but the most popular are the large, mowed grassy sites for RVs with full hookups. Though there's a good view of the surrounding Green Mountains, some may find the campground too densely settled. A swimming pool is provided on the grounds, and there's also a large field for flying kites and playing. Downtown Rutland is only minutes from here. On U.S. 4 in town, the Norman Rockwell Museum has a comprehensive display of the artist's magazine covers, advertisements, and other published works—more than 2,000 pieces in all.

Open: May 1 through October 15.

89 Sugarhouse Campground

Location: North of Plymouth; Southern Vermont map page 281, grid c2.

Campsites, facilities: There are 45 sites for tents and RVs with full hookups. Hot showers, fire rings, picnic tables, and a playground are provided. Leashed pets are permitted.

Reservations, fees: Reservations are required in the winter. Sites are $12 to $15 a night in the summer, $20 a night in the winter. Weekly, monthly, and seasonal rates are available.

Contact: Sugarhouse Campground, Route 100, HCR 70, Box 44, Plymouth, VT 05056; (802) 672-5043.

Directions: From the junction of Routes 100 and 100A in Plymouth, travel half a mile north on Route 100 to the campground entrance on the left (west) side of the road.

Trip notes: Folks who like catching trout will like these sites near the Black River. The campground is shaded by sugar maples and is just up the road from historic Plymouth. A laid-back atmosphere and informal organized events make Sugarhouse popular with seasonal campers. Potluck suppers, the Strawberry Social, and theme dinners are just a few of the offerings. This is one of only a handful of central Vermont RV campgrounds open year-round with winterized services. At Sugarhouse, you are just minutes from the Killington Ski and Summer Resort—a grand six-mountain ski center—and are also close to Okemo and Pico, two midsize alpine ski areas. Multiuse trails are found to the north at Coolidge State Park (see campground number 90).

Open: Year-round.

90 Coolidge State Park

Location: In Plymouth; Southern Vermont map page 281, grid c3.

Campsites, facilities: There are 60 sites for tents and RVs including 35 lean-tos, all without hookups. Each site has a picnic table and fireplace. Metered hot showers, flush toilets, recycling bins, a dump station, picnic shelter, snack bar, and playground are provided. Leashed pets with rabies vaccination certification are permitted, but not in day-use areas.

Reservations, fees: Reservations are recommended. Sites are $11 to $15 a night for four people. Each additional person four years and older will be charged $3 at a tent site and $4 at a lean-to. The maximum allowable number of people at a site is eight, and there must be at least one person 18 years of age or older with each camping party. See also page 284.

Contact: Coolidge State Park, HCR 70, Box 105, Plymouth, VT 05056; (802) 672-3612.

Directions: From Route 100 in Plymouth, travel north for two miles on Route 100A to the park entrance on the right.

Trip notes: As part of Calvin Coolidge State Forest, the campground is wooded with spruce, hemlock, fir, birch, beech, and sugar maples. Hikes lead to Slack Hill from the campground where some primitive "wilderness" campsites are located. A network of trails explores the more than 16,000 acres of the preserve, including a route to Shrewsbury Peak northwest of Plymouth, one of the highest points in the forest. A trail leads to the summit, and connector trails meet up with the Long and Appalachian Trails. In nearby Plymouth is the birthplace of Calvin Coolidge, the 30th president of the United States and the man for whom the park was named. This campground was the site of the third Civilian Conservation Corps camp built in Vermont; CCC workers established the camp in June of 1933.

Open: Mid-May to Columbus Day.

91 Lake St. Catherine State Park

Location: South of Poultney; Southern Vermont map page 281, grid c1.

Campsites, facilities: There are 61 sites for tents and RVs including 10 lean-tos, all without hookups. Each site has a picnic table and fireplace. Facilities include a dump station, flush toilets, metered hot showers, a boat ramp, sports field, and playground. Firewood, boat rentals, and a snack bar are available. Ice and LP gas can be obtained nearby. Leashed pets with rabies vaccination certification are permitted, but not in day-use areas.

Reservations, fees: Reservations are recommended. Sites are $12 to $16 a night for four people. Each additional person four years and older will be charged $3 at a tent site and $4 at a lean-to. The maximum allowable number of people at a site is eight, and there must be at least one person 18 years of age or older with each camping party. See also page 284.

Contact: Lake St. Catherine State Park, RD 2, Box 1775, Poultney, VT 05764; (802) 287-9158.

Directions: From Poultney, travel three miles south on Route 30 to the state park entrance.

Trip notes: At seven miles long, Lake St. Catherine is a boater's paradise. You'll find a boat ramp at this campground, where sites are set right on the shore and a sandy beach welcomes swimmers. Anglers can try for a variety of species including smallmouth and largemouth bass, perch, pike, and walleye. The aptly named Big Trees Nature Trail traverses the campground as it meanders through stately pines, maples, and a few red oaks.

Open: Mid-May through mid-October.

---

⑨⑦ Camp Plymouth State Park

Location: South of Plymouth on the east side of Echo Lake; Southern Vermont map page 281, grid c3.

Campsites, facilities: There are two cottages with flush toilets and hot showers. A playground and boat rentals are provided. Ice is available. No pets are allowed.

Reservations, fees: Reservations are necessary. Cottages are $400 a week. See also page 284.

Contact: Camp Plymouth State Park, RR 1, Box 489, Ludlow, VT 05149; (802) 228-2025.

Directions: From Ludlow, head north on Route 100 to Tyson. Once in town, turn right and drive east on Route 140 toward South Reading for one mile, then turn left and continue another mile to the park entrance.

Trip notes: Not everyone would call this camping. The state rents out two cottages in Tyson at the edge of Echo Lake, which is open to boating, fishing, canoeing, and swimming. Hiking trails follow the shore and traverse about 300 acres of woodlands.

Open: Mid-May through early September.

---

⑨③ Mount Ascutney State Park

Location: Northwest of Ascutney; Southern Vermont map page 281, grid d3.

Campsites, facilities: There are 39 sites for tents and trailers with no hookups. Ten additional sites have lean-tos. Facilities include a dump station, rest rooms, metered hot showers, piped water, a playground, fireplaces, and tables. Firewood is available on site, and ice and LP gas can be obtained nearby in Ascutney. No generators or firearms are allowed, and only two vehicles are permitted at each campsite. Leashed pets with rabies vaccination certification are permitted, but not in day-use areas.

Reservations, fees: Reservations are accepted after January 1 for specific sites if you're staying four or more consecutive nights; there is a nonrefundable $3 reservation fee. The maximum allowable stay is three weeks. Tent sites are $10 a night and lean-tos are $14 a night for four people. Each additional person four years and older will be charged $3 at a tent site and $4 at a lean-to. The maximum allowable number of people at a site is eight, and there must be at least one person 18 years of age or older with each camping party. See also page 284.

Contact: Mount Ascutney State Park, RR 1, Box 33, North Springfield, VT 05150; (802) 886-2434.

Directions: From Interstate 91 at Ascutney, take exit 8 and drive two miles north on U.S. 5. Head northwest on Route 44A for one mile to Mount Ascutney Road. The park entrance is about a mile ahead on the left.

Trip notes: Because of the excellent hiking opportunities at the park and the panoramic views from the summit of Mount Ascutney, these campsites are in high demand. In addition to the wooded, spacious sites at the campground, trailside camping is permitted. The trails here are well established—some historians claim this was the first American mountain with a developed footpath—and moderate in difficulty for the most part, with some steep sections. Several routes lead to the 3,144-foot summit. There is also an auto road ($3.50 per vehicle plus a per-person fee) that ends about half a mile from the summit and a trail that leads from the main parking lot to the top. You'll see some notable sights as you hike, including the Steam Donkey—a machine used for logging in the early 1900s—on the Futures Trail and Crystal Cascade Falls, an 84-foot waterfall on the Weathersfield Trail. The mountain is a monadnock, not part of any ridge or chain, and thus provides an ideal launch for hang gliders. You can hike to the gliders' takeoff points and observe their flights, or bring your own set of wings. An observation tower and other communication towers are atop Ascutney's summit.

Open: Mid-May through early October.

⑨④ Running Bear Camping Area

Location: In Ascutney; Southern Vermont map page 281, grid d3.

Campsites, facilities: There are 101 sites, 43 with full hookups, 38 with water and electric, and 20 with none. Each site has a table, fire ring, and grill. Facilities include a dump station, hot showers, rest rooms, and a rec hall. Also on the property are a heated pool, a sports field, and horseshoe pits. LP gas, groceries, ice, and firewood are available. Leashed pets are permitted.

Reservations, fees: Reservations are recommended and in winter are necessary. Sites are $13 to $16 a night for two people.

Contact: Phil and Brenda Aylward, Running Bear Camping Area, Route 5, Ascutney, VT 05030; (802) 674-6417.

Directions: From Interstate 91 at Ascutney, take exit 8 and travel half a mile east on Route 131 to U.S. 5. Drive one mile north to the campground entrance on the right (east) side of U.S. 5.

Trip notes: Set in hilly woodlands, this campground is less than a mile from the Connecticut River. The area is densely formatted—sites are only about 25 feet wide—but it is fully equipped for RVers who want a spot close to the interstate. Some sites are rented seasonally in summer and in winter. A short drive inland on Route 44A leads to Mount Ascutney State Park. There, in summer, the summit hike is a good way to spot hawks; in winter, the privately owned ski area is a fun family destination with plenty of easy and moderate terrain. Since the freestanding mountain is not part of any range, it affords sweeping views in all directions.

Open: Year-round.

⑨⑤ Wilgus State Park

Location: South of Ascutney on the Connecticut River; Southern Vermont map page 281, grid d4.

Campsites, facilities: There are 29 sites for tents and RVs including nine lean-tos, all without hookups. Facilities include a dump station, flush toilets, metered hot showers, a group area, playground, tables, and fireplaces. Firewood is available, and ice and supplies can be obtained in Ascutney. Leashed pets with rabies vaccination certification are permitted at sites, but not in day-use areas.

Reservations, fees: Reservations are recommended. Sites are $11 to $15 a night for four people. Each additional person four years and older will be charged $3 at a tent site and $4 at a lean-to. The maximum allowable number of people at a site is eight, and there must be at least one person 18 years of age or older with each camping party. See also page 284.

Contact: Wilgus State Park, RR 1, Box 196, Ascutney, VT 05030; (802) 674-5422 in the summer or (802) 886-2434 in the winter.

Directions: From Interstate 91 in Ascutney, take exit 8 and travel half a mile east on Route 131 to U.S. 5. Drive two miles south to the park entrance on the left (east) side of U.S. 5.

Trip notes: You'll be pitching your tent along the Connecticut River at Wilgus State Park. Trout, walleye, pike, bass, and shad make their home in the river and are fair game for anglers. If you plan on canoeing the Connecticut, you'll want a good guide (AMC publishes a river guide for the New Hampshire and Vermont section) because certain areas, such as one spot near Bellows Falls, cannot be run. The abundant wildlife here includes river otters, beavers, and various birds. Within the park are two foot trails, each less than a mile long, leading to the 600-foot Pinnacle. This peak offers a view of the Connecticut River and across to New Hampshire. To the north, the town of Windsor lays claim to the longest covered bridge in the United States; it crosses the Connecticut River and connects New Hampshire and Vermont.

Open: Mid-May through early October.

96 Getaway Mountain and Campground

Location: South of Ascutney on Route 5; Southern Vermont map page 281, grid d4.

Campsites, facilities: There are 27 sites for tents and RVs, 17 with full hookups and 10 with water and electric. Flush toilets, metered hot showers, a dump station, playground, and rec room are provided. Ice and firewood are available. Leashed pets are permitted.

Reservations, fees: Reservations are recommended. Sites start at $15 a night.

Contact: Getaway Mountain and Campground, P.O. Box 372, Ascutney, VT 05030; (802) 674-2812.

Directions: From Interstate 91 in Ascutney, take exit 8 and travel half a mile east on Route 131 to U.S. 5. Drive south on this road to the campground two miles ahead on the left (east).

Trip notes: Only a few years in operation, this campground offers full RV amenities and clean, partially shaded sites. New facilities include a pool, canoe rentals, and miniature golf. Some sites look out over the Connecticut River. Boaters and anglers who want to get out on the water should head a short distance north to Wilgus State Park (see campground number 95). In addition to hiking and nature trails, the state-owned parcel includes frontage on the Connecticut River and boat access.

Open: Late May through late October.

97 Hideaway "Squirrel Hill" Campgrounds

Location: East of Ludlow; Southern Vermont map page 281, grid c3.

Campsites, facilities: There are 24 sites

for tents and RVs, 7 with full hookups, 7 with water and electric, and 10 with water only. Hot showers, a dump station, and a playground are provided. Firewood is available. Leashed pets are permitted.

Reservations, fees: Reservations are recommended. Sites are $10 to $15 a night.

Contact: Nelson and Hope DeRoo, Hideaway "Squirrel Hill" Campgrounds, P.O. Box 176, Ludlow, VT 05149; (802) 228-8800.

Directions: From Ludlow, travel 1.5 miles southeast on Route 103 to Bixby Road. Turn left and go to the campground entrance about 500 feet ahead on the left.

Trip notes: Small, quiet, and unadorned, this wooded campground is host to many seasonal campers. Be sure to call ahead if you want a spot. Located near the Green Mountain National Forest and the town of Ludlow, Hideaway is convenient to both wilderness and nightlife. Okemo State Forest is home to Okemo Ski Mountain, and the town of Ludlow at its base bustles with shops and restaurants. While the skiers wait for the white stuff to appear, hikers can venture to the 3,343-foot summit of Okemo, also known as Ludlow Mountain, in spring, summer, and fall.

Open: Mid-May through mid-October.

98 Otter Creek Campground

Location: North of Danby; Southern Vermont map page 281, grid d2.

Campsites, facilities: There are 50 sites for tents and RVs, 35 with water and electric hookups and 15 with none. Each site has a fire ring, grill, and table. Facilities include a dump station and laundry. Also provided are a rec hall, swimming pool, boat rentals, badminton and volleyball courts, a sports field, and horseshoe pits. Limited

groceries, LP gas, ice, and firewood are available. Leashed pets are permitted.

Reservations, fees: Reservations are recommended, especially in summer and fall. There are no refunds. Sites start at $14 a night per family.

Contact: Otter Creek Campground, Route 7, Danby, VT 05739; (802) 293-5041.

Directions: From the northern town limits of Danby, travel north on U.S. 7 for three-quarters of a mile to the campground entrance.

Trip notes: Though these sites are located directly on Otter Creek, they lose some of their scenic value due to the "wheel-to-wheel" feel: sites are only about 20 feet wide. The river flows north to Lake Champlain and is ripe for quick-water canoeing in springtime when it's swollen from snowmelt and runoff. There are some small swimming holes at the campground, as well as warm-water fishing for smallmouth bass and northern pike.

Open: Year-round; fully operational May 1 through October 1.

99 Greendale Campground

Location: West of Ludlow in the Green Mountain National Forest; Southern Vermont map page 281, grid d2.

Campsites, facilities: There are 11 sites for tents and trailers. Pit toilets, piped water, grills, and tables are provided. A picnic area also serves as a group tenting area. Leashed pets are permitted.

Reservations, fees: Sites are available on a first-come, first-served basis. The maximum stay is 14 days. Self-service payment is $5 a night.

Contact: Green Mountain National Forest, Manchester Ranger District, RR 1, Box 1940,

Manchester Center, VT 05255; (802) 362-2307.

Directions: From Weston, head north on Route 100 for three miles. Turn left on Forest Service Road 18 and drive northwest for two miles to the campground.

Trip notes: Spacious, wooded campsites are strung out along Greendale Brook. The waterway is inhabited by native trout and is also the target of an effort to reintroduce the endangered Atlantic salmon. Along the brook, you'll notice logs or rocks deliberately placed to create and cover deep pools for the protected fish; the salmon are off-limits, but you can cast for trout with a valid Vermont fishing license. The campground is at the edge of the White Rocks National Recreation Area, which is traversed by an extensive trail system and is home to the Big Branch and Peru Peak Wilderness Areas.

Open: Spring, summer, and fall. The access road is not maintained for winter travel.

100 Emerald Lake State Park

Location: On Emerald Lake in Dorset; Southern Vermont map page 281, grid d2.

Campsites, facilities: There are 105 sites for tents and RVs including 36 lean-tos, all without hookups. Facilities include a dump station, metered hot showers, picnic tables, fireplaces, boat rentals, a snack bar, and playground. Firewood is available. Small grocery stores are located in Danby and East Dorset. Leashed pets with rabies vaccination certification are permitted, but not in day-use areas.

Reservations, fees: Reservations are recommended. Tent sites start at $12 a night and lean-tos start at $16 a night for four people. Each additional person four years and older will be charged $3 at a tent

site and $4 at a lean-to. The maximum allowable number of people at a site is eight, and there must be at least one person 18 years of age or older with each camping party. See also page 284.

Contact: Emerald Lake State Park, RD 485, East Dorset, VT 05253; (802) 362-1655 in the summer or (802) 483-2001 in the winter.

Directions: From the junction of U.S. 7 and Route 7A in Dorset, travel four miles north on U.S. 7 to the state park entrance on the left.

Trip notes: This park is located in the narrowest stretch of the Valley of Vermont, the groove that separates the Taconic Range (which continues into New York) from the Green Mountains. Campsites are set atop a heavily wooded ridge above Emerald Lake, the headwaters of Otter Creek. There are two no-pet zones near the day-use area of the park, so campers with animals in tow will need to stay in Area B. Area A is closest to the lake beach, but the other two sections have hiking trails that lead to the water through a forest of ash and hickory. The lake is open to nonmotorized boating and is a haven for quiet-water canoeing. A wheelchair-accessible beach house and play area are provided by the water.

Open: Mid-May through mid-October.

101 Hapgood Pond Recreation Area

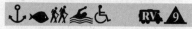

Location: West of Londonderry in the Green Mountain National Forest; Southern Vermont map page 281, grid d2.

Campsites, facilities: There are 28 sites for tents and trailers. Pit toilets, piped water, tent pads, grills, and tables are provided. Also on the property are an amphitheater, pavilion, and rest rooms. Leashed pets are permitted.

Reservations, fees: Sites are available on a first-come, first-served basis. The maximum stay is 14 days. Sites are $10 a night for up to six people.

Contact: January through April—Vermont Youth Conservation Corps, 103 South Main Street, Waterbury, VT 05671; (802) 241-3699. May through October—Hapgood Pond Recreation Area, General Delivery, Peru, VT 05152; (802) 824-6456. November through December—Green Mountain National Forest, Manchester Ranger District, RR 1, Box 1940, Manchester Center, VT 05255; (802) 362-2307.

Directions: From Manchester, travel east on Route 11 for six miles, bearing left into Peru. Continue two miles north of town on Hapgood Pond Road to the campground.

Trip notes: Hapgood Pond offers a wilderness camping experience for families. Wooded, private sites are set back from the pond in the woods. Down at the water there's a beach and a boat launch for your canoe or rowboat (inflatable floats are not allowed). A lifeguard is on duty between 10 A.M. and 5 P.M. from Memorial Day through Labor Day. This is a trout-stocked water, and with a Vermont fishing license, you can hook up to five fish a day. A short nature trail winds around the north edge of the pond and crosses Flood Brook. Hapgood Pond Recreation Area is operated by members of the Vermont Youth Conservation Corps who utilize the amphitheater and grounds for nature walks and musical programs. The Vermont Institute of Natural Science also conducts weekly nature programs.

Open: Memorial Day through Columbus Day.

102 Horseshoe Acres

Location: Between Weston and Andover; Southern Vermont map page 281, grid d3.

Campsites, facilities: There are 135 sites for tents and RVs, 17 with full hookups and 98 with water and electric. Each site has a table, fire ring, and grill. Facilities include a dump station, laundry, rec hall, pavilion, pool, playground, sports field, an adult lounge, a game room and arcade, and horseshoe pits. Limited groceries, ice, firewood, RV supplies, RV storage, cable TV, and LP gas are available. Leashed pets are permitted.

Reservations, fees: Reservations are recommended in summer and winter. Sites start at $15 a night.

Contact: Horseshoe Acres, RD 1, Box 206, Andover, VT 05143; (802) 875-2960.

Directions: From Interstate 91, take exit 6 and travel north on Route 103 to Chester. Head west on Route 11 for four miles, then turn right and go north on the Andover-Weston Road for 3.5 miles to the entrance.

Trip notes: Horseshoe Acres is set deep in the woods and has a pond and a swimming pool to cool off in during the summer. Utilizing a pavilion and a large lawn, the campground specializes in hosting camping safaris, reunions, receptions, and other group functions. In winter, the lodge becomes the center of activity for campers who wish to cross-country ski and snowmobile on trails that leave from the campground. Inside you'll find a fireplace, heated rest rooms, showers, and hot tubs. A limited number of sites are available in the winter, so reservations are suggested. This is an ideal spot for RVers who want to hit the slopes at nearby Nordic and alpine centers.

Open: Year-round; fully operational May 1 through Columbus Day.

103 Hidden Valley Campgrounds

Location: West of Springfield; Southern Vermont map page 281, grid d3.

Campsites, facilities: There are 36 sites for tents and RVs, 20 with water and electric hookups and 16 with none. A dump station, metered hot showers, a playground, and volleyball court are provided. Firewood is available on site, and ice is for sale nearby. Leashed pets are permitted.

Reservations, fees: Reservations are recommended. Sites start at $14 a night.

Contact: Andy and Peggy Rogstad, Hidden Valley Campgrounds, Mattson Road, Chester, VT 05143; (802) 886-2497.

Directions: From Interstate 91 near Bellows Falls, take exit 6 and follow Route 103 north to Chester. Continue north through town on the same road for 4.5 miles to Gassetts. Turn right on Route 10, heading east for one mile, then turn right on Mattson Road and bear left at the fork. The campground is two miles ahead.

Trip notes: Seasonal campers dominate these shaded sites on or near a freshwater pond where they can swim and fish. The North Springfield Lake and Stoughton Pond Recreation Areas just to the north are open to powerboating.

Open: May 1 through October 15.

104 Tree Farm Campground

Location: East of Springfield; Southern Vermont map page 281, grid d3.

Campsites, facilities: There are 118 sites for tents and RVs, 85 with full hookups and 33 with water and electric. Each site has a table and fire ring. There's also an open camping area for clubs and groups. Sixty-six sites are open for winter camping. Facilities include a pavilion, heated rec room, rest rooms, and free hot showers. Also on the property are a playground, horseshoe pits, a sports area, and dump station. Firewood, ice, cable TV, limited groceries, RV storage, and LP gas are available. Leashed pets are permitted.

Reservations, fees: Reservations are recommended. Sites with full hookups including cable TV are $17 a night per family. Ask about special rates for groups and clubs.

Contact: Bert and Bill Wilson, Tree Farm Campground, 53 Skitchewaug Trail, Springfield, VT 05156; (802) 885-2889.

Directions: From Interstate 91 at Springfield, take exit 7 and travel three miles west on Route 11. Turn right at Bridge Street and drive about half a mile, crossing the Black River, then turn right again on Route 143 and drive another half mile northeast to the campground entrance on the right.

Trip notes: Tree Farm Campground is nestled at the foot of one of Vermont's famous green hillsides. Sites are shaded by a canopy of tall pine trees and are surrounded by more than 100 acres of pine forest crisscrossed by a multiuse trail system. In the summer, mountain bikers and hikers fill the paths. Then in the winter, skiers and snowmobilers enjoy the white woods; the campground also serves as a registration station for snowmobiles. A fireplace in the heated log cabin lodge and rec room welcomes campers in the winter. Nearby is the Baltimore Covered Bridge, which links Springfield to Baltimore and was built over Great Brook in 1870.

Open: Year-round. The winter season is November 1 through May 1.

105 Winhall Brook Camping Area

Location: On Ball Mountain Lake in South Londonderry; Southern Vermont map page 281, grid d3.

Campsites, facilities: There are 109

sites for tents and RVs, all without hookups. Each site has a table and fire grill. Facilities include a dump station, showers, piped water, horseshoe pits, picnic areas, and rest rooms. Firewood is sold at the campground office. Leashed pets with rabies vaccination certification are permitted.

Reservations, fees: Reservations are not accepted. Sites start at $10 a night for four people.

Contact: Upper Connecticut River Basin Office, RR 1, Box 164B, Perkinsville, VT 05151; (802) 874-4881.

Directions: From South Londonderry, travel 2.5 miles south on Route 100 to the campground entrance on the left.

Trip notes: The handiwork of the U.S. Army Corps of Engineers gives these streamside campsites their no-nonsense appeal. Located north of the Ball Mountain Dam, which controls the West River, the wooded sites are surrounded by reservoir lands open to hunting in season. The West River provides fishing for brown trout downstream of the dam and is stocked with Atlantic salmon as part of a restoration program. Smallmouth bass inhabit the 75-acre reservoir. The surrounding forest is traversed by multiuse trails that are open year-round.

Open: Mid-May through early September.

---

106 Jamaica State Park

Location: On the West River in Jamaica; Southern Vermont map page 281, grid d3.

Campsites, facilities: There are 59 sites for tents and RVs including 17 lean-tos, all without hookups. Facilities include a dump station, metered hot showers, flush toilets, a picnic shelter, playground, horseshoe pits, and recycling bins. Ice and firewood are available. Leashed pets with rabies vaccination certification are permitted, but not in day-use areas.

Reservations, fees: Reservations are recommended. Sites are $12 to $16 a night for four people. Each additional person four years and older will be charged $3 at a tent site and $4 at a lean-to. The maximum allowable number of people at a site is eight, and there must be at least one person 18 years of age or older with each camping party. See also page 284.

Contact: Jamaica State Park, P.O. Box 45, Jamaica, VT 05343; (802) 874-4600.

Directions: From Route 30 in Jamaica, head half a mile north on the town road to the park entrance.

Trip notes: Heavily wooded and right on the West River, these sites are popular with expert canoeists and kayakers. Upriver from the campground is Ball Mountain Dam; in the last weeks of April and September water releases turn the river into a gnarly rip of white water on which competitions are often held. A fine swimming hole at the campground bears some historical significance: during the French and Indian Wars, three Frenchmen and several Native Americans ambushed British soldiers at Salmon Hole. The most spectacular feature at the park is Hamilton Falls, the state's longest waterfall—a 125-foot cascade tumbling down a series of granite ledges. From the campground, the Overlook Trail leads to the summit of Little Bald Mountain. The trail then links up with an old railroad bed that leads along the river all the way to the dam. The trail is a good vantage point for watching paddlers during the spring and fall.

Open: Mid-May through mid-October.

---

107 Camping on the Battenkill

Location: In Arlington on the Batten Kill River; Southern Vermont map page 281, grid e1.

Campsites, facilities: There are 103 sites for tents and RVs, 45 with full hookups, 43 with water and electric, and 15 with none. Each site has a picnic table, garbage can, gravel pad, and fire ring. Air conditioners are allowed, but heaters are not. Facilities include a dump station, hot showers, and rest rooms. LP gas, ice, fishing licenses, and firewood are available. Groups can rent sites in May, June, and September. Leashed pets are permitted.

Reservations, fees: Reservations are recommended for holiday weekends and during July and August; a deposit of one day's fee is required. No single-day or weekend reservations are taken for July or August. Please call after 9 A.M. or before 7 P.M. Sites start at $16 a night for two people and $17 for families, with surcharges for guests, children, and hookups. Two camping units (a unit is a tent, van, or trailer) may occupy one site, but they will be charged as if each had its own site.

Contact: The Pratt Family, Camping on the Battenkill, Inc., RR 2, Box 3310, Arlington, VT 05250; (802) 375-6663.

Directions: From U.S. 7 north of Bennington, take exit 3 to Route 7A, heading west then north into the town of Arlington, then turn left on Route 313. The campground entrance is on the right, three-quarters of a mile from the junction of Routes 313 and 7A.

Trip notes: Seasonal campers make up about one-third of the summer population at Battenkill. Many of the wooded sites are located on the river and are favored by people who like to cast a fishing line from their campsite. The only drawback is the tight quarters along the riverfront, where sites are rarely more than 25 feet wide. The Batten Kill River (derived from an English word meaning "to grow prosperous" and the Dutch word for river) is a good choice for intermediate canoeists in search of

quick water, but you might want to tease the brook trout as well, so bring a fishing pole along with your paddles. From Manchester to the campground and on to the New York border, this stretch of water is narrow and challenging, especially where it meets Roaring Brook in the town of Arlington. The town is known for its association with artist Norman Rockwell, who lived there from 1939 to 1953. Arlington's town meeting is depicted in Rockwell's famous "Four Freedoms" series as representing Freedom of Speech, and visitors can view his work at the Norman Rockwell Exhibition on Main Street.

Open: Mid-April through mid-October.

108 Howell's Camping Area

Location: Southwest of Arlington; Southern Vermont map page 281, grid e1.

Campsites, facilities: There are 73 sites for tents and RVs, 40 with full hookups and 33 with water and electric. Dump stations, laundry facilities, LP gas, and firewood are available. The property also has a rec room, boat rentals, horseshoe pits, picnic tables, and fire rings. Leashed pets are permitted.

Reservations, fees: Reservations are recommended. Sites start at $16 a night for four people.

Contact: Howell's Camping Area, School Street, Arlington, VT 05250; (802) 375-6469.

Directions: From U.S. 7 north of Bennington, take exit 3 and travel two miles west then one mile north on Route 7A. Turn left on Route 313 and make a quick left (after 200 feet) onto School Street, heading south. Continue to the road's end and the campground entrance.

Trip notes: Campsites are set beside a small pond that is open to fishing, swimming, and boating with electric motors only. Campers have use of a sandy beach as well as a boat ramp where they can launch their own vessels. Several canoes and paddleboats are also available for rent. Canoeing on the pond is a quiet affair, but the Batten Kill River is a short drive to the north and offers quick-water adventures. There's a put-in at downtown Arlington, a classic Vermont village full of historic charm.

Open: Mid-April through mid-October.

109 Lake Shaftsbury State Park

Location: South of Arlington; Southern Vermont map page 281, grid e1.

Campsites, facilities: There are 15 sites for tents and trailers, all with lean-tos. There are no hookups or dump stations. Pit toilets, fireplaces, tables, a playground, and a boat ramp are provided. Boat and canoe rentals are available, as is a snack bar. No pets are allowed.

Reservations, fees: Reservations are recommended. Sites start at $10 a night for four people. Each additional person four years and older will be charged $3 at a tent site and $4 at a lean-to. The maximum allowable number of people at a site is eight, and there must be at least one person 18 years of age or older with each camping party. See also page 284.

Contact: Lake Shaftsbury State Park, RD 1, Box 266, Shaftsbury, VT 05262; (802) 375-9978.

Directions: From Arlington, travel two miles south on Route 7A to the state park entrance.

Trip notes: The cool waters of Lake Shaftsbury border this handful of campsites. A snack bar, boat rentals, and a boat ramp make the area popular for day use,

but because of the primitive plumbing, the sites are less popular than some of the other state parks in the southern part of the state. A short nature trail circumnavigates the lake and crosses through several types of terrain, including swamp and hardwood forest, as well as passing over a glacial esker, or curious rogue ridge.

Open: Mid-May through Labor Day.

110 Grout Pond

Location: West of Stratton in the Green Mountain National Forest; Southern Vermont map page 281, grid e2.

Campsites, facilities: There are nine primitive campsites, four accessible by canoe, one suitable for wheelchair users, and three with lean-tos. A cabin with a fireplace is available year-round. Water can be obtained from a hand pump but should be treated before drinking. Outhouses are provided. Leashed pets with rabies vaccination certification are permitted.

Reservations, fees: Sites are available on a first-come, first-served basis. There is no fee.

Contact: Green Mountain National Forest, Manchester Ranger District, RR 1, Box 1940, Manchester Center, VT 05255; (802) 362-2307.

Directions: From West Wardsboro east of Arlington, travel seven miles west through the town of Stratton on Route 100. Turn left on Grout Pond Road and proceed to the campsites.

Trip notes: Like pearls, these tent sites are strung along the shoreline of small, pristine Grout Pond. Aside from fire rings and a few lean-tos, there are no amenities. But you will find an abundance of peace and quiet disturbed only by the sounds of frogs, birds, and other wildlife. Beavers have established a lodge at the south end of the pond, while other nooks and crannies house sunfish, yellow perch, and a few wise bass. Easy hiking trails circle the pond and lead south to Somerset Reservoir. If you are looking for a backwoods respite without having to backpack in, this is a good choice.

Open: Year-round.

---

111 Townshend State Park

Location: On the West River north of Townshend; Southern Vermont map page 281, grid e3.

Campsites, facilities: There are 34 sites for tents and RVs, four with lean-tos. There are no hookups or dump stations. Flush toilets, metered hot showers, picnic tables, and fire rings are provided. Ice and firewood are available. Leashed pets with rabies vaccination certification are permitted, but not in day-use areas.

Reservations, fees: Reservations are recommended. Sites are $10 to $14 a night for four people. Each additional person four years and older will be charged $3 at a tent site and $4 at a lean-to. The maximum allowable number of people at a site is eight, and there must be at least one person 18 years of age or older with each camping party. See also page 284.

Contact: Townshend State Park, RR 1, Box 2650, Townshend, VT 05353; (802) 365-7500.

Directions: From Brattleboro, take exit 2 to Route 30 and travel north for 15 miles. Turn left on State Forest Road, bearing right after four-tenths of a mile. The state park road is ahead on the left.

Trip notes: Set along the West River, the campsites in Townshend State Park are favored by canoeists and anglers alike. Rainbow and brown trout live in this waterway. The U.S. Army Corps of Engineers maintains a dam and recreation area north of the state forest, and during water releases in spring and fall, the river offers exciting white-water canoeing for intermediate and expert paddlers. A loop trail leads from the campground to the summit of Bald Mountain (1,680 feet) through a forest of hemlock, white pine, and mixed hardwoods. Along the trail are waterfalls, chutes, and pools. Views to the north, south, and east await on the summit. The Scott Covered Bridge spans the West River on the approach to the campground and is open to foot traffic only. There's a beach for swimming and a boat ramp for larger vessels at the recreation area north of the forest.

Open: Mid-May through early October.

---

112 Bald Mountain Campground

Location: On the West River in Townshend; Southern Vermont map page 281, grid e3.

Campsites, facilities: There are 200 sites for tents and RVs, 16 with full hookups and 184 with water and electric hookups. Each site has a picnic table and fire ring. There are group sites for tents and RVs, and a separate tenting area. Air conditioners are allowed, but heaters are not. Facilities include a dump station, laundry machines, hot showers, rest rooms, a rec hall, playground, horseshoe pits, a swimming pool, volleyball and badminton, and a basketball hoop. RV storage, LP gas, limited groceries, ice, and firewood are available. Leashed pets are permitted.

Reservations, fees: Reservations are accepted. Sites are $16 to $18 a night per family.

Contact: Bald Mountain Campground, RR 1, Box 2658, State Park Road, Townshend, VT 05353; (802) 365-7510.

Directions: From Brattleboro, take exit 2 to Route 30 and travel north for 15 miles. Turn left on State Forest Road, bearing right after four-tenths of a mile. The campground is 1.3 miles ahead.

Trip notes: Meadows and forest make up the landscape at Bald Mountain Campground. Formerly used for farming, this parcel offers sites on the West River or beside a beaver pond, sites in wooded areas, and open spaces with mountain views. Swimming, tubing, and fishing are popular river activities here. Miles of dirt roads ideal for mountain biking surround the campground and neighboring Townshend State Park, and two hiking trails leave the park and ascend Bald Mountain. The hike climbs 1,100 vertical feet and features waterfalls, chutes, and pools along the way. The Scott Covered Bridge, built in 1870, spans the West River just north of the campground and state park.

Open: Late April through Columbus Day.

⑬ Camperama Family Campground

Location: On the West River in Townshend; Southern Vermont map page 281, grid e3.

Campsites, facilities: There are 218 sites for tents and RVs, 52 with full hookups and 166 with water and electric hookups. Each site has a table and fire ring. Air conditioners are allowed, but heaters are not. Facilities include a dump station, laundry, grocery store, free hot showers, rest rooms, a rec hall, playground, horseshoe pits, two shuffleboard courts, a pool, volleyball and badminton, and a basketball hoop.

Cable TV, RV supplies, LP gas, ice, and wood are available. Leashed pets are permitted.

Reservations, fees: Reservations are recommended; call (800) 63CAMPS. Sites start at $18 a night per family.

Contact: Camperama Family Campground, Depot Road, Townshend, VT 05353; (802) 365-4315.

Directions: From the junction of Routes 30 and 35 in Townshend, travel three-quarters of a mile south on Route 30, then turn right and drive a quarter mile west on Depot Road. The campground is just ahead after you cross the river.

Trip notes: With cows for company, you'll camp alongside a river and have access to full RV amenities at Camperama. Bordered by a barnyard on one side and the West River on another, the campsites are well shaded, and many enjoy mountain views. Sites 148 through 175 are right on the river, and all campers are encouraged to fish and swim in the refreshing current. A short drive to the north is Townshend State Park, complete with hiking trails. From the dam above the park to Interstate 91 in Brattleboro, the river offers white-water canoeing for intermediate or better paddlers during water releases in the spring and fall.

Open: Mid-April through mid-October.

⑭ Kenolie Village

Location: In Newfane on the West River; Southern Vermont map page 281, grid e3.

Campsites, facilities: There are 100 sites for tents and RVs, 80 with water and electric hookups, and six sites just for tents. Flush toilets, hot showers, a dump station, playground, pavilion, rec hall, and laundry facilities are provided. LP gas, limited groceries, ice, and firewood are available. Leashed pets are permitted.

Reservations, fees: Reservations are recommended. Sites start at $12 a night for two people.

Contact: Stella and Ken Dowley, Kenolie Village, Route 30, Newfane, VT 05345; (802) 365-7671.

Directions: From Townshend, travel southeast on Route 30 for 3.5 miles to the campground entrance on the left.

Trip notes: Designed with RVers in mind, these sites are located in the West River Valley, and many look out onto the surrounding Green Mountains. Campers can fish and swim in the refreshing West River or take a short drive north to Townshend State Park, where multiuse trails attract bikers and hikers. The U.S. Army Corps of Engineers maintains a dam and recreation area north of the state forest, and when they release water in the spring and fall the river is an exciting place for intermediate and expert paddlers to canoe.

Open: April 1 through December 1.

115 Brattleboro North KOA

Location: South of Putney on U.S. 5; Southern Vermont map page 281, grid e3.

Campsites, facilities: There are 42 sites for tents and RVs, 12 with full hookups, 29 with water and electric hookups, and 1 with none. Each site has a shade tree, picnic table, and charcoal grill. Use of air conditioners and heaters is allowed. Facilities include a dump station, laundry, a pool, limited groceries, free hot showers, rest rooms, a rec hall, playground, horseshoe pits, volleyball court, and basketball hoop. Ice and wood are available. Leashed pets are permitted.

Reservations, fees: Reservations are strongly recommended. Sites are $23 to $26 a night for two people.

Contact: Brattleboro North KOA, RFD 2, Box 560, Putney, VT 05346; (802) 254-5908 or reservations (800) 562-5909.

Directions: From Interstate 91 north of Brattleboro, take exit 3 and travel 3.5 miles north on U.S. 5 to the campground entrance on the right.

Trip notes: Against a backdrop of Vermont's famous green hills, each of these campsites has a manicured plot of grass and a shade tree. The roomy sites are separated by gravel roads but have no natural buffers, so privacy is at a minimum. Super-clean facilities add to the civilized feel; this is a good choice for travelers who want to regroup before heading to wilder destinations. Nearby tourist attractions include Basketville, a specialty store featuring all manner of woven works, and Santa's Land, a theme park with rides, elves, Santa's workshop, and real reindeer to feed; both are just north of Putney.

Open: Mid-April to late October.

116 Hidden Acres Campground

Location: North of Brattleboro; Southern Vermont map page 281, grid e3.

Campsites, facilities: There are 87 sites for tents and RVs, 11 with full hookups, 56 with water or water and electric, and 20 with none. Each site has a picnic table and fire ring. Group sites are available for tents and RVs. Use of air conditioners and heaters is allowed. Facilities include a dump station, hot showers, and rest rooms. Also on the property are a pool, miniature golf, nature trails, shuffleboard, basketball and volleyball courts, and horseshoe pits. RV storage, limited groceries, ice, and firewood are available. Leashed pets are permitted.

Reservations, fees: Reservations are

recommended and require a nonrefundable deposit. Tent sites are $17 to $19 a night for two people, and RV and trailer sites are $21 to $23 a night for two people. Monthly and seasonal rates are available.

Contact: The Shorts, Hidden Acres Campground, Route 5, Box 401A, Brattleboro, VT 05301; (802) 254-2098 or (802) 254-2724.

Directions: From Interstate 91 north of Brattleboro, take exit 3 and travel 2.5 miles north on U.S. 5 to the campground entrance on the left.

Trip notes: This full-service RV park has mostly open and many pull-through sites near the interstate. It's a good choice for travelers heading north who need to stop for the night. Families can keep busy with all the on-site recreation and nearby tourist attractions, especially the Santa's Land theme park a short drive north. The Connecticut River is conveniently close for people who enjoy fishing and boating. For those who like river cruising in a more leisurely style, there's the *Belle of Brattleboro*, a small-scale, open-air, motor-driven cruise boat that offers a variety of tours on the river separating Vermont and New Hampshire. Knowledgeable captains share history about the town of Brattleboro and the river itself.

Open: May 1 through mid-October.

⑪⑦ Red Mill Campground

Location: East of Bennington in the Green Mountain National Forest; Southern Vermont map page 281, grid e2.

Campsites, facilities: There are 31 tent sites, some of which will accommodate small trailers. Pit toilets, piped water, tent pads, grills, and tables are provided. Sites are wheelchair accessible with assistance.

Reservations, fees: Sites are available on a first-come, first-served basis. There is no fee, but donations are accepted.

Contact: Green Mountain National Forest, Manchester Ranger District, RR 1, Box 1940, Manchester Center, VT 05255; (802) 362-2307.

Directions: From Bennington, travel east on Route 9 for 10 miles to the campground entrance.

Trip notes: Wooded campsites are set along Red Mill Brook in an area known for its many beaver ponds that are home to native brook trout. At-risk youth from Bennington help maintain the area in summertime to earn high school credits through the ACE (Alternative Community Experience) program. Just to the west of the campground is the Long Trail, which makes this a good base camp for backpacking excursions into the Green Mountains.

Open: May 15 through late fall.

⑪⑧ Woodford State Park

Location: East of Bennington; Southern Vermont map page 281, grid e2.

Campsites, facilities: There are 103 sites for tents and RVs including 20 lean-tos, all without hookups. Facilities include a dump station, flush toilets, metered hot showers, piped water, picnic tables, fireplaces, a playground, and boat ramp. Firewood is available, and there's a store nearby. Leashed pets with rabies vaccination certification are permitted, but not in day-use areas.

Reservations, fees: Reservations are recommended. Sites are $12 to $16 a night for four people. Each additional person four years and older will be charged $3 at a tent site and $4 at a lean-to. The maximum allowable number of people at a site is eight, and there must be at least one person 18 years of age or older with each camping party. See also page 284.

Contact: Woodford State Park, HCR 65, Box 928, Bennington, VT 05201; (802) 447-7169.

Directions: From Bennington, travel 10 miles east on Route 9 to the park entrance.

Trip notes: Adams Reservoir, which is open to nonmotorized boating and swimming, is the focal point of Woodford State Park. Campsites are set in two heavily wooded areas east of the reservoir. The park is perched on a plateau at an elevation of 2,400 feet and supports stands of high-elevation spruce, fir, and birch trees. A 2.7-mile trail loops around the reservoir, while more trails are available in the surrounding Green Mountain National Forest.

Open: Mid-May through early October.

119 Greenwood Lodge and Campsites

Location: East of Bennington; Southern Vermont map page 281, grid e2.

Campsites, facilities: There are 26 sites for tents and RVs, six of which have water and electric hookups. Each site has a fire ring, picnic table, and trash container. Flush toilets, hot showers, and a dishwashing sink are provided. Also on the property are horseshoe pits, a playing field, and a volleyball court. Supplies can be purchased across the street at True's General Store. Quiet, leashed pets are allowed, but their owners must pick up after them.

Reservations, fees: Reservations are recommended. A 100 percent deposit is required for the first three nights and 50 percent for each consecutive night. Sites start at $13 a night for two people with surcharges for extra campers, firewood, and hookups.

Contact: Ed and Ann Shea, Greenwood

Lodge and Campsites, P.O. Box 246, Bennington, VT 05201; (802) 442-2547.

Directions: From Bennington, travel eight miles east on Route 9 to the Prospect Mountain Ski Area sign on the south side of the road. The entrance to the campground is off the ski area entrance; follow the signs.

Trip notes: Two ponds on the property are open to swimming, boating, fishing, and canoeing. The campground is operated in conjunction with a lodge that offers rooms and meal plans in a rustic, home-style atmosphere. Campsites are secluded, set in a wooded, mountaintop glen; some are right on the ponds, and a small number of sites near the lodge have water and electric hookups. The facility is adjacent to the Green Mountain National Forest and is three miles from the Appalachian Trail, both of which offer excellent hiking and backpacking. If you're a history buff, head north to Bennington: the town's museum houses what is thought to be the oldest surviving Stars and Stripes, flown at the Battle of Bennington in 1777.

Open: May through the fall foliage season.

120 Pine Hollow Campground

Location: South of Bennington; Southern Vermont map page 281, grid f1.

Campsites, facilities: There are 50 sites for tents and RVs, 16 with full hookups and 34 with water and electric. Each site has a picnic table and fire ring. A dump station, playground, cable TV hookups, rest rooms, metered hot showers, boat rentals, and group areas are available. On the property you'll find shuffleboard and badminton courts, a sports field, volleyball, and horseshoe pits. Quiet, leashed pets are allowed.

Reservations, fees: Reservations are recommended and require a nonrefundable deposit. Sites start at $12 to $16 a night.

Contact: Ronald and Rachel Lauzon, Pine Hollow Campground, RD 1, Box 343, Pownal, VT 05261; (802) 823-5569.

Directions: From the junction of Route 9 and U.S. 7 in Bennington, travel six miles south on U.S. 7, then 1.5 miles east on Barbers Pond Road. Turn right on Old Military Road and drive three-quarters of a mile south, then turn right again and continue half a mile west to the campground.

Trip notes: Grassy meadows and mixed hardwoods meet at this campground on a spring-fed pond. Sites are compact and close together but have ample shade. Trout may be caught and released from the pond, which is also open to swimming and nonmotorized boating. Nearby is the southern starting point of the Long Trail, the country's first long-distance hiking route. Extending from the Massachusetts border into Canada, the Long Trail accesses 265 miles of rugged, scenic terrain. This southernmost section is shared with the 2,158-mile Appalachian Trail (see below) before it forks northeast in Sherburne Center.

Open: Mid-May through mid-October.

⑫ Appalachian Trail

Location: The trail runs north-south along the southern ridge of the Green Mountains to Sherburne Pass near Pico Peak, then veers west toward Hanover, New Hampshire, where it crosses the Connecticut River; Southern Vermont map page 281, grid f2.

Campsites, facilities: There are several dozen campsites along the 100-mile section of the Appalachian Trail (AT) that joins with the Long Trail at the Massachusetts border, none more than a moderate day hike apart. Some of these have lodges with

wood stoves, many have Adirondack-style lean-tos, and others are wooded tent sites. Primitive toilets are provided at most sites. On the 40-mile stretch from Sherburne Pass to Hanover, New Hampshire, Adirondack-style shelters are located no more than a moderate day hike apart. Most of the sites offer some kind of water source, as indicated in guides and on topographic maps, but not all are reliable or pure. Off-trail camping is allowed in the Green Mountain National Forest and on state-owned lands under an elevation of 2,500 feet. Leashed pets are permitted.

Reservations, fees: All sites are available on a first-come, first-served basis. Use of any overnight facility operated by the Green Mountain Club is limited to three consecutive nights. In the summer months, some of the more heavily used sites on the Long Trail portion of the AT are manned by caretakers and charge fees of $3 a night for Green Mountain Club members and $4 for nonmembers. Some of the sites on Green Mountain National Forest property charge a nightly fee.

Contact: The Green Mountain Club, Route 100, RR 1, Box 650, Waterbury Center, VT 05677; (802) 244-7037. Appalachian Trail Conference, P.O. Box 807, Harper's Ferry, WV 25425; (304) 535-6331. The nonprofit Appalachian Trail Conference publishes 10 sectional guides, which are accompanied by topographic maps.

Directions: To reach the southern starting point of the Appalachian Trail, from the junction of U.S. 7 and Route 2 at the traffic circle in Williamstown, Massachusetts, travel three miles east to a traffic light at Phelps Avenue. There is no parking at the trailhead; parking is available with permission at the Greylock Community Club one-tenth mile east of the trail or at the Holy Family Catholic Church adjacent to the AT.

Trip notes: From Springer Mountain in

Georgia to Mount Katahdin in Maine, the Appalachian Trail traverses the Appalachian Mountain chain on a 2,158-mile continuous, marked footpath. The trail and its adjacent lands—about 270,000 acres—link more than 75 parks and forests in 14 states, including eight units of the national forest system and six units of the national park system. Countless wild, scenic, historic, and pastoral settings are enjoyed along the footpath by "through-hikers"—those who typically start in Georgia and make a six-month trek to Maine—day hikers, and overnight backpackers. On average, fewer than 200 through-hikers complete the 2,000-mile journey each year.

For the first 100 miles north of the Vermont-Massachusetts border, the Appalachian Trail and Vermont's Long Trail (see campground number 33) share a common path. The Long Trail is the oldest long-distance hiking route in America and served as the inspiration for the Appalachian Trail; the 270-mile track follows the main ridge of the Green Mountains from the state line north to the Canadian border. At Sherburne Pass near Pico Peak, the trails diverge and the Appalachian Trail leads east while the Long Trail continues north. Most of the 100-mile stretch shared by the two trails is located in the Green Mountain National Forest. On a south-to-north route, the first major summit encountered is Glastonbury Mountain. From there, the trail ascends several peaks dominated by spruce groves and descends into a number of hardwood valleys. After topping out at Pico Peak, the trail travels across the low hills of the Green Mountains, passing through former farms and reverting woodlands. The trail crosses into New Hampshire from Norwich, Vermont, on a small bridge over the Connecticut River near the Dartmouth College boathouses.

Open: The Long Trail portion of the Appalachian Trail is open in summer, fall, and winter. Travel is discouraged during mud season, usually between late March and early May. The rest of the AT is open year-round. Hikers should note that use of the trail during mud season abets erosion.

122 Molly Stark State Park

Location: East of Wilmington; Southern Vermont map page 281, grid f2.

Campsites, facilities: There are 34 sites for tents and RVs including 10 lean-tos, all without hookups. Each site has a fireplace and picnic table. On the grounds are a dump station, playground, volleyball court, horseshoe pits, and a large group picnic pavilion. Ice, firewood, flush toilets, and metered hot showers are available. A general store and laundry facilities are located in Wilmington. Leashed pets with rabies vaccination certification are permitted; they are not allowed in day-use areas and may be restricted to certain areas within the campground.

Reservations, fees: Reservations are recommended. Sites are $10 a night and lean-tos are $14 a night for four people. Each additional person four years and older will be charged $3 at a tent site and $4 at a lean-to. The maximum allowable number of people at a site is eight, and there must be at least one person 18 years of age or older with each camping party. See also page 284.

Contact: Molly Stark State Park, Route 9, Wilmington, VT 05363; (802) 464-5460.

Directions: From Wilmington, travel east on Route 9 for three miles. Turn right into the state park entrance.

Trip notes: Open lawns, the surrounding woods, and Mount Olga to the east are part of the striking landscape at Molly Stark.

From the campground, a short hiking trail ascends Mount Olga (2,145 feet), where a fire tower on the summit is a popular destination during peak foliage season. The park's first structures (fireplaces and a toilet building) were built by the Civilian Conservation Corps in the 1930s. Route 9 and the park were named for Molly, the famous wife of General John Stark, a Revolutionary War hero who led troops to the Battle of Bennington in Vermont; it's said that she followed him to nurse the sick and wounded. On the 158-acre preserve, Beaver Brook offers the best cold-water fishing.

Open: Early May through mid-October.

123 Moss Hollow Campground

Location: West of Brattleboro; Southern Vermont map page 281, grid f3.

Campsites, facilities: There are 50 sites for tents and RVs with water and electric hookups. Each site has a fire ring and table. Flush toilets, hot showers, horseshoe pits, a dump station, and small store are provided. Ice and firewood are available. Leashed pets are permitted.

Reservations, fees: Reservations are recommended. Sites are $12 to $16 a night.

Contact: Mike Drummey, Moss Hollow Campground, RD 4, Box 723, Brattleboro, VT 05301; (802) 368-2418.

Directions: From Interstate 91 near Brattleboro, travel west on Route 9 for 1.4 miles. Turn left on Greenleaf Street and follow the paved road to its end. Cross the bridge to continue on the dirt road. After crossing three more concrete bridges, take the first right and drive to the campground entrance 300 feet ahead on the right.

Trip notes: A swimming hole and pools where campers can fish for trout are some of the perks at these rustic and private sites near a stream. On some weekends the owners offer hayrides through the countryside. Mountain bikers and hikers will find an abundance of dirt roads and trails that leave from the campground. In the summer, Mount Snow north of Wilmington swaps boards for bikes and becomes a fat-tire mecca. With more than 140 miles of trails, guided tours, lessons, and chairlift rides to the top (3,600 feet), the Mount Snow Mountain Bike Center appeals to riders of all skill levels; for information, call (802) 464-3333.

Open: May 15 through October 15.

124 Fort Dummer State Park

Location: Near the Connecticut River in Brattleboro; Southern Vermont map page 281, grid f3.

Campsites, facilities: There are 60 sites for tents and RVs including 10 lean-tos, all without hookups. Each site has a table and fireplace. A dump station, flush toilets, metered hot showers, and a playground are provided. Firewood is available. Leashed pets with rabies vaccination certification are permitted, but not in day-use areas.

Reservations, fees: Reservations are recommended. Sites are $10 to $14 a night. Each additional person four years and older will be charged $3 at a tent site and $4 at a lean-to. The maximum allowable number of people at a site is eight, and there must be at least one person 18 years of age or older. See also page 284.

Contact: Fort Dummer State Park, 434 Old Guilford Road, Brattleboro, VT 05301; (802) 254-2610.

Directions: From Interstate 91 in Brattleboro, take exit 1 and travel a tenth of a mile north on U.S. 5. Turn right on Fairground

Road and drive half a mile east. Take another right on Main Street and continue south for one mile to Old Guilford Road. The park entrance is just ahead.

Trip notes: Fort Dummer is a small park, only 217 acres. These sites are mostly open with some shade and afford access to nearby historic sites in Brattleboro as well as fishing and boating on the Connecticut River. There are hiking trails around the park.

Open: Mid-May through early September.

125 Connecticut River Canoe Sites

For more information on a series of canoe campsites along the Connecticut River, which forms the border between Vermont and New Hampshire, see campground number 25 on page 187 in the New Hampshire section.

Massachusetts

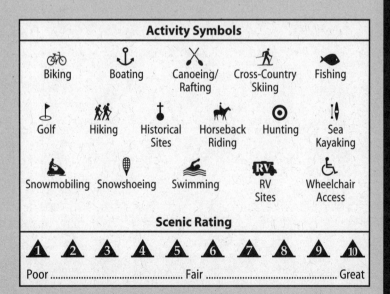

Activity Symbols

Biking	Boating	Canoeing/ Rafting	Cross-Country Skiing	Fishing
Golf	Hiking	Historical Sites	Horseback Riding	Hunting	Sea Kayaking
Snowmobiling	Snowshoeing	Swimming	RV Sites	Wheelchair Access

Scenic Rating

Poor .... Fair .... Great

Western Massachusetts

Adjoining Maps: North: Southern New Hampshire ...... *page 169*
Southern Vermont .... *page 281*
East: Eastern Massachusetts .... *page 355*
South: Connecticut .... *pages 448–449*

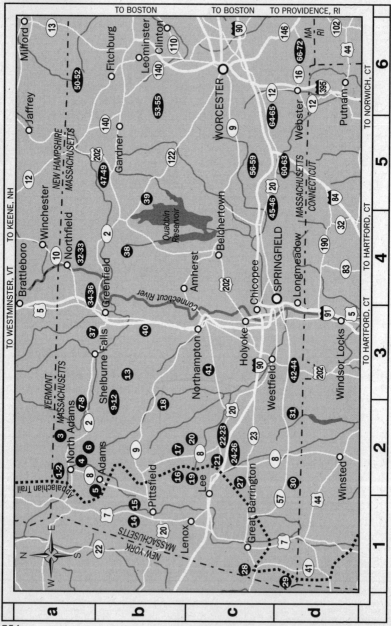

Eastern Massachusetts

Adjoining Maps: North: Southern New Hampshire .... *page* 169
East: Cape Cod/Martha's Vineyard ..... *page* 356
West: Western Massachusetts .... *page* 354

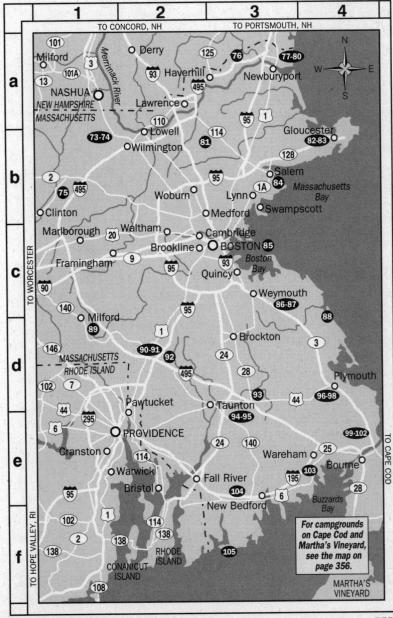

For campgrounds on Cape Cod and Martha's Vineyard, see the map on page 356.

355

Cape Cod/Martha's Vineyard

Adjoining Maps: East: Eastern Massachusetts .... *page 355*

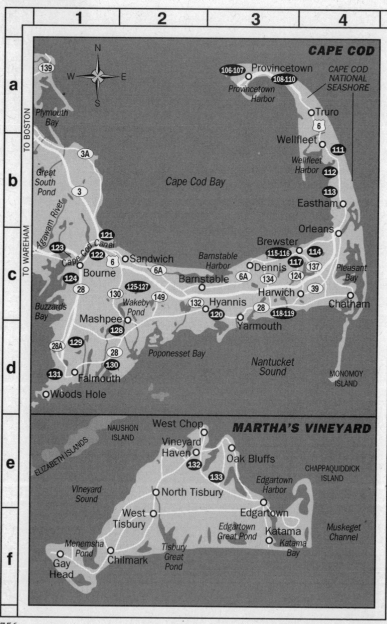

CAPE COD

139

N
W E
S

Plymouth
Bay

3A

Great
South
Pond

3

TO BOSTON

106-107 Provincetown
108-110

Provincetown
Harbor

CAPE COD
NATIONAL
SEASHORE

Truro
6

Wellfleet
111

Wellfleet
Harbor
112

113
Eastham

Cape Cod Bay

Orleans

Agawam River

TO WAREHAM

121
123
Cape Cod Canal
122
6 Sandwich

6A

Barnstable
Harbor

Brewster
115-116 114
117 137
Dennis
134 124

Pleasant
Bay

124
28
130

125-127
149

Wakeby
Pond

6A
Barnstable

132 Hyannis
120

Harwich
28 118-119

39

Chatham

Buzzards
Bay

Mashpee
128

Yarmouth

28A 129

28
130

Poponesset Bay

Nantucket
Sound

MONOMOY
ISLAND

131 Falmouth

Woods Hole

MARTHA'S VINEYARD

NAUSHON
ISLAND

West Chop

Vineyard
Haven
132

Oak Bluffs

CHAPPAQUIDDICK
ISLAND

ELIZABETH ISLANDS

133

Edgartown
Harbor

Vineyard
Sound

North Tisbury

West
Tisbury

Edgartown

Edgartown
Great Pond

Katama

Muskeget
Channel

Menemsha
Pond

Chilmark

Tisbury
Great
Pond

Katama
Bay

Gay
Head

Massachusetts features:

❶ Appalachian Trail

Location: From the Connecticut border in the south, the Appalachian Trail leads north through the Berkshires, over Mount Grey-lock, and on to the Vermont border where it intersects with the Long Trail; Western Massachusetts map page 354, grid a2.

Campsites, facilities: Lean-tos are located all along the Massachusetts portion of the trail, never more than a moderate day hike apart. Primitive toilets are provided. Current topographic maps show reliable and seasonal water sources. You'll find formal campsites at October Mountain and Beartown State Forests, Clarksburg State Park, and Mount Greylock State Reservation. Pets are permitted.

Reservations, fees: Lean-to sites are available on a first-come, first-served basis. Sometimes a nominal nightly fee is charged in summer. Check with the Appalachian Trail Conference for up-to-date fees and conditions.

Contact: Appalachian Trail Conference, P.O. Box 807, Harper's Ferry, VW 25425; (304) 535-6331. This nonprofit group publishes 10 sectional guides, which are accompanied by topographic maps.

Directions: In the western part of the state, the trail extends northward from Mount Everett State Reservation near the Connecticut border to Clarksburg State Park on the Vermont border. Easily accessible trailheads are on U.S. 7 in Sheffield, Route 8 south of Washington, Route 9 east of Dalton, Route 8 north of Cheshire, and Route 2 at Blackinton.

Trip notes: Some say the Berkshires are a state unto themselves. Geographically this is true, as the region is separated from the rest of Massachusetts by the low hills for which the area is named. This 87-mile-long portion of the Appalachian Trail hits the highlights of the Berkshires. Geologists claim that this region and the Green Mountains to the north are remnants of an ancient Cambrian sea, making them one of the oldest lands on earth, emerging some half a billion years ago. You may sense this timelessness when walking through second-growth forests, passing by chipper brooks and impromptu gorges, and summiting on Mount Greylock, which affords a sweeping view of western Massachusetts—all of which you'll experience on the Appalachian Trail.

Open: Year-round.

❷ Clarksburg State Park

Location: On the Vermont border in Clarksburg; Western Massachusetts map page 354, grid a2.

Campsites, facilities: There are 47 sites for tents and RVs, all without hookups. Each site has a picnic table and fire grill. Piped water, flush toilets, and hot showers are provided. Leashed pets are permitted.

Reservations, fees: Reservations aren't usually necessary except in late fall during leaf-peeping season. Sites are $6 a night.

Contact: Clarksburg State Park, Middle Road, Clarksburg, MA 02155; (413) 663-8469.

Directions: From Route 8 north of North Adams, turn left on Middle Road. Signs will lead you to the campground entrance on the right.

Trip notes: You'll fall asleep among a smorgasbord of hardwoods and red and white pines at this heavily forested campground. Clarksburg State Park consists mainly of mountain uplands overlooking the Hoosic River, which runs parallel to Route 8. The Appalachian Trail crosses the westernmost portion of the forest, and a network of trails carries hikers to altitudes between 1,000 and 2,000 feet. The hardwood mix makes this a popular spot during leaf season. Campers can fish, swim, and boat in nonmotorized craft (canoes and kayaks) on Mauserts Pond next to the campground. Trout fishing is excellent in the many streams that wind through the forestlands. Another plus is the newly built rest rooms.

Open: Mid-May through mid-October.

❸ Monroe State Forest

Location: East of North Adams; Western Massachusetts map page 354, grid a2.

Campsites, facilities: There are three hike-in sites with shelters but no facilities. Pets are allowed in the park.

Reservations, fees: Reservations are recommended. Sites are $5 a night.

Contact: Monroe State Forest Headquarters, c/o Mohawk Trail State Forest, P.O. Box 7, Charlemont, MA 01339; (413) 339-5504.

Directions: From North Adams, travel about four miles east on Route 2 to Tilda Hill Road. Continue east to the forest entrance two miles ahead.

Trip notes: Your backcountry camping experience in Monroe State Forest will most likely result in wildlife sightings. Campers here share the mountainous hardwood forest with deer, snowshoe hares, raccoons, woodcocks, and other small game and birds, as well as the occasional black bear. Nine miles of designated trails cross more than 4,000 acres at elevations up to 2,730 feet. Raycroft Lookout is a good vantage point from which to see the Deerfield River gorge. Dunbar Brook, which traverses the forest, is known for its many small falls and rapids. In the winter months, these trails are frequented by cross-country skiers and snowmobilers. Hunting and fishing are allowed in season, and the streams are stocked with trout.

Open: Year-round.

❹ Historic Valley Campground

Location: Southeast of North Adams on Windsor Lake; Western Massachusetts map page 354, grid a2.

Campsites, facilities: There are 103 large, wooded, and shaded sites for tents and RVs with water and electric hookups, plus a special wilderness section set aside for tents. Use of air conditioners and heaters is allowed. Facilities include rest rooms, laundry, a dump station, boat and canoe rentals, a lake beach with lifeguards, a pavilion, arcade, and scheduled activities. Firewood and ice are available. Motorcycles are prohibited. Dogs and cats are allowed but must be leashed at all times.

Reservations, fees: Reservations are recommended. Sites are $11 to $23 a night. Visitors, pets, air conditioners, and heaters are $2 extra per day. Weekly, monthly, and seasonal rates are available.

Contact: Historic Valley Campground, 10 Main Street, North Adams, MA 01247; (413) 662-3198.

Directions: From Route 2 approaching downtown North Adams from the east, turn onto East Main Street at Ed's Variety. After a quarter mile, take a quick left on Kemp Avenue. The campground is 1.5 miles ahead.

Trip notes: Windsor Lake is open to nonmotorized boating only, making it a peaceful spot to fish, canoe, and swim. Hiking trails surround the campground. Some of the RV sites are a little crowded, but the wilderness areas offer relief for tenters. The campground is centrally located to many attractions in western Massachusetts including the Mohawk Trail and Mount Greylock State Reservation. One bizarre wonder can be found at Natural Bridge State Park a half mile north of North Adams: a natural marble bridge spans Hudson Brook—beautiful evidence of 550 million years of erosion.

Open: May 15 through October 15.

❺ Mount Greylock State Reservation

Location: West of Adams; Western Massachusetts map page 354, grid a2.

Campsites, facilities: There are 35 sites for tents and RVs with no hookups or sewage disposal. Primitive toilets, piped water, picnic tables, and fireplaces are provided. Five group sites open to nonprofit organizations only can accommodate 25 people each. Backcountry lean-tos are open to backpackers for wilderness camping with no facilities. Leashed pets are permitted.

Reservations, fees: Reservations are recommended; lean-tos are first come, first served. Sites are $4 a night. Group sites must be reserved.

Contact: Mount Greylock State Reservation, P.O. Box 138, Route 7, Lanesborough, MA 01237; (413) 499-4262.

Directions: From the Massachusetts Turnpike (Interstate 90), take exit 2 to U.S. 20/7 west/north. Take this road north to Lanesborough and follow signs to the park.

Trip notes: This rustic setting at the foot of Stony Ledge is scenic and quiet. The campsites are located next to the Hopper, a protected region of old-growth forest with trees as old as 150 years. The Money Brook Trail crosses the Hopper from north to south and leaves from the campground.

Mountain biking is allowed on designated trails only; one route departs from West Mountain Road and connects to a paved road just before the summit of Mount Greylock, the state's tallest peak. Atop the mountain, you'll find the 92-foot War Veterans Memorial Tower. On a clear day, you can see the Green Mountains of Vermont to the north and the Adirondacks to the far west in New York. Since you can drive to the top, the summit gets crowded in the summer. The Appalachian Trail bisects the reservation, and there are several shelters for backpackers. Make sure you have a blueberry pail with you if you're here in late July.

Open: Memorial Day weekend through mid-October.

❻ Savoy Mountain State Forest

Location: North of Savoy; Western Massachusetts map page 354, grid a2.

Campsites, facilities: There are 45 sites for tents and RVs, all without hookups. Flush toilets, showers, piped water, picnic tables, and fireplaces are provided. A group site open to nonprofit organizations only can accommodate up to 50 people. Three cabins are also available. Leashed pets are permitted.

Reservations, fees: Reservations are recommended for cabins, which cost $16 a night and can sleep four people. Campsites are $6 a night. The group site must be reserved.

Contact: Savoy Mountain State Forest, RFD 2, North Adams, MA 02147; (413) 663-8469.

Directions: From Route 2 east of North Adams, travel south on Central Shaft Road and follow signs to the park entrance and the campground.

Trip notes: Encompassing more than 11,000 acres of forestland, Savoy Mountain is one of the state's largest undeveloped parcels. Its extensive system of trails designated for various uses attracts many kinds of outdoor enthusiasts. The terrain is rugged—most of the park is at an elevation of 2,000 feet or better—and trails lead to several peaks and points of interest such as Crooked Forest, a stand of misshapen trees most likely contorted by a severe ice storm. Colonists settled this tract of land, as evidenced by the cellar holes, stone walls, and family graveyards found throughout the forest. Campsites are set in an old apple orchard, so campers wake to the heady scent of apple blossoms in springtime. The woods also have a fruitful understory of blackberry, raspberry, and mountain laurel. You'll be camped out next to South Pond, one of two swimming ponds in the forest, which has a boat ramp. Streams and ponds in the area are stocked with trout for fishing.

Open: Memorial Day through mid-October. Cabins may be rented year-round.

---

❼ Mohawk Trail State Forest

Location: East of North Adams; Western Massachusetts map page 354, grid a2.

Campsites, facilities: There are 56 sites for tents and RVs, all without hookups. Sixteen sites are open for self-contained RVs year-round. One group site open to nonprofit organizations only can accommodate up to 50 people. Five cabins are also available. Flush toilets, showers, picnic tables, piped water, and fireplaces are available. Leashed pets are permitted.

Reservations, fees: Reservations are recommended for cabins, which are $16 to $20

a night. Campsites are $12 a night. The winter fee for self-contained RVs is $5 a night.

Contact: Mohawk Trail State Forest, P.O. Box 7, Route 2, Charlemont, MA 01339; (413) 339-5504.

Directions: From Charlemont, travel four miles west on Route 2 and follow signs to the campground.

Trip notes: Wooded sites by the Cold River offer campers plenty of wilderness and privacy. There's a swimming beach near the campground and good trout fishing in the Cold and Deerfield Rivers. Hiking trails leave from the far end of the campground and ascend both Clark and Todd Mountains. These trails are used by myriad woodspeople: horseback riders, bicyclists, hikers, anglers, and hunters. Hikers must yield to everybody, and bicyclists are asked not to skid to avoid startling horses. In addition to the thick forest of beech, birch, maple, oak, and assorted softwoods, the park is colored by seasonal wildflowers such as violets, orchids, and lilies of the valley. Mountain laurel, blueberries, and wild roses embellish the landscape in season. Bears inhabit these woods, as do foxes and raccoons, so be sure to securely pack up your foodstuff at night.

Open: Year-round for cabins and self-contained RVs, May 1 through Columbus Day for all other sites.

---

❽ Country Aire

Location: East of North Adams; Western Massachusetts map page 354, grid a2.

Campsites, facilities: There are 100 sites for tents and RVs, both open and shaded, all with water and electric hookups and 70 with additional sewer connections. Each site has a table and fire ring. Laundry facilities, hot showers, rest rooms, LP gas, and a dump station are provided. You'll find a pavilion, concrete swimming pool, horseshoe pits, a playground, and a camp store on site. Leashed pets are permitted.

Reservations, fees: Reservations are recommended. Sites are $16 to $20 a night.

Contact: Country Aire, P.O. Box 286, Charlemont, MA 01339; (413) 625-2996.

Directions: From Interstate 91 near Greenfield, take exit 26 and travel 13 miles west on Route 2 to Charlemont. The campground is directly behind the Oxbow Motel and Restaurant.

Trip notes: Homogeneous RV sites in mostly open fields are what you'll find at Country Aire. There are nature trails on the grounds, and the nearby Deerfield River offers swift water for canoeing, rafting, and tubing as well as spots for fishing.

Open: Year-round; fully operational May 15 through October 15.

⑨ Shady Pines Campground

🚶🏃🚣🎾🏊♿ 🚐 ⑥

Location: Northeast of Savoy; Western Massachusetts map page 354, grid b2.

Campsites, facilities: There are 150 sites for tents and RVs in a mix of grassy, open, and partially open settings, 38 with full hookups and the rest with water and electric. Each site has a picnic table and fire ring. You'll find RV storage, group sites, rest rooms, dump stations, laundry facilities, a limited grocery store, rec hall, pavilion, pool, and sports courts on the property. Ice and firewood are available. Group activities are planned on weekends. Seasonal sites are available. Leashed pets are permitted.

Reservations, fees: Reservations are recommended June 1 through Labor Day. Sites start at $20 a night for two people.

Contact: Bill and Edna Daniels, Shady Pines Campground, 547 Loop Road, Savoy, MA 02156; (413) 743-2694.

Directions: From the west junction of Routes 8A and 116, travel three miles east on Route 116 to the campground entrance on the left.

Trip notes: Campers are packed in a bit tightly at Shady Pines, where the open landscape of the grounds puts privacy at a minimum. Nature trails from the campground access thousands of acres of surrounding state-run forestlands and are used year-round by hikers, cross-country skiers, and snowmobilers. Dubuque Memorial State Forest lies to the north, Savoy Mountain State Forest to the northwest, and to the south is Windsor State Forest. On the weekends, the adults-only lounge on the premises features live bands and dancing.

Open: Year-round; fully operational May 1 through November 1.

⑩ Dubuque Memorial State Forest

🚴🏔🥾🎣🌽 ⑨
🚶🏇🎯🚣🌽

Location: South of West Hawley; Western Massachusetts map page 354, grid b2.

Campsites, facilities: There are three hike-in sites at designated backcountry pavilions with no facilities. Leashed pets are permitted.

Reservations, fees: Sites are available on a first-come, first-served basis; you should check in at forest headquarters off Route 8A to let them know about your overnight plans and to make sure there is room. There is no fee.

Contact: Dubuque Memorial State Forest, P.O. Box 7, Charlemont, MA 01339; (413) 339-5504.

Directions: From Route 2 near Charlemont, take Route 8A south to the park entrance on the left.

Trip notes: Backcountry enthusiasts will

love these sites set on rugged, heavily wooded land crossed by several brooks. Nearly 8,000 acres of forest are protected here and the camping pavilions are several miles into the thick of it, accessed via little-used roads. There are eight miles of designated hiking trails and another 35 miles of woods roads and bridle paths used by snowmobilers, mountain bikers, and skiers. Several ponds and streams can be fished for trout, perch, and pickerel. The forest is home to plentiful wildlife, including the occasional bear and coyote, so hunters flock here in season; know when to wear your blaze orange.

Open: Year-round.

⑪ Berkshire Green Acres

Location: Northeast of Plainfield Center; Western Massachusetts map page 354, grid b2.

Campsites, facilities: There are 190 sites, 180 with full hookups. Each site has a picnic table, fireplace, and concrete patio. Use of air conditioners and heaters is allowed. Seasonal sites are available, as are group sites for tents and RVs. Facilities include RV storage, a dump station, rec hall, sports fields and courts, a pool, and horseshoe pits. Some limited groceries, LP gas, gasoline, ice, and firewood are available. Motorcycles and leashed pets are permitted.

Reservations, fees: Reservations are recommended May through October. Sites start at $20 a night per family with surcharges for heaters and air conditioners.

Contact: The Bolduc Family, Berkshire Green Acres, Grant Street, Plainfield, MA 01019; (413) 634-5385.

Directions: From the east junction of Routes 116 and 8A, travel four miles southeast on Route 116 through Plainfield. Turn left on Bow Street. The campground en-

trance is one mile ahead.

Trip notes: Things can get pretty boisterous at this campground. You'll see groups of motorcyclists here in summer before the snowmobile clubs take over in winter. The many raucous planned activities include mud bog races, demolition derbies, and pig roasts in season. Sites—either open or partially shaded—aren't too private, as they're at the edge of open fields, but they are apropos for the kind of group antics enjoyed by most campers who frequent the place. Large banquet facilities, a restaurant, and a cocktail lounge are on the property.

Open: Year-round; fully operational May 1 through October 15.

⑫ Windsor State Forest

Location: Southeast of Savoy; Western Massachusetts map page 354, grid b2.

Campsites, facilities: There are 24 sites for tents and RVs with no hookups or dump stations. Primitive toilets, piped water, picnic tables, and fireplaces are provided. A group site open to nonprofit organizations only can accommodate up to 25 people. Leashed pets are permitted.

Reservations, fees: Reservations are recommended. Sites are $4 a night. The group site must be reserved.

Contact: Windsor State Forest, River Road, Windsor, MA 01270; (413) 663-8469.

Directions: From Interstate 91 at Northampton, take Route 9 west to West Cummington. Follow signs to River Road, which leads north into the forest.

Trip notes: Of the three large state forests in the immediate area—the other two are Dubuque Memorial and Savoy Mountain—Windsor is the smallest and affords the most privacy. You can easily drive or bike to the others to take advantage of their extensive trail systems, but for the most peace and quiet, you'll want to return here at the end of the day. Most RVers shy away from the campground with its unimproved facilities, so your neighbors will most likely be tenters. The forest is known for the Windsor Jambs, a gorge formed by the brook that is the outlet of Windsor Pond. It's also a popular spot to fish, swim, and canoe.

Open: Memorial Day weekend through Columbus Day.

⑬ D.A.R. State Forest

Location: Northwest of Northampton in Goshen; Western Massachusetts map page 354, grid b3.

Campsites, facilities: There are 50 sites for tents and RVs with no hookups or dump stations. Flush toilets, showers, piped water, picnic tables, and fireplaces are provided. A group site open to nonprofit organizations only can accommodate up to 75 people. Leashed pets are permitted.

Reservations, fees: Some sites can be reserved. Reservations should be made in person or by telephone between Monday and Friday, 9 A.M. to 4 P.M.; no reservations are taken for holidays. You can reserve up to six months in advance for stays of seven to 14 days and three months in advance for stays of two to six days. A deposit must be paid within two weeks of making the reservation. Sites are $6 a night. The group site is $16 and must be reserved. For self-contained RVs, the fee is $5 a night from mid-October through May 1.

Contact: D.A.R. State Forest, 555 East Street, Williamsburg, MA 01096; (413) 268-7098.

Directions: From Northampton, take Route 9 west to Goshen. Just past town, turn right and head north on Route 112,

following signs to the park entrance on the right side of the road.

Trip notes: Second-growth forest with an understory of mountain laurel, ferns, witch hazel, and blueberry makes up the attractive surroundings at the D.A.R. Campground, one of the state's most popular. Campsites are located next to Upper Highland Lake, complete with a large swimming beach and boat launch. Both Upper and Lower Highland Lakes are open for non-motorized boating. Bass, perch, and trout live in these waters, while deer, mink, and weasel make their home in the surrounding forest, which is traversed by hiking trails, dirt roads, and bridle paths. A trail leads from the far end of the campground to a fire tower. The campground is also near a nature center that conducts evening walks in the woods and around the pond. This is also the starting point for a three-mile self-guided nature trail.

Open: May 1 through Columbus Day; sites are open to self-contained RVs and groups year-round.

⑭ Pittsfield State Forest

Location: South of Hancock on the New York border; Western Massachusetts map page 354, grid b1.

Campsites, facilities: There are 31 sites for tents and RVs with no hookups or dump stations. Flush and primitive toilets, piped water, picnic tables, and fireplaces are provided. Two group sites open to nonprofit organizations only can accommodate up to 20 and 50 people, respectively. Leashed pets are permitted.

Reservations, fees: Reservations are required for group sites, which cost $16 a night. For regular sites, reservations are recommended in summer and the fee is $4 to $5 a night.

Contact: Pittsfield State Forest, Cascade Street, Pittsfield, MA 01201; (413) 442-8992.

Directions: From Pittsfield Center, take U.S. 20 west toward the New York border and follow signs to the park entrance on the right side of the road.

Trip notes: Hikers especially will enjoy camping at Pittsfield State Forest, where sites are woodsy and rustic. In all, about 30 miles of trails lead through woods punctuated by streams, waterfalls, and flowering shrubs. Mount Lebanon stands at the south end of the park; the Taconic Skyline Trail runs the entire length of the ridge, providing lots of ledges from which to enjoy the scenic, rolling Berkshire hills. Caves and rocky outcrops are one reason why bears seem to like it here. Berry Pond is stocked with trout, and a dam holds the water of Lulu Brook in a basin for swimming near the campground. At the campground there's also a three-quarter-mile paved trail that's popular with wheelchair users. In the northeast corner of the forest is Balance Rock, a 165-ton limestone rock balanced on a point of bedrock only three feet wide.

Open: Mid-May to mid-October, but 10 sites for self-contained RVs are available year-round.

⓯ Bonnie Brae Cabins and Campsites

Location: North of Pittsfield near Pontoosuc Lake; Western Massachusetts map page 354, grid b1.

Campsites, facilities: There are 42 sites for tents and RVs in a mix of open and shaded settings, 25 with full hookups and 17 with water and electric. Each site has a table and fireplace. On site you'll find a dump station, laundry facilities, a pool, and rest rooms. Leashed pets are permitted.

Reservations, fees: Reservations are recommended. Sites start at $23 a night for two people; each extra adult is $3, and each child is $1.

Contact: Richie and Sandy Halkowicz, Bonnie Brae Cabins and Campsites, 108 Broadway Street, Pittsfield, MA 01201; (413) 442-3754.

Directions: From Pittsfield, head north on U.S. 7 for three miles. Pontoosuc Lake will be on your left. Turn right on Broadway Street and drive to the campground.

Trip notes: If "nothing fancy" describes what you're looking for, give Bonnie Brae a try. There are no amenities to speak of, nor any disruptive group activities. This is low-key camping particularly suited to RVers. It's within striking distance of many of the area's major attractions, including Tanglewood (summer home of the Boston Pops Symphony Orchestra) in Lenox and the Hancock Shaker Village in Pittsfield. Also in Pittsfield is Arrowhead, Herman Melville's home from 1850 to 1863. This National Historic Landmark has an outstanding view of Mount Greylock to the north. Melville wrote that the mountain's shape reminded him of a whale and inspired him to write his epic tale *Moby Dick*.

Open: May 1 through October 31, but self-contained RVs are allowed year-round.

⓰ Fernwood Forest

Location: West of Hinsdale; Western Massachusetts map page 354, grid b2.

Campsites, facilities: There are 29 secluded woodland sites for tents and RVs, 20 with water and electric hookups. Each site has a fireplace and table. Rest rooms, free hot showers, a dump station, playground, horseshoe pits, sports fields, and game courts are available on the property. Ice and firewood are sold on the premises. Leashed pets are permitted.

Reservations, fees: Reservations are recommended. Tent sites are $12 a night, and sites with water and electric hookups are $15 a night.

Contact: Ward and Marion Tinney, Fernwood Forest, Box 896, Hinsdale, MA 01235; (413) 655-2292.

Directions: From Hinsdale proper, drive west on Michael's Road. Turn left on Plunkett Reservoir Road and continue to the campground.

Trip notes: Not only is Fernwood clean, quiet, and private, but the prices are just about the lowest in the Berkshires for sites with hookups. You can walk to a trout-stocked fishing hole, or swim and boat on Plunkett Reservoir.

Open: May 1 through October 15.

⓱ Bissellville

Location: South of Hinsdale; Western Massachusetts map page 354, grid b2.

Campsites, facilities: There are 35 sites for tents and RVs, all with water and electric hookups and 13 with additional sewer connections. Use of air conditioners and heaters is allowed. A pool, ballpark, laundry facilities, free hot showers, and dump station are located on the property. Campfires are allowed. Leashed pets are permitted.

Reservations, fees: Reservations are recommended. Sites start at $15 a night for two people with surcharges for air conditioners and heaters.

Contact: Eugene and Lorraine Brunet, Bissellville, 1109 Washington Road, Hinsdale, MA 01235; (413) 655-8396.

Directions: From the junction of Routes

8 and 143 in Hinsdale, head south for three miles on Route 8 to the campground.

Trip notes: Here's another tidy, quiet, private campground in the heart of the Berkshire hills. Sites are set on rural, wooded flatlands. These folks cater to visitors seeking the combination of arts, culture, history, and scenic beauty that the area offers, from the Shakespeare festivals held at The Mount (novelist Edith Wharton's home) in Lenox to the One Cell Town Jail in Chester. Bissellville remembers Israel Bissell, who is buried in a cemetery on Route 143 in Hinsdale. This unsung patriot outdid Paul Revere, galloping for five days to carry the news of Lexington to Connecticut, New York, and Philadelphia.

Open: Mid-May through mid-October.

⓲ Berkshire Park Camping Area

Location: Southeast of Worthington Corners; Western Massachusetts map page 354, grid b2.

Campsites, facilities: There are 90 sites for tents and RVs, 25 with water and electric hookups and the rest with none. Each site has a table and fireplace. There is no dump station. Facilities include sports courts, a playground, horseshoe pits, laundry, rest rooms, and free hot showers. Firewood is available on the premises. Leashed pets are permitted.

Reservations, fees: Reservations are recommended. Sites start at $12.50 a night for two people. Seasonal rentals are encouraged; prices are available on request.

Contact: Bob and Dawn Brimmer, Berkshire Park Camping Area, P.O. Box 531, Harvey Road, Worthington, MA 01098; (413) 238-5918 or (800) 727-0067.

Directions: From the junction of Routes

112 and 143 at Worthington Corners, travel 1.2 miles southeast on Old Post Road to the campground.

Trip notes: Cool and woodsy, the campsites at Berkshire Park are well distanced from the kind of noise and traffic congestion that can clog the area in summer. Campers sleep beside a small pond where they can swim and fish. Nature trails leave from the campground. Right down the road at Chesterfield Gorge spectacular glacial action is evidenced by a 30-foot-deep canyon through which the waters of the Westfield River tumble past granite cliffs.

Open: May 1 through mid-October.

⑲ October Mountain State Forest

Location: East of Lenox; Western Massachusetts map page 354, grid c2.

Campsites, facilities: There are 50 sites for tents and RVs, all without hookups. Each site has a table and fireplace. Flush toilets, showers, piped water, and a dump station are provided. Leashed pets are permitted.

Reservations, fees: Reservations are accepted for the one wheelchair-accessible site; the rest are available on a first-come, first-served basis. Sites are $12 a night.

Contact: October Mountain State Forest, RR 2, Box 193, Lee, MA 01238-9563; (413) 243-1778.

Directions: From the Massachusetts Turnpike (Interstate 90) near Lee, take exit 2 and travel west on U.S. 20. Turn right on Center Street, which leads into the forest, following the signs.

Trip notes: October Mountain is the state's largest protected tract. On more than 16,000 acres you'll find trails for every level of experience, including a challenging section of the Appalachian Trail, which crosses

the forest. Campsites dot a sunny hillside and are broken out into three levels. The second and third levels are reserved for tents; hiking trails leave directly from the two upper areas. One of the most scenic hikes in the forest leads to Schermerhorn Gorge. Nonmotorized boating and fishing are best at Finerty Pond and Lake Felton. Once a privately owned game preserve, the forest remains a popular hunting destination, so wear blaze orange in season.

Open: Mid-May through mid-October.

⑳ Summit Hill Campground

Location: East of Becket; Western Massachusetts map page 354, grid c2.

Campsites, facilities: There are 106 sites for tents and RVs, 80 with water and electric hookups and 13 with additional sewer connections. Heaters and air conditioners are prohibited. On site you'll find a heated pool, rec hall, free hot showers, rest rooms, an adult lounge, sports courts, a dump station, and horseshoe pits. LP gas, ice, and firewood can be purchased on the premises. RV supplies and storage are available. Leashed pets are permitted.

Reservations, fees: Reservations require a $20 deposit. Sites start at $18 a night for two people.

Contact: Summit Hill Campground, Summit Hill Road, Washington, MA 01235; (413) 623-5761.

Directions: From Route 8 at Washington, get on Stonehouse Road by the town hall and continue until it turns into Summit Hill Road. From there, the campground is 1.7 miles away.

Trip notes: Summit Hill caters to seasonal campers, so you'll be rubbing elbows (literally, since sites are typically about 24 feet wide) with people who stay here every year. Backpackers have their own area, which is more private and natural. Sites are shaded and grassy, set in mountain woodlands, and there are nature trails on and around the property.

Open: May 1 through September 30.

㉑ Bonnie Rigg Camping Club

Location: In Becket; Western Massachusetts map page 354, grid c2.

Campsites, facilities: There are 210 wooded and open sites for tents and RVs with water and electric hookups. A dump station and honey wagon services are provided. Facilities include four rest rooms with free hot showers, a pool, TV lounge, rec hall, general store, playground, game room, and horseshoe pits. LP gas, ice, and firewood are sold on the premises. Leashed pets are permitted.

Reservations, fees: Reservations are recommended. Tent sites are $16 a night and RV sites are $20.

Contact: Bonnie Rigg Camping Club, P.O. Box 14, Chester, MA 01011-0014; (413) 623-5366.

Directions: From the Massachusetts Turnpike (Interstate 90) west of Springfield, take exit 3. Follow Route 10/202 south for two miles, then turn right onto U.S. 20 heading west. Continue to the junction with Route 8. The campground is at the crossroads.

Trip notes: Located at the intersection of two well-traveled roads, Bonnie Rigg is a member-owned campground that's open to nonmembers also. Most of the sites are in the woods, with 45 labeled as "safari sites"—open and grassy. Organized activities such as hayrides, horseshoe tour-

naments, a men's beauty contest in the summer, and a winter carnival in January make this a tight-knit community and encourage campers to meet one another.

Open: Year-round.

㉒ Walker Island Camping

Location: Just south of downtown Chester; Western Massachusetts map page 354, grid c2.

Campsites, facilities: There are 85 sites for tents and RVs; 60 have water and electric hookups, and 28 of those also have sewer connections. Each site has a table and fireplace. Facilities include a dump station, laundry, free hot showers, a heated pool, miniature golf, horseshoe pits, a store, rec hall, game room, snack bar, and RV storage. LP gas and firewood are available on site. Cable TV is also offered. Leashed pets are permitted.

Reservations, fees: Reservations are recommended in July and August. Sites start at $20 a night for two people.

Contact: Walker Island Camping, P.O. Box 131, Chester, MA 01011; (413) 354-2295.

Directions: From the junction of Route 8 and U.S. 20, travel east on U.S. 20 for 2.25 miles to the campground.

Trip notes: Mountain streams border the campsites at Walker Island. Choose from secluded tent sites or equipped RV sites shaded by maple trees and other hardwoods, and, if you have a sweet tooth, sample the syrup (made from trees on the property) in the sugar shack by the office. Swimmers can take a dip in the streams or in the heated pool on the premises. Trails leave the campground and ascend rocky ledges and mountain lookouts. Organized activities are offered all season long, many especially for kids, from parades to theme meals.

Open: April 15 through October 15.

㉓ Chester-Blandford State Forest

Location: In Chester; Western Massachusetts map page 354, grid c2.

Campsites, facilities: There are 15 campsites in mountainous woodlands. Primitive toilets, piped water, picnic tables, and fireplaces are provided. Leashed pets are permitted.

Reservations, fees: Sites are available on a first-come, first-served basis and cost $4 a night.

Contact: Chester-Blandford State Forest, P.O. Box 371, Huntington, MA 01050; (413) 354-6347.

Directions: From the Massachusetts Turnpike (Interstate 90) west of Springfield, take exit 3. Follow Route 10/202 south for two miles, then turn right on U.S. 20 heading west. Pass through Huntington and follow signs to the state forest entrance.

Trip notes: You'll hear some traffic noise as you fall asleep under the mixed hardwood canopy, since the campground is located directly off U.S. 20. Once you penetrate the 2,000-plus acres of Chester-Blandford, however, those sounds will soon be forgotten. Trails and forest roads offer challenging and sometimes steep hiking. A paved road leads to Sanderson Brook, which is graced with a 100-foot cascade about a quarter mile from the parking area. This small campground is popular in spring and early summer with anglers who come to try their luck in the trout-stocked streams. You'll need to arrive early then to secure a spot.

Open: Mid-May through Columbus Day.

㉔ Laurel Ridge Camping Area

Location: West of the Otis Reservoir in East Otis; Western Massachusetts map page 354, grid c2.

Campsites, facilities: There are 140 sites for tents and RVs, all with water and electric hookups. Each site has a picnic table and fireplace. Facilities include a dump station, hot showers, rest rooms, a store, pool, rec hall, game room, playground, and snack bar. There's also a basketball court and horseshoe pits. LP gas, firewood, and RV storage are available. Campers can borrow sports equipment. Leashed pets are permitted.

Reservations, fees: Reservations are recommended in July and August. Sites start at $17 a night for two people, with surcharges for guests and children.

Contact: Laurel Ridge Camping Area, P.O. Box 519, East Otis, MA 01029; (413) 269-4804.

Directions: From East Otis Center on Route 23, take Old Blandford Road south for three-quarters of a mile.

Trip notes: Large, flat, wooded campsites near the Otis Reservoir and on the border of Tolland State Forest are perfect for family camping. Some open, grassy safari sites are available, too. Campers can take motorboats out on the reservoir, using a boat ramp located one mile from Laurel Ridge. See the listing for Tolland State Forest (campground number 25) for information on fishing and hiking in the area.

Open: Mid-May through Columbus Day.

㉕ Camp Overflow

Location: West of the Otis Reservoir in

East Otis; Western Massachusetts map page 354, grid c2.

Campsites, facilities: There are 100 sites for tents and RVs, 50 with water and electric hookups. Each site has a picnic table and fireplace. Facilities include dump stations, hot showers, a camp store, firewood, a rec hall, playground, snack bar, sports courts, and boat rentals. Seasonal rentals are available, but there is no on-site RV storage. Leashed pets are permitted.

Reservations, fees: Reservations are recommended. Sites start at $16 a night for two people, plus 50 cents for each child under 18. There are $3 surcharges for overnight visitors and electric hookups.

Contact: Camp Overflow, P.O. Box 645, Otis, MA 01253; (413) 269-4036.

Directions: From the Massachusetts Turnpike (Interstate 90) in Westfield, take exit 3 and drive south on Route 10/202. After a short distance, turn right and head west on Route 23. Continue to Reservoir Road and follow signs to the campground down Tolland Road. The entrance will be on your right.

Trip notes: Overflow has some open safari-type sites as well as more wooded spots, though they tend to be close together. A large contingent of seasonal campers makes up the clientele of this campground each year. That's because the Otis Reservoir is right across the street, offering excellent fishing and waters that are open to motorboating, and the streams and hills of Tolland State Forest are right down the road. Boats are available for rent at the campground.

Open: May 15 through October 1.

㉖ Tolland State Forest

Location: Near the Otis Reservoir; Western Massachusetts map page 354, grid c2.

Campsites, facilities: There are 90 sites for tents and RVs with no hookups. Facilities include a dump station, flush toilets, showers, piped water, picnic tables, and fireplaces. Five group sites are open to nonprofit organizations. There's a boat ramp on the reservoir. Leashed pets are permitted.

Reservations, fees: Reservations are recommended, and are required for groups; reserve by phone or in person. Sites are $6 a night.

Contact: Tolland State Forest, P.O. Box 342, East Otis, MA 01029; (413) 269-6002.

Directions: From the Massachusetts Turnpike (Interstate 90) in Westfield, take exit 3 and drive south on Route 10/202. After a short distance, turn right and head west on Route 23. Follow signs to Reservoir Road and the campground.

Trip notes: This woodsy campground set in the north end of the state forest enjoys a locale on a lake peninsula. Thirty-five of the sites are right on the shore, and all campers have access to a beach and boat ramp. Anglers can try for trout, bass, bluegill, perch, and pickerel, while boaters with motorized craft can zip around the reservoir unhindered by speed limits. Ten miles of multiuse trails border the forest. A wide variety of birds lives in the area, including owls, blue herons, purple finches, and ruby-throated hummingbirds.

Open: Mid-May through mid-October.

㉗ Beartown State Forest

Location: Southeast of Stockbridge; Western Massachusetts map page 354, grid c2.

Campsites, facilities: There are 12 sites for tents and RVs with no hookups. Primitive toilets, piped water, and picnic tables are provided. One group site open to non-profit organizations only can accommodate up to 100 people; groups are required to bring a commercial, portable toilet. Leashed pets are permitted.

Reservations, fees: Reservations are required for the group site. All others are available on a first-come, first-served basis. Sites are $4 a night.

Contact: Beartown State Forest, P.O. Box 97, Blue Hill Road, Monterey, MA 01245; (413) 528-0904.

Directions: From the Massachusetts Turnpike (Interstate 90) near Lee, take exit 2 and head east on U.S. 20. Get on Route 102 and drive west to Stockbridge, then take U.S. 7 south to Route 23 heading east. Turn left on Blue Hill Road and follow signs to the forest.

Trip notes: Spacious and wooded, these campsites in the foothills of the Hoosac Range are in high demand in spring and early summer; get here early if you want to spend the night. RVs tend to have trouble ascending the winding road to the campground, so you'll find mostly backpackers here. At the forest center, Mount Wilcox (2,150 feet) stands surrounded by trout-filled streams that lure anglers to their banks. You can swim in Benedict Pond below the campsites; the 1.5-mile loop trail around the shore is picturesque in any season. All-terrain vehicles and snowmobiles are permitted on the forest's multiuse trails, so skiers and hikers should use caution. The Appalachian Trail crosses the forest on a north-south track for five miles.

Open: Mid-May through Columbus Day; self-contained RVs are welcome year-round.

28 Prospect Lake Park

Location: In North Egremont; Western Massachusetts map page 354, grid c1.

Campsites, facilities: There are 120 sites for tents and RVs with water and electric hookups, 15 of which have additional sewer connections. Each site has a fire ring and picnic table. Facilities include dump stations, laundry, a rec hall, playground, sports courts, boat rentals, and snack bar. Metered LP gas; a camp store selling firewood, ice, and bait; RV storage; and seasonal sites are available. You'll find hot showers and rest rooms at four locations. Leashed pets are permitted.

Reservations, fees: Reservations are recommended. Sites range from $22 to $26 a night for two people. Monthly and seasonal rates are available.

Contact: Prospect Lake Park, Prospect Lake Road, North Egremont, MA 02152; (413) 528-4158.

Directions: From the junction of Routes 71 and 23 in southwestern Massachusetts, travel three miles west on Route 71 to Prospect Lake Road. Turn left here and drive less than a mile to the park entrance on the right.

Trip notes: Some of the either open or shaded sites are right on Prospect Lake, making this a good choice for campers who enjoy swimming, boating, or fishing. A lovely picnic area is shaded by tall cathedral pines. Scheduled activities include bingo, dances, potluck suppers, and live music.

Open: Early May through Columbus Day.

29 Mount Washington State Forest

Location: West of Route 41 in the southwesternmost corner of the state; Western Massachusetts map page 354, grid d1.

Campsites, facilities: There are 15 wilderness campsites for tents with no facilities. The park does have rest rooms. Leashed pets are permitted.

Reservations, fees: Sites are available on a first-come, first-served basis; you should check in at forest headquarters on East Street in Mount Washington to let them know about your overnight plans and to make sure there is room. Sites are $3 a night.

Contact: Mount Washington State Forest, East Street, Mount Washington, MA 01258; (413) 528-0330.

Directions: From the Massachusetts Turnpike (Interstate 90) near Lee, take exit 2 and head east on U.S. 20. Get on Route 102 and drive west. Head south on U.S. 7, then take Route 23 west to Route 41. Drive south on Route 41 for about 300 feet to the park entrance.

Trip notes: The rocky ledges and steep slopes of this forest attract campers in summertime, when the sites tend to fill up. Bash Bish Falls, a cascade of water that tumbles through a series of gorges and drops 60 feet over the falls and into a sparkling pool, is a tourist magnet in these parts. Just east of the forest boundary is Bartholomew's Cobble, a limestone cobble foundation that supports boulder ledges, craggy outcrops, and stone sculptures. Here, foot trails wind along hemlock-covered slopes. For a million-dollar view of western Massachusetts at a bargain basement "price," make an ascent of 2,624-foot Mount Everett in an auto: from the village of Mount Washington, follow signs to the Mount Everett Reservation past Guilder Pond, one of the highest lakes in the state.

Open: Year-round.

🉑 Sandisfield State Forest

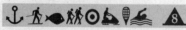

Location: West of Sandisfield; Western Massachusetts map page 354, grid d2.

Campsites, facilities: There are 10 wilderness campsites with no facilities. Rest rooms are available at York Lake. Leashed pets are permitted.

Reservations, fees: Sites are available on a first-come, first-served basis; you should check in at forest headquarters on West Street in Sandisfield to let them know about your overnight plans and to make sure there is room. Sites are $3 a night.

Contact: Sandisfield State Forest, West Street, Sandisfield, MA 01255; (413) 528-0904.

Directions: From the Massachusetts Turnpike (Interstate 90) near Lee, take exit 2 to Route 102 and drive west. Head south on U.S. 7, then take Route 23 east to Route 57. Head south on Route 57, following signs to the forest entrance.

Trip notes: These "wilderness" campsites are just a short hike from the parking area. Surrounding hills and forests are laced with 20 miles of multiuse trails. Swimmers can plunge into York Lake, which is also open to nonmotorized boating and has a public boat ramp.

Open: Year-round.

🉛 Granville State Forest

Location: South of West Granville on the Connecticut border; Western Massachusetts map page 354, grid d2.

Campsites, facilities: There are 33 tent sites at two locations within the state forest. Halfway Brook offers hot showers, flush toilets, fireplaces, piped water, and picnic tables. Hubbard River has primitive toilets, piped water, fireplaces, and tables. Leashed pets are permitted.

Reservations, fees: Sites are available on a first-come, first-served basis. Halfway Brook sites are $6 a night, and those at Hubbard River are $4.

Contact: Granville State Forest, West Harland Road, Route 57, Granville, MA 01034; (413) 357-6611.

Directions: From the Massachusetts Turnpike (Interstate 90) at Westfield, take exit 3 and head south on Route 10/202. At the junction with Route 57, exit and drive west, following signs to the park entrance on West Harland Road.

Trip notes: If you're in the mood for more of a wilderness experience, definitely opt for the state forest's Hubbard River Camping Area, where sites are right on the shore with a backdrop of towering hemlocks growing on steep slopes flanking the brook. Swimming is allowed. The 2,000-plus-acre forest has been sculpted by streams that created ravines and drainages as they flowed to the Hubbard River. Hunters track deer, snowshoe hare, grouse, and woodcock, and the waterways are stocked with trout. The relatively easy Hubbard River Trail parallels the riverbed.

Open: May 1 through Columbus Day.

recommended June 15 through Labor Day. Sites start at $17 a night per family.

Contact: Al and Midge Williams, Wagon Wheel Camping Area, 909 Wendell Road, Warwick, MA 01378; (508) 544-3425.

Directions: From the junction of Routes 2 and 2A west of Orange, travel three-quarters of a mile east on Route 2A. Turn left and head north on Wendell Road for two miles to the campground entrance.

Trip notes: Lofty pines and simple, home-style attitudes make for an agreeable atmosphere at Wagon Wheel. In summer, the owners regularly book musical acts, comedians, and other performers who entertain in the recreation barn, while swingers young and old enjoy teeing off at the 18-hole miniature golf course on the property. Sites are clean and spacious, and the campground is surrounded by 5,000-acre Erving State Forest, which is traversed with a multiuse trail and road system.

Open: May 1 through Columbus Day.

32 Wagon Wheel Camping Area

Location: Northwest of Orange near Erving State Forest; Western Massachusetts map page 354, grid a4.

Campsites, facilities: There are 102 sites for tents and RVs, 91 with water and electric hookups and 31 with additional sewer connections. Each site has a table and fire ring. Dump stations and services are provided. Use of air conditioners and heaters is allowed. Facilities include laundry, sports courts and athletic fields, a store, pool, rec hall and game room, and RV storage. RV supplies, LP gas, ice, and firewood are available. There's also a traffic control gate. Well-behaved, leashed pets are allowed.

Reservations, fees: Reservations are

33 Erving State Forest

Location: East of Greenfield; Western Massachusetts map page 354, grid a4.

Campsites, facilities: There are 32 sites for tents and RVs with no hookups or dump station. Piped water, picnic tables, fireplaces, and primitive toilets are provided. Some of the day-use facilities are wheelchair accessible. There's also a boat ramp. Leashed pets are permitted.

Reservations, fees: Sites are available on a first-come, first-served basis and cost $4 a night.

Contact: Erving State Forest, RFD 1, Route 2A, Erving, MA 01364; (508) 544-3939.

Directions: From the town of Erving on

Route 2, travel half a mile east to Church Street. Turn left and follow signs to the campground.

Trip notes: Mountain bikers, you will find 12 miles of prime dirt roads in Erving State Forest that leave right from this campground; just be aware that you'll be sharing the paths with equestrians and hikers. Sites are spread out along a camp road in a mixed forest of oaks, white pines, and hemlocks. Next to the campground is Laurel Lake, a trout-stocked beauty that's open to motorboating, fishing, and swimming. A boat ramp is situated at one end of the lake, away from the swimming beach.

Open: May 1 through Columbus Day.

34 Traveler's Woods of New England

Location: Directly north of Greenfield; Western Massachusetts map page 354, grid a4.

Campsites, facilities: There are 79 sites for tents and RVs, seven with full hookups and 57 with water and electric. Dump stations and services are available. Facilities include a playground, laundry, rec hall, and game room. Firewood, ice, and RV supplies are available on the premises. Leashed pets are permitted.

Reservations, fees: Reservations are recommended. Sites are $10 to $16 a night.

Contact: Traveler's Woods of New England, P.O. Box 88, Bernardston, MA 01337; (413) 648-9105.

Directions: From Interstate 91 north of Greenfield, take exit 28 south and make a right turn onto Route 10. A quick left on River Road (after the Bernardston Auto Exchange) takes you to the campground entrance seven-tenths of a mile ahead.

Trip notes: These grassy sites beside the Falls River are in close proximity to the interstate. Anglers can cast a fishing line into the stream from the campground, though canoeists will have to look elsewhere for a put-in. Seasonal campers, too, will have to find someplace else to park their RVs; the campground is only for short-term stays.

Open: May 1 through the third week in October.

35 Barton Cove

Location: North of Greenfield on the Connecticut River; Western Massachusetts map page 354, grid a4.

Campsites, facilities: There are 23 family sites and two group sites for tents only. Showers, a rec area, ice, firewood, and canoe and rowboat rentals are available on the property. Leashed pets are permitted.

Reservations, fees: Reservations are recommended. Sites start at $12 a night.

Contact: Barton Cove, c/o Northfield Mountain, 99 Millers Falls Road, Northfield, MA 01360; (413) 863-9300.

Directions: From Interstate 91 at Greenfield, take exit 27 and travel four miles east on Route 2. Watch for the campground sign on your right.

Trip notes: Lovely, natural campsites are set along a wooded peninsula on the Connecticut River, part of a parcel of land that's maintained by the Northfield Mountain Recreation and Environmental Center. Campers have access to a nature trail featuring dinosaur footprints and nesting bald eagles. Another 25 miles of trails at the center are open for mountain biking and hiking. Staff members teach outdoor courses in orienteering, guide riverboat cruises and power-station tours, and operate a museum.

Open: The third weekend in May through Labor Day.

36 Connecticut River Canoe Sites

Location: Along the Connecticut River; Western Massachusetts map page 354, grid a4.

Campsites, facilities: There are no officially designated sites on the Massachusetts section of the river, though the state's Department of Environmental Management is currently working to establish some. Facilities differ from site to site, but most have primitive toilets.

Reservations, fees: Sites are available on a first-come, first-served basis. Fees are charged at private sites.

Contact: Massachusetts Department of Environmental Management, 40 Cold Storage Drive, Amherst, MA 01004; (413) 545-5993.

Directions: The Connecticut River flows south through western Massachusetts from where it forms the New Hampshire–Vermont border to the Connecticut border, running roughly parallel to Interstate 91.

Trip notes: The state of Massachusetts is in the process of developing formal campsites on its stretch of the Connecticut River. Many people now camp on the banks and islands, but the official word is that permission from private landowners must be obtained first. The following campsites (listed from north to south) are either "semiauthorized"—people camp there on a regular basis and these sites will likely be formalized as the state gains land rights and easements—or privately owned.

Barton Cove (north of Greenfield): There are 23 family sites and two group sites, all for tents. Showers, a recreation area, ice, firewood, and canoe and rowboat rentals are available on the property. Leashed pets are permitted. Sites start at $12 a night, and

reservations are recommended. The campground is open from the third weekend in May through Labor Day. For further information, see campground number 35.

Gill Campsites (in Greenfield): Set on a long peninsula and maintained by New England Utilities, these sites offer fire pits, grills, a dock, and a showerhouse.

Whately (below a bridge on the west bank at Whately): This is a primitive site on county property. It is adjacent to a soccer field where chemical toilets are available to the public.

Elwell Island (in Northampton, just before the Coolidge Bridge): You will find no sanitary facilities at this semiauthorized site.

Mitch's Island and Marina (in Hadley, three miles south of Elwell Island): Sites are on a 20-acre, privately owned island. Rest rooms, a snack bar, dockage for all types of boats, and supplies are available.

Brunelle's Marina (seven miles south of Mitch's Island): On the west shore, this marina has a boat launch and sells supplies. Camping is by permission only.

Swim at your own risk and use good judgment; you'll see a number of popular beaches from your canoe. To take fish from the river you need a Massachusetts license. More than 60 native species live in the river including American shad, striped bass, trout, and the short-nosed sturgeon. The latter is on the federal list of endangered species, and anyone in possession of the fish may be fined up to $20,000. Know your species and check the laws before you throw in a line. Some sections of the river are heavily used by powerboaters, so use caution if you are in a smaller vessel. The river is a major migration route for waterfowl, hawks, and songbirds. In summer you will likely see bald eagles, ospreys, herons, owls, cormorants, and many other birds. Along the shore you may spy deer, fox, muskrat, beaver, woodchucks, and perhaps even a mink or two.

Open: Year-round as weather and river conditions permit.

㊲ Springbrook Family Camping Area

Location: North of Shelburne Falls; Western Massachusetts map page 354, grid a3.

Campsites, facilities: There are 98 sites for tents and RVs, 90 with water and electric hookups. Each site has a table and fire ring. A dump station and pump service are available, as are LP gas, ice, and firewood. On site you'll find a traffic control gate, swimming pool, rec and game rooms, a playground, sports courts and athletic fields, and RV storage. Leashed pets are permitted.

Reservations, fees: Reservations are recommended in summer. Sites start at $20 a night for two people.

Contact: Springbrook Family Camping Area, RFD 1, 32 Tower Road, Shelburne, MA 01370; (413) 625-6618.

Directions: From Interstate 91 at Greenfield, take exit 26 and head west on Route 2 for 5.5 miles. Turn right on Little Mohawk Road. Travel 1.5 miles to the Patten Road sign and turn left; take the next left onto Tower Road and go to the campground entrance on the left.

Trip notes: Farmland stretches forth in the panorama before you at Springbrook. Set atop a cleared hill, the campground looks out upon the Holyoke Range to the south and Mount Monadnock to the north. Picturesque farms and meadows dot the landscape of the fertile Connecticut River Valley below. Springbrook is popular with seasonal campers, though there are some developed short-term RV sites and a secluded tent area for overnighters. Most sites have some shade but are grassy, spacious, and open. Hikers and mountain bikers will find trails and dirt roads that leave from the campground. One two-mile route leads to High Ledges, the Audubon Society Sanctuary, where the Lady Slipper Trail is especially memorable in the spring. The village of Shelburne Falls is a popular tourist destination in itself. The "Bridge of Flowers" spans the Deerfield River there, and streets are lined with artisans' studios, shops, and restaurants. Also worthy of note are a series of glacial potholes in the riverbed below the falls for which the town is named.

Open: May 1 through October 15.

㊳ Lake Wyola Park and Campground

Location: Northwest of the Quabbin Reservoir in Lock Village; Western Massachusetts map page 354, grid b4.

Campsites, facilities: There are 48 sites for tents and RVs. No hookups are available, but there is a dump station. Springwater, showers, washrooms, a rec hall, and laundry facilities are provided. No pets are allowed.

Reservations, fees: Reservations are recommended. Sites start at $18 a night for two people.

Contact: Lake Wyola Park and Campground, P.O. Box 83, Montague, MA 01351; (413) 367-2627.

Directions: From U.S. 202 north of Amherst, take the Shutesbury exit heading west. Turn right and continue north at the town junction toward Lock Village and Lake Wyola. Follow signs to the campground.

Trip notes: Stay at this primitive campground in the Quabbin Reservoir district and you'll enjoy plentiful fishing and wildlife viewing in a protected watershed. The roomy campsites are set in a pine forest by Lake Wyola. Campers enjoy the use of a four-acre beach on the lakeshore as well as a boat basin.

Open: May 1 through mid-September.

㉟ Federated Women's Club State Forest

Location: South of Athol on the Quabbin Reservoir; Western Massachusetts map page 354, grid b5.

Campsites, facilities: There are six primitive campsites with no facilities. Leashed pets are permitted.

Reservations, fees: Sites are available on first-come, first-served basis and cost $3 a night.

Contact: Federated Women's Club State Forest, c/o Otter River State Forest, U.S. 202, Baldwinville, MA 01436; (508) 939-8962.

Directions: From South Athol, drive south on U.S. 202 to Route 122. Turn left and head east for about three miles to the campground entrance on the right.

Trip notes: Encompassing more than a thousand acres, this state forest is located in the Quabbin Reservoir watershed. Hunting is permitted in season, and the streams here are stocked with trout.

Open: April through December, weather permitting.

㊵ White Birch Campground

Location: North of Whately; Western Massachusetts map page 354, grid b3.

Campsites, facilities: There are 40 sites for tents and RVs, all with water and electric hookups. Dump stations and services are provided. LP gas, laundry facilities, a store, rec hall, game room, playground, and snack bar are available. Leashed pets are permitted.

Reservations, fees: Reservations are available and should be accompanied by a $20 deposit. Sites start at $20 a night for two people.

Contact: White Birch Campground, 122 North Street, Whately, MA 01093; (413) 665-4941.

Directions: From Greenfield, head south on Interstate 91. Take exit 25. Bear right on Route 116 and take the first left onto Whately Road. The campground is two miles ahead.

Trip notes: Open fields surrounded by a forest of mixed hardwoods greet visitors to White Birch. Campsites are set on grassy plots at the edge of the woods. There is a stream for fishing on the property, and trails for hiking through the surrounding woods.

Open: May through November 1.

㊶ Windy Acres Campground

Location: West of Northampton; Western Massachusetts map page 354, grid c3.

Campsites, facilities: There are 150 sites for tents and RVs, all with water and electric hookups and 18 with additional sewer connections. Dump stations and pumping services are available. Air conditioners are allowed, but heaters are not. Facilities include laundry, rec and game rooms, hot showers, a traffic control gate, sports courts, a pavilion, athletic fields, a playground, and a camp store. Firewood, ice, LP gas, and on-site RV storage are available. Leashed pets are permitted.

Reservations, fees: Reservations are recommended in the summer. Sites start at $19 a night per family.

Contact: Windy Acres Campground, 139 South Street, Westhampton, MA 01027; (413) 527-9862.

Directions: From the junction of Routes 66 and 9 in Northampton, travel west on Route 66 for nine miles. Turn right on South Road and drive one block north to the campground.

Trip notes: Roomy sites are set on a hillside in the small, rural town of Westhampton. A spring-fed swimming pond here has a small beach that's usually overrun with families in summer. You'll find hometown hospitality at organized events ranging from hayrides to horseshoe tournaments. Seasonal sites are landscaped, and some have permanent structures on them. There's also a safari field for group camping. If you want to get a sense of the history of these hills, stop in at the restored Westhampton Blacksmith Shop Museum. Largely donated by area families, the museum's collection includes furniture, toys, books, photos, clothing, tools, and other town memorabilia handed down through the ages.

Open: May 1 through October 15.

㊷ Sunledge/West Granville KOA

Location: West of Springfield in Granville; Western Massachusetts map page 354, grid d3.

Campsites, facilities: There are 155 sites for tents and RVs, all with water and electric hookups and 24 with additional sewer connections. Each site has a table and fire ring. Dump stations and pumping services are available. Facilities include laundry, rec and game rooms, hot showers, a traffic control gate, snack bar, sports courts, a pavilion, playground, heated pool, athletic fields, and a camp store. Firewood,

ice, LP gas, and on-site RV storage are available. Leashed pets are permitted.

Reservations, fees: Reservations are recommended. There is a three-day minimum stay on holiday weekends. Sites start at $25 a night for two people.

Contact: Sunledge/West Granville KOA, Route 57, West Granville, MA 01034; (413) 357-6494.

Directions: From Interstate 91 south of Springfield, take exit 5 and follow U.S. 5 through North Agawam. This road turns into Route 57. Follow Route 57 west through Southwick to Granville Center, then continue another four miles to the campground entrance, which will be on your left.

Trip notes: Mountaintop campsites at this KOA offer great views. Two fishing ponds are located on the premises, one with sites on it: sites 39 through 50 and 60 through 65 are on the shore of Peter's Pond. For hikers, several miles of walking trails lead through the surrounding hilly woods. Special dinners, bingo, dances, and theme weekends are part of the long list of planned activities coordinated seven days a week by a full-time recreation professional in season. The abundance of amenities and activities tends to attract RVers, so tenters might want to consider heading farther down Route 57 to Granville State Forest (see campground number 31). The 2,000-plus-acre forest has been sculpted by streams that created ravines and drainages en route to the Hubbard River; a relatively easy hike parallels the riverbed.

Open: May 1 through October 15.

㊸ Sodom Mountain Campground

Location: West of Springfield in Southwick; Western Massachusetts map page 354, grid d3.

Campsites, facilities: There are 125 sites for tents and RVs, all with water and electric hookups and 15 with additional sewer connections. Each site has a fire ring and picnic table. Dump stations and pumping services are available. Facilities include laundry, rec and game rooms, hot showers, sports courts, a pool, athletic fields, a playground, and a camp store. Firewood, ice, LP gas, and on-site RV storage are available. Leashed pets are permitted.

Reservations, fees: Reservations are recommended. Sites start at $20 a night per family.

Contact: Janice LaFrance, Sodom Mountain Campground, 227 South Loomis Street, P.O. Box 702, Southwick, MA 01077; (413) 569-3930.

Directions: From Interstate 91 south of Springfield, take exit 5 and follow U.S. 5 through North Agawam. This road turns into Route 57. Follow Route 57 west to Southwick Center, then continue another 3.5 miles to South Loomis Street. Turn left and go a quarter mile to the campground entrance.

Trip notes: Families flock to this campground because of its proximity to the Riverside Amusement Park in Agawam and the Eastern States Expo (site of fairs, trade shows, horse shows, big-name entertainers, circuses, etc.) in West Springfield, so reservations are necessary in the summertime. Discount tickets to the amusement park are available through the campground. Campsites are situated on a plateau on the side of Sodom Mountain and are spacious and mostly wooded, though some open areas do exist. Hiking trails lead from the campground to the top of the mountain; the summit hike is moderate, with some steep sections, and takes about an hour. Planned activities—including pig roasts and live entertainment—fill the weekends.

Open: May 1 through Columbus Day.

44 Southwick Acres

Location: South of Southwick; Western Massachusetts map page 354, grid d3.

Campsites, facilities: There are 65 sites for tents and RVs with water and electric hookups. Each site has a fire ring and picnic table. Dump stations and pumping services are available. Facilities include laundry, a rec hall, and clean rest rooms. Firewood and ice are available, and there's a grocery store nearby for supplies. Seasonal campers can get cable TV hookups. There's also on-site RV storage. Leashed pets are permitted.

Reservations, fees: Reservations are recommended. Sites start at $21 a night for two people.

Contact: Southwick Acres, P.O. Box 984, College Highway, Southwick, MA 01077; (413) 569-6339.

Directions: From Southwick Center, take Route 10/202 south for two miles to the campground entrance on the left.

Trip notes: Facilities are tailored to senior citizens at Southwick. Older campers appreciate the oversized sites (up to 60 feet) and the large L-shaped pool with stairs and a generous shallow end. Price discounts are also given to seniors. Though right off a major thoroughfare, Route 10/202, these wooded campsites are set back far enough to escape most of the traffic noise.

Open: May 1 through October 1.

45 Sunsetview Farm Camping Area

Location: South of Palmer; Western Massachusetts map page 354, grid c5.

Campsites, facilities: There are 120 sites for tents and RVs, 30 with full hookups and 70 with water and electric. Each site has a fire ring, grill, and picnic table. Air conditioners are allowed, but heaters are not. Dump stations and pumping services are available. Facilities include laundry, a store, rec and game rooms, sports courts, athletic fields, and a playground. Firewood, ice, RV supplies, and RV storage are available on site. There's also a traffic control gate. Leashed pets are permitted.

Reservations, fees: Reservations are recommended Memorial Day through Labor Day. Sites start at $19 a night for two people. Seasonal rates are available. There are extra charges for air conditioners, guests, and additional vehicles.

Contact: Sunsetview Farm Camping Area, 57 Town Farm Road, Monson, MA 01057; (413) 267-9269.

Directions: From the junction of U.S. 20 and Route 32 in Palmer, travel south on Route 32 for three-quarters of a mile to Fenton Road. Turn left and travel east; after half a mile turn right on Town Farm Road. Drive 1.5 miles south to the campground entrance.

Trip notes: Seasonal campers dominate the population at Sunsetview. Many return to enjoy the sites by the woods in the shade of an apple orchard and to participate in a host of activities from country line dancing to Monte Carlo weekends. Some sites are available to overnight guests, but be sure to call ahead. A swimming pond and a small fishing pond are on the grounds, and a short hiking trail leads through the woods. Hop over to Brimfield State Forest on Monson Road for a day of trout fishing and hiking on 3,250 acres of protected land.

Open: April 15 through October 15.

㊻ Partridge Hollow

Location: On Dean Pond in Monson;

Western Massachusetts map page 354, grid c5.

Campsites, facilities: There are 272 sites for tents and RVs, 125 with full hookups and 133 with water and electric. Each site has a fire ring, grill, and picnic table. Dump stations and pumping services are available. Air conditioners are allowed, but heaters are not. Facilities include laundry, a store, rec and game rooms, sports courts, athletic fields, and a playground. Firewood, ice, RV supplies, and RV storage are available on site. There's also a traffic control gate. Leashed pets are permitted.

Reservations, fees: Reservations are recommended Memorial Day through Labor Day. Sites start at $19 to $22 a night.

Contact: Partridge Hollow, P.O. Box 41, Munn Road, Monson, MA 01057; (413) 267-5122.

Directions: From the junction of U.S. 20 and Route 32 in Palmer, travel 5.4 miles east on U.S. 20, then head south for three-quarters of a mile on Monson Road. At the Brimfield State Park sign, turn left on Dean Pond Road and go 2.5 miles southeast to the campground.

Trip notes: You'll be camping in the company of young oak and pine trees at Partridge Hollow. The campground has been developed with RVers in mind, but some areas have been set aside for tenters. Summer weekends get a little wild with all the planned events, such as bingo, hayrides, parades, dances, theme dinners, and scavenger hunts. To escape the festivities, head down the road into Brimfield State Forest, where there are multiuse trails for hiking, biking, hunting, and horseback riding. Fast-flowing streams are home to abundant trout populations. And though no boats are permitted on Dean Pond, the largest of several ponds in the forest, swimming is allowed.

Open: April 15 through October 15.

⑰ Lake Dennison State Recreation Area

Location: South of Winchendon; Western Massachusetts map page 354, grid b5.

Campsites, facilities: There are 151 sites for tents and RVs with a dump station but no hookups. Flush toilets, showers, picnic tables, piped water, and fireplaces are provided. Leashed pets are permitted.

Reservations, fees: Reservations are recommended. Sites are $6 a night.

Contact: Lake Dennison State Recreation Area, c/o Otter River State Park, Baldwinville, MA 01436; (508) 939-8962.

Directions: From Fitchburg, take Route 12 north to Winchendon and head south on U.S. 202 to the park on the right (west) side of the road.

Trip notes: Lakeside sites underneath the pines provide campers with a tranquil setting. Nonmotorized boating, fishing, and swimming are permitted on Lake Dennison, which has a public boat ramp. Multiuse trails leave the campground and access more than 4,000 acres of forest and meadowlands.

Open: Memorial Day to Columbus Day.

⑱ Otter River State Forest

Location: South of Winchendon; Western Massachusetts map page 354, grid b5.

Campsites, facilities: There are 100 sites for tents and RVs with no hookups. Flush toilets, picnic tables, piped water, and fireplaces are provided. Three group sites open to nonprofit organizations only can accommodate up to 25 people each. Leashed pets are permitted.

Reservations, fees: Reservations are necessary for group campsites, which cost $8 a night. Regular sites are first come, first served and cost $5 a night.

Contact: Otter River State Forest, Baldwinville, MA 01436; (508) 939-8962.

Directions: From Fitchburg, take Route 12 north to Winchendon and head south on U.S. 202 to the park on the right (west) side of the road.

Trip notes: Camping along the Otter River is cool and comfortable even in the dog days of August. Because there are no hookups, this campground is better suited to tenters; RVers will be more comfortable at Lake Dennison (see campground number 16). Better than 1,000 acres of state forestland is open to hiking, horseback riding, and hunting, while the quiet waters of the river await your canoe.

Open: Memorial Day to Columbus Day.

⑲ Lamb City Campground

Location: East of Athol; Western Massachusetts map page 354, grid b5.

Campsites, facilities: There are 150 sites for tents and RVs, 115 with full hookups and the rest with water and electric. Fourteen pull-through sites, seasonal lots, and cable TV are available. On site you'll find a dump station, free hot showers, rest rooms, laundry facilities, a full-service store, LP gas, ice, firewood, three swimming pools, a boat ramp and rentals, sports courts, a rec hall with game room, a playground, and horseshoe pits. Leashed pets are permitted.

Reservations, fees: Reservations are accepted. Sites start at $17 a night per family.

Contact: Lamb City Campground, Royalston Road, Phillipston, MA 01331; (508) 249-2049 or (800) 292-5262.

Directions: From Route 2, take exit 19 and turn left on Route 2A. Travel 300 feet, then turn right on Royalston Road. The campground will be half a mile ahead on the left.

Trip notes: This is the ultimate RV option for campers who want access to fishing, swimming, and nonmotorized boating on Lake Dennison. Level and shaded sites are either right on or near the lake. You can rent canoes and paddleboats at the campground. Lamb City also coordinates many group activities including live entertainment.

Open: Year-round.

㊾ The Pines

Location: In Ashby near the New Hampshire border; Western Massachusetts map page 354, grid a6.

Campsites, facilities: There are 56 sites for tents and RVs, 32 with full hookups and 17 with water and electric. Each site has a table and fireplace. Facilities include a dump station, camp store, swimming pool, rec hall, hot showers, and playground. Firewood is for sale. Sites can be rented seasonally, but there is no on-site RV storage. Leashed pets are permitted.

Reservations, fees: Reservations are recommended. Sites are $15 to $17 a night for four people.

Contact: Pat and Paul Fiola, The Pines, 49 Davis Road, Ashby, MA 01431; (508) 386-7702.

Directions: From the junction of Routes 119 and 31 in Ashby, follow Route 31 north for three miles to Davis Road. Turn right and drive a short distance to the campground entrance.

Trip notes: Old-fashioned country-style camping 'neath tall pines is the order of the day here. There's a stream on the property for fishing and a pool to cool off in on hot summer days. Sites are roomy and shaded and can accommodate all but supersize RVs. Tenters will feel at home in this small-town atmosphere, though RVers do dominate the scene. Just down the road is Townsend State Forest with its easy and moderate hiking trails.

Open: May 1 through October 15.

㊿ Pearl Hill State Park

Location: North of Fitchburg; Western Massachusetts map page 354, grid a6.

Campsites, facilities: There are 51 sites without hookups; the maximum RV length is 20 feet. Tables, fire rings, and flush toilets are provided. Leashed pets are permitted.

Reservations, fees: Reservations are recommended. Sites are $5 a night.

Contact: Pearl Hill State Park, c/o Willard Brook State Forest, Route 119, West Townsend, MA 01474; (508) 597-8802.

Directions: From Route 2 in Leominster, take Route 13 north to Townsend. Make a left onto Route 119, drive west, and look for New Fitchburg Road on the left about 1.5 miles from the turnoff. The signs are faded. Follow the road to Pearl Hill State Park.

Trip notes: Campers enjoy the use of a small swimming beach at the entrance to the park at Pearl Hill Pond, not to mention acres of wooded hillsides over which they can stroll. Generous campsites are scattered on top of a hill amid an expanse of tall pines with ample room in between. Up the road apiece in Willard Brook State Forest are 18 miles of hiking trails and a river stocked with trout.

Open: Memorial Day through Labor Day.

⑤ Willard Brook State Forest

Location: North of Fitchburg; Western Massachusetts map page 354, grid a6.

Campsites, facilities: There are 21 wooded sites for tents and RVs with a 20-foot maximum length, all without hookups. Grills, tables, and flush toilets are provided. Supplies can be purchased in Townsend. Leashed pets are permitted.

Reservations, fees: Reservations are recommended. Sites are $5 a night.

Contact: Willard Brook State Forest, Route 119, West Townsend, MA 01474; (508) 939-8962.

Directions: From Marlborough, take Interstate 495 north to exit 31 and drive west on Route 119 toward Ashby. Follow signs to the campground entrance.

Trip notes: Inside the state park you'll find a good swimming spot at Damon Pond, brooks for trout fishing, 18 miles of hiking trails that are suitable for horseback riding, and lovely riverside spots where you can sit back and simply relax. The road through the forest winds along parallel to the river and can be crowded in the summer months, but the campground is tucked far enough into the trees to provide peace and quiet. Mountain bikers should head north on Route 13 and thrash themselves on the trails in Townsend State Forest, located to the west of the road on the New Hampshire border.

Open: May 1 through Columbus Day.

⑤ Pout and Trout Family Campground

Location: Northwest of Worcester; Western Massachusetts map page 354, grid b6.

Campsites, facilities: There are 156 sites for tents and RVs, 70 with full hookups and 75 with water and electric. Each site has a fireplace and picnic table. Air conditioners are allowed, but heaters are not. A dump station, laundry facilities, small grocery store, RV storage, LP gas, ice, and free firewood are available on the property. There's also a traffic control gate. You'll find a rec hall, swimming pool, sports courts and fields, and horseshoe pits on the property. Leashed pets are permitted.

Reservations, fees: Reservations are recommended June 15 through Labor Day. Sites start at $16 a night per family. Weekly, monthly, and seasonal rates are available.

Contact: The Lockes, Pout and Trout Family Campground, 94 River Road, North Rutland, MA 01543; (508) 886-6677.

Directions: From Rutland Center, travel four miles north on Route 56 to Route 68. Just north of the junction, turn and continue one mile east on River Road to the campground.

Trip notes: Most sites at Pout and Trout are occupied by seasonal campers who return each year to participate in a season of group activities such as line dancing, fishing contests, and treasure hunts. A quieter "Adult Leisure Time Area" is tucked away from the center of activity. Anglers can fish for trout in the private pond on the property (no state fishing license required) or in a river that runs through here.

Open: March 17 through Columbus Day.

⑤ Coldbrook Country Club and Campground

Location: West of the Quabbin Reservoir; Western Massachusetts map page 354, grid b6.

Campsites, facilities: There are 110

sites for tents and RVs, 30 with full hook-ups and 80 with sewer and electric. Each site has a picnic table and fireplace. Rest rooms, showers, laundry facilities, a snack bar, picnic grove, poolside lounge, and country store are on the property. You'll also find sports courts and fields, two pools, a children's play area, rec hall, restaurant, and game room. Leashed pets are permitted.

Reservations, fees: Reservations are recommended. Sites are $15 to $18 a night per family.

Contact: Coldbrook Country Club and Campground, 864 Old Coldbrook Road, Barre, MA 01005; (508) 355-2090.

Directions: From Worcester, take Route 122 north to Barre. In town, turn right on Fruitland Road, then take another right at the stop sign onto Old Coldbrook Road. The campground is 1.2 miles ahead.

Trip notes: Country club camping is the motif of Coldbrook Resort. On the site of former farmland, the campground offers spacious grassy and wooded sites atop rolling hills next to a family restaurant, a nine-hole golf course, and a 400-seat banquet facility. Tenters enjoy a separate wilderness area. On the grounds are both a swimming pool and a wading pool, a trout-stocked fishing pond, and multiuse trails that cut through woods and fields. The 350-acre resort abuts land controlled by the Massachusetts Water Resources Authority around the Quabbin Reservoir, which is replete with hiking trails.

Open: April 15 through October 15.

55 Pine Acres Family Camping Area

Location: Northwest of Worcester; Western Massachusetts map page 354, grid b6.

Campsites, facilities: There are 350 sites for tents and RVs, nearly 300 of which have water, electric, and sewer hookups. Each site has a picnic table and fire ring. A dump station, LP gas, laundry facilities, camp store, firewood, rec hall and game room, playground, and seasonal storage are available on the property. On site you'll also find tennis courts, sports courts, heated rest rooms with showers, horseshoe pits, a lodge, bait shop, and RV service station. Leashed pets are permitted.

Reservations, fees: Reservations require a 50 percent deposit; to obtain a waterfront site in July and August, reservations must be prepaid in full. Sites start at $17 a night for two people, with waterfront sites priced at $25. There are surcharges for children, guests, pets, air conditioners, heaters, boat launching, and use of boat slips.

Contact: Pine Acres Family Camping Area, 203 Bechan Road, Oakham, MA 01068; (508) 882-9509.

Directions: From Worcester, travel north on Route 122 for approximately 15 miles. Turn left on Route 148 (North Brookfield Road) and continue for 1.5 miles. Turn left after you pass the lake, then follow signs to the campground entrance.

Trip notes: Set beside 67-acre Lake Dean, these campsites are generally shaded and spacious. Some are right on the water, and there's also a secluded hill for wilderness tent camping. Launch your own boat and dock it by Pine Acres' long, sandy beach for a fee, or rent a boat from the campground. More than a mile in length, Lake Dean is popular with water-skiers, while anglers can appreciate the resident population of bass and horned pout. If you're in the mood for socializing, a recreation director plans group activities that range from crafts classes and dances to gambling field trips and tennis tournaments.

Open: Year-round.

56 Highview Vacation Campground

Location: West of Worcester in West Brookfield; Western Massachusetts map page 354, grid c5.

Campsites, facilities: There are 160 sites for tents and RVs, 140 with full hookups. Each site has a table and fireplace. Facilities include a dump station, hot showers, flush toilets, laundry, a camp store, and RV storage. There's also a rec hall, playground, and swimming pool, as well as scheduled activities. Firewood and ice are available. Leashed pets are permitted.

Reservations, fees: Reservations are recommended in summer. Sites start at $18 a night for four people; extra adults are $4 per person.

Contact: The Frizell Family, Highview Vacation Campground, RD Box 173, West Brookfield, MA 01585; (508) 867-7800.

Directions: From West Brookfield center on Route 9, travel two miles north on John Gilbert Road.

Trip notes: Most campers at Highview rent sites seasonally, but overnight and short-term visitors are welcome, too. Sites are shaded and cool, set at an elevation of 906 feet on a wooded hillside. There's a pond on site for fishing and trails that traverse the surrounding lands. With dirt roads and country hospitality, this is an old-fashioned type of campground. It's quiet despite the wide selection of planned activities.

Open: April 15 through October 15.

57 Old Sawmill Campground

Location: West of Worcester in West Brookfield; Western Massachusetts map page 354, grid c5.

Campsites, facilities: There are 125 sites for tents and RVs, 50 with full hookups and 60 with water and electric. Each site has a table and fire ring. Air conditioners and heaters are not allowed. Facilities include a dump station, laundry, hot showers, flush toilets, a camp store, rec hall, and RV storage. Firewood, ice, LP gas, and planned activities are available. A playground, game room, swimming pool, wading pool, and horseshoe pits are provided. Leashed pets are permitted.

Reservations, fees: Reservations are recommended; there are no refunds for cancellations. Sites are $16 to $20 a night for two people. Weekly, monthly, and seasonal rates are available.

Contact: Old Sawmill Campground, P.O. Box 377, Long Hill Road, West Brookfield, MA 01585; (508) 867-2427.

Directions: From West Brookfield Center on Route 9, head south at the traffic light on Central Street to the road's end. Turn right and head south on Front Street, then turn right on Long Hill Road and continue three-quarters of a mile to the campground, crossing a railroad bridge on the way.

Trip notes: You might feel a little crowded at Old Sawmill because the sites are typically less than 30 feet apart. Most are shaded by trees, but there's not much separating you from your neighbors. Chances are you'll meet them anyway if you're here on a weekend, as Friday, Saturday, and Sunday are loaded with planned activities such as bingo, dancing, cribbage tournaments, and hayrides. From the campground, a nature trail leads to a bubbling brook where you can fish, while other trails explore the wooded hills around the campground. If you're looking for serenity and privacy, this isn't your best bet.

Open: May 1 through Columbus Day.

58 Lakeside Resort

Location: West of Worcester in Brookfield; Western Massachusetts map page 354, grid c5.

Campsites, facilities: There are 118 sites for tents and RVs, 100 with full hookups and the rest with water and electric. Sites are available on an overnight, seasonal, or for-sale basis, and there are some group sites. Air conditioners are allowed, but heaters are not. Facilities include RV storage, a dump station, hot showers, a hot spa, and laundry. Tables, fire rings, and a guard service are provided. Ice and firewood are available on site, and there's a store nearby. Campers can use a dance pavilion, sundeck, clubhouse, sports courts, swimming pool, and horseshoe pits. Leashed pets are permitted.

Reservations, fees: Reservations are recommended in July and August. Tent sites are $20 a night; sites with full hookups are $25 a night for two people.

Contact: Lakeside Resort, 12 Hobbs Avenue, Brookfield, MA 01560; (508) 867-2737.

Directions: From the junction of Routes 9 and 49 in East Brookfield, continue 3.9 miles west on Route 9 to Quaboag Street and turn left. Follow Quaboag Street for eight-tenths of a mile to Hobbs Avenue. The campground will be straight ahead.

Trip notes: Lakeside Resort is located across the street from Quaboag Lake, a 540-acre freshwater pool open to motorboating, sailing, windsurfing, fishing, and swimming. Boat moorings are available near the resort-owned clubhouse on the shore. In addition, three rivers that are accessible from the lake offer quiet waters for canoeing. The grounds are neatly landscaped, and some of the sites are owned outright—you'll see travel trailers, motor homes, park models, and even cabins sporting flower beds and with permanent structures attached to them. Designated areas have been set aside for overnight visitors, so you won't be pitching your tent next to a vacation home. Still, RVers will feel more comfortable here than tenters.

Open: May 1 through Columbus Day.

59 Wells State Park

Location: North of Sturbridge; Western Massachusetts map page 354, grid c5.

Campsites, facilities: There are 59 sites for tents and RVs, all without hookups. Facilities include flush toilets, showers, picnic tables, a dump station, fireplaces, and piped water. Leashed pets are permitted at the campground.

Reservations, fees: Sites are available on a first-come, first-served basis and cost $6 a night.

Contact: Wells State Park, Route 49, Sturbridge, MA 01436; (508) 347-9257.

Directions: From Interstate 84 near the Connecticut border, head north to exit 3, then drive a short distance east on U.S. 20 to Route 49 north. Follow the signs to the park entrance off Route 49.

Trip notes: Low prices and easy access to historic Sturbridge and its surrounding attractions lure campers to Wells State Park. Shaded sites offer plenty of privacy, and Quacumquasit Pond is open to motorboating, fishing, canoeing, and swimming. Multiuse trails thread their way through the mixed forest in the park. Whether you're looking for a base camp from which to venture or a home base for an outdoor adventure, Wells State Park is a good choice. This park is also the best option for tenters in the Sturbridge region.

Open: Mid-May through mid-October.

60 Village Green Family Campground

Location: West of Sturbridge; Western Massachusetts map page 354, grid d5.

Campsites, facilities: There are 128 sites for tents and RVs, most with water and electric hookups and none with sewer connections. Each site has a table and fire ring. There are group sites for both tents and RVs. Air conditioners are allowed, but heaters are not. Facilities include dump stations and service, laundry, a camp store, playgrounds, rec hall, LP gas, game room, boat rentals, and RV storage. Firewood and ice are available. Courts for volleyball, basketball, and badminton are on the property, as are horseshoe pits. Leashed pets are permitted.

Reservations, fees: Reservations are recommended in July and August; they are taken over the phone and must be paid by personal check, with a $5 service charge for cancellations. Holiday weekends require a minimum reservation of three days. Sites starts at $20 a night for four people.

Contact: Lester and Meg Twarowski, Village Green Family Campground, 228 Sturbridge Road, Brimfield, MA 01010; (413) 245-3504.

Directions: From the junction of Interstate 84 and U.S. 20, travel 4.75 miles west on U.S. 20 to the campground entrance; Village Green is operated in conjunction with a motel.

Trip notes: Set on a small spring-fed pond, Village Green offers campers a chance to enjoy nonmotorized boating, freshwater fishing and swimming, and a family atmosphere. Weekends are studded with group activities, including talent shows, hayrides, beach parties, and cardboard boat races. Walking trails lead through the woods behind the pond. Sites are mostly spacious and wooded but lose some of their natural flavor by being located next to a motel.

Open: April 1 through October 31.

61 Yogi Bear's Sturbridge Jellystone Park

Location: Southwest of Sturbridge; Western Massachusetts map page 354, grid d5.

Campsites, facilities: There are 399 sites for tents and RVs, 350 with water and electric hookups and 60 with additional sewer connections. Each site has a picnic table and fire ring. Facilities include a dump station and service, laundry, a snack bar, grocery store, RV supplies, LP gas, and a traffic control gate and guard. For recreation, there's a miniature water park with waterslide and Jacuzzi, miniature golf, paddleboats, shuffleboard, movies, horseshoe pits, and sports fields and courts. Ice and firewood are available. Leashed pets are permitted.

Reservations, fees: Reservations are recommended Memorial Day through Labor Day; there are no refunds. Sites are $27 to $40 a night for two people.

Contact: Yogi Bear's Sturbridge Jellystone Park, P.O. Box 600, Sturbridge, MA 01566; (508) 347-9570.

Directions: From Interstate 84, take exit 2 and drive west on U.S. 20 toward East Brimfield. Follow signs to the campground.

Trip notes: Roving costumed characters from the Yogi Bear show are part of the package at this theme park packed with entertainment for the whole family. From fishing in the camp's private pond (no license required) to nightly entertainment by hypnotists and magicians, this is a high-energy camping experience. Horse-drawn hay wagons and a petting zoo are located on the property, as is an aquacenter, where, for an extra charge, campers can enjoy a waterslide and Jacuzzi. This is the closest place to camp near Old Sturbridge Village, a living history museum. It's not for those who want peace, quiet, and privacy.

Open: Year-round.

⑫ Quinebaug Cove

Location: West of Sturbridge; Western Massachusetts map page 354, grid d5.

Campsites, facilities: There are 125 sites for tents and RVs, 110 with water and electric hookups and 45 with additional sewer connections. Each site has a table and fire ring. Air conditioners and heaters are allowed. Facilities include dump stations and service, laundry, LP gas, a swimming pool, rec hall, game room, playgrounds, snack bar, boat rentals, and RV storage. There's also a traffic control gate and a boat launch. Courts for basketball, shuffleboard, volleyball, and badminton are located on the property. A camp store carries ice and firewood. Leashed pets are permitted with proof of rabies vaccination, but they must stay off the beach.

Reservations, fees: Reservations are recommended. There's a three-day minimum stay during holiday weekends. Sites start at $20 a night for two people.

Contact: Quinebaug Cove, 49 East Brimfield–Holland Road, Brimfield, MA 01010; (413) 245-9525.

Directions: From the intersection of Interstate 84 and U.S. 20, travel three miles west on U.S. 20 to East Brimfield–Holland Road. The campground is half a mile ahead.

Trip notes: Brimfield Reservoir and Long Pond are the focal points of this lakeside campground in the woods near Old Sturbridge Village. Powerboating and swimming are popular summertime pursuits. Anglers will find perch, northern pike, bass, and pickerel in the several ponds, lakes, and streams that are part of the watershed; licenses are required and are available nearby. The Massachusetts Department of Environmental Management maintains a canoe trail that extends from Quinebaug Cove to the Tolland Pond Recreation Area five miles south—just rent a canoe at the campground and you're set. There are hiking trails around the reservoir that hunters use in season. Planned weekend activities include visits from Chippy the Chipmunk and Barney the Dinosaur for the kids, karaoke, live bands, and sports tournaments.

Open: Year-round.

⑬ Oak Haven Campground

Location: West of Sturbridge; Western Massachusetts map page 354, grid d5.

Campsites, facilities: There are 90 sites for tents and RVs, 70 with full hookups and 20 with water and electric. Each site has a table and fire ring. Heaters and air conditioners are allowed. On site you'll find laundry facilities, group sites for tents and RVs, RV storage, LP gas, and RV supplies. Ice and firewood are available. A swimming pool, rec hall, game room, playground, snack bar, pavilion, sports fields, and courts are provided for use by campers. Leashed pets are permitted.

Reservations, fees: Reservations are recommended Memorial Day through Labor Day. Sites start at $20 a night for two people with water and electric hookups.

Contact: Alan and Penny Jalbert, Oak Haven Campground, Route 19, Wales, MA 01081; (413) 245-9525.

Directions: From the junction of Route 19 and U.S. 20 in West Brimfield, travel south on Route 19 for 4.5 miles to the campground entrance on the left.

Trip notes: Many of the sites at Oak Haven are rented by seasonal campers who enhance their "second homes" with landscaping, decks, and other permanent fixtures. The park is impeccably clean and neat, bordered with wood fencing, dotted with rustic bridges, and landscaped with perennial gardens. A large swimming pool and recreation area are centrally located to the open and wooded sites set on 90 acres of rolling farmland with a small petting zoo. Five minutes away is the Norcross Wildlife Sanctuary. Located in Wales and Monson, the 3,000-acre preserve is home to rare wildflowers and indigenous wildlife. Two museums and a self-guided nature trail help visitors interpret what they see. The preserve is open year-round, and entrance is free.

Open: May 1 through Columbus Day.

---

⑥⑤ The Woodlot Campground

Location: Near the Massachusetts Turnpike north of Charlton; Western Massachusetts map page 354, grid c5.

Campsites, facilities: There are 92 sites for tents and RVs, most with water and electric hookups. Each site has a table and fire ring. Air conditioners are allowed, but heaters are not. Facilities include dump stations, laundry, a limited grocery store, RV storage, RV supplies, LP gas, ice, and firewood. A traffic control gate stands at the campground entrance. Courts for basketball, volleyball, and badminton are located on site, as are a playground, swimming and wading pools, and horseshoe pits. Free movies are included. Leashed pets are permitted.

Reservations, fees: Reservations are recommended in July and August. Sites start at $21 a night for two people. Weekly and monthly rates are available.

Contact: The Woodlot Campground, P.O. Box 968, Charlton, MA 01508; (508) 248-5141.

Directions: From the Massachusetts Turnpike (Interstate 90), take exit 9 and follow Interstate 84 south to exit 3A. Drive east on U.S. 20 for 5.5 miles to Route 31. Turn left (north) at the traffic light and turn right on Stafford Street after one-tenth mile. The campground is a quarter mile ahead.

Trip notes: Beneath a canopy of old oaks and pines you'll find large, wooded sites with plenty of privacy. Pools and sports courts keep everyone busy, and planned events on the weekends only add to the fun. For an excellent family day trip, head six miles west to Old Sturbridge Village, a living history museum designed to re-create an 1830s New England community. Costumed interpreters answer questions, while special events and tours target visitors of every age group.

Open: May 15 through Columbus Day.

⑥⑤ Applewood Campground

Location: South of Charlton; Western Massachusetts map page 354, grid c6.

Campsites, facilities: There are 60 sites for tents and RVs, all with water and electric hookups, plus two group safari areas. Each site has a table and fireplace. Facilities include dump stations, a rec hall, laundry, metered hot showers in a modern rest room facility, and sports fields. Motorcycles, minibikes, and mopeds are prohibited. Leashed pets weighing less than 35 pounds are permitted.

Reservations, fees: Reservations are recommended in July and August and require a nonrefundable deposit. Group sites must be reserved. Sites start at $18 a night for tents and $20 for trailers.

Contact: Walt and Elaine Daubney, Applewood Campground, 44 King Road, Charlton, MA 01507; (508) 248-7017.

Directions: From the junction of U.S. 20 and Route 31 near Charlton, travel 4.5 miles south on Route 31 to the Dresser Hill Farm ice cream stand and turn right. Drive half a mile downhill to King Road on the left. The campground is just ahead.

Trip notes: Applewood is a great place to bring the family. Extra-large sites in the woods afford maximum privacy, and there's a separate primitive tent area. The playground and group sites are surrounded by forestland that is accessed by stone-bordered pathways. Less than 10 miles away is the living history museum of Old Sturbridge Village.

Open: Mid-May through Columbus Day.

---

66 Indian Ranch Campground

Location: Near Webster on Webster Lake; Western Massachusetts map page 354, grid d6.

Campsites, facilities: There are 110 sites for use by seasonal campers only, all with water and electric hookups. Dump stations and services are provided. On site you'll find an outdoor amphitheater, a camp store, rec hall with game room, playground, snack bar, boat rentals, and RV storage. LP gas and laundry facilities are available in Webster. Leashed pets are permitted.

Reservations, fees: Reservations are required. Rates are available upon request.

Contact: Indian Ranch Campground, Route 16, P.O. Box 1157, Webster, MA 01570; (508) 943-3871.

Directions: From the junction of Interstate 395 and Route 16 in Webster, travel one mile east on Route 16 to the camp-

ground entrance on the right (south) side of the road.

Trip notes: Indian Ranch does not accommodate overnight guests on its lakeside property, as all sites are rented seasonally. Webster Lake is surrounded by pine forests and is open to powerboating, fishing, and swimming. A country-and-western all-star show is presented every other weekend in the outdoor amphitheater near the shore. The lake is widely known by its native name, Chargoggagogmanchauggagoggchaubunagungamaugg, the longest geographical name in the United States. Translated, it means "I fish on my side of the lake, you fish on yours, and no one fishes in between."

Open: May 1 through October 1.

---

67 Sturbridge/Webster KOA Family Kampground

Location: East of Webster near Webster Lake; Western Massachusetts map page 354, grid d6.

Campsites, facilities: There are 150 sites for tents and RVs, 102 with water and electric hookups and 48 with none. A dump station is provided. On site you'll find laundry facilities, a limited grocery store, LP gas, a rec room, playground, sports courts, and horseshoe pits. Leashed pets are permitted.

Reservations, fees: Reservations are recommended in the summer. Sites start at $21 a night for two people.

Contact: Sturbridge/Webster KOA Family Kampground, Route 16, Webster, MA 01570; (508) 943-1895.

Directions: From the junction of Interstate 395 and Route 16 in Webster, travel 2.5 miles east on Route 16 to the campground entrance.

Trip notes: This rural, wooded campground is close to Webster Lake, where visitors can fish, powerboat, and swim in a freshwater setting. Sites are close together—most are about 25 feet wide—so privacy is at a minimum. Tenters have a separate primitive area of their own. Short trails lead through the wooded hillsides.

Open: Year-round; fully operational from April 1 through December 1.

68 Sutton Falls Camping Area

Location: Southeast of Worcester; Western Massachusetts map page 354, grid d6.

Campsites, facilities: There are 95 sites for tents and RVs, nearly all with water and electric hookups and 80 with additional sewer connections. On-site services include RV storage, boat rentals, and dump stations. Hot showers, a playground, camp store, and events pavilion are located on the property. You'll also find group camping areas, laundry facilities, sports courts, and a lake for swimming. Leashed pets are permitted.

Reservations, fees: Prepaid reservations are a must for holiday weekends. Sites start at $15 a night for two people. Weekly, monthly, and seasonal rates are available.

Contact: Tom and Betty Therrien, Sutton Falls Camping Area, Manchaug Road, West Sutton, MA 01590; (508) 865-3898 in the summer or (508) 476-2653 in the winter.

Directions: From Interstate 395 south of Worcester at Oxford, take exit 4A to Sutton Avenue. Continue four miles to Manchaug Road on the right. Turn and drive to the campground eight-tenths of a mile ahead on the right.

Trip notes: Aldrich Pond is the centerpiece of this quiet, woodsy campground. Most sites are staked out by seasonal campers, but some are set aside for overnight guests. Electric motors are the only kind allowed on the pond, making this a peaceful place for swimming and fishing. Saturday night movies in the rec hall are among the many planned activities.

Open: Mid-April through Columbus Day.

69 Old Holbrook Place

Location: On Lake Manchaug; Western Massachusetts map page 354, grid d6.

Campsites, facilities: There are 66 sites for tents and RVs up to 28 feet long, each with water and electric hookups and 35 with additional sewer connections. No dump station or service is provided. Available amenities include rowboat rentals, hot showers, a playground, ice, and firewood. Leashed pets are permitted.

Reservations, fees: Reservations are recommended. Sites are $14 to $20 a night.

Contact: The Nelson Family, Old Holbrook Place, 114 Manchaug Road, West Sutton, MA 01590; (508) 248-5141.

Directions: From Interstate 395 south of Worcester at Oxford, take exit 4A to Sutton Avenue. Continue four miles to Manchaug Road on the right, then turn. The campground is one mile ahead on the right, just past the Sutton Falls entrance.

Trip notes: Nearly half the campsites are located right on the shore of Lake Manchaug, a convenient setup for those who want to swim, powerboat, or fish. Though seasonal rentals are offered, this campground restricts the building of any permanent structure, maintaining a natural appearance throughout the park. The long, sandy beach, boat dock, ramp, and swim raft make this an ideal spot for boaters and young families.

Open: Memorial Day through Labor Day.

70 King's Campground

Location: On Lake Manchaug; Western Massachusetts map page 354, grid d6.

Campsites, facilities: There are 120 sites for tents and RVs, 110 with full hookups and 10 with water and electric. Each site has a table and fire ring. A dump station is provided on site. Also on the property are laundry facilities, metered LP gas, a store, rec hall, game room, playground, snack bar, and RV storage. Ice and firewood are available at the camp store. No pets are allowed.

Reservations, fees: Reservations are recommended. Sites start at $20 a night for two people.

Contact: Paul Boutiette, King's Campground, P.O. Box 302, Manchaug, MA 01526; (508) 476-2543.

Directions: From Route 146 just north of the Rhode Island border, take the Manchaug exit and continue 2.2 miles to Manchaug Center. Go straight through the stop sign, turn left at the fork, travel half a mile, crossing the dam, then turn left again. Take the first right onto Holt Road to get to the campground.

Trip notes: Wooded and open sites are set either on or near the shore of Lake Manchaug, where campers can swim, powerboat, and fish. The campground runs a marina on the lake and provides boat rentals. Planned family activities round out the fun.

Open: Mid-April through mid-October.

71 Lake Manchaug Camping

Location: On Lake Manchaug; Western Massachusetts map page 354, grid d6.

Campsites, facilities: There are 192 sites for seasonal and monthly campers, 180 of which have full hookups. Dump stations and honey wagon service are available. Also on the property are a playground and RV storage. Leashed pets are permitted.

Reservations, fees: Reservations are required. Rates are available on request.

Contact: Joe and Jan Staruk, Lake Manchaug Camping, 76 Oak Street, East Douglas, MA 01516; (508) 476-2471 in the summer or (508) 476-2328 in the winter.

Directions: From Route 146 just north of the Rhode Island border, take the Manchaug exit and continue 2.2 miles to Manchaug Center. Go straight through the stop sign, turn left at the fork, travel half a mile, crossing the dam, then turn left again. Take the first right onto Holt Road and proceed half a mile to the campground.

Trip notes: Lake Manchaug Camping welcomes campers who want to stay for a month or an entire season either on or near its half mile of lake frontage.

Open: May 1 through September 15.

72 Winding Brook Family Campground

Location: North of the Rhode Island border in Douglas; Western Massachusetts map page 354, grid d6.

Campsites, facilities: There are 145 sites for tents and RVs, 80 with full hookups and 45 with water and electric. Each site has a table and fire ring. Air conditioners are allowed, but heaters are not. Facilities include a dump station, new swimming pool, store, rec hall, game room, playground, snack bar, phone connections, and RV storage. Ice, firewood, and church services are available at the campground. Campers can also use sports courts and fields. Dancing is one of many planned group activities. Leashed pets are permitted.

Reservations, fees: Reservations are recommended July through Labor Day. Sites start at $18 a night per family.

Contact: Ray Cardogno, Winding Brook Family Campground, P.O. Box 1011, South Street, Route 90, East Douglas, MA 01516; (508) 476-7549.

Directions: From the junction of Routes 16 and 96 east of Webster, travel two miles south on Route 96 to the campground entrance on the right.

Trip notes: Some 5,000 acres of protected woodlands abut this campground, where the sites are spacious lots shaded by tall pines. Douglas State Forest, a wheelchair-accessible park, offers lake swimming, powerboating, hunting, and miles of maintained multiuse trails for use by hunters, hikers, mountain bikers, and horseback riders.

Open: May 15 through October 1.

Wyman's Beach

Location: East of Groton; Eastern Massachusetts map page 355, grid b1.

Campsites, facilities: There are 227 lakeside sites for tents and RVs, all with hookups. Fire rings, grills, tables, RV supplies, sewage disposal, LP gas, sports courts, flush toilets, metered hot showers, ice, and firewood are available on the property. There's also a convenience store and rec hall. Leashed pets are permitted.

Reservations, fees: Reservations are recommended in summer. Sites start at $18 a night for two people.

Contact: Wyman's Beach, Wyman's Beach Road, Westford, MA 01886; (508) 692-6287.

Directions: From U.S. 3, take exit 33 to Route 40. Travel three miles west on Route

40, then turn right on Dunstable Road. The campground is one mile ahead.

Trip notes: RVers predominate at this campground. Shaded sites are packed in close to the waterfront of spring-fed Long Sought-for Pond. With planned activities throughout the summer and a lake open for fishing, swimming, and boating, Wyman's Beach campers have plenty to do on site. But only seven miles away is Lowell National Historic Park, offering exhibits on water-power, mill girls, immigrants, and labor history, as well as walking tours. In summertime, a barge and trolley tour the Merrimack River, famed for its role in New England's early mill history.

Open: Memorial Day through Labor Day.

Minuteman KOA

Location: In Littleton; Eastern Massachusetts map page 355, grid b1.

Campsites, facilities: There are 95 sites for tents and RVs, 30 with full hookups, 51 with water and electric, and 14 with none. Fire rings, hot showers, LP gas, picnic tables, laundry facilities, a dump station, pool, and rec hall are available on the grounds. Groceries, firewood, and ice are sold on site. Leashed pets are permitted.

Reservations, fees: Reservations are required for group sites. Single sites are $23 a night with no hookups and $29 with hookups.

Contact: Ted and Maureen Nussdorfer, Minuteman KOA, P.O. Box 2122, Littleton, MA 01460; (508) 772-0042 or (800) 562-7606.

Directions: From Interstate 495 north of Marlborough, take exit 30. Travel west on Route 2A/110 for 2.5 miles. The campground will be on your left.

Trip notes: If you're looking for a good

place to park the ark and take in the historic sites of Lexington, this is it. Though you're right next to a busy road, sites are wooded and spacious, the grounds are clean, and the services are excellent. Oak Hill and Tophet Chasm offer easy family hiking only three miles away. Anglers will want to seek out nearby Oxbow National Wildlife Refuge. Take Route 110 west for about seven miles to the small Still River Post Office; turn right at the post office and continue until you see the refuge sign. You'll find level hiking trails, as well as fishing for pickerel and bullhead on the Nashua River, which is also a good choice for canoeing. Just be on the lookout for any metal bomb-type surprises in the woods. This was once a blasting range for the Defense Department.

Open: May 1 through October.

75 Crystal Springs Campground

Location: West of Interstate 495 in Bolton; Eastern Massachusetts map page 355, grid b1.

Campsites, facilities: There are 219 sites for tents and RVs, 101 with full hookups and another 114 with water and electric. On site there's a dump station, laundry facilities, hot showers, rest rooms, a grocery store, RV supplies, LP gas, ice, and firewood. A swimming pool, game room, sports courts, tennis courts, miniature golf, picnic tables, fireplaces, and a snack bar are provided. Leashed pets are permitted.

Reservations, fees: A deposit must accompany reservations. Sites are $17 to $21 a night for two people.

Contact: Bill and Mary Ann Doucette, Crystal Springs Campground, P.O. Box 279, Bolton, MA 01740; (508) 779-2711.

Directions: From the Massachusetts Turn-

pike (Interstate 90) west of Framingham, take Interstate 495 north. At exit 27, get on Route 117 and travel west for two miles. The campground will be on your right.

Trip notes: Sites at Crystal Springs are placed fairly close together underneath tall pines. The general setup is suited more to RVers, though tenters are welcome. There's a small pond on the property as well as a full-sized pool for swimming. Campers are entertained every weekend in season by the country sounds of the Goodtime Band. Activities are organized for every age group, so families are the predominant campers. From arts and crafts to bingo, two recreation directors on staff make sure there's something for everyone to do and ensure that there's never a dull moment.

Open: April 1 through mid-October.

76 Powow Cove Campground

Location: In Amesbury; Eastern Massachusetts map page 355, grid a3.

Campsites, facilities: There are 74 sites for tents and RVs, 45 with full hookups and 25 with water and electric. You'll find dump stations, laundry facilities, a camp store, rec hall, playground, snack bar, boat rentals, and RV storage on the property. Picnic tables, fireplaces, a security gate, and rest rooms are provided. No pets are allowed.

Reservations, fees: Call the campground for information on rates and reservations.

Contact: Powow Cove Campground, 43 Newton Road, Amesbury, MA 01913; (508) 388-4022.

Directions: From Interstate 495 east of Haverhill, take exit 54 and travel north on Route 150 through the traffic lights. In half a mile, turn left on Highland Road, proceed to Lions Mouth Road, and bear left. The campground is three miles from Route 150.

Trip notes: Powow Cove offers mostly shaded sites by a small lake. The majority of campers here rent space for the entire season, so call to find out if there is any space available. If you find yourself in the area, the Bartlett Museum in Amesbury features Native American artifacts, natural science collections, and a display of antique carriages.

Open: May 5 through September.

77 Black Bear Campground

Location: North of Salisbury Beach; Eastern Massachusetts map page 355, grid a3.

Campsites, facilities: There are 200 sites for tents and RVs, all with water and electric hookups and 175 with additional sewer connections. Facilities include fireplaces, picnic tables, coin-op showers, flush toilets, a dump station, laundry, RV storage, a game room, playground, sports courts, adult clubhouse, and pool. Leashed pets are permitted.

Reservations, fees: Reservations are recommended in July and August. Tent sites are $22 a night and RV sites are $25 a night for two people.

Contact: Black Bear Campground, 116 Main Street, Salisbury, MA 01952; (508) 462-3183.

Directions: From Interstate 95 north of Newburyport, take exit 60 and travel east on Route 286. Turn left at the first set of lights onto Main Street and continue to the campground 200 feet ahead on the left.

Trip notes: Wooded and open sites at Black Bear are close to the interstate, just three miles north of Salisbury Beach and three miles south of New Hampshire's Hampton Beach. Tenters will enjoy spaces that are roomier than the sardinelike RV sites. Explore the area's tidal bogs on trails leading from the campground. When you tire of surf casting and lying on white sand beaches, visit the Seacoast Science Center just over the New Hampshire border in Rye. Exhibits, programs, and trails explore Odiorne Point's scenery. Discover how this Native American fishing ground became the site of the first European settlement in New Hampshire. There's also lots of wildlife—snakes, frogs, turtles, crabs, and starfish, to name a few—for kids to handle.

Open: May 15 through October 1.

78 Rusnik Campground

Location: North of Salisbury Beach; Eastern Massachusetts map page 355, grid a3.

Campsites, facilities: There are 150 sites for tents and RVs, 140 with water and electric hookups. Facilities include dump stations, fireplaces, picnic tables, hot metered showers, flush toilets, a rec hall, game room, and laundry. Firewood and ice are available. Leashed pets are permitted.

Reservations, fees: Reservations are recommended. Sites are $24 a night in season.

Contact: Rusnik Campground, P.O. Box 5441, Salisbury, MA 01952-0441; (508) 462-9551 in the summer or (508) 465-5295 in the winter.

Directions: From Interstate 495 near Amesbury, take exit 55 and travel 3.5 miles east on Route 110. Take a left on U.S. 1 and drive one mile north to the campground.

Trip notes: Bring your bathing suit and surf casting rod because the beach is just a stone's throw from this campground. Campsites are large, wooded, and set back far enough from the highway that you won't be bothered by traffic noise. There's a miniature golf course on the property and full-scale courses nearby. Five-mile-long Salisbury Beach lies three miles north of here and is open to the public. Newburyport, just five minutes away, offers numerous "urban" seaside attractions: whale watch cruises, deep-sea fishing, shopping, summer theater—even greyhound races. When you tire of the ocean, head inland to 480-acre Maudslay State Park in Newburyport where you'll find freshwater fishing and trails for hiking, biking, and horseback riding. A two-mile hike along the Merrimack River offers ocean views from Castle Hill.

Open: May 15 through October 1.

⑦⑨ Pines Camping Area

Location: South of Salisbury Beach; Eastern Massachusetts map page 355, grid a3.

Campsites, facilities: There are 160 open and shaded sites for tents and RVs, 16 with full hookups and 115 with water and electric. Each site has a table and fire ring. Use of heaters and air conditioners is not allowed. On site you'll find a small playground, horseshoe pits, and a basketball hoop. Group sites for tents and RVs, sewage disposal, firewood, ice, and flush toilets are available. Leashed pets are permitted.

Reservations, fees: Reservations are recommended. Sites are $17 to $21 a night.

Contact: Pines Camping Area, Sand Hill Road, Salisbury, MA 01952; (508) 465-0013.

Directions: From the junction of U.S. 1 and Route 1A north of Newburyport, travel half a mile north on Route 1A, then turn right on Sand Hill Road and drive half a mile south.

Trip notes: Self-billed as a "no-frills family campground," Pines offers just the basics, meaning campers must travel to find recreation and amenities. Sites are quiet enough,

set among—you guessed it—pine trees. Salisbury Beach is right down the road, and just south of there lies Newburyport, known for Plum Island, a spit of land that's home to the 3,200-acre Parker River Wildlife Refuge. Though boats cannot launch or land on the refuge, it is accessible by car and draws birdwatchers by the thousands. More than 300 species have been sighted in the area, which is a pit stop for migratory fowl. Hunting and fishing are permitted in designated areas, but swimming can be a bit dangerous: Beware of cold temperatures, rough surf, and aggressive tides. Six miles of barrier shoreline await sunbathers in search of undeveloped beach.

Open: Mid-May through Columbus Day.

⑧⓪ Salisbury Beach State Reservation

Location: On Salisbury Beach; Eastern Massachusetts map page 355, grid a3.

Campsites, facilities: There are 483 tent and RV sites, 324 of which have water and electric hookups. The maximum allowable RV length is 31 feet. A boat ramp, grills, tables, dump station, showers, flush toilets, a rec pavilion, and playground are located on site. Leashed pets are permitted.

Reservations, fees: Reservations are recommended in the summer. Sites are $7 to $9 a night.

Contact: Salisbury Beach State Reservation, P.O. Box 5303, Salisbury, MA 01952; (508) 462-4481.

Directions: From Interstate 95 north of Newburyport, take exit 60 and head east on Route 286, crossing U.S. 1, to the intersection with Route 1A. Follow Route 1A two miles east to the water. The campground will be on your right.

Trip notes: Here's that oceanfront property you've been looking for. Sites at Salisbury Beach—part of a 520-acre state-owned reservation—are on or near the shore. This boat-friendly campground is the perfect spot for sportfishing. A good outing for families with seaworthy craft is the seven-mile boat ride to the Isles of Shoals. Star Island, one member of this rocky string, is home to a hospitable inn and several historic religious structures. It is the largest, most accommodating port in the chain and is also accessible by chartered boats from Salisbury and Hampton, New Hampshire. Another island, Smuttynose, is rumored to harbor pirates' buried treasure. From the campground, a short paddle up the Merrimack River in a canoe will bring you to a good spot to try for striped bass. In the fall, this point where the river meets the sea is prime waterfowl-hunting territory.

Open: April through mid-October.

(81) Harold Parker State Forest

RV 7

Location: In North Andover; Eastern Massachusetts map page 355, grid b2.

Campsites, facilities: There are 125 wooded tent and RV sites without hookups. Fireplaces, picnic tables, flush toilets, showers, and a dump station are provided. Leashed pets are permitted.

Reservations, fees: Reservations are recommended. Sites are $6 a night.

Contact: Harold Parker State Forest, 1951 Turnpike Road, North Andover, MA 01845; (508) 686-3391.

Directions: From Boston, take Interstate 95 north. Get on Route 114 and drive west for 10 miles. Follow signs to the park.

Trip notes: Set among mixed hardwoods, the sites at Harold Parker are mostly shaded, private, and ideal for tents and tent trailers. The 3,500-acre state forest is crisscrossed with trails suitable for horseback riding and hiking. Ten ponds keep anglers busy: Berry Pond is stocked with trout, while the rest support populations of bass. Hunting is also permitted in season. The campground is only 26 miles from downtown Boston.

Open: May through October.

(82) Cape Ann Campsite

RV 8

Location: North of Route 128 on Cape Ann; Eastern Massachusetts map page 355, grid b4.

Campsites, facilities: There are 250 campsites for tents and RVs, 42 with full hookups, 90 with water and electric, and 118 with none. Fire rings, tables, sewage disposal, laundry, RV supplies, flush toilets, showers, a snack bar, and ice are available on the premises. Leashed pets are permitted.

Reservations, fees: Reservations are recommended June through Labor Day. Sites start at $15 a night for two people.

Contact: Cape Ann Campsite, 80 Atlantic Street, West Gloucester, MA 01930-1699; (508) 283-8683.

Directions: From Interstate 95, take Route 128 north to exit 13. Travel northeast on Concord Street, then turn right on Atlantic Street and continue to the campground.

Trip notes: Campsites are set on 100 acres of woodlands overlooking saltwater inlets. They are less than a mile from the white sands and dunes of Wingaersheek Beach. Be sure to explore Halibut Point State Park at the northernmost tip of Cape Ann. This bluff is an abandoned granite quarry, and on clear days visitors enjoy views all the way to Maine. Just to the south is the town of Rockport, a veritable artists colony boasting winding streets lined with galleries and studios.

Open: May 1 through November 1.

(83) Annisquam Campground

Location: South of Route 128 on Cape Ann; Eastern Massachusetts map page 355, grid b4.

Campsites, facilities: There are 35 sites for tents and RVs, all with electric hookups. Facilities include showers, picnic tables, and laundry. An Olympic-sized pool, a store, and rec hall are located on the property. Leashed pets are permitted.

Reservations, fees: Reservations are recommended. Sites start at $15 a night for two people in season plus $3 for water and electric hookups.

Contact: Annisquam Campground, Stanwood Point, Gloucester, MA 01930; (508) 283-2992.

Directions: From Interstate 95, take Route 128 north to exit 14. Turn right on Route 133 and travel east for 1.25 miles, then turn left on Stanwood Avenue. Cross the railroad tracks and continue to the campground at the end of the road.

Trip notes: Open-field camping by the ocean is the specialty of Annisquam. Amble from the pool to the volleyball court, or head down to the beach and stroll over sandy dunes tufted with sea grass. You're in the heart of an area that's rich in seafaring history: For more than 300 years, the city of Gloucester has thrived on the fruits of the ocean. Learn more at the Cape Ann Historical Museum in Gloucester or stop by the Schooner Adventure in Gloucester Harbor and stand at the wheel of a real "Gloucesterman"—America's last dory trawler. Another must-see is the Rocky Neck Art Colony off Main Street. It's the country's oldest working art colony.

Open: Early May through September.

(84) Winter Island Park

Location: Near the ocean in Salem; Eastern Massachusetts map page 355, grid b3.

Campsites, facilities: There are 41 sites, eight with water and electric hookups and two with just electric. A water shuttle, boat launch, bathhouse, hot showers, grills, picnic tables, and snack bar are available. The recreation area is open to the public. Leashed pets are permitted.

Reservations, fees: Reservations are recommended. Sites are $15 to $18 a night. Group and weekly rates are available upon request.

Contact: Winter Island Park, 50 Winter Island Road, Salem, MA 01970; (508) 745-9430.

Directions: From the junction of Interstate 95 and Route 128, take exit 25 to Gardner Parkway. Travel toward Salem on North Street. At the junction of Fort Avenue and Derby Street in town, take Fort Avenue northeast to Winter Island Road. Follow signs to the park.

Trip notes: Windsurfers, kayakers, and scuba divers will find Winter Island an ideal place to camp. From here, you can access Salem Harbor as well as a number of coves to the north and south. Right out your front door, there are opportunities to swim in the ocean or surf cast on the site of historic Fort Pickering and its lighthouse. Off the water, there's even more to do in historic Salem. For a spook, check out the Salem Witch Museum. Literary-minded travelers must pay a visit to the House of the Seven Gables, which inspired Nathaniel Hawthorne's book of the same name. Heritage trails, maritime history tours, museums, and cemeteries are some of the other offerings. Your best bet is to stop first at the Chamber of Commerce in the Old Town Hall in downtown Salem's Derby Square. They'll help you narrow down the choices and suggest those which best suit your interests.

Open: May 1 through October 31.

---

85 Boston Harbor Islands State Park

Location: In Boston Harbor; Eastern Massachusetts map page 355, grid c3.

Campsites, facilities: There are 41 individual sites and two group areas for tents only on four of the park's 17 islands: Lovells, Peddocks, Bumpkin, and Grape. Freshwater is not available on any of the islands, but there are toilets. No open fires are allowed in the camping areas, but beach fires are permitted below the tide line. A free water taxi shuttle runs between the islands. No pets are allowed.

Reservations, fees: Reservations are required. Sites are free.

Contact: Boston Harbor Islands State Park, Lincoln Street, Building 45, Hingham, MA 02043; (617) 740-1605.

Directions: Ferries to the islands depart regularly from Long Wharf in downtown Boston. Additional ferries leave from Hingham: Take Interstate 93 south out of Boston, then take Route 3A along the south shore to Hingham. Follow signs to the ferry.

Trip notes: Boston Harbor Islands State Park encompasses a group of islands that are rich in history and natural treasures. Peddocks Island, at 134 acres, is one of the largest and most diverse: You can see the remains of Fort Andrews, which was active from 1904 through World War II, at East Head; foot trails pass by a salt marsh, pond,

and coastal forest, and a visitors center has displays on the natural and military history of the island. Lovells Island was once home to Fort Standish.

Grape Island used to be cultivated by Native Americans and colonial farmers, and now wild blackberries, bayberries, and rose hips proliferate, attracting many species of birds. Bumpkin Island is lined with slate and shell beaches and dotted with open fields. Fort Warren, a National Historic Landmark, dominates Georges Island (there's no camping, but ferries do stop here daily); this granite fort, constructed between 1833 and 1869, was used during the Civil War for training Union soldiers and later as a prison for captured Confederates. Sites differ from island to island, but most are partially shaded. No matter where you end up, you'll enjoy million-dollar views of Boston.

Open: May through Columbus Day.

---

86 Wompatuck State Park

Location: South of Hingham; Eastern Massachusetts map page 355, grid c3.

Campsites, facilities: There are 400 campsites, 140 with electric hookups. Facilities include flush toilets, rest rooms, showers, picnic tables, piped water, fireplaces, and dump stations. Leashed pets are permitted.

Reservations, fees: Reservations are accepted. Sites are $6 and $8 a night.

Contact: Wompatuck State Park, Union Street, Hingham, MA 02043; (617) 749-7160.

Directions: From Route 3 south of Boston, take exit 14. Drive northeast on Route 228 and follow signs to the park entrance.

Trip notes: Campers can access 10 miles of trails within Wompatuck State Park. Don't miss the two-mile interpretive trail that leads through old-growth forest. The Forest Sanctuary Climax Grove harbors large white pine, hemlock, and American beech trees, some nearly 200 years old. If you venture out to the coast just minutes away, you'll find the World's End Reservation on the peninsula at the end of Martin's Lane in Hingham; it was landscaped by Frederick Law Olmsted, renowned designer of New York City's Central Park. Seven miles of carriage roads and footpaths traverse the reservation's drumlin—an ancient pile of glacial silt. From atop Planter's Hill you can look out across Hingham Bay and see the Boston skyline.

Open: Mid-April to mid-October.

87 Norwell Campsites

Location: South of Hingham in Norwell; Eastern Massachusetts map page 355, grid c3.

Campsites, facilities: There are 75 RV sites, all with hookups. Free hot showers, flush toilets, and LP gas are available, and there's a swimming pool on the grounds. Leashed pets are permitted.

Reservations, fees: Reservations are recommended. Sites start at $15 a night.

Contact: Norwell Campsites, 239 Washington Street, Norwell, MA 02061; (617) 871-0527.

Directions: From Interstate 93 south of Boston, take Route 3 south to exit 13. Travel 1.5 miles north on Route 53 to the campground entrance.

Trip notes: Tenters will find no accommodations here, as only RVers are welcome. Sites are mostly shaded, but are located amid urban surroundings. Just 20 miles from downtown Boston via bus, Norwell is an ideal jumping-off point for big-city adventures. Two self-guided tours worthy

of note are the Black Heritage Trail and the Freedom Trail. On the former you'll see the oldest standing black church building and the first public school for black children; for information, call (617) 742-1854. The Freedom Trail traces 350 years of American history along a 2.5-mile red line on a sidewalk. Begin at the Boston Common Information Center or the Boston National Historical Park Visitor Center; call (617) 242-5462 for information. To unwind in a more pastoral setting, the 3,500-acre Wompatuck State Park in Hingham is open to boating, biking, fishing, and horseback riding. And South Shore beaches are just a short drive to the east.

Open: Year-round, with limited winter sites; fully operational April 1 through December 1.

88 Fourth Cliff Recreation Area

Location: South of Scituate on an ocean spit; Eastern Massachusetts map page 355, grid d4.

Campsites, facilities: There are 31 sites for tents and RVs, 11 with RV hookups. The campground is open to military personnel only. Sewage disposal, ice, tables, grills, a rec hall, and bathhouse are available. Leashed pets are permitted.

Reservations, fees: Reservations are necessary. Sites are $12 a night for RVs and $8 for tents.

Contact: Pat Ames, Fourth Cliff Recreation Area, P.O. Box 479, Humarock, MA 02047; (617) 837-9269 or (800) 468-9547.

Directions: From Interstate 93 south of Boston, take Route 3 south to exit 12 and turn right at the bottom of the exit. Travel 1.5 miles to Furnace Street and turn left. When you reach the T intersection, turn left on Ferry Street. Turn right on Sea Street, going over the bridge, then left on Central

Avenue. At the fork, bear left and continue to Fourth Cliff.

Trip notes: The campground overlooks the Atlantic Ocean at the end of the Fourth Cliff peninsula, with the North River on the inside. Sites are right on the ocean, so you can surf cast from your front door. An information display booth at the office posts the latest news on local points of interest and entertainment. Discount tickets and season passes for area events are sometimes available.

89 Circle C. G. Farm Campground

Location: North of the Rhode Island border in Bellingham; Eastern Massachusetts map page 355, grid d1.

Campsites, facilities: There are 135 wooded sites for tents and RVs, 90 with full hookups. Group safari sites are available. You'll find dump stations, tables, fireplaces, ice, firewood, RV supplies, and a grocery store on site. There are also many sports courts, miniature golf, two swimming pools, and a pond for fishing. Small pets are allowed.

Reservations, fees: Reservations are recommended, and are necessary for holiday weekends. Sites start at $21 a night for two people.

Contact: Circle C. G. Farm Campground, 1131 North Main Street, Bellingham, MA 02019; (508) 966-1136.

Directions: From Interstate 95 southwest of Boston, take Interstate 495 north to exit 18. From there, travel a mile south on Route 126 to the campground entrance on the left.

Trip notes: Bring your spurs, for Circle C. G. takes you west. Some of the popular planned activities include country-and-western bands, cowboy breakfasts, wagon rides, and chuck wagon suppers and shows. All summer long, Boston group tours—including visits to the John Hancock Tower and Fanueil Hall—leave and return directly from the campground. Nearby in Uxbridge, the 1,005-acre Blackstone River National Heritage Corridor offers canoeing, hiking, and hunting in season.

Open: Year-round.

90 Normandy Farms Campground

Location: North of Foxboro; Eastern Massachusetts map page 355, grid d2.

Campsites, facilities: There are 355 wooded sites for tents and RVs, 95 with full hookups and 260 with water and electric. Each site has a concrete patio, fireplace, and picnic table. Use of air conditioners and heaters is allowed. Some facilities are wheelchair accessible. Church services, laundry facilities, dump stations, hot showers, four swimming pools, a rec hall, sports courts, and a traffic control gate are provided. Firewood and ice are available, and there's a store on the property. Leashed pets are permitted.

Reservations, fees: Reservations are recommended during the summer. Sites start at $25 a night.

Contact: Normandy Farms Campground, 72 West Street, Foxboro, MA 02035; (508) 543-7600.

Directions: From the junction of Interstate 495 and U.S. 1 southwest of Boston, travel one mile north on U.S. 1 then 1.5 miles east on Thurston and West Streets to the campground.

Trip notes: Offering unrivaled amenities—including four swimming pools, one of which is indoor, developed sites, and wooded sites in rolling terrain—Normandy

Farms is an RVers' paradise. There are several safari sites for group camping and a separate tent area by a pond. Multiuse trails leave the campground. Nearby, the F. Gilbert Hills State Forest, also in Foxboro, has nearly 1,000 acres of hiking, cross-country skiing, and horseback riding trails, should you need to get away from the organized recreation philosophy of Normandy Farms. Typical events at the campground include teen pool parties, bingo, dances, and live entertainment.

Open: Year-round.

(91) Boston Hub KOA

Location: South of Foxboro near Wrentham State Forest; Eastern Massachusetts map page 355, grid d2.

Campsites, facilities: There are 140 wooded sites for tents and RVs, most with hookups. Each site has a table and fire ring. Use of air conditioners and heaters is allowed. Group sites, free hot showers, propane, LP gas, and dump stations are available. Also on the property are miniature golf, a game room, billiards, pools, a playground, petting zoo, sports courts, and laundry facilities. Firewood and ice are available. Leashed pets are permitted.

Reservations, fees: Reservations are recommended for June through Labor Day. Sites start at $23 a night for two people.

Contact: Boston Hub KOA, 1095 South Street, P.O. Box 505, Wrentham, MA 02093-0505; (508) 384-8930 or (800) KOA-2173.

Directions: From Interstate 495 west of Foxboro, take exit 15 to Route 1A. Travel 200 yards south to the campground entrance.

Trip notes: Oak trees provide shade and privacy for campers who snag the spacious sites at Boston Hub. A plethora of recreational opportunities abounds on site, from pools to petting zoos, as well as organized events such as bus tours and theme dinners. Because of its proximity to a main interstate highway, this facility tends to be more popular with RVers, but there are sites especially for tents.

This is not a peaceful campground, since the focus is on activity—and that's fitting given its location in Wrentham, a town that was established as a frontier settlement in 1660. You'll find the rolling green hills and clear lakes that attracted the first pioneers to this spot. Here and at nearby Wrentham State Forest, there are trails for hiking and biking; hikers can also head to Joe's Rock (off Route 1A), a set of high cliffs affording views of Boston. You can fish and swim at Lake Pearl Park, established in 1885, also in Wrentham.

Open: April through October.

(92) Canoe River Campground

Location: East of Mansfield; Eastern Massachusetts map page 355, grid d2.

Campsites, facilities: There are 120 wooded sites for tents and RVs. Flush toilets, hot showers, boat rentals, two pools, ice, firewood, propane, picnic tables, and fireplaces are available. Leashed pets are permitted.

Reservations, fees: Reservations are recommended. Sites are $16 to $20 a night for two people.

Contact: Canoe River Campground, 137 Mill Street, East Mansfield, MA 02031; (508) 339-6462.

Directions: From Interstate 495, take exit 10 and head east on Route 123. Turn left on Newland Street and continue about two miles to the campground.

Trip notes: Geese and ducks call Mill Pond

home, and young campers love to keep them well fed. Sites are situated on wooded, flat terrain near the pond, which is open to nonmotorized boating and fishing but not swimming; two heated pools on the property are provided for those who want to take the plunge. Families will also appreciate the large playgrounds here. When in Mansfield, you ought to check out the entertainment line-up at the Great Woods Center for the Performing Arts. Big names in jazz, rock, folk, and classical music are booked at the outdoor theater all summer long; call (508) 339-2333 for information.

Open: April 15 through October 15.

93 Plymouth Rock KOA

Location: North of Middleboro; Eastern Massachusetts map page 355, grid d3.

Campsites, facilities: There are 276 sites for tents and RVs, 132 with full hookups, plus safari areas for groups. Small fire rings, picnic tables, hot showers, modern toilets, sanitary dump stations, laundry facilities, and mail services are provided. You'll also find game and rec rooms, a playground, and off-season RV storage. Leashed pets are permitted.

Reservations, fees: Reservations are recommended. Sites are $21 to $31 a night.

Contact: Plymouth Rock KOA, 438 Plymouth Street, P.O. Box 616, Middleboro, MA 02346; (508) 947-6435 or (800) 638-6435.

Directions: From Interstate 495, take exit 6 onto U.S. 44. Travel 2.5 miles east to the campground entrance.

Trip notes: This campground is designed for RVers, though tenters will find their own separate area nearby, complete with water. Most sites are open, roomy, and grassy and offer some kind of shade. Seventy acres of woods on the premises await hikers. There

are organized activities as well as bus tours of all the major attractions of Boston and the South Shore. At nearby Massasoit State Park (see campground number 94) southeast of Taunton, you'll find 1,500 acres of parkland where you can swim, fish, boat, hunt, hike, and canoe.

Open: April 1 through October.

94 Massasoit State Park

Location: Southeast of Taunton; Eastern Massachusetts map page 355, grid e3.

Campsites, facilities: There are 126 sites for tents and RVs up to 21 feet in length; 24 sites have full hookups and another 81 are equipped with electricity. A dump station, boat ramp, piped water, showers, picnic tables, flush toilets, and fireplaces are provided. Leashed pets are permitted.

Reservations, fees: Sites are available on a first-come, first-served basis. Depending on services, fees are $6, $8, and $9 a night.

Contact: Massasoit State Park, 1361 Middleboro Avenue, East Taunton, MA 02718; (508) 822-7405.

Directions: From Interstate 495 north of Middleboro, take exit 5 onto Route 18/105 heading south. Signs will indicate the entrance to the park.

Trip notes: Despite its proximity to the urban center of Taunton, Massasoit State Park offers quiet, wooded, natural sites beside a freshwater pond that's open to nonmotorized boating. Hunting, swimming, and fishing are permitted throughout the 1,500-acre park. Named for the Wampanoag Indian chief who negotiated a peace treaty with the Pilgrims in 1621, the park displays historic markers telling the story of the first people to inhabit this land.

Open: Mid-April through Columbus Day.

95 Forge Pond Campground

Location: North of Fall River in Assonet; Eastern Massachusetts map page 355, grid e3.

Campsites, facilities: There are 65 sites for tents and RVs with hookups. Dump stations, metered hot showers, a rec hall, firewood, a game room, and playground are provided. Leashed pets are permitted.

Reservations, fees: Reservations are recommended. Call for rates. Seasonal sites are available.

Contact: Forge Pond Campground, 62 Forge Road, Assonet, MA 02702; (508) 644-5701.

Directions: From Fall River, take Route 24 north to Assonet, then travel northeast on Route 79 to the railroad crossing. Turn left on Forge Road, go a quarter mile west, and turn right at the sign for "A Camper's Campground."

Trip notes: Large, wooded sites are set on freshwater Forge Pond. This campground is close to the city of Fall River, which boasts many historical sights including the battleship *Massachusetts*. Just down Route 79 from the campground, Freetown State Forest offers more than 5,000 acres of woodlands with multiuse trails for biking, hiking, and horseback riding, as well as wheelchair-accessible facilities.

Open: May 1 through October 15.

full hookups. Use of air conditioners and heaters is allowed. Open fireplaces, breakfast, a restaurant, LP gas, RV service, RV supplies, laundry facilities, a camp store, ice, firewood, rowboat and canoe rentals, dump stations, and a bathhouse are available. On site you'll also find a playground, courts for badminton and volleyball, and horseshoe pits. No pets are allowed.

Reservations, fees: Reservations are recommended in the summer. Sites are $18 to $25 a night.

Contact: Pinewood Lodge Campground, 190 Pinewood Road, Plymouth, MA 02360; (508) 746-3548.

Directions: From Boston, follow Interstate 93 south to Route 3 and continue driving south. Take exit 6 to U.S. 44 and go three miles west to Pinewood Lodge.

Trip notes: Tall pines surround campsites overlooking a freshwater lake at Pinewood Lodge. Motorized boats are not allowed on the water, so swimming and fishing are the preferred pursuits. On weekends, the recreation director plans events with such themes as Western Weekend or Christmas in July. In Plymouth, pay homage to the native American berry at the Cranberry World Visitors Center on the waterfront. It's free, and not only will you learn the history of this native crop, you'll get to sample the tart treat as well. From the campground, you can also walk to the Plymouth Colony Winery on Pinewood Road for tastings.

Open: April 1 through November 1.

96 Pinewood Lodge Campground

Location: West of Plymouth; Eastern Massachusetts map page 355, grid d4.

Campsites, facilities: There are 250 shaded sites for tents and RVs, most with

97 Ellis Haven Family Campground

Location: South of Plymouth; Eastern Massachusetts map page 355, grid d4.

Campsites, facilities: There are 420 open and wooded sites, 380 with water and electric hookups. Dump stations, laundry facilities, hot showers, tables, and flush toilets are provided. A camp store sells ice, firewood, and LP gas. Also on site are boat rentals, sports fields and courts, a playground, miniature golf, a pavilion, and snack bar. Leashed pets are permitted.

Reservations, fees: Reservations are recommended. Base rates are $19 to $23 a night. Weekly, monthly, and seasonal rates are available.

Contact: Ellis Haven Family Campground, 531 Federal Furnace Road, Plymouth, MA 02360; (508) 746-0803.

Directions: From Boston, follow Interstate 93 south to Route 3 and continue driving south. Take exit 6 to U.S. 44 and drive one mile west. Bear left at the lights onto Seven Hills–Federal Furnace Road. Follow signs to the campground entrance on the right.

Trip notes: Set in the woods by a spring-fed lake, Ellis Haven offers campers a place to enjoy a variety of water sports that don't involve motorized boating. Most sites are rented seasonally, but some are available to overnight campers. A trip to Plymouth wouldn't be complete without a visit to Plymouth Rock, the very spot where America's first Pilgrims reportedly landed aboard the *Mayflower* in 1620. To get a real sense of what life was like for the Pilgrims, stroll around the Plimoth Plantation, a living history museum re-creating village life in 1627. It's also located in Plymouth; for information call (508) 746-1679.

Open: May 1 through October 1.

98 Shady Acres Campground

Location: Southwest of Plymouth; Eastern Massachusetts map page 355, grid d4.

Campsites, facilities: There are 127 sites for tents and RVs, 112 with water and electric hookups and 40 with additional sewer connections. Each site has a fire ring and table. Dump stations, laundry facilities, a camp store, rec hall, playground, flush toilets, free hot showers, and on-site off-season RV storage are provided. LP gas, firewood, and ice are available. Leashed pets are permitted.

Reservations, fees: Reservations are recommended. Sites are $18 to 22 a night. Seasonal sites are available.

Contact: Shady Acres Campground, P.O. Box 128, South Carver, MA 02366; (508) 886-4040.

Directions: From Interstate 495 south of Boston, take exit 6. Travel east on U.S. 44 to Route 58 and turn right, heading south. In four miles, turn left on Mayflower Road. The Shady Acres entrance is at the end of Mayflower Road on Tremont Street.

Trip notes: Here you'll find quiet, shady sites on rolling hills beside a pond. Most are fully prepared for RVs, though there's also a less-developed area for tents. Myles Standish State Forest is right down the road from the campground. In winter, miles of trails there are maintained for use by cross-country skiers and snowmobilers. In warmer months, 35 glacial kettle ponds nurture a community of rare and uncommon plants.

Open: Year-round.

99 Myles Standish State Forest

Location: South of Plymouth; Eastern Massachusetts map page 355, grid e4.

Campsites, facilities: Several campgrounds within the forest offer a total of 475 campsites. Some areas have hot showers, and all have rest rooms, water, picnic tables, fireplaces, and dump stations. Group sites are available to nonprofit organizations. Leashed pets are permitted.

Reservations, fees: Reservations are recommended for summer weekends. Sites are $5 to $6 a night.

Contact: Myles Standish State Forest, P.O. Box 272, Cranberry Road, South Carver, MA 02366; (508) 866-2526.

Directions: From Route 3 south of Plymouth, take exit 5 and travel west on Long Pond Road. Follows signs to the forest entrance.

Trip notes: Myles Standish is the largest recreation area in Massachusetts and attracts similarly sized crowds, especially in the summertime. There are 15 miles of trails for bikes, 20 miles for equestrians, and 35 miles for recreational vehicles—and motorcycles are allowed! Three miles of trails are devoted to hikers only. You'll find bass, perch, and pickerel in several stocked ponds as well as fire towers from which you can get an overview of the entire park. The forest sprawls across more than 14,000 protected acres in Plymouth and Carver, which was once part of the Indian village of Patuxet. Within the park is the Pine Barrens, one of the largest contiguous pitch pine/scrub oak communities north of Long Island. Open seeded fields attract hawks, owls, waterfowl, juncos, and many other winged wonders. In season, hunters can bag pheasants, quail, grouse, and rabbit deer. Snowmobilers and cross-country skiers make their way here in the winter months.

Open: Mid-April through Columbus Day, but 44 sites are open year-round for self-contained units.

100 Indianhead Resort

Location: South of Plymouth near the ocean; Eastern Massachusetts map page 355, grid e4.

Campsites, facilities: There are 220 sites with water and electric hookups. Each site has a fire ring, grill, and picnic table. Use of air conditioners and heaters is allowed. Facilities include metered hot showers, flush toilets, a dump station, insect control, a rec hall, game room, camp store, sports courts, and a playground. LP gas, firewood, and ice are available on site. Leashed pets are permitted.

Reservations, fees: Reservations are recommended in the summer. Sites start at $21 a night.

Contact: Indianhead Resort, 1929 State Road/Route 3A, Plymouth, MA 02360; (508) 888-3688.

Directions: From Route 3 south of Boston, take exit 2 and travel two miles north on Route 3A to the campground entrance on the left.

Trip notes: Lakeside sites are tucked into the woods at Indianhead Resort. Campers can frolic in freshwater Savory Pond, which is open to all types of nonmotorized boating, swimming, and fishing. Pedalboats, rowboats, and canoes may be rented at the campground. What's great about this place is that you can walk to the ocean beach through tiny Ellisville Harbor State Park, which is just across the street from the campground entrance. It's less than a mile to the protected stretch of beach where saltwater fishing enthusiasts can cast out a line.

Open: April through Columbus Day.

101 Maple Park Family Campground

Location: North of the Cape Cod Canal in East Wareham; Eastern Massachusetts map page 355, grid e4.

Campsites, facilities: There are 400 wooded sites, 300 with full hookups. Dump stations, hot showers, boat rentals, horseshoe pits, planned activities, and fireplaces are available. Use of heaters and air conditioners is prohibited, as are minibikes and motorcycles. Males are required to have short hair. Leashed pets are permitted.

Reservations, fees: Reservations are recommended in the summer, but are absolutely necessary during the Cranberry Harvest Festival on Columbus Day weekend. Sites start at $18 to $20 a night.

Contact: Maple Park Family Campground, RFD 1, East Wareham, MA 02538; (508) 295-4945.

Directions: From the junction of U.S. 6 and Route 28 north of the Bourne Bridge, travel two miles north to the campground entrance on Glen Charlie Road.

Trip notes: This secluded campground overlooks cranberry bogs and borders a freshwater pond where campers can swim. Even though the sites are wooded, they are squished together and lack privacy. Strict rules about noise and visitors keep the place very quiet despite its size. Between all the towns and villages in the area, there are more than 13,000 acres of cranberry bogs. Depending on what time of year you visit, you'll get to observe this native plant being fertilized, harvested, or maintained. Be aware that it's illegal to venture onto a bog.

Open: May 1 through October 15.

102 Sandy Pond Campground

Location: North of the Cape Cod Canal in Plymouth; Eastern Massachusetts map page 355, grid e4.

Campsites, facilities: There are 129 wooded sites for tents and RVs, most with hookups. Each site has a table and fire ring. A dump station, canoe rentals, hot showers, flush toilets, a camp store, firewood, ice, and playgrounds are available. Leashed pets are permitted; big, aggressive dogs are not allowed during the summer.

Reservations, fees: Reservations are recommended and must be accompanied by a 50 percent deposit. Sites start at $20 to $24 a night for two people, with surcharges for boats and extra cars.

Contact: The Doonans, Sandy Pond Campground, Bourne Road, South Plymouth, MA 02360; (508) 759-9336 in season, or (508) 224-3707 during the off-season.

Directions: From Boston, take Route 3 south to exit 3. Make a right turn at the end of the ramp, drive about 1,000 feet, then turn left on Long Pond Road. After 1.7 miles, turn right on Halfway Pond Road, and after seven-tenths of a mile, turn left on Bourne Road. The campground is 5.5 miles ahead on the right.

Trip notes: The campground's 2,000 feet of shoreline on freshwater Sandy Pond offer opportunities for fishing and swimming. Sites are surrounded by towering pines, and the grounds are impeccably neat. There are different areas for different tastes so be sure to ask; for instance, some sites overlook the second hole of the Atlantic Country Club golf course, while remote tent sites provide solitude-seekers with ample privacy. The campground is within easy distance of both Cape Cod and Plymouth. To reflect on our nation's history, amble into Plymouth proper and look for the National Monument to the Forefathers. Perched on a hilltop overlooking Plymouth Harbor, where the *Mayflower* pulled up more than 375 years ago, this 81-foot structure was built in 1889 to honor the virtues that carried the Pilgrims to the New World: Morality, Law, Education, and Liberty.

Open: April 15 through October 15.

103 Knight and Look Campground

Location: In Rochester, south of Wareham and close to Buzzards Bay; Eastern Massachusetts map page 355, grid e4.

Campsites, facilities: There are 135 tent and RV sites among tall pine and oak trees, most with water and electric hookups. Each site has a fire ring and table. Group sites are available. You'll find a small grocery store, RV storage, laundry facilities, sewage disposal, hot showers, and flush toilets on the premises. Leashed pets are permitted at the campground.

Reservations, fees: Reservations are recommended in the summer. Sites are $22 to $25 a night.

Contact: Knight and Look Campground, Route 105, Rochester, MA 02770; (508) 763-2454.

Directions: From Interstate 195 near Rochester, take exit 20. Travel about 1.5 miles northwest on Route 105 to the campground entrance.

Trip notes: Just a stone's throw from Buzzards Bay, this campground is a good choice for people who want access to all that Cape Cod has to offer but don't want to be engulfed by throngs of tourists. Campsites at Knight and Look are peaceful and level, and a small pond on the property is stocked with fish. Only nonmotorized boating is allowed. Seafarers can launch their craft, people-powered or motorized, at the public docks in the nearby seaside town of Marion. Buzzards Bay and the Cape Cod Canal offer plenty of protected water for many types of aquatic recreation. The canal makes it a breeze—quite literally for sailors—to access the north shore of the Cape.

Open: Mid-April through October 1.

104 Westport Camping Grounds

Location: South of Fall River in Westport; Eastern Massachusetts map page 355, grid e3.

Campsites, facilities: There are 100 sites for tents and RVs, all with water and electric hookups and 80 with additional sewer connections. Dump stations, fire rings, tables, sports courts, flush toilets, hot showers, and some groceries are available. There's also a game room, rec hall, billiard room, snack bar, and security gate. No pets are allowed.

Reservations, fees: Reservations are recommended; there are no refunds. Sites start at $20 a night for two people.

Contact: Westport Camping Grounds, 346 Old County Road, Box N112, Westport, MA 02790; (508) 636-2555.

Directions: From Interstate 195 east of Fall River, take exit 10 toward Horseneck Beach. Follow Route 88 south for three miles then turn left at the second set of traffic lights. The campground is a quarter mile from the intersection on Old County Road.

Trip notes: This secluded and woodsy campground is the right choice for RVers who want to be close to Horseneck Beach and other waterside locales in the Fall River/ New Bedford region, but desire more amenities than the state park can offer. Sites are a little close together—each is about 30 feet wide—but natural barriers maintain a measure of privacy. Lovely beaches are a short drive south, including Horseneck Beach State Reservation. If you have an interest in the whaling history of New England, make a trek to the Whaling Museum in New Bedford, where you can board a half-scale replica of a whaling bark.

This is the largest museum devoted to America's whaling past.

Open: April 1 through October 31.

---

105 Horseneck Beach State Reservation

Location: On the ocean in Westport Point; Eastern Massachusetts map page 355, grid f3.

Campsites, facilities: There are 100 sites for tents and RVs without hookups, but a dump station is provided. Facilities include tables, grills, a boat ramp, piped water, hot showers, and fireplaces. Leashed pets are permitted.

Reservations, fees: Reservations are accepted. Sites are $6 a night.

Contact: Horseneck Beach State Reservation, Route 88, P.O. Box 328, Westport, MA 02791; (508) 636-8816.

Directions: From Interstate 195 east of Fall River, take exit 10 toward Horseneck Beach. Follow Route 88 south to the ocean. Signs will direct you to the campground.

Trip notes: If you're a boater who wants to explore Buzzards Bay and the Elizabeth Islands or port-hop down to Newport, Rhode Island, this is the ideal campground. Sites are open and most have views of the ocean. There's a boat ramp at the state reservation. You can surf cast for saltwater species from the campground or head out on the water. Ocean swimming and sunbathing are other popular pursuits here.

Open: Memorial Day weekend through Columbus Day weekend.

---

106 Coastal Acres Camping Court

Location: At the tip of the Cape, west of

Provincetown; Cape Cod and Martha's Vineyard map page 356, grid a3.

Campsites, facilities: There are 120 sites for tents and RVs, 80 with full hookups. Each site has a table and concrete patio. Use of air conditioners and heaters is not allowed. Seasonal sites, RV storage, RV supplies, a grocery store, LP gas, ice, and a dump station are available. Leashed pets are permitted.

Reservations, fees: Reservations are recommended in July and August. Sites are $20 to $27 a night for two people.

Contact: Coastal Acres Camping Court, P.O. Box 593, Provincetown, MA 02657; (508) 487-1700.

Directions: Follow U.S. 6 to its end, then turn left at Herring Cove onto Route 6A. Continue to the Bradford Street extension.

Trip notes: This is one of the few private outer Cape campgrounds that allows pets during the busy season. There are virtually no amenities at the campground itself, so you have to venture into nearby Provincetown for laundry, showers, and supplies. It is, however, the closest campground to Province Lands Park at the tip of the Cape. Here you'll find a visitors center, foot and bike paths, beaches, a naturalist program, and excellent birding; you'll likely see a number of hawks, cardinals, owls, and kingfishers, to name a handful of the winged locals. This is quintessential Cape Cod, the perfect spot to stake a claim in the sand dunes and read a trashy novel, take a strenuous trek in the soft sand, or pick some wild cranberries.

Open: April 1 through November 1.

---

107 Dunes' Edge Campground

Location: At the tip of the Cape, northwest of Provincetown between Race Point Beach and Pilgrim Lake; Cape Cod and Martha's Vineyard map page 356, grid a3.

Campsites, facilities: There are 100 wooded sites, 15 suitable for trailers and the rest for tents. Only 22 sites have hookups, and all have tables. Use of air conditioners and heaters is not allowed. You'll find a dump station, hot showers, laundry facilities, and a limited grocery store that sells ice on the property. Leashed pets are permitted.

Reservations, fees: Reservations are recommended in July and August and require a nonrefundable deposit. Credit cards and personal checks are not accepted. Sites start at $20 a night for two people.

Contact: Dunes' Edge Campground, P.O. Box 875, Route 6, Provincetown, MA 02657; (508) 487-9815.

Directions: On U.S. 6 heading toward Provincetown, look for the "Entering Provincetown" sign. Travel two miles past the sign and turn right at mile marker 116. The campground will be on your right.

Trip notes: Quiet and family oriented, Dunes' Edge is a tenter's oasis in the treed dunes of the outer Cape. Most sites afford privacy—they are nestled between the Cape Cod National Seashore and Horses Head, one of the tallest hills on the outer Cape—and once you park your car, you can bike or walk to most of the attractions in Provincetown. In town, you'll find some of the best restaurants and a slew of quaint galleries and shops. Hiking trails to the national seashore and Race Point Beach leave right from the campground. At nearby Race Point you can enjoy saltwater fishing and swimming. Just down the road, Beech Forest is a prime birding spot and one of the last remaining stands of the beech trees that once covered the entire Cape. Most of the area was heavily forested until European settlers cleared the land for farming in the mid-1600s. Once the trees were gone, wind and sand collaborated on a successful dune-making enterprise. Race Point Beach is the epitome of Cape Cod, with rolling dunes, an endless expanse of ocean, and infinite beachfront.

Open: Early May through late September.

108 North of Highland Camping Area

Location: In North Truro on the east shore of the outer Cape; Cape Cod and Martha's Vineyard map page 356, grid a3.

Campsites, facilities: There are 237 sites for tents and tent trailers with no hookups. Picnic tables, free cold showers, metered hot showers, flush toilets, and a rec building are available. Pets and wood fires are prohibited.

Reservations, fees: Reservations are encouraged. Sites are $18 a night.

Contact: North of Highland Camping Area, P.O. Box 297, North Truro, MA 02652; (508) 487-1191.

Directions: Take U.S. 6 to North Truro then turn right on Head of Meadow Road. The campground is on the left.

Trip notes: Surrounded by the Cape Cod National Seashore, this campground with sites set amid scrub pines is designed for beach-lovers. Wood fires are permitted on the beach, and just south of here is Highland Light. To better enjoy the shoreline, check in at the National Seashore's Salt Pond Visitors Center in Eastham where you can learn about the 40 miles of sandy beaches and obtain a map of the area's biking and nature trails. Films and exhibits will help you interpret what this 27,000-acre site has to offer.

Open: Mid-May through mid-September.

109 North Truro Camping Area

🚴 🚶🏃 **RV** ⚠7

Location: In North Truro on the east shore of the outer Cape; Cape Cod and Martha's Vineyard map page 356, grid a3.

Campsites, facilities: There are 350 sites for tents, tent trailers, and RVs; 105 have full hookups, 125 have water and electric, and 100 have none. Facilities include a store, laundry, LP gas, a dump station, rest rooms, free cable TV, and metered hot showers. Town ordinances prohibit campfires. Dogs are not allowed mid-June through Labor Day and must be leashed at all other times.

Reservations, fees: Reservations require a deposit. No credit cards are accepted. Sites are $7.50 a night per person with a $15 minimum.

Contact: North Truro Camping Area, Highland Road, North Truro, MA 02652; (508) 487-1847.

Directions: Follow U.S. 6 east, passing through Truro. Watch for Highland Road (there's also a South Highland Road) and turn right. The campground is a short distance ahead.

Trip notes: Families are the dominant campers at North Truro, where sites are set in native scrub pines. The facility affords easy access to the hiking and biking trails of the 27,000-acre Cape Cod National Seashore to the south, and beaches for sunbathing, swimming, and fishing are just minutes away. One interesting and historical ramble leaves from Truro proper to the south: Look for the Pilgrim Heights area. A path leads to the site of a spring where Pilgrims may have first quenched their thirst in New England. The moderate walk is under a mile in length and has some log steps.

Open: Year-round; fully operational mid-June through Labor Day.

110 Horton's Camping Resort

🚶🏃♿ **RV** ⚠8

Location: In North Truro, just inland from the Highland Light; Cape Cod and Martha's Vineyard map page 356, grid a3.

Campsites, facilities: There are 222 open and wooded sites near the ocean with separate sections for tents and RVs; 76 sites have hookups. Each site has a picnic table. A dump station, water faucets, laundry facilities, camp store, playground, snack bar, rest rooms, metered showers, horseshoe pits, and a volleyball court are provided. Fires are prohibited by town ordinance. No dogs are allowed.

Reservations, fees: Reservations are requested during July and August and require a deposit. Sites are $16 to $22 a night.

Contact: Horton's Camping Resort, P.O. Box 308, 71 South Highland Road, North Truro, MA 02652; (508) 487-1220 or (800) 252-7705.

Directions: From U.S. 6 at North Truro, take South Highland Road east for one mile to the campground.

Trip notes: Scrub pines and a golf course are all that stand between you and the Atlantic Ocean when you camp at Horton's. Most RV sites are grassy and open, while tenters are nestled into wooded lots. There's also an adults-only area where children aren't welcome. A path from the campground leads to the Highland Golf Links course and down to the Highland Light. Saltwater fishing and swimming are possible at the nearby beaches of the Cape Cod National Seashore, where you can hike the coastline to your heart's content.

Open: Early May through mid-October.

⟮111⟯ Paine's Campground

🚲🏃🚶   🚐 ⛺ 10

Location: North of Marconi Beach in South Wellfleet; Cape Cod and Martha's Vineyard map page 356, grid b4.

Campsites, facilities: There are 150 sites primarily for tents and tent trailers, with a separate RV area that has 25 sites with water and electric hookups. Ice and a dump station are available. Metered hot showers, approved drinking water, and picnic tables are provided. Cookstoves and charcoal grills, but not campfires, are permitted. Pets are not allowed in July and August and must be leashed at all other times.

Reservations, fees: Reservations are recommended in July and August and cost $5. Sites are $15 to $20 a night for two people, plus $4 with hookups. Children and dogs are $3 extra each.

Contact: Bob and Cynthia Paine, Paine's Campground, Box 201, South Wellfleet, MA 02663; (508) 349-3007.

Directions: From the junction of U.S. 6 and Old Country Road one mile north of the Marconi Beach access, travel three-quarters of a mile east on Old Country Road to the campground.

Trip notes: Paine's Campground is a tenter's paradise, with sites divided into sections catering to the different needs of campers. Family sites accommodate multiple tents, vans, and small tent trailers, while the "quiet couples" area is devoid of children. Sites for singles and young couples are more open and thus conducive to meeting neighboring campers. "Lug-in" sites are reached via private, shaded footpaths and are restricted to tents only. A small RV section offers large, deep, shaded sites with water and electric hookups. There are even group sites that are available by reservation only.

Hiking and biking trails lead from the campground to the beaches of the Cape Cod National Seashore. A mile to the south, scenic sandstone cliffs provide a backdrop to the white sands of Marconi Beach. In South Wellfleet, the Massachusetts Audubon Society operates the Wellfleet Bay Wildlife Sanctuary—800 acres of marsh, pine woods, fields, brooks, and moors laced with five miles of foot trails. Enter the sanctuary on the west side of U.S. 6 just north of the Eastham/Wellfleet town line.

Open: Mid-May through late September.

⟮112⟯ Maurice's Campground

🚲⚓🎣🏊   🚐 6

Location: Near the bay in Wellfleet; Cape Cod and Martha's Vineyard map page 356, grid b4.

Campsites, facilities: There are 240 sites for tents, trailers, and RVs, more than half with full hookups. You'll find a camp store equipped with a deli on the property. A dump station and LP gas are also available. Pets are not welcome.

Reservations, fees: Reservations are recommended for July and August. Sites start at $19 a night for two people.

Contact: Maurice M. Gauthier, Maurice's Campground, RR 2, Box 1, Wellfleet, MA 02667; (508) 349-2029.

Directions: Follow U.S. 6 past the Orleans rotary heading toward Provincetown. At the Eastham/Wellfleet town line, you'll see the Wellfleet Drive-In Theater on the left. Maurice's Campground is on the right, 200 yards down the road. Enter at the driveway to Ann's Motor Court/Maurice's Campground.

Trip notes: This campground is located on the Cape's main access road and thus doesn't offer much natural privacy, though sites are set in a pine grove. Saltwater swimming, fishing, and boating are all possible nearby. A bike trail leads from the campground to the beaches of the national seashore, so you can bypass the heavy summer traffic.

Open: May 24 through October 15.

---

113 Atlantic Oaks Campground

Location: North of Eastham; Cape Cod and Martha's Vineyard map page 356, grid b4.

Campsites, facilities: There are 100 sites for RVs with full hookups as well as a small tenting area. Free hot showers, cable TV, laundry, nightly movies in season, tables, and sewage disposal are available. Campfires are prohibited. Pets are not recommended.

Reservations, fees: Reservations are recommended. Winter season camping is available by reservation. Sites are $22 to $29 a night depending on the season.

Contact: Atlantic Oaks Campground, Route 6, Eastham, MA 02642; (508) 255-1437.

Directions: From Route 3 heading south out of Boston, get on the Cape by following U.S. 6. The campground is half a mile north of the national seashore entrance in Eastham.

Trip notes: Atlantic Oaks' large, wooded sites are custom tailored to meet the needs of RVers, including free cable TV hookups and pull-through sites. Only half a mile south of here, you can enter the outer Cape: The Cape Cod National Seashore encompasses and protects some 40 miles of wind-polished dunes, kettle ponds, scrub forests, marshes, and bogs. And some of the Cape's most serene beaches for strolling on are found on this spit of land. Windsurfing is allowed in waters outside of the life-guarded beaches. Don't forget to bring your bike, since the 25-mile-long Cape Cod Rail Trail runs directly behind the campground. Surf, bay, or freshwater swimming and fishing are all possible close by. Several nearby harbors offer boat ramps for public use.

Open: May 1 through November 1.

---

114 Nickerson State Park

Location: East of Brewster; Cape Cod and Martha's Vineyard map page 356, grid c4.

Campsites, facilities: There are 420 open, wooded, and shaded sites, split between seven areas, for tents and RVs with no hookups. Each site has a fireplace and picnic table. Dump stations, piped water, hot showers, telephones, recycling bins, and an amphitheater are available throughout the park, and there are boat ramps on the larger ponds. Two group sites open to nonprofit organizations only can accommodate up to 30 people each. Pets with rabies vaccination certification are allowed on a leash.

Reservations, fees: Reservations can be made over the phone up to two weeks before arrival for stays of two to 14 days between Memorial Day and Labor Day. Most sites are reserved for the entire summer by May 15. Payment is required within 10 days of making a reservation and can be made by sending a personal, bank, or traveler's check to the address below. Sites are $6 a night.

Contact: Nickerson State Park, 3488 Main Street, Brewster, MA 02631-1521; (508) 896-4615.

Directions: From U.S. 6 near Brewster,

take exit 12. Turn left at the bottom of the ramp and travel one mile to the park entrance on the left.

Trip notes: More than a dozen freshwater kettle ponds, formed some 60,000 years ago by retreating glaciers, are open to swimming, boating, and fishing at Nickerson State Park, and several are even stocked with trout year-round. Trails for hiking, biking, cross-country skiing, and horseback riding traverse the park's 1,955 acres, making this one of the most popular places to camp in all of Massachusetts. Campsites are spacious and natural, and trails lead from them to all the larger ponds. Powerboating is allowed on Cliff Pond, the largest body of water in the park. Resident wildlife include red foxes, white-tailed deer, eagles, woodland birds, hawks, and waterfowl. The land was owned until 1934 by the estate of Roland C. Nickerson, who was the largest private owner of forestland on Cape Cod in the twentieth century.

Open: Year-round; fully operational mid-April through mid-October.

⑮ Shady Knoll Campground

Location: North of Brewster near the Cape's north shore; Cape Cod and Martha's Vineyard map page 356, grid c3.

Campsites, facilities: There are 100 sites—some shaded, others open and grassy—for tents and RVs, 49 with full hookups, 31 with water and electric, and 20 with none. Each site has a table and fire grill. Use of air conditioners and heaters is allowed. You'll find free hot showers, rest rooms, a dump station, laundry facilities, firewood, ice, and RV supplies available on site. There's also a game room, basketball hoop, and playground. Pets are not recommended.

Reservations, fees: Reservations are requested. Sites are $16 to $22 a night for two people.

Contact: Shady Knoll Campground, 1709 Route 6A, Brewster, MA 02631; (508) 896-3002 or (800) 332-2267.

Directions: From U.S. 6 south of Brewster, take exit 11 and follow Route 137 north to its end. Shady Knoll Campground is directly across Route 6A.

Trip notes: In-town camping is the motif at Shady Knoll. Brewster's ocean beaches are one mile away, and liquor and grocery stores are within walking distance. There's not much in the way of on-site recreation, so most campers tend to make their way to the beach. Boat ramps are available for public use locally at Sesuit and Rock Harbors. To access a bit of wilderness, head west toward Dennis on Route 6A, turn left at Stony Brook Road (there's a blinking light), and take a second left onto Run Hill Road. You'll find a sign and parking for the town-owned Punkhorn Parklands. Once a sheep-grazing area and cranberry farm, the land is now laced with a network of trails open for use by mountain bikers, horseback riders, and hikers. Single- and double-track trails crisscross mixed hardwood groves and circle around ponds.

Open: May 15 through October 15.

⑯ Jolly Whaler Trailer Park

Location: West of Brewster; Cape Cod and Martha's Vineyard map page 356, grid c3.

Campsites, facilities: There are 28 RV-only sites adjacent to a small hotel, 23 with full hookups and the remainder with water and electric. A beauty salon, swimming pool, two shuffleboard courts, and a barbecue pit are on the property. Pets are negotiable.

Reservations, fees: A $25 deposit is required for reservations. Sites are $24 a night for three people and $2 a night for each additional person. Weekly and seasonal rates are available on request.

Contact: Jolly Whaler Trailer Park, Route 6A, Brewster, MA 02631; (508) 896-3474.

Directions: From U.S. 6 south of Brewster, take exit 11 and head north on Route 137 for four miles. Turn left on Route 6A and travel 1.5 miles west to the campground.

Trip notes: You'll camp on a lawn under the trees at Jolly Whaler, where most of the clientele rents space for the entire summer season. Cape Cod Bay beaches are a five-minute walk from the park. And just down the road from Jolly Whaler you'll find the 18-hole Captains Golf Course—reportedly rated among America's top 10 courses. Also next door is the New England Fire and History Museum, with its collection of early fire engines and a working blacksmith shop.

Open: May 15 through October 1.

117 Sweetwater Forest

Location: A few miles south of Brewster, just north of Pleasant Lake; Cape Cod and Martha's Vineyard map page 356, grid c3.

Campsites, facilities: There are 250 sites for tents and RVs, 50 with full hookups and 150 with water and electric, plus a separate tenting area with water faucets throughout. Each site has a picnic table. Free hot showers, dump stations, a security gate, five playgrounds, horseshoe pits, pony rides, boat and bike rentals, babysitting, LP gas, an RV showroom and repair service, video arcade, and adult clubhouse are available on the property. A camp store sells bait, tackle, ice, stamps, and groceries. No open fires are allowed, but charcoal grills and cookstoves are permitted. Pets with rabies vaccination certification are allowed on a leash.

Reservations, fees: Reservations are advised in July and August. Sites start at $20 a night for two people.

Contact: Sweetwater Forest, P.O. Box 1797, Brewster, MA 02631; (508) 896-3773.

Directions: From U.S. 6 south of Brewster, take exit 10 and head north on Route 124 for 2.8 miles to the campground entrance on the left.

Trip notes: Amenities abound at Sweetwater Forest, but this wooded campground manages to remain peaceful. Sites are spacious and well screened by a pine and hardwood forest. The use of motorboats is restricted on spring-fed Sweetwater Lake, but at nearby Long Pond you'll find a boat ramp and open, fresh water ripe for waterskiing. There's also a trail leading from the campground to the Cape Cod Rail Trail, a paved bike and in-line skating path that extends from South Dennis to South Wellfleet.

Open: May through October, but self-contained units are allowed year-round.

118 Campers Haven

Location: On Nantucket Sound, east of Hyannis in Dennisport; Cape Cod and Martha's Vineyard map page 356, grid c3.

Campsites, facilities: There are 265 RV-only sites with full hookups. Each site has a table and fire grill. Facilities include laundry, hot showers, exercise equipment, a grocery store, dump station, rec hall, and sports courts. RV supplies, ice, and planned group activities are also available. Pets are not allowed June 25 through Labor Day.

Reservations, fees: Reservations are recommended. Sites start at $30 a night per family.

Contact: Campers Haven, 184 Old Wharf Road, Dennisport, MA 02639; (508) 398-2811.

Directions: From U.S. 6 south of Dennis, take exit 9. Keep right and follow Route 134 south to the stop sign at Lower County Road. Turn left and drive half a mile, then turn right onto Old Wharf Road. Continue one mile to the campground on the left.

Trip notes: The sites at Campers Haven are a little crowded, as the average width is only 24 feet. It's also an "RV exclusive" spot, meaning there is no tenting and only full-hookup units are accepted. In this light, the campground offers shuttle services to the bustling town of Hyannis for campers who haven't towed along their car. The campground is located across the street from the ocean, but the facility's private beach down the road is available for fishing and swimming in the average 80-degree summer surf. Free shuttles also run to the beach.

You can pick up the Cape Cod Rail Trail a few miles away in South Dennis. This 50-mile round-trip bike path is paved and flat and ends in South Wellfleet to the north. Once the bed of the Penn Central Railroad, the path tends to be crowded in the summer months with amateur in-line skaters, dogs, and families, but it does afford an opportunity to see the noncoastal Cape countryside sans auto. Of course, you don't have to go all the way to South Wellfleet; the South Dennis portion provides a short, lovely jaunt through farmland.

Open: Mid-April through mid-October.

(119) Grindell's Ocean View Park

Location: On Nantucket Sound, east of Hyannis in Dennisport; Cape Cod and Martha's Vineyard map page 356, grid c3.

Campsites, facilities: There are 160 RV-only sites on sandy knolls by the ocean, all with full hookups. Each site has a concrete patio and space for one car. Use of heaters and air conditioners is not allowed. A small grocery store, RV supplies, LP gas, and ice are available on the property. Many of the lots are rented for the entire season. No pets are allowed.

Reservations, fees: Reservations are recommended in July and August. Sites start at $30 a night per family. Guests cost $9 a day per car. Weekly and seasonal rates are available.

Contact: Clyde and Phyllis Grindell, Grindell's Ocean View Park, 61 Old Wharf Road, Dennisport, MA 02639; (508) 398-2671.

Directions: From U.S. 6 south of Dennis, take exit 9. Keep right and follow Route 134 south to the stop sign at Lower County Road. Turn left and drive half a mile, then turn right onto Old Wharf Road and continue about 1.4 miles to the campground on the right.

Trip notes: You can cast for stripers and bluefish right out your front door at Grindell's, where some sites are actually right next to the water, among them T116 b–e and T18–29. And the rest are only a short walk from the beach. Some strict regulations help keep the peace here, including a town ordinance prohibiting alcohol on the beach and rules about where you can hang wet laundry. One rainy day rescue for family campers is the Discovery Days Children's Museum on Main Street in Dennisport, which offers lots of hands-on exhibits and fun activities. For a view across the whole of Cape Cod Bay on a clear day, make the short excursion north to Dennis and climb the Scargo Hill Observation Tower off Route 6A. From your perch, you'll see all the way to Provincetown.

Open: May 1 through Columbus Day.

(120) Bass River Trailer Park

Location: East of Hyannis in West Yarmouth; Cape Cod and Martha's Vineyard map page 356, grid c3.

Campsites, facilities: There are 125 sites for RVs only, with water, electric, and cable TV hookups. Shopping, miniature golf, and restaurants are just half a mile away. Leashed pets are permitted at the campground.

Reservations, fees: Reservations are recommended. Sites start at $20 a night.

Contact: Bass River Trailer Park, Route 28, Bass River, MA 02664; (508) 398-2011.

Directions: From U.S. 6 south of Yarmouth, take exit 8. At the bottom of the ramp, turn right and travel two miles through three sets of lights. After the third light, continue one mile to the park on the left side of the road behind the Bass River Car Wash.

Trip notes: Though this may not be the most scenic campground in the area—it's located right off the main drag behind a car wash—it is just a mile from the beach, where campers can while away the hours swimming, boating, and fishing. Since so many services are available nearby, the only amenity offered at Bass River is a dump station; you must go off site for all other services, including laundry and firewood. Still, the reasonable prices reflect the spare offerings. JFK buffs will want to pay a visit to the John F. Kennedy Museum in Hyannis, the next town to the west. The collection includes photos and video relating to the president's life on Cape Cod. Also in Hyannis are ferries to Martha's Vineyard and Nantucket, giving campers an abundance of day-trip options.

Open: May 1 through October 31.

(121) Scusset Beach State Reservation

Location: Bordering the Cape Cod Canal in Sandwich, on the northwesternmost portion of the Cape; Cape Cod and Martha's Vineyard map page 356, grid c1.

Campsites, facilities: There are 103 open, flat sites for tents and RVs, all with electric hookups and shared water hookups. Each site has a picnic table and fireplace. Flush toilets, showers, and a dump station are available. A group camping area open to nonprofit organizations only can accommodate 50 people. Safari camping is available for other groups with self-contained units. Leashed pets are permitted.

Reservations, fees: Reservations are accepted. Sites are $8 a night.

Contact: Scusset Beach State Reservation, P.O. Box 1292, Buzzards Bay, MA 02532; (508) 888-0859.

Directions: Take Route 3 south from Boston to the Sagamore Bridge traffic circle. Follow signs to the campground.

Trip notes: Anglers can cast a lure into the Cape Cod Canal right from this campground, and they don't need a fishing license to do so. Ocean swimming is another on-site activity, and interpretive programs are presented during the summer months. The campsites are clean but homogeneous on this rather flat stretch of land. From here you can hop on your bike and boat-watch along the canal or head into Sandwich to check out the Currier & Ives collection at the Heritage Plantation on Pine and Grove Streets. The museum also boasts trails and gardens as well as an exhibit of antique and classic cars.

Open: Mid-April to mid-October, but self-contained vehicles are permitted year-round.

122 Shawme Crowell State Forest

Location: Near the historic town of Sandwich; Cape Cod and Martha's Vineyard map page 356, grid c1.

Campsites, facilities: There are 280 sites without hookups, so only self-contained units are allowed. Each site has a table and grill. A dump station and public phone are available. Leashed pets are permitted.

Reservations, fees: Reservations are accepted. Sites are $6 a night.

Contact: Shawme Crowell State Forest, P.O. Box 621, Route 130, Sandwich, MA 02563; (508) 888-0351.

Directions: From U.S. 6 near Sagamore, take exit 1 and turn right at the traffic light onto Route 6A. Turn right again onto Route 130 and follow signs to the state forest.

Trip notes: Shawme Crowell's 742 acres are studded with walking and biking trails. In winter, these same paths become havens for cross-country skiers. Campers can also access the coast—the campground fee includes day-use privileges at Scusset Beach State Reservation on the west side of the canal (see campground number 121). The near-by town of Sandwich is definitely worth a visit: Historic homes, the oldest church on the Cape, and the Sandwich Glass Museum are just a few of the attractions. The latter has an interesting exhibit of antique glass made in this town during the mid- to late 1800s.

Open: Year-round; fully operational mid-April through mid-October.

123 Bourne Scenic Park Campground

Location: On the west side of the Cape Cod Canal in Bourne; Cape Cod and Martha's Vineyard map page 356, grid c1.

Campsites, facilities: There are 476 sites for tents and RVs, all with water and electric hookups except for one area with 39 sites. Each site has a fire ring, grill, and picnic table. Facilities include free hot showers, rest rooms, a dump station, rec hall, pavilion, coin games, a swimming pool, and sports fields and courts. Groceries, firewood, ice, and RV supplies are available. Bikes are welcome but must be on the campsite after dusk. Leashed pets are permitted.

Reservations, fees: Sites are filled on a first-come, first-served basis. Fees are $20 to $22 a night; weekly rates are available.

Contact: Bourne Scenic Park Campground, 231 Sandwich Road, Bourne, MA 02532-3622; (508) 759-7873.

Directions: From Route 3 south of Boston, take a right turn onto U.S. 6 heading west toward Buzzards Bay. Just before you reach the Bourne Bridge (to the Cape), you'll see the park entrance on the left.

Trip notes: Located on the banks of the Cape Cod Canal, Bourne Scenic Park offers unique opportunities for boat-watching, as vessels of every kind cruise by between Buzzards Bay and the north shore. Stairways lead down to the canal, and anglers can cast a fishing line from the park into the salty waters of the canal—without needing a license. Regulations restrict semipermanent campground improvements such as plantings and added structures, so you won't find many seasonal dwellings here.

On the property there's a 450-foot saltwater swimming pool with a lifeguard; it's located in Area P–X, the only section of the campground south of the Bourne Bridge. If you're bothered by the sound of traffic, consider choosing a site in Area C, the farthest from the busy span. In summer, the bridge is often clogged with traffic, so sometimes the best way to get onto the

Cape is via bicycle. On either shore, the canal service road doubles as a 7.2-mile hiking and biking trail. If you are interested in learning about the Cape's first inhabitants, stop in at the Aptucxet Trading Post and Museum on Aptucxet Road in Bourne on the other side of the canal. In addition to a replica of the Pilgrim-Dutch trading post, there are Native American artifacts on display.

Open: April 1 through mid-October.

---

⑫④ Bay View Campgrounds

Location: In Bourne, on Buzzards Bay, on the south shore of Cape Cod; Cape Cod and Martha's Vineyard map page 356, grid c1.

Campsites, facilities: There are 415 sites for tents and RVs, with an average site width of 40 feet. Full and partial hookups are available. Each site has a picnic table and fire ring. Rest rooms, hot showers, laundry facilities, a rec hall, dump station, tennis courts, three swimming pools, horseshoe courts, and two playgrounds are provided on the grounds. A camp store sells firewood, ice, gas, and RV supplies. Skateboards, in-line skates, and motorcycles are prohibited. Leashed pets are welcome, but owners are responsible for clean-up.

Reservations, fees: Reservations must be accompanied by a one-night nonrefundable deposit per week, and no personal checks will be accepted upon arrival. Sites are $22 to $25 a night for two people, with a $3 surcharge per child under 18.

Contact: Bay View Campgrounds, 260 MacArthur Boulevard, Bourne, MA 02532; (508) 759-7610.

Directions: From Boston, follow Route 3 south to the Sagamore Bridge. After crossing the bridge, take exit 1. At the traffic light, turn left and follow Canal Road to the Bourne Bridge rotary. Follow Route 28 south for one mile to the campground entrance.

Trip notes: Bay View welcomes family campers only, so even though there are more than 400 sites, you won't find too much chaos. What you will find are peaceful campsites on a wooded plateau near the ocean bay, ideal for RVers who want the choice of sampling the fruits of Cape Cod only minutes away or partaking of the recreational offerings close to home. At Cape Cod Canal and Buzzards Bay, you can enjoy fishing, boating, and ocean beach swimming. While out and about, don't forget to dine on fresh seafood—there's a bounty of take-out restaurants by the Bourne Marina. Recreation and leisure opportunities abound within Bay View, including an ice cream parlor, organized activities, and entertainment during the summer months. If you decide to take a day trip out on the water, the campground conveniently serves as a ticket agent for local ferry boats.

Open: May 1 through October 15.

---

⑫⑤ Lawrence Pond Village

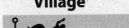

Location: East of Sandwich on Lawrence Pond; Cape Cod and Martha's Vineyard map page 356, grid c2.

Campsites, facilities: There are 24 spacious sites for RVs, 20 with full hookups and four with just sewer. A camp store sells groceries as well as lottery tickets and deli meats. Rustic cabins are also available for rent. Leashed pets are permitted.

Reservations, fees: Reservations are accepted. Sites start at $15 a night; seasonal rates are available on request.

Contact: Bob and Diane Cotter, Lawrence Pond Village, 45 Great Hill Road, Sandwich, MA 02563; (508) 428-6225.

Directions: From U.S. 6 in East Sandwich, take exit 4. Travel two miles south on Chase Road, which turns into Great Hill Road, to the campground on the left.

Trip notes: Not only does Lawrence Pond offer great fishing for trout and bass, it tends to be quiet since boaters are subject to a 10 mph speed limit on the 138-acre lake. This is a small campground with few amenities—aside from peace and quiet. In nearby Barnstable, a killer mountain bike ride called the Trail of Tears awaits: Take U.S. 6 to exit 5 and head south on Route 149 for a matter of moments before turning right on the service road for the Barnstable Conservation Lands. There, test your endurance on this strenuous series of hills running underneath power lines, perfect for gluttonous single-track seekers.

Open: March 17 through Columbus Day.

126 Dunroamin' Trailer Park

Location: South of Sandwich on Peters Pond; Cape Cod and Martha's Vineyard map page 356, grid c2.

Campsites, facilities: There are 64 mostly shaded sites for RVs up to 28 feet in length, all with full hookups. Picnic tables are provided at each site, and rubbish containers are centrally located. A private beach, play area, horseshoe pits, and public pay phone are on the property. Pets are not allowed on the beach and must otherwise be restrained.

Reservations, fees: Reservations are requested. Sites start at $25 a night.

Contact: Dunroamin' Trailer Park, 5 John Ewer Road, RR 3, Sandwich, MA 02563; (508) 477-0541 or (508) 477-0859.

Directions: From U.S. 6, take exit 2, turn right on Route 130, and drive 1.5 miles. Turn

left on Cotuit Road, and after 2.3 miles, make a right onto John Ewer Road. The campground will be on your right.

Trip notes: Quiet, sandy beachfront for swimming and sunning is the main attraction at Dunroamin', which is restricted to family campers. Sites are set in a wooded area beside a 137-acre lake that is stocked with trout and bass and is open to all types of boating.

Open: April through October.

127 Peters Pond Park

Location: In Sandwich on Peters Pond; Cape Cod and Martha's Vineyard map page 356, grid c2.

Campsites, facilities: There are 500 sites for tents and RVs, 278 with full hookups, 100 with water and electric, and 122 with none. Tent, tepee, cottage, and trailer rentals are available. Rest rooms, laundry facilities, metered hot showers, a convenience store, RV supplies, propane, ice, an adult clubhouse, a teen rec hall, playgrounds, playing fields, sports courts, and a special events tent are on the property. Group activities include bonfires, fishing derbies, and theme dinners. Campfires are not allowed at sites but can be lit in a picnic area and are also started nightly by the staff. Pets are not allowed between July 1 and Labor Day except by special arrangement, and all pets must have rabies vaccination certification.

Reservations, fees: Reservations are recommended July 1 through Labor Day. Sites are $17 to $31 a night.

Contact: Peters Pond Park, 185 Cotuit Road, P.O. Box 999, Sandwich, MA 02563; (508) 477-1775.

Directions: From the Sagamore Bridge, follow U.S. 6 to exit 2. Turn right on Route

130 and travel about three miles, then turn left at the first set of lights onto Quaker Meeting House Road. Turn right at the next set of lights onto Cotuit Road. Peters Pond Park is half a mile ahead on the right.

Trip notes: Boasting a mile-long stretch of sandy beach for swimming and water sports, Peters Pond Park offers campers full access to the 137-acre freshwater lake. Campsites are generous—the most common width is 40 feet—and each is carpeted with wood chips or pine needles and landscaped with split rail fencing and shrubbery. You'll be sleeping in a pine forest but will still be able to smell the salty ocean air. Some campsites are located directly on the lake, which is stocked with bass and trout. Also on the property is a 20-acre conservation area.

Open: Mid-April through mid-October.

128 Otis Trailer Village/ John's Pond Campground

Location: South of Mashpee on John's Pond; Cape Cod and Martha's Vineyard map page 356, grid d1.

Campsites, facilities: There are 90 open and shaded sites for tents and RVs, most with full hookups. Each site has a picnic table. Fireplaces are not furnished, but you may bring your own grill. Toilets, metered hot showers, laundry facilities, LP gas, and a playground are provided. Supplies are available in Mashpee, about 10 minutes away. Leashed pets are permitted.

Reservations, fees: Reservations require a minimum deposit. Fees start at $18 a night for sites with no hookups and $20 with hookups. There are surcharges for trailered boats and extra vehicles.

Contact: The MacDonald Family, Otis

Trailer Village, P.O. Box 586, Falmouth, MA 02541; (508) 477-0444.

Directions: From Bourne, drive south on Route 28 and take the exit for Route 151 heading east to North Falmouth. Continue 3.75 miles to Currier Road and turn left. At Hoophole Road, turn right and continue straight for two miles to the end of the road. Turn right at the intersection and you'll see Otis Trailer Village.

Trip notes: Campers share space with year-round mobile home residents at Otis Trailer Village. This is a popular place, as the campsites are set in wooded terrain beside one of the Cape's largest natural lakes. At 314 acres, John's Pond can accommodate any kind of boat; there's even a state-run boat ramp right next to the campground. The clear waters of the loch are stocked with trout and bass, and the campground owns a long, natural sandy beach. Hikers can explore cranberry bogs and a wildlife sanctuary bordering the facility. About 15 minutes away by car is South Cape Beach State Park, with ocean beaches providing a place to escape and enjoy saltwater swimming, boating, and fishing.

Open: April 15 through October 15.

129 Cape Cod Campresort

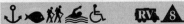

Location: In Falmouth; Cape Cod and Martha's Vineyard map page 356, grid d1.

Campsites, facilities: There are 185 wooded sites for tents and RVs, 145 with full hookups. Each site has a picnic table. You'll find rest rooms, hot showers, a clubhouse, badminton nets, horseshoe pits, a swimming pool, boat rentals, and planned group activities. Ice is available on site. Fires are allowed only in specially designated fireplaces. Leashed pets are permitted.

Reservations, fees: Reservations are not required. Sites start at $24 a night.

Contact: Cape Cod Campresort, 176 Thomas Landers Road, East Falmouth, MA 02536; (508) 548-1458 or (800) 777-2175.

Directions: From the Bourne Bridge, go south on Route 28A to the exit for Thomas Landers Road. Turn left off the exit; in 2.5 miles you'll see the campground entrance.

Trip notes: Nearly half the sites at this campground are rented by seasonal campers who return year after year to swim and fish in the crystal-clear pond on the pine-forested property. Those same folks will make you and your family feel at home in the clubhouse and during group events. In addition to the pond, the swimming pool is a favorite watery haunt for kids. The resort is a good jumping-off point for those planning to visit the islands, as the ferries are a short drive away in Falmouth. Some hiking trails lead through the property, but naturalists will want to stop in at the Ashumet Holly and Wildlife Sanctuary on Ashumet Road in East Falmouth to take advantage of self-guided nature walks and a holly trail. The sanctuary also is home to a colony of barn swallows.

Open: April 15 through October 15.

⑬⓪ Waquoit Bay National Estuarine Research Reserve

Location: On the coast in Mashpee, south of Waquoit Village; Cape Cod and Martha's Vineyard map page 356, grid d1.

Campsites, facilities: Ten beachfront sites are accessible by private boat only. Primitive facilities are provided. Leashed pets are permitted.

Reservations, fees: Call the number below for rates and reservations.

Contact: Waquoit Bay National Estuarine Research Reserve, Route 28, Mashpee, MA 02541; (508) 457-0495.

Directions: From Route 3 heading south out of Boston, drive onto the Cape via the Sagamore Bridge. Take U.S. 6 south to exit 2 and travel east on Route 130 to Great Neck Road, which you then follow to the Mashpee rotary. Get off the rotary on Route 28 and head west. The park is 3.5 miles ahead to the south. To reach the campsites, you must launch a boat from the park.

Trip notes: You will feel like you've discovered your own private paradise when you camp at the Waquoit Bay National Estuarine Research Reserve. These wilderness campsites can only be accessed by private boat, so you'll be with like-minded company once you pull up on shore. From the campground, you have access to the reserve's nearly 1,800 acres. Kayaking in the estuary is a spectacular affair, with views of undisturbed land where the river meets the ocean. You can also canoe or kayak across the estuary to Washburn Island State Park. Interpretive programs are conducted at the Waquoit Reserve in season.

Open: Mid-April through mid-October.

⑬① Sippewissett Campground and Cabins

Location: South of West Falmouth and north of Woods Hole, near Buzzards Bay; Cape Cod and Martha's Vineyard map page 356, grid d1.

Campsites, facilities: There are 120 sites for tents and RVs, half with hookups. Each site has a fire ring and picnic table. Use of air conditioners and heaters is not allowed. Facilities include RV storage, dump stations, laundry, rest rooms, free hot showers, and a traffic control gate. Also on site are a volleyball court, playground, rec hall, and video games. Group tent camping is available. No dogs are permitted from Memorial Day through Labor Day.

Reservations, fees: A $20 deposit is required for all reservations. Sites start at $27 a night for two people.

Contact: The Tessier Family, Sippewissett Campground and Cabins, 836 Palmer Avenue, Falmouth, MA 02540; (508) 548-1971 or (800) 957-CAMP.

Directions: From the Bourne Bridge, take Route 28 south for 11.2 miles to the Route 28A/Sippewissett exit. Make an immediate right at the blinking light and continue half a mile to the campground on the left.

Trip notes: Shade is plentiful in the terraced and well-groomed sites at Sippewissett. If you like clean facilities, you'll find them in fine order here. The campground also offers free shuttle service to the Martha's Vineyard ferries and warm-water public beaches just a mile or two away. If you're interested in Cape Cod sea life, stop in at the National Marine Fisheries Aquarium in Woods Hole. Surf casters should head out to Nobska Point, southeast of Woods Hole proper.

Open: Mid-May through mid-October.

⓲ Martha's Vineyard Family Campground

Location: In Vineyard Haven on Martha's Vineyard; Cape Cod and Martha's Vineyard map page 356, grid e2.

Campsites, facilities: There are 180 sites for tents and RVs, 50 with full hookups and 110 with water and electric. Each site has a picnic table and fire grill. Use of air conditioners and heaters is allowed. Some sites are rented seasonally. RV storage, sewage disposal, laundry facilities, piped water, rest rooms, a grocery store, firewood, ice, a playground, rec hall, and RV supplies are available on the property. Dogs and motorcycles are prohibited.

Reservations, fees: Prepaid reservations are advised for July and August. Credit cards are accepted; personal checks may be used only for advance reservations. Sites start at $26 to $28 a night for two people. Children are $2 extra each, and additional adults pay $9.

Contact: Martha's Vineyard Family Campground, 569 Edgartown Road, P.O. Box 1557, Vineyard Haven, MA 02568; (508) 693-3772.

Directions: Ferries to the island sail from Woods Hole, Falmouth, Hyannis, and New Bedford. The Steamship Authority in Woods Hole operates seven days a week and carries campers, cars, and trucks of any size. Advance reservations are recommended and can be obtained by calling (508) 477-8600 or (508) 693-9130. If you cannot get a reservation, drive to the ferry and take a turn in the standby line. Any driver arriving at either the Woods Hole terminal or the Vineyard Haven terminal on the island before 2 P.M. is guaranteed passage that day. Travel is by reservation only on holiday and busy summer weekends; be sure to inquire. Passengers without vehicles (not including bicycles) do not need reservations.

From Woods Hole on the mainland, take a 45-minute ferry ride to Vineyard Haven. Head out of town on Main Street and turn left on Edgartown Road. Travel one mile to the campground on your right.

Trip notes: Of the two campgrounds on the island, this is the least quiet. Families dominate the scene, but sites are wooded, so there is some measure of privacy. Campers can access 25 miles of bike paths from the campground, and public ocean beaches for swimming and fishing are just minutes away. Take a few swings at the Farm Neck Golf Club in Oak Bluffs or head out on a fishing boat or whale watch cruise. Families usually swim and sun at State Beach while the single, rowdy set cools off at Katama Beach near Edgartown.

Open: Mid-May through mid-October.

⒀ Webb's Camping Area

Location: At Lagoon Pond in Vineyard Haven on Martha's Vineyard; Cape Cod and Martha's Vineyard map page 356, grid e3

Campsites, facilities: There are 150 sites in a pine forest, a few with water and electric hookups and some with water views. Each site has a fire ring and picnic table. Facilities include a dump station, laundry, rec room, playground, sports fields, piped water, rest rooms, hot showers, pay phones, recycling center, and volleyball court. A camp store carries ice and firewood. Dogs and motorcycles are prohibited.

Reservations, fees: Reservations are strongly recommended. A deposit of one week's fee is required for stays of a week or longer; shorter stays require full prepayment. Lagoon-view or "private" sites are $29 a night for two people and any children under five. Regular sites start at $27. Hookups cost $2 a night, children over five are $1, and additional adults are $8. Group and weekly rates are available.

Contact: Webb's Camping Area, RD 3, Box 100, Vineyard Haven, MA 02568; (508) 693-0233.

Directions: Ferries to the island sail from Woods Hole, Falmouth, Hyannis, and New Bedford. The Steamship Authority in Woods Hole operates seven days a week and carries campers, cars, and trucks of any size. Advance reservations are recommended and can be obtained by calling (508) 477-8600 or (508) 693-9130. If you cannot get a reservation, drive to the ferry and take a turn in the standby line. Any driver arriving at either the Woods Hole terminal or the Vineyard Haven terminal on the island before 2 P.M. is guaranteed passage that day. Travel is by reservation only on holiday and busy summer weekends; be sure to inquire. Passengers without vehicles (not including bicycles) do not need reservations.

From the Oak Bluffs ferry, travel a quarter mile west on Oak Bluff Road, then half a mile southwest on Circuit Avenue. Cross over Country Road and continue another 1.5 miles on Barnes Road to the campground entrance on your left.

Trip notes: Peace, quiet, and clean facilities are the hallmarks of Webb's, where private campsites in a secluded pine forest overlook Lagoon Pond. Birders should visit the Felix Neck Wildlife Sanctuary in Vineyard Haven on Edgartown Road. Four miles of self-guided trails and a nature center there are maintained by the Massachusetts Audubon Society and support native waterfowl and nesting ospreys. The Audubon Society also arranges activities such as cruises and snorkeling excursions. Mountain bikers will want to explore the seemingly infinite tracks and fire roads of the 4,000-acre Manuel F. Correllus State Park, set smack-dab in the middle of Martha's Vineyard. Another of the island's big draws is the Gay Head Cliffs, with its bright rainbows of layered sediment that command $10 per visitor.

Open: Mid-May through mid-September.

Rhode Island

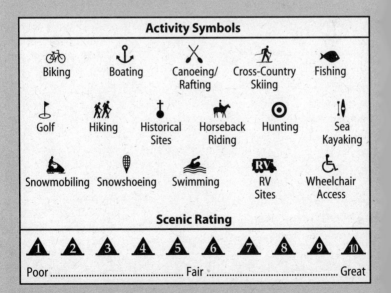

Activity Symbols

Biking	Boating	Canoeing/ Rafting	Cross-Country Skiing	Fishing
Golf	Hiking	Historical Sites	Horseback Riding	Hunting	Sea Kayaking
Snowmobiling	Snowshoeing	Swimming	RV Sites	Wheelchair Access

Scenic Rating

1 2 3 4 5 6 7 8 9 10

Poor .... Fair .... Great

Rhode Island

Adjoining Maps:
North: Eastern Massachusetts .... *page 355*
East: Eastern Massachusetts .... *page 355*
West: Eastern Connecticut .... *page 449*

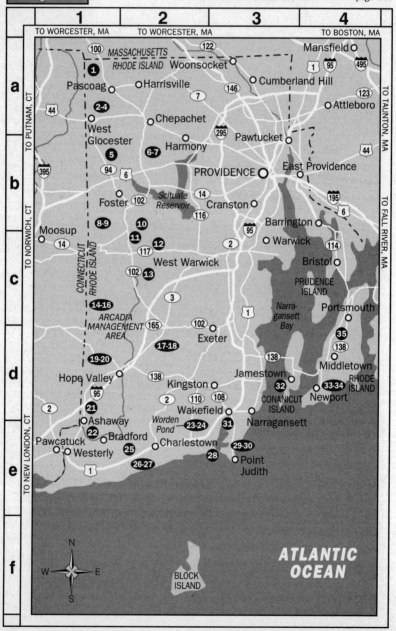

TO WORCESTER, MA — TO WORCESTER, MA — TO BOSTON, MA

1 **2** **3** **4**

MASSACHUSETTS
RHODE ISLAND
Woonsocket
Mansfield
100
122
146
1 95 495
Pascoag
Harrisville
Cumberland Hill
7
123
Attleboro
44
2-4
Chepachet
295
West Glocester
Harmony
6-7
Pawtucket
44
5
94 6
PROVIDENCE
East Providence
395
195
6
Foster
102
Scituate Reservoir
14
Cranston
Barrington
Moosup
8-9
116
95
Warwick
14
10
11
117
12
2
114
Bristol
West Warwick
102 13
PRUDENCE ISLAND
3
Narra-gansett Bay
Portsmouth
14-16
ARCADIA MANAGEMENT AREA
165
102
1
35
138
17-18
Exeter
138
Middletown
19-20
Jamestown
RHODE ISLAND
Hope Valley
138
Kingston
32
33-34
Newport
95
2 110 108
CONANICUT ISLAND
2
21
Ashaway
Wakefield
31
Narragansett
22
Bradford
Worden Pond
23-24
29-30
Pawcatuck
25
Charlestown
28
Point Judith
Westerly
26-27
1

ATLANTIC OCEAN

N
W E
S

BLOCK ISLAND

TO PUTNAM, CT
TO NORWICH, CT
TO NEW LONDON, CT
CONNECTICUT / RHODE ISLAND
TO TAUNTON, MA
TO FALL RIVER, MA

a
b
c
d
e
f

428

Rhode Island features:

❶ Buck Hill Family Campground

Location: West of Pascoag near the Buck Hill Management Area; Rhode Island map page 428, grid a1.

Campsites, facilities: There are 98 sites for tents and RVs, 58 with water and electric hookups and 40 with none. Each site has a picnic table and fireplace. Flush toilets, hot showers, laundry facilities, a dump station, and a store are provided. Recreation facilities include canoe rentals, a rec room, playground, crafts, a rifle range, and an archery program. Leashed pets are permitted.

Reservations, fees: Reservations are accepted. Sites are $15 to $24 a night.

Contact: Buck Hill Family Campground, 464 Wakefield Road, Pascoag, RI 02859; (401) 568-0456.

Directions: From the junction of Route 100 and Buck Hill Road, drive 1.75 miles west on Buck Hill Road. Turn left (south) on Croff Road and continue 1.5 miles to the campground.

Trip notes: Visitors to Buck Hill Family Campground have access to a lake where they may swim, fish, or float lazily in a canoe. You'll find the campground near the absolute northwest corner of Rhode Island, just south of the Buck Hill Management Area, a 2,100-acre upland hardwood forest that stands on what was once cleared pastureland. The management area is bordered to the west by Connecticut and to the north by Massachusetts, and numerous hiking trails lead into both states. An attractive part of Rhode Island, this land consists of rural farming country dotted with small towns and classic Yankee villages—many of which make interesting day trips.

Open: May 1 through October 31.

❷ Echo Lake Campground

Location: In Pascoag; Rhode Island map page 428, grid a1.

Campsites, facilities: There are 150 sites for tents and RVs with full, partial, and no hookups. Each site has a picnic table and fireplace. Flush toilets, hot showers, laundry facilities, a dump station, and a store are provided. Also on the grounds are a rec room, pavilion, volleyball and badminton nets, and horseshoe pits. No pets are allowed.

Reservations, fees: Reservations are accepted. Sites are $20 a night.

Contact: Echo Lake Campground, Box 4, Moroney Road, Pascoag, RI 02859; (401) 568-5000.

Directions: From the intersection of Route 102 and U.S. 44 at Chepachet, drive two miles west on U.S. 44. Turn right (north) on Jackson Schoolhouse Road and go one mile, then bear right on Moroney Road and head northeast for half a mile to the campground.

Trip notes: Echo Lake Campground is located along the shore of Pascoag Reservoir, the recreational focal point for campers who enjoy swimming, boating, waterskiing, and fishing. The park, which is very popular with seasonal campers, is set in a rural, scenic part of the state near the George Washington Management Area and the Buck Hill Management Area.

Open: May 1 through September 1.

❸ Bowdish Lake Camping Area

Location: Adjacent to the George Washington Management Area; Rhode Island map page 428, grid a1.

Campsites, facilities: There are 325

sites for tents and RVs with water and electric hookups. Each site has a picnic table and fireplace. Flush toilets, hot showers, a dump station, and a store are provided. You'll also find canoe and rowboat rentals, a rec room, horseshoe pits, and hiking trails. Leashed pets are permitted.

Reservations, fees: Reservations are accepted. Sites are $20 to $30 a night.

Contact: Bowdish Lake Camping Area, P.O. Box 25, Chepachet, RI 02814; (401) 568-8890.

Directions: From the intersection of Route 102 and U.S. 44 at Chepachet, drive 5.5 miles west on U.S. 44 to the campground on the right.

Trip notes: A very large campground has been established on the shores of Bowdish Reservoir some five miles west of Chepachet, a small New England village close to the Connecticut border. The campground lies adjacent to the George Washington Management Area—at 3,200 acres the largest public landholding in this part of the state—with its numerous ponds in which visitors can swim and fish. There are hiking loops ranging from two to eight miles in length, and in season the area is open for deer, grouse, woodcock, waterfowl, and small game hunting. The terrain is wooded, with open forests and many rocky outcrops and ledges.

Open: April 30 through October 10.

---

❹ George Washington Management Area

Location: West of Chepachet; Rhode Island map page 428, grid a1.

Campsites, facilities: There are 45 sites for tents or self-contained trailers, plus two shelters. Non-flush toilets, picnic tables, fireplaces, and water are provided. For recreation, there are hiking trails, a swimming beach, and a boat ramp. No pets are allowed.

Reservations, fees: Sites are allocated on a first-come, first-served basis. Fees for regular sites are $8 a night for residents of Rhode Island and $12 a night for nonresidents. Shelters are $20 a night.

Contact: George Washington Management Area, 2185 Putnam Pike, Chepachet, RI 02814; (401) 568-2013.

Directions: From the intersection of Route 102 and U.S. 44 at Chepachet, drive west on U.S. 44 for five miles. Follow signs to the George Washington Management Area.

Trip notes: Just across the border from Connecticut in the northwest corner of Rhode Island is this rather large collection of state-owned lands. George Washington Management Area, along with its well-maintained campground, is nestled in the rolling, hilly terrain that typifies this part of the state. The main draw of the campground is Bowdish Reservoir, a spot where both campers and day visitors retreat to swim, boat, and fish. Powerboating and waterskiing are two popular pursuits. Things get busy here during the summer, as the area is a popular gathering place for local folks. In addition to day visitors to the management area, many private residences line the north and west shores of the reservoir. Three hiking loops—with distances of two, six, and eight miles—lead throughout the area.

Open: Mid-April to mid-October.

---

❺ Oak Leaf Family Campground

Location: South of West Glocester; Rhode Island map page 428, grid b1.

Campsites, facilities: There are 60 sites for tents and RVs with full hookups. Flush toilets, hot showers, picnic tables, fireplaces, and a store are provided. For recreation, the campground offers a swimming pool, rec room, playground, volleyball, and horseshoes. Leashed pets are permitted.

Reservations, fees: Reservations are accepted. Sites are $18 a night.

Contact: Oak Leaf Family Campground, P.O. Box 521, Chepachet, RI 02814; (401) 568-4446.

Directions: From the intersection of Route 94 and Old Snake Hill Road in Glocester, drive half a mile east on Old Snake Hill Road to the campground.

Trip notes: Oak Leaf Family Campground is a pleasant little trailer park set in rural, wooded terrain in western Rhode Island, just shy of the Connecticut border. Several management areas to the near north offer opportunities to spend time hiking, boating, fishing, and swimming. While here, be sure to visit the Brown and Hopkins Country Store to the northeast in Chepachet. Dating back to 1809, it's one of the country's oldest continuously operating general stores and sells such wares as antiques and country furnishings, excellent food, and coffee.

Open: April 15 through October 31.

---

❻ Holiday Acres Campground

Location: West of the town of Harmony; Rhode Island map page 428, grid b2.

Campsites, facilities: There are 225 sites for tents and RVs, 200 with full hookups and 25 with none. Each site has a picnic table and fireplace. Facilities include flush toilets, hot showers, laundry, a dump station, and a store. For recreation, there are canoe, rowboat, and paddleboat rentals, a rec room and pavilion, volleyball, basket-

ball, badminton, miniature golf, and horseshoes. Leashed pets are permitted.

Reservations, fees: Reservations are accepted. Sites are $15 to $25 a night.

Contact: Holiday Acres Campground, 591 Snake Hill Road, North Scituate, RI 02857; (401) 934-0789.

Directions: From the intersection of U.S. 44 and Route 116 near Harmony, drive 1.5 miles south on Route 116, then bear right on Snake Hill Road and continue 2.75 miles west to the campground on the left.

Trip notes: Hilly, wooded countryside west of Providence is where you'll find Holiday Acres. This large, full-service campground is situated on a freshwater lake and offers many sites with waterfront and water views. Motorboats are not permitted on the lake, but there are plenty of other opportunities for water-based recreation, including canoeing, swimming, and fishing.

Open: Year-round.

---

❼ Camp Ponaganset

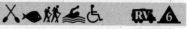

Location: West of Providence; Rhode Island map page 428, grid b2.

Campsites, facilities: There are 40 sites for tents and RVs with full or partial hookups. Each site has a picnic table and fireplace. Flush toilets, hot showers, laundry facilities, a dump station, and a store are provided. For recreation, there is a swimming pool, tennis court, ball field, and rec room. Leashed pets are permitted.

Reservations, fees: Reservations are accepted. Sites are $15 a night.

Contact: Camp Ponaganset, P.O. Box 399, Chepachet, RI 02814; (401) 647-7377.

Directions: From the intersection of U.S. 44 and Route 102 in Chepachet, drive four miles south on Route 102 to the campground on the left (east) side of the road.

Trip notes: Ponaganset is in the northwestern part of the state in high, rolling rural countryside. It's not far from Jerimoth Hill, which at 812 feet is the highest "peak" in Rhode Island. Also nearby is the Ponaganset Public Fishing Area, where anglers can cast a line for trout in a swift, woodsy stream. The campground specializes in seasonal camping for elderly and retired campers, so if you fit that description, this just might be the place you're looking for.

Open: April 15 through October 15.

❽ Dyer Woods Nudist Campground

Location: Near Foster; Rhode Island map page 428, grid b1.

Campsites, facilities: There are 16 sites for RVs with water and electric hookups. Each site has a picnic table and fireplace. Facilities include flush toilets, hot showers, laundry, a dump station, and a store. Also provided are a hot tub and sauna, a heated clubhouse, hiking trails, volleyball and badminton nets, and a bocce court. Leashed pets are permitted.

Reservations, fees: Reservations are accepted. Sites are $10 a night.

Contact: Dyer Woods Nudist Campground, 114 Johnson Road, Foster, RI 02825; (401) 397-3007.

Directions: From the junction of U.S. 6 and Boswell Road near the Connecticut border, drive 1.5 miles south on Boswell Road. Turn left and travel half a mile east on South Killingly Road, then turn right on Johnson Road and go another mile south to the campground.

Trip notes: Looking for a place where you can shed your clothes and your inhibitions? At this campground set in the rolling farm country of northwest Rhode Island, you can join fellow free spirits in an environment that allows you to discover who you really are underneath that external veneer. While you're in Foster be sure to stop by the Foster Townhouse at 180 Howard Hill Road. Constructed in 1796, the building is the nation's oldest house still being used for that New England Yankee tradition, the town meeting.

Open: May 1 through October 1.

❾ Ginny-B Family Campground

Location: Near Foster; Rhode Island map page 428, grid b1.

Campsites, facilities: There are 200 sites for RVs, some with full hookups and others with water and electric. Each site has a picnic table and fireplace. Flush toilets, hot showers, laundry facilities, a dump station, and a store are on the grounds. There's also a swimming pool, canoe rentals, teen and adult rec rooms, a pond for swimming and fishing, volleyball and basketball courts, and horseshoe pits. Leashed pets are permitted.

Reservations, fees: Reservations are accepted. Sites are $15.50 to $17.50 a night.

Contact: Ginny-B Family Campground, 46 Johnson Road, Foster, RI 02825; (401) 397-9477.

Directions: From the intersection of U.S. 6 and Route 94 near the Connecticut border, drive 3.25 miles west on U.S. 6, then turn left on Cucumber Hill Road and travel another 3.5 miles south. At Harrington Road, turn left and drive half a mile east to the campground.

Trip notes: The wooded, rolling countryside that characterizes western Rhode Island surrounds Ginny-B Family Campground, which lies not too far from the Connecticut border. Swimmers can take a dip in the pool on the grounds or plunge into a pond while others cast their fishing lines into the water. For those who want to get in a few rounds of golf, there's a public course conveniently located adjacent to this large, grassy campground.

Open: May 1 through September 30.

ogy, and hikers will discover old building foundations, mill ruins, and other points of interest. Hikers will enjoy the trails that cut through the woodlands, running up and over some moderately steep slopes and alongside streams that are punctuated with deep pools and waterfalls.

Open: April 15 through September 30.

⑩ Whippoorwill Hill Family Campground

Location: West of Scituate Reservoir near the George B. Parker Woodland; Rhode Island map page 428, grid b2.

Campsites, facilities: There are 150 sites for tents and RVs, 70 with full hookups, 70 with water and electric, and 10 with none. Each site has a picnic table and fireplace. Flush toilets, hot showers, laundry facilities, a dump station, and a store are provided. For recreation, you will find a spring-fed pond for swimming, a rec room, playing field, miniature golf, volleyball and badminton nets, and horseshoe pits. Leashed pets are permitted.

Reservations, fees: Reservations are accepted. Sites are $15 to $17 a night.

Contact: Whippoorwill Hill Family Campground, 106 Old Plainfield Pike, Foster, RI 02825; (401) 539-7011.

Directions: From the southern junction of Routes 14 and 102 in Foster, drive two miles east on Old Plainfield Pike to the campground.

Trip notes: Tall pine trees provide shade for the sites at Whippoorwill Hill, a family campground set in the rolling, wooded hills of the state's west-central region. Nearby is the George B. Parker Woodland, a 550-acre preserve owned by the Audubon Society of Rhode Island. The preserve's land was set aside for the study of historical archaeol-

⑪ Hickory Ridge Family Campground

Location: West of Scituate Reservoir near the George B. Parker Woodland; Rhode Island map page 428, grid c2.

Campsites, facilities: There are 200 sites for RVs, 60 with full hookups and 140 with water and electric. Each site has a picnic table and fireplace. Facilities include flush toilets, hot showers, laundry, a dump station, and a camp store. For recreation, there's a swimming pool, a lake for fishing, a rec room, volleyball and badminton nets, and horseshoe pits. Leashed pets are permitted.

Reservations, fees: Reservations are accepted. Sites are $15 a night.

Contact: Hickory Ridge Family Campground, 584 Victory Highway, Greene, RI 02827; (401) 397-7474.

Directions: From the intersection of Routes 117 and 102 west of Coventry, drive 1.25 miles north on Route 102/Victory Highway to the campground on the right (east) side of the road.

Trip notes: The full-hookup sites at Hickory Ridge are rented primarily by seasonal campers from the area. The campground is located in rolling, rural countryside near the George B. Parker Woodland, a 550-acre state-owned tract where visitors can hike through abandoned farms on miles of trails. These routes wander past old building foundations, mills, and other artifacts of early colonial settlement. A nearby lake is open for fishing and boating.

Open: May 1 through October 10.

⑫ Colwell's Campground

Location: On Flat River Reservoir in Coventry; Rhode Island map page 428, grid c2.

Campsites, facilities: There are 75 sites for tents and RVs with partial hookups. Each site has a picnic table and fireplace. Flush toilets, hot showers, laundry facilities, a dump station, and a store are provided. Leashed pets are permitted.

Reservations, fees: Reservations are accepted. Sites are $11 to $15 a night.

Contact: Colwell's Campground, 119 Peckham Lane, Coventry, RI 02816; (401) 397-4614.

Directions: From Interstate 95 near Warwick, take exit 10 and drive west on Route 117 for 8.5 miles to the campground in Coventry.

Trip notes: Campsites for tenters and RVers line the shore of Flat River Reservoir, also known as Johnson's Pond. Set almost smack-dab in the center of the state, this long and sinuous reservoir has a boat ramp and is open for fishing, swimming, and waterskiing. When in Coventry be sure to visit the home of General Nathanael Greene, George Washington's second-in-command during the American Revolution, at 50 Taft Street. Also within the town's boundaries is the George B. Parker Woodland, an Audubon Society of Rhode Island wildlife refuge encompassing 550 acres of woodlands, fields, and streams. The Audubon Society maintains hiking trails, conducts natural history programs and field trips, and offers maps and field guides for self-guided archaeology hikes.

Open: May 1 through September 30.

⑬ Westwood Family Campground

Location: Near the Quidnick Reservoir; Rhode Island map page 428, grid c2.

Campsites, facilities: There are 70 sites for tents and RVs, 60 with water and electric hookups and 10 with none. Each site has a picnic table and fireplace. Flush toilets, hot showers, and a dump station are provided. Recreational facilities include a rec hall; tennis, volleyball, and basketball courts; soccer and softball fields; and horseshoes. Leashed pets are permitted.

Reservations, fees: Reservations are accepted. Sites are $90 a week.

Contact: Westwood Family Campground, 2093 Harkney Hill Road, Coventry, RI 02816; (401) 397-7779.

Directions: From Coventry, drive four miles west on Harkney Hill Road to the campground.

Trip notes: Sports lovers will feel at home here. The park is located along the Quidnick Reservoir, which offers ample opportunities to engage in such water sports as swimming, boating, canoeing, windsurfing, sailing, and fishing. And for golf aficionados there's a golf course just down the road. If that's not enough activity to wear you out, stop in at Lakeview Amusements on Tiogue Avenue in Coventry, where you will find a 19-hole miniature golf course as well as hardball and softball batting cages.

Open: May 1 through September 30.

⑭ Pine Valley RV Campground

Location: On the Connecticut border near

the Arcadia Management Area; Rhode Island map page 428, grid c1.

Campsites, facilities: There are 70 sites for tents and RVs, 20 with water and electric hookups and 50 with none. Each site has a picnic table and fireplace. Flush toilets, hot showers, laundry facilities, honey wagon service, and a store are provided. For recreation, you'll find a swimming pool, tennis court, game field, rec hall with fireplace, volleyball, and horseshoes on the property, in addition to three nearby lakes. Leashed pets are permitted.

Reservations, fees: Reservations are accepted. Sites are $9 a night.

Contact: Pine Valley RV Campground, 64 Bailey Pond Road, West Greenwich, RI 02817; (401) 397-7972.

Directions: From the junction of Routes 3 and 165 in Austin, go 5.25 miles west on Route 165. Turn right on Bailey Pond Road and continue north to the campground.

Trip notes: The park is located just east of the Connecticut border within a network of public lands that includes the Arcadia Management Area and Beach Pond State Park. This rural region is covered with rolling hills, woods, rocky ledges, and several lakes, three of which are adjacent to the campground—convenient for folks who enjoy fishing, boating, swimming, and canoeing. The surrounding terrain is simply great for hiking, cross-country skiing, and mountain biking.

Open: Year-round.

⑮ Oak Embers Campground

Location: On the Connecticut border near the Arcadia Management Area; Rhode Island map page 428, grid c1.

Campsites, facilities: There are 60 sites for tents and RVs, 37 with water and electric hookups and 23 with none. Each site has a picnic table and fireplace. Flush toilets, hot showers, laundry facilities, a dump station, and a store are provided. For recreation, there is a swimming pool, rec room, pavilion, playing field, volleyball, badminton, and horseshoes. Leashed pets are permitted.

Reservations, fees: Reservations are accepted. Sites are $16 to $18 a night.

Contact: Oak Embers Campground, 219 Escoheag Hill Road, West Greenwich, RI 02817; (401) 397-4042.

Directions: From the junction of Routes 3 and 165 in Austin, drive 5.25 miles west on Route 165. Turn right on Escoheag Hill Road and continue 1.5 miles north to the campground.

Trip notes: Oak Embers is located just east of the Connecticut border and directly adjacent to the Arcadia Management Area, at 13,000 acres the state's largest tract of public wildlands. That puts campers within striking distance of two popular swimming lakes and great freshwater fishing and boating, as well as 40 woodland trails for hiking and mountain biking. This part of the state is absolutely beautiful, featuring rolling, wooded hills and high rocky ledges. Note that the campground is open nearly year-round for those who wish to explore this part of the country during the off-season, maybe by strapping on their cross-country skis.

Open: November 1 through September 30.

⑯ Legrand G. Reynolds Horsemen's Camping Area

Location: On the Connecticut border near the Arcadia Management Area; Rhode Island map page 428, grid c1.

Campsites, facilities: There are 20 tent sites with picnic tables and fireplaces. Non-flush toilets and piped water are provided, as are a show ring and riding trails. Leashed pets are permitted.

Reservations, fees: Sites are available on a first-come, first-served basis, with a maximum stay of four days. The fee is $3 a night, plus $10 a day for use of the show ring.

Contact: Legrand G. Reynolds Horsemen's Camping Area, 260 Arcadia Road, Hope Valley, RI 02832; (401) 539-2356 or (401) 277-1157.

Directions: From Interstate 95 near Austin, take exit 5A and follow Route 102 south. Turn right on Route 3, travel south to Route 165, and turn right again. After driving west for several miles, turn right (north) on Escoheag Hill Road and continue to the campground.

Trip notes: A one-of-a-kind place, this campground welcomes only people with horses. Riders may spend time practicing with their mounts in the show ring or exploring the extensive trail system within the campground proper. Or head into the adjacent Arcadia Management Area—Rhode Island's largest public landholding at 13,000 acres—with its 65-mile network of trails. When you or your horse need a break, Beach Pond State Park on the Rhode Island–Connecticut border is a good place for a refreshing swim. In other words, if you want to take an inexpensive vacation with your horse in tow, this might be the answer.

Open: Year-round.

⑰ Wawaloam Campground

Location: Just east of the Arcadia Management Area; Rhode Island map page 428, grid d2.

Campsites, facilities: There are 250 sites, 70 with full hookups and 180 with water and electric. Each site has a picnic table and fireplace. Facilities include flush toilets, hot showers, a dump station, laundry, and a store. For recreation, there's a swimming pool, rec room, pavilion, miniature golf, a sports field, volleyball, badminton, and horseshoes. Leashed pets are permitted.

Reservations, fees: Reservations are accepted. Sites are $20 to $21 a night.

Contact: Wawaloam Campground, Exeter, RI 02822; (401) 294-3039.

Directions: From Interstate 95 near Austin, take exit 5A and drive three miles south on Route 102. Turn right and drive half a mile southwest on Town Hall Road, then take Gardiner Road south for two miles to the campground.

Trip notes: Yet another rather large campground in the west-central part of Rhode Island, Wawaloam is located pretty close to the Arcadia Management Area, the state's largest public landholding. There is good fishing, hiking, boating, and bicycling in the area, and the park is also within easy reach of the state's renowned sandy beaches.

Open: Year-round.

⑱ Peeper Pond Campground

Location: West of Exeter; Rhode Island map page 428, grid d2.

Campsites, facilities: There are 31 sites for tents and RVs, 28 with water and electric hookups and three with none. Each site has a picnic table and fireplace. Flush toilets, hot showers, a dump station, a camp store, volleyball and badminton nets, and horseshoes are provided. Leashed pets are permitted.

Reservations, fees: Reservations are accepted. Sites are $12 to $16 a night.

Contact: Peeper Pond Campground, P.O. Box 503, Exeter, RI 02822; (401) 294-5540.

Directions: From the junction of Routes 102 and 2 in Exeter, drive 3.5 miles south on Route 2 to Mail Road, where you turn right and drive 1.5 miles west. Turn right when you reach Liberty Church Road and continue eight-tenths of a mile north to the campground.

Trip notes: Peeper Pond lies hidden away in the woods of central Rhode Island yet is still close to the attractions of Providence, the coastal beaches, and the Great Swamp Management Area. While you're here, be sure to check out the Fisherville Brook Wildlife Refuge: miles of hiking trails at the state's newest Audubon Society preserve wind through 700 acres of beautiful forests, ponds, and waterfalls. Also in Exeter is the Tomaquag Indian Memorial Museum, filled with artifacts, information, and exhibits about local tribes.

Open: May 1 through September 30.

accepted. Sites are $17 to $26 a night, depending on the season.

Contact: Whispering Pines Campground, P.O. Box 425, 41 Sawmill Road, Hope Valley, RI 02832; (401) 539-7011.

Directions: From Interstate 95, take exit 3B and drive three miles west on Route 138. Turn right on Sawmill Road and go half a mile north to the campground.

Trip notes: A 50-acre grove of towering pine trees surrounds this campground. It's located in a rural part of the state yet is close to many major attractions. Just 20 minutes from Rhode Island's famed ocean beaches, the campground is within easy reach of the Arcadia Management Area and within 12 miles of the Mashantucket Pequot Indian tribe's Foxwoods Casino, the nation's largest and most lucrative gambling establishment. Campers can fish for trout in a stocked brook, plunk a canoe into the nearby Wood River, or head into the Arcadia preserve or Beach Pond State Park for a few hours of hiking, biking, or swimming.

Open: March 1 through December 31.

⑲ Whispering Pines Campground

Location: Near the Connecticut border in Hope Valley; Rhode Island map page 428, grid d1.

Campsites, facilities: There are 180 sites for tents and RVs with full, partial, and no hookups. Each site has a picnic table and fireplace. Flush toilets, hot showers, laundry facilities, a dump station, and a store are provided. Recreational facilities include a sports field, swimming pond, canoe rentals, a rec room, tennis court, shuffleboard courts, volleyball, basketball, badminton, and horseshoes. Leashed pets are permitted.

Reservations, fees: Reservations are

⑳ Greenwood Hill Campground

Location: Near the Arcadia Management Area in Hope Valley; Rhode Island map page 428, grid d1.

Campsites, facilities: There are 50 sites for tents and RVs, 40 with water and electric hookups and 10 with none. Each site has a picnic table and fireplace. Flush toilets, hot showers, a dump station, and a store are provided. For recreation, there's a swimming pond, playing field, rec room, volleyball, basketball, badminton, and horseshoes. Leashed pets are permitted.

Reservations, fees: Reservations are accepted. Sites are $17 to $20 a night.

Contact: Greenwood Hill Campground, Box 141, 13A Newberry Lane, Hope Valley, RI 02832; (401) 539-7154.

Directions: From Interstate 95, take exit 3B and drive 3.5 miles west on Route 138 to the campground.

Trip notes: The campground is located in the wooded, rolling hills of western Rhode Island, not far from the hiking trails, swimming beaches, and mountain biking routes of the 13,000-acre Arcadia Management Area, Rhode Island's largest public landholding. The management area is a hilly, rocky upland laced with streams and bejeweled with waterfalls. More than 65 miles of hiking trails make it a very popular destination for outdoor recreationists throughout the year. Anglers will also want to check out the fishing at the Rockville Management Public Fishing Area, with accessible shoreline on both Blue and Ashville Ponds.

Open: May 15 through October 15.

㉑ Frontier Family Camper Park

Location: Northeast of Westerly in southern Rhode Island; Rhode Island map page 428, grid d1.

Campsites, facilities: There are 218 sites for RVs, 100 with partial hookups and 118 with none. Each site has a picnic table and fireplace. Flush toilets, hot showers, laundry facilities, a dump station, and a store are provided. For recreation, there's a swimming pool, canoe rentals, a rec room, volleyball, basketball, badminton, and horseshoes. Leashed pets are permitted.

Reservations, fees: Reservations are accepted. Rates are available upon request.

Contact: Janet and Bill Thompson, Frontier Family Camper Park, RR 1, P.O. Box 180A,

Maxon Hill Road, Ashaway, RI 02804; (401) 377-4510.

Directions: From the intersection of Interstate 95 and Route 3 near the Connecticut border, drive a tenth of a mile south on Route 3 to Frontier Road. Turn left (east) on Frontier Road and follow signs to the campground.

Trip notes: Busy Interstate 95 is less than a minute away from Frontier Family Camper Park, making this campground in the southwest corner of Rhode Island near the Connecticut border a good choice for those who just want a convenient place to stop as they travel through the area. Nearby are western Rhode Island's sand beaches, where you can play in the surf or go deep-sea fishing. And just over the state line in Connecticut is the Foxwoods Casino, owned and operated by the Mashantucket Pequot Indians.

Open: May 1 through October 1.

㉒ Holly Tree Camper Park

Location: Northeast of Westerly in southern Rhode Island; Rhode Island map page 428, grid e1.

Campsites, facilities: There are 139 sites for RVs with full, partial, and no hookups. Each site has a picnic table and fireplace. Flush toilets, hot showers, laundry facilities, a dump station, a rec room, and a camp store are provided. Leashed pets are permitted.

Reservations, fees: Reservations are accepted. Sites are $15 to $20 a night.

Contact: Holly Tree Camper Park, P.O. Box 61, 109 Ashaway Road, Ashaway, RI 02804; (401) 596-2766.

Directions: From the intersection of Interstate 95 and Route 3 near the Connecticut border, drive south on Route 3 to Ashaway.

Turn left on Route 216 and travel two miles southeast to the campground.

Trip notes: Set up camp at Holly Tree Camper Park and you'll be just inland from the great swimming, surfing, and fishing beaches of the southern Rhode Island coast. An added attraction for those who enjoy games of chance is the campground's proximity to the Foxwoods Casino, the country's largest, operated by the Mashantucket Pequot Indians just across the state line in Connecticut.

Open: May 15 through October 1.

㉓ Card's Camp

Location: Just south of the Great Swamp Management Area; Rhode Island map page 428, grid e2.

Campsites, facilities: There are 278 trailer-only sites with partial hookups. Each site has a picnic table and fireplace. Flush toilets, hot showers, and a dump station are provided. Leashed pets are permitted.

Reservations, fees: Reservations are accepted. Sites are $22 a night.

Contact: Card's Camp, 1065 Worden Pond Road, Wakefield, RI 02879; (401) 783-7158.

Directions: From the intersection of Route 110 and Worden Pond Road in Tuckertown, drive a short distance west on Worden Pond Road to the campground on the left (south).

Trip notes: Card's Camp is a very large trailer park with no sites for tent campers. Just to the north is the Great Swamp Management Area, a 3,000-acre preserve that includes Worden Pond, the state's largest freshwater lake; covering some 1,000 acres, the pond is a popular spot for birdwatching, fishing, and canoeing. Several good canoe routes and hiking trails weave their way through the preserve. This is also one of the state's most popular hunting areas for deer, grouse, waterfowl, and small game. A mere 10 minutes away from Card's Camp are the long sandy beaches of Rhode Island's south coast, which attract surfers, anglers, swimmers, and sunbathers alike. Another boon for bird-watchers is that the campground is close to several other federal wildlife refuges and conservation areas situated along the Rhode Island shore.

Open: April 15 through October 15.

㉔ Worden Pond Family Campground

Location: In Wakefield, just south of the Great Swamp Management Area; Rhode Island map page 428, grid e2.

Campsites, facilities: There are 200 sites for tents and RVs, some with water and electric hookups and some with none. Each site has a picnic table and fireplace. Flush toilets, hot showers, a dump station, and a store are provided. For recreation, there's a lake, rec room, pavilion, playground, volleyball, badminton, and horseshoes. Leashed pets are permitted.

Reservations, fees: Reservations are accepted. Sites are $17 to $20 a night.

Contact: Worden Pond Family Campground, 416A Worden Pond Road, Wakefield, RI 02879; (401) 789-9113.

Directions: From the junction of U.S. 1 and Route 110 in Perryville, drive two miles north on Route 110, then turn left on Worden Pond Road and continue one mile west to the campground.

Trip notes: Worden Pond is the state's largest freshwater lake—a thousand-acre gem open to boating, canoeing, fishing, and waterskiing—and this campground is situated right near its southern shore. Campers enjoy water access and a sandy beach. Another plus is that the Great Swamp Management Area, a 3,000-acre nature preserve encompassing much of the land abutting the lake's northern end, is nearby, waiting to be explored. This is also where the Indian uprising known as King Philip's War came to a bloody end in 1675. The campground is within a 10-minute drive of many of the state's finest ocean beaches and within 20 minutes of the deep-sea fishing and excursion boats based near Point Judith.

Open: May 1 through October 15.

㉕ Burlingame State Park

Location: Near the ocean in Charlestown; Rhode Island map page 428, grid e2.

Campsites, facilities: There are 755 sites for tents and RVs, all without hookups. Each site has a picnic table and fireplace. Flush toilets, hot showers, a grocery store, and a dump station are provided. For recreation, you'll find a rec room on the grounds, a swimming beach and boat ramp on Watchaug Pond, and hiking trails in the park. No pets are allowed.

Reservations, fees: Sites are available on a first-come, first-served basis, with a two-week maximum stay. Fees are $8 a night for residents of Rhode Island and $12 a night for nonresidents.

Contact: The Rhode Island Division of Parks and Recreation, 2321 Hartford Avenue, Johnston, RI 02919; (401) 322-7994 or (401) 322-7337.

Directions: From Charlestown, travel southwest on U.S. 1 for four miles. Turn right (north) on Cookestown Road and follow the signs to the park.

Trip notes: The biggest of Rhode Island's state parks is 2,100-acre Burlingame State Park. Its centerpiece and main attraction is

Watchaug Pond, covering some 600 acres and boasting a sandy swimming beach. Small motorboats and canoes are permitted on the water, and fishing for trout is a popular pursuit. Also within park boundaries is the Kimball Wildlife Refuge, a 29-acre preserve on Watchaug Pond that is overseen by the Audubon Society of Rhode Island. A trail system winds around the area, affording good vantage points for spotting waterfowl and migrating birds. For saltwater swimmers, boaters, and deep-sea fishing enthusiasts, several Atlantic coast beaches are a short drive away. The Ninigret National Wildlife Refuge and Park is also within close driving distance; for more details on activities there, see the trip notes for the Ninigret Conservation Area (campground number 26).

Open: April 15 to October 31.

㉖ Ninigret Conservation Area

Location: On the beach near Charlestown; Rhode Island map page 428, grid e2.

Campsites, facilities: There are 20 primitive sites for self-contained camping units only. Tenting is not permitted. The campsites are located in two areas accessed by a sand trail requiring a four-wheel-drive vehicle. Pack in your water. No pets are allowed.

Reservations, fees: Sites are available on a first-come, first-served basis. The maximum stay is four days, with a three-day break in between stays. Fees are $8 a night for residents of Rhode Island and $12 a night for nonresidents.

Contact: The Rhode Island Division of Parks and Recreation, 2321 Hartford Avenue, Johnston, RI 02919; (401) 322-0450.

Directions: From Charlestown, travel south on U.S. 1 for approximately five miles.

Turn left on East Beach Road and continue to the end of the road. Access to the camping area is to the left.

Trip notes: Camping on a spit of sand at the ocean's edge is what people do at the Ninigret Conservation Area. With a campsite bordered on one side by Ninigret Pond (the largest saltwater pond in the state) and on the other side by the Atlantic Ocean, a water lover can't go wrong. The surf casting, swimming, ocean kayaking—and anything else you like to do near the ocean—are all terrific. This place is far from the madding crowds, a real haven.

Open: Mid-April to October 31.

㉗ Charlestown Breachway

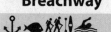

Location: On the beach near Charlestown; Rhode Island map page 428, grid e2.

Campsites, facilities: There are 75 sites for self-contained camping units only, all without hookups. There are no tent sites. Flush toilets and water are provided. For recreation, there's a swimming beach and a boat ramp. No pets are allowed.

Reservations, fees: Sites are available on a first-come, first-served basis. The maximum stay is one week, with a four-day break in between stays. Fees are $8 a night for residents of Rhode Island and $12 a night for nonresidents.

Contact: The Rhode Island Division of Parks and Recreation, 2321 Hartford Avenue, Johnston, RI 02919; (401) 364-7000.

Directions: From Charlestown, travel south on the Charlestown Beach Road. When the road ends, turn right and proceed to the breachway and the campground.

Trip notes: This campground is basically a sand parking lot near the ocean. With vast areas of wetlands, a large saltwater pond,

numerous small islands, and Block Island Sound all surrounding the breachway, birders will find plenty of opportunities to observe waterfowl and migrating species. The swimming is terrific on either the pond or the sound side. And for surf casters, this is nothing but paradise. While it would be difficult to imagine why someone would want to leave this spot, plenty of recreational options are available nearby. A hike in the Kimball Wildlife Refuge, a visit to a shoreline community such as Matunuck, and a deep-sea fishing excursion are just three easy day-trip possibilities. The only downside is the plethora of cheap seaside development that you must pass on the drive to the breachway.

Open: April 15 to October 31.

㉘ Wakamo Park Resort

Location: South of Wakefield near the ocean; Rhode Island map page 428, grid e3.

Campsites, facilities: There are 30 trailer sites with full hookups. A gift store, dock space, paddleboat and canoe rentals, a game room, and planned activities are available. No pets are allowed.

Reservations, fees: Reservations are accepted. Sites are $40 a night.

Contact: Wakamo Park Resort, 697 Succotash Road, South Kingston, RI 02879; (401) 783-6688.

Directions: From the junction of U.S. 1 and Succotash Road in South Kingston, turn south on Succotash Road and follow signs for East Matunuck State Beach. You'll find the campground right next to the beach.

Trip notes: Wakamo Park Resort enjoys a prime location on the water near East Matunuck State Beach, one of the fine stretches of sand and surf that have made Rhode Island a favorite vacation spot for beach lovers. Here you can spend your days clamming, fishing, swimming, or boating. Be sure to visit the Great Swamp Management Area while you're here in South Kingston. One of the state's great public lands, this is where the New England–wide Indian uprising known as King Philip's War came to a bloody end in 1675. The waterways of the preserve offer good canoeing and fine trout fishing.

Open: April 15 through October 15.

㉙ Fishermen's Memorial State Park

Location: Near the ocean in Narragansett; Rhode Island map page 428, grid e3.

Campsites, facilities: There are 182 sites for tents and RVs, 40 with full hookups, 107 with water and electric, and 35 with none. Facilities include flush toilets, hot showers, picnic tables, a dump station, tennis and basketball courts, horseshoe pits, and a children's playground. No pets are allowed.

Reservations, fees: Reservations are available by mail only. You must submit your request on an official form, available at the park, and it must be postmarked no earlier than January 14. Sites are $8 to $12 a night for residents of Rhode Island and $12 to $16 a night for nonresidents.

Contact: The Rhode Island Division of Parks and Recreation, 1011 Old Point Judith Road, Narragansett, RI 02882; (401) 789-8374.

Directions: From the intersection of Route 108 and U.S. 1 in Narragansett, travel south on Route 108 (Old Point Judith Road) to the park.

Trip notes: The well-manicured campground at Fishermen's Memorial State Park has an almost suburban feel, with its tract

"neighborhoods" connected by winding asphalt lanes. From the park, you only have to stroll a short distance to find great swimming spots at Wheeler Memorial Beach or Salty Brine State Beach. If you want to spend a day on Block Island to the south—with its beaches, lighthouse, and national wildlife refuge—head to nearby Galilee, where you can hop a ferry. Or you can explore Point Judith Pond and the Galilee Bird Sanctuary. Fishing enthusiasts might want to take a deep-sea fishing trip or cast from the shore or the state piers. One other site that's well worth a visit is the octagonal brick lighthouse built in 1816 at Point Judith.

Open: Year-round.

㉚ Breakwater Village Campground

Location: Near the ocean in Narragansett; Rhode Island map page 428, grid e3.

Campsites, facilities: There are 38 sites for RVs with partial hookups. A dump station and a snack bar are provided. Leashed pets are permitted.

Reservations, fees: Reservations are accepted. Sites are $30 a night.

Contact: Breakwater Village Campground, P.O. Box 563, Narragansett, RI 02882; (401) 783-9527.

Directions: From the junction of U.S. 1A and Ocean Road in Narragansett, drive approximately four miles south on Ocean Road to the campground.

Trip notes: Breakwater Village Campground is the place to go if you love surf, sand, and sun. Located on Ocean Road in Narragansett, the campground offers easy access to the town's beaches, all five of them. Narragansett is a great summer resort community, one that can satisfy the needs of various beachgoers, from families with kids to sunbathers to surf casters looking for a little solitude. Should you tire of the beach, head to the north end of town to check out Canochet Farm, a nineteenth-century working farm with a historic cemetery dating back to 1700, a fitness trail, nature trails, picnic areas, and the South County Museum. Also be sure to visit the Point Judith Lighthouse, erected in 1816 on the site of a tower beacon maintained during the American Revolution.

Open: April 15 through October 15.

㉛ Long Cove Marina Campsites

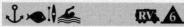

Location: On a saltwater cove in Narragansett; Rhode Island map page 428, grid e3.

Campsites, facilities: There are 180 sites for tents and RVs with full, partial, and no hookups. Flush toilets, hot showers, picnic tables, fireplaces, and a dump station are provided. There's also a boat launch, a ramp, and docks. Leashed pets are permitted.

Reservations, fees: Reservations are accepted. Sites are $16 to $19 a night.

Contact: The Kivisto Family, Long Cove Marina Campsites, 325 Old Point Judith Road, Narragansett, RI 02882; (401) 783-4902.

Directions: From the intersection of U.S. 1 and Route 108, drive one mile south on Route 108 (Old Point Judith Road) to the campground.

Trip notes: Long Cove is a saltwater bay fed by the Atlantic Ocean. From this campground you can launch your boat and be out on the open sea within a matter of minutes. Or stick close to shore if you enjoy surf casting or saltwater swimming. This is a very attractive campground with a sampling of sites in the woods, in open fields,

and along the water. Many of the sites are either right on the waterfront or at least afford water views. This part of the state is known for its great beaches, interesting villages, and spectacular ocean scenery. Be sure to visit the lighthouse at Point Judith, about four miles south of here.

Open: May 1 through October 15.

㉜ Fort Getty Recreation Area

Location: On Conanicut Island in Jamestown, in Narragansett Bay; Rhode Island map page 428, grid d3.

Campsites, facilities: There are 125 sites for tents and RVs, 100 with water and electric hookups and 25 with none. Each site has a picnic table and fireplace. Flush toilets, hot showers, a dump station, boat ramp, and fishing dock are provided. Leashed pets are permitted.

Reservations, fees: Reservations are not accepted. Sites are $17 to $22 a night.

Contact: Fort Getty Recreation Area, P.O. Box 377, Jamestown, RI 02835; (401) 423-7264.

Directions: Take either the Jamestown Bridge from the mainland or the Newport Bridge from Newport to Route 138 and turn south onto North Main Road. Turn west onto Narragansett Avenue, then south onto Southwest Avenue, which merges into Beavertail Road. Continue to Fort Getty Road, turn right, and drive west to the campground.

Trip notes: Fort Getty State Park is located near the historic town of Jamestown on Conanicut Island in Narragansett Bay. Tall suspension bridges link this tiny island with the mainland to the west and with the city of Newport on the island of Rhode Island to the east. From your campsite at the recreation area, you'll be able to savor spectacular views of Rhode Island's Atlantic coastline across the water. Equally stunning views are to be had at nearby Beavertail State Park to the south. Water lovers will be in their element here, with all the great shoreline access and plentiful swimming and boating opportunities close at hand. Be sure to visit the lighthouse at Beavertail Point at the southern tip of the island.

Open: May 18 through October 1.

㉝ Meadowlark RV Park

Location: In Middletown on Rhode Island; Rhode Island map page 428, grid d4.

Campsites, facilities: There are 40 sites for RVs only, all with full hookups. Flush toilets, hot showers, picnic tables, fireplaces, a dump station, and an RV supply store are provided. Leashed pets are permitted.

Reservations, fees: Reservations are accepted. Sites are $22 a night.

Contact: Joe and Mae Rideout, Meadowlark RV Park, 132 Prospect Avenue, Middletown, RI 02840; (401) 846-9455.

Directions: From the Newport Bridge, drive 2.5 miles north on Route 138, then turn right on Route 138A and drive two miles south to Prospect Avenue. Continue half a mile east to the campground on the right side of the road.

Trip notes: Meadowlark, a mobile home park for RVers only, is situated very close to the attractions of Newport, one of America's best known and perhaps most historic resort communities. From here, you can walk to the famous beaches of Newport, watch a tennis match at the Tennis Hall of Fame, hike the Cliff Walk past the mansions of nineteenth-century robber barons, peruse the myriad shops and boutiques on Bannister Wharf, and visit the harbor where,

on and off for over a century, America's Cup races have been held. There's also a golf course nearby.

Open: April 15 through October 30.

㉞ Paradise Mobile Home Park

Location: In Middletown on Rhode Island; Rhode Island map page 428, grid d4.

Campsites, facilities: There are 16 sites for RVs with full hookups. Tents are not allowed, and only self-contained units may use this park. Flush toilets, hot showers, and picnic tables are provided. No pets are allowed.

Reservations, fees: Reservations are accepted. Sites are $23 a night.

Contact: Paradise Mobile Home Park, 265 Prospect Avenue, Middletown, RI 02842; (401) 847-1500.

Directions: From the intersection of Routes 138A and 214 in Middletown, drive a quarter mile north on Route 138A to the campground.

Trip notes: This mobile home park offers a great location in the heart of the Newport resort area, within walking distance of beaches, shops, wharves, and turn-of-the-century mansions. For more information about what makes this area so special, see the trip notes for the Meadowlark RV Park (campground number 33).

Open: May 1 through October 15.

㉟ Melville Pond Campground

Location: In Portsmouth on Rhode Island; Rhode Island map page 428, grid d4.

Campsites, facilities: There are 123

sites for tents and RVs, 33 with full hookups, 33 with water and electric, and 57 with none. Flush toilets, hot showers, picnic tables, and fireplaces are provided. For recreation there are volleyball nets, a playground, a playing field, and hiking trails. Leashed pets are permitted.

Reservations, fees: Reservations are accepted. Sites are $13 to $22 a night.

Contact: Melville Pond Campground, 181 Bradford Avenue, Portsmouth, RI 02871; (401) 849-8212.

Directions: From the Newport Bridge, drive north on Route 138 to Route 114 and continue north toward Portsmouth. Turn left on Stringham Road and go half a mile west, then turn right on Sullivan Road and proceed another half mile north to the campground. If you're entering the island from the north, from the junction of Routes 24 and 114 in Portsmouth, drive 1.7 miles south on Route 114, then turn right on Stringham Road and proceed as above.

Trip notes: Owned and operated by the city of Portsmouth, Melville Pond is set at the northern end of the island of Rhode Island in Narragansett Bay and offers campers easy water access. There's a nearby lake where you can spend some time swimming, canoeing, or boating with an electric motor (no gas-powered craft are allowed). The campground is pretty close to some interesting historical sites, including Butts Hill Fort, the site of the only major land battle of the American Revolution to be fought in Rhode Island. Look for the Memorial to Black Soldiers, dedicated to the men of the First Rhode Island Regiment who made a heroic stand against British troops during that 1778 battle. The regiment was composed mainly of African American soldiers.

Open: April 1 through November 1.

Connecticut

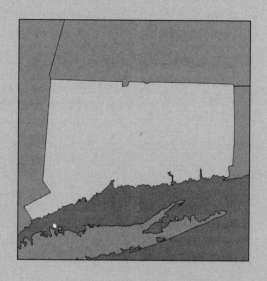

Activity Symbols

🚲 Biking	⚓ Boating	✕ Canoeing/ Rafting	🎿 Cross-Country Skiing	🐟 Fishing
⛳ Golf	🥾 Hiking	Historical Sites	🐴 Horseback Riding	◉ Hunting	Sea Kayaking
Snowmobiling	Snowshoeing	🏊 Swimming	**RV** RV Sites	♿ Wheelchair Access

Scenic Rating

▲1 ▲2 ▲3 ▲4 ▲5 ▲6 ▲7 ▲8 ▲9 ▲10

Poor .... Fair .... Great

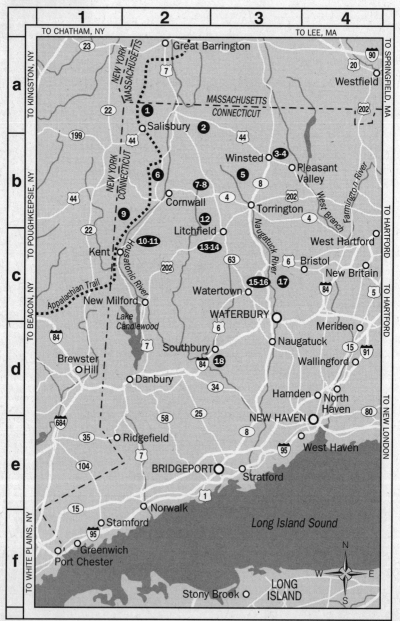

Western Connecticut

Adjoining Maps: North: Western Massachusetts .... *page* 354
East: Eastern Connecticut .... *page* 449

	1	**2**	**3**	**4**

TO CHATHAM, NY

TO LEE, MA

23

Great Barrington

NEW YORK

MASSACHUSETTS

7

90

20

TO KINGSTON, NY

TO SPRINGFIELD, MA

Westfield

a

22

1

MASSACHUSETTS
CONNECTICUT

Salisbury

2

202

199

44

44

44

Winsted

3-4

Pleasant
Valley

b

6

5

8

TO POUGHKEEPSIE, NY

44

7-8

Farmington River

22

Cornwall

4

202

9

Torrington

West Branch

Kent

12

Litchfield

4

West Hartford

TO HARTFORD

10-11

Housatonic River

13-14

202

63

6

Bristol

c

New Britain

Appalachian Trail

Watertown

15-16

17

84

5

TO BEACON, NY

84

New Milford

WATERBURY

Meriden

TO HARTFORD

Brewster
Hill

Lake
Candlewood

6

Naugatuck

15

91

d

7

Southbury

84

18

Wallingford

Danbury

34

Hamden

North
Haven

80

TO NEW LONDON

684

58

25

NEW HAVEN

35

Ridgefield

8

104

7

West Haven

e

BRIDGEPORT

95

Stratford

15

1

TO WHITE PLAINS, NY

Norwalk

Long Island Sound

95

Stamford

Greenwich
Port Chester

N

W   E

S

LONG
ISLAND

Stony Brook

f

448

Eastern Connecticut

Adjoining Maps: North: Western Massachusetts .... *page* 354
East: Rhode Island .... *page* 428
West: Western Connecticut .... *page* 448

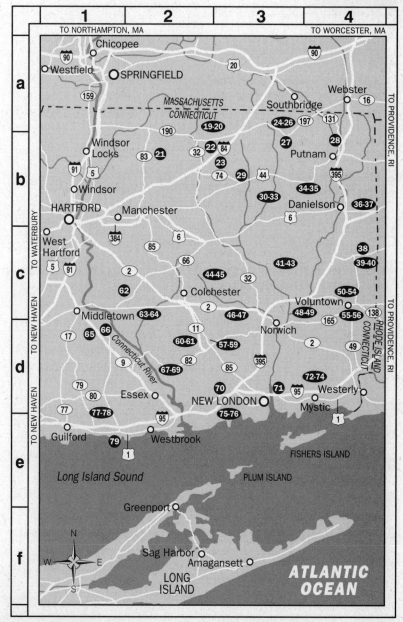

| | **1** | **2** | **3** | **4** |

TO NORTHAMPTON, MA   TO WORCESTER, MA

a

90 Chicopee
Westfield
90
90
SPRINGFIELD
20
159
Webster
16
MASSACHUSETTS
CONNECTICUT
Southbridge
19-20
24-26
197
131
TO PROVIDENCE, RI

b

190
Windsor
Locks
83
21
32
22
84
27
28
91
5
23
Putnam
395
Windsor
74
29
44
HARTFORD
Manchester
30-33
34-35
6
Danielson
36-37

c

384
West
Hartford
85
6
38
5
91
66
39-40
2
44-45
32
41-43
62
Colchester
50-54
Middletown
63-64
2
46-47
48-49
Voluntown
55-56
138
17
65
66
11
Norwich
165
CONNECTICUT
TO NEW HAVEN

d

Connecticut River
60-61
57-59
49
9
67-69
82
395
85
2
72-74
79
70
71
95
Westerly
80
Essex
NEW LONDON
95
Mystic
77
77-78
75-76
1
RHODE ISLAND
TO NEW HAVEN

e

79
Guilford
1
Westbrook
FISHERS ISLAND
Long Island Sound
PLUM ISLAND
Greenport

f

N
W E
S
Sag Harbor
Amagansett
ATLANTIC OCEAN
LONG ISLAND

449

Connecticut features:

Connecticut State Parks

The State Parks Division of Connecticut strongly urges reservations for its campsites. Reservations must be made by mail for Memorial Day through Labor Day, and are accepted beginning January 15 for stays during that year. The official park season is April 19 through Labor Day, but many of the parks don't open until May 15 and many stay open through mid-October. Blank permit forms may be obtained by contacting the State Parks Division, Bureau of Outdoor Recreation, Department of Environmental Protection, 79 Elm Street, Hartford, CT 06106-5127; (860) 424-3200. There's a two-night minimum stay for reservations. Unreserved spots are available on a first-come, first-served basis. Send completed permit applications to the campground where you intend to stay; a validated permit will be returned to you.

❶ Appalachian Trail

Location: In the northwest corner of Connecticut; Western Connecticut map page 448, grid a2.

Campsites, facilities: There are about

a dozen lean-tos on the Connecticut stretch of the Appalachian Trail, none of which are more than a moderate day hike apart. Primitive toilets are provided at each site. Current topographic maps show reliable and seasonal water sources. You'll find formal campsites at Macedonia Brook, Mohawk Mountain, and Housatonic Meadows State Parks.

Reservations, fees: Lean-to sites are available on a first-come, first-served basis. Sometimes a nominal nightly fee is charged in summer. Check with the Appalachian Trail Conference (see address below) for up-to-date fees and conditions.

Contact: Appalachian Trail Conference, P.O. Box 807, Harper's Ferry, WV 25425; (304) 535-6331. This nonprofit group publishes 10 sectional guides, which are accompanied by topographic maps.

Directions: In the northwestern part of Connecticut, the Appalachian Trail extends northward from Kent to Salisbury before crossing into Massachusetts. There are easily accessible trailheads on U.S. 44 just east of Salisbury and on U.S. 7 north of Cornwall.

Trip notes: The 56-mile stretch of the Appalachian Trail in Connecticut offers some of the best hiking opportunities in the state. Low-slung hills and mountains and rolling, wooded terrain are what you'll discover as you hike, along with the occasional spectacular view of the Litchfield Hills. Rivers, brooks, and small clear lakes provide plenty of scenic beauty as well as good habitat for wild turkeys, and bald eagles have even been spotted near the Housatonic River. In autumn, the colorful mix of hardwood trees (forests of oak and hickory) draw leaf-peepers (peak foliage is usually around Columbus Day), while 200-year-old pine trees in Cornwall are an attraction in themselves.

Open: Year-round.

❷ Lone Oak Campsites

Location: In East Canaan; Western Connecticut map page 448, grid a2.

Campsites, facilities: There are 500 sites with full hookups in a mix of open and wooded settings. Cabins and trailers can be rented. Recreation facilities include two pools, a hot tub, pub, rec halls, laundry facilities, an outdoor movie theater, hot showers, a market and deli, arcade, game fields, and sports courts. Also available on site are dump stations, free cable TV hookups, and a propane filling station. Leashed pets are permitted.

Reservations, fees: Reservations are recommended. Sites with full hookups are $30 a night or $162 a week. Cabins are $60 a night, and trailers are $80 a night, with additional charges for more than two people.

Contact: Lone Oak Campsites, U.S. 44, East Canaan, CT 06024; (860) 824-7051 or (800) 422-2267.

Directions: From Route 8 in Winsted, travel west on U.S. 44 to Norfolk. Continue four miles west to the campground entrance on the south side of the road.

Trip notes: Half of the sites at this self-described destination resort are rented by seasonal campers who set up shop for the summer. This is indeed a busy place; every weekend the recreation director organizes a flurry of events from bingo and kids' arts and crafts to DJ dances, parades, talent shows, and live music. There's even a PA system and a cable access channel to help spread the word on activities. Should you need a respite from all the action, many natural attractions are close by, including the Appalachian Trail to the west off Route 41, where you can take a scenic 5.5-mile loop hike. Campers may want to wet a fishing line in the Blackberry River at the campground, or head north to Campbell Falls State Park, which is open for fishing and picnicking as well as hiking on a winding, wooded trail that leads to some waterfalls.

Open: April 15 through October 15.

❸ White Pines Campsites

Location: Northeast of Winsted; Western Connecticut map page 448, grid b3.

Campsites, facilities: The 206 wooded or open sites have fire rings, picnic tables, and full hookups. RV rental units are available. In addition to a stocked fishing pond, the campground offers paddleboat rentals, a pool, sports facilities, and a camp store. RV supplies are sold. Pets are permitted.

Reservations, fees: A 50 percent non-refundable deposit is required for reservations. Sites are $24 a night in season; before Memorial Day and after Labor Day, they are $18.

Contact: White Pines Campsites, 232 Old North Road, Winsted, CT 06098; (860) 379-0124 or (800) 379-0124.

Directions: From Winsted, drive a mile west on U.S. 44. Bear right, heading north on Old Route 8. Turn right (east) on Route 20, then take an immediate hard right onto Old North Road. The campground will be one mile ahead on the left.

Trip notes: Named for the tall beauties that shade this 60-acre parcel of land, White Pines is a low-key, attractive campground. Natural-wood buildings and trim lawns help set the stage for good, clean fun. Social activities—from fishing derbies to arts and crafts—are geared toward families. Music and movies attract older campers, while sports tournaments are held for campers of all ages. Several large lakes nearby are open for freshwater boating and swimming.

Open: April 15 through October 15.

---

❹ Austin F. Hawes Memorial Campground

Location: Northeast of Winsted in the American Legion State Forest; Western Connecticut map page 448, grid b3.

Campsites, facilities: There are 30 sites for tents and RVs. A dump station, flush toilets, showers, and free firewood are provided. One leashed pet per site is allowed.

Reservations, fees: Reservations are recommended. Sites are $10 a night.

Contact: American Legion State Forest, P.O. Box 161, Pleasant Valley, CT 06063; (860) 379-0922.

Directions: From Winsted, take U.S. 44 east to the intersection with Route 318 in Pleasant Valley. Proceed north on West River Road to the campground entrance on the right.

Trip notes: Campground regulars include anglers and canoeists who are drawn to the Farmington River, which is stocked with several types of trout, perch, bass, and pickerel and is known for its challenging white water. Class I–III rapids dominate the 12-mile stretch from a put-in at Riverton on Route 20 south to New Hartford. Across the river from the campground is Peoples State Forest. To reach the forest entrance from Pleasant Valley, cross the bridge over the river and take a left heading north on East River Road. From there, the yellow-marked Jessie Gerard Trail starts near the old Indian Settlement known as Barkhamsted Lighthouse. At the fork, the trail to the right goes through the lighthouse site and continues north to the Chaugham Lookouts; the left fork climbs more directly to the overlooks via 299 stone steps.

Open: Mid-April through October.

❺ Taylor Brook Campground

Location: North of Torrington; Western Connecticut map page 448, grid b3.

Campsites, facilities: Each of the 40 wooded sites has a fire ring and picnic table. Hot showers, a dump station, and flush toilets are provided. Beer kegs are prohibited. No pets are allowed.

Reservations, fees: Reservations are recommended. Sites are $10 a night.

Contact: Taylor Brook Campground, (860) 379-0172. Burr Pond State Park, 385 Burr Mountain Road, Torrington, CT 06790; (860) 482-1817.

Directions: From the intersection of Routes 4 and 8 in Torrington, head six miles north on Route 8 to exit 46. Take West Highland Lake Road to Burr Mountain Road and continue to the campground on the right. This road loops around by the park entrance before reentering West Highland Lake Road.

Trip notes: Rowdy campers like Taylor Brook because the sites are set in a dense forest, affording maximum privacy and a buffer zone for outdoor reveling. To control the fun, park officials have imposed a no-keg rule. From the far loop of the campground, a trail leads along Taylor Brook to Burr Pond State Park, where a wide lakeshore beach and freshwater fishing attract campers and many day-users. Just west of the campground on Burr Mountain Road is Indian Lookout. Overlooking Burr Pond, this 60-plus-acre wildlife sanctuary is home to a spectacular grove of mountain laurel, the state flower.

Open: April 19 through September 30.

❻ Housatonic Meadows State Park

Location: Northwest of Litchfield on the Housatonic River; Western Connecticut map page 448, grid b2.

Campsites, facilities: There are 95 wooded tent and RV sites, all without hookups. Picnic tables and fire rings are provided, as are hot showers, flush toilets, a dump station, and piped water. Maximum RV length is 35 feet. No pets are allowed.

Reservations, fees: Reservations are highly recommended. There's a two-night minimum stay for reservations. Sites are $10 a night.

Contact: Housatonic Meadows State Park, Cornwall Bridge, CT 06754; (860) 672-6772 (campground) or (860) 927-3238 (park office).

Directions: From New Milford, head north on U.S. 7. Or, follow Route 4 west from Torrington. The campground is located on U.S. 7 approximately one mile north of the intersection with Route 4.

Trip notes: At this fly fisher's paradise, most campsites are set beneath tall pines just a cast's distance from the mighty Housatonic River, which flows another 132 miles from here to Long Island Sound. Housatonic Meadows State Park is part of a nine-mile trout management area, and the lower half of the protected zone has been set aside for fly-fishing only; check with rangers about boundaries and restrictions. A hydroelectric power station to the north in Falls Village causes the water level of the Housatonic to fluctuate: it rises in mid-morning and doesn't go back down until late afternoon. Clarke Outdoors, a kayak and canoe rental shop up the road from the park entrance, offers white-water instruction (call 860/672-6365). From below Falls Village to the campground, canoeists will find Class I, II, and III white water on a 12-mile stretch of the river.

Open: May through October.

❼ Valley in the Pines

Location: West of Torrington; Western Connecticut map page 448, grid b2.

Campsites, facilities: The campground holds 30 well-buffered, wooded sites, all with hookups. Two-thirds of the sites are rented seasonally by RVers. Facilities include a bathhouse with hot showers and flush toilets, a rec hall, and a swimming pool. Leashed pets are permitted.

Reservations, fees: Reservations are required. Sites are $24 a day, $125 a week. A cabin is available for $10 extra daily. Winter camping is offered seasonally for $350. Seasonal rates for summer are available on request.

Contact: Valley in the Pines, P.O. Box 5, Goshen, CT 06756; (860) 491-2032.

Directions: From the intersection of Routes 4 and 63 in Goshen Center, travel west on Route 4 for approximately two miles. Where Route 4 makes a sharp right and a camping sign indicates to stay on that road, turn left on Milton Road. The campground is two miles ahead on the right.

Trip notes: Valley in the Pines is occupied primarily by seasonal campers. Sites are set in thick woodland hills traversed by foot trails. Anglers can try for brown and rainbow trout at the stocked pond on the property. Down the road is Mohawk State Forest, which is crossed by the 35-mile Mattatuck Trail in its northernmost reaches. At the forest headquarters off Route 4, nature lovers can stroll along a bog trail and boardwalk to view bog flora such as mountain holly and sundew.

Open: Year-round; fully operational April 15 through October 15.

❽ Mohawk Campground

Location: West of Torrington; Western Connecticut map page 448, grid b2.

Campsites, facilities: There are 80 partially wooded sites with full hookups. Air conditioners and heaters are allowed. Picnic tables, fireplaces, flush toilets, hot showers, a dump station, rec hall, a pool, and a sports field are provided. Leashed dogs are permitted; horses are not allowed.

Reservations, fees: Reservations are recommended. Sites are $15 a day per adult; add $3 more each day for visitors, electric heaters, and air conditioners.

Contact: Mohawk Campground, P.O. Box 488, West Goshen, CT 06756; (860) 491-2231.

Directions: From Route 8 north of Torrington, take exit 44 and drive west on Route 4. Continue through the intersection of Route 63 in Goshen. Follow signs to the campground entrance on the north side of the road.

Trip notes: Set out in an orderly grid fashion, the campsites here are open and grassy with a backdrop of trees. The atmosphere is pleasant, tidy, and quiet. Catering to RVers, Mohawk Campground is popular with travelers who come to Goshen for a range of summertime events including the Goshen Fair, a balloon festival, and several dog shows and trials.

Open: Early May through early October.

❾ Macedonia Brook State Park

Location: South of Sharon on the New

York border; Western Connecticut map page 448, grid b2.

Campsites, facilities: There are 84 rustic sites for tents and RVs in open or wooded settings. Each campsite has a fire ring and a picnic table. Piped water and pit toilets are provided, and there is a group shelter on the grounds. Supplies and laundry facilities are available four miles away in Kent. The maximum RV length is 35 feet. No pets are allowed.

Reservations, fees: Reservations are highly recommended. There's a two-night minimum stay for reservations. Sites are $9 a night.

Contact: Macedonia Brook State Park, 159 Macedonia Brook Road, Kent, CT 06757; (860) 927-4100 (campground) or (860) 927-3238 (park office).

Directions: From Interstate 84 north of Danbury, take exit 7 and follow U.S. 7 north to Kent. Turn left on Route 341 and continue to Macedonia Brook Road, on the right about three miles ahead. Signs lead directly into the park.

Trip notes: Macedonia Brook sings a joyful song as it tumbles by these wooded campsites. Birders favor this location for the many woodland species that overnight here during their migrations, and both groups tend to be up at dawn. Be sure to bring your mountain bike, for an extensive network of dirt roads leads through the park and the surrounding forest. From the park you can hop on a section of the Appalachian Trail and hike to spectacular viewpoints over the Connecticut countryside. Hit this section of the trail in late September and you'll likely meet up with some through-hikers, folks who make a six-month pilgrimage from the trail's origin in Georgia to its terminus atop Mount Katahdin in Maine.

Open: Mid-April through early October.

⑩ Treetops Camp Resort

Location: East of Kent on North Spectacle Lake; Western Connecticut map page 448, grid c2.

Campsites, facilities: There are 262 sites for tents and RVs, 25 with full hookups, 207 with water and sewer, and 30 with none. Several mobile units are available for rent. Picnic tables, fire rings, hot showers, and flush toilets are provided. Also available are laundry facilities, a camp store, miniature golf, basketball, horseshoes, volleyball, and beach parking. Leashed pets are permitted.

Reservations, fees: Reservations are recommended. Sites start at $20 a night.

Contact: Treetops Camp Resort, Route 341, Kenico Road, Kent, CT 06757; (860) 927-3555.

Directions: From Litchfield Center, drive approximately eight miles west on U.S. 202 to Woodville, then turn right (west) on Route 341. Proceed to Warren, where Route 45 splits from this road; take a left and stay on Route 341. In three miles, turn right on Kenico Road and continue to the campground on the left.

Trip notes: Campsites dot the hillside above spring-fed North Spectacle Lake, known for its healthy population of bass and open to all kinds of boating, fishing, and swimming. Many sites are rented seasonally, and campers can choose from Serenity Hill, where alcohol is prohibited; Hemlock Hill, for sites without hookups; or Willow Green, which is closest to the beach and is equipped with sewer connections. From May through October, there are many planned activities, from bingo to hayrides to game tournaments. Just north of here on U.S. 7 is Kent Falls State Park, home to spectacular waterfalls: Kent Falls Brook drops about 200 feet in a series of cascades.

Three miles south of town, also on U.S. 7, is Bull's Covered Bridge, one of two covered bridges still open to traffic in Connecticut. Take a right onto Bull's Bridge Road, cross the first bridge, go through the covered bridge, and cross a third bridge to access the Appalachian Trail. From here a challenging stretch of the trail follows the Housatonic River, with views of Ten Mile Gorge along the way, then continues on to Ten Mile Hill overlooking the rolling hills of Litchfield.

Open: May 15 through October 15.

⑪ Lake Waramaug State Park

Location: Between Kent and Litchfield; Western Connecticut map page 448, grid c2.

Campsites, facilities: There are 77 sites for tents and RVs. Amenities include picnic tables, concrete fireplaces, hot showers, flush toilets, a sheltered group picnic area, recycling, and a dump station. The campground rents canoes and paddleboats for use on the lake, or you can launch your own cartop boat. The maximum RV length is 35 feet. No pets are allowed.

Reservations, fees: Reservations are highly recommended. There's a two-night minimum stay for reservations. Sites are $10 a night.

Contact: Lake Waramaug State Park, 30 Lake Waramaug Road, New Preston, CT 06777; (860) 868-0220.

Directions: From Litchfield, take U.S. 202 west to New Preston. Turn left (north) on Route 45 and drive about a mile until you see the lake. Turn on Lake Waramaug Road, which will be on your left, and drive to the campground. The road circles the lake and reenters Route 45 to the north.

Trip notes: A quiet road is all that separates these campsites from charming Lake Waramaug. Stately homes with sweeping lawns decorate the opposite shoreline, and your property is just as pretty. Sites are fairly open, shaded by tall hardwood trees; numbers 65 and above, at the far end of the park, offer the most privacy. Campers can swim or launch a boat from the campground's beach. By bike or foot, you can circumnavigate the lake on eight miles of country roads. Be sure to stop at Hopkins Vineyard a few miles downshore from the state park. It's one of six vineyards that comprise the Connecticut Wine Trail, a bike and auto tour. The vineyard offers free wine tasting and tours of the facility.

Open: Mid-May through September 30.

⑫ Hemlock Hill Camp Resort

Location: North of Litchfield; Western Connecticut map page 448, grid b2.

Campsites, facilities: There are 135 sites for tents and RVs, 125 with full hookups and 10 with none. Each has a fire pit and picnic table. This full-service campground has two pools, a hot tub, a bocce court, bingo, and laundry facilities. A pavilion, RV storage, sports courts, a playground, and rec hall are also on site. Leashed pets are permitted.

Reservations, fees: Telephone reservations are accepted with a deposit equal to the price of one night's stay. Tent sites are $20 a night from July through September, with discounts for stays of a week or longer. RV sites start at $29 a night from July through September; there's an extra charge for the use of air conditioners. Some sites are cooperatively owned: you can purchase your own campsite and pay annual dues for maintenance. Ownerships are available.

Contact: Jerry and Mary Hughes, Hemlock

Hill Camp Resort, P.O. Box 828, Hemlock Road, Litchfield, CT 06759; (860) 567 2267.

Directions: From Route 8 north of Plymouth, take exit 42 and follow Route 118 west to Litchfield Center. Head west on U.S. 202 for one mile. Turn right on Milton Road and follow signs to the campground entrance on the right.

Trip notes: Hemlock Hill is a favorite destination of many campers because of its recreation schedule. Every weekend, the cooperative campground organizes family-oriented activities, from Christmas in July and an Italian festival to bingo bonanzas and pumpkin picking. The spacious, clean sites are on a hillside shaded by towering hemlock trees, and some are available for overnight guests. You can paddle a canoe on the brook that flows through here. The nearby town of Litchfield is full of colonial charm. Driving north along Route 63, you'll pass several historic sites including the birthplace of Harriet Beecher Stowe and Sheldon's Tavern, where George Washington lodged for a night in 1781.

Open: Late April through late October.

⑬ Looking Glass Hill

Location: Five miles west of Litchfield Center; Western Connecticut map page 448, grid c3.

Campsites, facilities: There are 50 sites for tents and RVs. Fire pits, flush toilets, hot showers, a rec hall, and picnic tables are provided. Leashed pets are permitted.

Reservations, fees: Reservations are recommended. Sites start at $15 a night.

Contact: Madelyn and Kurt Paskiewicz, Looking Glass Hill, P.O. Box 1610, Litchfield, CT 06759; (860) 567-2050.

Directions: From Litchfield Center, take U.S. 202 west for 5.1 miles. The camp-ground entrance is on the south side of the road and can be easily missed, so watch your odometer closely.

Trip notes: Looking Glass Hill provides a combination of quiet, rustic campsites with modern, clean facilities on a forested hillside. Mountain bikers favor the campground for its no-nonsense air and prime location in the heart of the Litchfield hills, a very popular biking area. Winding roads meander through rolling terrain in every direction. It's a good option for RVers when the White Memorial Conservation Center is full.

Open: Mid-April through mid-October.

⑭ White Memorial Foundation Family Campgrounds

Location: West of Litchfield; Western Connecticut map page 448, grid c3.

Campsites, facilities: Between two locations, there are 47 sites for tents and RVs and 18 tent-only sites. Pit toilets, fire rings, and a dump station are provided, but there are no showers or hookups. A store and marina are located at the entrance. No pets are allowed.

Reservations, fees: Reservations are recommended; reserve by writing to the address below before Memorial Day and in person at the campground store thereafter. Unreserved sites are available on a first-come, first-served basis. There's a two-day minimum stay—three days on holiday weekends. Tent sites are $8 a night at Windmill Hill and $11 a night at Point Folly (waterfront); sites for camping vehicles are $12.75 a night.

Contact: White Memorial Foundation, P.O. Box 368, Litchfield, CT 06759; (860) 567-0089.

Directions: From Route 8 north of Plymouth, take exit 42 and follow Route 118 south to U.S. 202 in Litchfield. Continue two miles through town to the entrance for the White Memorial Conservation Center on the left. The entrance to Point Folly Campground is about a quarter mile farther down the road, also on the left.

Trip notes: The White Memorial Conservation Center owns and operates these two campgrounds, along with 4,000 acres of sanctuary lands on Bantam Lake. Point Folly Campground is set on a peninsula on the lake, offering many sites right on the water. Water-skiers will want to reserve lot number 21 there—it has a perfect view of the Bantam Lake Ski Club's ski jump. All sites have some shade but tend to be sloped or bumpy, and many will not accommodate very large RVs; the camp manager makes decisions about allowable vehicle length depending on which sites are open, so owners of large RVs need to call ahead.

Eighteen tent-only sites are at Windmill Hill, a peaceful, wooded area with a walking trail to the White Memorial Conservation Center. An additional 35 miles of hiking, horseback riding, and nature trails weave throughout the preserve. Bird-watchers will delight in the many species that make their home at Bantam Lake, the state's largest natural body of water. The center's Holbrook Bird Observatory overlooks a landscaped area, and 30 sheltered viewing stations are perfectly situated for bird-watchers and photographers.

Open: Memorial Day through Labor Day.

⓯ Black Rock State Park

Location: North of Watertown; Western Connecticut map page 448, grid c3.

Campsites, facilities: The 95 mostly wooded campsites are for tents and RVs.

There's a dump station but no hookups. A food concession operates at the beach, and supplies can be obtained in nearby Thomaston or Watertown. Hot showers, picnic tables, fire grills, recycling bins, and a horseshoe pit are provided. A nature center and ball field are on park grounds. Black Rock is a dry campground—alcoholic beverages are not permitted in the park. The maximum RV length is 35 feet. No pets are allowed.

Reservations, fees: Reservations are recommended for Memorial Day through Labor Day. There's a two-night minimum stay for reservations. Sites are $10 a night.

Contact: Black Rock State Park, Route 6, Thomaston, CT 06787; (860) 283-8088.

Directions: From Interstate 84 in Waterbury, take exit 20 and drive north on Route 8. When you reach exit 38, turn and follow U.S. 6 south. On the last mile, signs will lead you to the state park entrance.

Trip notes: Boating, swimming, and fishing on Black Rock Pond are the main attractions at this campground. The mostly grassy, partially shaded sites are perched on a hillside above the water. Across from the park entrance you'll find a road leading into Mattatuck State Forest, where multiuse trails provide excellent hiking and mountain biking opportunities. Through these very woods, Indian chief King Philip pursued colonial farmers along a footpath—now the 35-mile-long Mattatuck Trail—in an attempt to discourage settlement. The wooded trail also leads past Leatherman's Cave, named for a famed mountain recluse whose former home you are welcome to explore.

Open: Mid-April through September 30.

⓰ Branch Brook Campground

Location: North of Watertown near Black

Rock State Park; Western Connecticut map page 448, grid c3

Campsites, facilities: There are 63 sites for RVs and tents, 55 with full hookups. Picnic tables, fire rings, and wheelchair-accessible rest rooms are provided. The site has a pool, laundry facilities, a rec hall, and an RV repair service. LP gas, ice, and firewood are available. RV rental units are also available. Leashed pets are permitted.

Reservations, fees: Reservations are recommended. There is a three-day minimum stay during holiday weekends. Sites start at $20 a night per family.

Contact: Kip and Denise Brammer, Branch Brook Campground, 435 Watertown Road, Thomaston, CT 06787; (860) 283-8144.

Directions: From Interstate 84 in Waterbury, take exit 20 and head north on Route 8. When you reach exit 38, turn and follow U.S. 6 south. Over the last mile, signs will lead you to Black Rock State Park; the campground entrance is directly across the street.

Trip notes: Set beside Branch Brook, this campground is popular with seasonal campers, so you'll find some permanent structures with a lived-in, and not very scenic, appearance. The brook offers great fishing from the campground all the way up to Black Rock Dam. Just down the road is Mattatuck State Forest, with its wooded roads and trails that are ideal for mountain biking and nature walks.

Open: April 1 through October 31.

⑰ Gentile's Golden Hill Campground

Location: South of Plymouth; Western Connecticut map page 448, grid c3.

Campsites, facilities: There are 110 hilly, wooded sites for tents and RVs of any length. Each site has a picnic table and fire ring. Full hookups (including cable TV), a pool, LP gas, a store, and a large rec hall are provided. The grounds also hold a miniature golf course and a chapel. Leashed pets are permitted.

Reservations, fees: Reservations are required. Rates are available upon request.

Contact: Irene and Ray Gentile, Gentile's Golden Hill Campground, Route 262/ Mount Tobe Road, Plymouth, CT 06782; (860) 283-8437.

Directions: From Interstate 84 in Waterbury, take exit 20 and head north on Route 8. When you reach exit 39, turn on U.S. 6 and drive two miles. At the light, turn right on Route 262 and head south for three miles. The campground is on the left; there is a large sign at the front entrance.

Trip notes: If you don't mind close quarters (these sites are only about 20 feet apart), try Gentile's for a good selection of RV amenities and on-site recreation including tennis courts and a swimming pool. You can set up a tent, but the majority of sites are rented seasonally by RVers; that means you'll see many vehicles parked here for good. The campground abuts Mattatuck State Forest, which boasts trout-stocked streams and multiuse trails. For a challenging and rewarding hike, head east to Bristol and strike out on the Tunxis Blue Trail, a 6.5-miler featuring a mile of ledges, beaver lodges, and a scenic lookout over the Bristol Reservoir. To reach the trailhead at the Bristol Nature Center, get on U.S. 6 and follow it east to Route 69. Travel 2.5 miles north on Route 69, then take a right onto Shrub Road.

Open: April 1 through November 15.

⑱ Kettletown State Park

Location: South of Southbury; Western Connecticut map page 448, grid d3.

Campsites, facilities: There are 72 open and wooded sites for tents and RVs, all without hookups. Rest rooms, hot showers, an outdoor amphitheater, group picnic areas, fire grills, recycling, a dump station, and horseshoe pits are provided. The camp office sells firewood, worms, and ice. The maximum RV length is 26 feet. No pets are allowed.

Reservations, fees: Reservations are highly recommended for Memorial Day through Labor Day. There's a two-night minimum stay for reservations. Sites are $10 a night.

Contact: Kettletown State Park, 175 Quaker Farms Road, Southbury, CT 06488; (203) 264-5678.

Directions: From Interstate 84 in Southbury, take exit 15 and drive less than a tenth of a mile east on Route 67. Following the signs, make an immediate right on Kettletown Road and continue approximately five miles to the park entrance and the campground.

Trip notes: At Kettletown State Park, campsites are located in the hills above and directly on Lake Zoar, which is fed by clear, cool Kettletown Brook. There's something here for outdoor-lovers of many different persuasions: Cast a line in either the stream or the lake—both are stocked with bass—or launch a cartop boat at the park. Hikers can head out on the Pomperaug Blue Trail from the trailhead at the park entrance. This four-mile woodland walk offers sweeping ridgetop views of the lake and surrounding hills. Wildlife-viewing opportunities at Kettletown include the endangered wood turtle and the less-innocuous copperhead snake. An extensive network of interpretive nature trails near the campground is perfect for ecology-minded kids. Fresh local honey is sold at a farm just outside the park entrance.

Open: April 19 through October 14.

⑲ Mineral Springs Family Campground

Location: North of Stafford; Eastern Connecticut map page 449, grid a2.

Campsites, facilities: The campground holds 150 sites for tents and RVs in a mix of wooded and open settings. All offer water and electric hookups, picnic tables, and fire rings. Use of RV air conditioners and heaters is allowed. Recreation facilities include horseshoe pits, a rec hall, large playground, and pool. Also available are hot showers, flush toilets, laundry facilities, a group tenting area, and a store selling ice, firewood, and LP gas. Leashed pets are permitted.

Reservations, fees: Reservations are recommended June through September. Sites start at $17 a night.

Contact: The Goodale Family, Mineral Springs Family Campground, 135 Leonard Road, Stafford Springs, CT 06076; (860) 684-2993.

Directions: From Interstate 84 northeast of Tolland, take exit 70 and drive north on Route 32 to Stafford Springs. At the junction of Routes 32 and 190, head right (east) on Route 190 for a quarter mile, then turn north on Route 19. In two miles bear left at the fork and cross a steel bridge onto Leonard Road. The campground is one mile north, on the right.

Trip notes: Though rural, this campground is not always peaceful; its close proximity to Stafford Motor Speedway makes it a favorite of NASCAR race fans, who tend to be a little rowdy. The nearby New England States Civilian Conservation Corps Museum, in Stafford Springs on Route 190, makes for an interesting rainy-day outing. Exhibits at the museum focus on early forestry tools and techniques.

Open: May 1 through October 15.

⑳ Roaring Brook Campground

㉑ Del-Aire Family Campground

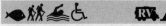

Location: Southeast of Stafford; Eastern Connecticut map page 449, grid a3.

Campsites, facilities: More than 400 sites fill this co-op campground. Most are reserved on a seasonal basis by the owner-members, though some overnight spots are available to nonowners. All sites feature full hookups, picnic tables, and fire rings. Facilities include flush toilets, hot showers, a pool, store, and recreation area. Leashed pets are permitted.

Reservations, fees: Reservations are recommended. Fees are $150 a week. Nightly rates are available on request, but the campground is geared to longer-term stays. Monthly and seasonal rates are available, as are ownership options.

Contact: Roaring Brook Campground, 8 South Road, Route 190, Stafford Springs, CT 06076; (860) 684-7086.

Directions: From Interstate 84 near the Massachusetts border, take exit 72 to Route 89 north. Follow Route 89 to Route 190 and turn left (west). The campground is two miles up the road, on the right.

Trip notes: The campers at Roaring Brook—predominantly owner-members—tend to stay a while, thanks to the area's abundant recreation and relaxation opportunities. A stocked pond on the grounds offers trout and bass fishing as well as a white sandy beach for swimming or sunbathing. Nipmuck State Forest is close by for long hikes through the woods. And the Nipmuck Laurel Sanctuary is just off Route 190—don't miss it when it's in full bloom in late June. The campground also offers group activities ranging from community meals to sporting competitions.

Open: Mid-April through October 15.

Location: North of Tolland; Eastern Connecticut map page 449, grid b2.

Campsites, facilities: Each of the 125 mostly wooded sites has a picnic table and stone fireplace; 100 sites have water and electric hookups. Facilities include metered hot showers, flush toilets, and a small store selling ice, firewood, and limited groceries. A rec hall, playground, and sports fields are also located on the premises. Leashed pets are permitted.

Reservations, fees: Reservations are recommended July 1 through Labor Day. Tent sites are $14 a night, and sites with hookups are $18 a night; weekly and seasonal rates are available.

Contact: Del-Aire Family Campground, Shenipsit Lake Road, Tolland, CT 06084; (860) 875-8325.

Directions: From Interstate 84 east of Vernon, take exit 67 and travel north on Route 31 for a quarter mile to Route 30. Make a right at the light and follow Route 30 for four miles to Brown's Bridge Road. At the intersection with Shenipsit Lake Road (a dirt road) turn right; the campground entrance is on the right.

Trip notes: This tidy, quiet campground enjoys an established seasonal clientele. Most sites are flat, close together, and wooded; a less-developed section is available for tents. Two clear brooks run through the grounds, while nearby Shenipsit Lake offers powerboating, fishing, and swimming. Expect to see many species of birds at the lake, including cranes and cormorants. Also nearby, an easy trail up Soapstone Mountain leads to a summit lookout tower and great river-valley views.

Open: May 1 through October 15.

㉒ Rainbow Acres Campground

Location: South of Stafford Springs; Eastern Connecticut map page 449, grid b2.

Campsites, facilities: Of the 135 sites, some are wooded, some are open, and more than half are equipped with hookups. A special area for tents lies by the lake. Amenities include picnic tables, fire rings, hot showers, flush toilets, a snack bar, paddleboat rentals, and a dump station. Furnished trailers are available for rent. Leashed pets are permitted.

Reservations, fees: Reservations are recommended. Sites are $18 a night without hookups and $20 a night with water and electricity.

Contact: Rainbow Acres Campground, 150 Village Hill Road, Willington, CT 06279; (860) 684-5704.

Directions: From Interstate 84 northeast of Tolland, take exit 70 and travel north on Route 32 for about 300 feet. Take a right onto Village Hill Road and continue 1.5 miles to the campground.

Trip notes: Rainbow Acres lies in a well-forested region home to abundant wildlife, including turkey, deer, pheasant, and rabbit. The peaceful, shaded campground sits beside a 30-acre spring-fed lake ringed by white sandy beaches—perfect for long, relaxing afternoons. Only electric- or people-powered boats are allowed on the lake; paddleboat rentals are available. Every weekend the campground sponsors social events ranging from barbecues and wine tastings to fishing derbies and dancing. Hikers can follow an easy, one-mile trail right from the campground to the top of Beacon Light Hill, where the Carbide Light Tower once stood. When it was erected in 1921, this tower was the country's first air-navigation aid. Race-car enthusiasts will want to check out Stafford Motor Speedway, only three miles away.

Open: May to October.

㉓ Moosemeadow Camping Resort

Location: East of Tolland; Eastern Connecticut map page 449, grid b3.

Campsites, facilities: There are 200 sites for tents and RVs, most with cooking grills. Recreation facilities include horseshoe pits, a miniature golf course, and courts for shuffleboard, basketball, volleyball, and tennis. Hot showers, flush toilets, and laundry facilities are available, as are ice, firewood, and LP gas. Leashed pets are permitted.

Reservations, fees: Reservations are recommended, and a nonrefundable deposit is required. Sites start at $24 a night with no hookups and $27 with water and electric hookups.

Contact: Moosemeadow Camping Resort, P.O. Box 38, West Willington, CT 06279; (860) 429-7451.

Directions: From Interstate 84 east of Tolland, take exit 69 and travel four miles east on Route 74, then turn left on Moosemeadow Road and drive one mile north to the campground entrance.

Trip notes: Grassy meadowlands provide the setting for this full-service RV campground. A pond on the property offers fishing and swimming, and nearby Shenipsit Lake is open to powerboats. A primitive area is available for tenting. Not too far south of West Willington in Coventry is Nutmeg Vineyards Farm Winery, featuring weekend walking tours of the vineyard and samples of European-style wines. The route from the campground to the winery follows quiet country roads, making the excursion ideal for bicyclists.

Open: Mid-April through mid-October.

24 Manna Campground

Location: East of Bigelow Hollow State Park; Eastern Connecticut map page 449, grid a3.

Campsites, facilities: The 26 wooded sites are equipped with fire pits and picnic tables. Some sites have water, electric, and sewer hookups. An additional field is available for group camping, while a conference building has hot showers and heated rest rooms. Leashed pets are permitted.

Reservations, fees: Reservations are recommended. Sites start at $15 a night per family. Seasonal rates are available.

Contact: Manna Campground, 1728 Route 198, Woodstock, CT 06281; (203) 974-3910.

Directions: From Interstate 84 near the Massachusetts border, take exit 73. Travel east on Route 190 for 1.9 miles to Union. Just north of town, turn right on Route 171S/197. Continue east for 2.2 miles and take a left on Route 197. Follow Route 197 to Route 198 and turn left (north). The campground is 1.7 miles ahead on the left.

Trip notes: The campground occupies 33 acres of wooded hillsides punctuated by fields, brooks, and ponds and surrounded by Nipmuck State Forest lands; trails lead into the forest from the campground. Kids will enjoy swimming or fishing in a small pond right on the property. In addition to campsites, Manna holds a photomobile model museum displaying models of solar-powered boats, cars, planes, trains, and hovercraft. Visitors may also ride in the museum's full-scale solar-powered golf cart and canoe. At nearby Bigelow Hollow State Park (off Route 171S/197), Mashapaug Pond offers a public boat ramp and is open for powerboating, fishing, and swimming.

Open: May 1 through October 31.

25 Solair Recreation League Campground

Location: Near the Massachusetts border in North Woodstock; Eastern Connecticut map page 449, grid a3.

Campsites, facilities: There are 150 sites for tents and RVs at this nudist park. Recreation facilities include boat rentals, sports fields, and a rec hall. Among other amenities are a coffee shop, laundry facilities, hot showers, and a dump station. LP gas and firewood are available. Leashed pets are permitted.

Reservations, fees: Reservations are recommended. Sites start at $20 a night.

Contact: Solair Recreation League Campground, 65 Ide Perrin Road, Woodstock, CT 06281; (860) 928-9174.

Directions: Please call the above number for directions.

Trip notes: Set on Potter Pond, Solair Recreation League—a family-oriented nudist park in operation since 1934—offers boating, fishing, and swimming, as well as a full program of social events and children's activities. The well-established campground draws many returning campers each year. Worth visiting in nearby Woodstock is Roseland Cottage (circa 1846) on Route 169. The Gothic Revival summer home was built by merchant and publisher Henry Bowen, who hosted presidents Grant, Hayes, Harrison, and McKinley at his lavish Fourth of July parties. His barn contains what is believed to be the country's oldest surviving indoor bowling alley.

Open: April to November.

㉖ Chamberlain Lake Campground

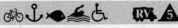

Location: On Chamberlain Lake in Woodstock; Eastern Connecticut map page 449, grid a3.

Campsites, facilities: There are 120 campsites with fire pits and picnic tables. Most have full hookups, and some are right on the lakeshore. A shower house also holds laundry facilities. Other amenities include a snack bar, rec hall, sports courts, a group camping area, and dump stations. Boat rentals are available, as are ice, firewood, and propane. Leashed pets are permitted.

Reservations, fees: Reservations are recommended. Tent sites without hookups are $19 a night; sites with water and electricity start at $22.

Contact: Chamberlain Lake Campground, 1397 Route 197, Woodstock, CT 06281; (860) 974-0567.

Directions: From Interstate 84 near the Massachusetts border, take exit 73. Travel east on Route 190 for 1.9 miles to Union. Just north of town, turn right on Route 171S/197. Continue east for 2.2 miles and take a left on Route 197. The campground is 3.4 miles down the road, on the left.

Trip notes: The wooded sites are either on the lakeshore or above it on a slight slope. They're only about 30 feet wide but have plenty of shade and natural buffers. Another plus is that the owners and staff are friendly and accessible. The campground owns Chamberlain Lake, so you don't need a fishing license to pull out largemouth bass from the waters. Be aware, however, that all fishing here is catch-and-release, and only electric- or people-powered boats are allowed on the lake. Summertime brings scheduled weekend activities including fishing derbies, horseshoe tournaments, group meals, and entertainment. And there are plenty of dirt roads throughout the campground for mountain bikers. Chamberlain Lake is also a favorite among auto-racing fans since it's located midway between Stafford Motor Speedway and Thompson International Speedway.

Open: May 1 through October 15.

㉗ Black Pond Campsites

Location: On Black Pond in Woodstock; Eastern Connecticut map page 449, grid b3.

Campsites, facilities: There are 12 wooded sites open for seasonal rentals. Only self-contained RVs are allowed—no tents or pop-ups. Each site has full hookups but no other facilities. Supplies are available in Woodstock. Leashed pets are permitted.

Reservations, fees: Reservations are required. Rates are available upon request.

Contact: Black Pond Campsites, Woodstock, CT 06281; (203) 974-2065.

Directions: From Interstate 84 near the Massachusetts border, take exit 73. Go east on Route 190 for 1.9 miles to Union. Just north of town, turn right on Route 171S/197. Take Route 197 to the junction with Route 198, then drive two miles farther east on Route 197 to the campground.

Trip notes: Trout-stocked Black Pond lies alongside this small RV park. The sites are well shaded, as they're set within a thick forest. In addition to fishing, swimming and boating are allowed on the pond.

Open: May 15 through October 15.

㉘ West Thompson Lake Campground

Location: West of Thompson on West

Thompson Lake; Eastern Connecticut map page 449, grid b4.

Campsites, facilities: There are 27 wooded sites for tents and RVs, some with hookups. Each has a picnic table and fire ring. Facilities include clean showers, flush toilets, and a dump station, as well as a playground and horseshoe pit. Piped water is available, and firewood is for sale. Leashed pets are permitted.

Reservations, fees: Reservations are not accepted. Sites are $10 a night for tents, $20 with water and electric hookups, and $16 for one of the two Adirondack shelter campsites.

Contact: West Thompson Lake Campground, RFD 1, North Grosvenor Dale, CT 06255-9801; (203) 923-2982.

Directions: From Interstate 395 near the Massachusetts border, take exit 99. Follow Route 200 east to Thompson Center, then make a right onto Route 193. Follow this road west underneath the interstate and continue straight across Route 12 at the traffic light. Turn right on Reardon Road after crossing the French River; the campground entrance will be a half mile ahead on the left.

Trip notes: Wooded, rustic, and neat as a pin, these spacious, private campsites next to West Thompson Lake are absolute gems. A short drive past the campground entrance brings you to the lake and a boat ramp. Operated by the U.S. Army Corps of Engineers, West Thompson Lake is a dam-controlled impoundment of the Quinebaug River. The river is stocked with brown, rainbow, and brook trout while the 200-acre lake supports a healthy population of warm-water species such as bass and perch. Hiking and interpretive trails lace the woods around the dam and lake. Dam tours are given every other weekend in summer and are an attraction in themselves. Also on weekends, nature programs are conducted

in the campground amphitheater to discuss the area's flora and fauna. Deer, raccoon, red fox, grouse, and quail are among the critters inhabiting the surrounding forest of eastern white pine, northern red oak, and shagbark hickory. The wetlands area is also a popular stopover for mallards, geese, and black ducks. This is a naturalist's paradise, and the facilities are so well kept even the most fastidious camper will be impressed.

Open: Third Friday in May through the second Sunday in September.

㉙ Brialee RV and Tent Park

Location: East of Willington; Eastern Connecticut map page 449, grid b3.

Campsites, facilities: There are 176 grassy or wooded sites for tents and RVs. Most sites have full hookups, including cable TV. All come with fire pits and picnic tables. Recreation facilities include a pool, stocked trout pond, boat rentals, nature trails, horseshoe pits, and shuffleboard courts. Also on the premises are a store, laundry facilities, hot showers, and flush toilets. Leashed pets are permitted.

Reservations, fees: Reservations are recommended. Sites start at $29 a night per family with hookups, $25 without hookups. Group and seasonal rates are available.

Contact: Brialee RV and Tent Park, 174 Laurel Lane, P.O. Box 125, Ashford, CT 06278-0125; (860) 429-8359 or (800) 303-2267 (CAMP).

Directions: From Interstate 84 east of Tolland, take exit 69 and head east on Route 74. After eight miles, take a left onto U.S. 44 east and continue one mile to Route 89. Turn left (north) on Route 89, take the first left onto Perry Hill Road, then the second right onto Laurel Lane. Follow Laurel Lane to the campground entrance.

Trip notes: This full-service RV park is geared toward a seasonal clientele. During the summer months, Brialee features outdoor movies, rollerskating, live music, wagon tours through the countryside, and other special events. Look for the Miss Brialee pageant in June. Events also take place on selected weekends in spring and fall. On Easter weekend, for example, campers can learn crafts, attend community dinners, and participate in an Easter-egg hunt.

Open: April 1 to December 1.

---

⑳ Charlie Brown Campground

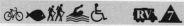

Location: On the Natchaug River in Phoenixville; Eastern Connecticut map page 449, grid b3.

Campsites, facilities: There are 97 primary tent and RV sites and another 26 sites in a group camping area. All sites have picnic tables and fire barrels, and most have electric and water hookups. Fourteen sites have sewer hookups. Use of RV air conditioners and heaters is allowed. Recreation facilities include a rec hall, sports courts, and athletic fields. Other amenities include a picnic pavilion, a centrally located bath and laundry facility, dump stations, a camp store, and an RV supply shop. Some facilities are designed for wheelchair access. Leashed pets are permitted.

Reservations, fees: Reservations are recommended. Sites start at $21 a night.

Contact: Charlie Brown Campground, Route 198, Phoenixville, CT 06242; (860) 974-0142.

Directions: From Interstate 84 east of Tolland, take exit 69 and drive east on Route 74. Turn left (east) on U.S. 44, drive past Ashford to Route 198, and turn south on this road. The campground is on the east side of Route 198, three-quarters of a mile south of the turnoff.

Trip notes: This full-service RV park in the heart of the Natchaug State Forest lies at the confluence of the Still, Natchaug, and Bigelow Rivers. Brook trout abound in these parts—the state stocks the Natchaug River—and a first-rate swimming hole is right on the grounds. The state forest borders the campground, beckoning with miles of hiking and mountain biking trails. Charlie Brown also offers a full activities schedule including performances by country bands in the rec hall every weekend in the summer. Shrubs, fences, and grassy areas separate the campground's shaded, flat sites.

Open: Mid-April through mid-October.

㉛ Peppertree Camping

Location: On the Natchaug River in Phoenixville; Eastern Connecticut map page 449, grid b3.

Campsites, facilities: Of the 55 tent and RV sites, 40 offer full hookups and 15 have water and electric hookups. Fire rings and tables are provided, and a small store sells ice, firewood, and LP gas. Amenities include hot showers, laundry facilities, sports courts, and a group picnic site. Leashed pets are permitted.

Reservations, fees: Reservations are recommended. Sites are $19 or $20 a night.

Contact: Peppertree Camping, Route 198, Eastford, CT 06242; (203) 974-1439.

Directions: From Interstate 84 east of Tolland, take exit 69 and drive east on Route 74. Turn left (east) on U.S. 44, drive past Ashford to Route 198, and turn south on this road. The campground is on the east side of Route 198, 1.25 miles south of the turnoff.

Trip notes: Natchaug means the "land between the rivers," an accurate description of Peppertree's location at the junction of the Bigelow and Still Rivers in Phoenixville. Sites are heavily wooded and private; many are rented seasonally. The 12,500-acre Natchaug State Forest, once part of the hunting grounds of the Wabbaquasset Indians, borders the campground. Multiuse trails web the forest, following riverways, crossing hilly woodlands, and traversing marshes with excellent bird-watching and berry-picking opportunities.

Open: Mid-April through mid-October.

32 Silvermine Horse Camp

Location: In the southern half of Natchaug State Forest; Eastern Connecticut map page 449, grid b3.

Campsites, facilities: This wooded 28-site campground is reserved for equestrians only. Facilities include primitive toilets and a central water pump. Leashed pets are permitted.

Reservations, fees: Reservations are required. Sites are free.

Contact: Natchaug State Forest, Star Route Pilfershire Road, Eastford, CT 06242; (860) 974-1562.

Directions: From Interstate 84 east of Tolland, take exit 69 and drive east on Route 74. Turn left (east) on U.S. 44, drive past Ashford to Route 198, and turn south on this road. Follow signs to the state forest entrance on the east side of Route 198, about three miles south of U.S. 44. Obtain a map at forest headquarters and follow directions to Silvermine; it's several miles into the state forest backcountry.

Trip notes: Open to equestrians only, Silvermine is a primitive campground

reached via dirt roads in the state forest. The grassy, spacious sites are nestled in a private glen. Each has its own hitching post but little else. The extensive Natchaug horse-trail system begins here and traverses many marshlands. Loops in the trail network permit rides of various lengths. The trails are mostly gravel logging roads without extreme grades.

Open: Mid-April through Thanksgiving.

33 Nickerson Campground and RV Supply

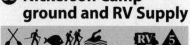

Location: South of Natchaug State Forest on Route 198; Eastern Connecticut map page 449, grid b3.

Campsites, facilities: There are 112 sites, some just for tents, others with full RV hookups including cable TV. Fire rings and tables are provided, and shower and laundry facilities are centrally located. Other amenities include a full-service RV supply store and a rec hall. Leashed pets are permitted.

Reservations, fees: Reservations are always recommended and are required on holiday weekends, when a three-day minimum stay requirement is also in effect. Tent sites are $15 a night, and sites with hookups are $18.

Contact: Nickerson Campground and RV Supply, 1036 Phoenixville Road, Route 198, Chaplin, CT 06235; (860) 455-0007.

Directions: From Interstate 84 east of Tolland, take exit 69 and drive east on Route 74. Turn left (east) on U.S. 44, drive past Ashford to Route 198, and turn south on this road. Drive 4.5 miles to the campground.

Trip notes: Of the three privately owned campgrounds on this stretch of road, Nickerson is the least expensive and the only one open year-round. Sites are wooded, but are spaced a bit too close together. The Natchaug River flows through the campground, and nonmotorized boating is permitted. Adjacent Natchaug State Forest is a great place to fish and hunt in season, and Nickerson is an ideal base camp for those activities. In the winter months, miles of roads and trails in the state forest are open for ski-touring.

Open: Year-round.

㉞ Mashamoquet Brook Campground

Location: East of Abington in Mashamoquet Brook State Park; Eastern Connecticut map page 449, grid b4.

Campsites, facilities: The 20 wooded sites accommodate tents and RVs up to 35 feet long. Facilities are primitive: outhouses, concrete fireplaces, piped water, and picnic tables. No pets are allowed.

Reservations, fees: Reservations are highly recommended. There's a two-night minimum stay for reservations. Sites are $9 a night.

Contact: Mashamoquet Brook Campground, Mashamoquet Brook State Park, Pomfret Center, CT 06259; (860) 928-6121.

Directions: From the intersection of U.S. 44 and Route 198 in Phoenixville, continue east on U.S. 44 through Abington. Signs for the campground will lead you to its entrance on the south side of the road, while state park signs will direct you farther west to the park's main entrance.

Trip notes: This is the smaller of two campgrounds at 781-acre Mashamoquet Brook State Park. The other, Wolf's Den (see campground number 35), is near the park office farther west down U.S. 44. Sites here are set in the woods above meandering, trout-stocked Mashamoquet Brook, but can

be noisy due to traffic on the nearby highway. Personal outhouses at each site are a welcome convenience. This parcel was once owned by the Daughters of the American Revolution, which preserved several historic dwellings on the property. At the entrance to the campground stands the Old Red Mill, as well as the flood-damaged remains of an old cider mill, a gristmill, and a wagon shop. The Old Red Mill is maintained by the Pomfret Historical Society, whose members provide interpretive programs for visitors. Several good hikes leave from the state park, but if you're looking for a short side trip, try the two-mile hike at the Nature Conservancy's Dennis Farm, off Route 97 in Pomfret.

Open: May to October.

㉟ Wolf's Den Campground

Location: East of Abington in Mashamoquet Brook State Park; Eastern Connecticut map page 449, grid b4.

Campsites, facilities: This 35-site campground offers hot showers, flush toilets, a dump station, and a small camp store selling firewood and ice. Other supplies can be obtained close by in Dayville. The maximum RV length is 35 feet. No pets are allowed.

Reservations, fees: Reservations are highly recommended. There's a two-night minimum stay for reservations. Sites are $9 a night.

Contact: Wolf's Den Campground, Mashamoquet Brook State Park, Pomfret Center, CT 06259; (860) 928-6121.

Directions: From the intersection of U.S. 44 and Route 198 in Phoenixville, continue east on U.S. 44 through Abington. You'll see a sign for Mashamoquet Brook Campground, but continue east on U.S. 44 and follow signs for the state park. These signs will lead you a little farther down the road to the main entrance. Take a right on the park road and follow it to the campground.

Trip notes: Campsites here are open, surrounded by woods, and, unlike Mashamoquet Brook Campground, have modern rest rooms. Mashamoquet Brook flows through the park, offering good fishing and some tempting swimming holes. Hiking trails lace the park, winding through scenic hardwood forests crisscrossed by old stone walls. One of the trails leaves from the state park and gradually ascends a hillside to the eponymous Wolf's Den. In 1742, farmer Israel Putnam crept into the den and shot what was believed to be the last wolf in Connecticut. According to the plaque at the site, the animal had been feeding on Putnam's livestock. Nearby are several rock formations including Table Rock and Indian Chair; all three sites can be reached on a four-mile loop from the campground.

Open: May to October.

36 Hide-A-Way Cove Family Campground

Location: Near Killingly Pond State Park on the Rhode Island border; Eastern Connecticut map page 449, grid b4.

Campsites, facilities: The 300 sites have full hookups, picnic tables, and fire rings. In addition to laundry, rest room, and shower facilities, the campground offers a rec hall, swimming pool, camp store, horseshoe pits, and volleyball court. LP gas, ice, and firewood are available. Leashed pets are permitted.

Reservations, fees: Reservations are recommended, and a nonrefundable deposit is required. Sites are $18 a night, $90 a week. Seasonal rates are available.

Contact: Hide-A-Way Cove Family Campground, P.O. Box 129, East Killingly, CT 06234; (860) 774-1128.

Directions: From Interstate 395 at Dayville, take exit 93 onto Route 101 and drive 3.5 miles east to North Road. Turn left on North Road just before the blinking light. The campground is ahead on the right.

Trip notes: Hide-A-Way is located on Middle Lake, an otherwise undeveloped body of water. Many of the closely spaced sites are permanently occupied by seasonal RV campers. The campground's section of lakeshore offers a sandy beach and a boat ramp; motors up to seven horsepower are allowed on the lake. A smorgasbord of organized activities—a cribbage league, bingo, and crafts classes, to name a few—keeps campers busy.

Open: May 1 through mid-October.

37 Stateline Campresort

Location: Near Killingly Pond State Park on the Rhode Island border; Eastern Connecticut map page 449, grid b4.

Campsites, facilities: There are 200 sites for tents and RVs. Most are shaded, and all have fire rings, tables, and water and electric hookups. Recreation facilities include sports courts, playing fields, a rec hall, and boat rentals. A store sells ice, firewood, and LP gas. Dump stations and laundry facilities are provided. Leashed pets are permitted.

Reservations, fees: Reservations are encouraged. Sites start at $22 a night. Most sites are owned through a membership program, but overnight guests are welcome.

Contact: Stateline Campresort, Route 101, East Killingly, CT 06234; (860) 774-3016.

Directions: From Interstate 395 at Dayville, take exit 93 and follow Route 101 east for five miles to the campground entrance on the north side of the road.

Trip notes: The campground's owner-members occupy most of the choice, shaded sites beside Killingly Pond, but other sites are usually available, so call ahead. A boat ramp allows you to slip your trusty vessel into the pond, but be aware that no motors are allowed. Swimmers can splash about in the lake or the campground pool. Killingly Pond State Park is also on the pond, and hikers will discover several foot trails weaving through the surrounding state-owned woods. For an unbeatable view of Rhode Island, Massachusetts, and Connecticut, stop in at Palazzi Orchard, on North Road in East Killingly. It's open through fall, beginning September 1. The 150-acre hilltop orchard offers hayrides across the property and tours of the cider-making operation.

Open: April 15 through October 15.

❸❽ Sterling Park Campground

Location: East of Sterling on the Rhode Island border; Eastern Connecticut map page 449, grid c4.

Campsites, facilities: The 100 sites have tables, fireplaces, and full hookups including cable TV. Among the extensive recreation facilities are a swimming pool, rec hall, radio-control race car track, miniature golf course, horseshoe pits, and sports courts. Laundry facilities are provided, and a small store sells RV supplies as well as ice, firewood, and LP gas. Leashed pets are permitted.

Reservations, fees: Reservations are recommended and require a nonrefundable deposit. Sites are $22 to $26 a night per family.

Contact: Sterling Park Campground, 177 Gibson Hill Road, Sterling, CT 06377; (860) 564-8777.

Directions: From Interstate 395 north of Plainfield, take exit 89 and travel east on Route 14 for approximately six miles. Turn left on Gibson Hill Road; the campground is one mile ahead on the left.

Trip notes: Peace reigns at this rural campground. Sites are mostly grassy and shaded but are close together, averaging just 25 feet wide. Weekend events and various recreational facilities, including a large swimming pool and a miniature golf course, make this a good choice for families.

Open: May 1 through October 15.

❸❾ River Bend Campground

Location: South of Oneco; Eastern Connecticut map page 449, grid c4.

Campsites, facilities: The 160 sites occupy a mix of wooded, open, and grassy areas. All sites offer picnic tables, fireplaces, and full hookups. Trailer rentals are available. Recreation facilities include boat rentals, sports courts, a miniature golf course, pool, and playgrounds. Other amenities include a camp store, group area, movies, showers, flush toilets, and a riverbank beach. Leashed pets are permitted.

Reservations, fees: Prepaid reservations are recommended. Sites start at $23 a night.

Contact: River Bend Campground, P.O. Box 23, Oneco, CT 06373; (860) 564-3440.

Directions: From Interstate 395 near Plainfield, take exit 88 and travel 5.5 miles east on Route 14A to Oneco. Make a right turn at the River Bend sign just before the bridge.

Trip notes: River Bend is a canoeist's paradise. It's located on the gentle Moosup River, which winds its way through a forested landscape. The river is well stocked with fish, and flows are easy enough for any family member to paddle. The campground rents and sells canoes, but you're welcome to bring your own.

Open: April 19 through October 7.

---

⑩ Circle C Campground

Location: South of Sterling Hill; Eastern Connecticut map page 449, grid c4.

Campsites, facilities: There are 82 sites for tents and RVs, some with partial hookups. Each has a picnic table and fire pit. Use of RV air conditioners and heaters is allowed. A central bath and laundry facility holds hot showers and flush toilets. Other amenities include a group camping area, rec hall, adult lounge, playground, arcade, and sports courts. A small camp store sells ice and firewood. Leashed pets are permitted.

Reservations, fees: Reservations are recommended. Tent sites are $18 a night or $106 a week; sites with water and electric hookups are $21 a night or $126 a week.

Contact: Circle C Campground, 21 Bailey Pond Road, Voluntown, CT 06384; (860) 564-4534.

Directions: From Interstate 395 north of Norwich, take exit 85 and travel east on Route 138 to the intersection with Route 49. Travel 2.25 miles north on Route 49 and turn right on Brown Road. Travel 2.75 miles northeast on Brown Road, then take a right on Gallop Homestead Road. In one mile take another right on Bailey Pond Road and continue three-quarters of a mile to the campground.

Trip notes: Finding this campground can be a challenge, so follow the directions carefully. Sites are either set beneath tall pines or are open and grassy. Bailey Pond and two other small ponds on the property provide places for fishing and swimming.

Bailey Pond is also open to powerboating (subject to a 10 mph speed limit) and canoeing. Planned activities, including theme weekends such as Murder Mystery weekend and Las Vegas weekend, parades, water Olympics, luaus, and pizza parties, make this a fun place for the whole family. For an adults-only afternoon of fun, visit the Plainfield Greyhound Park (at exit 87 off Interstate 395), featuring year-round pari-mutuel racing.

Open: Mid-April through mid-October.

---

⑪ Highland Campground

Location: North of Norwich in Scotland; Eastern Connecticut map page 449, grid c3.

Campsites, facilities: There are 160 wooded sites for tents and RVs, all with water and electric hookups, picnic tables, and fireplaces. Recreational facilities include a swimming pool, sports fields and game courts, a stocked fishing pond, rec hall, and hiking trails. Also available are free hot showers, laundry facilities, a camp store that sells firewood and ice, a snack bar, adult lounge, and safari group camping area. Leashed pets are permitted.

Reservations, fees: Reservations are recommended. Sites start at $21 a night.

Contact: Highland Campground, P.O. Box 305, Scotland, CT 06264; (203) 423-5684.

Directions: From Interstate 395 near Plainfield, take exit 89 and travel west on Route 14 to Scotland Center. Turn left (south) on Route 97 and drive one mile, then turn right on Toleration Road. The campground entrance is directly ahead.

Trip notes: Forested, roomy campsites are set on rolling terrain, far back from Toleration Road. A small stream feeds a pond on the grounds where anglers can practice catch-and-release fishing. If you prefer hiking, footpaths lead through the surrounding woodlands. The facilities are modern and clean, and scheduled weekend activities include golf-cart parades, bingo, dancing, and hayrides.

Open: Year-round; weekends only from November 1 through April 30.

42 Salt Rock Campground

Location: North of Baltic near Mohegan State Forest; Eastern Connecticut map page 449, grid c3.

Campsites, facilities: There are 125 sites for tents and RVs, 65 with full hookups, 33 with water and electric, and 27 with none. Each has a concrete patio, fire ring, grill, and picnic table. On-site facilities include a swimming pool, dump stations, showers, sports fields, and horseshoe pits. There's also a pavilion for group activities. Ice and firewood are available. Leashed pets are permitted.

Reservations, fees: Reservations are recommended, and a nonrefundable deposit is required. Sites start at $21 a night without hookups and $25 a night for full services.

Contact: Salt Rock Campground, 120 Scotland Road, Route 97, Baltic, CT 06330; (203) 822-8728.

Directions: From Interstate 395 northeast of Norwich, take exit 83 and travel north on Route 97 to Baltic. The campground is two miles north of town.

Trip notes: Perched on a hillside, the wooded sites at this quiet, family-oriented campground are bordered by the Shetucket River, where campers can fish for trout or float in an inner tube. Footpaths lead along the river and throughout Mohegan State Forest just north of here. The on-site croquet court is reportedly one of the world's largest.

Open: April 15 through October 15.

43 Ross Hill Park

Location: North of Jewett City; Eastern Connecticut map page 449, grid c3.

Campsites, facilities: There are 250 sites for tents and RVs, 120 with full hookups, 105 with water and electric, and 25 with none. Each has a fire ring and picnic table. Dump stations, laundry facilities, a grocery store, LP gas, ice, firewood, a rec hall, boat rentals, a swimming pool, and sports fields and courts are provided. Leashed pets are permitted.

Reservations, fees: Reservations are recommended. Sites start at $20 a night.

Contact: Ross Hill Park, 170 Ross Hill Road, Lisbon, CT 06531; (860) 376-9606.

Directions: From Interstate 395 at Jewett City, take exit 84 and travel north on Route 12 to Route 138. Turn left, follow Route 138 west to Ross Hill Road, then take a right. The campground is 1.5 miles ahead on the right side of the road.

Trip notes: Neat and friendly, this campground takes full advantage of its location on the Quinebaug River where the Aspinook Dam has created Aspinook Pond. You can rent rowboats, canoes, and paddleboats at the campground, and boats with motors up to 5 horsepower are welcome. There is a large beach for swimming and sunning, as well as docks and a boat ramp. Every Saturday night, live bands turn up the volume; planned family activities include fishing derbies and theme weekends. Sites are either on the water or on a wooded hillside overlooking the pond.

Open: Year-round; fully operational April 1 through October 31.

44 Lake Williams Campground

Location: On Williams Pond north of Colchester; Eastern Connecticut map page 449, grid c2.

Campsites, facilities: There are 87 sites for RVs, 62 with full hookups and 25 with water and electric. A few sites are suitable for tents. Tables and fire rings are provided. A store, rec hall, game room, laundry facilities, hot showers, ice, firewood, a pavilion, horseshoe pits, and a volleyball court are on site. Leashed pets are permitted.

Reservations, fees: Reservations are recommended in the summer and are necessary on holiday weekends. Sites start at $23 a night.

Contact: Lake Williams Campground, 1742 Exeter Road, Route 207, Lebanon, CT 06249; (860) 642-7761.

Directions: From Route 2 in Marlborough, take exit 13 and travel east on Route 66 to Route 85. Turn right and continue south on Route 85 for 1.5 miles. Turn left on Route 207 and drive 2.4 miles east to the campground entrance on the left.

Trip notes: Open and shaded sites are available on and near Williams Pond, where campers keep busy fishing for bass, water-skiing, swimming, and boating. Planned events include visits from Santa, barbecues, hayrides, and potluck suppers. When you tire of water sports, check out the historical attractions to the east in Lebanon. On the town green is the Governor Jonathan Trumbell House (circa 1735), home of the only colonial governor to support the Revolutionary War. Nearby on West Town Street stands the Revolutionary War Office, which

was built in 1727 and served as the Trumbell family store. Years later, the Council of Safety met in that office to plan the supply lifeline for troops fighting the war for independence from England.

Open: April 15 through October 15.

45 Water's Edge Family Campground

Location: North of Colchester; Eastern Connecticut map page 449, grid c3.

Campsites, facilities: There are 170 wooded, lakeview, and safari campsites with picnic tables, fire rings, and water and electric hookups; six additional sites have no hookups. Use of air conditioners and heaters is allowed. Hot showers, laundry facilities, propane, and dump stations are provided. The grounds offer an arcade, store, rec hall, boat rentals, playground, sports courts, and athletic fields. Leashed pets are permitted.

Reservations, fees: Reservations are recommended. Sites are $23 to $26 a night ($15 during the off-season).

Contact: Water's Edge Family Campground, 271 Leonard Bridge Road, Lebanon, CT 06249; (860) 642-7470.

Directions: From the junction of Routes 207 and 87 in Lebanon, travel five miles west on Route 207. Make a left on Leonard Bridge Road and continue to the campground entrance a half mile ahead.

Trip notes: The campground borders a 10-acre spring-fed lake stocked with large bass that are bred here. Sites are overdeveloped and close together, so there isn't much privacy, but the ultra-friendly staff makes for a comfortable stay. The lake is a major attraction, offering nonmotorized boating, swimming, and fishing. Weekends are filled with planned activities such as theme bingo, DJ dancing, visits from Rocky the campground mascot, and special dinners. One nearby historical oddity is the Dr. William Beaumont House on West Town Street on the green in Lebanon. This eighteenth-century cottage was the birthplace of Dr. Beaumont, known as the Father of Digestion Physiology, and now displays an intriguing collection of early surgical instruments.

Open: April 15 through October 15.

46 Acorn Acres

Location: Northwest of Norwich near Gardner Lake; Eastern Connecticut map page 449, grid c3.

Campsites, facilities: There are 200 sites for tents and RVs with full hookups. Each has a table and stone fireplace. On site you'll find an Olympic-sized swimming pool, shuffleboard, bingo, sports courts, and horseshoe pits. Hot showers, a camp store, laundry facilities, and a rec hall are available. Pets are allowed.

Reservations, fees: Reservations are recommended. Sites start at $25 a night.

Contact: Acorn Acres, 135 Lake Road, Bozrah, CT 06334; (203) 859-1020.

Directions: From Norwich, travel six miles west on Route 82. Make a right on Route 163 and drive north for one mile, then turn left on Lake Road. The campground is one mile ahead; follow the signs to the entrance.

Trip notes: Gardner Brook feeds a two-acre pond on the property where you can fish for bass and trout. Primarily occupied by RVs, the naturally landscaped sites here are roomy and attractive, and most have shade trees. With a wide array of recreational facilities—tennis courts, shuffleboard, playgrounds, a pool—and nearby Gardner Lake open to boating and water-

skiing, this is a hot spot for families. Land that used to be the hunting grounds for Mohegan Indians surrounds the campground and can be explored on foot trails.

Open: May 1 through Columbus Day.

47 Odetah Campground

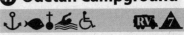

Location: Northwest of Norwich; Eastern Connecticut map page 449, grid c4.

Campsites, facilities: There are 250 wooded sites for tents and RVs, many with full hookups. Each has a fireplace and picnic table. Use of air conditioners and heaters is allowed. Hot showers, flush toilets, a snack bar, laundry facilities, a grocery store, swimming pool, group area, miniature golf, movies, and sports facilities are located on the property. There's also a guarded traffic control gate. Ice and firewood are available. Leashed pets are permitted.

Reservations, fees: Reservations are recommended. There is a two-day minimum stay on weekends. Fees start at $19 a night for primitive sites and $25 a night for full hookups.

Contact: Odetah Campground, P.O. Box 151, 38 Bozrah Street Extension, Bozrah, CT 06334; (860) 889-4144 or (800) 448-1193.

Directions: From Interstate 395 north of Norwich, take exit 81 and drive west on Route 2. Turn left at exit 23 on Route 163 and continue about 1,000 feet to the campground entrance.

Trip notes: Campers who stay at Odetah have access to a private sandy beach on a 30-acre lake. Nonmotorized boating is allowed, and rowboats, canoes, and paddleboats can be rented at the campground. Organized activities, including pancake breakfasts, relay contests, pony rides, and live entertainment, keep the place hopping. Formerly the home of E. Judson Miner, a delegate to the Constitutional Convention at the turn of the century, Odetah was most likely a stopover point on the Underground Railroad.

Open: April 15 through October 15.

48 Hidden Acres Family Campground

Location: Northeast of Norwich; Eastern Connecticut map page 449, grid c3.

Campsites, facilities: There are 180 sites for RVs, 125 with full hookups, 40 with water and electric, and 15 with none. Each has a table and fire ring. Air conditioners are allowed, but heaters are not. Cabins and mobile units are also available for rent. On the grounds are a store, group areas, a snack bar, laundry facilities, RV storage, a rec hall, petting zoo, metered hot showers, flush toilets, LP gas, and a dump station. Sports facilities include a bocce court. Ice and firewood are available, and there is a traffic control gate. Leashed pets are permitted.

Reservations, fees: Reservations are recommended Memorial Day through Labor Day. Sites range from $20 a night with water to $26 with full hookups.

Contact: Hidden Acres Family Campground, 47 River Road, Preston, CT 06365; (860) 887-9633.

Directions: From Interstate 395 at Jewett City, take exit 85 and travel south on Route 164 for one mile. Turn right on George Palmer Road and continue three miles, bearing right at the fork, to the campground.

Trip notes: Aptly named, this campground is tucked away in the woods of Preston and borders the Quinebaug River. June is the month to bring your inner tube for a wild ride down the swollen river. This developed campground offers small, level sites under large trees; many are rented

seasonally. Sites 5 through 15, 17 and 18, and 40 through 50 are right next to the water. Families with boisterous kids dominate the landscape, and planned activities, including Christmas in July and weekend dance parties, create a fun kind of chaos all summer long.

Open: May 1 through Columbus Day.

49 Strawberry Park Campground

Location: North of the Mashantucket Pequot Reservation; Eastern Connecticut map page 449, grid c4.

Campsites, facilities: There are 440 sites, 160 with full hookups and 270 with water and electric, in a mix of settings—open, wooded, grassy, and shaded. Each has a table and fire pit. The campground has three swimming pools, an exercise facility, arcade, store, restaurant, hot showers, flush toilets, laundry facilities, an amphitheater and stage, and a 20,000-square-foot rec hall. For recreation, there's a regulation softball diamond, soccer field, horseshoe pits, extensive sports courts, hiking trails, and movies. A cooperative ownership program is available. Leashed pets are permitted.

Reservations, fees: Reservations are necessary during the summer months. On holiday weekends, there is a three-day minimum stay. Sites are $17 to $39 a night for two people.

Contact: Strawberry Park Campground, P.O. Box 830, Norwich, CT 06360; (860) 886-1944.

Directions: From Interstate 395 near Jewett City, take exit 85 and head south on Route 164. Drive five miles to the intersection with Route 165. Turn left and drive east to Pierce Road; you'll see a large red sign for the campground. Follow Pierce Road to the campground entrance on the right.

Trip notes: At the resort destination of Strawberry Park, campers get the antithesis of a wilderness experience. All kinds of sports and athletics can be practiced at the 77-acre campground, from softball and horseback riding to aerobics and aquacise. Live entertainment, teen dances, movies, three playgrounds, several pools, and a spa are among the offerings. The Strawberry Grill and Creamery, a full-service restaurant and ice cream parlor, operates right on the grounds. There's also a cooperative ownership program and an RV sales office. A must-see is the Foxwoods Casino, run by the Mashantucket Pequot Indians less than five miles away; in addition to gambling, it has several restaurants, shopping, lodging, movies, and bingo.

Open: Year-round.

---

⑤⓪ Hopeville Pond State Park

Location: East of Jewett City; Eastern Connecticut map page 449, grid c4.

Campsites, facilities: The 82 wooded tent and RV sites have fire rings, grills, and picnic tables but no hookups. A central bathhouse with a dump station, flush toilets, and hot showers is augmented by periphery outhouses. Other amenities include canoe and paddleboat rentals, a boat launch, and group recreation facilities. Ice and firewood are available. The maximum RV length is 35 feet. No pets are allowed.

Reservations, fees: Reservations are highly recommended. There's a two-night minimum stay for reservations. Sites are $10 a night.

Contact: Hopeville Pond State Park, 193 Roode Road, Jewett City, CT 06351; (860) 376-0313 (campground) or (860) 376-2920 (park office).

Directions: From Interstate 395 at Hopeville, take exit 86 and travel east on Route 201. Follow signs to the campground entrance on the south side of the road.

Trip notes: The campground's flat, wooded sites are on or near Hopeville Pond, which the state stocks with fish. Sandy swimming beaches invite a cooling dip, and a large day-use area with athletic fields might be just the place for a round of Frisbee golf. Nearby Pachaug State Forest, the state's largest, offers 35 miles of multiuse trails, seven lakes, many streams, and white cedar swamps. Wildlife is abundant in the area, and the campground showers are an entomologist's dream, infested with insects of every size, shape, and color.

Open: Mid-May to mid-October.

---

⑤① Camper's World

Location: On the south side of Hopeville Pond near Hopeville; Eastern Connecticut map page 449, grid c4.

Campsites, facilities: This adults-only park offers 92 RV-only sites with full hookups. Facilities—some wheelchair accessible—include metered showers, beach access, and, oddly enough, a playground. Leashed pets are permitted.

Reservations, fees: Reservations are recommended. Fees are $16 a night or $90 per week.

Contact: George Barr, Camper's World, P.O. Box 333, Jewett City, CT 06351; (203) 376-3944.

Directions: From Interstate 395 at Hopeville, take exit 86 and follow Route 201 east for about half a mile. Make a right on Edmund Road and a left on Nowakowski Road, following the large signs. The campground is straight ahead.

Trip notes: Seasonal campers dominate

this park, and despite rules prohibiting permanent structures from being added on to RVs, most are decked out with tacky accoutrements such as misshapen screen porches and old lawn furniture. Sardinelike sites line the waterfront of south Hopeville Pond here. Some sites have their own docks, and most have shade trees. Recreation opportunities abound. You can launch your boat from the campground, bask on a postage-stamp beach, or go swimming or fishing on the pond.

Open: May through October.

52 Frog Hollow Horse Camp

Location: North of Voluntown in Pachaug State Forest; Eastern Connecticut map page 449, grid c4.

Campsites, facilities: The 18 sites have fire pits, picnic tables, and horse tethers, but no hookups. A water pump and primitive toilets are available. One horse and one leashed dog per site are allowed.

Reservations, fees: Reservations are required. Sites are $9 a night.

Contact: Pachaug State Forest, P.O. Box 5, Voluntown, CT 06063; (860) 376-4075.

Directions: From Interstate 395 north of Norwich, take exit 85 and drive east on Route 138. Past Voluntown, turn left (north) on Route 49 and follow it to the state park entrance on the left. Follow signs to Mount Misery Campground (see campground number 53), then continue past that campground another 1.5 miles on a dirt road to Frog Hollow.

Trip notes: The secluded campground is reserved for use by campers with horses as well as those with mountain bikes. Sites are grassy and shaded, and are close to a swamp. An extensive system of equestrian

trails leaves from the campground and explores the mixed pine and hardwood forests of Pachaug. Mountain bikers are allowed on these routes, but they should take care not to startle the horses.

Open: May through October.

53 Mount Misery Campground

Location: North of Voluntown in Pachaug State Forest; Eastern Connecticut map page 449, grid c4.

Campsites, facilities: There are 22 wooded sites for tents and RVs. All sites hold picnic tables and fire pits. Piped water and primitive toilets are provided. Leashed pets and one horse per site are permitted.

Reservations, fees: Reservations are not accepted, and the sites are available on a first-come, first-served basis. The fee is $9 a night.

Contact: Pachaug State Forest, P.O. Box 5, Voluntown, CT 06063; (860) 376-4075.

Directions: From Interstate 395 north of Norwich, take exit 85 and drive east on Route 138. Past Voluntown, turn north on Route 49 and follow it to the state park entrance on the left. Once in the park, follow signs to Mount Misery Campground.

Trip notes: The Nehantic and Pachaug hiking trails run right through Mount Misery Campground. Horses are permitted at the camp itself and on the multiuse trails, which are also open to mountain bikers and hikers. From the campground, an easy trail leads through stands of cedars and oaks to the rocky summit of Mount Misery, an ideal picnic spot. The Pachaug River is open to canoeing; you'll find a boat launch at forest headquarters, just a short drive away. Across from the campground is the Rhododendron Sanctuary, an especially colorful treat in early July.

Open: May through October.

54 Nature's Campsites

Location: East of Pachaug State Forest; Eastern Connecticut map page 449, grid c4.

Campsites, facilities: This hilly campground offers 185 wooded or open sites for tents and RVs with full or partial hookups. Each has a picnic table and fire pit. Recreation facilities include a playground, basketball court, volleyball area, two swimming pools, and canoe rentals. A group camping area and a barbecue pit are also available. Other amenities include modern rest rooms, a general store, and dump stations. One pet is allowed per site.

Reservations, fees: Reservations are recommended. Tent sites are $20 a night, and sites with hookups range from $22 to $24 a night.

Contact: Nature's Campsites, Route 49 North, Voluntown, CT 06384; (860) 376-4203.

Directions: From Interstate 395 north of Norwich, take exit 85 and drive east on Route 138. Past Voluntown, turn left (north) onto Route 49. The campground is a half mile ahead on the right.

Trip notes: The rustic sites are well shaded by tall pines, though they're somewhat close together (35 feet wide). The campground is located on the state-stocked Pachaug River, which offers excellent bass and trout fishing. A group camping area and a pavilion with a barbecue pit cater to large parties of happy campers. Pachaug State Forest borders the campground, providing on-site access to 23,000 acres of woodlands linked by hiking, biking, and nature trails leading to seven lakes and numerous streams.

Open: May 1 through October 15.

55 Ye Olde Countryside Campground

Location: In Voluntown near Pachaug State Forest; Eastern Connecticut map page 449, grid c4.

Campsites, facilities: All 68 wooded tent or RV sites have picnic tables and stone fireplaces. Facilities include flush toilets, a dump station, and hot showers. Firewood is available on the premises. Leashed pets are permitted.

Reservations, fees: Reservations are recommended and require a nonrefundable deposit. Tent sites are $18 a day; RV sites with electric and water hookups are $20 a day.

Contact: Linda Mackin, Ye Olde Countryside Campground, P.O. Box 80B, Voluntown, CT 06384; (860) 376-0029.

Directions: From Interstate 395 north of Norwich, take exit 85 and drive east on Route 138 toward Voluntown. Make a right on Route 201, travel one mile south, and turn left on Cook Hill Road. The campground will be a short distance ahead on the right.

Trip notes: Natural, wooded campsites surround a spring-fed swimming pond, while trees and understory flora provide maximum privacy. A fishing pond is also on site. If all the state campgrounds are full, this makes an excellent alternative base camp for Pachaug State Forest recreation.

Open: May 1 through October 15.

56 Green Falls Campground

Location: On Green Falls Pond in Pachaug State Forest, south of Voluntown; Eastern Connecticut map page 449, grid c4.

Campsites, facilities: There are 18 wooded sites with primitive toilets and piped water. Each site offers picnic tables and fire rings. Keg beer is prohibited. One pet is allowed per site.

Reservations, fees: Reservations are not accepted. Sites are $10 a night.

Contact: Pachaug State Forest, P.O. Box 5, Voluntown, CT 06063; (860) 376-4075.

Directions: From Interstate 395 north of Norwich, take exit 85 and drive east on Route 138. Continue three miles east past Voluntown and follow signs to the park and campground.

Trip notes: Most sites have rocky outcroppings and are well shaded. All are located just across a dirt road from Green Falls Pond. The Narragansett, Pachaug, and Nehantic hiking trails cross through Green Falls Campground, making this a good starting point for backpacking trips on those three state trails. The clear waters of undeveloped Green Falls Pond offer pleasurable swimming, fishing, and nonmotorized boating. All things considered, it's no surprise that this campground fills up fast in good weather.

Open: Mid-April through mid-October.

---

⑤⑦ Laurel Lock Family Campground

Location: West of Norwich on Gardner Lake; Eastern Connecticut map page 449, grid d2.

Campsites, facilities: Most of the 130 sites are for RVs, with cable, water, electric, and sewage hookups. Picnic tables and fireplaces are provided. A safari area is suitable for tents and group camping. A rec hall, store, laundry facility, flush toilets, metered hot showers, and boat docks are on the property. No pets are allowed.

Reservations, fees: Reservations are recommended. Sites are $22 a night.

Contact: Laurel Lock Family Campground, 15 Cottage Road, Oakdale, CT 06370; (860) 859-1424.

Directions: From Route 2 at Colchester, head south on Route 354. Drive five miles to the first caution light, then turn left on Winter Road. At the end of the road, turn right on Lake Road and take the first right onto Cottage Road. The campground is ahead on the left.

Trip notes: Occupied mostly by seasonal renters, the sites at Laurel Lock—from open and grassy to wooded and waterfront—are set on a hill above Gardner Lake. The campground boasts 1,000 feet of shoreline where all types of water sports can be played. Rest rooms are passably clean. The property abuts Hopemead State Park, which has some foot trails. This region of the state is rich in Native American history. To learn more about this heritage, check out the Tantaquidgeon Indian Museum in Uncasville to the south. The facility focuses on the native peoples of the eastern woodlands and contains a unique collection of stone, bone, and wood items.

Open: April 15 through October 15.

---

⑤⑧ Pequot Ledge Campground and Cabins

Location: West of Norwich on Gardner Lake; Eastern Connecticut map page 449, grid d2.

Campsites, facilities: There are 92 beachfront and wooded sites for tents and RVs. All sites offer water and electric hookups, picnic tables, and fire rings; most have sewer connections, too. Furnished cottages near the water are available for rent. A showerhouse with flush toilets is on the property. There's also a boat launch and docks, a dump station, snack bar, two rec halls with stone fireplaces, and pool tables. Organized events are held for children and adults. Leashed pets are permitted.

Reservations, fees: Reservations are recommended. Sites start at $25 a night.

Contact: Pequot Ledge Campground and Cabins, 157 Doyle Road, Oakdale, CT 06370; (860) 859-2949.

Directions: From Interstate 395 south of Norwich, take exit 80 and start driving west on Route 82. After about five miles (a gas station will be on your left), turn right on Church Road. At the end of Church Road, stay left at the fork. The campground is just ahead on the right.

Trip notes: The campground is perched above Gardner Lake in rolling woodlands. Though there are numerous seasonal sites with permanent structures attached, old pine trees help maintain a natural appearance. The lodge owns 900 feet of shoreline where campers can swim, fish, and launch a boat. One mile wide and three miles long, spring-fed Gardner Lake provides great fishing for largemouth and smallmouth bass, calico, and trout. Organized activities for children and adults include dances, bingo games, lollipop hunts, and arts and crafts.

Open: April 15 to October 15.

---

59 Witch Meadow Lake Family Campground

Location: South of Colchester in Salem; Eastern Connecticut map page 449, grid d2.

Campsites, facilities: There are 280 wooded sites for tents and RVs with full hookups. Each has a picnic table and fireplace. A rec hall, adult lounge, group pavilion, convenience store, laundry facilities,

bathhouse, LP gas, and dump stations are also provided. Pets are allowed, but they must remain on their owner's campsite at all times.

Reservations, fees: Reservations are recommended, and a nonrefundable deposit is required. Sites are $23 a night.

Contact: Witch Meadow Lake Family Campground, 139 Witch Meadow Road, Salem, CT 06420; (860) 859-1542.

Directions: From Route 2 in Colchester, take exit 20 and head south on Route 11 to exit 5. Turn left on Witch Meadow Road and travel a short distance east to the campground entrance, which is just ahead on the right after you cross a bridge.

Trip notes: Witch Meadow Lake is a 14-acre pond where campers can spend their days swimming, boating in nonmotorized craft, and taking advantage of great fishing. The campground is situated on the hillsides above the lake. Note that although the sites are in the woods, they are overdeveloped and in no way private. The facility offers boat rentals, a miniature golf course, and theme weekends. From the Great Texas Steakout to Mardi Gras, all events are geared toward families.

Open: Late April through late October.

---

60 Salem Farms Campground

Location: South of Colchester near Devils Hopyard State Park; Eastern Connecticut map page 449, grid d2.

Campsites, facilities: There are 180 RV sites and six tent sites. All have picnic tables and fireplaces, and most come with hookups. Metered hot showers, on-site trailer rentals, dump stations, and a camp store are provided. There are two pools, a petting zoo, sports courts, athletic fields, a large recreation barn with games, and an adult lounge. Leashed pets are permitted.

Reservations, fees: Reservations are recommended. Sites are $21 a night.

Contact: Salem Farms Campground, Inc., 39 Alexander Road, Salem, CT 06420; (860) 859-2320 or (800) 479-9238.

Directions: From Route 2 in Colchester, head south on Route 11 via exit 19. At exit 5, turn right and drive west on Witch Meadow Road. At the first intersection the road turns into Alexander Road. The campground entrance is ahead on the left.

Trip notes: Kiddie rides on an antique fire engine are among the many special activities at Salem Farms, where both open and shaded sites are offered in a quiet, rural setting. Dances and sporting competitions are frequently held, and costumed characters make appearances in the spirit of family fun. For an outing your whole tribe will enjoy, head to Gardner Lake Park, a privately owned beach at the corner of Routes 82 and 354 in Salem. You can rent wave runners, paddleboats, and bumper boats there, or take a dip in the fresh water. The park also offers inflatable rafts, food, an arcade, and kiddie rides—all at only $2 a head for visitors over the age of six.

Open: May 1 through October 1.

---

61 Devils Hopyard State Park

Location: South of Colchester; Eastern Connecticut map page 449, grid d2.

Campsites, facilities: There are 21 sites for tents and RVs, all without hookups. Each has a picnic table and concrete fireplace. A central water pump and primitive toilets are provided. The maximum RV length is 35 feet. No pets are allowed.

Reservations, fees: Reservations are highly recommended. There's a two-night minimum stay for reservations. Sites are $9 a night.

Contact: Devils Hopyard State Park, 366 Hopyard Road, East Haddam, CT 06423; (860) 873-8566.

Directions: From Route 9 south of Haddam, take exit 7. Follow Route 82 across the Connecticut River and through East Haddam to the junction with Route 151. Continue driving east (Route 82 veers south here), and the road will eventually enter the park; signs clearly indicate the route to the campground.

Trip notes: Spanning a section of the Eight Mile River, the park was named for the pothole formations found in the rocks in the riverbed. According to folklore, these holes were made by the devil's footpads as he stomped down the river, angry at having gotten his tail wet. From the campground you can explore the river, which is stocked with brook trout, via the 2.5-mile Vista Trail. In all, about 15 miles of foot trails are maintained by the state park. The campground is a stone's throw from Chapman Falls, a lovely cascade that tumbles down a 60-foot escarpment. Due to its small size and off-the-beaten-path locale, the campground is quiet, even in the thick of summer. Sites are flat and shaded by young trees.

Open: Mid-April through early October.

---

62 Nelson's Family Campground

Location: North of East Hampton; Eastern Connecticut map page 449, grid c1.

Campsites, facilities: There are 280 sites for tents and RVs, 255 with water and electric hookups. Each has a picnic table and fireplace. On the grounds are sports courts, a playground, paddleboat rentals, laundry facilities, miniature golf, a dump station, and a pool. Leashed pets are permitted.

Reservations, fees: Reservations are strongly recommended in the summer, especially on weekends. Holiday weekends require a three-day minimum stay. Sites start at $23 a night.

Contact: Nelson's Family Campground, 71C Mott Hill Road, East Hampton, CT 06424; (860) 267-5300.

Directions: From the stoplight on Route 66 in downtown East Hampton, travel two miles north on Main Street to Mott Hill Road. Turn left and continue half a mile to the campground.

Trip notes: While many of the sites here are rented seasonally, grassy, open spaces are available for overnighters. Families will appreciate the accessible pool, playgrounds, and recreation facilities that are always abuzz with organized events. More sedate campers should request a site far from the action if they desire a little peace. One nearby notable is the Comstock Covered Bridge, located off Route 16. One of the few such bridges left in Connecticut, it crosses the Salmon River and is open to pedestrian traffic only. A full afternoon outing would include a visit to the bridge and to Salmon River State Forest, also off Route 16 in East Hampton.

Open: April 15 through Columbus Day.

⑥③ Markham Meadows Campground

Location: West of East Hampton near Salmon River State Forest; Eastern Connecticut map page 449, grid c2.

Campsites, facilities: There are 100 grassy and wooded sites for tents and RVs, most with hookups. Each has a picnic table and fireplace. You'll find a rec hall, group

pavilion, laundry facilities, and a bathhouse on site, as well as sports courts and a library. One dog per site is allowed.

Reservations, fees: Reservations are recommended. Sites are $22 a night, and $80 for holiday weekends.

Contact: Markham Meadows Campground, 7 Markham Road, East Hampton, CT 06424; (860) 267-9738.

Directions: From Route 2 at Colchester, take exit 18 and head west on Route 16. Travel seven miles to Tartia Road and turn left. The campground entrance is one mile ahead on the left.

Trip notes: The sites at this developed family campground are either open and grassy or wooded. A full slate of organized activities is offered every weekend, from the Strawberry Festival in June to the Twilight Family Swim and Bonfire in August. Just down the road is Salmon River State Forest, offering hiking and nature trails and a chance to fish for trout in the Salmon River. Be sure to check current regulations because some sections are for fly-fishing only. The hatchery at the park entrance turns out salmon that are genetically engineered to go forth to the Atlantic then return to spawn and die.

Open: May through October.

⑥④ Sunrise Resort

Location: In Moodus, north of East Haddam; Eastern Connecticut map page 449, grid c2.

Campsites, facilities: There are 66 sites for tents and RVs, 16 with water and electric hookups and 50 with none. Each has a picnic table and fire ring. Laundry facilities, a dump station, rec hall, group pavilion, paddleboat rentals, miniature golf, sports courts, a pool, and a playground are available. Leashed pets are permitted.

Reservations, fees: Reservations are required. Rates are available upon request.

Contact: Sunrise Resort, Route 151, Moodus, CT 06469; (860) 873-8681.

Directions: From Route 9 in Haddam, drive south to exit 7. Turn left on Route 82 and go across the East Haddam Bridge, then turn left and continue three miles north on Route 149. At the intersection with Route 151, turn left and drive north on Route 151 for one mile to the resort entrance.

Trip notes: In addition to the pleasant, grassy sites, campers will enjoy dining on the American Plan (all meals included) at this resort campground. A host of activities—from hiking on trails to swimming in a river or a pool to planned events—is available on the grounds. The resort is centrally located to many attractions in the Haddam area, including the Goodspeed Opera House in East Haddam. This historic Victorian facility overlooking the Connecticut River hosts nationally acclaimed musicals. In season, daily tours of the opera house explain the history of the 1876 structure built by shipping magnate William Goodspeed.

Open: Memorial Day weekend through Labor Day.

⑥⑤ Little City Campground

Location: North of Higganum; Eastern Connecticut map page 449, grid d1.

Campsites, facilities: There are 50 sites for tents and RVs, most with hookups. Each has a picnic table and fireplace. The campground also has a bathhouse, rec hall, swimming pond, sports fields and courts, a dump station, and LP gas. Leashed pets are permitted.

Reservations, fees: Reservations are recommended. Rates are available on request.

Contact: Little City Campground, 741 Little City Road, Higganum, CT 06441; (860) 345-8469.

Directions: From Interstate 91 south of Rocky Hill, take exit 22 and head south on Route 9. Follow this road to exit 10, then continue south on Route 154. Just before the light in Higganum, take a sharp right onto Candlewood Hill Road and go 3.4 miles. Turn left on Little City Road and follow signs to the campground.

Trip notes: This out-of-the-way campground is close to the Connecticut River, which affords boundless opportunities for fishing and boating. Spacious, hilly sites and a variety of activities make it popular with seasonal renters, so be sure to call ahead and reserve a spot. The sites are either in open or wooded settings. There's a swimming pond on the property and the area abuts Millers Pond State Park, where you'll find hiking trails and ponds and streams that are open to fishing. One nearby spot on the Connecticut River is Haddam Meadows State Park, a short drive south of Higganum Center on Route 154. This 175-acre meadowland lies in the river floodplain.

Open: May 1 through October 1.

⑥⑥ Hurd State Park

Location: On the Connecticut River north of Haddam; Eastern Connecticut map page 449, grid d2.

Campsites, facilities: The riverside tent sites can accommodate as many as 12 campers traveling via canoe. There are fireplaces and pit toilets but no mooring or docking facilities. Campers must break camp by 9 A.M. No pets are allowed.

Reservations, fees: Reservations are required. The fee is $4 a night per person.

Contact: Supervisor, Gillette Castle State Park, 67 River Road, East Haddam, CT 06423; (203) 526-2336.

Directions: Accessible by boat only, these sites are on the Connecticut River, 47 miles downstream from the Connecticut/Massachusetts border.

Trip notes: Located just north of George D. Seymour State Park, the Hurd State Park canoe sites offer access to river woodlands and hiking trails. If you debark before nightfall or rise early enough, make the short hike through the park to Split Rock and on to White Mountain for a great view of the river.

Open: May 1 through September 30.

67 Gillette Castle State Park

Location: On the Connecticut River south of East Haddam; Eastern Connecticut map page 449, grid d2.

Campsites, facilities: The riverside tent sites can accommodate as many as 20 campers traveling via canoe. There are fireplaces and pit toilets but no mooring or docking facilities. Campers must break camp by 9 A.M. No pets are allowed.

Reservations, fees: Reservations are required. The fee is $4 a night per person.

Contact: Supervisor, Gillette Castle State Park, 67 River Road, East Haddam, CT 06423; (203) 526-2336.

Directions: Accessible by boat only, these sites are on the Connecticut River, 56 miles downstream from the Connecticut/Massachusetts border.

Trip notes: Along with Hurd and Selden Neck State Parks, this is one of three camps on the Connecticut River designated for use by canoeists only (see also campgrounds 66

and 69). The surrounding parcel of land was named for the mansion of William Gillette, who won fame as a stage actor by playing Sherlock Holmes and, in 1919, built his 24-room fieldstone home overlooking the river. You can access the castle and the rest of the 184-acre park by following a path from the campground. The park offers tours of the castle for a fee; use of the walking and nature trails is free.

Open: May 1 through September 30.

68 Wolf's Den Family Campground

Location: South of East Haddam near Gillette Castle State Park; Eastern Connecticut map page 449, grid d2.

Campsites, facilities: There are 205 mostly grassy sites for tents and RVs with water and electric hookups. Each has a picnic table and fireplace. Campers also have use of a rec hall, camp store, laundry facilities, flush toilets, and hot showers. On site you'll find dump stations, two pavilions, and a group camping area. Leashed pets are permitted.

Reservations, fees: Reservations are recommended. Sites are $23 a night.

Contact: Wolf's Den Family Campground, 256 Town Street, Route 82, East Haddam, CT 06423; (860) 873-9681.

Directions: From Interstate 91 south of Hartford, take exit 22 and head south on Route 9. When you reach exit 7, turn and travel east on Route 82, driving over the Connecticut River. At the junction with Route 151, bear right and continue south on Route 82, looking for signs to Gillette Castle State Park. The entrance to Wolf's Den is on the left, four miles from Route 9, just before the state park entrance on the right.

Trip notes: If a private adult lair is what

you seek, Wolf's Den is not the answer. Geared toward kids and families, the campground features a sizable pool, a swimming pond and beach, miniature golf, and an overwhelming array of organized activities, including kids' beauty pageants, pig roasts, and auctions. Gillette Castle State Park across the street from the campground features the 24-room fieldstone mansion of William Gillette, a famous stage actor from the early 1900s.

Open: May 1 through October 1.

⑥⑨ Selden Neck State Park

Location: On the Connecticut River east of Chester; Eastern Connecticut map page 449, grid d2.

Campsites, facilities: Four separate sites are available: Cedars Camp is located on Selden Creek, while Hogback, Springledge, and Quarry Knob are on the Connecticut River. Cedars can accommodate 20 tent campers; Hogback, 6; Springledge, 8; and Quarry Knob, 12. The sites are open to river travelers in any kind of boat. There are fireplaces and pit toilets but no mooring or docking facilities. No pets are allowed.

Reservations, fees: Reservations are required. There's a two-night minimum stay. The fee is $4 a night per person.

Contact: Supervisor, Gillette Castle State Park, 67 River Road, East Haddam, CT 06423; (203) 526-2336.

Directions: Accessible by boat only, these sites are on the Connecticut River, 58 miles downstream from the Connecticut/Massachusetts border.

Trip notes: These riverside campsites are for the adventuresome canoeist. A short paddle up Selden Creek gets you to a trailhead that will take you to Observatory Hill,

a great vantage point for expansive views for miles around. One good aspect of the Selden Neck sites is that you don't have to break camp by 9 A.M., as you do at the two other canoe campsites to the north (see campgrounds 66 and 67).

Open: May 1 through September 30.

⑦⓪ The Island

Location: In East Lyme on Lake Pattagansett; Eastern Connecticut map page 449, grid d3.

Campsites, facilities: There are 35 sites for tent trailers and RVs, all with water and electric hookups. Each site has a table and is near hot showers and flush toilets. A private beach and play area are on the island. Leashed pets are permitted.

Reservations, fees: Reservations are recommended. Sites start at $18 a night.

Contact: The Island, 20 Islanda Court, East Lyme, CT 06333; (860) 739-8316.

Directions: From Interstate 95 in Lyme, take exit 74 and head north on Route 161 for a short distance. Turn left, head a mile west on U.S. 1, then take Islanda Court to the right. The road ends on the island.

Trip notes: This offbeat little island on Lake Pattagansett seems as if it were made for relaxing. Sites either overlook the lake or are just nearby, and all are shaded. When you set up camp in this oasis, the hubbub of the Mystic area to the east is a world away. Just relax on the beach, catch a fish or two, and forget your troubles.

Open: May 15 through October 15.

⑦① Trailer Haven

Location: North of Groton; Eastern Connecticut map page 449, grid d3.

Campsites, facilities: Five RV sites with hookups are located in the rear of a Super 8 motel parking lot. Each has a concrete pad, tree, and picnic table, but there are no rest rooms. Leashed pets are permitted.

Reservations, fees: Reservations are recommended. Sites are $25 a night, plus $10 for sewer and water hookups.

Contact: Trailer Haven, Route 12, Groton, CT 06340; call Chip at (860) 445-4931.

Directions: From Interstate 95 in Groton, take exit 86 and drive north on Route 12 for 100 yards. Pull into the Super 8 motel parking lot. The campground is behind the building.

Trip notes: Nothing special, this campground is located on a strip of grass at the far end of a motel parking lot. It is, however, near several historic sites in Groton. At Fort Griswold on Fort Street, there's the Ebenezer Avery House, an eighteenth-century home built by a naval ensign wounded in the 1781 battle of Groton Heights. Fort Griswold Battlefield Park bears a monument to that massacre, in which colonial defenders were bested by British troops under Benedict Arnold's direction. The USS *Nautilus* Memorial and Submarine Force Library and Museum are also in town. Here, the world's first nuclear-powered submarine has been refitted to accept visitors on self-guided tours. The museum provides a visual account of the history of submarines in this country.

Open: Year-round.

---

⑫ Seaport Campgrounds

Location: North of Mystic; Eastern Connecticut map page 449, grid d4.

Campsites, facilities: There are 130 sites for tents and RVs, most with water and electric hookups. Each site has a picnic table and fire pit. Dump stations and service are provided. Recreational facilities include a full-sized swimming pool, miniature golf course, rec room, and fishing pond. Also available on the premises are laundry facilities, a store, bathhouse, pavilion, LP gas, firewood, ice, and RV supplies. There is a traffic control gate and a guard. Leashed pets are permitted.

Reservations, fees: Reservations are recommended Memorial Day through Labor Day. Tent sites with no utilities are $26 a night, and sites with hookups are $29.

Contact: Seaport Campgrounds, P.O. Box 104, Route 184, Old Mystic, CT 06372; (860) 536-4044.

Directions: From Interstate 95 north of Mystic, take exit 90 and go 1.25 miles north on Route 27. Turn right and drive a half mile east on Route 184. The campground is on the left.

Trip notes: Set in a mostly grassy field with a few shade trees, Seaport Campgrounds' sites are generous and open. There is a separate tenting area. Campers have all the amenities, including a swimming pool and fishing pond on the grounds as well as access to nearby Mystic. One oft-overlooked attraction is the Pequotsepos Nature Center on Pequotsepos Road in Old Mystic. The 125-acre sanctuary has more than seven miles of hiking trails that weave through four distinct habitats and offers excellent birding. The Mystic Seaport is a world-famous indoor/outdoor maritime museum that tells America's seaside story. Historic ships, working craftspeople, period homes, and exhibits help to make New England's rich coastal past come alive. The town bustles all summer long with tourists who flock to the museum and other attractions.

Open: Mid-April to late October.

⓭ MHG RV Park

RV 🔺 **4**

Location: In North Stonington; Eastern Connecticut map page 449, grid d4.

Campsites, facilities: There are five RV sites with hookups. LP gas, laundry facilities, and cable TV and telephone hookups are available. Leashed pets are permitted.

Reservations, fees: Reservations are recommended. Rates are available on request.

Contact: MHG RV Park, Route 184, Box 374, North Stonington, CT 06359; (860) 535-0501.

Directions: From Interstate 95 north of Pawcatuck, take exit 93. Drive a short distance north on Route 216, then make a quick left onto Route 184 heading south. The campground entrance is about five miles ahead on the left.

Trip notes: Rented to seasonal campers only, these sites are coveted for their proximity to ocean beaches. They're partially shaded and grassy, so there is something of a buffer zone from the sound of traffic on Route 184. This small trailer haven is a good choice for gambling aficionados, as the Foxwoods Casino is only six miles away.

Open: Year-round.

⓮ Highland Orchards Resort Park

 RV 🔺 **6**

Location: In North Stonington near the Rhode Island border; Eastern Connecticut map page 449, grid d4.

Campsites, facilities: There are 260 mostly pull-through sites for RVs and some secluded and group areas for tent campers; all have picnic tables and fireplaces. Use of air conditioners and heaters is allowed. Campers have the use of a swimming pool, sports courts, a fishing pond, rec hall, free hot showers, miniature golf, laundry facilities, dump stations, and a covered pavilion. There is a traffic control gate. On-site RV service and sales are offered, and LP gas, ice, and firewood are available. Leashed pets are permitted.

Reservations, fees: Reservations are recommended Memorial Day through Labor Day. Sites are $26 to $33 a night.

Contact: Highland Orchards Resort Park, P.O. Box 222, Route 49, North Stonington, CT 06359; (860) 599-5105 or (800) 624-0829.

Directions: From Interstate 95 north of Pawcatuck, take exit 92 and turn north onto Route 49. The campground entrance is the first driveway on the right; watch for signs.

Trip notes: With a full slate of organized activities (such as line dancing and theme dinners) and a wide assortment of sports and athletic facilities, this full-service RV park caters to families. It's located on one of the state's first farms, and the landscape includes manicured lawns and century-old maple trees. Campsites are open and grassy, offering little natural buffer between neighbors. Ocean beaches are a short drive to the south. A bonus for campers is free shuttle service to the nearby Foxwoods Casino.

Open: Year-round.

⓯ Camp Niantic by the Atlantic

⚓ 🏕️ 🏃 🍴 🏊 **RV** 🔺 **5**

Location: West of Niantic; Eastern Connecticut map page 449, grid d3.

Campsites, facilities: There are 100 open or slightly wooded sites for tents and RVs. Each has full hookups, a fireplace, and picnic tables. A common bathhouse, rec hall, sports courts, and hiking trails are provided. Leashed pets are permitted.

Reservations, fees: Reservations are

recommended. Sites are $20 a night in the off-season, $25 a night midseason.

Contact: Camp Niantic by the Atlantic, 271 West Main Street, Niantic, CT 06357; (203) 739-9308.

Directions: From Interstate 95 west of Waterford, take exit 72 and travel south on the turnpike connector to Route 156. Turn left and head southeast. The campground is 800 feet ahead on the right.

Trip notes: This RVers mecca is set on a wooded hillside close to ocean beaches. Home-style hospitality and a creative activity schedule make this a popular park. Bingo, dart tournaments, theme weekends, and cookouts are typical events. Campers can get a free pass to McCook Point Beach, about five minutes from the campground by car. Also nearby is Rocky Neck State Park, featuring a half-mile-long crescent-shaped beach open to every form of saltwater recreation.

Open: April through October.

76 Rocky Neck State Park

Location: On the ocean, between Waterford and Old Lyme; Eastern Connecticut map page 449, grid d3.

Campsites, facilities: There are 160 sites for tents and RVs, all without hookups. Each site has a picnic table but no fireplace; campfires are permitted only in camper-supplied containers or in several community fireplaces. Hot showers and flush toilets are available at centrally located bathhouses. There is a dump station. The maximum RV length is 35 feet. No pets are allowed.

Reservations, fees: Reservations are required. There's a two-night minimum stay. Sites are $12 a night.

Contact: Rocky Neck State Park, Box 676, Niantic, CT 06357; (203) 739-5471.

Directions: From Interstate 95 west of Waterford, take exit 72 and travel south on the turnpike connector to Route 156. Turn left and go east to the park entrance just ahead on the right.

Trip notes: Ocean fishing and water sports are the main attractions at Rocky Neck State Park, where a half-mile-long crescent-shaped beach offers saltwater recreation at its best. A bike path leads from the campground, which offers sites in a mix of open and wooded settings, to the beach. Niantic is home to the Millstone Information and Science Center, which has exhibits on nuclear and other energy sources. The center also houses an aquarium, multimedia shows, and computer games, making it a good side trip for family campers on a rainy Rocky Neck day.

Open: Mid-May to mid-October.

77 Riverdale Farm Campsites

Location: North of Clinton near the Hammonasset River; Eastern Connecticut map page 449, grid d1.

Campsites, facilities: There are 250 sites for RVs, 100 with full hookups and 150 with water and electric. Use of air conditioners and heaters is allowed. Tables and fireplaces are provided at each site. On the grounds are flush toilets, hot showers, laundry facilities, a store, dump stations, and LP gas. There are sports courts, a swimming pool, group pavilion, rec hall, and planned activities. Leashed pets are permitted.

Reservations, fees: Reservations are recommended. Sites start at $23 a night.

Contact: Riverdale Farm Campsites, 245 River Road, Killingworth, CT 06419; (860) 663-1639.

Directions: From Interstate 95 in Clinton,

take exit 62 and drive north to the first road on the right, about 200 feet up. Go a half mile east on Duck Hole Road, turn left over the bridge, and bear left onto River Road. The camp is 1.5 miles ahead on the left.

Trip notes: If you are a neatnik, you'll appreciate Riverdale, where the yards are manicured and the facilities are spotless. Sites, many of which are rented seasonally, are spacious and flat with natural buffers. A spring-fed pond for swimming and fishing is on the grounds, as is a pool, and the Hammonasset River is close by for fishing. Just three miles away are Long Island Sound and its beaches. Though tenters are welcome here, more suitable tent camping can be found near the ocean at Hammonasset Beach State Park. In the town of Clinton, the Opera Theater of Connecticut is a popular destination. So is the Stanton House, circa 1790, on Main Street; site of Yale University's first classroom, the house holds a collection of antique American and Staffordshire dinnerware and a general store display of period items.

Open: April 15 through October 1.

78 River Road Campground

Location: North of Clinton near the Hammonasset River; Eastern Connecticut map page 449, grid d2.

Campsites, facilities: There are 50 rustic sites for tents and RVs, all with water and electric hookups. Each has a table, fire ring, and grill. A dump station, playground, and camp store are on the property. Ice and firewood are available. The maximum RV length is 33 feet. Leashed pets are permitted.

Reservations, fees: Reservations are recommended. There is a three-day minimum stay on holiday weekends. Sites are $18 a night.

Contact: River Road Campground, 13 River Road, Clinton, CT 06413; (860) 669-2238.

Directions: From Interstate 95 in Clinton, take exit 62 and travel north to the first road on the right, about 200 feet up. Drive a half mile east on Duck Hole Road, take a left turn over the bridge, and bear left onto River Road. The campground is one mile ahead on the right.

Trip notes: Set next to the Hammonasset River, the hilly, wooded sites here are a good pick for canoeists, not to mention those who like to swim or wet a fishing line in a river. The campground itself is unkempt, but the waterside sites are scenic. The river lets out into the Atlantic Ocean at Hammonasset Beach State Park. There, the public has access to a two-mile beach, swimming, scuba diving, fishing, a nature center, and interpretive programs. The state park is a short drive or paddle away.

Open: April 15 through October 15.

79 William F. Miller Campground

Location: In Hammonasset Beach State Park in Clinton; Eastern Connecticut map page 449, grid e1.

Campsites, facilities: There are 558 open sites for tents and RVs, all without hookups. The grounds offer a snack concession, community fireplaces, a dump station, flush toilets, and showers. Piped water and several buildings with electrical outlets are available. No pets are allowed.

Reservations, fees: Reservations are required. There's a two-night minimum stay. Sites are $12 a night.

Contact: Hammonasset Beach State Park, Box 271, Madison, CT 06443; (203) 245-1817.

Directions: From Interstate 95 at Clinton,

take exit 62 and follow the turnpike connector south to the park entrance.

Trip notes: With the most sites of any campground in Connecticut, Hammonasset Beach State Park lacks privacy in the busy season. Still, it does afford access to all saltwater recreation. Hiking and interpretive trails weave through the park—just watch out for natural preserve areas, which are off-limits. On the grounds, there's a public boat ramp with trailer parking, a nature center, and an amphitheater. Located at the mouth of the Hammonasset River, the campsites overlook marshlands that are home to herons and various waterfowl species.

Open: Mid-May through October 31.

Index

FOGHORN OUTDOORS

Founded in 1985, Foghorn Press has quickly become one of the country's premier publishers of outdoor recreation guidebooks. Through its unique Books Building Community program, Foghorn Press supports community environmental issues, such as park, trail, and water ecosystem preservation. Foghorn Press is also committed to printing its books with soy-based inks on 100 percent recycled paper.

Foghorn Press books are available throughout the United States in bookstores and some outdoor retailers. If you cannot find the title you are looking for, visit Foghorn's Web site at http://www.foghorn.com or call 1-800-FOGHORN.

The Complete Guide Series

- *New England Hiking* (416 pp) $18.95
- *Utah & Nevada Camping* (384 pp) $18.95
- *Southwest Camping* (544 pp) $17.95
- *Baja Camping* (294 pp) $12.95
- *California Camping* (848 pp) $19.95
- *California Hiking* (688 pp) $20.95—New 3rd edition
- *California Waterfalls* (408 pp) $17.95
- *California Fishing* (768 pp) $20.95—New 4th edition
- *California Beaches* (640 pp) $19.95
- *California Boating and Water Sports* (608 pp) $19.95
- *California In-Line Skating* (480 pp) $19.95
- *Tahoe* (704 pp) $18.95
- *Pacific Northwest Camping* (720 pp) $19.95
- *Pacific Northwest Hiking* (648 pp) $20.95—New 2nd edition
- *Washington Fishing* (528 pp) $19.95
- *Alaska Fishing* (640 pp) $19.95

The National Outdoors Series

- *America's Secret Recreation Areas—Your Recreation Guide to the Bureau of Land Management's Wild Lands of the West* (640 pp) $17.95
- *America's Wilderness—The Complete Guide to More Than 600 National Wilderness Areas* (592 pp) $19.95
- *The Camper's Companion—The Pack-Along Guide for Better Outdoor Trips* (464 pp) $15.95
- *Wild Places: 20 Journeys Into the North American Outdoors* (305 pp) $15.95

A book's page length and availability are subject to change.

For more information, call 1-800-FOGHORN,
e-mail: foghorn@well.com, or write to:
Foghorn Press
P.O. Box 77845
San Francisco, CA 94107

Acknowledgments

Thanks to my sister and mom, Josie and Mary Ann,
for moral support, and to Marilyn Simons for her
research on Vermont campgrounds.

—*C. C.*

I am grateful to the sons and daughters of Thoreau who
have struggled to keep the wild in New England.
Each of us with an interest in this book
owes you a large debt.

—*S. G.*

Credits

Editor in Chief	Donna Leverenz
Developmental Editor	Rebecca Poole Forée
Editor	Karin Mullen
Production Coordinator	Alexander Lyon
Production Assistant	Leigh Anna Mendenhall
Acquisitions Editor	Judith Pynn
Contributing Editor	Don Root
Cover Photo	Stephen Gorman Gulf of Maine

The chapters on Maine and Rhode Island were written by
Stephen Gorman, and those on New Hampshire, Vermont,
Massachusetts, and Connecticut were written by Carol Connare.

Both authors contributed to the Camping Tips section.

About the Authors

Carol A. Connare is a travel editor at *Yankee Magazine* in Dublin, New Hampshire, and writes frequently about New England, music, and the outdoors.

A native of the Granite State, she worked as a general news reporter after graduating from the University of New Hampshire. In 1990 she drove to Alaska to live and work on the Yukon River, where she cared for 90 sled dogs and fished for salmon while outwitting hordes of mosquitoes and avoiding bears. For two winters, she returned to New Hampshire and worked for a logging operation on land bordering the White Mountain National Forest.

After returning home for good, Connare started a desktop publishing company, Idea Outfitters, Inc., wrote a historical cookbook about Portsmouth, New Hampshire, scouted fishing and hunting spots as the traveling outdoorswoman for the *New Hampshire Sportsman,* and wrote on assignment for regional and national publications. Now she lives, hikes, bikes, and skis in the shadow of Mount Monadnock.

Stephen Gorman's work appears in *Men's Journal, Outside, Sierra, Wildlife Conservation,* and other national magazines. He is a principal author of Houghton-Mifflin's *Insight Guides: National Parks of the Eastern U.S.,* and his book *Winter Camping* is a bestselling sports/adventure title.

Gorman holds a master's degree in Environmental Studies from Yale and a bachelor's degree in American Studies from Wesleyan. A former Registered Maine Guide and Outward Bound instructor, he worked as a cowboy in Wyoming and as an exploration geologist in Alaska and Nevada. Prior to devoting himself full-time to writing and photography, Gorman conducted Wild and Scenic River studies in New England for the National Park Service. He and his wife, Mary, live in Exeter, New Hampshire.

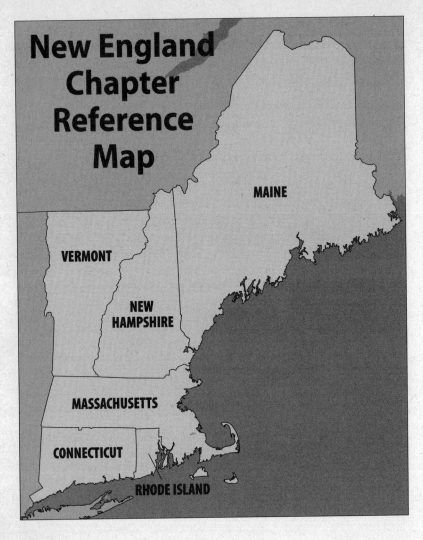

New England
Chapter
Reference
Map

MAINE

VERMONT

NEW
HAMPSHIRE

MASSACHUSETTS

CONNECTICUT

RHODE ISLAND